CLARENCE BYRD
Clarence Byrd Inc.

IDA CHEN
Clarence Byrd Inc.

With contributions by
GARY DONELL

Study Guide
to accompany

Byrd & Chen's
Canadian
Tax
Principles

2020–2021 EDITION

Pearson

Please contact https://support.pearson.com/getsupport/s/contactsupport with any queries on this content.

Pearson Canada Inc., 26 Prince Andrew Place, North York, Ontario M3C 2H4.

ISBN 978-0-13-674487-0

1 2020

CONTENTS

PREFACE

Complete Preface In Volume I

The complete preface to this three volume set of *Canadian Tax Principles* can be found in Volume I.

This Study Guide

Contents

Your two volume textbook is accompanied by this Study Guide. The chapters of this Study Guide correspond to the chapters of **Byrd & Chen's Canadian Tax Principles.** Each of these Study Guide chapters contains the following:

- A list of learning objectives for the material in the chapter.
- Detailed guidance on how to work through the text and problems in the chapter.
- Detailed solutions to the Exercises in the textbook for the chapter and the Self Study Problems available online.
- Two sample personal tax returns and two Self Study Tax Software Problems in Chapters 4 and 11.
- A sample corporate tax return in Chapter 13.

Glossary

At the back of this Study Guide is a comprehensive Glossary that carefully defines more than 500 tax terms that are used throughout the text. Tied to this important resource, at the end of each chapter you will find a list of the Key Terms, without definitions, that were used in that chapter. This provides an additional resource for reviewing the text material in that, by reviewing this list, you can ensure that you are familiar with all of the concepts that are presented in the chapter.

To assist in this review, Glossary Flashcards for each Chapter are also available on MyLab.

Using The Solutions

We encourage you to try to solve each Exercise and Self Study Problem before consulting these solutions. It is our opinion that one of the most unfortunate misconceptions that many students have is the belief that simply reading through a solution is a good learning experience. It is not!

MyLab Accounting

MyLab Accounting for *Canadian Tax Principles* contains a great deal of additional material that will provide significant assistance to users of this text. Instructions on how to access MyLab can be found on the access card provided with this package. The URL for MyLab is:

http://www.pearsonmylabandmastering.com

Chapter 1 Learning Objectives

After completing Chapter 1, you should be able to:

1. List some of the different bases that can be used by the various levels of government to assess taxes (paragraph [P hereafter] 1-1 through 1-6).
2. List all of the types of entities that are subject to paying federal income taxes and GST (P 1-7 through 1-12).
3. Explain the relationship between the assessment of taxes at the federal level and the assessment of taxes at the provincial level (P 1-13 through 1-25).
4. List some of the ways that taxation is used to achieve economic objectives (P 1-26).
5. Describe the differences between progressive, regressive, and flat tax systems, including some of the advantages and disadvantages of each system (P 1-27 through 1-34).

6. Discuss the issue of who ultimately pays the cost of various types of taxes (P 1-35 and 1-36).
7. Explain the nature of tax expenditures (P 1-37 through 1-40).
8. Evaluate issues in tax policy on the basis of the qualitative characteristics of tax systems (P 1-41 through 1-43).
9. Describe the reference materials that are available on income tax databases (P 1-44 through 1-48).
10. Describe the general structure of the *Income Tax Act* (P 1-49 through 1-60).

11. List and explain the nature of other sources of income tax legislation (P 1-61 through 1-70).
12. Describe other sources of income tax information (P 1-71 through 1-75).
13. Describe the charging provisions of the *Income Tax Act* for residents and non-residents (P 1-76 through 1-93).
14. Determine the residence of an individual based on an evaluation of primary and secondary residential ties (P 1-94 through 1-101).
15. Evaluate the residency status of an individual who is temporarily absent from Canada or is only resident for part of the year (P 1-102 through 1-108).

16. Identify the types of individuals who will be deemed to be Canadian residents without regard to their actual physical location (P 1-109 through 1-122).
17. Determine the residence of corporations and trusts (P 1-123 through 1-132).
18. Describe, in general terms, the various views of income that are held by economists, accountants, and tax authorities (P 1-133 through 1-141).
19. Calculate Net Income For Tax Purposes by applying the rules found in Section 3 of the *Income Tax Act* (P 1-142 through 1-167).
20. Explain how Net Income For Tax Purposes is converted to Taxable Income (P 1-168 and 1-169).

21. Explain the principles of tax planning (P 1-170 through 1-173).
22. Explain and provide examples of tax avoidance or reduction and tax deferral (P 1-174 through 1-181).
23. Explain and provide examples of income splitting (P 1-182 through 1-188).

How to Work Through Chapter 1

MyLab Accounting for this book can be found at:

http://www.pearsonmylabandmastering.com

We suggest you access MyLab before using the text to familiarize yourself with the useful student resources available there. In particular, review the corrections and updates to the textbook and Study Guide that are posted there to save yourself unnecessary frustration.

We recommend the following approach in dealing with the material in this chapter:

The Canadian Tax System
- Read paragraph 1-1 to 1-12 (in the textbook).
- Do Exercises One-1 and One-2 (in the textbook) and check the solutions in this Study Guide. All solutions to Exercises and Self Study Problems can be found in this Study Guide and the page numbers all start with the prefix S-.
- Read paragraph 1-13 to 1-17.
- Do Exercise One-3 and check the solution in this Study Guide.
- Read paragraph 1-18 to 1-25.

Tax Policy Concepts And Qualitative Characteristics Of Tax Systems
- Read paragraph 1-26 to 1-28.
- Do Exercise One-4 and check the solution in this Study Guide.
- Do Self Study Problem One-1 which is available on MyLab and check the solution in this Study Guide.
- Read paragraph 1-29 to 1-34.
- Do Self Study Problem One-2 and check the solution in this Study Guide.
- Read paragraph 1-35 to 1-43.
- Do Self Study Problem One-3 and check the solution in this Study Guide.

Income Tax Reference Materials
- Read paragraph 1-44 to 1-75.
- Do Self Study Problem One-4 and One-5 and check the solution in this Study Guide.

Liability For Income Tax
- Read paragraph 1-76 to 1-93.
- Do Exercise One-5 and check the solution in this Study Guide.

Residence Of Individuals, Including Part Year, Sojourner, And Deemed Residents
- Read paragraph 1-94 to 1-101.
- Do Exercise One-6 and check the solution in this Study Guide.
- Read paragraph 1-102 to 1-106.
- Do Exercise One-7 and check the solution in this Study Guide.
- Read paragraph 1-107 and 1-108.
- Do Exercises One-8 and One-9 and check the solutions in this Study Guide.
- Read paragraph 1-109 to 1-115.
- Do Exercise One-10 and check the solution in this Study Guide.

Individuals With Dual Residency
- Read paragraph 1-116 to 1-119.
- Do Exercise One-11 and check the solution in this Study Guide.
- Read paragraph 1-120 to 1-122.
- Do Self Study Problems One-6 to One-8 and check the solutions in this Study Guide.

Residence Of Corporations And Trusts
- Read paragraph 1-123 to 1-129.
- Do Exercises One-12 to One-14 and check the solutions in this Study Guide.
- Do Self Study Problems One-9 and One-10 and check the solutions in this Study Guide.
- Read paragraph 1-130 to 1-132.
- Do Self Study Problem One-11 and check the solution in this Study Guide.

Alternative Concepts Of Income
- Read paragraph 1-133 to 1-141.

Net Income For Tax Purposes
- Read paragraph 1-142 to 1-167.
- Do Exercises One-15 to One-17 and check the solutions in this Study Guide.
- Do Self Study Problems One-12 to One-14 and check the solutions in this Study Guide.

Net Income To Taxable Income
- Read paragraph 1-168 and 1-169.
- Do Self Study Problem One-15 and check the solution in this Study Guide.

Principles Of Tax Planning
- Read paragraph 1-170 to 1-188.
- Do Exercises One-18 and One-19 and check the solutions in this Study Guide.

Abbreviations To Be Used
- Read paragraph 1-189.

To Complete This Chapter
- If you would like more practice in problem solving, do the Supplementary Self Study Problems for the chapter. These problems and solutions are available on MyLab.
- Review the Key Terms Used In This Chapter in the textbook at the end of Chapter 1. Consult the Glossary for the meaning of any key terms you do not know.
- Test yourself with the Chapter 1 Glossary Flashcards available on MyLab.
- Ensure you have achieved the Chapter 1 Learning Objectives listed in this Study Guide.
- As a review, we recommend you view the PowerPoint presentation for Chapter 1 that is on MyLab.

Practice Examination
- Write the Practice Examination for Chapter 1 that is on MyLab. Mark your examination using the Practice Examination Solution that is on MyLab.

Solutions to Chapter 1 Exercises

Exercise One - 1 Solution
Max Jordan, the Jordan family trust, and Jordan Enterprises Ltd. could be required to file income tax returns. Jordan's Hardware, Jordan & Jordan, and the Jordan Foundation are not taxable entities for income tax purposes.

Exercise One - 2 Solution
Under the GST legislation, all of the listed entities could be required to file a GST return. Where only individuals, corporations, and trusts can be required to file an income tax return, the definition of a person (i.e., taxable entity) is much broader for GST purposes. As is explained in detail in Chapter 21, whether an entity is required to file a GST return is dependent on the level of commercial activity.

Exercise One - 3 Solution

Federal Tax Payable [(15%)($27,000)]	$4,050
Provincial Tax Payable [(7.5%)($27,000)]	2,025
Total Tax Payable [(15% + 7.5%)($27,000)]	$6,075

Exercise One - 4 Solution

Margie's HST paid totals $22,360 [(13%)($172,000)]. Based on her Taxable Income of $895,000, this would represent an effective rate of 2.5 percent ($22,360 ÷ $895,000).

Jane's HST paid totals $3,575 [(13%)($27,500)]. On her Taxable Income of $18,000, this would be an effective rate of 19.9 percent ($3,575 ÷ $18,000).

Exercise One - 5 Solution

She is not correct. Under ITA 2(3) she would be subject to Canadian taxes on employment income earned in Canada.

Exercise One - 6 Solution

While the situation is not completely clear, it is likely that the CRA would conclude that Simon is no longer a Canadian resident. By retaining his residence, he has maintained one of the primary residential ties. However, the fact that he was not able to sell the property, accompanied by the long-term lease to a third party, would probably be sufficient evidence that this is not a significant residential tie. The retention of his membership in the CPA would be viewed as a secondary residential tie. However, S5-F1-C1 indicates that it would be unusual for a single secondary tie to be sufficient for an individual to be considered a Canadian resident.

Exercise One - 7 Solution

Jane did, in fact, sever most of her residential ties with Canada. This would suggest that she would not be considered a Canadian resident during the 26 months that she worked in Florida. However, the fact that she returned frequently to visit her boyfriend might lead the CRA to assess her on the basis of being a Canadian resident during this period, but it is not clear that such an assessment would be successful.

Exercise One - 8 Solution

Mark would be taxed on his worldwide income for the part of the year that he was resident in Canada. This would be the period January 1 through June 15, the date that his wife and children fly to the U.S. June 15 would be latest of the date that Mark leaves Canada (February 1), the date that Mark establishes U.S. residency (February 1), and the date that his wife and children depart Canada (June 15). It is unlikely that the fact that his house was not sold until a later date would influence his residence status.

Exercise One - 9 Solution

Mr. Kirsh will be a part year resident and liable for Canadian taxes on his worldwide income, including any income on the U.S. bank accounts, for the period September 1 through December 31 of the current year.

Exercise One - 10 Solution

While Ms. Blakey is the child of a Canadian high commissioner, it appears that she is no longer a dependant of this individual. It would also appear that she has income in excess of the base for the basic personal tax credit for 2020 of $12,069. As a consequence, she would not be considered a deemed resident under ITA 250(1).

Exercise One - 11 Solution

Case 1   As it appears that Dizzy has a permanent home in Los Angeles, the tie-breaker rules would indicate that he is a resident of the United States. As he has been in Canada for more than 183 days in 2020, the sojourner rules might have made him a deemed Canadian resident. However, the tie-breaker rules in the international tax treaty would override this.

The boarding rooms and hotels would not be considered a permanent home given that Dizzy never intended to stay for a long period of time.

Case 2 As Donna was in Canada for more than 183 days in 2020, she is a deemed resident through the application of the sojourner rule, and therefore a dual resident. In applying the tie-breaker rules, the first factor that is considered is in which country the individual has a permanent home. With respect to this criteria, Donna would not be considered to have a permanent home in either country. She gave up her lease on the New York property and, given that she only planned to stay for a short period of time, the Toronto apartment would not be considered a permanent home. In the absence of a permanent home in either country, the next factor to consider would be the location of Donna's "centre of vital interests". This would appear to be the U.S. and, given this, the tie-breaker rules would make Donna a resident of the U.S. and a non-resident of Canada.

Exercise One - 12 Solution

Roswell Ltd. is a U.S. resident because it was incorporated in that country. It is also a Canadian resident under the mind and management test. In such dual residency cases, the tie-breaker rule in the Canada/U.S. tax treaty indicates that the taxes will be assessed in the country of incorporation. That means that Roswell Ltd. would be considered a resident of the U.S. and a non-resident of Canada.

Exercise One - 13 Solution

As the company was incorporated in Canada after April 26, 1965, it would be deemed to be a Canadian resident under ITA 250(4). While the problem does not provide enough information to determine this, it is possible that the company has dual residency with the country or countries where it does business. This could result in the application of one or more international tax treaties. Note that, in general, where a corporation does business is not relevant to the residency decision.

Exercise One - 14 Solution

Case 1 Taxco would be considered a deemed resident of Canada by ITA 250(4) since it was incorporated in Canada after April 26, 1965. Taxco would also be considered a factual resident of the U.S. since its mind and management are located there. Article IV(3) of the Canada/U.S. tax treaty, however, breaks the tie in favor of the place of incorporation. Taxco would therefore be considered a resident of Canada and a non-resident of the U.S.

Case 2 Junko would be considered a factual resident of Canada since its mind and management are situated in Canada. Junko would also be considered a resident of the U.S. since it was incorporated there. Article IV(3) of the Canada/U.S. tax treaty, however, breaks the tie in favor of the place of incorporation. Junko would therefore be considered a resident of the U.S. for treaty purposes and a non-resident of Canada.

Exercise One - 15 Solution

Mr. Blanton's Net Income For Tax Purposes is calculated as follows:

Income Under ITA 3(a):		
Net Employment Income		$42,000
Income Under ITA 3(b):		
Taxable Capital Gains	$24,000	
Allowable Capital Losses	Nil	24,000
Balance From ITA 3(a) And (b)		$66,000
Subdivision e Deductions		(13,000)
Balance Under ITA 3(c)		$53,000
Deduction Under ITA 3(d):		
Business Loss		(15,000)
Net Income For Tax Purposes (Division B Income)		**$38,000**

Exercise One - 16 Solution

Ms. Stodard's Net Income For Tax Purposes would be calculated as follows:

Income Under ITA 3(a):		
Interest Income		$33,240
Income Under ITA 3(b):		
Taxable Capital Gains	$24,750	
Allowable Capital Losses	(19,500)	5,250
Balance From ITA 3(a) And (b)		$38,490
Subdivision e Deductions		Nil
Balance Under ITA 3(c)		$38,490
Deduction Under ITA 3(d):		
Rental Loss		(48,970)
Net Income For Tax Purposes (Division B Income)		**Nil**

She would have a non-capital loss carry over of $10,480 ($38,490- $48,970).

Exercise One - 17 Solution

Mrs. Bergeron's Net Income For Tax Purposes would be calculated as follows:

Income Under ITA 3(a):		
Net Employment Income		$42,680
Income Under ITA 3(b):		
Taxable Capital Gains	$27,400	
Allowable Capital Losses	(33,280)	Nil
Balance From ITA 3(a) And (b)		$42,680
Subdivision e Deductions		(8,460)
Balance Under ITA 3(c)		$34,220
Deduction Under ITA 3(d):		
Business Loss		(26,326)
Net Income For Tax Purposes (Division B Income)		**$ 7,894**

She would have an allowable capital loss carry over of $5,880 ($27,400 - $33,280).

Exercise One - 18 Solution

Mr. Chung is involved in income splitting, tax deferral, and possibly tax avoidance. He is getting the deduction from taxable income now and his wife will be taxed on the income in the future. All RRSP contributions normally create a tax deferral. The contribution will be deductible and the earnings on the contribution will accumulate on a tax free basis. However, all of these amounts will be taxable when they are withdrawn from the plan. There may also be tax avoidance. This will happen if his spouse is taxed at a lower rate than is currently applicable to Mr. Chung when the funds become taxable to her.

Exercise One - 19 Solution

As the dental plan is a benefit that can be received by Mr. Green without being taxed (private health care), tax avoidance is illustrated.

Solution for Self Study Problem One - 1

The HST is based on certain specified expenditures, not on the income level of the individual making the expenditure. In most cases, the proportion of an individual's income that is spent declines as the individual's level of income increases. This means that when a flat rate of tax is applied to a decreasing portion of the individual's income, the rate of taxation as a percentage of that income will decline.

For example, a 13 percent HST applied to $150,000 in expenditures made by a person with $250,000 in income would amount to only 7.8 percent of that person's income ($19,500 ÷ $250,000).

In contrast, that same 13 percent HST applied to $25,000 in expenditures made by a person with $20,000 in income would reflect a tax rate of 16.3 percent ($3,250 ÷ $20,000) of that person's income.

Solution for Self Study Problem One - 2

If tax simplification was the only objective, Mr. Right's proposal would be appropriate. However, such a system would be in conflict with other possible objectives of tax policy. For example, it would almost certainly be in conflict with the objective of fairness in that it would not provide for treating different types of income (capital gains vs. employment income) or people (the poor vs. the rich) in a suitable manner.

His system would also conflict with other objectives such as the goal of equity and after-tax income stability and the need for redistribution of income. In other words, in meeting the objective of simplicity, Mr. Right's system would ignore other possible objectives of a taxation system.

Solution for Self Study Problem One - 3

Note The descriptions of these tax measures are significantly simplified. The objective of this problem is to present the basic ideas so they can be understood without a detailed knowledge of tax, while still providing a basis for discussion. The following analysis is intended to be no more than suggestive of possible points that could be made. There are, of course, many alternative solutions.

Increase In Lifetime Capital Gains Deduction
Possible comments here would be as follows:

Neutrality The increase in the amount of the deduction for farmers and fishermen is not neutral. It favours farmers and fishermen with no benefits for any other group.

Simplicity The determination of what properties are considered to be qualified for this deduction involves some very complex legislation.

Home Accessibility Tax Credit
Possible comments here would be as follows:

Neutrality This provision is not neutral. Its benefits accrue exclusively to seniors, disabled individuals, and their families. Other individuals do not benefit from this provision.

Equity Or Fairness Disabled seniors face accessibility challenges that are not present for most other individuals. Given this, it can be argued that helping this particular group involves fairer treatment of these individuals.

Increase In Tax Free Savings Account Limits
Possible comments here would be as follows:

Equity Or Fairness It was clear that this change would not benefit low-income individuals. If an individual is making $20,000 per year, it is highly unlikely that this individual would have the first $5,500, much less an extra $4,500, to contribute. The reversal of the increase in 2016 was due in large part to its lack of fairness.

Simplicity This change gets high marks for simplicity. Amounts earned on the assets in the account are not subject to tax, either while the assets are in the plan or when the earnings are removed from the plan.

Solution for Self Study Problem One - 4

The principal other sources of information can be described as follows:

1. **Draft Legislation**   This legislation often provides the only information available with respect to announced budget changes that require application in the current taxation year. Explanatory notes are included with released draft legislation but are always set out separately.

2. **Income Tax Regulations**   These Regulations provide detailed guidance with respect to the implementation and administrative enforcement of the provisions of the *Income Tax Act*.

3. **International Tax Treaties**   These are a group of bilateral tax treaties between Canada and other countries. They are designed to avoid double taxation of taxpayers who pay taxes in more than one jurisdiction and to prevent international tax evasion.

4. **Income Tax Folios**   Income Tax Folios are a series of publications, introduced in 2013, that deal with technical issues. They are scheduled to replace existing Interpretation Bulletins (see item 5). The publications are organized into seven Series with each Series divided into Folios that contain Chapters on specific topics. As new Folios are introduced, the Interpretation Bulletins and Income Tax Technical Newsletters they are replacing are being cancelled.

5. **Interpretation Bulletins**   These IT-Bulletins give the CRA's interpretations of particular sections of the law that it administers and provide a vehicle for announcing significant changes in departmental interpretation. These Bulletins are being replaced by Income Tax Folios (see item 4).

6. **Income Tax Application Rules, 1971 (ITARs)**   These are a set of transitional rules that were introduced when the *Income Tax Act* was heavily revised at the end of 1971. The rules were largely designed to ensure that the provisions of the new *Act* were not applied retroactively. Although they continue to be of some significance in a limited number of situations, their general importance has been greatly diminished over time.

7. **Income Tax Technical News**   These newsletters were an occasional publication of the CRA that provided detailed guidance on various current issues. Existing newsletters are being cancelled as new Income Tax Folios (see item 4) are gradually incorporating their content.

8. **Information Circulars**   These Circulars provide information with respect to procedural matters related to both the *Income Tax Act* and the Canada Pension Plan.

9. **CRA News Releases, Tax Tips, and Fact Sheets**   The CRA provides News Releases, tax tips, and fact sheets on a variety of current subjects on its website.

10. **Guides And Pamphlets**   These non-technical publications provide guidance for the public on a variety of income tax issues (e.g., treatment of rental income).

11. **Advance Income Tax Rulings**   For a fee, the CRA will provide an Advance Income Tax Ruling on how it will tax a proposed transaction, subject to certain limitations and qualifications. These are rulings that are provided in response to requests from taxpayers.

12. **Technical Interpretations**   The CRA provides both written and telephone Technical Interpretations to the public free of charge. These Interpretations provide technical information on various current issues.

13. **Court Decisions**   Decisions by the Tax Court of Canada, the Federal Court, and the Supreme Court on income tax cases serve to establish precedents for dealing with particular tax issues.

Solution for Self Study Problem One - 5

Note to students: The purpose of this problem is to give you some practical examples of how to identify that part of the Income Tax Act where you are likely to find guidance on the income tax outcome. Specific references have been added for information purposes only. You will not be required to reference any provisions of the *Income Tax Act* in this tax course, although we will continue to provide income tax references.

(a) You spent $15,000 to landscape around the building in which your business is carried on. **Answer:** Subdivision b (paragraph 20(1)(aa))

(b) Someone told you that you could only deduct 50% of any business related meals. **Answer:** Subdivision f (section 67.1)

(c) You became a member of a partnership this year and want to contribute some land you own to it. **Answer:** Subdivision j (section 97)

(d) Your employer advises you that you now qualify for the company stock option plan. **Answer:** Subdivision a (section 7)

(e) Your spouse was unemployed and received employment insurance payments. **Answer:** Subdivision d (subparagraph 56(1)(a)(iv))

(f) One of your parents passed away and you have been named as the executor. **Answer:** Subdivisions f (section 70) and k (section 104)

(g) Your employer provides you with a company owned car for you to use in your employment duties. **Answer:** Subdivision a (Paragraphs 6(1)(e) and (k) and subsection 6(2))

(h) You sold the home you have lived in for the last 10 years and purchased another one. **Answer:** Subdivision c (paragraph 40(2)(b) and the definition of "principal residence" in section 54)

(i) You were audited by the CRA. It cost you $2,000 to have advisors represent you in dealing with the CRA. You wonder if you can deduct the fees. **Answer:** Subdivision e (paragraph 60(o))

(j) You purchased some shares of a major Canadian public company last year and made money selling them this year. You also received dividends from the company earlier this same year. **Answer:** Subdivision b and h for the dividends received (paragraph 12(1)(j) and section 82) and Subdivision c for the sale of the shares (sections 38, 39, and 40)

(k) Your parents created a family trust years ago and named you a beneficiary. You received a cheque from the trust this year for your part of the trust income. **Answer:** Subdivision b and k (paragraph 12(1)(m) and section 104)

(l) You own shares in a family operated company. The company redeemed half of your shares this year. **Answer:** Subsection b and h (paragraph 12(1)(j) and subsection 84(3))

(m) You paid $4,500 in child care expenses this year for your four-year-old daughter. **Answer:** Subdivision e (section 63)

(n) You received $6,000 in Canada Child Benefit payments from the federal government. **Answer:** You would look to subdivision d. If the Canada Child Benefit is to be included in income and taxed, it must be found in that subdivision. Since it is not in that subdivision the amount is not required to be included in income

(o) A family friend asked for your help. She had lost her job after 10 years of service but had been given a large cheque in recognition of those years of service. **Answer:** Subdivision d (subparagraph 56(1)(a)(ii))

Solution for Self Study Problem One - 6

S5-F1-C1 indicates that, in general, the CRA will view an individual as becoming a non-resident on the latest of three dates:

- The date the individual leaves Canada.
- The date the individual's spouse or common-law partner and dependants leave Canada.
- The date the individual becomes a resident of another country.

As Paul's wife and daughter did not leave Canada, it would appear that the CRA would take the position that Paul did not stop being a resident of Canada.

As he purchased a house in the U.S., it is possible that he will also be viewed as a resident of that jurisdiction. If this is the case, the tie-breaker rules that are contained in the tax treaty between Canada and the U.S. tax treaty must be applied. As Paul has a permanent home available in both locations, we need to apply the centre of vital interests criterion. The personal ties appear to be stronger in Canada, so it is likely that the CRA would conclude that the centre of vital interests is Canada. Given this, Paul would not be considered to be resident in the U.S.

Based on this conclusion, Paul should report his worldwide income in Canada and claim a foreign tax credit for any U.S. tax paid on his employment income while he was living and working in the U.S.

Solution for Self Study Problem One - 7

Mr. Aiken And Mr. Baker
Assuming that their respective moves were permanent in nature, both Mr. Aiken and Mr. Baker would be treated as part year residents. This means that they would be considered residents of Canada only for that portion of the year that they were actually in Canada. As a result, they will be liable for Canadian taxes only for a part of the current year. The prorating of deductions and credits are determined in accordance with ITA 114 and ITA 118.91.

Mr. Chase
While Mr. Chase was in Canada for the same number of days as the other individuals, the fact that he was present only on a temporary basis makes him subject to the sojourning rule. Under this rule [see ITA 250(1)(a)], he will be considered a resident for the full year if he sojourns in Canada for 183 days or more during any calendar year. As Mr. Chase was present for 192 days, he would be viewed as a Canadian resident throughout the year.

However, as he appears to also be a resident of the U.S., his dual residency status would be resolved by the tie-breaker rules in the Canada/U.S. tax treaty. As he only has a permanent home in the U.S., the tie-breaker rules would deem Mr. Chase not to be a resident of Canada. This means that he would be taxed in the U.S.

Solution for Self Study Problem One - 8

A. Jane Smith would be deemed a Canadian resident because she is a dependent child of a Canadian ambassador [ITA 250(1)(f)].

B. Marvin Black would not be considered a resident of Canada as he does not live in Canada. He would not be a deemed resident as S5-F1-C1 makes it clear that days spent commuting to Canada to earn employment income do not count as sojourning in Canada. However, he would likely be subject to Canadian taxation on the employment income earned in Canada [ITA 2(3)(a)].

C. John Leather would be considered a resident of Canada for the part of the year until September 12. As his presence in Canada during the first part of the year was not on a part time basis, he would not fall under the sojourning rules.

D. Members of the Canadian Armed Forces are deemed to be Canadian residents without regard to where they actually live. As Francine Donaire is exempt from French taxation due to her relationship to a deemed resident, she is a deemed resident of Canada [ITA 250(1)(g)].

E. More information would be required here. Depending on the nature of his stay in Canada, Robert could either be a part year resident of Canada or, alternatively, a non-resident earning employment income in Canada. If he established sufficient residential ties in Canada, it is possible that he would be viewed as a resident during his short stay. The importance of this is that, under this interpretation of the facts, he would be subject to Canadian income tax on his worldwide income during his stay. Alternatively, if he is not considered a resident during his stay in Canada, he is likely to be subject to Canadian tax on only his Canadian employment income.

F. The fact that Susan Allen is a Canadian citizen is irrelevant to the determination of residency. Since she appears to have no residential ties with Canada, she would not be considered a Canadian resident.

Solution for Self Study Problem One - 9

A. As AMT Ltd. was incorporated prior to April 27, 1965, it is not automatically considered to be a resident of Canada. However, under Canadian legislation the company would be deemed a Canadian resident based on the fact that the mind and management was in Canada subsequent to that date. [ITA 250(4)(a) and(c)].

   As the mind and management is now in the U.S., it would also be considered a U.S. resident. Given this dual residency, the tie-breaker rules in the Canada/U.S. tax treaty resolve the situation by making the company a resident of its country of incorporation. This would result in AMT being considered a resident of Canada.

B. UIF Inc. was not incorporated in Canada and its mind and management are not currently within Canada. Therefore, UIF Inc. would not be considered a Canadian resident.

C. BDT Ltd. would be deemed a Canadian resident. This is because it was incorporated in Canada subsequent to April 26, 1965. [ITA 250(4)(a)]. However, as the mind and management is now in the U.S., it would also be considered a U.S. resident. Given this dual residency, the tie-breaker rules in the Canada/U.S. tax treaty resolve the situation by making the company a resident of its country of incorporation. This would result in BDT being considered a resident of Canada.

D. While QRS Inc. was not incorporated in Canada, it would appear that its mind and management are located in Ontario. However, as it was incorporated in New York state, it will also be considered a resident of the U.S. As noted previously, in such cases, the tie-breaker rules in the Canada/U.S. tax treaty would make the company a resident of the U.S. as that is the country of incorporation and not a Canadian resident.

Solution for Self Study Problem One - 10

Case A
Mr. Salazar is not a resident of Canada. Commuting across the border for employment purposes is not considered sojourning (S5-F1-C1). However, unless he is exempted by the Canada/U.S. tax treaty, he would be subject to Canadian taxation on the employment income he earns in Windsor.

With respect to the treaty exemption, his employment income exceeds $10,000 and he is physically present in Canada for more than 183 days in the year. Given these facts, he would not qualify for the treaty exemption.

Case B

The information suggests that Mr. Wills made a clean break with Canada on September 1 of the current year. As a consequence, he would be considered a Canadian resident for the portion of the current year prior to his departure and would be taxed on his worldwide income for this period. For the portion of the year subsequent to his departure, he would no longer be considered a Canadian resident.

Case C

Joan Brothers would be deemed to be a Canadian resident under ITA 250(1)(f) because she is a dependent child of an officer or servant of Canada who is deemed to be a resident of Canada under ITA 250(1)(c)(i).

Case D

Brogan Inc. was not incorporated in Canada and its mind and management are not currently within Canada. As a result, the company is not a Canadian resident and none of its income would be subject to Canadian taxes.

Case E

Mercer Ltd. was incorporated prior to April 27, 1965, and, if it had not resided in or done business in Canada subsequent to that date, it would not be considered a resident of Canada. However, the fact that directors' meetings were held in Canada until May 1997 makes it a Canadian resident. As the mind and management are now in the U.S., it would also be considered a resident of that country.

In cases of dual residency for corporations, where a corporation could be considered a resident of both countries, the Canada/U.S. tax treaty indicates that the corporation will be deemed to be a resident only in the country in which it is incorporated. Mercer Ltd. would be a resident of Canada and its worldwide income would be subject to tax in Canada.

Case F

The Booker Manufacturing Company would be considered resident in Canada because of the location of its mind and management. However, as Booker was incorporated in the U.S., it would also be considered a resident of that country. In cases of dual residency for corporations, where a corporation could be considered a resident of both countries, the Canada/U.S. tax treaty indicates that the corporation will be deemed to be a resident only in the country in which it is incorporated. As a result, the company is not a Canadian resident and none of its income would be subject to Canadian taxes.

Solution for Self Study Problem One - 11

Solution to Case 1

Jim is a factual resident of the U.S. since his current family, home, social, and economic life is in the U.S. However, because of the 183 day sojourner rule of ITA 250(1)(a) Jim is also initially considered a deemed resident of Canada. This deemed residency status results in Jim being considered a dual resident of both Canada and the U.S. When this occurs you need to consider the tax treaty between the two countries, one of the purposes of which is to determine which country has the priority to tax that individual. The tie-breaker rule was briefly discussed at paragraph 1-119 and is easily resolved in this case using the first criteria of the "permanent home". Since Jim has a permanent home in the U.S. and none in Canada, the tax treaty resolves the dual residency problem in favour of the U.S. ITA 250(5) (discussed at paragraph 1-118) applies when a tax treaty resolved dual residency in favour of another country by then deeming the person to be a non-resident of Canada. This final step of the analysis overrides the sojourner rule.

Conclusion – Case 1

Jim is a deemed non-resident of Canada.

Solution to Case 2

U.S. federal tax law considers any corporation incorporated in the U.S. to be a resident of the U.S. Therefore, Sitcom will be a factual resident of the U.S. For Canadian tax purposes a corporation will be considered a deemed resident of Canada by either (1) incorporating in Canada after April 26, 1965 (ITA 250(4)(a)) or (2) by being factually resident in Canada, which can only occur if the majority of the members of the board of directors actually make decisions on behalf of the company in Canada. Since the majority of the directors meet in Canada to make decisions, the corporation is initially considered to be factually resident in Canada. We refer to this factual concept as the "mind and management" rule in paragraph 1-127.

Based on the facts, Sitcom Inc. is a dual resident – both a factual resident of the U.S. and Canada. When this occurs we must turn to the tax treaty. The tie-breaker rule in the Canada/US tax treaty resolves residency in favour of the country in which the company was incorporated. As a result, Sitcom is considered a resident of Canada. Since the tax treaty treats the company as only a resident of the U.S., ITA 250(5) once again applies to deem Sitcom to be a non-resident of Canada, overriding the mind and management factual residency determination.

Conclusion – Case 2

Sitcom Inc. is a deemed non-resident of Canada.

Solution to Case 3

There are no deemed residency rules in Canada for trusts. The determination of trust residency has been somewhat of a grey area until the 2012 decision of the Supreme Court of Canada in Fundy Settlement. In that decision the Supreme Court applied a factual residency test to trusts that is comparable to that of corporations. The test looks to where the important decisions are made, which is where the mind and management actually takes place. With corporations you look to the board of directors, and with trusts you look to the trustee or trustees where there are more than one. The creation of a trust outside Canada may result in the trust being considered a resident of that country and potentially liable to its tax subject to a tax treaty. Most tax treaties do not contemplate trust residence, meaning that decisions to determine which country has priority to tax are made by the competent authority, which is mentioned briefly in paragraph 1-119. If no tax treaty exists then a trust could potentially be resident in both countries.

In this case the sole trustee clearly has no real authority to make decisions with regard to the trust as they are made by Jan and Dean. Since Jan and Dean reside in Canada nd direct the trustee from Canada the trust would be considered a factual resident of Canada.

Conclusion – Case 3

The family trust is a factual resident of Canada.

Note for Case 3: We have purposefully avoided discussion of the non-resident trust rules of ITA 94, which is well beyond the scope of an introductory course on federal income taxation. Those complex rules, however, would only apply if the trust was a non-resident of Canada. Since our analysis has concluded that the trust is a resident of Canada, those rules would not have applied in any case.

Solution for Self Study Problem One - 12

Case A

The Case A solution would be calculated as follows:

Income Under ITA 3(a):		
Employment Income	$50,000	
Interest Income	12,000	$62,000
Income Under ITA 3(b):		
Taxable Capital Gains	$95,000	
Allowable Capital Losses	(73,000)	22,000
Balance From ITA 3(a) And (b)		$84,000
Subdivision e Deductions		(8,000)
Balance From ITA 3(c)		$76,000
Deductions Under ITA 3(d):		
Business Loss		(23,000)
Net Rental Loss		(5,000)
Net Income For Tax Purposes (Division B Income)		$48,000

In this Case, Mr. Dorne has no carry overs available.

Case B

The Case B solution would be calculated as follows:

Income Under ITA 3(a):		
Employment Income	$45,000	
Net Rental Income	23,000	$68,000
Income Under ITA 3(b):		
Taxable Capital Gains	$25,000	
Allowable Capital Losses	(46,000)	Nil
Balance From ITA 3(a) And (b)		$68,000
Subdivision e Deductions		(10,500)
Balance From ITA 3(c)		$ 57,500
Deduction Under ITA 3(d):		
Business Loss		(51,000)
Net Income For Tax Purposes (Division B Income)		$ 6,500

In this Case, Mr. Dorne has a carry over of unused allowable capital losses in the amount of $21,000 ($46,000 - $25,000). The lottery prize is not considered to be income for tax purposes.

Solution for Self Study Problem One - 13

Case A
The Case A solution would be calculated as follows:

Income Under ITA 3(a):		
Employment Income	$73,300	
Rental Income	8,300	$ 81,600
Income Under ITA 3(b):		
Taxable Capital Gains	$42,400	
Allowable Capital Losses	(18,600)	23,800
Balance From ITA 3(a) And (b)		$105,400
Subdivision e Deductions		(6,200)
Balance From ITA 3(c)		$ 99,200
Deduction Under ITA 3(d):		
Business Loss		(14,700)
Net Income For Tax Purposes (Division B Income)		$ 84,500

In this Case, Mr. Marks has no loss carry overs at the end of the year.

Case B
The Case B solution would be calculated as follows:

Income Under ITA 3(a):		
Employment Income	$41,400	
Rental Income	5,900	$47,300
Income Under ITA 3(b):		
Taxable Capital Gains	$ 7,800	
Allowable Capital Losses	(11,600)	Nil
Balance From ITA 3(a) And (b)		$47,300
Subdivision e Deductions		(2,800)
Balance From ITA 3(c)		$44,500
Deduction Under ITA 3(d):		
Business Loss		(4,700)
Net Income For Tax Purposes (Division B Income)		$39,800

In this Case, Mr. Marks has an allowable capital loss carry over of $3,800 ($7,800 - $11,600).

Case C
The Case C solution would be calculated as follows:

Income Under ITA 3(a):		
Employment Income	$89,400	
Rental Income	5,300	$ 94,700
Income Under ITA 3(b):		
Taxable Capital Gains	$23,700	
Allowable Capital Losses	(21,200)	2,500
Balance From ITA 3(a) and (b)		$ 97,200
Subdivision e Deductions		(22,400)
Balance From ITA 3(c)		$ 74,800
Deduction Under ITA 3(d):		
Business Loss		(112,600)
Net Income For Tax Purposes (Division B Income)		Nil

In this Case, Mr. Marks would have a business loss carry over in the amount of $37,800 ($74,800 - $112,600).

Case D

The Case D solution would be calculated as follows:

Income Under ITA 3(a):		
Employment Income		$34,300
Income Under ITA 3(b):		
Taxable Capital Gains	$24,700	
Allowable Capital Losses	(26,300)	Nil
Balance From ITA 3(a) And (b)		$34,300
Subdivision e Deductions		(6,400)
Balance From ITA 3(c)		$27,900
Deduction Under ITA 3(d):		
Business Loss		(47,800)
Rental Loss		(20,100)
Net Income For Tax Purposes (Division B Income)		Nil

Mr. Marks would have a carry over of business and rental losses in the amount of $40,000 ($27,900 - $47,800- $20,100) and of allowable capital losses in the amount of $1,600 ($24,700- $26,300).

Solution for Self Study Problem One - 14

Case 1

The Case 1 solution would be calculated as follows:

Income Under ITA 3(a):		
Net Employment Income	$123,480	
Interest Income	4,622	$128,102
Income Under ITA 3(b):		
Taxable Capital Gains	$ 24,246	
Allowable Capital Losses	(4,835)	19,411
Balance From ITA 3(a) And (b)		$147,513
Child Care Costs		(9,372)
Balance From ITA 3(c) And Net Income For Tax Purposes		$138,141

In this Case, Mr. Comfort has no loss carry overs at the end of the year.

Case 2

The Case 2 solution would be calculated as follows:

Income Under ITA 3(a):		
Net Business Income		$72,438
Income Under ITA 3(b):		
Taxable Capital Gains	$4,233	
Allowable Capital Loss	(7,489)	Nil
Balance From ITA 3(a) And (b)		$72,438
RRSP Contributions		(22,000)
Balance From ITA 3(c)		$50,438
Deduction Under ITA 3(d):		
Net Rental Loss		(9,846)
Net Income For Tax Purposes (Division B Income)		$40,592

In this Case, Mr. Comfort has a carry over of $3,256 ($7,489- $4,233) in unused allowable capital losses.

Case 3

The Case 3 solution would be calculated as follows:

Income Under ITA 3(a):		
Net Employment Income		$47,234
Income Under ITA 3(b):		
Taxable Capital Gains [(1/2)($12,472)]	$6,236	
Allowable Capital Losses [(1/2)($9,332)]	(4,666)	1,570
Balance From ITA 3(a) and (b)		$48,804
Child Care Costs		(3,922)
Balance From ITA 3(c)		$44,882
Deduction Under ITA 3(d):		
Net Business Loss		(68,672)
Net Income For Tax Purposes (Division B Income)		Nil

In this Case, Mr. Comfort would have a business loss carry over in the amount of $23,790 ($68,672 - $44,882).

Case 4

The Case 4 solution would be calculated as follows:

Income Under ITA 3(a):		
Interest Income	$ 6,250	
Net Business Income	43,962	$50,212
Income Under ITA 3(b):		
Taxable Capital Gains [(1/2)($12,376)]	$ 6,188	
Allowable Capital Losses		
[(1/2)($23,874)]	(11,937)	Nil
Balance From ITA 3(a) And (b)		$50,212
Moving Expenses		(7,387)
Balance From ITA 3(c)		$42,825
Deduction Under ITA 3(d):		
Net Rental Loss		(72,460)
Net Income For Tax Purposes (Division B Income)		Nil

Mr. Comfort would have a rental loss carry over in the amount of $29,635 ($72,460 - $42,825) and unused allowable capital losses in the amount of $5,749 ($11,937 - $6,188).

Solution for Self Study Problem One - 15

Part 1
Required: Determine Vincent's income for the 2020 year – follow the ITA 3 format shown in Figure 1-4 in Chapter 1. Also indicate whether or not there are any loss carryovers.

Solution

ITA 3(a)

Employment income ($82,000 – 7,100)	$74,900	
Business income ($105,000 – 49,000)	56,000	$130,900

ITA 3(b)

Taxable Capital Gains		$58,000	
Less:			
Allowable capital losses	$104,000		
Less: ABIL	37,000	67,000	Nil
Total of ITA 3(a) and 3(b)			$130,900
Subdivision e deduction			
Deductible RRSP Contributions		$22,000	
Deductible moving expenses		9,200	31,200

ITA 3(c) $ 99,700

Rental loss ($37,000 – 12,000)	$25,000	
Investment loss dividends ($19,000 – 10,000)	9,000	
Allowable business investment loss	37,000	71,000

ITA 3(d) – Income for the year $ 28,700

Net Capital loss Carryover = $ 11,000 ($67,000 - $58,000)

There are no other loss carryovers

Part 2

Required – The CRA subsequently audited Vincent and determined that the amount reported as an ABIL was a regular capital loss. What are the results?

Solution

ITA 3(a)

Employment income ($82,000 – 7,100)	$74,900	
Business income ($105,000 – 49,000)	56,000	$130,900

ITA 3(b)

Taxable Capital Gains		$58,000	
Less:			
Allowable capital losses	$104,000		
Less: ABIL	Nil	104,000	Nil
Total of ITA 3(a) and 3(b)			$130,900
Subdivision e deduction			
Deductible RRSP Contributions		$22,000	
Deductible moving expenses		9,200	31,200

ITA 3(c) $ 99,700

Rental loss ($37,000 – 12,000)	$25,000	
Investment loss dividends ($19,000 – 10,000)		9,000
Allowable business investment loss	Nil	34,000

ITA 3(d) – Net income for the year $ 65,700

Net Capital loss Carryover = $ 46,000 ($104,000- $58,000)

There are no other loss carryovers

You can see that the reclassification of the ABIL to a regular capital loss results in $37,000 of additional net income and an increase in the net capital loss of $37,000.

Part 3
Required – Assume that the CRA never audited Vincent but the accountant spotted three errors as follows:

1. The deductible business expenses should have been $149,000 not $49,000;
2. Deductible spousal support in the amount of $24,000 was missed;
3. Taxable capital gains were overstated by $17,000 because of certain reserves.

Solution

ITA 3(a)

Employment income ($82,000 – 7,100)		$74,900

ITA 3(b)

Taxable Capital Gains		$41,000	
Less:			
Allowable capital losses	$104,000		
Less: ABIL	37,000	67,000	Nil
Total of ITA 3(a) and 3(b)			$74,900
Subdivision e deduction			
Deductible RRSP Contributions		$22,000	
Spousal Support		24,000	
Deductible moving expenses		9,200	55,200
ITA 3(c)			$19,700

Business loss ($149,000 – 105,000)	$56,000	
Rental loss ($37,000 – 12,000)	25,000	
Investment loss dividends ($19,000 – 10,000)	9,000	
Allowable business investment loss	37,000	127,000

ITA 3(d) – Income for the year		$ Nil

Net Capital loss Carryover = $ 26,000 ($67,000 - $41,000)

Non-capital loss Carryover = $ 107,300 ($127,000 – $19,700)

Chapter 2 Learning Objectives

After completing Chapter 2, you should be able to:

1. Explain when an individual is required to file an income tax return (paragraph [P here-after] P 2-8 to 2-15).
2. List the dates on which income tax returns must be filed by living and deceased individuals (P 2-16 to 2-21).
3. Explain the nature of, and need for, withholding for income tax (P 2-22 to 2-28).
4. Explain the circumstances which result in an individual having to make income tax instalment payments (P 2-29 to 2-33).
5. Calculate the amount of any income tax instalment payments required for individual taxpayers and determine their due date (P 2-34 to 2-44).

6. Explain how the prescribed interest rates are used to calculate interest on amounts owing to and from the CRA (P 2-45 to 2-51).
7. Calculate the penalties that will be assessed for the late filing of income tax returns and large late and deficient instalments (P 2-52 to 2-56).
8. Identify the dates on which balances owing by living and deceased individuals are due (P 2-57 and 2-61).
9. Identify the dates on which income tax returns must be filed by corporations and the filing alternatives that are available (P 2-62 to 2-68).
10. Calculate the amount of income tax instalment payments required for corporations, including small CCPCs (P 2-69 to 2-74).

11. Identify the dates on which balances owing by corporations are due (P 2-75 and 2-76).
12. Calculate the interest and penalties that will be assessed on late tax payments and for the late filing of corporate income tax returns (P 2-77 to 2-80).
13. Explain the general filing and payment requirements for testamentary and inter vivos trusts (P 2-81 to 2-88).
14. Explain the circumstances in which a taxpayer is required to file an information return (P 2-89).
15. Describe the record keeping requirements of the CRA (P 2-90 and 2-91).

16. Briefly describe the My Account and My Business Account services available on the CRA website (P 2-92).
17. Describe the Notice of Assessment, Notice of Reassessment and explain the reassessment period (P 2-93 to 2-95).
18. Explain when interest is paid on refunds and how it is calculated (P 2-96 to 2-101).
19. Explain how to make adjustments to previously filed tax returns (P 2-102 to 2-105).
20. Explain the initial procedures for disputing an assessment and the procedures for filing a notice of objection (P 2-106 to 2-1 21).

21. Describe further appeals procedures, including those made to the Tax Court of Canada, the Federal Court of Appeals, and the Supreme Court of Canada (P 2-1 22 to 2-131).
22. Explain the difference between tax evasion, avoidance and planning, including the concepts involved in the General Anti-Avoidance Rule (P 2-132 to 2-141).
23. Describe the collection and enforcement procedures available to the CRA (P 2-142 to 2-147).
24. Describe some of the penalties that can be assessed including those applicable to tax advisors and tax return preparers (P 2-148 to 2-153).
25. Briefly describe the taxpayer relief provisions (P 2-154 to 2-157).

How to Work Through Chapter 2

We recommend the following approach in dealing with the material in this chapter:

Administration Of The Department

- Read paragraph 2-1 to 2-7 (in the textbook).

Filing Requirements For Living And Deceased Individuals

- Read paragraph 2-8 to 2-18.
- Do Exercise Two-1 (in the textbook) and check the solution in this Study Guide.
- Read paragraph 2-19 to 2-21.
- Do Exercise Two-2 and check the solution in this Study Guide.

Withholdings For Income Tax

- Read paragraph 2-22 to 2-28.

Instalment Payments For Individuals

- Read paragraph 2-29 to 2-44.
- Do Exercises Two-3 to Two-5 and check the solutions in this Study Guide.
- Do Self Study Problem Two-1 which is available on MyLab and check the solution in this Study Guide.

Interest, Penalties And Balance Due Dates For Living And Deceased Individuals

- Read paragraph 2-45 to 2-56.
- Do Exercise Two-6 and check the solution in this Study Guide.
- Read paragraph 2-57 to 2-61.

Returns And Payments, Including Instalments, For Corporations

- Read paragraph 2-62 to 2-74.
- Do Exercises Two-7 and Two-8 and check the solutions in this Study Guide.

Balance Due Dates For Corporations

- Read paragraph 2-75 and 2-76.
- Do Exercise Two-9 and check the solution in this Study Guide.

Interest And Penalties For Corporations

- Read paragraph 2-77 to 2-80.
- Do Self Study Problems Two-2 to Two-4 and check the solutions in this Study Guide.

Returns And Payments For Trusts

- Read paragraph 2-81 to 2-88.
- Do Self Study Problem Two-5 and check the solution in this Study Guide.

General Administrative Issues, Including The "My Account" Service, Assessments, Refunds, And Adjustments To Returns

- Read paragraph 2-89 to 2-105.

Appeals And Notices Of Objection

- Read paragraph 2-106 to 2-121.
- Do Exercise Two-10 and check the solution in this Study Guide.
- Read paragraph 2-122 to 2-131.
- Do Self Study Problem Two-6 and check the solution in this Study Guide.

Tax Evasion, Avoidance, And Planning

- Read paragraph 2-132 to 2-141.

Collection And Enforcement

- Read paragraph 2-142 to 2-153.
- Do Self Study Problem Two-7 and check the solution in this Study Guide.

Taxpayer Relief Provisions

- Read paragraph 2-154 to 2-157.

To Complete This Chapter

- If you would like more practice in problem solving, do the Supplementary Self Study Problems for the chapter. These problems and solutions are available on MyLab.
- Review the Key Terms Used In This Chapter in the text book at the end of Chapter 2. Consult the Glossary for the meaning of any key terms you do not know.
- Test yourself with the Chapter 2 Glossary Flashcards available on MyLab.
- Ensure you have achieved the Chapter 2 Learning Objectives listed in this Study Guide.
- As a review, we recommend you view the PowerPoint presentation for Chapter 2 that is on MyLab.

Practice Examination

- Write the Practice Examination for Chapter 2 that is on MyLab. Mark your examination using the Practice Examination Solution that is also on MyLab.

Solutions to Chapter 2 Exercises

Exercise Two - 1 Solution
While Mr. Katarski's 2020 tax return does not have to be filed until June 15, 2021, his tax liability must be paid by April 30, 2021, in order to avoid the assessment of interest.

Exercise Two - 2 Solution
Sally Cheung's 2020 tax return must be filed by the later of six months after the date of her death and her normal filing date. As her husband has business income, her normal filing date is June 15, 2021. The later of the two dates would be August 15, 2021, six months after the date of her death. Her final return for 2021 would be due on June 15, 2022.

Exercise Two - 3 Solution
She is not required to make instalment payments as long as her current year (2020) net tax owing is less than $3,000.

Exercise Two - 4 Solution
As his net tax owing in the current year and one of the two preceding years is in excess of $3,000, he is required to make instalment payments. The minimum amount would be based on the preceding taxation year's net tax owing of $1,500, and would be $375 ($1,500 ÷ 4) per quarter. They are due on March 15, June 15, September 15, and December 15.

Exercise Two - 5 Solution

The net tax owing amounts can be calculated as follows:

2018 $1,000 ($53,000 − $52,000)
2019 $7,000 ($59,000 − $52,000)
2020 $4,000 ($64,000 − $60,000)

As the net tax owing exceeds $3,000 in the current year and the first preceding year, instalments are required. The three alternatives for calculating instalment payments are as follows:

- Based on the estimate for the current year, the instalments would be $1,000 ($4,000 ÷ 4).
- Based on the estimate for the preceding year, the instalments would be $1,750 ($7,000 ÷ 4).
- Based on the second preceding year, the first two instalments would each be $250 ($1,000 ÷ 4). The second two instalments would each be $3,250 {[1/2][$7,000 − ($250)(2)]}. The instalments would total $7,000, the same amount as under the preceding year alternative.

While the first two instalments are lower under the second preceding year alternative, the total for all the instalments under this alternative is $7,000, higher than the $4,000 total under the current year alternative. The current year alternative would be the best. They are due on March 15, June 15, September 15, and December 15. Note, however, that if the estimated taxes payable are below actual taxes payable for 2020, instalment interest may be charged.

Exercise Two - 6 Solution

Given the size of her net tax owing, ITA 163.1 will not be applicable and there will be no penalties for late instalments. The penalty for late filing will be based on the number of **complete** months of non-payment, which is two. It will be equal to 7 percent of taxes payable (5 percent, plus 1 percent per month). If in one of the three preceding taxation years she has also late filed, the penalty could be 14 percent (10 percent, plus 2 percent per month) if the CRA has already sent a formal demand to file a return.

Interest will be assessed on the deficient instalments, calculated from the date on which the instalment was due and continuing until the balance due date. Interest will also be assessed on the balance owing on her filing date, along with the penalty for late filing. This interest will be assessed for the period May 1 through July 20, 2021. All of the interest will be calculated at the prescribed rate plus 4 percent.

Exercise Two - 7 Solution

Not Small CCPC   If we assume that Madco Ltd. is not a small CCPC, the first two instalments would be due on the last day of January and February 2020. They would be based on the second preceding year and would be $2,667 each ($32,000 ÷ 12). The remaining 10 instalments would be based on the preceding year, less the $5,334 paid in the first two instalments. The amount would be $5,367 [($59,000 − $5,334) ÷ 10] and the instalments would be due on the last day of each month for March to December, 2020.

Small CCPC   If we assume that Madco Ltd. is a small CCPC, the first instalment would be due on March 31, 2020. The amount would be based on the second preceding year and would equal $8,000 ($32,000 ÷ 4). The remaining three instalments would be based on the preceding year, less the amount paid in the first instalment. These payments would be equal to $17,000 [($59,000 − $8,000) ÷ 3]. These payments would be due on the last days of June, September, and December 2020.

Note that when the initial instalment(s) are based on the second preceding year, the total amount of instalments will be the same as when all of the instalments are based on the first preceding year. However, using the second preceding year is preferable in that it provides some deferral of taxes.

Exercise Two - 8 Solution

Not Small CCPC If we assume that Fadco is not a small CCPC, the minimum instalments would be based on the estimated taxes payable for the taxation year ending November 30, 2020. The amount would be $1,417 ($17,000 ÷ 12) and the instalments would be due on the last day of each month beginning in December 2019 and continuing to November 2020. Note that if the estimate of tax payable for 2020 is too low, interest may be assessed on the deficiency.

Small CCPC If we assume that Fadco is a small CCPC, the instalments would be based on the estimated taxes payable for the taxation year ending November 30, 2020. The amount would be $4,250 ($17,000 ÷ 4). These amounts would be due on the last days of February, May, August, and November 2020.

Exercise Two - 9 Solution

Radco Inc.'s tax return is due six months after the fiscal year end, on July 31, 2020. Unless Radco is able to claim the small business deduction, the final payment on their taxes is due two months after the year end, on March 31, 2020. If Radco is eligible for the small business deduction, the final payment can be deferred for an additional month, to April 30, 2020, provided the Taxable Income for the preceding taxation year did not exceed $500,000.

Exercise Two -10 Solution

The notice of objection must be filed by the later of:

- 90 days after the date on the Notice of Reassessment (August 13, 2022); or
- one year after the due date for filing the return that is being reassessed (April 30, 2022).

The later of these two dates is August 13, 2022.

Solution to Self Study Problem Two - 1

Need For Instalments

Instalments are required when an individual's "net tax owing" exceeds $3,000 in the current year and in either of the two preceding years. In somewhat simplified terms, "net tax owing" is defined as the combined federal and provincial taxes payable, less amounts withheld under ITA 153. Mr. Grafton's net tax owing figures are as follows:

2018 = $1,700 ($31,500 − $29,800)
2019 = $8,400 ($14,600 − $6,200)
2020 = $3,100 ($27,400 − $24,300) Estimated

As Mr. Grafton's net tax owing in 2020 (the current year) and his net tax owing in 2019 (one of the two preceding years) is greater than $3,000, he is required to make instalment payments.

Amounts

If Mr. Grafton bases the first two quarterly payments on the 2018 net tax owing, they would only be $425 each ($1,700 ÷ 4). However, the payments for the last two quarters would be $3,775 each {[$8,400 − (2)($425)] ÷ 2}, resulting in total instalment payments of $8,400.

A preferable alternative would be to base the payments on the net tax owing for 2020. These payments would be $775 each ($3,100 ÷ 4), for a total of $3,100.

Payment Dates

The quarterly payments would be due on March 15, June 15, September 15, and December 15.

Solution to Self Study Problem Two - 2

Case One

1. As the corporation's tax payable for both the current and the preceding year exceeds $3,000, instalments are required. As the corporation is a small CCPC, instalments will be quarterly.

2. The three acceptable alternatives would be as follows:

   - Quarterly instalments of $27,405 ($109,620 ÷ 4) based on the current year estimate.
   - Quarterly instalments of $31,290 ($125,160 ÷ 4) based on the first preceding year.
   - One instalment of $25,305 ($101,220 ÷ 4) based on the second preceding year, followed by three instalments of $33,285 [($125,160 − $25,305) ÷ 3] for a total of $125,160.

3. The best alternative in terms of minimum instalments would be four instalments of $27,405, for total payments of $109,620.

   The instalments are due on March 31, June 30, September 30, and December 31, 2020.

Case Two

1. As the corporation's tax payable for both the current and the preceding year exceeds $3,000, instalments are required. As the corporation is a small CCPC, instalments will be quarterly.

2. The three acceptable alternatives would be as follows:

   - Quarterly instalments of $27,405 ($109,620 ÷ 4) based on the current year estimate.
   - Quarterly instalments of $26,075 ($104,300 ÷ 4) based on the first preceding year.
   - One instalment of $25,305 ($101,220 ÷ 4) based on the second preceding year, followed by three instalments of $26,331.67 [($104,300 − $25,305) ÷ 3] for a total of $104,300.

3. The best alternative would be one payment of $25,305, followed by three payments of $26,331.67. While the total instalments are the same, $104,300, in both the second and third alternatives, the third alternative is preferable because the first payment is lower. This provides a small amount of tax deferral.

   The instalments are due on March 31, June 30, September 30, and December 31, 2020.

Case Three

1. As the corporation's tax payable for both the current and the preceding year exceeds $3,000, instalments are required. As the corporation is not a small CCPC, monthly instalments are required.

2. The three acceptable alternatives would be as follows:

   - Monthly instalments of $9,135 ($109,620 ÷ 12) based on the current year estimate.
   - Monthly instalments of $10,430 ($125,160 ÷ 12) based on the first preceding year.
   - Two monthly instalments of $8,435 ($101,220 ÷ 12) based on the second preceding year, followed by 10 monthly instalments of $10,829 {[$125,160 − (2)($8,435)] ÷ 10} for a total of $125,160.

3. The best alternative in terms of minimum instalments would be 12 instalments of $9,135, resulting in a total of $109,620 in instalment payments.

   The instalments would be due on the last day of each month, beginning in January 2020.

Case Four

1. As the corporation's tax payable for both the current and the preceding year exceeds $3,000, instalments are required. As the corporation is not a small CCPC, monthly instalments are required.

2. The three acceptable alternatives would be as follows:

   - Monthly instalments of $9,135 ($109,620 ÷ 2) based on the current year estimate.
   - Monthly instalments of $8,691.67 ($104,300 ÷ 12) based on the first preceding year.
   - Two monthly instalments of $8,435 ($101,220 ÷ 12) based on the second preceding year, followed by 10 monthly instalments of $8,743 {[$104,300 − (2)($8,435)] ÷ 10} for a total of $104,300.

3. The best alternative would be 2 payments of $8,435, followed by 10 payments of $8,743. While the total instalments are the same, $104,300, in both the second and third alternatives, the third alternative is preferable because the first two payments are lower. As indicated in Case Two, this provides a small amount of tax deferral.

   The instalments would be due on the last day of each month, beginning in January 2020.

Solution to Self Study Problem Two - 3

Case One

1. The individual's net tax owing in each of the three years is as follows:

   2018 = Nil ($72,300 − $73,700)
   2019 = $6,200 ($89,400 − $83,200)
   2020 = $3,300 ($78,300 − $75,000)

   As the net tax owing exceeds $3,000 in the current year and one of the two preceding years, instalments are required.

2. The three alternatives would be:

   - Quarterly instalments of $825 ($3,300 ÷ 4) based on the current year estimate.
   - Quarterly instalments of $1,550 ($6,200 ÷ 4) based on the first preceding year.
   - Based on the second preceding year, the first two instalments would be nil. The remaining two instalments would be $3,100 each [($6,200 - Nil) ÷ 2] for a total of $6,200.

3. The best alternative to minimize instalments would be four quarterly instalments of $825 for a total of $3,300.

   The instalments are due on March 15, June 15, September 15, and December 15.

Case Two

1. The individual's net tax owing in each of the three years is as follows:

   2018 = $7,200 ($72,300 − $65,100)
   2019 = Nil ($89,400 − $90,100)
   2020 = $6,400 ($78,300 − $71,900)

   As the net tax owing exceeds $3,000 in the current year and one of the two preceding years, instalments are required.

2. The three alternatives would be:

   - Quarterly instalments of $1,600 ($6,400 ÷ 4) based on the current year estimate.
   - Quarterly instalments of nil based on the first preceding year.
   - Two quarterly instalments of $1,800 ($7,200 ÷ 4) based on the second preceding year. No further instalments would be required.

3. The best alternative would be quarterly instalments of nil based on the first preceding year.

Case Three

1. As the corporation's tax payable for both the current and the preceding year exceeds $3,000, instalments are required. As the corporation is a small CCPC, instalments will be quarterly.

2. The three acceptable alternatives would be as follows:

   - Quarterly instalments of $19,575 ($78,300 ÷ 4) based on the current year estimate.
   - Quarterly instalments of $22,350 ($89,400 ÷ 4) based on the first preceding year.
   - One instalment of $18,075 ($72,300 ÷ 4) based on the second preceding year, followed by three instalments of $23,775 [($89,400 − $18,075) ÷ 3] for a total of $89,400.

3. The best alternative would be four instalments of $19,575 for total payments of $78,300.

   The instalments are due on March 31, June 30, September 30, and December 31.

Case Four

1. As the corporation's tax payable for both the current and the preceding year exceeds $3,000, instalments are required. As the corporation is not a CCPC and is not eligible for the small business deduction, monthly instalments are required.

2. The three acceptable alternatives would be as follows:

   - Monthly instalments of $6,525 ($78,300 ÷ 2) based on the current year estimate.
   - Monthly instalments of $6,208.33 ($74,500 ÷ 2) based on the first preceding year.
   - Two monthly instalments of $6,025 ($72,300 ÷ 2) based on the second preceding year, followed by 10 monthly instalments of $6,245 {[($74,500 − (2)($6,025)] ÷ 10} for a total of $74,500.

3. In terms of minimizing instalment payments, both the second and third alternatives involve paying $74,500, which is less than the payment of $78,300 under the first alternative. While the problem does not ask you to take into consideration deferral, the third alternative would be the best in that the first two payments are lower.

   The instalments would be due on the last day of each month, beginning in January.

Solution to Self Study Problem Two - 4

Case A

The individual's actual and estimated net tax owing is equal to the Tax Payable in each of the three years as follows:

2018 = $18,000
2019 = $14,400
2020 = $13,500 (Estimated)

As the estimated tax payable for the current year and the actual tax payable for the preceding year exceeds $3,000, instalments are required.

Using the estimated Tax Payable for the current year would result in the minimum instalment payments. Based on this year, the required quarterly instalments would be $3,375 ($13,500 ÷ 4).

They would be due on March 15, June 15, September 15, and December 15 and would total $13,500.

Since the actual federal and provincial taxes payable for 2020 of $16,000 is higher than the tax payable of $14,400 of the preceding year, the instalments should have been based on $14,400. The instalments should have been $3,600 ($14,400 ÷ 4) for each quarter.

Interest at the prescribed base rate plus 4 percent is charged on any portion of a required instalment payment that is not remitted on the required instalment due date. The interest is charged from the date the instalment is due until an offset occurs, or until the due date for the balance owing.

Case B
The individual's net tax owing in each of the three years is as follows:

2018 = $11,000 ($18,000 − $7,000)
2019 = Nil (Withholdings exceed tax payable. Note this is nil, not a negative amount.)
2020 = $4,500 ($1 3,500 − $9,000) (Estimated)

As the individual's net tax owing is expected to exceed $3,000 in 2020 and was more than $3,000 in 2018, the payment of instalments is required.

Using the 2019 net tax owing would result in minimum instalment payments. Based on this year, the required quarterly instalments would be nil.

The fact that the actual federal and provincial taxes payable for 2020 are higher than were estimated is not relevant in this Case.

Case C
The corporation's Tax Payable for the three years is as follows:

2018 = $18,000
2019 = $14,400
2020 = $13,500 (Estimated)

As the corporation's tax payable for both the current and the preceding year exceeds $3,000, instalments are required.

Using the estimated Tax Payable for the current year would result in the minimum instalment payments. As the corporation is a small CCPC, the required instalments would be quarterly. The amount would be $3,375 ($13,500 ÷ 4).

They would be due on the last days of March, June, September, and December 2020.

Like Case A, since the actual federal and provincial taxes payable for 2020 of $16,000 is higher than the tax payable of $14,400 of the preceding year, the instalments should have been based on $14,400. The instalments should have been $3,600 ($14,400 ÷ 4) for each quarter.

Interest at the prescribed base rate plus 4 percent is charged on any portion of a required instalment payment that is not remitted on the required instalment due date. The interest is charged from the date the instalment is due until an offset occurs or until the due date for the balance owing.

Case D
The corporation's Tax Payable for the three years is as follows:

2018 = $18,000
2019 = $14,400
2020 = $16,000 (Estimated and actual)

As the corporation's tax payable for both the current and the preceding year exceeds $3,000, instalments are required.

Using the estimated Tax Payable for 2019 would result in minimum instalment payments. Because the corporation is not a CCPC and is not eligible for the small business deduction, the required instalments would be monthly. The amount would be $1,200 ($14,400 ÷ 2). They would be due on the last day of each month, beginning in January 2020.

Solution to Self Study Problem Two - 5

The three taxable entities are individuals, corporations, and trusts. The required information for each is as follows:

Individuals   For individuals, the taxation year is the calendar year. For individuals without business income, the filing deadline is April 30 of the following year. Individuals with business income, and their spouse or common-law partner, have an extended filing deadline of June 15.

If an individual dies after October, the due date of the return for the year of death is extended to 6 months after the date of death. Instalment payments for all individuals, if required, are to be made quarterly on March 15, June 15, September 15, and December 15.

Corporations   Corporations can choose any fiscal year that does not exceed 53 weeks. The filing deadline is six months after the fiscal year end. In general, corporations must make instalments on the last day of each month. However, if the corporation qualifies as a small CCPC, quarterly instalments are required on the last day of the last month of each 3 month period in the corporation's taxation year.

Trusts - Inter Vivos   Inter vivos trusts must use the calendar year as their taxation year. As the required tax return must be filed within 90 days of the taxation year end, returns for inter vivos trusts will be due March 31 (March 30 in leap years). Legislation requires that quarterly instalments be made on March 15, June 15, September 15, and December 15. Note, however, the CRA has generally not enforced this requirement.

Trusts - Testamentary   The rules are the same for most testamentary trusts. However, the exception to this is a testamentary trust that has been designated a graduated rate estate (CRE). Such CREs can use a non-calendar fiscal year for up to three years subsequent to the death of the settlor. CRE returns are due 90 days after the date that has been selected as the taxation year end. Quarterly instalments are required, with the specific dates determined by the choice of taxation year end. It is likely that the CRA will not enforce the instalment requirement.

Solution to Self Study Problem Two - 6

Since Mr. Coffee has been your client for many years, there should be a signed Consent Form, T1013, filed with the CRA that authorizes you to represent him in his affairs. If you have not already been authorized to represent him online, it would be advantageous for you to request that Mr. Coffee take the steps needed to authorize you to access his file through the online Represent a Client service. This will enable you to deal with this dispute and any future disputes more quickly.

With respect to resolving this dispute, the first step would be a call to the CRA to discuss the matter. If there has been a misunderstanding of the facts, an error on your or the CRA's part, or missing information, this may be the only step required and the matter can be resolved.

However, if more formal steps are necessary they can be outlined as follows:

Notice of Objection   As the reassessment relates to the previous year's tax return, it is within the normal 3 year time limit for reassessment. This means that notice of objection can be filed within 90 days of the date on the Notice of Reassessment or (as Mr. Coffee is an individual) one year from the due date for the return under reassessment. This can be done through the mail by letter or using Form T400A, or online through the Represent A Client service. It should explain the facts and reasons why the reassessment is not justified.

Tax Court of Canada   If there is an adverse decision on the notice of objection, Mr. Coffee has up to 90 days after the mailing date of the response to the notice of objection to appeal to the Tax Court of Canada. Alternatively, if he does not receive a response to his notice of objection within 90 days, he will then be able to appeal to the Tax Court of Canada. As the amount involved is only $5,000, it would probably be advisable for Mr. Coffee to choose the informal procedures.

Federal Courts   If Mr. Coffee has elected the informal Tax Court of Canada procedures, no appeal of an adverse decision is possible. An appeal to the Federal Court - Appeals Division would, however, be possible if an adverse decision was rendered under the general procedures. In theory, an adverse decision by the Federal Court could be appealed to the Supreme Court of Canada. However, this can only happen if the Federal Court recommends it or the Supreme Court authorizes such action. This would be extremely unlikely given the amount involved.

Solution to Self Study Problem Two - 7

Note To Instructor   These Cases have been based on examples found in IC 01-1.

Case A
In view of the business that the taxpayer is in, there was nothing in the income statement that would have made the accountant question the validity of the information provided. Therefore, the accountant could rely on the good faith reliance exception and would not be subject to the preparer penalty.

Case B
The prospectus prepared by the company contains a false statement (overstated fair market value of the software) that could be used for tax purposes. The company knew or would reasonably be expected to know, but for culpable conduct, that the fair market value of the software was a false statement. Since the company is engaged in an excluded activity, it cannot rely on the good faith reliance exception with respect to the valuation. The CRA would consider assessing the company with third-party civil penalties in the amount of $2,000,000 (i.e., the gross entitlements). The CRA would also consider assessing the appraiser with third-party civil penalties. The amount of the penalty would be his gross entitlements from the valuation activity, which is $75,000.

Case C
Although the tax return contains one or more false statements, the tax return preparer would be entitled to the good faith defence since she relied, in good faith, on information (the financial statements that were not obviously unreasonable) provided by another professional on behalf of the client. Therefore, she would not be subject to the preparer penalty.

The third-party penalties may be applied to the other accountant if he knew or would be expected to know, but for circumstances amounting to culpable conduct, that the financial statements contained false statements.

Case D
The accountant would not be subject to the penalties for participating or acquiescing in the understatement of a tax liability. The facts were highly suspect until the accountant asked questions to clear up the doubt in his mind that the client was not presenting him with implausible information. The response addressed the concern and was not inconsistent with the knowledge he possessed.

Case E

Since the tax return preparer efiled the taxpayer's return without obtaining the charitable donation receipt, the CRA would consider assessing the tax return preparer with the preparer penalty. Given that the size of the donation is so disproportionate to the taxpayer's apparent resources as to defy credibility, to proceed unquestioningly in this situation would show wilful blindness and thus an indifference as to whether the ITA is complied with.

Case F

The issue here is whether the accountant is expected to know that GST is not payable on wages, interest expense, and zero-rated purchases. It is clear that the accountant should have known that no GST could be claimed on these items. Given this, in filing a claim that includes a GST refund on the preceding items, the accountant made a false statement, either knowingly, or in circumstances amounting to culpable conduct. Consequently, the CRA would consider assessing the accountant with the third-party civil penalty, specifically, the preparer penalty.

Chapter 3 Learning Objectives

After completing Chapter 3, you should be able to:

1. Explain the basic concept of employment income (paragraph [P hereafter] 3-1 to 3-6).
2. Explain the reasons for using, and rules associated with, bonus arrangements for employees (P 3-7 to 3-13).
3. Distinguish between an employee and a self-employed individual earning business income and list the advantages and disadvantages of both classifications (P 3-14 to 3-44).
4. Explain how salaries and fringe benefits in general are taxed (P 3-45 to 3-55).
5. List the benefits that can be excluded from employment income under ITA 6(1)(a) and the benefits that must be included in income under the other Paragraphs in ITA 6(1) (P 3-56 to 3-59).

---

6. Apply the content of IT Folio S2-F3-C2 or the CRA Employers' Guide with respect to the tax status of the various employee benefits described within the publications (P 3-60 to 3-63).
7. Explain the basic elements of tax planning for employee benefits (P 3-64 to 3-76).
8. Describe the effects of GST/HST/PST on taxable benefits (P 3-77 and 3-78).
9. Calculate the standby charge and operating cost benefits that apply to employees who are provided with an automobile that is leased or owned by their employer (P 3-79 to 3-122).
10. Explain basic tax planning for company cars (P 3-123 and 3-124).

---

11. Explain the tax treatment of allowances that are provided by employers to their employees for travel costs (P 3-125 to 3-142).
12. Describe the tax status of various types of insurance benefits that are provided by employers to their employees (P 3-143 to 3-148).
13. Calculate the tax consequences of low rate or interest free loans to employees (P 3-149 to 3-156).
14. Calculate the tax consequences that result from employees receiving and exercising stock options and from the subsequent sale of the acquired shares (P 3-157 to 3-176).
15. List and describe other inclusions in employment income (P 3-177 to 3-185).

---

16. List and describe specific deductions against employment income that are listed in ITA 8 (P 3-186 to 3-206).
17. Explain how deductible work space in the home costs for employees are calculated (P 3-207 to 3-212).

How to Work Through Chapter 3

We recommend the following approach in dealing with the material in this chapter:

Employment Income Defined

- Read paragraph 3-1 to 3-11 (in the textbook).
- Do Exercise Three-1 (in the textbook) and check the solution in this Study Guide.
- Do Self Study Problem Three-1, which is available on MyLab, and check the solution in this Study Guide.
- Read paragraph 3-12 to 3-13.

Employee Versus Self-Employed

- Read paragraph 3-14 to 3-44.
- Do Self Study Problem Three-2 and check the solution in this Study Guide.

Salaries And Fringe Benefits

- Read paragraph 3-45 to 3-63.
- Do Exercises Three-2 and Three-3 and check the solutions in this Study Guide.
- Read paragraph 3-64 to 3-76.
- Do Exercise Three-4 and check the solution in this Study Guide.

GST/HST/PST On Taxable Benefits

- Read paragraph 3-77 to 3-78.
- Do Exercise Three-5 and check the solution in this Study Guide.

Automobile Benefits (Standby Charge And Operating Cost Benefit)

- Read paragraph 3-79 to 3-116.
- Do Exercise Three-6 and check the solution in this Study Guide.
- Read paragraph 3-117 to 3-122.
- Do Exercise Three-7 and check the solution in this Study Guide.
- Read paragraph 3-123 and 3-124.
- Do Self Study Problems Three-3 to Three-5 and check the solutions in this Study Guide.

Allowances

- Read paragraph 3-125 to 3-137.
- Do Exercises Three-8 and Three-9 and check the solutions in this Study Guide.
- Read paragraph 3-138 to 3-142.
- Do Exercise Three-10 and check the solution in this Study Guide.

Employee Insurance Benefits

- Read paragraph 3-143 to 3-148.
- Do Exercise Three-11 and check the solution in this Study Guide.

Loans To Employees

- Read paragraph 3-149 to 3-151.
- Do Exercise Three-12 and check the solution in this Study Guide.
- Read paragraph 3-152 to 3-156.
- Do Exercise Three-13 and check the solution in this Study Guide.
- Do Self Study Problem Three-6 and check the solution in this Study Guide.

Stock Option Benefits

- Read paragraph 3-157 to 3-171.
- Do Exercise Three-14 and check the solution in this Study Guide.
- Read paragraph 3-172 to 3-176.

- Do Exercise Three-15 and check the solution in this Study Guide.
- Do Self Study Problems Three-7 to Three-9 and check the solutions in this Study Guide.

Other Inclusions
- Read paragraph 3-177 to 3-185.

Specific Deductions Including Salesperson's Expenses And Work Space In The Home Costs
- Read paragraph 3-186 to 3-202.
- Do Exercise Three-16 and check the solution in this Study Guide.
- Read paragraph 3-203 to 3-212.
- Do Self Study Problems Three-10 to Three-14 and check the solutions in this Study Guide.

To Complete This Chapter
- If you would like more practice in problem solving, do the Supplementary Self Study Problems for the chapter. These problems and solutions are available on MyLab.
- Review the Key Terms Used In This Chapter in the textbook at the end of Chapter 3. Consult the Glossary for the meaning of any key terms you do not know.
- Test yourself with the Chapter 3 Glossary Flashcards available on MyLab.
- Ensure you have achieved the Chapter 3 Learning Objectives listed in this Study Guide.
- As a review, we recommend you view the PowerPoint presentation for Chapter 3 that is on MyLab.

Practice Examination
- Write the Practice Examination for Chapter 3 that is on MyLab. Mark your examination using the Practice Examination Solution that is also on MyLab.

Solutions to Chapter 3 Exercises

Exercise Three - 1 Solution
The bonus will be taxed in Mr. Neelson's hands in the year of receipt. This means that it will be included in his 2021 tax return. With respect to Neelson Inc., the bonus is not payable until more than 180 days after the September 30 fiscal year end. Note that the limit is 180 days from the fiscal year end, not the date on which the bonus was declared.

As a consequence, the company will not be able to deduct the bonus in the year ending September 30, 2020, the year of declaration. It will be deducted in the year ending September 30, 2021, the year of payment.

Exercise Three - 2 Solution
The tax consequences associated with each of the listed items are as follows:

Gift	Tax Consequence
$15 T-Shirt	No consequences as value is immaterial
$75 Birthday Gift	Taxable as it is a near cash gift
$400 Performance Reward	Taxable as it is performance related
$275 10-Year Award	Non-taxable as it is under $500
$300 Wedding Gift	These remaining three gifts qualify as non-taxable. However, their total value is $700 ($300 + $250 + $150).
$250 Weight Loss Award	
$150 Holiday Season Gift	The $200 excess over $500 will be taxable.

Exercise Three - 3 Solution

The tax consequences of the various items would be as follows:

- Discounts on merchandise do not create a taxable benefit provided they are available to all employees and do not reduce the price below the employer's cost.
- It could be argued that these tuition fees are related to business activity. If the argument is successful, the payment would not be taxable to John. If unsuccessful, the $2,000 would be a taxable benefit.
- Special clothing is not a taxable benefit if it is distinctive and the employee is required to wear it at work, or if it is required to protect the employee from some type of employment related hazard. It is unlikely that business clothing would fall into this category as it could be used for personal purposes. The $8,500 should be included in John's income as a taxable benefit.
- The $450 gift would not be taxable to John.
- Employer paid premiums for private health care plans are not a taxable benefit.

Exercise Three - 4 Solution

From Jill's point of view, the best alternative is probably the dental plan. Its value is significantly enhanced by the fact that it can be received without tax consequences. The annual vacation trip is clearly a taxable benefit. With respect to the $4,000 birthday gift, the $3,500 excess over the limit of $500 will be taxable. Note that the desirability of the dental plan would be affected by whether her spouse has a dental plan.

Exercise Three - 5 Solution

Ms. Correli's taxable benefit would be $4,725, the $4,500 cost of the trip plus the additional $225 in GST.

Exercise Three - 6 Solution

As Mrs. Lee's employment related use is more than 50 percent of the total (16,000 out of 28,000), she is eligible for a reduction in the full standby charge. She is also eligible for the alternative one-half of the standby charge calculation of the operating cost benefit. Given these factors, the taxable benefit would be calculated as follows:

Standby Charge	
[(2%)(12)($25,000 + $1,250 + $2,000)(12,000 ÷ 20,004*)]	$4,067
Operating Cost Benefit - Lesser Of:	
• [($0.28)(12,000)] = $3,360	
• [(1/2)($4,067)] = $2,034	2,034
Total Benefit	$6,101

*[(12 Months)(1,667)]

Exercise Three - 7 Solution

The actual operating costs paid by the employer do not affect these calculations. Rounded to the nearest whole number, 325 days results in 11 months of availability. As Mr. Forthwith's employment related use is more than 50 percent, he is eligible for a reduction in the full standby charge. He is also eligible for the alternative one-half of the standby charge calculation of the operating cost benefit. Given these factors, the taxable benefit would be calculated as follows:

Standby Charge [(2/3)($525 + $68)(11)(3,000 ÷ 18,337*)]	$ 711
Operating Cost Benefit - Lesser Of:	
• [($0.28)(3,000)] = $840	
• [(1/2)($711)] = $356	356
Total Benefit	$1,067

*[(11)(1,667)]

Exercise Three - 8 Solution

Because the allowance is not based on kilometres driven, she will have to include the $3,600 allowance in her income. Because the allowance has been included in income, she can deduct the employment-related portion of her actual automobile costs against this amount. This would be $1,936 [($7,150)(6,500 ÷ 24,000)]. The net inclusion would be $1,664 ($3,600 - $1,936).

Exercise Three - 9 Solution

As the milage allowance paid by the employer was based on the number of employment-related kilometres driven, the $3,500 [(35,000 km.)($0.10)] will not be included on his T4 Information Return and, as a consequence, it does not have to be included in his employment income. However, he will not be able to deduct his actual costs of owning and operating the automobile.

Mr. Lorenz's actual deductible costs total $11,900 [($5,400 + $15,000)(35,000/60,000)], well in excess of the allowance of $3,500. While Mr. Lorenz could attempt to include the allowance in income and deduct the actual costs, this approach could be disallowed by the CRA.

Exercise Three - 10 Solution

The hotel allowance would appear to be reasonable and would not be included in Ms. Ohm's T4. Given this, it will not be included in her net employment income. Even though her actual costs of $18,300 are in excess of the $16,400 allowance, it would be difficult for Ms. Ohm to argue that the $200 figure is not reasonable. Given this, she does not have the choice of including the $16,400 in income and deducting the actual amount of $18,300.

As the milage charge is based on kilometres, it will not be included in her T4. In addition, since the amount appears to be reasonable in terms of actual costs, she does not have the choice of including it in income and deducting the actual costs. In fact, it would not be to Ms. Ohm's advantage to do so as her actual costs would be $2,880 [($7,200)(9,400/23,500)], which is less than the $3,854 payment she received.

No amounts would be included in Ms. Ohm's net employment income and no amounts would be deductible.

Exercise Three - 11 Solution

As his employer contributes to the plan and the contributions do not create a taxable benefit, the $5,250 in benefits received during the year will be included in his employment income. This will be reduced by the $525 ($300 + $225) in non-deductible contributions that he made during 2019 and 2020, leaving a net inclusion of $4,725 ($5,250 - $525).

Exercise Three - 12 Solution

The ITA 80.4(1) benefit is calculated as follows:

The Lesser Of:
- [($100,000)(2%)(1/4) + ($100,000)(3%)(1/4) + ($100,000)(1%)(2/4)] = $1,750
- [($100,000)(2%)] = $2,000 $1,750

Less Interest Payment [($100,000)(1%)]   (1,000)

Net Benefit $ 750

As this is a home purchase loan, the annual benefit cannot exceed the benefit that would result from applying the 2 percent rate that was in effect when the loan was made. Note that the 2 percent rate is not compared to the prescribed rate on a quarter-by-quarter basis, but on an annual basis. The lower figure of $1,750 would then be reduced by the $1,000 in interest paid.

Exercise Three - 13 Solution

In the absence of the interest free loan, the employee would borrow $125,000 at 5 percent, requiring an annual interest payment of $6,250. The after tax cash outflow associated with the employer providing sufficient additional salary to carry this loan would be calculated as follows:

Required Salary [$6,250 ÷ (1 - 0.42)]	$10,776
Corporate Tax Savings From Deducting Salary [($10,776)(26%)]	(2,802)
Employer's After Tax Cash Flow - Additional Salary	$ 7,974

Alternatively, if the loan is provided, the employee will have a taxable benefit of $2,500 [(2%)($125,000)], resulting in taxes payable of $1,050 [(42%)($2,500)]. To make this situation comparable to the straight salary alternative, the employer will have to provide the employee with both the loan amount and sufficient additional salary to pay the taxes on the imputed interest benefit. The amount of this additional salary would be $1,810 [$1,050 ÷ (1 - 0.42)]. The employer's after tax cash flow associated with providing the additional salary and the loan amount would be calculated as follows:

Required Salary [$1,050 ÷ (1 - 0.42)]	$1,810
Corporate Tax Savings From Deducting Salary [($1,810)(26%)]	(471)
After Tax Cost Of Salary To Cover Taxes On Benefit	$1,339
Employer's Lost Earnings [(7%)(1 - 0.26)($125,000)]	6,475
Employer's After Tax Cash Flow - Loan	$7,814

Given these results, providing the loan appears to be the better alternative.

Exercise Three - 14 Solution

At time of exercise, Mr. Guise will have an employment income benefit of $21,250 [($31.50 - $23.00)(2,500 shares)]. As the option price at issue exceeded the fair market value at issue, Mr. Guise will be able to deduct $10,625 [(1/2)($21,250)] in the determination of Taxable Income. These results are summarized in the following table:

Fair Market Value Of Shares Acquired [(2,500)($31.50)]	$78,750
Cost Of Shares [(2,500)($23)]	(57,500)
ITA 7(1)(a) Employment Income Inclusion = **Increase In Net Income For Tax Purposes**	**$ 21,250**
ITA 110(1)(d) Deduction [(1/2)($21,250)]	(10,625)
Increase In Taxable Income	**$ 10,625**

When the shares are sold, there will be an allowable capital loss, calculated as follows:

Proceeds Of Disposition [($28.00)(2,500)]	$ 70,000
Adjusted Cost Base [($31.50)(2,500)]	(78,750)
Capital Loss	($ 8,750)
Inclusion Rate	1/2
Allowable Capital Loss	($ 4,375)

Mr. Guise will only be able to deduct this loss in 2020 to the extent that he has taxable capital gains on other dispositions. It cannot be deducted against the employment income inclusion.

Exercise Three - 15 Solution

There will be no tax consequences in either 2018, when the options are received, or in 2019, when the options are exercised. This latter result reflects the fact that the acquired shares are those of a Canadian controlled private corporation.

At the time the shares are sold in 2020, there will be an employment income benefit of $58,500 [($75.00 - $42.50)(1,800 shares)]. As the option price of $42.50 was below the fair market value of $45 at the time the options were issued, there is no deduction under ITA 110(1)(d). Although she could have been eligible for the deduction under ITA 110(1)(d.1), she did not hold the shares for the required two years. These results are summarized in the following table:

Deferred Employment Income:	
Fair Market Value Of Shares Acquired [(1,800)($75)]	$135,000
Cost Of Shares [(1,800)($42.50)]	(76,500)
ITA 7(1)(a) Employment Income Inclusion =	
Increase In **Net Income For Tax Purposes**	**$ 58,500**
ITA 110(1)(d) Deduction (Option Price < FMV)	N/A
ITA 110(1)(d.1) Deduction (Held Less Than 2 Years)	N/A
Increase In **Taxable Income**	**$ 58,500**

When she sells the shares in 2020, Ms. Van will have an allowable capital loss calculated as follows:

Proceeds Of Disposition [($49)(1,800)]	$ 88,200
Adjusted Cost Base [($75)(1,800)]	(135,000)
Capital Loss	($ 46,800)
Inclusion Rate	1/2
Allowable Capital Loss	($ 23,400)

Ms. Van will only be able to deduct this loss in 2020 to the extent that she has taxable capital gains on other dispositions. It cannot be deducted against the employment income inclusion.

Exercise Three - 16 Solution

The potential deduction is $27,100 [$8,000 + (1/2)($12,000) + $13,100]. However, this total exceeds his commissions and, if these amounts are deducted under ITA 8(1)(f), his deduction will be limited to the commissions of $12,200.

Alternatively, if he uses ITA 8(1)(h), he cannot deduct the advertising or the entertainment, limiting the amount of this deduction to $13,100.

As the two provisions cannot be used simultaneously, Morton would use the larger figure of $13,100 that is available under ITA 8(1)(h).

Solution to Self Study Problem Three - 1

The required information for the four Cases included in this problem is as shown in the following table:

	Deduction - Empire Inc. Year Ending October 31	Inclusion-Ms. Betz Calendar Year
Case A	2020	2020
Case B	2020	2021
Case C	2021	2021
Case D	2020	2020

In Case A, the bonus is deducted when accrued because it is paid within 180 days of Empire's 2020 year end. It is taxed when received.

In Case B, the bonus is deducted when accrued because it is paid within 180 days of Empire's 2020 year end. It is taxed when received.

In Case C, the bonus is not paid within 180 days of Empire's year end. As a consequence, it cannot be deducted until the year ending October 31, 2021. However, as it is paid within three years of Empire's 2020 year end it is not a salary deferral arrangement. This means it does not have to be included in Ms. Betz's Taxable Income until 2021.

In Case D, the bonus is not paid until more than three years after the end of the calendar year in which Ms. Betz rendered the services. This makes it a salary deferral arrangement, resulting in Ms. Betz having to include it in her 2020 Taxable Income. Empire will deduct the bonus in the fiscal year ending October 31, 2020.

Solution to Self Study Problem Three - 2

Quantitative Considerations

If the individual's services are acquired as an employee, the 2020 costs would be as follows:

Basic Salary	$250,000
Company Benefits [($250,000)(8%)]	20,000
CPP (Maximum)	2,898
Employer's Share Of EI [(1.4)(1.58%)($54,200)]	1,198
Payroll Tax [(2%)($250,000)]	5,000
Total Cost	$279,096

This is very close to the $280,000 that would have to be paid to the individual if he is classified as an independent contractor.

Other Considerations

While the quantitative factors slightly favour employee classification, this is probably not the best choice. Other factors that should be considered include the following:

- self-employed status relieves the company from any ongoing commitment beyond the period specified in the contract,
- Farnham Ltd. would not be legally responsible for any errors in the work of the engineer if he is self-employed,
- the fact that employment contracts usually require that salary and related benefits grow over time, and
- the added administrative costs of withholding amounts from his salary if he is an employee.

It would appear to be more advantageous to structure the arrangement so that this individual qualifies as an independent contractor.

Solution to Self Study Problem Three - 3

Ms. Marianne Dorsey   The taxable benefit to be allocated to the president of the company would be calculated as follows:

Standby Charge [(2%)(11)($185,000)]	$40,700
Operating Cost Benefit [(53,000 - 18,000)($0.28)]	9,800
Total Benefit	$50,500

As less than 50 percent of Marianne's kilometres were employment related, she cannot reduce the standby charge or use the alternative calculation of the operating cost benefit, based on one-half of the standby charge, even if it were more advantageous.

Mr. John Dorsey   The taxable benefit to be allocated to the vice president of finance would be calculated as follows:

Standby Charge [(2%)($71,500)(10)(16,670/16,670*)]	$14,300
Operating Cost Benefit - Lesser Of:	
• [(22,000)($0.28)] = $6,160	
• [(1/2)($14,300)] = $7,150	6,160
Total Benefit	$20,460

*The numerator cannot exceed the denominator, which is equal to [(10)(1,667)]

While John is eligible for the reduced standby charge calculation, his personal use is more than 1,667 kilometres per month of availability. This means that the reduction formula leaves the standby charge unchanged. While he is eligible for the alternative calculation of the operating cost benefit, it would produce a larger taxable benefit in this situation.

Ms. Misty Dorsey   The taxable benefit to be allocated to the vice president of design would be calculated as follows:

Standby Charge [(2/3)(12)($620 - $100)]	$ 4,160
Operating Cost Benefit [(51,000 - 14,000)($0.28)]	10,360
Reimbursement [(12)($200)]	(2,400)
Total Benefit	$12,120

As less than 50 percent of the kilometres are employment related, there is no reduction in the standby charge. In addition, the alternative calculation of the operating cost benefit cannot be used.

Mr. Saul Dorsey   The taxable benefit that would be allocated to the vice president of marketing would be calculated as follows:

Standby Charge [(2/3)(8)($1,200)(1,700/13,336*)]	$ 816
Operating Cost Benefit - Lesser Of:	
• [(1,700)($0.28)] = $476	
• [(1/2)($816)] = $408	408
Total Benefit	$1,224

*[(8)(1,667)]

As more than 50 percent of the use was employment related, there is a reduction in the standby charge. As the car was driven more than 50 percent for employment related purposes, Saul can calculate the operating cost benefit as one-half of the standby charge, which results in a lower benefit.

Solution to Self Study Problem Three - 4

Mr. Sam Stern

The taxable benefit for the president of the company would be calculated as follows:

Standby Charge [(2%)($78,000)(8)]	$12,480
Operating Cost Benefit [(32,000)($0.28)]	8,960
Taxable Benefit	$21,440

As Mr. Stern did not drive the car more than 50 percent for employment related purposes, no reduction in the standby charge is available. Since his employment related use was not more than 50 percent, he cannot use the alternative calculation of the operating cost benefit.

Ms. Sarah Blue

The taxable benefit for the marketing vice president would be calculated as follows:

Standby Charge [(2/3)(12)($900)(5,000/20,004)]	$1,800
Operating Cost Benefit - Lesser Of:	
• [(5,000)($0.28)] = $1,400	
• [(1/2)($1,800)] = $900	900
Taxable Benefit	$2,700

As employment related driving was more than 50 percent of the total, Ms. Blue can reduce the standby charge on the basis of actual personal usage. As the car was driven more than 50 percent for employment related purposes, Ms. Blue can calculate the operating cost benefit as one-half of the standby charge, which results in a lower benefit.

Mr. John Stack

The taxable benefit for the finance vice president would be calculated as follows:

Standby Charge [(2%)($48,000)(12)(10,000/20,004]	$5,759
Operating Cost Benefit - Lesser Of:	
• [(10,000)($0.28)] = $2,800	
• [(1/2)($5,759)] = $2,880	2,800
Payment For Use Of Company Car	(7,000)
Taxable Benefit	$1,559

Mr. Stack's employment related driving was more than 50 percent of the total and, as a consequence, he can reduce his standby charge on the basis of actual personal mileage. Mr. Stack could have calculated the operating cost benefit as one-half of the standby charge, but this would have resulted in a higher benefit.

Mr. Alex Decker

The taxable benefit for the industrial relations vice president would be calculated as follows:

Standby Charge [(2/3)(10)($500)(8,500/16,670)]	$1,700
Operating Cost Benefit - Lesser Of:	
• [(8,500)($0.28)] = $2,380	
• [(1/2)($1,700)] = $850	850
Taxable Benefit	$2,550

As Mr. Decker's employment related driving is more than 50 percent of the total, he can reduce his standby charge on the basis of actual personal mileage. While the $10,000 deposit will affect the deductibility of the lease payments by the employer, it does not influence the calculation of the taxable benefit to Mr. Decker. As the car was driven more than 50 percent for employment related purposes, Mr. Decker can calculate the operating cost benefit as one-half of the standby charge, which results in a lower benefit.

Tax Planning

With respect to the tax planning of management compensation, two points can be made. First, the question of providing company cars as a method of compensation should be examined on a case-by-case basis.

In situations where a car is owned by the company and provided to an executive for a fairly long period of time, the taxable benefit assessed may exceed the value of the benefit. For example, over five years, the taxable benefit without regard for operating costs on Mr. Stern's Mercedes could total $93,600 [(2%)(60)($78,000)]. This is more than $15,000 in excess of the cost of the car.

With the limitations on the deductibility of CCA and leasing costs on cars, the after tax cost to the company of owning and leasing luxury cars can be very high. While a complete analysis of this issue will depend on a number of variables, it is possible that some of these executives would be better off receiving additional amounts of salary and billing the company for employment related mileage driven in their own cars.

The second point to be made here is that, except in situations where the car is kept for very short periods of time, the employee will be allocated a smaller taxable benefit if the company were to lease the car rather than buy it. In general, monthly lease payments on a three year lease will tend to be between 2 percent and 2.5 percent of the capital cost of the cars.

As the leasing standby charge is based on two-thirds of the monthly lease payment, it is clear that the standby charge under this type of arrangement will be less than the 2 percent per month that is assessed when the company owns the car. However, for shorter lease terms, the lease payment will be a greater percentage of the capital cost, and this relationship may reverse.

Other tax planning techniques would involve any procedure that would reduce the capital cost of purchased cars or the lease payments on leased cars. Such procedures would include high residual values on leasing arrangements and low trade in values assigned to old cars when new ones are purchased. In addition, it might be possible to reduce a taxable benefit, such as the one being allocated to Mr. Stern, by selling his car to a leasing company with an immediate leaseback arrangement. Although large refundable deposits on leasing arrangements would reduce the lease payment and therefore the standby charge, there would be a tax cost to the employer (see Chapter 6).

Solution to Self Study Problem Three - 5

Employer Continues To Provide Automobile
If the employer continues to provide the car, John's only cash outflow will be the taxes assessed on the taxable benefit that results from his having the car available. This outflow under the two Cases would be calculated as follows:

	Case A $35,000 Cost	Case B $70,000 Cost
Standby Charge		
[(2%)($35,000)(12)]	$ 8,400	
[(2%)($70,000)(12)]		$16,800
Operating Cost Benefit [(40,000 Kilometres)($0.28)]	11,200	11,200
Total Annual Benefit	$19,600	$28,000
Number Of Years	2	2
Total Benefit	$39,200	$56,000
John's Marginal Tax Rate	48%	48%
Total Taxes On Taxable Benefit	$18,816	$26,880

Note that, because John's use of the car is not primarily (more than 50 percent) for employment purposes, he cannot use the alternative one-half of standby charge calculation of the operating cost benefit.

John Purchases The Automobile
If John purchases the car and pays his own operating costs, the total cash outflow in both Cases would be calculated as follows:

Purchase Price	$ 20,000
Estimated Resale Value	(12,000)
Operating Costs [(2)(40,000 Kilometres)($0.20)]	16,000
Total Cash Outflow	$24,000

Conclusion - Case A ($35,000)

On the basis of non-discounted cash flows, the best alternative would be to have John's employer continue to provide him with the car. If the cash flows were discounted, the results would be even more favourable for this alternative.

Conclusion - Case B ($70,000)

Since the original cost of the car was $70,000, on the basis of non-discounted cash flows, the best alternative would be to have John purchase the car since the taxable benefit is so high.

Although the requirements of the problem ask that only the cash flows be considered, we would note that the alternative of purchasing the car carries more uncertainty. Both the resale value and the actual operating costs are estimates. If there was a large variation from the estimate for either or both of these amounts, it could substantially affect the total cash outflow of the purchase alternative.

Solution to Self Study Problem Three - 6

Alternative 1 - Provide Additional Salary

In the absence of the interest free loan, Ms. Monson would borrow $300,000 at 4.5 percent, requiring an annual interest payment of $13,500. In determining the amount of salary needed to carry this loan, consideration has to be given to the fact that additional salary will be taxed at 46 percent.

As the interest is not deductible, additional salary of $25,000 [$13,500 ÷ (1 - 0.46)] is needed.

Using this figure, the employer's after tax cash flow required to provide sufficient additional salary for the Ms. Monson to carry a conventional $300,000 mortgage would be calculated as follows:

Required Salary [$13,500 ÷ (1 - 0.46)]	$25,000
Tax Savings From Deducting Salary [($25,000)(28%)]	(7,000)
Employer's After Tax Cash Flow - Additional Salary	$18,000

Alternative 2 - Provide The Loan

If the loan is provided, Ms. Monson will have a taxable benefit of $6,000 [(2% - Nil)($300,000)], resulting in additional taxes payable of $2,760 [(46%)($6,000)]. To make this situation comparable to the straight salary alternative, Elmwood Inc. will have to provide Ms. Monson with both the loan amount and sufficient additional salary to pay the $2,760 in taxes on the benefit that will be assessed.

The required amount would be $5,111 [$2,760 ÷ (1 - 0.46)].

Elmwood Inc.'s cash flow associated with the after tax cost of providing the additional salary as well as the after tax lost earnings on the $300,000 loan amount would be calculated as follows:

Required Salary [$2,760 ÷ (1 - 0.46)]	$ 5,111
Tax Savings From Deducting Salary [($5,111)(28%)]	(1,431)
After Tax Cost Of Salary To Cover Taxes On Benefit	$ 3,680
Employer's Lost Earnings [(7%)(1 - 0.28)($300,000)]	15,120
Employer's After Tax Cash Flow - Loan	$18,800

Conclusion

Given these results, on the basis of cash flows only, payment of additional salary appears to be the better alternative. However, the difference between the alternatives is relatively small. As Ms. Monson is a highly valued employee, there could be non-financial advantages to providing the loan, such as employee loyalty and the retention of her services, especially if the loan is for a longer period of time.

Solution to Self Study Problem Three - 7

Case A
2018 In 2018, the year in which the options are issued, there would be no tax consequences for Ms. Wu.

2019 The tax consequences in 2019 would be as follows:

Fair Market Value At Exercise [(12,000)($31)]	$372,000
Cost Of Shares [(12,000)($22)]	(264,000)
Employment Income Inclusion	
= Increase In **Net Income For Tax Purposes**	$108,000
Deduction Under ITA 110(1)(d) [(1/2)($108,000)]	(54,000)
Increase In **Taxable Income**	$ 54,000

2020 When the shares are sold in 2020, the tax consequences would be as follows:

Proceeds Of Disposition [(12,000)($28)]	336,000
Adjusted Cost Base [(12,000)($31)]	(372,000)
Capital Loss	($ 36,000)
Inclusion Rate	1/2
Allowable Capital Loss	($ 18,000)

Ms. Wu will only be able to deduct this loss in 2020 to the extent that she has taxable capital gains on other dispositions.

Case B
2018 There are no tax consequences in 2018.

2019 There are no tax consequences in 2019.

2020 In 2020, the employment income inclusion would be as follows:

Fair Market Value At Exercise [(12,000)($31)]	$372,000
Cost Of Shares [(12,000)($22)]	(264,000)
Employment Income Inclusion	
= Increase In **Net Income For Tax Purposes**	$108,000
Deduction Under ITA 110(1)(d) [(1/2($108,000)]	(54,000)
Increase In **Taxable Income**	$ 54,000

In addition, there would be an allowable capital loss calculated as follows:

Proceeds Of Disposition [(12,000)($28)]	$336,000
Adjusted Cost Base [(12,000)($31)]	(372,000)
Capital Loss	($ 36,000)
Inclusion Rate	1/2
Allowable Capital Loss	($ 18,000)

Ms. Wu will only be able to deduct this loss in 2020 to the extent that she has taxable capital gains on other dispositions.

Solution to Self Study Problem Three - 8

Part A

There would be no tax effects resulting from the granting of the options in 2018.

Since the option price was below the fair market value at the time the shares were issued, there is no deduction available under ITA 110(1)(d) in the calculation of Taxable Income. As Patricia's employer is a public company, the exercise of the options in 2019 will result in the following addition to Net Income For Tax Purposes and Taxable Income:

Fair Market Value At Exercise [(1,500)($50)]	$75,000
Option Price [(1,500)($45)]	(67,500)
Employment Income (Increase In **Net** And **Taxable Income)**	$ 7,500

In 2020, when the shares are sold, there is the following addition to **Net Income For Tax Purposes** and **Taxable Income**:

Proceeds Of Disposition [(1,500)($55)]	$82,500
Adjusted Cost Base [(1,500)($50)]	(75,000)
Capital Gain	$ 7,500
Inclusion Rate	1/2
Taxable Capital Gain	$ 3,750

Part B

There would be no tax effects resulting from the granting of the options in 2018.

If the 2018 trading value for the shares had been $44, the option price would have been above fair market value and the ITA 110(1)(d) deduction would be available. On this basis, the 2019 results would be as follows:

Fair Market Value At Exercise [(1,500)($50)]	$75,000
Option Price [(1,500)($45)]	(67,500)
Employment Income	
Increase In **Net Income For Tax Purposes**	$ 7,500
ITA 110(1)(d) Deduction [(1/2)($7,500)]	(3,750)
Increase In **Taxable Income**	$ 3,750

The results for 2020 would be unchanged from Part A.

Part C

If Patricia's employer had been a Canadian controlled private company, there would be no tax effects in either 2018 or 2019.

There is no deduction available under either ITA 110(1)(d) or ITA 110(1)(d.1) when the shares are sold. The option price was below the fair market value when the options were issued. Further, Patricia did not hold the shares for the two years required for the ITA 110(1)(d.1) deduction. When the shares are sold in 2020, there is the following addition to Net Income For Tax Purposes and Taxable Income:

Fair Market Value At Exercise [(1,500)($50)]	$75,000
Option Price [(1,500)($45)]	(67,500)
Taxable Capital Gain [(1/2)(1,500)($55 - $50)]	3,750
Increase In **Net Income For Tax Purposes**	
And **Taxable Income**	$11,250

Solution to Self Study Problem Three - 9

Salary From Maritime Trust [(6/12)($105,000)]		$ 52,500
Salary From Bolten [(6/12)($90,000)]		45,000
Total Salaries		$ 97,500
Maritime Trust Stock Options (Note 1):		
Market Price Of Shares [(5,000)($16)]	$80,000	
Option Price [(5,000)($15)]	(75,000)	5,000
Bolten Financial Services Stock Options (Note 1)		Nil
Automobile Benefit (Note 2):		
Standby Charge [(2%)($40,000)(4)(6,668/6,668)]	$ 3,200	
Operating Cost Benefit - Lesser Of:		
• [(10,000)($0.28)] = $2,800		
• [(1/2)($3,200)] = $1,600	1,600	4,800
Loan Benefit (Note 3)		2,000
Net Employment Income		$109,300

Notes:

1. As Bolten Financial Services is a Canadian controlled private corporation, the exercise of the option to purchase its common stock does not result in a taxable benefit at the time of exercise. Since Maritime Trust Inc. is a public company, the exercise of the option to purchase its common stock does result in a taxable benefit at the time of exercise. Mr. Jurgens has a stock option deduction equal to $2,500 [(1/2)($5,000)] under ITA 110(1)(d) created by the exercise of the Maritime Trust stock option. However, the stock option deduction would reduce Taxable Income and would not affect net employment income. The Bolten stock option income inclusion of $2,000 [(1,000)($22 - $20)] and deduction of $1,000 [(1/2)($2,000)] are both deferred until the shares are sold.

2. As Mr. Jurgens' employment-related milage is more than 50 percent of the total milage, he can make use of the reduced standby charge formula. In this case, however, his personal usage exceeded the 6,668 [(4)(1,667)] kilometre maximum usage allowed by the reduction, so the reduction is nil. His employment-related milage is more than 50 percent of the total and, as a consequence, he can elect to calculate the operating cost benefit as one-half of the standby charge. Since this is less than the amount determined through the usual calculation, it would be the operating cost benefit.

3. The imputed interest on the interest free loan must be included in employment income under the requirements of ITA 6(9), a benefit that is defined in ITA 80.4(1). The amount of the benefit is $2,000 [(2%)($200,000)(6/12)]. Note that there is a deduction under ITA 110(1)(j) for the amount of this benefit that relates to an interest free home relocation loan of $25,000. However, this is a deduction in the calculation of Taxable Income and will not affect the amount of net employment income.

4. The interest and dividend income is not included in the calculation of net employment income.

Solution to Self Study Problem Three - 10

Ms. Kline's net employment income for the year would be calculated as follows:

Gross Salary	$73,500
Registered Pension Plan Contributions	(2,400)
Automobile Benefit (Note One)	270
Contributions To Group Disability Plan (Note Two)	Nil
Disability Insurance Benefit (Note Two)	1,400
Professional Dues	(1,650)
Stock Option Benefit [(200)($70 - $50)] (Note Three)	4,000
Net Employment Income	$75,120

Note One Based on the fact that Ms. Kline's employment-related usage is more than 50 percent of total usage, the automobile benefit is calculated as follows:

Standby Charge [(2/3)(11)($700 - $50)(3,000/18,337*)]	$ 780
Operating Cost Benefit - Lesser Of:	
• [(3,000)($0.28)] = $840	
• [(1/2)($780)] = $390	390
Total Before Payments	$1,170
Payments For Personal Use [(3,000)($0.30)]	(900)
Taxable Benefit	$ 270

*[(11)(1,667)]

As Ms. Kline's employment-related usage is more than 50 percent, she can elect to use one-half of the standby charge as the operating cost benefit.

Note Two The contributions to the group disability plan are not deductible, but can be applied against the $1,800 received under the plan during the year. Since the employer's contributions to this plan are not a taxable benefit, the $1,800 in benefits received must be included in employment income. However, this benefit can be reduced by the $400 ($225 + $175) in total contributions that she has made in 2019 and 2020.

Note Three Although Ms. Kline would qualify for the deduction of one-half of the stock option benefit under ITA 110(1)(d), it is a deduction from Taxable Income and would not affect the calculation of the required figure in this problem, net employment income.

Solution to Self Study Problem Three - 11

As Ms. Firth paid all of her own operating expenses, there is no taxable benefit for vehicle operating costs. However, she has to include the $7,200 car allowance in income. Given this, she can deduct a pro rata share of her actual expenses. The deduction would be $5,728 [($6,200) (85,000 km ÷ 92,000 km)].

Ms. Firth's total entertainment, meal, and travel expenses that would be deductible under ITA 8(1)(f) are as follows:

Entertainment Expenses [(1/2)($6,500)]	$ 3,250
Travel Meals [(1/2)($1,300)]	650
Lodging	3,500
Automobile Operating Costs [($6,200)(85,000 ÷ 92,000)]	5,728
Total Salesperson Expenses	$13,128

As this total is less than her commission income of $14,000, they can all be deducted under ITA 8(1)(f).

Ms. Firth's net employment income for the year would be calculated as follows:

Gross Salary			$72,000
Commission Income			14,000
Additions:			
Disability Insurance Receipts,			
Less Employee's Premium ($2,000 - $250)	$	1,750	
Car Allowance		7,200	
Automobile Benefit (Note 1)		2,471	
Term Life Insurance Benefit [($1,350)(2/3)]		900	
Low Interest Loan Benefit [($400,000)(2%) - $3,000]		5,000	
Gift (Note 2)		Nil	
Stock Option Benefit [(1,000)($7 - $5)] (Note 3)		2,000	
Tennis Club Membership (Note 4)		Nil	
Travel Allowance		3,600	22,921
Deductions:			
Registered Pension Plan Contributions (Note 5)	($	3,200)	
Salesperson Expenses (Preceding Calculation)	(	13,128)	(16,328)
Net Employment Income			$92,593

Note 1 The personal benefit on the company car would be calculated as follows:

Reduced Standby Charge [(2%)($58,000)(11)(7,000/18,337*)]	$4,871
Operating Costs Benefit	Nil
Total Benefit	$4,871
Less: Payments Withheld By Employer	(2,400)
Taxable Benefit	$2,471

*[(1,667)(11)]

Note 2 Employers can provide their employees with a non-cash gift with a value of less than $500 without creating a taxable benefit. The mini iPad costs less than $500.

Note 3 Although Ms. Firth would qualify for the deduction of one-half of the stock option benefit under ITA 110(1)(d), it is a deduction from Taxable Income and would not affect the calculation of net employment income.

Note 4 The $2,500 membership to the Mountain Tennis Club paid by the company for Ms. Firth is not a taxable benefit since the primary beneficiary appears to be the company.

Note 5 Contributions made to a registered pension plan under the terms of the plan are deductible. The matching contributions made by the employer are not a taxable benefit.

Other Excluded Items Other items not included and the reason for their exclusion:

- Federal and provincial income taxes withheld are not deductible.

Solution to Self Study Problem Three - 12

Mr. Jones' net employment income would be calculated as follows:

Salary			$25,800
Taxable Benefit From Fishing Trip			2,450
Commission Income			
Sales Commissions		$47,700	
Deductions:			
Airline Tickets	($ 2,350)		
Office Supplies	(415)		
Client Entertainment			
[(50%)($1,750)]	(875)		
CCA (Note 1)	(7,560)		
Operating Costs (Note 2)	(5,040)	(16,240)	31,460
Net Employment Income			$59,710

Note 1 The deductible capital cost allowance on the car would be calculated as follows:

Full Capital Cost Allowance*	$10,800
Employment Related Usage Proportion (35,000/50,000)	70%
Deductible Amount	$ 7,560

*While this subject is not covered until Chapter 5, the maximum capital cost allowance would be calculated as follows:

$$\$10,800 = [(\$24,000)(30\%)(150\%)]$$

Note 2 As the car was used 30 percent on personal matters, only $5,040 [(70%)($7,200)] in operating costs would be deductible.

Other Notes

- The laptop computer is a capital expenditure and is not deductible as an expense. Since an employee cannot deduct CCA except for an automobile, musical instrument, or aircraft, the purchase of the laptop computer would not have any effect on either employment income or taxes payable.
- The payment for Blue Cross would be eligible for the medical expenses tax credit, but would not be deductible in the calculation of net employment income. The life insurance premiums would not have any effect on either employment income or taxes payable.
- Discounts for employees on merchandise normally sold by an employer are not generally considered to be a taxable benefit.

Solution to Self Study Problem Three - 13

Part A

As Mr. Worthy's income includes commissions, he has a choice of deducting his expenses under a combination of ITA 8(1)(f), (i), and (j) or, alternatively, under a combination of ITA 8(1)(h), (h.1), (i), and (j).

Deductions under ITA 8(1)(f) are limited to the amount of commissions earned. Alternatively, traveling costs and motor vehicle costs other than capital costs can be deducted under ITA 8(1)(h) and ITA 8(1)(h.1). Deductions under these provisions are not limited to commission income. As discussed in the text, he cannot use both ITA 8(1)(f) and the combination of ITA 8(1)(h) and (h.1).

As the deduction under ITA 8(1)(f) is limited by commission income, alternative calculations are required to determine the maximum deduction. In the calculations that follow, we have minimized the effect of the commission income limit by listing any item that can be deducted under either ITA 8(1)(f) or ITA 8(1)(i) or (j) under the ITA 8(1)(i) and (j) column.

For example, house utilities and maintenance could be deducted under either ITA 8(1)(f) or 8(1)(i). We have included them under ITA 8(1)(i) to minimize the deductions that are limited by commission income.

The required calculations are as follows:

	ITA 8(1)(f) (Limited To $11,000)	ITA 8(1) (h) and (h.1)	ITA 8(1) (i) and (j)
Work Space In The Home Costs			
Monthly Charge For Residential Line	-	-	-
Long Distance Telephone Charges	-	-	$ 400
Cellular Phone Airtime	-	-	800
Office Supplies	-	-	295
House Utilities	-	-	485
House Maintenance	-	-	255
House Insurance	$ 70	-	-
Property Taxes	265	-	-
Capital Cost Allowance - House	-	-	-
Mortgage Interest	-	-	-
Automobile Costs:			
Operating Costs [(80%)($2,700)]	2,160	2,160	-
Car Interest [(80%)($2,300)]	-	-	1,840
Car CCA [(80%)($2,450)]	-	-	1,960
Entertainment			
Deductible Portion [(50%)($2,550)]	1,275	-	-
Travel Costs			
Hotels	2,850	$2,850	-
Deductible Portion Of Meals [(50%)($900)]	450	450	-
Office Furniture			
Interest	-	-	-
Capital Cost Allowance	-	-	-
Total	$7,070	$5,460	$6,035

Using the preceding calculations, Mr. Worthy's minimum net employment income can be calculated as follows:

Salary		$65,000
Commissions	$11,000	
Expenses Under ITA 8(1)(f) - Limited To Commissions	(7,070)	3,930
Total		$68,930
Expenses Under ITA 8(1)(i) and (j)		(6,035)
Net Employment Income		$62,895

Expenses in excess of commission income cannot be deducted under ITA 8(1)(f). Since the total of the expenses is less than the commissions of $11,000, they can all be deducted. The deduction of automobile capital costs (CCA and financing costs) under ITA 8(1)(j) is permitted without regard to other provisions used.

Notes:

1. The monthly telephone charge is not deductible. The long distance charges and cellular telephone airtime to clients can be deducted. The deduction for supplies can be deducted under ITA 8(1)(f) or (i). They have been deducted under ITA 8(1)(i), which is not limited by the commission income.

2. Only 50 percent of entertainment and meals when traveling are deductible.

3. ITA 8(1)(f) prohibits the deduction of amounts associated with capital assets except as they are permitted under ITA 8(1)(j) and ITA 8(1)(p). These latter Paragraphs only permit interest or capital cost allowance to be deducted when it is related to an automobile, aircraft, or musical instrument. Therefore, the interest and the capital cost allowance on the house and the office furniture would not be deductible against employment income. This is a good illustration of the importance of distinguishing between employment income and business income. While these amounts cannot be deducted against employment income, they would likely be deductible against business income.

4. As the car is used 20 percent for personal purposes, this proportion of the operating costs, capital cost allowance, and interest costs will not be deductible.

5. The deduction for work space in the home costs has been split between ITA 8(1)(i) and (f). Since the maintenance portion can be deducted under ITA 8(1)(i) by any employee, it is not limited by the commission income. The insurance and property tax components are limited as they can only be deducted under ITA 8(1)(f). A limitation, which is not illustrated in this problem, prevents the deduction of work space in the home costs from creating an employment loss. If any of these costs had not been deductible during the current year, they could be deducted against employment income in any subsequent year as long as a loss is not created or increased by their deduction.

6. Mr. Worthy's employer must sign Form T2200 certifying that Mr. Worthy is required to incur travel expenses and maintain his own work space. Mr. Worthy must retain this signed form with his records in order to deduct car and home office expenses.

Part B

If Mr. Worthy deducted the ITA 8(1)(f) expenses, they would be limited to his commission income of $4,000. Alternatively, he can use the combination of ITA 8(1)(h) and (h.1). His minimum net employment income under both alternatives can be calculated as follows:

	ITA 8(1)(f)	ITA 8(1)(h)(h.1)
Salary	$65,000	$65,000
Commissions	4,000	4,000
Expenses Under ITA 8(1)(f) - Limited To Commissions	(4,000)	Nil
Subtotal	$65,000	$69,000
Expenses Under ITA 8(1)(h) and (h.1)	Nil	(5,460)
Expenses Under ITA 8(1)(i) and (j)	(6,035)	(6,035)
Net Employment Income	$58,965	$57,505

Using the combination of ITA 8(1)(h), (h.1), (i), and (j) produces a lower net employment income figure. Note that when this approach is used, work space in the home costs are limited to utilities and maintenance. Further, there is no deduction for entertainment costs. However, this approach results in deductions totalling $1,460 ($5,460 - $4,000) more than the amount available using ITA 8(1)(f), (i), and (j) due to the effect of the commission income limit.

Solution to Self Study Problem Three - 14

Mitch Lesner's net employment income would be calculated as follows;

Item 1 - Signing Bonus (Note 1)	$10,000
Item 1 - Salary Received (Note 1)	62,550
Item 1 - RPP Contributions Withheld	(1,200)
Item 1 - Other Items (Note 1)	Nil
Item 2 - Bonus Received (Note 2)	2,000
Item 3 - Counseling Services (Note 3)	Nil
Item 4 - Group Medical Coverage (Note 4)	Nil
Item 5 - Employer Contribution To RPP (Note 5)	Nil
Item 6 - Professional Dues Paid (Note 6)	(785)
Item 6 - Employer Reimbursement Of Professional Dues (Note 6)	628
Item 7 - Wedding Gifts (Note 7)	Nil
Item 8 - Squash Club Membership (Note 8)	Nil
Item 9 - Housing Loss Reimbursement (Note 9)	1,300
Item 10 - Imputed Interest On Housing Loan (Note 10)	170
Item 11 - Stock Option Benefit (Note 11)	1,280
Item 12 - Automobile Benefit (Note 12)	741
Item 13 - Stationery And Supplies	(129)
Item 13 - Long Distance Calls	(74)
Item 13 - Home Office (Note 13)	(563)
Item 14 - Home Office Allowance (Note 14)	1,500
Net Employment Income	$77,418

Note 1 Amounts received prior to, during, or after employment are required to be included in employment income when received.

Salary and other forms of remuneration such as bonuses are included in income when received regardless of when earned.

Income taxes, CPP, and EI withheld are not deductible. Note, however, that the CPP and EI are eligible for a non-refundable tax credit that will reduce Tax Payable.

Note 2 Only the $2,000 amount of the bonus that was received in 2020 will be included in that year's Net Income For Tax Purposes. The remaining $5,450 will not be included in Net Income For Tax Purposes until it is received in 2021.

Note 3 Employer provided mental health counseling services are not considered to be a taxable benefit.

Note 4 Group medical plans are generally referred to as Private Health Insurance Plans. Employer paid premiums for such plans are not considered to be a taxable benefit.

Note 5 Employer contributions to RPPs are not considered to be a taxable benefit.

Note 6 The reimbursement of employee professional dues is considered a taxable benefit, but the employee is generally entitled to an employment expense deduction for annual professional membership dues under ITA 8(1)(i).

Note 7 Non-cash gifts from employers that total less than $500 per year are not considered taxable benefits. The employer's share of the wedding gifts was $425.

Note 8 Fees for club memberships where the primary advantage is to the employer are not considered to be a taxable benefit.

Note 9 Employer reimbursed housing losses fall into two categories – regular housing losses and eligible housing losses. Eligible housing losses occur when there is an eligible relocation, which generally means a relocation or move the expenses of which would qualify for a moving expense deduction had they been paid by the employee. In this case the move is an eligible relocation meaning that the reimbursement qualifies as an eligible housing loss. The employer reimbursed $17,600 [(80%)($22,000)]. The taxable portion of the loss reimbursement is $1,300 [(1/2)($17,600 - $15,000)]. The remaining tax free amount of $16,300 can be calculated as ($17,600 - $1,300) or [$15,000 + (1/2)($17,600 - $15,000)].

Note 10 When an employee receives an interest free or low interest loan an imputed interest benefit is calculated. The interest benefit is $170 [(1%)($200,000)(31/365)]. Note that the alternative calculation, based on months outstanding, would result in a value of $167 [(1%)($200,000) ÷ 12]. It appears that this value would be accepted by the CRA.

There is no reduction in that amount since Mitch is not required to repay any of the interest. As this loan would qualify as a home relocation loan, Mitch will claim a home relocation loan deduction in the calculation of Taxable Income. However, this would have no effect on the required net employment income calculation.

Note 11 Despite the fact that the option price was 20 percent below fair market value, the issuance of the stock options does not create employment income. However, when he exercises the option by purchasing shares, there is a benefit as follows:

Market Value At Exercise Date ($12,800 ÷ 80%)	$16,000
Option Price	(12,800)
Value of Benefit (200 shares)	$ 3,200
Per Share Benefit ($3,200 ÷ 200)	$16 Per Share

As Oxford Associates is a CCPC, this benefit can be deferred until the shares are sold. As 80 shares are sold, there will be a 2020 net employment income inclusion of $1,280 [(80)($16)]. Note that, while this is not relevant to the determination of net employment income, no deduction would be available under either ITA 110(1)(d) or 110(1)(d.1) as the option price will always be less than the fair market value at the time the option was granted.

In addition to the employment income inclusion, there is a taxable capital gain of $1,280 {[1/2][$8,960 - (80/200)($16,000)]}. However, capital gains are not a component of net employment income.

Note 12 The kilometres driven in the year total 19,252 (19,414 − 162), of which 5,198 are personal and 14,054 (19,252 - 5,198) are employment related. Since the employment-related driving accounts for more than 50 percent (14,054 ÷ 19,252 = 73%), a reduced standby charge is available. The automobile benefit would be calculated as follows:

Standby Charge [(2/3)(8)($430)(5,198 ÷ 13,336*)]	$ 894
Operating Cost Benefit - Lesser Of:	
• [($0.28)(5,198)] = $1,455	
• [(1/2)($894) = $447	447
Total Benefit	$1,341
Reimbursement To Employer [(8)($75)]	(600)
Net Benefit	$ 741

*[(8)(1,667)]

Note 13   Based on floor space, the home office occupies 8.5 percent of the apartment [100 ÷ 1,176]. The work space in the home expenses that may be claimed for the period June 1 to November 30 are the following:

Rent Paid [(6)($960)]	$5,760
Electricity Paid [($870)(6 ÷ 8.5 Months)]	614
Paint	253
Total Eligible Expenses	$6,627
Home Office Use	8.5%
Deductible Expense	$ 563

Note 14   Allowances received are included in employment income unless the allowance is specifically excluded by ITA 6(1)(b). There is no exclusion for this allowance. The amount is $1,500 [(6)($250)].

Chapter 4 Learning Objectives

Note Regarding Rates And Credits

A schedule of rates, brackets, credit amounts, and other data is available at the beginning of both Volumes of this textbook (but not this Study Guide) and on MyLab. We expect you to refer to this information when calculating the credits covered in this chapter (i.e., you are not expected to memorize the rates, brackets, and credit bases).

After completing Chapter 4, you should be able to:

1. Calculate Taxable Income when an individual has basic deductions against Net Income For Tax Purposes. (paragraph [P hereafter] 4-1 to 4-9).
2. Calculate federal and provincial Tax Payable before the consideration of any tax credits (P 4-10 to 4-32).
3. Calculate the personal tax credits described in ITA 118(1), which include the:
    *   spousal,
    *   eligible dependant,
    *   Canada caregiver for a child,
    *   basic, and
    *   Canada caregiver credits (P 4-33 to 4-73).
4. Calculate the age tax credit (P 4-74 and 4-75).
5. Calculate the pension income tax credit (P 4-76 to 4-80).

6. Calculate the Canada employment tax credit (P 4-81 to 4-83).
7. Calculate the adoption expenses tax credit (P 4-84 to 4-88).
8. Calculate the digital news subscriptions credit that is effective in 2020 (P 4-89 to 4-90).
9. Calculate the home accessibility tax credit (P 4-91 to 4-101).
10. Calculate the first-time home buyer's tax credit (P 4-102 to 4-104).

11. Calculate the volunteer firefighters and search and rescue workers tax credit (P 4-105 to 4-108).
12. Calculate the charitable donations tax credit when the donation is in the form of cash (P 4-109 to 4-120).
13. Calculate the medical expense tax credit (P 4-121 to 4-131).
14. Calculate the disability tax credit (P 4-132 to 4-142).
15. Calculate the tax credits related to tuition fees, examination fees, ancillary fees, and student loan interest. (P 4-143 to 4-150).

16. Calculate the amount of education related tax credits that can be carried forward or transferred to another individual (P 4-151 to 4-160).
17. Calculate the Employment Insurance and Canada Pension Plan credits (P 4-161 to 4-167).
18. List the types and amounts of tax credits that can be transferred to a spouse or common-law partner (P 4-168 to 4-170).
19. Calculate the political contributions tax credit (P 4-171 to 4-174).

20. Calculate the labour sponsored venture capital corporation tax credit (P 4-175 to 4-179).

21. Explain the basic provisions of the refundable GST credit (P 4-180 to 4-187).
22. Calculate the refundable medical expense supplement (P 4-188 to 4-191).
23. Calculate the Canada Workers Benefit (P 4-192 to 4-195).
24. Calculate the refundable teacher and early childhood educator school supply tax credit (P 4-196 to 4-198).
25. Explain the Climate Action Incentive payments (refundable credit) (P 4-199 to 4-206).

26. Calculate the Canada Training Credit (P 4-207 to P-211).
27. Calculate the OAS and EI clawbacks (P 4-212 to 4-222).
28. Complete a simple personal tax return using the ProFile T1 tax preparation software program.

How to Work Through Chapter 4

We recommend the following approach in dealing with the material in this chapter:

Taxable Income Of Individuals
- Read the beginning of the Chapter to paragraph 4-9 (in the textbook).

Federal And Provincial Tax Payable Before Credits
- Read paragraph 4-10 to 4-22.
- Do Exercise Four-1 and check the solution in this Study Guide.
- Read paragraph 4-23 to 4-27.

Credits Against Tax Payable - Calculating The Amount
- Read paragraph 4-28 to 4-32.

Basic Personal Amount (BPA) and Spousal Tax Credits
- Read paragraph 4-33 to 4-49.
- Do Exercise Four-2 and check the solution in this Study Guide.
- Do Self Study Problem Four-1, which is available on MyLab, and check the solution in this Study Guide.

Eligible Dependant, Canada Caregiver For Child And Caregiver Tax Credits
- Read paragraph 4-50 to 4-71.
- Do Exercises Four-3 to Four-5 and check the solutions in this Study Guide.
- Read paragraph 4-72 and 4-73.
- Do Exercise Four-6 and check the solution in this Study Guide.

Age, Pension, Canada Employment, And Adoption Expenses Tax Credits
- Read paragraph 4-74 and 4-75.
- Do Exercise Four-7 and check the solution in this Study Guide.
- Read paragraph 4-76 to 4-88
- Do Exercise Four-8 and check the solution in this Study Guide.

Digital News Subscriptions Credit
- Read paragraph 4-89 to 4-90.

Home Accessibility Tax Credit
- Read paragraph 4-91 to 4-101.
- Do Exercise Four-9 and check the solution in this Study Guide.

First-Time Home Buyer's And Volunteer Firefighters And Search And Rescue Workers Tax Credits
- Read paragraph 4-102 to 4-108

Charitable Donations Credit
- Read paragraph 4-109 to 4-116.
- Do Exercise Four-10 and check the solution in this Study Guide.
- Read paragraph 4-117 to 4-120.
- Do Exercise Four-11 and check the solution in this Study Guide.

Medical Expense Credit
- Read paragraph 4-121 to 4-131.
- Do Exercise Four-12 and check the solution in this Study Guide.

Disability Credit
- Read paragraph 4-132 to 4-139.
- Do Exercise Four-13 and check the solution in this Study Guide.
- Read paragraph 4-140 to 4-142.

Education Related Credits Including Carry Forwards And Transfers
- Read paragraph 4-143 to 4-150.
- Do Exercise Four-14 and check the solution in this Study Guide.
- Read paragraph 4-151 to 4-160.
- Do Exercise Four-15 and check the solution in this Study Guide.

Employment Insurance And Canada Pension Plan Tax Credits
- Read paragraph 4-161 to 4-167.

Credit Transfers To A Spouse Or Common-Law Partner
- Read paragraph 4-168 to 4-170.
- Do Exercise Four-16 and check the solution in this Study Guide.
- Do Self Study Problems Four-2 and Four-3 and check the solutions in this Study Guide.

Political Contributions Credit
- Read paragraph 4-171 to 4-174.
- Do Exercise Four-17 and check the solution in this Study Guide.

Labour Sponsored Venture Capital Corporation (LSVCC) Credit
- Read paragraph 4-175 to 4-179.
- Do Self Study Problems Four-4 and Four-5 and check the solutions in this Study Guide.

Refundable Credits - GST And Refundable Medical Expense Supplement
- Read paragraph 4-180 to 4-191.
- Do Exercise Four-18 and check the solution in this Study Guide.

Refundable Credits - Canada Workers Benefit And Teacher School Supply
- Read paragraph 4-192 to 4-198.

Refundable Credits - Climate Action Incentive Payments
- Read paragraph 4-199 to 4-206.

Refundable Credits - Canada Training Credit (Proposed)
- Read paragraph 4-207 to 4-211.

EI And OAS Repayment (Clawback)
- Read paragraph 4-212 to 4-222.
- Do Exercise Four-19 and check the solution in this Study Guide.

Comprehensive Example
- Read paragraph 4-223.
- Do Self Study Problems Four-6 to Four-8 and check the solutions in this Study Guide.

Sample Personal Tax Return For Chapter 4
- Read the Sample Personal Tax Return For Chapter 4 found in this Chapter of this Study Guide. The complete tax returns are available on MyLab in two formats, a T1 ProFile return file and a .PDF file.

Tax Software Self Study Problem
- Read the Suggestions For Working With ProFile Software found in this Chapter of this Study Guide.
- Do Tax Software Self Study Problem - Chapter 4 using the ProFile T1 Software. The Self Study Problem is found in this Chapter of this Study Guide. The complete tax return is available on MyLab.

To Complete This Chapter
- If you would like more practice in problem solving, do the Supplementary Self Study Problems for the chapter. These problems and solutions are available on MyLab.
- Review the Key Terms Used In This Chapter in the textbook at the end of Chapter 4. Consult the Glossary for the meaning of any key terms you do not know.
- Test yourself with the Chapter 4 Glossary Flashcards available on MyLab.
- Ensure you have achieved the Chapter 4 Learning Objectives listed in this Study Guide.
- As a review, we recommend you view the PowerPoint presentation for Chapter 4 that is on MyLab.

Practice Examination
Write the Practice Examination for Chapter 4 that is on MyLab. Mark your examination using the Practice Examination Solution that is also on MyLab.

Sample Personal Tax Return For Chapter 4

The following example contains a T1 individual income tax return completed using the ProFile T1 Personal Income Tax Program for 2019 tax returns from Intuit Canada. As software for 2020 is not yet available, this example contains 2019 rates and credits.

The updated 2020 filing version of the ProFile software will be available in January 2021. Non-filing versions will be available prior to that date, but include a number of 2020 draft forms that have not yet been updated. On installation, the program defaults to check for updates, so non-filing versions may be installed automatically. In January 2021, after the first 2020 filing version is released, the updated 2020 version of this sample return will be available on MyLab at:

http://www.pearsonmylabandmastering.com

This example is expanded in Chapter 11 to contain other components of Taxable Income and Tax Payable. In the following example, the relevant T1 schedule or ProFile form name is provided in square brackets to make it easier for users to find where the information is input.

A Word on the CRA Redesign of the T1 Individual Income Tax Return for 2019
The CRA has redesigned the T1 individual income tax return for 2019. The new return has doubled in size increasing to eight pages from four. The most significant changes are (1) the addition of new questions concerning whether any income received is exempt under the *Indian Act*; (2) the change of line numbers from 3 or 4 digits to 5 - for example net income was previously line 236 and is now line 23600; and (3) the elimination of Schedule 1 (tax calculations including tax credits) and the related worksheet, which are now incorporated into the income tax return. The CRA further explains in the introductory pages to the 2019 Federal Income Tax and Benefit Guide that additional changes include the increased use of plain language, increasing the font size, adding white space, and updating worksheets to simplify calculations.

Sample Files On MyLab
To View The Tax Return Files
The complete sample tax returns are available on MyLab in two versions, a T1 ProFile return file and a .PDF file.

To view the ProFile return files (files with a .19T extension), you must have the ProFile program installed. For information on how to obtain the program for free, see MyLab.

To view the .PDF files, you must have the Adobe Reader program installed. This program can be installed for free from the Adobe website (www.adobe.com).

Tips To Increase The Benefits From Viewing The ProFile Files

When viewing the sample return ProFile file, we suggest the following:

- Press <F1> on any ProFile form or field to display related information in the help system. In ProFile dialog boxes, click the [?] symbol in the top right corner, then click any element for help on that item.
- By pressing <F4> you will open the Form Explorer. In the categories of forms appearing in the shaded box on the left, if you choose "A. Used" near the bottom of the column, all the forms that have calculations for the return will be shown. You can then double click on the form itself to view it.
- Right clicking on a number in a field shows a variety of options, including the form or schedule where the amount originated from.
- Clicking on "Show Auditor" under the "Audit" list will display any warnings or potential errors.

For students who would like more assistance in using the software, we have provided "Suggestions For Working With ProFile Software" in this Study Guide following this example.

Sample T1 Tax Return Data

DISCLAIMER: All characters appearing in this example are fictitious. Any resemblance to real persons, living or dead, is purely coincidental.

George Pilot (SIN 527-000-145) is a married, semi-retired air force pilot living in Banff, Alberta. His wife, Deborah (SIN 130-692-544), was mauled by a grizzly bear while hiking three years ago. The attack left her blind and limited her mobility. [Schedule 2 - Yes to disability amount]

They have been your clients for many years. George was born on February 24, 1968, and Deborah was born on April 10, 1972. They are both Canadian citizens.

After some discussion with George and Deborah, you confirm that they have never owned any foreign property. They both authorize the CRA to provide information to Elections Canada and authorize you to e-file their returns. They are currently living at 69 BBB Street in Banff, Alberta, T9Z 0C0. Their home phone number is (403) 111-1111.

George and Deborah have three children who are all in good health:

- Bryan (SIN 527-000-947) was born on March 12, 2012, and had no income during the year.
- Janice (SIN 527-000-269) was born on June 6, 2006, and is in high school. She had income from babysitting totaling $400 during 2019.
- Willa (SIN 527-000-228) was born on January 22, 2000, and is attending university in Edmonton. Willa had Net Income of $3,300 during 2019.

George has a passion for flying and was hired in February to fly fire bombers from June 1 to September 30 for the provincial forest service fire control squad located in Banff.

George informs you that on February 12, 2019, he received $2 million from his mother's estate. Using some of these funds, George bought a house in Banff. The remainder of the funds were invested with his stockbroker, $$$$ Inc. In this Chapter 4 version of the example, assume there is no investment income from these funds.

Deborah had no income during the year. [Info - Spousal information - Yes to the question "Is spouse's Net Income zero?"]

George brings you the following receipts and documents:

1. A T4 (included in this example).
2. A T2202A "Tuition And Enrollment Certificate" for himself from Athabasca University. It showed he was a part time student for six months and paid $591 in tuition for 2019. [T2202]

3. Two charitable donation receipts. One in George's name for $1,000 from the Canadian Wildlife Federation dated April 10, 2019. A second receipt in Deborah's name for $100 from the Canadian National Institute for the Blind (CNIB) dated December 3, 2019. [Donations]

4. A statement from the Banff Dental Clinic that George paid a total of $1,650 during 2019. This consisted of $850 for himself on November 24, and $200 each for Deborah, Bryan, Willa, and Janice on December 15. [Medical]

5. An invoice from the CNIB in Deborah's name for $375 dated December 26, 2019, for computer peripherals designed exclusively for a person who is blind to use a computer. She had obtained a prescription from her doctor specifying her need for this equipment. [Medical]

6. George spent $14,700 during 2019 on various permanent modifications to the house. His goal for these changes was to allow Deborah to be more mobile inside and outside the house (e.g., outside ramps and railings in the halls and stairways) and to reduce the risk of harm to her (a walk-in bathtub). George has detailed invoices for the renovations. Since Deborah's mobility impairment is not severe, these expenditures do not qualify as allowable medical expenses. [Schedule 12]

7. An agreement of purchase and sale for a house at 69 BBB St. in Banff. The purchase price was $800,000 and the invoice for legal fees totaled $1,200. The deal closed March 31, 2019, and George paid the purchase price of the house in cash. George and his family had been living in a rented townhouse for the last five years. Prior to that George had owned a house, but it went to his ex-wife in the divorce settlement. Deborah has never owned a principal residence. [OtherCredits for the Home Buyers' Credit.]

8. An instalment statement for 2019 that showed that George had paid the CRA instalments of $1,500 on September 14 and December 14 ($3,000 in total). These were the instalments requested by the CRA for the year due to his self-employed income in the previous year. [OtherCredits]

Sample T1 Tax Return Notes
General Notes

- Inheritances are not taxable.
- Due to his low Net Income For Tax Purposes, George is eligible for the refundable medical expense supplement and the Canada Workers Benefit.
- Although George could consider carrying forward his medical expenses because his non-refundable tax credits are greater than his Tax Payable, if he did so, he would not receive the refundable medical expense supplement.
- Since Willa is over 17 years of age, her medical expenses are reduced by 3 percent of her Net Income For Tax Purposes.
- Due to his nil Tax Payable, George's charitable donation credit and his tuition credit are both carried forward.
- As a resident of Alberta George qualifies for the refundable Climate Action Incentive payment for 2019. This refundable credit is available to individuals who are residents of Ontario, Manitoba, Saskatchewan, and Alberta in 2019. The maximum credit for a family of four in Alberta is $888.
- George's 2019 CPP contribution of $790.50 is calculated as 5.1 percent of insurable earnings, which are equal to his employment income of $19,000 minus a basic exemption of $3,500. There are two components to the CPP contribution rate of 5.1 percent. The first is a <u>basic</u> contribution rate of 4.95 percent and the second an additional amount of 0.15 percent referred to as an <u>enhancement</u>. The enhancement represents an effort by the Federal government to provide increased CPP retirement pension benefits. The basic 4.95 percent or $767.25 is treated as a non-refundable tax credit and the enhanced portion of $23.25 is allowed as a deduction (new line 22215).

Item Specific Notes

- (Item 3) For couples, the CRA's administrative practices permit either spouse to claim some or all of the donations made by the couple. This is not relevant in this version as the donations are carried forward. Complete Schedule 9.

- (Item 5) Both ITA 118.2 and Income Tax Folio S1-F1-C1 clearly state that medical expenses can only be deducted by the individual who paid for them. However, in the T1 Guide, this rule is contradicted for couples. According to this Guide, either spouse can claim the medical expense credit, without regard to who actually paid for the expenses. This administrative position is used in practice. As a result, George is claiming the amount Deborah paid for the computer peripherals.
- (Item 6) George's receipts for the expenses eligible for the Home Accessibility Credit total more than the $10,000 maximum for the year on "the worksheet for the return". As a result the maximum credit of $1,500 [(15%)($10,000)] is available. However, since George's non-refundable tax credits already exceed his Tax Payable, he cannot take advantage of this credit and it cannot be carried forward.
- (Item 7) The Home Buyers' Tax Credit of $750 [(15%)($5,000)] is available since George had been living in a rented town house for five years and neither he nor Deborah had another principal residence. However, since George's non-refundable tax credits already exceed his Tax Payable, he cannot take advantage of this credit either and it cannot be carried forward.

Tax Planning Points

- Willa should file a return in order to receive the GST credit and to help her keep track of her tuition credit carry forward.
- (Item 8) George has paid instalments based on the CRA's Instalment Reminders. Given the amount of his refund, they were unnecessary. George should review his estimated net tax owing periodically in the future to determine whether instalments should be paid.

Completed Tax Returns

The complete sample tax returns are available on MyLab in two versions, a T1 ProFile return file and a .PDF file.

Suggestions For Working With ProFile Software

Before You Start

To get the maximum benefit from using the ProFile tax software program, we strongly advise that you do the tutorial "Getting Started" included within the program under the Training tab. The data in the sample tax returns can be used in the tutorial. Also on the Training tab is access to "Other Training Options", which include online training and many how-to videos.

Creating A New T1 Return

To provide some guidance on how to use ProFile to create a simple new personal tax return, we suggest the following approach.

1. Start the ProFile software. Open a new file. Ensure that you have chosen the new file in the correct software (T1) and year (2019 or 2020 if the updated data are available).

2. By default, ProFile will open on the form "Info". Fill in the highlighted cells and answer all questions that are applicable. If you do not fill in the highlighted areas, ProFile will generate an audit message. At a minimum, you will need the following information:

   - Taxpayer's Social Insurance Number (SIN)
   - Taxpayer's first and last name
   - Address, city, province, and postal code
   - Telephone number
   - Taxpayer's birth date

If applicable, you will also need to enter any relevant information for the spouse on the "Info" form. At a minimum, the following information will be necessary:

- Spouse's Social Insurance Number (SIN)
- Spouse's first and last name
- Address, city, province, and postal code
- Telephone number
- Spouse's birth date

3. Using the Form Explorer (F4), go to the Dependant form and enter all relevant information about any dependants. At a minimum, the following information will be necessary:

- Dependant's Social Insurance Number (SIN) if there is one
- Dependant's first and last name
- Dependant's relationship to the taxpayer
- Dependant's birth date
- Dependant's Net Income
- Address, city, province, and postal code

Note that if there are child care expenses, the information will flow here from T778. If the dependant has tuition fee amounts, the tuition fee information should be entered on the Dependant form.

4. Using the Form Explorer (F4), open the relevant information slip form. Enter all relevant information in the appropriate forms. Some common information slip forms are:

- T3 - Statement of Trust Income
- T4 - Statement of Remuneration Paid
- T5 - Statement of Investment Income
- T2202A - Tuition Slips
- T4AOAS - Statement of Old Age Security

5. Enter any other relevant income information on the appropriate forms. These forms may include the following:

- S3Details - Capital Gains Entry
  (this form, not Schedule 3, must be used to input details on capital dispositions)
- T2125 - Statement of Business or Professional Activities
- T2125Asset - T2125 Asset Details
- T2125CCA - T2125 CCA Details
- T776 - Statement of Real Estate Rentals
- T776Asset - T776 Asset Details
- T776CCA - T776 CCA Details

6. Enter any relevant deduction information on the appropriate forms. These forms may include the following:

- RRSP - RRSP Deduction
- T777 - Statement of Employment Expenses (Use the jump link to T777Details in the upper right hand corner of form if applicable)
- T778 - Child Care Expense Deduction
- Support - Support Payments
- T777 Auto - Motor Vehicle Expenses
- Investment income such as interest and taxable dividends was formerly included on Schedule 4, which no longer exists. This information together with the deduction of carrying charges is now included on the "worksheet for the return".
- LossNetCap - Net Capital Losses (carry forward information)
- LossNonCap - Non-Capital Losses (carry forward information)

7. Enter any relevant tax credit information on the appropriate forms. These forms may include the following:

    - Donations - Charitable Donations Schedule 9
    - Medical - Medical Expenses

8. Enter any remaining relevant information in the appropriate schedule. These schedules may include the following:

    - S2 - Federal Amounts Transferred From Your Spouse or Common-Law Partner (primarily used if spouse or common-law partner is not filing a tax return)
    - T1032 - Joint Election To Split Pension Income

9. Use the function "Show Auditor" under the "Audit" list to check for warnings or potential errors.

Tips For Using ProFile Software

- Press the <F5> key or choose Spouse from the Form menu to display the return of the spouse.
- If you cannot determine where a specific slip or other information should be input, one way to search for the correct form is to open the Form Explorer (<F4>) and choose the "Key" mode icon in the top right corner of the menu. If you type a key word into the line above the listing of key words, the appropriate form may be found.
- Press the <F4> key to view the Form Explorer. Choose the form "Summary" to see the tax data of both spouses on the same one page summary. (Second column will be blank for a single taxpayer.)
- If you want to print only the form you have on the screen, use the print icon identified with 1 in the tool bar. The other print icon opens the print selection screen for printing complete returns. If you want to print just one copy of the return, deselect the print sets you don't want on the print selection screen. Before you print the return, review the forms that have been selected in the print set to ensure that you will not be printing forms you do not require. If it is a coupled return, the print settings for the spouse should be reviewed before clicking on Print as both returns will be printed.
- Review marks can be used to flag information that should be reviewed. The cell with the review mark will be listed when the Show Auditor feature is turned on.
- A memo and/or a tape can be attached to a cell to provide backup information.
- If you are having problems with a specific issue, go to the Training tab, "Other Training Options", to access the online how-to videos, which may help solve your problems.

Tax Software Self Study Problem - Chapter 4

Note The following problem contains 2019 (not 2020) information as software for 2020 is not yet available. If you have an updated 2020 version of ProFile installed on your computer, ensure that when you begin you open a file for 2019, not 2020, as this data is for 2019. Shortly after the first filing version of the 2020 Intuit ProFile software is available in January 2021, the updated 2020 version of this problem will be available on MyLab at:

http://www.pearsonmylabandmastering.com

This Tax Software Self Study Problem is expanded in Chapter 11 to contain other components of Taxable Income and Tax Payable.

DISCLAIMER: All characters appearing in this problem are fictitious. Any resemblance to real persons, living or dead, is purely coincidental.

Ms. Eleanor Victoria's husband died two years ago. After her husband died, she moved from her house in Prince George, B.C., to a rented house in Victoria, B.C.

Ms. Victoria's widowed mother, Marjorie Vancouver, lives with Ms. Victoria and takes care of the house, Ms. Victoria's younger daughter, Amy, and all of the household cooking. In addition to OAS benefits, Marjorie has a very small income from her deceased husband's life insurance policy. She has never filed a tax return and she is not infirm.

Diane Victoria, Eleanor's older daughter, is studying psychology at McGill University in Montreal. Her field is addiction research with a special emphasis on gambling. She does volunteer work at a gambling addiction treatment centre in Montreal in the summers. As Eleanor has paid for her tuition and living costs, Diane has agreed that the maximum tuition amount should be transferred to her mother.

Diane has decided not to file a tax return this year as she knows she does not owe any taxes. Her income was earned driving for a client of the addiction treatment centre who had lost his licence after being charged with impaired driving.

Information concerning Ms. Victoria for 2019 is given on the following pages.

Required: With the objective of minimizing Ms. Victoria's Tax Payable, prepare the 2019 income tax return of Eleanor Victoria using the ProFile tax software program. List any assumptions you have made, and any notes and tax planning issues you feel should be discussed with Ms. Victoria. Ignore HST implications in your solution by assuming that Ms. Victoria does not qualify for the GST/HST rebate.

Personal Information

Title	Ms.
First Name	Eleanor
Last Name	Victoria
SIN	527-000-087
Date of birth (Y/M/D)	1972-05-15
Marital Status	Widowed
Canadian citizen?	Yes
Provide information to Elections Canada?	Yes
Own foreign property of more than $100,000 Canadian?	No

Taxpayer's Address

111 VVV Street Victoria, B.C. V4H 3W4
Phone number (250) 111-1111

Dependants

Dependants	Child 1	Child 2	Mother
First Name	Diane	Amy	Marjorie
Last Name	Victoria	Victoria	Vancouver
SIN	527-000-293	None	527-000-483
Date of birth (Y/M/D)	1999-05-14	2007-10-11	1947-05-21
Net income	$2,300	Nil	$8,000

T4	Box	Amount
Issuer - 1750 Canada Inc.		
Employment income	14	60,201.80
Employee's CPP contributions	16	2,748.90
Employee's EI premiums	18	856.36
RPP contributions	20	2,406.16
Pension adjustment	52	7,829.00
Income tax deducted	22	6,408.00
Employment commissions	42	0
Union dues	44	748.59
Charitable donations	46	175.00

Eleanor has a signed T2200 from her employer specifying her work requires her to have an office in the home. She meets the conditions required to deduct work space in the home expenses. Of the 1,800 square feet in the house, her office, waiting area and storage space totals 310 square feet. She doesn't qualify for the GST rebate.

During 2019 she paid the following:

Rent for the year (No GST charged)	$30,000
Utilities (hydro and gas) for the year	2,500
Cleaning services (No GST charged)	1,200
Insurance for household effects (No GST charged)	400
Car insurance (No GST charged)	700

Eleanor and her family had the following medical expenses, all of which Eleanor paid for:

Patient	(Y/M/D)	Medical Expenses	Description	Am't
Eleanor	2019-08-15	Grace Hospital	Ambulance charge	392
Eleanor	2019-08-18	Paramed Home Health	Nursing care	1,350
Marjorie	2019-05-20	Dr. Zhang (Optometrist)	Contact lenses	110
Marjorie	2019-07-06	Pharmacy	Prescription	75
Diane	2019-09-01	Dr. Glassman	Physiotherapist	100
Amy	2019-05-11	Walk Right Foot Clinic	Orthotics	450
Amy	2019-01-23	Dr. Tamo	Dental Fees	1,120

T2202A - (Diane)	Box	Amount
Tuition fees - for Diane Victoria (daughter)	A	7,000
Number of months in school - part time	B	2
Number of months in school - full time	C	8

Donor	Charitable Donation Receipts	Am't
Eleanor	Heart and Stroke	375
Eleanor	Terry Fox Foundation	50
Diane	Addiction Research Council of Canada	100

Solutions to Chapter 4 Exercises

Exercise Four - 1 Solution

The required Tax Payable would be calculated as follows:

Tax Payable On First $48,535 At 20.05 Percent (15.00% + 5.05%)	$ 9,731
Tax Payable On Next $8,165 ($56,700 - $48,535)	
At 29.65 Percent (20.5% + 9.15%)	2,421
Total Tax Payable Before Credits	$12,152

Her average rate of tax is 21.4 percent ($12,152 ÷ $56,700).

Exercise Four - 2 Solution

Assuming Johan's wife does not have a mental or physical infirmity, the required amount would be calculated as follows:

Basic Personal Amount (Johan)	$13,229
Spousal Amount ($13,229 - $2,600)	10,629
Credit Base	$23,858
Rate	15%
Personal Tax Credits - No Infirmity	$ 3,579

If there were a mental or physical infirmity, the amount would be calculated as follows:

Basic Personal Amount (Johan)	$13,229
Spousal Amount ($13,229 + $2,273 - $2,600)	12,902
Credit Base	$26,131
Rate	15%
Personal Tax Credits - With Infirmity	$ 3,920

Exercise Four - 3 Solution

As her father is not infirm, Joan would not be entitled to a Canada caregiver credit for him. She is entitled to a Canada caregiver credit for her mother who is infirm. The credit would be:

$$[15\%][\$7,276 - (\$21,400 - \$17,085)] = \$444$$

Exercise Four - 4 Solution

Marcia will be entitled to the spousal tax credit, including the additional amount for an infirm spouse. In addition, she can claim the Canada caregiver credit for her infirm adult son. The total credits would be calculated as follows:

Spousal Including Infirm Amount	
($13,229 + $2,273 - $5,600)	$ 9,902
Canada Caregiver ($7,276 - Nil)	7,276
Total Base	$17,178
Rate	15%
Marcia's Tax Credits Related To Spouse And Son	$ 2,577

Exercise Four - 5 Solution

Darcy would claim the Canada caregiver amount for a child under ITA 118(1)(b.1). He would also claim the eligible dependant credit for Janice. Because he claims the Canada caregiver amount for a child, he cannot claim the additional amount for an infirm eligible dependant. His total credits would be as follows:

$$[(15\%)(\$2,273) + (15\%)(\$13,229 + Nil)] = \$2,325$$

Exercise Four - 6 Solution

The base for Sandy's eligible dependant credit for her mother would be nil ($13,229 + $2,273 - $18,000), resulting in an eligible dependant tax credit of nil. Her calculation of the Canada caregiver amount would result in a base of $6,361 [$7,276 - ($18,000 - $17,085)]. As the eligible dependant tax credit was nil, the additional amount is $6,361 ($6,361 - Nil), resulting in a credit of $954 [(15%)($6,361)].

Exercise Four - 7 Solution

Mr. Smythe's age credit would be $853 {[15%][$7,637 - (15%)($51,500 - $38,508)]}.

Exercise Four - 8 Solution

The adoption expenses tax credit would be calculated as follows:

Cost Of First China Trip	$ 4,250
Cost Of Second China Trip	6,420
Chinese Orphanage Fee	1,600
Canadian Adoption Agency Fee	3,200
Legal Fees	2,700
Medical Costs (Qualify For Medical Expense Credit)	Nil
Total Eligible Expenses	$18,170

Since the $5,000 employer reimbursement is a taxable benefit and included in employment income, it does not reduce the total eligible adoption expenses.

The adoption period begins at the time that an application is made for registration with an adoption agency licensed by a provincial government. This means that all of the expenses listed in the preceding table would be eligible expenses made during the adoption period. However, for 2020, there is an overall limit of $16,563 and the maximum credit that can be claimed is $2,484 [(15%)($16,563)].

Exercise Four - 9 Solution

The snow removal contract would not be a qualifying expenditure. The base for the home accessibility tax credit would be limited to the lesser of $10,000 and the qualifying expenditures of $8,500. This will result in a credit of $1,275 [(15%)($8,500)].

Either spouse can claim the credit and it will be worth the same amount to either spouse. Since it is non-refundable, whoever claims the credit should have at least $1,275 in federal Tax Payable. Alternatively, the $8,500 base amount can be split between the two spouses.

Exercise Four - 10 Solution

With Net Income For Tax Purposes of $350,000, the maximum base for Mr. Hoffman's credit is $262,500 [(75%)($350,000)]. As his eligible charitable gifts are less than this, he can use the full amount as the base for his credit. Given this, the calculation of the credit is as follows:

$$[(15\%)(A)] + [(33\%)(B)] + [(29\%)(C)], \text{ where}$$

A = $200
B = The Lesser Of:
  • $225,000 - $200 = $224,800
  • $325,000 - $214,368 = $110,632 (Note Taxable Income is used here)
C = $114,168 [$225,000 - ($200 + $110,632)]

The charitable donation credit would be equal to $69,647, calculated as [(15%)($200)] + [(33%) ($110,632)] + [(29%)($114,168)].

Exercise Four - 11 Solution

With Net Income For Tax Purposes of $350,000, the maximum base for Ms. Hoffman's credit is $262,500 [(75%)($350,000)]. As her donation credit carry forward is less than this, she can use the full amount as the base for her credit. Given this, the calculation of the credit is as follows:

$$[(15\%)(A)] + [(33\%)(B)] + [(29\%)(C)], \text{ where}$$

A = $200
B = The Lesser Of:
• $225,000 - $200 = $224,800
• $250,000 - $214,368 = $35,632 (Note Taxable Income is used here)
C = $189,168 [$225,000 - ($200 + $35,632)]

The charitable donation credit would be equal to $66,647, calculated as [(15%)($200)] + [(33%)($35,632)] + [(29%)($189,168)]. If she had any unused portions of her 2020 donation, it would be available until 2024.

Exercise Four - 12 Solution

Amount B Qualifying Expenses ($4,330 + $4,600)		$ 8,930
Amount C - Lesser Of:		
• [(3%)($150,000)] = $4,500		
• 2020 Threshold Amount = $2,397		(2,397)
Subtotal		$ 6,533
Amount D		
Max's Medical Expenses	$ 8,425	
Reduced By The Lesser Of:		
• $2,397		
• [(3%)($8,250)] = $248	(248)	8,177
Matt's Medical Expenses	$ 120	
Reduced By The Lesser Of: $2,397		
• [(3%)($6,000)] = $180	(180)	Nil*
Allowable Amount Of Medical Expenses		$14,710
Amount A The Appropriate Rate (Minimum Rate)		15%
Medical Expense Tax Credit		2,207

*As medical expenses can only be reduced to nil, the net result cannot be negative in this calculation.

Exercise Four - 13 Solution

As Keith has no income, his disability credit can be transferred to John. As Keith is over 17, the disability child supplement is not available. In addition to the disability credit, John will be able to take the Canada caregiver credit, as well as a credit for Keith's medical expenses.

The total credits related to Keith would be as follows:

Transfer Of Keith's Disability Amount		$ 8,576
Canada Caregiver	$ 16,240	7,276
Keith's Medical Expenses		
Reduced By The Lesser Of:		
• 2020 Threshold Amount = $2,397		
• [(3%)(Nil)] = Nil	Nil	16,240
Total Credit Base		$32,092
Rate		15%
Total Credits Related To Keith		$ 4,814

Exercise Four - 14 Solution

Ms. Bright's education related tax credits would be calculated as follows:

Tuition Amount:		
Total (Including $1,000 Prepayment)	$3,200	
Ineligible Ancillary Fees ($400 - $250)	(150)	$3,050
Interest On Student Loan		325
Total Credit Base		$3,375
Rate		15%
Total Available Credits		$ 506

Exercise Four - 15 Solution

The available tuition credit would be calculated as follows:

Tuition Amount (Maximum Transfer = $5,000)	$23,500
Rate	15%
Tuition Credit (Maximum Transfer = $750)	$ 3,525

Note that the transfer and carry forward amounts calculated in the following alternative approaches ignore his medical expense credit.

Income Tax Act Approach The $750 maximum transfer of the tuition credit must be reduced by Jerry's Tax Payable, before deducting his medical expense credit of $266 [(15%)($15,000 - $13,229)]. This will leave a maximum transfer of $484 ($750 - $266) and a carry forward credit of $2,775 ($3,525 - $266 - $484).

Tax Return Approach The $5,000 maximum transfer of the tuition credit must be reduced by $1,771 ($15,000 - $13,229)], the excess of Jerry's Taxable Income over his basic personal amount. This results in a maximum transfer of $3,229 ($5,000 - $1,771) and a carry forward amount of $18,500 ($23,500 - $1,771 - $3,229). Multiplying this by 15 percent gives the same $2,775 that we calculated under the alternative approach.

Exercise Four - 16 Solution

His tax credits would be calculated as follows:

Basic Personal Amount	$13,229
Spousal Including Infirm Amount ($13,229 + $2,273 - Nil)	15,502
Age [$7,637 - (15%)($42,000 - $38,508)]	7,113
Pension Income*	2,000
Transfer Of Spouse's Age	7,637
Transfer Of Spouse's Disability	8,576
Transfer Of Spouse's Tuition - Lesser Of:	
• Actual Tuition = $2,200	
• Maximum Transfer = $5,000	2,200
Credit Base	$56,257
Rate	15%
Total Credits	$ 8,439

*A payment from a life annuity purchased with funds in an RRSP is eligible pension income.

Exercise Four - 17 Solution

Ms. Unger's $487 credit would be calculated as follows:

	Contributions	Credit Rate	Tax Credit
First	$400	3/4	$300
Next	350	1/2	175
Remaining	35	1/3	12
Maximum Credit	$785		$487

Exercise Four - 18 Solution

The regular medical expense credit would be calculated as follows:

Medical Expenses		$6,250
Lesser Of:		
• [(3%)($28,400)] = $852		
• 2020 Threshold Amount = $2,397		(852)
Allowable Amount Of Medical Expenses		$5,398
Rate		15%
Medical Expense Credit		$ 810

The refundable supplement would be calculated as follows:

Lesser Of:	
• $1,272 (2020 Maximum)	
• [(25/15)($810)] = $1,350	$1,272
Reduction [(5%)($28,400 - $28,164)]	(12)
Refundable Medical Expense Supplement	$1,260

Ms. Brunt's total Tax Payable (Refund) would be calculated as follows:

Tax Payable Before Credits [(15%)($28,400)]		$4,260
Non-Refundable Credits:		
Basic	$13,229	
Common-Law Partner	13,229	
Allowable Medical Expenses	5,398	
Total	$31,856	
Rate	15%	(4,778)
Tax Before Refundable Supplement		$ Nil*
Refundable Medical Expense Supplement		(1,260)
Tax Payable (Refund)		($1,260)

*As Tax Before Refundable Supplement can only be reduced to nil, the net result cannot be negative for this subtotal.

Exercise Four - 19 Solution

Ms. Jacobi's income before deducting either the EI or OAS repayments would be as follows:

Net Employment Income	$65,000
EI Benefits	10,000
OAS Benefits	7,400
Income Before Deductions	$82,400

Dealing first with the EI repayment, Ms. Jacobi would have to repay $3,000, the lesser of:

- $3,000 [(30%)($10,000)]
- $4,395 [(30%)($82,400 - $67,750)]

Using this deduction, the clawback of her OAS payments would be the lesser of:

- $7,400, the OAS payments included in income, and
- $52 [(15%)($82,400 - $3,000 - $79,054)].

As a result, her Net Income For Tax Purposes would be as follows:

Income Before Deductions	$82,400
ITA 60(v.1) Deduction (EI)	(3,000)
ITA 60(w) Deduction (OAS)	(52)
Net Income For Tax Purposes	$79,348

Solution to Self Study Problem Four - 1

Case One
In Case One, the combined Tax Payable would be calculated as follows:

Barbra's Tax Payable		
Federal Tax Before Credits [(15%)($42,000)]	$ 6,300	
Basic Personal Credit [($13,229)(15%)]	(1,984)	$ 4,316
Sally's Tax Payable		
Tax On First $150,473	$ 31,115	
Tax On Next $29,527 ($180,000 - $150,473) At 29%	8,563	
Federal Tax Before Credits	$39,678	
Basic Personal Credit [($12,799*)(15%)]	(1,920)	37,758
Combined Tax Payable		$ 42,074

*The base for Sally's basic personal amount is calculated as follows:

$13,229 - [$931][$180,000 - $150,473) ÷ $63,895]

Case Two
In Case Two, the Tax Payable for each individual would be the same and the combined Tax Payable would be calculated as follows:

Barbra's Tax Payable		
Tax On First $97,069	$ 17,230	
Tax On Next $13,931 ($111,000 - $97,069) At 26%	3,622	
Federal Tax Before Credits	$20,852	
Basic Personal Credit [($13,229)(15%)]	(1,984)	$18,868
Sally's Tax Payable		
Tax On First $97,069	$ 17,230	
Tax On Next $13,931 ($111,000 - $97,069) At 26%	3,622	
Federal Tax Before Credits	$20,582	
Basic Personal Credit [($13,229)(15%)]	(1,984)	18,868
Combined Tax Payable		$37,736

Case Three

In Case Three, only Barbra would have Tax Payable, which would be calculated as follows:

Tax On First $214,368	$49,645
Tax On Next $7,632 ($222,000 - $214,368) At 33%	2,519
Federal Tax Before Credits	$52,164
Basic Personal Credit [($12,298*)(15%)]	(1,845)
Common-Law Partner Credit [($12,298)(15%)]	(1,845)
Barbra's Tax Payable	$48,474

*Both Barbra's basic personal credit and her common-law partner credit would be calculated as follows:

$$\$13,229 - [\$931][(\$214,368 - \$150,473) \div \$63,895]$$

Solution to Self Study Problem Four - 2

Case 1

Leonard Wilkins will qualify for the following credits:

Basic Personal Amount	$13,229
Spousal ($13,229 - $8,720)	4,509
Canada Caregiver	7,276
Total Credit Base	$25,014
Rate	15%
Total Credits	$ 3,752

Case 2

Pete Webb will qualify for the following credits:

Basic Personal Amount	$13,229
Spousal ($13,229 - $3,920)	9,309
EI (Maximum)	856
CPP (Maximum)	2,732
Canada Employment	1,245
Total Credit Base	$27,371
Rate	15%
Total Credits	$ 4,106

Case 3

Candace Hall will qualify for the following tax credits:

Basic Personal Amount	$13,229
Spousal ($13,229 - $5,130)	8,099
Age [$7,637 - (15%)($69,420 - $38,508)]	3,000
Pension Income	2,000
Total Credit Base	$26,328
Rate	15%
Total Credits	$ 3,949

Note that, because her income is below the $79,054 income threshold, there will be no clawback of Ms. Hall's OAS receipts.

Case 4

Gladys Crawford will qualify for the following tax credits:

Basic Personal Amount	$13,229
Spousal ($13,229 - $2,600)	10,629
Medical Expenses (See Note)	20,819
Total Credit Base	$44,677
Rate	15%
Total Credits	$ 6,702

Note The claim for medical expenses is determined as follows:

Expenses For Gladys, Her Spouse, And Under 18 Children		
($5,150 + $4,240 + $2,040 + $3,220)		$14,650
Reduced By The Lesser Of:		
• [(3%)($126,470)] = $3,794		
• 2020 Threshold Amount = $2,397		(2,397)
20 Year Old's Medical Expenses	$8,840	
Reduced By The Lesser Of:		
• [(3%)($9,130)] = $274		
• $2,397	(274)	8,566
Allowable Medical Expenses		$20,819

Case 5

Austin Schneider will qualify for the following credits:

Basic Personal Amount	$13,229
Eligible Dependant (See Note)	13,229
Total Credit Base	$26,458
Rate	15%
Total Credits	$ 3,969

Note The eligible dependant credit can be taken for any child. It should not be claimed for the 14 year old as the amount of the credit would be reduced because of his income.

Solution to Self Study Problem Four - 3

The amount of the personal tax credits would be as follows:

1. **Ms. Jones** will qualify for the following credits:

Basic Personal Amount	$13,229
Spousal ($13,229 - $3,750)	9,479
Total Credit Base	$22,708
Rate	15%
Total Credits	$ 3,406

There is no tax credit available for her son.

2. **Ms. Martin** will qualify for the following credits:

Basic Personal Amount	$ 13,229
Spousal Including Infirm Amount	
($13,229 + $2,273)	15,502
Age	7,637
Pension	2,000
Spouse's Disability	8,576
Total Credit Base	$46,944
Rate	15%
Total Credits	$ 7,042

As Ms. Martin's Net Income For Tax Purposes is less than the relevant income thresholds, there will be no reduction in her age credit or clawback of her OAS benefits.

3. **Mr. Sharp** will qualify for the following credits:

Basic Personal Amount	$ 13,229
Spousal	13,229
Canada Caregiver Amount (20 Year Old Child)	7,276
Total Credit Base	$33,734
Rate	15%
Total Credits	$ 5,060

4. **Mr. Barton** will qualify for the following credits:

Basic Personal Amount	$ 13,229
Eligible Dependant (Any Child)	13,229
Total Credit Base	$26,458
Rate	15%
Total Credits	$ 3,969

5. **Ms. Cole** will qualify for the following credits:

Basic Personal Amount	
$13,229 - [$931][($175,000 - $150,473) ÷ $63,895]	$12,872
Spousal ($12,872 - $36,000)	Nil
EI (Maximum)	856
CPP (Maximum)	2,732
Canada Employment	1,245
Total Credit Base	$ 17,705
Rate	15%
Total Credits	$ 2,656

Her husband's income will have to be considered for the entire year and, with him having total income of $36,000 ($33,000 + $3,000), the spousal credit will be eliminated.

6. **Mr. Smead** will qualify for the following credits:

Basic Personal Amount	$13,229
Eligible Dependant - Son	13,229
Canada Caregiver - Mother	
[$7,276 - ($18,500 - $17,085)]	5,861
Total Credit Base	$32,319
Rate	15%
Total Credits	$ 4,848

Given the mother's high level of income, the eligible dependant credit should be claimed for the son. This will allow for the Canada caregiver credit to be claimed for the mother.

Solution to Self Study Problem Four - 4

Mr. Lane's federal tax payable (refund) would be calculated as follows:

Net Income For Tax Purposes And Taxable Income		$70,000
Tax On First $48,535		$ 7,280
Tax On Next $21,465 ($70,000 - $48,535) At 20.5 Percent		4,400
Federal Tax Before Credits		$11,680
Basic Personal Amount	($ 13,229)	
Eligible Dependant (Note 1)	(13,229)	
CPP (maximum)	(2,732)	
Canada Employment	(1,245)	
Medical Expenses (Note 2)	(2,300)	
Credit Base	($33,591)	
Rate	15%	(5,039)
Federal Political Tax Credit [(3/4)($400) + (1/2)($50)]		(325)
Federal Tax Payable		6,316
CPP Overpayment ($2,933 - $2,898)		(35)
Federal Tax Withheld (Given)		(10,100)
Federal Tax Payable (Refund)		($ 3,819)

Note 1 The eligible dependant amount can be claimed for either his 10 or 12 year old child. His 15 year old son would not be selected as he has Net Income For Tax Purposes of $8,200.

Note 2 Allowable medical expenses are as follows:

Minor Child's Medical Expenses	$4,400
Reduced By The Lesser Of:	
• [(3%)($70,000)] = $2,100	
• 2020 Threshold Amount = $2,397	(2,100)
Allowable Medical Expenses	$2,300

Since his 15 year old son is under 18 years of age, his allowable medical expenses are not affected by his Net Income For Tax Purposes. If he was 18 or older, they would be.

Solution to Self Study Problem Four - 5

Part A
The Tax Payable calculation for Marg is as follows:

Taxable Income	$15,300
Basic Personal Amount	(13,229)
EI	(242)
CPP [(4.95%)($15,300 - $3,500)]	(584)
Canada Employment	(1,245)
Subtotal	$ Nil

Note 1   Marg has a tuition amount available of $6,300. Because her Tax Payable is nil, she cannot use any of this credit. This means the maximum of $5,000 can be transferred to her father. This will leave her with a carry forward amount of $1,300 ($6,300 - $5,000).

Since Marg's medical expenses were paid for by her father, she cannot claim them herself and they must be claimed by her father. Even if she had paid for them herself and claimed them, she would not increase the transfer to her father as the medical expense tax credit is not taken into consideration in determining the tuition amount that can be transferred.

Part B
Mr. Barth's minimum Net Employment Income for the year would be calculated as follows:

Gross Salary	$ 82,500
Additions:	
Bonus (Note 2)	20,000
Automobile Benefit (Note 3)	7,580
Counseling Benefit (Note 4)	1,500
Imputed Interest Benefit (Note 5)	375
Stock Option Benefit [($18 - $15)(1,000)] (Note 6)	3,000
Deductions:	
Registered Pension Plan Contributions	(3,200)
Professional Dues	(1,800)
Net Employment Income	$109,955

Note 2   As the bonus is not payable until more than three years after the end of the employer's taxation year, it is a salary deferral arrangement and must be included in income under ITA 6(11).

Note 3   Since Mr. Barth's employment-related usage is not more than 50 percent, there is no reduction of the full standby charge. In addition, he cannot use the alternative calculation of the operating cost benefit. Given this, the automobile benefit is calculated as follows:

Standby Charge [(2%)($47,500)(10)]	$9,500
Operating Cost Benefit [(6,000)($0.28)]	1,680
Payments Withheld	(3,600)
Taxable Benefit	$7,580

Note 4   Counseling services, with the exception of those items specified under ITA 6(1), are considered taxable benefits. The items specified under ITA 6(1)(a)(iv) are counseling with respect to mental or physical health or with respect to re-employment or retirement. As a consequence, the counseling on personal finances is a taxable benefit.

Note 5   The imputed interest benefit is calculated as follows:

Taxable Benefit [($150,000)(2%)(3/12)]	$750
Reduction For Interest Paid	(375)
Net Addition To Employment Income	$375

Note 6   As the option price was greater than the market price at the time the options were issued, one-half of this amount can be deducted in the determination of Taxable Income. The adjusted cost base of the stock option shares is equal to their fair market value at the exercise date ($18 per share). Since they were sold for $18 per share, there is no capital gain or loss.

Taxable Income

Mr. Barth's Taxable Income would be calculated as follows:

Net Employment Income	$109,955
Deductible CPP ($2,898 - $2,732)	(166)
Net Income For Tax Purposes	109,789
Stock Option Deduction [(1/2)($3,000)] (Note 6)	(1,500)
Taxable Income	$108,289

Tax Payable

Mr. Barth's Tax Payable would be calculated as follows:

Tax On First $97,069		$17,230
Tax On Next $11,220 ($108,289 - $97,069) At 26 Percent		2,917
Federal Tax Before Credits		$20,147
Basic Personal Amount	($13,229)	
Spousal Including Infirm Amount		
($13,229 + $2,273 - $1,250)	(14,252)	
Spouse's Disability	(8,576)	
EI	(856)	
CPP	(2,732)	
Canada Employment	(1,245)	
Medical Expenses (Note 7)	(1,614)	
Marg's Tuition Transfer (See Part A)	(5,000)	
Credit Base	($47,504)	
Rate	15%	(7,126)
Charitable Donations (Note 8)		
[(15%)($200) + (29%)($2,000 - $200)]		(552)
Net Federal Tax		$12,469
Federal Income Tax Withheld During Year		(16,000)
Federal Tax Payable (Refund)		($ 3,531)

Note 7   Allowable medical expenses are as follows:

John And Spouse Medical Expenses ($200 + $3,550)		$ 3,750
Reduced By The Lesser Of:		
• [(3%)($109,955)] = $3,297		
• 2020 Threshold Amount = $2,397		(2,397)
Marg's Medical Expenses	$ 720	
Reduced By The Lesser Of:		
• [(3%)($15,300)] = $459		
• $2,397	(459)	261
Allowable Medical Expense		$ 1,614

Note 8   As none of his income is taxed at 33 percent, this rate will not be applicable to the calculation of the charitable donations tax credit.

Solution to Self Study Problem Four - 6

Mr. Kern's minimum Net Employment Income for the year would be calculated as follows:

Gross Salary	$ 67,600
Additions:	
Automobile Benefit (Note 1)	857
Disability Insurance Benefit (Note 2)	1,300
Stock Option Benefit [($83 - $75)(200)]	1,600
Deductions:	
Registered Pension Plan Contributions	(1,800)
Contributions To Group Disability Plan	Nil
Professional Dues	(1,233)
Net Employment Income	$68,324

Note 1   Based on the fact that Mr. Kern's employment-related usage is more than 50 percent of total usage, the automobile benefit is calculated as follows:

Standby Charge [(2/3)(9)($815 - $89)(3,000/15,003*)]	$ 871
Operating Cost Benefit - Lesser Of:	
• [(3,000)($0.28)] = $840	
• [(1/2)($871)] = $436	436
Total Before Payments	$1,307
Payments For Personal Use [($50)(9)]	(450)
Taxable Benefit	$ 857

*[(9)(1,667)]

As Mr. Kern's employment-related usage is more than 50 percent, he can elect to use one-half the standby charge as the operating cost benefit.

Note 2 As his employer contributed to the plan and the contributions did not create a taxable benefit, the $1,650 in benefits received during the year must be included in employment income. However, this benefit is reduced by the $350 ($200 + $150) in total contributions that he has made in 2019 and 2020.

Net And Taxable Income

Taxable Income would be calculated as follows:

Net Employment Income	$68,324
Deductible CPP	(166)
Net Income For Tax Purposes	68,158
Stock Option Deduction [(1/2)($1,600)]	(800)
Taxable Income	$67,358

Tax Payable

Tax Payable would be calculated as follows:

Tax On First $48,535		$ 7,280
Tax On Next $18,823 ($67,358 - $48,535) At 20.5 Percent		3,859
Federal Tax Before Credits		$11,139
Basic Personal Amount	($13,229)	
Spousal ($13,229 - $3,660)	(9,569)	
EI	(856)	
CPP	(2,732)	
Canada Employment	(1,245)	
Medical Expenses (Note 3)	(3,907)	
David's Transfer Of Tuition (Note 4)	(5,000)	
Credit Base	($36,538)	
Rate	15%	(5,481)
Charitable Donations Carried Forward (Note 5)		
[(15%)($200) + (29%)($500 - $200)]		(117)
Net Federal Tax		$ 5,541
Federal Amounts Withheld During Year (Given)		(7,200)
Federal Tax Payable (Refund)		($ 1,659)

Note 3 The allowable medical expenses would be calculated as follows:

Samuel And Spouse Medical Expenses ($2,100 + $770)		$ 2,870
Reduced By The Lesser Of:		
• [(3%)($68,324)] = $2,050		
• 2020 Threshold Amount = $2,397		(2,050)
David's Medical Expenses	$3,260	
Reduced By The Lesser Of:		
• $2,397		
• [(3%)($5,780)] = $173	(173)	3,087
Allowable Medical Expenses		$ 3,907

Note 4 The transfer from David is as follows:

Tuition Fees	$6,700
Maximum Transfer	(5,000)
Carry Forward (For David's Use Only)	$1,700

David's Tax Payable is completely eliminated by his basic personal credit. He can transfer a maximum of $5,000 of his tuition amount to his father. The remaining $1,700 can be carried forward indefinitely, but must be used by David.

Note 5   As none of his income is taxed at 33 percent, this rate will not be applicable to the calculation of the charitable donations tax credit.

Solution to Self Study Problem Four - 7

Part A

Ms. Van Horne's minimum Net Employment Income would be calculated as follows:

Salary	$126,000
Add:	
Commissions	32,000
Bonus [(1/2)($25,000)]	12,500
Employer's Life Insurance Contribution	550
Automobile Benefit (Note 1)	2,237
Stock Option Benefit (Note 2)	30,000
Deduct:	
RPP Contributions	(7,400)
Employment-Related Expenses (Note 3)	(17,700)
Net Employment Income	$178,187

Note 1   The automobile benefit would be calculated as follows:

Standby Charge [(2/3)(11)($728 - $50)(5,500 ÷ 18,337*)]	$1,491
Operating Cost Benefit - Lesser Of:	
• [(1/2)($1,491)] = $746	
• [($0.28)(5,500)] = $1,540	746
Total Benefits	$2,237

*[(11)(1,667)]

As Ms. Van Horne's employment-related use was more than 50 percent, there is a reduction in the standby charge and she can use the alternative calculation of the operating cost benefit.

Note 2   The employment income inclusion resulting from the exercise of the stock option is $30,000 [(5,000)($31 - $25)]. As the option price was equal to the market price at the time the options were issued, one-half of this amount can be deducted in the determination of Taxable Income.

Note 3   As Ms. Van Horne's commission income was $32,000, her deductible expenses are not limited by this constraint. They are calculated as follows:

Advertising	$ 5,600
Entertainment [(1/2)($9,000)]	4,500
Meals (reimbursed)	Nil
Hotels [(1/2)($8,400)]	4,200
Airline Tickets	3,400
Deductible Expenses	$17,700

Part B

Ms. Van Horne's minimum Taxable Income would be calculated as follows:

Net Employment Income	$178,187
Deductible CPP ($2,898 - $2,732)	(166)
Net Income For Tax Purposes	178,021
Stock Option Deduction [(1/2)($30,000)]	(15,000)
Taxable Income	$163,021

Part C

Based on the Taxable Income calculated in Part B, Ms. Van Horne's Tax Payable would be calculated as follows:

Tax On First $150,473		$31,115
Tax On Next $12,548 ($163,021 - $150,473) At 29 Percent		3,639
Tax Before Credits		$34,754
Basic Personal Amount (Note 4)	($13,046)	
Eligible Dependant - Son		
[($13,046 - $2,500)]	(10,546)	
Caregiver (Note 5)	(7,276)	
EI Premiums	(856)	
CPP Contributions	(2,732)	
Canada Employment	(1,245)	
Transfer Of Tuition (Note 6)	(5,000)	
Medical Expenses (Note 7)	(3,700)	
Credit Base	44,401)	
Rate	15%	(6,660)
Charitable Donations		
[(15%)($200) + (29%)($1,800 - $200)]		(494)
Federal Political Contributions		
[(3/4)($400) + (1/2)($350) + (1/3)($900 - $400 - $350)]		(525)
Federal Tax Payable		$27,075

Note 4   The Basic Personal Amount would be calculated as follows:

$$\$13,229 - [\$931][(\$163,021 - \$150,473 \div \$63,895)] = \$13,046$$

Note 5   The father's $8,000 income is below the threshold for the caregiver credit (his casino winnings are not included in his Net Income For Tax Purposes). This means that Ms. Van Horne can claim the full amount of the caregiver credit.

Note 6   The transfer from her daughter is as follows:

Tuition Fees	$7,000
Total Amount Available	$7,000
Maximum Transfer	(5,000)
Carry Forward (For Daughter's Use Only)	$2,000

Her daughter's Tax Payable is completely eliminated by her basic personal credit. She can transfer a maximum of $5,000 of her tuition amounts to her mother. The remaining $2,000 can be carried forward indefinitely, but must be used by her daughter.

Note 7 The base for Ms. Van Horne's medical expense credit can be calculated as follows:

Ms. Van Horne And Her Children ($850 + $1,480)	$2,330	
Reduced By The Lesser Of:		
[(3%)($178,187)] = $5,346		
2020 Threshold Amount = $2,397	(2,397)	Nil
Father's Medical Expenses	$3,940	
Reduced By The Lesser Of:		
$2,397		
[(3%)($8,000)] = $240	(240)	3,700
Allowable Medical Costs		$3,700

Solution to Self Study Problem Four - 8

Part A

Lydia's minimum Net Employment Income would be calculated as follows:

Salary	$73,500
Additions:	
Bonus (Note 1)	6,000
Stock Options (Note 2)	Nil
Automobile Benefit (Note 3)	1,176
Gifts (Note 5)	650
Interest Free Loan Benefit (Note 6)	1,333
Deductions:	
RPP Contributions	(2,600)
Professional Dues	(350)
Client Meals And Entertainment (Note 4)	Nil
Net Employment Income	$79,709

Note 1 The $4,000 that will be paid in 2021 is not included in Net Income For Tax Purposes until it is paid. However, the amount that will be paid in 2024 is a salary deferral arrangement and, given this, it will have to be included in 2020 Net Income For Tax Purposes.

Note 2 The stock option benefit would be calculated as follows:

$$[(200)($90 - $72)] = $3,600$$

Since the employer is a CCPC, the taxation of this benefit is deferred until the shares are sold. Note that, because the option price was less than the fair market value of the shares at the time the options were granted, no ITA 110(1)(d) deduction will be available in the determination of Taxable Income when they are sold. However, if she holds the shares for more than two years before selling, she will be eligible for the ITA 110(1)(d.1) deduction.

Note 3 The automobile benefit would be calculated as follows:

Standby Charge [(2/3)(11)($565 - $75)(4,000 ÷ 18,337*)]	$ 784
Operating Cost Benefit - Lesser Of:	
• [(1/2)($784)] = $392	
• [($0.28)(4,000)] = $1,120	392
Total Benefits	$1,176

    *[(11)(1,667)]

As Lydia's employment-related use was more than 50 percent, the reduced standby charge is available. In addition, she can use the alternative calculation of the operating cost benefit.

Note 4 Lydia's meal and entertainment costs exceed her employer's reimbursement by $2,400 ($5,600 - $3,200). However, as she has no commission income, she cannot deduct these out-of-pocket costs.

Note 5 The gift certificate for $150 is taxable because it is a near-cash gift. The first $500 of the long-service award will not be a taxable benefit. However, the excess of $500 ($1,000 - $500) will be a taxable benefit. As the value of the Christmas gift basket is under $500, it will not create a taxable benefit. The total taxable benefit for gifts is $650 ($150 + $500).

Note 6 The taxable benefit on the loan is calculated as follows:

$$[(2\%)(\$100,000)(8/12)] = \$1,333$$

Part B

Net and Taxable Income would be calculated as follows:

Net Employment Income	$79,709
Deductible CPP Contributions ($2,898 - $2,732)	(166)
Net Income For Tax Purposes And Taxable Income	79,543

As there are no Division C deductions, Lydia's Taxable Income would be equal to her Net Income For Tax Purposes of $79,543. There would be no stock option deduction as there was no stock option benefit.

Part C

Lydia's Tax Payable would be calculated as follows:

Tax On First $48,535		$ 7,280
Tax On Next $31,008 ($79,543 - $48,535) At 20.5 Percent		6,357
Federal Tax Before Credits		$13,637
Basic Personal Amount	($13,229)	
Spousal ($13,229 - $8,600)	(4,629)	
Canada Caregiver - Mary	(7,276)	
Transfer Of Harry's Tuition (Note 7)	(4,129)	
First-Time Home Buyers'	(5,000)	
EI Premiums	(856)	
CPP Contributions	(2,732)	
Canada Employment	(1,245)	
Medical Expenses (Note 8)	(18,993)	
Credit Base	($58,089)	
Rate	15%	(8,713)
Charitable Donations [(15%)($200)		
+ (29%)($2,000 - $200)] (Note 9)		(525)
Federal Tax Payable		$ 4,372

Note 7 Harry will have to reduce his own Tax Payable to nil before transferring any part of his tuition amount. He will require $871 ($14,100 - $13,229) of this amount and his transfer will be limited to $4,129 ($5,000 - $871). This will leave Harry with a carry forward of $6,300 ($11,300 - $871 - $4,129). The residence costs are not eligible for a credit.

Note 8 There are three medical expenses in the problem that do not qualify for the medical expenses tax credit: Botox treatment, hair replacement procedures, and liposuction. (These exclusions are listed in the textbook.) All of the allowable medical expenses of Lydia, Mark, and Barry are eligible for reimbursement from the health care plan and the reimbursement is deducted. As both Mary and Harry are older than 17, their expenses are not eligible for reimbursement.

The base for Lydia's medical expense credit can be calculated as follows:

Lydia - Prescriptions		$ 2,500
Lydia - Botox treatments		Nil
Mark - Dentist fees for root canals (3)		7,200
Mark - Hair replacement procedures		Nil
Barry - Dentist fees, including $1,000 for a tooth replacement		2,100
Allowable Medical Expenses		$ 11,800
Reimbursement [(50%)(11,800)]		(5,900)
Reduced By The Lesser Of:		
• [(3%)($79,709)] = $2,391		
• 2020 Threshold Amount = $2,397		(2,391)
Mary's Allowable Medical Expenses		
($8,400 + $3,900 + Nil)	$12,300	
Reduced By The Lesser Of:		
• $2,397		
• [(3%)($3,100)] = $93	(93)	12,207
Harry's Allowable Medical Expenses		
($1,500 + $2,200)	$ 3,700	
Reduced By The Lesser Of:		
• $2,397		
• [(3%)($14,100)] = $423	(423)	3,277
Allowable Medical Costs		$18,993

Note 9 As none of her income is taxed at 33 percent, this rate will not be applicable to the calculation of the charitable donations tax credit.

Solution to Tax Software Self Study Problem - Chapter 4

The complete tax return is available on MyLab in two versions, a T1 ProFile return file and a .PDF file. Note that prior to late January 2021, the returns will be for 2019, not 2020, as the 2020 filing version will not yet be available.

For more information on how to use the ProFile tax program, refer to the Chapter 4 sample tax return in this Study Guide.

Notes To Tax Return

- Diane transfers the $5,000 maximum tuition amount to Eleanor and carries forward the remaining $2,000 [$7,000 - $5,000]. The carry forward can only be used by Diane.
- Eleanor cannot claim the charitable donation made by Diane, but Diane can carry it forward for up to five years.

- Since Amy is under 18 and wholly dependent, Eleanor claimed the eligible dependant credit for Amy.
- Because Marjorie is not infirm, Eleanor can claim no credit for her.
- Since Diane and Marjorie are over 17 years of age, their medical expenses are reduced by 3 percent of their Net Income For Tax Purposes. This means that none of Marjorie's medical expenses can be claimed by Eleanor.
- In calculating work space in the home costs, the household insurance is not deductible as the T4 information shows she has no commission income. The car insurance is not relevant as there is no information that Eleanor uses her car for employment-related purposes.

Tax Planning Points

- Although she is not required to file, Marjorie should file a tax return, otherwise she will not be eligible for the GST credit.
- Although she is not required to file, Diane should file a tax return, otherwise she will not be eligible for the GST credit and she will not benefit from the RRSP deduction room created during the year. Filing a tax return will also make her tuition credit and charitable donation tax credit easier to keep track of for carry forward purposes.

Chapter 5 Learning Objectives

After completing Chapter 5, you should be able to:

1. Describe the differences between the accounting procedures used for depreciable assets and the tax procedures used for these assets (paragraph [P hereafter] 5-1 to 5-11).
2. Determine the types of costs that are included in the amounts that are added to depreciable asset classes (P 5-12 to 5-25).
3. Recall the basic available for use rules (P 5-26 to 5-28).
4. Recall the general rules for segregating depreciable assets into classes (P 5-29 to 5-31).
5. Recall the types of assets that must be allocated to separate classes (P 5-32).

6. Explain the basic elements of the CCA system (P 5-33 to 5-35).
7. Apply the rates and methods that are applicable to common CCA classes in order to determine the maximum CCA for the period (P 5-36).
8. Describe the half-year rules in the determination of maximum CCA for the period (P 5-37 to 5-41).
9. Describe the Accelerated Investment Incentive (AccII) (P 5-42 to 5-54).
10. Describe the application of the AccII to Classes 12, 13, 14, and 53 (P 5-55 to 5-60).

11. Describe the enhanced CCA provisions for zero emission vehicles in Class 54 and 55 (P 5-61 to 5-67).
12. Apply the short fiscal period rules in the determination of maximum CCA for the period (P 5-68 to 5-70).
13. Describe the additions to Class 14.1 and the special treatment for goodwill (P 5-71 to 5-79).
14. Explain the tax planning considerations that are involved when a business takes less than maximum CCA (P 5-80 to 5-84).
15. Determine the tax consequences associated with dispositions of depreciable assets, including recapture, terminal losses, and capital gains (P 5-85 to 5-102).

16. Explain the special disposition rules applicable to Class 54 (P 5-103 to 5-105).
17. Explain how the treatment of dispositions in Class 14.1 differs from that for other CCA classes (P 5-106 to 5-113).
18. Create the commonly used CCA schedule for a situation with depreciable assets (P 5-114 to 5-115).
19. Apply the provisions relating to separate class elections (P 5-116 to 5-125).
20. Apply the provisions relating to the change in use of automobiles and other special situations. (P 5-126 to 5-131).

How to Work Through Chapter 5

We recommend the following approach in dealing with the material in this chapter:

Tax And Accounting Procedures Compared
- Read the beginning of the chapter to paragraph 5-11 (in the textbook).

Additions To Capital Cost, Including Available For Use Rules
- Read paragraph 5-12 to 5-28.

Capital Cost Allowances - General Overview and Rates For Common Classes
- Read paragraph 5-29 to 5-36.
- Do Exercises Five-1 and Five-2 (in the textbook) and check the solutions in this Study Guide.

Half-Year (a.k.a. First Year) Rules
- Read paragraph 5-37 to 5-41.

Accelerated Investment Incentive (AccII)
- Read paragraph 5-42 to 5-54.
- Do Exercise Five-3 and check the solution in this Study Guide.

AccII Application - Classes 12 and 13
- Read paragraph 5-55 to 5-58.
- Do Exercise Five-4 and check the solution in this Study Guide.

AccII Application - Class 14
- Read paragraph 5-59.
- Do Exercise Five-5 and check the solution in this Study Guide.

AccII Application - Class 53
- Read paragraph 5-60.
- Do Exercise Five-6 and check the solution in this Study Guide.

Zero Emission Vehicles
- Read paragraph 5-61 to 5-67.

Short Fiscal Periods
- Read paragraph 5-68 to 5-70.
- Do Exercise Five-7 and check the solution in this Study Guide.

Class 14.1 (Including Goodwill)
- Read paragraph 5-71 to 5-79.

Tax Planning Considerations For CCA
- Read paragraph 5-80 to 5-84.
- Do Exercise Five-8 and check the solution in this Study Guide.

Dispositions Of Depreciable Assets
- Read paragraph 5-85 to 5-93.
- Do Exercise Five-9 and check the solution in this Study Guide.

Recapture of Capital Cost Allowance
- Read paragraph 5-94 to 5-97.
- Do Exercise Five-10 and check the solution in this Study Guide.

Terminal Losses
- Read paragraph 5-98 to 5-102.
- Do Exercises Five-11 and Five-12 and check the solutions in this Study Guide.

Dispositions of Class 54 Assets (Zero Emission Vehicles)
- Read paragraph 5-103 to 5-105.

Dispositions Of Class 14.1 - Differences From Other Classes
- Read paragraph 5-106 to 5-109.
- Do Exercise Five-13 and check the solution in this Study Guide.
- Read paragraph 5-110 to 5-112.

Summary Of Tax Consequences
- Read paragraph 5-113.

CCA Schedule - Example
- Read paragraph 5-114 to 5-115.
- Do Self Study Problems Five-1 to Five-7, which are available on MyLab, and check the solutions in this Study Guide.

Separate Class Election
- Read paragraph 5-116 to 5-123.
- Do Exercise Five-14 and check the solution in this Study Guide.
- Read paragraph 5-124 to 5-125.

Change In Use For Automobiles And Other Special Situations
- Read paragraph 5-126 to 5-131.

To Complete This Chapter
- If you would like more practice in problem solving, do the Supplementary Self Study Problems for the chapter. These problems and solutions are available on MyLab.
- Review the Key Terms Used In This Chapter in the textbook at the end of Chapter 5. Consult the Glossary for the meaning of any key terms you do not know.
- Test yourself with the Chapter 5 Glossary Flashcards available on MyLab.
- Ensure you have achieved the Chapter 5 Learning Objectives listed in this Study Guide.
- As a review, we recommend you view the PowerPoint presentation for Chapter 5 that is on MyLab.

Practice Examination
- Write the Practice Examination for Chapter 5 that is on MyLab. Mark your examination using the Practice Examination Solution that is also on MyLab.

Solutions to Chapter 5 Exercises

Exercise Five - 1 Solution

The correct classes for each of the assets would be as follows:

Asset	Class
Taxicab	16
Manufacturing and processing equipment	53
Franchise with a limited life	14
Passenger vehicle with a cost of $120,000*	10.1
Government licence with an unlimited life	14.1
Water storage tank	6
Photocopy machine (office equipment not specifically listed elsewhere)	8
Leasehold improvements	13
Rental building* (not including the land)	1

*These two assets would have to be allocated to separate classes. In addition, as covered later in the Chapter, the taxpayer could elect to include the photocopy machine in a separate class if its capital cost is $1,000 or more.

Exercise Five - 2 Solution

Ignoring the half-year rule, the impact would be calculated as follows:

Correct CCA [($326,000)(30%)]	$ 97,800
CCA Recorded In 2020 [($326,000)(4%)]	(13,040)
Understatement Of 2020 CCA	$84,760

Exercise Five - 3 Solution

The maximum CCA for 2020 and the January 1, 2021, UCC balance are calculated as follows:

January 1, 2020, UCC		$ 950,000
Add: Acquisitions During The Year	$300,000	
Deduct: Dispositions During The Year*	(144,000)	156,000
Add: AccII Adjustment [(1/2)($156,000)]		78,000
CCA Base (December 31, 2020, UCC)		$1,184,000
2020 CCA [(30%)($1,184,000)]		(355,200)
AccII Adjustment Reversal		(78,000)
January 1, 2021, UCC		$ 750,800

*The detailed coverage on dispositions is later in the Chapter. We have included dispositions during the year to more fully illustrate the calculation of the AccII adjustment. More accurately, dispositions are the lesser of the capital cost and the proceeds of disposition. To simplify the AccII calculations, this Exercise does not provide the capital cost of the cars disposed of.

Exercise Five - 4 Solution

The required CCA calculations for 2019 would be as follows:

On 2015 Improvements ($52,000 ÷ 15)	$3,467
On 2020 Improvements [(150%)($31,000 ÷ 10)]	4,650
2020 CCA	$8,117

The required CCA calculations for 2021 would be as follows:

On 2015 Improvements ($52,000 ÷ 15)	$3,467
On 2020 Improvements ($31,000 ÷ 10)	3,100
2021 CCA	$6,567

While this is not required by the Exercise, you should note that the 2029 CCA on the 2020 improvements would be limited to $1,550 ($31,000 - $4,650 - (8)($3,100)], the balance in the UCC for these improvements.

Exercise Five - 5 Solution

The required calculations are as follows:

Acquisition Amount	$375,000
CCA For 2020 [(150%)($375,000 ÷ 10)(275/365)]	(42,380)
January 1, 2021, UCC	$332,620

Exercise Five - 6 Solution

The required calculations are as follows:

January 1, 2020, UCC	$500,000
Acquisitions During The Year	100,000
AcclI Adjustment [(100%)($100,000)]	100,000
CCA Base	$700,000
2020 CCA [(50%)($700,000)]	(350,000)
AcclI Adjustment Reversal	(100,000)
January 1, 2021, UCC	$250,000

While this is not required, the ending UCC can be verified as follows:

January 1, 2020, UCC	$500,000
Acquisitions During The Year	100,000
Write-Offs:	
CCA On Opening UCC [(50%)($500,000)]	(250,000)
CCA On Additions [(100%)($100,000)]	(100,000)
January 1, 2021, UCC	$250,000

Exercise Five - 7 Solution

The required information is calculated as follows:

Capital Cost Of Additions	$115,000
AcclI Adjustment [(50%)($115,000)]	57,500
CCA Base	$172,500
2020 CCA [(20%)($172,500)(153/365)]	(14,461)
AcclI Adjustment Reversal	(57,500)
January 1, 2021, UCC	$100,539

Exercise Five - 8 Solution

Following the general rule that, when less than the maximum CCA is to be deducted, the amounts deducted should be taken from the class(es) with the lowest rates, the required calculations would be as follows:

Required Total		$45,000
Maximum CCA - Class 1 [(4%)($426,000)]	($17,040)	
Maximum CCA - Class 8 [(20%)($126,000)]	(25,200)	(42,240)
Required Balance		$ 2,760

As they are both 30 percent declining balance classes, the remaining $2,760 could be taken from either Class 10 or Class 10.1. It would be advisable to use Class 10.1, as recapture is not recorded for this class. In addition, if the Class 10.1 vehicle is going to be disposed of in the near future, it could be better tax planning to take the maximum CCA for Class 10.1 of $6,300 [(30%)($21,000)] and reduce the Class 8 CCA to $21,660 ($45,000 - $6,300 - $17,040). Since there is no recapture for Class 10.1, this could increase aggregate future deductions of the other classes. Whether this would be advantageous depends on the anticipated proceeds of disposition.

Exercise Five - 9 Solution

The only tax consequence would be a taxable capital gain of $2,500 [(1/2)($23,000 - $18,000)].

Following the basic rule for dispositions, we would subtract from the Class 8 UCC the lesser of the proceeds of disposition ($23,000) and the capital cost of the individual asset ($18,000). Subtracting the lesser figure of $18,000 would leave a large positive balance in Class 8. As there are no other dispositions during the year, we can conclude that the balance will be positive at the end of the year. This fact, combined with the presence of many other assets in Class 8, means that there will be no recapture and no terminal loss.

Exercise Five - 10 Solution

The required information would be calculated as follows:

UCC Of The Class At The Beginning Of The Year	$24,883
Add: Acquisitions During The Year	Nil
Deduct: Dispositions During The Year - Lesser Of:	
• Capital Cost = $27,000	
• Proceeds Of Disposition = $28,500	(27,000)
Deduct: One-Half Net Additions	N/A*
Negative Ending Balance	($ 2,117)
Recapture Of CCA	2,117
January 1, 2021, UCC Balance	Nil

*This adjustment for one-half of the excess of additions over disposal deductions is only made when the net amount is positive.

The effect would be an addition to business income of $2,117 in recaptured CCA. Note that, unlike terminal losses (see Exercise Five-11), the fact that there is still an asset in the class is irrelevant.

While there would also be a taxable capital gain of $750 [(1/2)($28,500 - $27,000)], this would not be included in business income.

Exercise Five - 11 Solution

The required information would be calculated as follows:

UCC Of The Class At The Beginning Of The Year	$24,883
Add: Acquisitions During The Year	Nil
Deduct: Dispositions During The Year - Lesser Of:	
• Capital Cost = $54,000	
• Proceeds Of Disposition = $18,000	(18,000)
Ending Balance With No Remaining Assets	$ 6,883
Terminal Loss	(6,883)
January 1, 2021, UCC Balance	Nil

As there is a positive balance in Class 8 at the end of the year, but no remaining assets, there would be a terminal loss of $6,883. This loss is deducted in the calculation of net business income.

Exercise Five - 12 Solution

The accounting results would be calculated as follows:

Proceeds Of Disposition	$126,000
Net Book Value	(43,500)
Accounting Gain	$ 82,500

For tax purposes, there would be a taxable capital gain calculated as follows:

Proceeds Of Disposition	$126,000
Capital Cost	(97,000)
Capital Gain	$ 29,000
Inclusion Rate	1/2
Taxable Capital Gain	$ 14,500

The capital cost of $97,000 would be subtracted from the UCC, leaving a balance of $2,365,000 ($2,462,000 - $97,000).

While this disposition would reduce the maximum CCA for the current and subsequent years, there would be no recapture (the balance in Class 8 is still positive) or terminal loss (there are still assets in Class 8).

Exercise Five - 13 Solution

CCA on Class 14.1 for 2020 would be calculated as follows:

January 1, 2020, Balance	Nil
2020 Additions ($85,000 + $105,000)	$190,000
AccII Adjustment [(1/2)($190,000)]	95,000
CCA Base	$285,000
2020 CCA [(5%)($285,000)]	(14,250)
AccII Adjustment Reversal	(95,000)
January 1, 2021, UCC	$175,750
Deduct: Dispositions During The Year - Lesser Of:	
Capital Cost = $190,000 (See Note)	
Proceeds Of Disposition =	
($65,000 + $105,000) = $170,000	(170,000)
UCC Subsequent To The Sales	$ 5,750

Note The capital cost of the single goodwill asset is $190,000 ($85,000 + $105,000).

There would be no immediate tax consequences resulting from the dispositions. Subsequent to the sales, Dextrin Inc. has a Class 14.1 UCC of $5,750 consisting of goodwill with a capital cost of $20,000 ($190,000 - $170,000).

Exercise Five - 14 Solution

Photocopiers would be included in Class 8, a 20 percent declining balance class. The following table compares the CCA if no election is made with the results if the separate class election is made.

	No Election 10 Copiers	With Election 2 Copiers	With Election 8 Copiers
January Acquisitions @ $20,000	$200,000	$40,000	$160,000
Dispositions	(6,000)	(6,000)	N/A
Terminal Loss		$34,000	
December Acquisitions @ $22,000	44,000	$44,000	
AccII Adjustments	119,000	22,000	80,000
CCA Base	$357,000	$66,000	$240,000
CCA Rate	20%	20%	20%
CCA	$ 71,400	$13,200	$ 48,000

If no election is made, there will be a deduction for CCA of $71,400. Alternatively, if each machine is allocated to a separate class, there will be a deduction for CCA of $61,200 ($13,200 + $48,000). In addition, there will be a terminal loss of $34,000. The use of the election increases the total deductible amount by $23,800 [($13,200 + $48,000) + $34,000 Terminal Loss- $71,400].

Solution to Self Study Problem Five - 1

The required calculation of the maximum CCA is as follows:

	Class 1	Class 8	Class 10
Opening Balance	$2,597,000	$718,000	$ 524,000
Additions	Nil	Nil	374,000
Dispositions			
Proceeds Of Disposition	Nil	Nil	(234,000)
AccII Adjustment			
[(1/2)($374,000 - $234,000)]	Nil	Nil	70,000
CCA Base	$2,597,000	$718,000	$ 734,000
CCA Rate	4%	20%	30%
Maximum CCA	$ 103,880	$143,600	$ 220,200

This gives a maximum amount for CCA of $467,680 for the taxation year ($103,880 + $143,600 + $220,200).

Part B

Since the company only has Net and Taxable Income before CCA of $328,000 and the problem states that loss carry overs should not be considered, maximum CCA would not be deducted as this would produce a loss. Only $328,000 in CCA should be taken in order to reduce the Taxable Income to nil.

Given that the CCA deduction is limited to $328,000, it would normally be deducted in the class or classes with the lowest rates. This would leave the unused amounts in classes with higher rates, which, in turn, would maximize the amount that could be deducted in the first profitable years. Taking this approach, the $328,000 would be deducted as follows:

Class 1 (Maximum Available)	$103,880
Class 8 (Maximum Available)	143,600
Class 10 (Required Balance)	80,520
Total CCA	$328,000

This CCA deduction would reduce Taxable Income to nil.

Note that if there were immediate plans to sell the building for more than its opening UCC, this could affect the choice of classes to deduct CCA from as any additional CCA taken on Class 1 would have to be added to income as recaptured CCA when the building is sold.

Solution to Self Study Problem Five - 2

Class 1

The required information is calculated as follows:

Opening Balance	$115,000
Additions	Nil
Dispositions - Lesser Of:	
• Cost = $190,000	
• Proceeds Of Disposition = $110,000	(110,000)
Ending Balance With No Remaining Assets In Class	$ 5,000
Terminal Loss	(5,000)
January 1, 2021, UCC Balance	Nil

Since the building sold is the last asset in the class, there is a terminal loss of $5,000, which is deducted in the determination of business income. The proceeds of disposition for the building total $110,000 ($260,000 - $150,000). As the adjusted cost base of the land is equal to the proceeds of disposition, there is no gain on the disposition of the land.

Class 8

The required information is calculated as follows:

Opening Balance		$ 96,000
Additions	$52,000	
Dispositions - Lesser Of:		
• Cost = $75,000		
• Proceeds Of Disposition = $35,000	(35,000)	17,000
AccII Adjustment [(1/2)($17,000)]		8,500
CCA Base		$121,500
CCA At 20 Percent		(24,300)
AccII Adjustment Reversal		(8,500)
January 1, 2021, UCC Balance		$ 88,700

Class 10

The required information is calculated as follows:

Opening Balance		$ 6,700
Additions	$ 8,000	
Dispositions - Lesser Of:		
• Cost = $20,000		
• Proceeds = $25,000	(20,000)	(12,000)
AccII Adjustment (Only If Net Additions Are Positive)		N/A
Negative Ending Balance		($ 5,300)
Recaptured CCA (i.e., Recapture)		5,300
January 1, 2021, UCC Balance		Nil

As the cost of the used car is less than $30,000, its cost is added to Class 10. With respect to the retirement, only the capital cost of the truck sold is deducted from Class 10. The excess of the $25,000 proceeds over the capital cost of $20,000 is a $5,000 capital gain, one-half of which would be taxable. The $12,000 net deduction creates a negative balance in the class and, as a consequence, no CCA will be taken for 2020. However, the negative balance of $5,300 will have to be taken into income as recapture.

Class 53
The required information is as follows:

Opening Balance	$75,000
CCA At 50 Percent	(37,500)
January 1, 2021, UCC Balance	$ 37,500

Summary Of Results (Required)
The preceding results can be summarized as follows:

Terminal Loss - Class 1	($ 5,000)
CCA - Class 8	(24,300)
Recapture - Class 10	5,300
CCA - Class 53	(37,500)
Decrease In Net Business Income	($61,500)
Taxable Capital Gain - Class 10 [(1/2)($25,000 - $20,000)]	2,500
Decrease In Net Income For Tax Purposes	($59,000)

Note that detailed coverage of capital gains is available in Chapter 8 of the text.

Solution to Self Study Problem Five - 3

2017 Solution
The required calculations are as follows:

Opening Balance	Nil
Additions To Class 10 [(20 Cars)($21,500)]	$430,000
One-Half Net Additions [(1/2)($430,000)]	(215,000)
CCA Base	$215,000
CCA [(30%)($215,000)(122/365)]	(21,559)
One-Half Net Additions	215,000
Class 10 UCC For January 1, 2018	$408,441

As the business was established on September 1, 2017, its operations were carried out for 122 days in 2017, and only a proportionate share of the annual CCA charge may be taken. We would call your attention to the fact that it is the length of the taxation year, not the period of ownership of the assets, that establishes the fraction of the year for which CCA is to be recorded.

2018 Solution

The required calculations are as follows:

Opening Balance For Class 10	$408,441
Additions [(6 Cars)($22,800)]	136,800
Dispositions - Lesser Of:	
• Capital Cost = 6 @ $21,500 = $129,000	
• Proceeds Of Disposition = 6 @ $11,400 = $68,400	(68,400)
One-Half Net Additions [(1/2)($136,800 - $68,400)]	(34,200)
CCA Base	$442,641
CCA [(30%)($442,641)]	(132,792)
One-Half Net Additions	34,200
Class 10 UCC For January 1, 2019	$344,049

2019 Solution

With respect to Class 10 cars, the required calculations are as follows:

Opening Balance For Class 10	$344,049
Additions [(18 Cars)($24,300)]	437,400
Dispositions - Lesser Of:	
• Capital Cost = 14 @ $21,500 = $301,000	
• Proceeds Of Disposition = $137,200	(137,200)
AccII Adjustment [(1/2)($437,400 - $137,200)]	150,100
CCA Base	$794,349
CCA [(30%)($794,349)]	(238,305)
AccII Adjustment Reversal	150,100
Class 10 UCC For January 1, 2020	$405,944

With respect to the BMW convertibles, each would have to be allocated to a separate Class 10.1. Further, the addition to each Class 10.1 would be limited to $30,000. The required calculations would be as follows:

	BMW 1 Class 10.1	BMW 2 Class 10.1
Acquisitions	$ 30,000	$ 30,000
AccII Adjustment	15,000	15,000
CCA Base	$ 45,000	$ 45,000
CCA [(30%)($45,000)]	(13,500)	(13,500)
AccII Adjustment Reversal	(15,000)	(15,000)
UCC For January 1, 2020	$16,5001	$ 16,500

2020 Solution

The required calculations for the Class 10 vehicles are as follows:

Opening Balance For Class 10	$405,944
Dispositions - Lesser Of:	
• Capital Cost = 18 @ $24,300 + 6 @ $22,800 = $574,200	
• Proceeds Of Disposition = 24 @ $8,300 = $199,200	(199,200)
Balance Before Terminal Loss	$206,744
Terminal Loss	(206,744)
UCC For January 1, 2021	Nil

After all of the assets in Class 10 have been retired there is still a $296,804 balance in the UCC. This results in a terminal loss that will be deducted in full from the Haddad brothers' other income. How this deduction will be shared by the two brothers will depend on the terms of their partnership agreement for the delivery business. The terminal loss will also be deducted from the UCC balance.

With respect to the two Class 10.1 assets, no recapture or terminal losses can be recorded on these assets. However, in the year of disposal, taxpayers are allowed to deduct one-half year of CCA. Given the short fiscal final year, this means that on each of the Class 10.1 vehicles there would be a CCA deduction of $2,861 [(1/2)(30%)($25,500)(273/365)] for a total of $5,722.

Solution to Self Study Problem Five - 4

Part A
The maximum CCA for the three years would be calculated as follows:

2018	Class 1	Class 10	Class 8
Opening Balance	Nil	Nil	Nil
Additions	$180,000	$150,000	$48,000
One-Half Net Additions	(90,000)	(75,000)	(24,000)
CCA Base	$ 90,000	$ 75,000	$24,000
Maximum CCA			
Class 1 [(6%)($90,000)(275 ÷ 365)]*	(4,068)		
Class 10 [(30%)($75,000)(275 ÷ 365)]		(16,952)	
Class 8 [(20%)($24,000)((275 ÷ 365)]			(3,616)
One-Half Net Additions	90,000	75,000	24,000
January 1, 2019, UCC	$175,932	$133,048	$44,384

*As the Class 1 building is being used 100 percent for non-residential purposes, it would qualify for the 6 percent CCA rate.

The total maximum CCA for 2018 would be $24,636 ($4,068 + $16,952 + $3,616).

2019	Class 1	Class 10	Class 8
Beginning UCC	$175,932	$133,048	$44,384
Additions	Nil	72,000	Nil
Disposition - Lesser Of:			
Capital Cost = $75,000			
Proceeds = [(3)($14,000)] = $42,000	Nil	(42,000)	Nil
AccII Adjustment			
[(1/2)($72,000 - $42,000)]	Nil	15,000	Nil
CCA Base	$175,932	$178,048	$44,384
Maximum CCA			
Class 1 [(6%)($175,932)]	(10,556)		
Class 10 [(30%)($178,048)]		(53,414)	
Class 8 [(20%)($44,384)]			(8,877)
One-Half Net Additions	Nil	(15,000)	Nil
January 1, 2020, UCC	$165,376	$109,634	$35,507

The total maximum CCA for 2019 would be $72,847 ($10,556 + $53,414 + $8,877).

2020	Class 1	Class 10	Class 10.1	Class 8
Beginning UCC	$165,376	$109,634	Nil	$35,507
Additions (Class Maximum)*	Nil	Nil	$30,000	Nil
Class 10 Disposition - Lesser Of:				
Capital Cost = $25,000				
Proceeds = $27,000	N/A	(25,000)	N/A	N/A
Class 8 Dispositions - Lesser Of:				
Capital Cost = $12,000				
Proceeds = Nil	N/A	N/A	N/A	Nil
AccII Adjustment				
[(50%)($30,000)]	N/A	N/A	15,000	N/A
Balance	$165,376	$ 84,634	$45,000	$35,507
Maximum CCA				
Class 1 [(6%)($165,376)]	(9,923)			
Class 10 [(30%)($84,634)]		(25,390)		
Class 10.1 [(30%)($45,000)]			(13,500)	
Class 8 [(20%)($35,507)]				(7,101)
AccII Adjustment Reversal	N/A	N/A	(15,000)	N/A
January 1, 2021, UCC	$155,453	$ 59,244	$16,500	$28,406

*Additions to Class 10.1 limited to $30,000.

The total maximum CCA for 2020 would be $55,914 ($9,923 + $25,390 + $13,500 + $7,101).

Part B
The tax effects of the unusual events would be as follows:

Theft Of Equipment This is, in effect, a disposition with nil proceeds. There will be no immediate tax effect as the equipment is not the last asset in the class.

Insurance Deductible The $7,770 in insurance proceeds would be included in income [ITA 12(1)(f)], and the full repair expenses of $8,270 would be a deductible expense. This results in the $500 in repairs that were not covered under the company's insurance policy being deducted as a repair or maintenance charge.

Car Sale As the car was sold for $2,000 more than its capital cost, there would be a capital gain of $2,000, resulting in a taxable capital gain of $1,000 [(1/2)($2,000)]. However, as there is still a balance in the class at the end of the year, no recapture would be recorded.

Solution to Self Study Problem Five - 5

Case One
For the year ending December 31, 2020, the maximum CCA, as well as the UCC balance for January 1, 2021, for Traxit's Class 14.1 would be as calculated as follows:

January 1, 2020, Balance	Nil
2020 Additions ($56,000 + $124,000)	$180,000
AccII Adjustment [(50%)($180,000)]	90,000
CCA Base	$270,000
2020 CCA [(5%)($270,000)]	(13,500)
AccII Adjustment Reversal	(90,000)
January 1, 2021, UCC	$166,500

The results for 2021 would be calculated as follows:

January 1, 2021, UCC	$166,500
Disposition - Lesser Of:	
Capital Cost = $180,000	
Proceeds Of Disposition = $97,000	(97,000)
CCA Base	$ 69,500
2021 CCA [(5%)($69,500)]	(3,475)
January 1, 2022, UCC	$ 66,025

There would be no immediate tax consequences resulting from the sale of goodwill, other than a reduction in the UCC. Note that the capital cost in the calculation is of the single goodwill property.

Case Two

For the year ending December 31, 2020, the maximum CCA, as well as the UCC balance for January 1, 2021, for Traxit's Class 14.1 would be as calculated as follows:

January 1, 2020, Balance	Nil
2020 Additions ($34,000 + $47,000)	$ 81,000
AccII Adjustment [(50%)($81,000)]	40,500
CCA Base	$121,500
2020 CCA [(5%)($121,500)]	(6,075)
AccII Adjustment Reversal	(40,500)
January 1, 2021, UCC	$ 74,925

The results for 2021 would be calculated as follows:

January 1, 2021, UCC	$74,925
Disposition - Lesser Of:	
Capital Cost = $81,000	
Proceeds Of Disposition = $85,000	(81,000)
Negative Ending Balance	($ 6,075)
Recapture Of CCA	6,075
January 1, 2022, UCC	Nil

Proceeds Of Disposition	$85,000
Capital Cost	(81,000)
Capital Gain	$ 4,000
Inclusion Rate	1/2
Taxable Capital Gain	$ 2,000

There would be an increase in Net Income For Tax Purposes of $8,075 ($6,075 + $2,000).

Solution to Self Study Problem Five - 6

Class 1 - Buildings (Existing And Separate Class)

As the new building has been allocated to a separate Class 1, two calculations are required here. The CCA on the existing Class 1 would be as follows:

Opening UCC Balance	$590,000
Disposition - Lesser Of:	
Proceeds = $290,000 ($440,000 - $150,000)	
Capital Cost = $300,000 ($475,000 - $175,000)	(290,000)
CCA Base	$300,000
CCA Rate	4%
Maximum CCA	$ 12,000

Since the replacement building is new, used 100 percent for non-residential purposes, and allocated to a separate Class 1, it qualifies for an enhanced CCA rate. As it is not used for manufacturing and processing, the enhanced rate is 6 percent. Using this rate, the CCA on the new building would be as follows:

Opening UCC Balance	Nil
Additions ($500,000 - $125,000)	$375,000
AccII Adjustment [(50%)($375,000)]	187,500
CCA Base	$562,500
CCA Rate	6%
Maximum CCA	$ 33,750

Class 8 - Furniture
The required calculation here would be as follows:

Opening UCC Balance	$570,000
Additions	14,000
AccII Adjustment [(50%)($14,000)]	7,000
CCA Base	$591,000
CCA Rate	20%
Maximum CCA	$ 118,200

Class 10 - Vehicles
The required calculations here would be as follows:

Opening UCC Balance	$61,000
Additions	22,000
AccII Adjustment*	Nil
CCA Base	$83,000
CCA Rate	30%
Maximum CCA	$24,900

*As the acquired truck was a depreciable property (it had a UCC balance) transferred from a non-arm's length person, the AccII provisions do not apply to this acquisition. The shareholder's UCC does not affect the CCA calculations for Bartel Ltd.

Summary (Not Required)
The maximum CCA is as follows:

Class 1	$ 12,000
Class 1	33,750
Class 8	118,200
Class 10	24,900
Maximum CCA	$188,850

Solution to Self Study Problem Five - 7

Class 1 - Building
There were no additions or dispositions in this class. As a consequence, the maximum 2020 CCA would be $25,000 [(4%)($625,000)]. The January 1, 2021, UCC of Class 1 would be $600,000 ($625,000 - $25,000).

Class 8 - Office Furniture And Equipment
The required calculations for this class would be as follows:

Opening UCC Balance		$155,000
Additions	$27,000	
Dispositions - Lesser Of:		
• Capital Cost = $22,000		
• Proceeds Of Disposition = $35,000	(22,000)	5,000
AccII Adjustment [(50%)($5,000)]		2,500
CCA Base		$162,500
2020 CCA [(20%)($162,500)]		(32,500)
AccII Adjustment Reversal		(2,500)
January 1, 2021, UCC Balance		$ 127,500

The sale of the furniture and equipment would result in a taxable capital gain that would be calculated as follows:

Proceeds Of Disposition	$35,000
Capital Cost	(22,000)
Capital Gain	$13,000
Inclusion Rate	1/2
Taxable Capital Gain	$ 6,500

Class 10 - Vehicles
The required calculations for this class would be as follows:

Opening UCC Balance		$118,000
Additions	$33,000	
Disposition of Truck - Lesser Of:		
• Capital Cost = $23,000		
• Proceeds Of Disposition = $8,500	(8,500)	
Disposition of Car - Lesser Of:		
• Capital Cost = $17,000		
• Proceeds Of Disposition = $8,000	(8,000)	16,500
AccII Adjustment [(50%)($16,500)]		8,250
CCA Base		$142,750
2020 CCA [(30%)($142,750)]		(42,825)
AccII Adjustment Reversal		(8,250)
January 1, 2021, UCC Balance		$ 91,675

Note that the amount received from the insurance company on the destroyed vehicle is treated as proceeds from a disposition.

Class 12 - Tools

Tools that cost $500 or less are allocated to Class 12 where they are not subject to the half-year rule or the AccII provisions. This means that they are eligible for a write-off rate of 100 percent in the year of acquisition. As a consequence, the entire $34,000 can be deducted as CCA for 2020, leaving a nil January 1, 2021, UCC balance.

Class 13 - Leasehold Improvements

In general, leasehold improvements will be written off over the term of the lease on a straight-line basis. For purposes of applying this calculation, the term of the lease would include the first renewal option, beginning in a period after the improvements were made. In the case of the original improvements, the period to be used is 12 years. With respect to the improvements during the current year, the write-off period will be 9 years. Also note that Class 13 assets are eligible for the AccII provisions on net additions. The required calculations are as follows:

Opening UCC Balance		$ 61,750
Additions		45,000
CCA Base		$106,750
CCA:		
• 2017 Improvements ($78,000 ÷ 12)	($6,500)	
• 2020 Improvements Including AccII Adjustment [($45,000 ÷ 9)(150%)]	(7,500)	(14,000)
January 1, 2021, UCC Balance		$ 92,750

Class 14.1 - Intangible Assets

The required calculations for this class are as follows:

Opening UCC Balance	Nil
Disposition - Lesser Of:	
• Capital Cost = Nil	
• Proceeds Of Disposition = $87,000	Nil
January 1, 2021, UCC Balance	Nil

Proceeds Of Disposition	$ 87,000
Capital Cost	Nil
Capital Gain	$ 87,000
Inclusion Rate	1/2
Taxable Capital Gain	$43,500

Class 50 - Computer Hardware

The required calculations are as follows:

Opening UCC Balance	$ Nil
Additions	28,000
AccII Adjustment [(50%)($28,000)]	14,000
CCA Base	$42,000
2020 CCA [(55%)($42,000)]	(23,100)
AccII Adjustment Reversal	(14,000)
January 1, 2021, UCC Balance	$ 4,900

Class 53 - Manufacturing Equipment

The required calculations are as follows:

Opening UCC Balance	$217,000
Dispositions - Lesser Of:	
• Capital Cost = $752,000	
• Proceeds Of Disposition = $188,000	(188,000)
Ending Balance With No Remaining Assets In Class	$ 29,000
Terminal Loss	(29,000)
January 1, 2021, UCC Balance	Nil

After all of the assets in Class 53 have been retired there is still a $29,000 UCC balance. This results in a terminal loss that will be deducted in full from the Net Income of Atlantic Manufacturing Company.

Other Income Effects

In addition, the following income effects resulted from the information provided in the problem:

Taxable Capital Gain On Class 8 Assets	$ 6,500
Taxable Capital Gain On Class 14.1 Assets	43,500
Terminal Loss On Class 53 Assets	(29,000)
Total Inclusion	$21,000

Summary Of CCA And UCC Results (Not Required)

The maximum 2020 CCA and the January 1, 2021, UCC balances can be summarized as follows:

	Maximum CCA	UCC
Class 1	$25,000	$600,000
Class 8	32,500	127,500
Class 10	42,825	91,675
Class 12	34,000	Nil
Class 13	14,000	92,750
Class 14.1	Nil	Nil
Class 50	23,100	4,900
Class 53	Nil	Nil

Solution to Self Study Problem Five - 8

Part A

The required calculation of the maximum CCA is as follows:

Class 8 [(20%)($163,000)]	$ 32,600
Class 10 (Note 1)	43,950
Class 12 (Note 2)	42,000
Class 13 (Note 3)	24,000
Class 14.1 [(5%)($132,330)]	6,617
Maximum Total	$149,167

Note 1   The Class 10 CCA would be calculated as follows:

Opening Balance	$ 112,000
Additions	52,000
Proceeds Of Disposition (Less Than Cost)	(29,000)
AccII Adjustment [(1/2)($52,000 - $29,000)]	11,500
CCA Base	$146,500
CCA Rate	30%
Maximum CCA	$ 43,950

Note 2   The rate for Class 12 is 100 percent. However, some additions to this class are subject to the half-year rules. The presence of an opening balance of $42,000 and the statement that maximum CCA has always been taken indicates that there must have been $84,000 of costs in 2019 that were subject to this rule. Given this, the entire balance can be deducted in 2020.

Note 3   The $204,000 balance in Class 13 is equal to 85 percent of $240,000. This means that during the two years 2018 and 2019, 15 percent of their cost was deducted as CCA. As the half-year rules are applicable to this class, this represents a half year for 2018 and a full year for 2019. Since Class 13 is a straight-line class, this indicates that the CCA rate is 10 percent (15 percent ÷ 1.5). Based on this analysis, maximum CCA for 2020 would be $24,000 [(10%)($240,000)].

Part B

Since the company only has Net and Taxable Income before CCA of $43,000, and the problem states that loss carry overs should not be considered, maximum CCA would not be deducted. Only $43,000 in CCA should be taken in order to reduce the Taxable Income to nil.

As to which CCA classes should be reduced, the usual procedure is to deduct the required amount from the balances with the lowest rates. By leaving the balances with higher rates untouched, larger amounts of CCA can be deducted in later periods as required.

Taking this approach, the recommended CCA would be as follows:

Class 14.1 (Maximum Available)	$ 6,617
Class 13 (Maximum Available)	24,000
Class 8 ($43,000 - $6,617 - $24,000)	12,383
Total CCA	$43,000

The deduction of this amount of CCA would serve to reduce Taxable Income to nil.

Chapter 6 Learning Objectives

After completing Chapter 6, you should be able to:

1. Classify property based on its use and determine what type of income will be produced while the asset is being held and when it is disposed of (paragraph [P hereafter] 6-1 to 6-16).
2. Describe the tax factors that can be affected by the classification of income as business or property (P 6-17 to 6-27).
3. Distinguish between business income and capital gains, including the criteria used by the courts in making this distinction (P 6-28 to 6-42).
4. Describe the major differences between net business income and Net Income as determined under GAAP (P 6-43 to 6-45).
5. Recall the various items that are included in net business income (P 6-46 to 6-53 and P 6-64 to 6-65).

---

6. Apply the system of reserves that can be used in determining net business income (P 6-54 to 6-63).
7. Apply the limitations on deductions that apply to business and property income, including those on home office costs (P 6-66 to 6-103).
8. Apply the limitations on deductions that apply to business, property, and employment income, including those related to meals and entertainment and automobile costs (P 6-104 to 6-132).
9. Apply the inventory valuation procedures that are used for determining net business income (P 6-133 to 6-141).
10. Recall the deductions that are specified in the Income Tax Act for calculating net business income (P 6-142 to 6-143).

---

11. Reconcile accounting Net Income with net business income (P 6-144 to 6-149).
12. Recall the rules for determining taxation years and calculate additional business income for non-calendar fiscal years (P 6-150 to 6-157).
13. Apply the special provisions related to farm activities and farm losses (P 6-158 to 6-169).
14. Apply the special rule for unbilled work in process applicable to the income of some professionals (P 6-170 to 6-174).
15. Apply the provisions related to the disposition of inventories and accounts receivable in situations where a business is being sold (P 6-175 to 6-181).

How to Work Through Chapter 6

We recommend the following approach in dealing with the material in this chapter:

Overview And Classification Of Business Income
- Read paragraph 6-1 to 6-16 (in the textbook).

Business Income Vs. Property Income
- Read paragraph 6-17 to 6-27.
- Do Exercise Six-1 (in the textbook) and check the solution in this Study Guide.

Business Income Vs. Capital Gains
- Read paragraph 6-28 to 6-42.
- Do Exercise Six-2 and check the solution in this Study Guide.

Business Income And GAAP
- Read paragraph 6-43 to 6-45.

Inclusions - Amounts Received And Receivable
- Read paragraph 6-46 to 6-53.

Reserves For Doubtful Debts, Undelivered Goods, And Unpaid Amounts
- Read paragraph 6-54 to 6-61.
- Do Exercise Six-3 and check the solution in this Study Guide.
- Read paragraph 6-62.
- Do Exercise Six-4 and check the solution in this Study Guide.
- Read paragraph 6-63.
- Do Exercise Six-5 and check the solution in this Study Guide.
- Do Self Study Problems Six-1 and Six-2, which are available on MyLab, and check the solutions in this Study Guide.

Other Inclusions
- Read paragraph 6-64 to 6-65.

Limitations On Deductions From Business And Property Income, Including Work Space In The Home Costs
- Read paragraph 6-66 to 6-93.
- Do Exercise Six-6 and check the solution in this Study Guide.
- Read paragraph 6-94 to 6-100.
- Do Exercise Six-7 and check the solution in this Study Guide.
- Do Self Study Problem Six-3 and check the solution in this Study Guide.
- Read paragraph 6-101 to 6-103.

Limitations On Deductions From Business, Property, And Employment Income, Including Reasonableness and Meals And Entertainment
- Read paragraph 6-104 to 6-112.

Restrictions On Automobile Costs
- Read paragraph 6-113 to 6-118
- Do Exercise Six-8 and check the solution in this Study Guide.
- Read paragraph 6-119 to 6-126.
- Do Exercise Six-9 and check the solution in this Study Guide.
- Do Self Study Problems Six-4 to Six-6 and check the solutions in this Study Guide.

Leasing Property
- Read paragraph 6-127 to 6-129.
- Do Exercise Six-10 and check the solution in this Study Guide.

Illegal Payments, Fines, And Penalties
- Read paragraph 6-130 and 6-132.

Specific Deductions From Business Income, Including Cost Of Sales
- Read paragraph 6-133 to 6-141.
- Do Exercise Six-11 and check the solution in this Study Guide.
- Do Self Study Problem Six-7 and check the solution in this Study Guide.
- Read paragraph 6-142 to 6-143.

Reconciliation Of Accounting Net Income And Net Income For Tax Purposes
- Read paragraph 6-144 to 6-149.
- Do Self Study Problems Six-8 to Six-10 and check the solutions in this Study Guide.

Taxation Year And Additional Business Income
- Read paragraph 6-150 to 6-157.
- Do Exercise Six-12 and check the solution in this Study Guide.
- Do Self Study Problem Six-11 and check the solution in this Study Guide.

Farming Income And Losses, Including Restricted Farm Losses
- Read paragraph 6-158 to 6-164.
- Do Exercise Six-13 and check the solution in this Study Guide.
- Read paragraph 6-165 to 6-169.

Professional Income (Billed Basis Of Recognition And Change in Legislation)
- Read paragraph 6-170 to 6-174.
- Do Exercise Six-14 and check the solution in this Study Guide.
- Do Self Study Problems Six-12 and Six-13 and check the solutions in this Study Guide.

Sale Of A Business, Including ITA 22 Election On Accounts Receivable
- Read paragraph 6-175 to 6-180.
- Do Exercise Six-15 and check the solution in this Study Guide.
- Do Self Study Problem Six-14 to Six-16 and check the solutions in this Study Guide.
- Read paragraph 6-181.

To Complete This Chapter
- If you would like more practice in problem solving, do the Supplementary Self Study Problems for the chapter. These problems and solutions are available on MyLab.
- Review the Key Terms Used In This Chapter in the textbook at the end of Chapter 6. Consult the Glossary for the meaning of any key terms you do not know.
- Test yourself with the Chapter 6 Glossary Flashcards available on MyLab.
- Ensure you have achieved the Chapter 6 Learning Objectives listed in this Study Guide.
- As a review, we recommend you view the PowerPoint presentation for Chapter 6 that is on MyLab.

Solutions to Chapter 6 Exercises

Exercise Six - 1 Solution
With a single transaction, Joan's activity clearly does not fall within the general definition of operating a business. However, the real question is whether this transaction would be considered an adventure or concern in the nature of trade. As she is not behaving like a dealer and does not appear to have an intent to sell the song rights, it is unlikely that this transaction would be viewed as an adventure or concern in the nature of trade. This means that the royalties would be treated as property income, rather than business income. While this classification would not be important as long as she holds the rights, if there is a disposition of these rights, any gain would be treated as a capital gain, rather than as a fully taxable business gain.

Exercise Six - 2 Solution

Provided that she can demonstrate that her intent was to operate the building as a rental property, the gain should qualify as a capital gain. The fact that the offer was unsolicited would support this conclusion.

Exercise Six - 3 Solution

The Bad Debt Expense would be as follows:

2020 Estimate Of Future Bad Debts (Credit Allowance)	($18,400)
Increase In Expense To Eliminate Debit Balance In Allowance	
($17,200 Actual Write-Offs - $16,000 Allowance)	(1,200)
2020 Bad Debt Expense For Accounting Purposes	($ 19,600)

For tax purposes, the net decrease for the year will be the same $19,600 calculated as follows:

Add: 2019 Reserve For Tax Purposes		$ 16,000
Deduct:		
2020 Actual Write-Offs	($ 17,200)	
2020 Reserve For Tax Purposes	(18,400)	(35,600)
2020 Net Deduction For Tax Purposes		($ 19,600)

Exercise Six - 4 Solution

The amount to be included in net business income would be calculated as follows:

Cash Sales	$53,400
Accounts Receivable	26,300
Reserve For Undelivered Services	(5,600)
Reserve For Doubtful Accounts	(425)
Total Increase	$73,675

Exercise Six - 5 Solution

As some of the proceeds are not receivable for more than two years after the date of sale, a reserve can be deducted under ITA 20(1)(n) for the years 2020, 2021, and 2022. As December 31, 2023, is more than 36 months after the sale was made, no reserve can be deducted for 2023 or 2024. Note that the previous year's reserve is added to income before deducting the new reserve. The maximum reserve is based on the gross profit of $65,000. None of this profit will be recognized in 2020 as no proceeds are received. In 2021 and 2022, 25 percent of the profit will be recognized, with the remainder being in 2023 when no reserve can be deducted.

The maximum reserve that can be deducted in each year, as well as the minimum income to be recognized in each year, is shown in the following schedule:

	Income	Proceeds Rec'd
2020 Reserve = [(100%)($65,000)] = $65,000	Nil	Nil
2021 Reserve = [(75%)($65,000)] = $48,750	$ 16,250	$ 30,000
2022 Reserve = [(50%)($65,000)] = $32,500	16,250	30,000
2023 Reserve = Nil (> 36 Months From Sale)	32,500	30,000
2024 Reserve = Nil (All Proceeds Received)	Nil	30,000
Totals	$65,000	$120,000

Note that the technically correct calculation of income involves adding back the previous year's reserve and deducting the new reserve. For example, the calculation for 2022 involves adding back the 2021 reserve of $48,750 and deducting the new reserve of $32,500 to calculate the income of $16,250 ($48,750 - $32,500).

Exercise Six - 6 Solution

As Ms. Johnson owns 30 percent of the common shares, she is clearly a specified shareholder under ITA 18(5). Her relevant equity balance would be $1,620,000 [(30%)($2,400,000) + (100%)($900,000)]. Given this, the disallowed interest would be calculated as follows:

Total Interest Paid To Ms. Johnson [(9%)($4,500,000)]	$405,000
Maximum Deductible Interest [(9%)(1.5)($1,620,000)]	(218,700)
Disallowed Interest	$186,300

Exercise Six - 7 Solution

The following work space in the home costs would be deductible in each of the three scenarios:

	Part A	Part B	Part C
Utilities	$2,400	$ 2,400	$ 2,400
Maintenance And Repairs	4,600	4,600	4,600
Property Taxes	Nil	5,200	5,200
House Insurance	Nil	2,300	2,300
Interest On Mortgage	Nil	Nil	7,800
House CCA	Nil	Nil	12,000
Subtotal	$ 7,000	$14,500	$34,300
Percentage	25%	25%	25%
Subtotal	$1,750	$ 3,625	$ 8,575
Repainting And Rewiring (100%)	1,000	1,000	1,000
Internet Service Fees [(95%)($960)]	Nil	Nil	912
Monthly Phone [(95%)($600)]	Nil	Nil	570
Long Distance Charges (100%)	390	390	390
Maximum Deduction	$3,140	$ 5,015	$11,447

Exercise Six - 8 Solution

With respect to the amount of CCA, since the business commenced operations on September 15, 2020, the CCA is limited to the proportion of the year the business was in operation (108/365) and the AccII provisions would apply. The fact that the car was purchased on October 1 does not affect the short fiscal year calculation.

The base amount for the CCA calculation is limited to the Class 10.1 maximum of $30,000. With respect to the interest, the car was financed for a total of 92 days with a limit of $10 per day. As a result, the amounts that can be deducted are as follows:

CCA [(150%)(108/365)(30%)($30,000)]	$3,995
Interest Costs - Lesser Of:	
• Amount Paid = $1,200	
• [($10)(92 Days)] = $920	920
Total Deduction	$4,915

Exercise Six - 9 Solution

The amount he can deduct is limited to $2,229, the least of:

- $4,925 [($985)(5)];
- $4,080 [($800)(153/30)];and
- $2,229 {[$4,925][$30,000 ÷ (85%)($78,000)]}.

Exercise Six - 10 Solution

For tax purposes, the lease would be treated as an operating lease, with the deduction being based only on the lease payments. Under GAAP, the lease would have to be treated as a purchase and capitalized. This is because during the lease term the lease transfers "substantially all of the benefits and risks of ownership related to the leased property from the lessor to the lessee". This means that the accounting deductions would be for amortization on the capitalized asset and interest costs on the associated liability.

Exercise Six - 11 Solution

The average per unit cost of $2.87 ($663,850 ÷ 231,000) is calculated as follows:

Price	Units	Total
$2.50	50,000	$ 125,000
$2.85	35,000	99,750
$2.95	62,000	182,900
$3.05	84,000	256,200
Totals	231,000	$ 663,850

The following calculations will be used in this solution.

Fair Market Value (Using Replacement Cost) [($3.10)(102,000)]	$316,200
Fair Market Value (Using Net Realizable Value) [(90%)($4.50)(102,000)]	413,100
FIFO Cost [(84,000)($3.05) + (102,000 - 84,000)($2.95)]	309,300
Average Cost [($2.87)(102,000)]	292,740

For tax purposes, the inventory value can be determined by any of the following methods.

Fair Market Value = Replacement Cost	$316,200
Fair Market Value = Net Realizable Value	413,100
Lower of FIFO Cost ($309,300) or Replacement Cost ($316,200)	309,300
Lower of FIFO Cost ($309,300) or Net Realizable Value ($413,100)	309,300
Lower of Average Cost ($292,740) or Replacement Cost ($316,200)	292,740
Lower of Average Cost ($292,740) or Net Realizable Value ($413,100)	292,740

Exercise Six - 12 Solution

Mr. Gelato's additional business income for 2020 will be $18,551 [($12,300)(184 Days ÷ 122 Days)]. The 184 days is for the period July 1 through December 31, while the 122 days is for the period March 1 through June 30. The total business income that Mr. Gelato will have to report for 2020 is $30,851 ($12,300 + $18,551).

Exercise Six - 13 Solution

For Ms. Morph, farming is clearly a secondary source of income. Given this, her farm losses will be restricted. The amount she can deduct for 2020 will be limited to $10,600 [$2,500 + (1/2)($18,700 - $2,500)]. The remaining $8,100 ($18,700 - $10,600) restricted farm loss is available for carry over.

Exercise Six - 14 Solution

Mr. Winters' income inclusion for the year ending December 31, 2020, would be calculated as follows:

January 1, 2020, Unbilled Work In Process [(100% - 40%)($35,000)]	$ 21,000
Billings For Work Done In 2020	185,000
December 2020 Unbilled Work In Process [(60%)($245,000 - $185,000)]	36,000
Total 2020 Income Inclusion	$242,000

Mr. Winters' income inclusion for the year ending December 31, 2021, would be calculated as follows:

Unrecognized Work In Process From 2020 [(100% - 60%)($245,000 - $185,000)]	$ 24,000
Billings For Work Done In 2021	247,000
December 2021 Unbilled Work In Process [(80%)($285,000 - $247,000)]	30,400
Total 2021 Income Inclusion	$301,400

Exercise Six - 15 Solution

Mr. Nero would include in his business income the 2019 reserve of $3,800. He could then deduct the $5,250 ($53,450 - $48,200) loss on the receivables. The net tax effect for Mr. Nero would be a deduction in the determination of business income of $1,450 ($5,250 - $3,800).

Mr. Labelle would have to include the $5,250 difference between the face value and the price paid in income. Subsequent to the sale, 100 percent of any difference between the $53,450 face value of the receivables and amounts actually collected will be deductible when calculating Mr. Labelle's net business income.

Mr. Labelle could establish a new reserve for doubtful debts related to any uncollected receivables that are outstanding at the end of the year.

Solution to Self Study Problem Six - 1

The net deduction for bad debts in the calculation of 2020 business income would be calculated as follows:

Add:	
2019 Reserve For Doubtful Debts	$ 11,500
Recoveries Of 2019 Bad Debts During 2020	1,500
Deduct:	
Actual Bad Debt Write-Offs During 2020 ($8,800 - $700)	(8,100)
2020 Reserve For Doubtful Debts ($15,900 + $700)	(16,600)
2020 Net Deduction From Business Income	($ 11,700)

Note that the $700 that was due from Dr. Allworth's personal friend has been treated as part of the reserve for doubtful debts, rather than as part of the write-offs for the period. The $190 recovery in 2019 would have been included in income in 2019 and would not affect 2020 income.

Solution to Self Study Problem Six - 2

The results for the two years would be as follows:

	2020	2021
Cash Collections ($259,000 - $88,000)	$171,000	
Cash Collections ($360,000 - $72,000)		$288,000
Ending Receivables	88,000	72,000
Reserve For Doubtful Debts:		
Add Prior Year Reserve	Nil	7,000
Deduct Current Year Reserve	(7,000)	(9,500)
Deduct Actual Write-Offs	Nil	(6,500)
Advances From Customers	27,000	21,000
Reserve For Undelivered Merchandise:		
Add Prior Year Reserve	Nil	27,000
Deduct Current Year Reserve	(27,000)	(21,000)
Gross Profit On Sale Of Unused Materials	15,000	Nil
Reserve For Unpaid Amounts:		
Add Prior Year Reserve		9,677
Deduct Current Year Reserve*		
{[$15,000][($62,000 - $22,000) ÷ $62,000]}	(9,677)	
{[$15,000][($62,000 - $42,000) ÷ $62,000]}		(4,839)
Net Effect	$257,323	$382,838

*As some of the proceeds on the sale of unused materials are not due until two years after the date of the sale, a reserve for unpaid amounts can be deducted. The three year time limit is not relevant as the full balance is paid off prior to the end of that period.

Solution to Self Study Problem Six - 3

Part A

Under ITA 18(12), the following conditions must be satisfied in order for expenses related to work space in a self-contained domestic establishment to be deductible:

- the work space is either the individual's principal place of business; or
- the work space is used exclusively for the purpose of earning income from business and is used on a regular and continuous basis for meeting clients, customers, or patients of the individual in respect of the business.

With respect to Ms. Hart's mail order business, the allocated space in her home would appear to be her principal place of business. This means that she would be able to deduct work space in home costs in determining her net business income.

Part B

The calculation of the minimum net business income to be reported in Veronica's personal tax return is as follows:

Revenues		$89,000
Less: Expenses Other Than Home Work Space Costs:		
Cost Of Merchandise Sold	($ 46,000)	
Packaging Materials	(1,547)	
Shipping Costs	(3,216)	
Miscellaneous Office Supplies	(825)	
Telephone	(210)	
Advertising Brochures	(156)	
CCA (Note 1)	(5,414)	(57,368)
Income Before Home Work Space Costs		$31,632
Less: Home Work Space Costs (Note 2)		(2,174)
Net Business Income		$29,458

Note 1 Maximum CCA amounts on the assets of the business (not including CCA on the house) for the short fiscal year would be calculated as follows (alternative calculations shown in the two columns):

		Short Fiscal Year
	100%	**(346/365)**
Class 8 [($14,000)(150%)(20%)]	$4,200	$3,981
Class 50 [($1,350)(150%)(55%)]	1,114	1056
Class 12 [($795)(1/2)(100%)]*	398	377
Total	$5,712	
Short Fiscal Year Factor	346/365	
Maximum CCA	$5,414	$5,414

*The AccII provisions do not apply to Class 12.

Note 2 The home work space costs would be calculated as follows:

Utilities For Home (Heat, Light, And Water)	$	2,850
Mortgage Interest Paid		4,183
House Insurance		400
Property Taxes		1,230
Repairs And Maintenance For Home		1,125
Total Out-Of-Pocket Costs	$	9,788
Class 1 CCA [($355,000 - $80,000)(1/2)(4%)]*		5,500
Total Costs For The Home	$	15,288
Percentage Of Floor Space		15%
Subtotal	$	2,293
Short Fiscal Year Factor		346/365
Deductible Home Work Space Costs	$	2,174

*As the residence was owned by Veronica prior to a portion being converted to business use, the AccII provisions would not be available.

Part C

There are two issues that should be discussed with Veronica.

- As this problem asks for "minimum" net business income, CCA must be deducted on Ms. Hart's home. The problem with this is that, if she takes CCA, it could jeopardize the principal residence exemption on this property, resulting in the payment of taxes on a portion of the taxable capital gain that might arise on any future sale of the property, assuming real estate prices are increasing. This is discussed in more detail in Chapter 8.

- Although it is not relevant for this year, Ms. Hart should be aware that the deduction of work space in home costs cannot be used to create a loss in the future. However, any amount not deductible because it is greater than her income can be deducted in any subsequent year provided there is sufficient income from the same business in that year. This provides for an unlimited carry forward of unused work space in home costs (see S4-F2-C2, *Business Use Of Home Expenses*).

Solution to Self Study Problem Six - 4

Part A

In Part A(i), Ms. Wise is an employee and, because her income includes commissions, she can deduct expenses related to the production of employment income under ITA 8(1)(f), provided no deduction is made under ITA 8(1)(h) or ITA 8(1)(h.1).

Deductions under ITA 8(1)(f) are limited to the amount of commissions earned. Alternatively, traveling costs and motor vehicle costs other than capital costs can be deducted under ITA 8(1)(h) and ITA 8(1)(h.1). Deductions under these provisions are not limited to commission income.

The deduction of dues and other expenses under ITA 8(1)(i) and automobile capital costs (CCA and financing costs) under ITA 8(1)(j) is permitted without regard to other provisions used.

	ITA 8(1)(f) (Limited To $15,000)	ITA 8(1) (h) and (h.1)	ITA 8(1) (i) and (j)	Part A(ii)
Professional Dues	-	-	$ 600	$ 600
Automobile Costs:				
Operating Costs				
[(35,000/50,000)($6,000)]	$ 4,200	$ 4,200	-	4,200
Financing Costs				
[(35,000/50,000)($2,500)]	-	-	1,750	1,750
CCA (See Note)	-	-	3,465	3,465
Home Office Costs:				
Utilities [(40%)($3,550)]	-	-	1,420	1,420
Maintenance [(40%)($1,500)]	-	-	600	600
Insurance [(40%)($950)]	380	-	-	380
Property Taxes [(40%)($4,700)]	1,880	-	-	1,880
Interest [(40%)($13,500)]	-	-	-	5,400
CCA [($140,000)(4%)]	-	-	-	5,600
Travel Costs	23,000	23,000	-	23,000
Non-Deductible Meals				
[(50%)($8,000)]	(4,000)	(4,000)	-	(4,000)
Country Club Charges	12,000	-	-	12,000
Non-Deductible Membership Fees	(2,500)	-	-	(2,500)
Non-Deductible Meals				
[(50%)($9,500)]	(4,750)	-	-	(4,750)
Total	$30,210	$23,200	$7,835	$49,045

Note The car will be allocated to Class 10.1 at a value of $30,000, the 2019 limit. The excess of $23,000 will not be deductible. Maximum CCA for 2019 would have been $13,500 [(30%)(1.5)($30,000)]. The deductible amount for 2019 would have been this amount multiplied by the portion of her total usage that was related to income producing activity.

The January 1, 2020, UCC would be $16,500 ($30,000 - $13,500) and maximum CCA for 2020 would have been $3,950 [(30%)($16,500)]. Note that, in determining the relevant UCC value, the full amount of maximum 2019 CCA was deducted, not just the portion that was actually deducted in that year. The deductible amount for 2020 equals $3,465 [(35,000/50,000)($4,950)].

The deduction for home office costs has been split between ITA 8(1)(i) and (f). Since the utilities and maintenance portion can be deducted under ITA 8(1)(i), it is not limited by the commission income. The insurance and property tax components are limited as they are deducted under ITA 8(1)(f). A limitation, which is not illustrated in this problem, prevents the deduction of home office costs from creating an employment loss.

As the ITA 8(1)(f) amount is limited to the $15,000 in commission income, the total deduction using ITA 8(1)(f), (i) and (j) is $22,835 ($15,000 + $7,835).

The total deduction using ITA 8(1)(h), (h.1), (i), and (j) is $31,035 ($23,200 + $7,835). Note that when this approach is used, home office costs are limited to utilities and maintenance. Further, there is no deduction for entertainment costs. However, this approach results in deductions totaling $8,200 ($31,035 - $22,835) more than the amount available using ITA 8(1)(f), (i), and (j) due to the effect of the commission income limit.

Comparing Parts A (i) and A (ii), there is a difference of $18,010 ($49,045 - $31,035) between the maximum employee and self-employed calculations, illustrating the importance of the difference between being an employee and being self-employed. This problem is, of course, somewhat unrealistic in that, if Ms. Wise was an employee, it is likely that she would be compensated or reimbursed for at least part of her employment-related expenses.

Part B
As will be discussed in Chapter 8, capital gains on an individual's principal residence are, in general, not subject to income taxes. While a strict application of the relevant rules would remove from principal residence status the portion of Ms. Wise's home that was used for income producing activities, the administrative procedures of the CRA do not follow this approach. It appears that, as long as no CCA is taken on the work space portion of the home, 100 percent of the property will qualify as a principal residence. Given this, and the assumption that real estate prices are increasing, it would not be wise for Ms. Wise to take CCA on her office space.

Solution to Self Study Problem Six - 5

Part A
Ford Focus The tax consequences resulting from the sale of the Ford Focus can be calculated as follows:

January 1, 2020, UCC	$12,980
Disposition - Lesser Of:	
Capital Cost = $23,600	
Proceeds Of Disposition = $18,200	(18,200)
Ending Balance With No Remaining Assets In Class	($ 5,220)
Recapture Of CCA	(5,220)
UCC - December 31, 2020	Nil

Because of its price, the new Mercedes will have to be allocated to a separate Class 10.1. This means that the Ford Focus was the last asset in Class 10. Given this, the negative balance of $5,220 will be added to income as recapture of CCA.

As no balance remains in this class, there will be no Class 10 CCA for 2020.

Mercedes E-Class Sedan   The maximum CCA deduction on the Mercedes would be calculated as follows:

Capital Cost (Limited To $30,000)	$30,000
AccII Adjustment [(50%)($30,000)]	15,000
CCA Base	$45,000
Rate	30%
Maximum CCA	$13,500

The net effect on income due to the two automobiles would be as follows:

Recapture Of CCA	$ 5,220
CCA	(13,500)
Operating Costs (Fully Deductible)	(17,460)
Total Deductible Costs	($25,740)

Part B

Because the Ford Focus was used primarily (more than 50 percent) for employment purposes, it is eligible for the reduced standby charge and the alternative operating cost benefit calculation. The minimum benefit on this vehicle would be calculated as follows:

Standby Charge: [(2%)($23,600)(4)(6,668 ÷ 6,668*)]	$1,888
Operating Cost Benefit - Lesser Of:	
• [($1,888)(1/2)] = $944	
• [(13,000)($0.28)] = $3,640	944
Ford Focus - Minimum Total Benefit	$2,832

*[(4)(1,667)] Also note that, as the personal use was greater than 1,667 kilometres per month, the numerator is equal to the denominator.

Less than one-half of the Mercedes' mileage was for employment-related activities. Given this, there is no reduction of the standby charge and no alternative calculation of the operating cost benefit available. The minimum total benefit is calculated as follows:

Standby Charge [(2%)($52,000)(8)]	$ 8,320
Operating Cost Benefit [(23,000)($0.28)]	6,440
Mercedes Sedan - Minimum Total Benefit	$14,760

The total benefit on the two vehicles would be calculated as follows:

Ford Focus	$ 2,832
Mercedes Sedan	14,760
Total Taxable Benefit	$17,592

Solution to Self Study Problem Six - 6

Analysis
The choice between the two alternatives will be based on the comparative tax flows of the two alternatives. The relevant calculations are provided in the sections that follow.

Employer Provides Automobile
If Jordan elects to have the employer provide the BMW, he will have a taxable benefit in each year. Since his employment-related mileage is greater than 50 percent, he is eligible for the reduced standby charge and the alternative operating cost benefit calculation. The after tax consequence of this choice would be as follows:

Standby Charge (Reduced)	
[(2%)(12)($125,000)(18,000 ÷ 20,004*)]	$26,995
Operating Cost Benefit - Lesser Of:	
• [(1/2)($26,995)] = $13,498	
• [($0.28)(18,000)] = $5,040	5,040
Total Automobile Benefit	$32,035
Marginal Tax Rate	50%
Annual Increase In Tax	$16,018

*[(12)(1,667)]

Jordan Buys the Automobile
The pre-tax cash inflows (outflows) associated with this alternative are as follows:

	2020	2021	2022
Loan Proceeds	$125,000	N/A	N/A
Automobile Purchase	(125,000)	N/A	N/A
Allowance Received [(12)($2,000)]	24,000	$24,000	$ 24,000
Loan Repayment	N/A	N/A	(125,000)
Proceeds From Sale Of Car	N/A	N/A	52,000
Operating Costs [($0.32)(65,000)]	(20,800)	(20,800)	(20,800)
Pre-Tax Cash Inflows (Outflows)	$ 3,200	$ 3,200	($ 69,800)

The tax savings (costs) associated with this alternative are as follows:

	2020	2021	2022
Operating Costs [($0.32)(65,000)]	($20,800)	($20,800)	($20,800)
CCA (Note 1)			
[(150%)(30%)($30,000)]	(13,500)		
[(30%)($16,500)]		(4,950)	
[(1/2)(30%)($11,550)]			(1,733)
Automobile Costs Before			
Imputed Interest	($ 34,300)	($ 25,750)	($ 22,533)
Employment Usage			
(47,000 ÷ 65,000)	72.3%	72.3%	72.3%
Deductible Amount	($ 24,799)	($ 18,617)	($ 16,291)
Allowance	24,000	24,000	24,000
Net Taxable Benefit On Loan (Note 2)	692	692	692
Inclusion In Taxable Income	($ 107)	$ 6,075	$ 8,401
Marginal Tax Rate	50%	50%	50%
Increase (Decrease) In Tax	($ 54)	$ 3,038	$ 4,201

Note 1 As a Class 10.1 asset is involved, the CCA base is limited to $30,000. When the asset is sold, no recapture or terminal loss can be recognized on Class 10.1. However, one-half year CCA can be deducted in the year of disposal.

Note 2 There will be a taxable benefit on the loan of $2,500 in interest per year [(2%)($125,000)]. However, ITA 80.5 deems such interest to be interest paid. As it is less than the limit of $10 of car loan interest per day, this would provide an interest deduction of $1,808 [($2,500)(47,000 ÷ 65,000)], based on the portion of the vehicle mileage that is used for employment-related purposes. As a result, the net benefit would be $692 ($2,500 - $1,808).

The net after tax cash outflow would be calculated as follows:

	2020	2021	2022
Pre-Tax Cash Inflow (Outflow)	$3,200	$ 3,200)	($69,800)
Tax Inflow (Outflow)	54	(3,038)	(4,201)
Net Cash Inflow (Outflow)	$3,254	$ 162	($ 74,001)

Best Alternative

A comparison of the two alternatives is as follows:

Net Cash Inflows (Outflows)	2020	2021	2022	Total
Employer Provided	($16,018)	($16,018)	($ 16,018)	($48,054)
Employee Purchase	3,254	162	(74,001)	(70,585)

Without consideration of the time value of money, the employer provided alternative is clearly preferable. The total cash outflow under this approach is $48,054 as compared to $70,585 under the employee purchase alternative.

Other Considerations

The preceding calculations could be quite different if any of the required estimates prove not to be accurate, such as if the actual number of kilometres driven or personal kilometres driven was different from the estimate, or if the resale value was not actually $52,000. However, given the much lower cash outflow under the employer provided alternative, it is unlikely that the conclusion would change.

Solution to Self Study Problem Six - 7

Market Determination - Two Possible Values

For tax purposes, the business can measure market using either replacement cost or net realizable value. These values would be as follows:

Replacement Cost [($16.75)(5,000)]	$ 83,750

Net Realizable Value [($18.30)(5,000)]	$ 91,500

While it is not an acceptable practice under GAAP, the CRA will accept the use of market values without regard to their relationship to cost.

Cost Determination - Two Possible Values

In the determination of cost, taxpayers are permitted to use specific identification (this would not appear to be practical here), a First In, First Out (FIFO) assumption, or average cost.

Using the First In, First Out method, the appropriate value for the ending inventory would be determined as follows:

1,500 Units At $16.50	$24,750
3,200 Units At $21.42	68,544
300 Units At $20.25	6,075
5,000 Units At FIFO Cost	$99,369

Based on average cost, the ending inventory value would be calculated as follows:

Number Of Units	5,000
Average Cost [($297,644 ÷ 15,300)]	19.45
5,000 Units At Average Cost	$97,250

Lower Of Cost And Market - Four Possible Values

For tax purposes, the possible values here would be as follows:

Lower Of Replacement Cost And FIFO Cost	$83,750
Lower Of Replacement Cost And Average Cost	83,750
Lower Of Net Realizable Value And FIFO Cost	91,500
Lower Of Net Realizable Value And Average Cost	91,500

For accounting purposes, only the last two values would be acceptable.

Solution to Self Study Problem Six - 8

The appropriate treatment for each of the listed items would be as follows:

1. Neither current nor future income taxes can be deducted in the calculation of Net Income For Tax Purposes. As a consequence, $123,000 would be added back to Net Income to arrive at the required tax figure.

2. Interest on late tax instalments is not deductible in the calculation of Net Income For Tax Purposes. As a consequence, $400 would be added back to Net Income to arrive at the required tax figure.

3. In the calculation of Net Income For Tax Purposes, amortization expense of $83,000 must be added back to accounting Net Income and CCA of $97,000 must replace it as the appropriate deduction for tax purposes.

4. The club dues of $2,500 are not deductible for tax purposes and must be added back to Net Income in the calculation of Net Income For Tax Purposes. In addition, 50 percent of the cost of entertaining clients would not be deductible. This means that the non-deductible portion of the $9,600 total would be $4,800. This amount would also be added back to Net Income in the calculation of Net Income For Tax Purposes.

5. The appropriate tax deduction for bad debts is $6,000 ($5,200 - $3,400 + $4,200). As only $5,200 was deducted in the accounting records, $800 ($6,000 - $5,200) must be deducted in the calculation of Net Income For Tax Purposes.

6. As this life insurance policy was required in order to obtain financing, the premiums would be deductible. No adjustment is required in the calculation of Net Income For Tax Purposes.

7. Provided that they are paid within 180 days of year end, bonuses are deductible when declared by a business. This means that the full amount would be deductible and no adjustment is required in the calculation of Net Income For Tax Purposes.

8. The bond discount amortization is not deductible for tax purposes. As a consequence, the $3,200 must be added back to Net Income in the calculation of Net Income For Tax Purposes.

9. While the landscaping costs were given the appropriate capitalization treatment for accounting purposes, ITA 20(1)(aa) specifically permits such costs to be deducted in the year in which they are paid. Therefore, a deduction of $27,000 will be required in the conversion of accounting Net Income to Net Income For Tax Purposes.

Solution to Self Study Problem Six - 9

The minimum net business income of Fairway Distribution would be calculated as follows:

Accounting Income As Reported	$ 273,000
Additions:	
Item 2 - Amortization	78,500
Item 3 - Cost Of Advertising In Foreign Newspaper (Note 1)	3,500
Item 3 - Donations To Charities (Note 2)	1,260
Item 3 - Cost Of Real Estate Appraisal (Note 3)	1,470
Item 3 - Cost Of Landscaping (Note 4)	5,260
Item 3 - Mrs. Fairway's Management Fee (Note 5)	123,000
Subtotal	$ 485,990
Deductions:	
Item 1 - Bad Debt Expense Adjustment (Note 6)	(4,200)
Item 2 - CCA (Given)	(123,600)
Net Business Income	$ 358,190

Note 1 In general, the cost of advertising in foreign media that is directed toward Canadian markets cannot be deducted for tax purposes. While there is an exception for foreign periodicals, it does not apply to foreign newspapers.

Note 2 Donations to charities cannot be deducted in the calculation of net business income. They will be the basis for a tax credit in the calculation of Tax Payable for Mr. Fairway.

Note 3 The cost of appraising a capital asset for purposes of sale is not deductible. Rather, it is an addition to the capital cost of the appraised asset.

Note 4 While landscaping costs related to business properties are deductible when incurred, the cost of improving non-business personal use property would not be.

Note 5 ITA 67 requires that business expenses be "reasonable in the circumstances". As Mrs. Fairway does not appear to do any work for the business, it would be difficult to view her management fee as reasonable. As a consequence, it would not be deductible.

Note 6 For tax purposes, the bad debt adjustment would be calculated as follows:

Last Year's Reserve	$ 15,000
Actual Write-Offs	(17,500)
This Year's Reserve	(19,200)
Total Deduction For Tax Purposes	($21,700)
Accounting Deduction (Actual Write-Offs)	17,500
Bad Debt Expense Adjustment	($ 4,200)

As $4,200 ($21,700 - $17,500) more than the amount that was written off for accounting purposes can be deducted for tax purposes, an adjustment is required. Note that the accounting procedures that were used in this case are not consistent with GAAP.

Solution to Self Study Problem Six - 10

The Net Income For Tax Purposes of Darlington Inc. would be calculated as follows:

Accounting Income		$ 596,000
Additions:		
Item 1 - Income Tax Expense		55,000
Item 3 - Foreign Advertising (Note 1)		Nil
Item 4 - Amortization Expense		623,000
Item 4 - Taxable Capital Gain On Class 8 Disposition		
[($550,000 - $400,000)(1/2)]		75,000
Item 5 - Non-Deductible Meals And Entertainment		
[(50%)($41,400)]		20,700
Item 6 - Club Fees		2,500
Item 7 - Property Taxes On Vacant Land (Note 4)		15,000
Subtotal		$1,387,200
Deductions:		
Item 2 - Landscaping Costs (Note 2)	(	95,000)
Item 4 - Accounting Gain On Class 8 Disposition	(	225,000)
Item 4 - CCA (Note 3)	(	1,017,250)
Terminal Loss (See Class 10 CCA Calculation)	(	113,000)
Net Income (Loss) For Tax Purposes	($	63,050)

Note 1 ITA 19.01 provides for the full deduction of advertising costs in foreign periodicals directed at the Canadian market, provided 80 percent or more of their non-advertising content is original editorial content. If the original editorial content is less than 80 percent, the deduction is equal to 50 percent of the costs. Note that this applies only to periodicals and not other print or broadcast media.

Note 2 Landscaping costs are fully deductible.

Note 3 The calculations for determining CCA are as follows:

Class 1 - Buildings The required calculations for this class would be as follows:

Headquarters Building

January 1, 2020, UCC Balance	$1,000,000
CCA At 4 Percent	(40,000)
January 1, 2021, UCC Balance	$ 960,000

New Building (Separate Class)

Addition ($650,000 - $125,000)	$ 525,000
AccII Adjustment [(50%)($525,000)]	262,500
CCA Base	$ 787,500
CCA At 6 Percent	(47,250)
AccII Adjustment Reversal	(262,500)
January 1, 2021, UCC Balance	$ 477,750

Class 8 - Office Furniture And Equipment The required calculations for this class would be as follows:

January 1, 2020, UCC Balance		$ 4,200,000
Additions	$ 700,000	
Dispositions - Lesser Of:		
• Proceeds = $550,000		
• Cost = $400,000	(400,000)	300,000
Accll Adjustment [(50%)($300,000)]		150,000
CCA Base		$ 4,650,000
CCA At 20 Percent		(930,000)
Accll Adjustment Reversal		(150,000)
January 1, 2021, UCC Balance		$ 3,570,000

With respect to the sale that occurred during the year, there would be a capital gain of $150,000 ($550,000 - $400,000). One-half, or $75,000, is included in the company's Net Income For Tax Purposes, and the accounting gain of $225,000 is deducted.

Class 10 - Vehicles The calculations for this class are as follows:

January 1, 2020, UCC Balance	$ 800,000
Disposition - Lesser Of:	
Capital Cost = $1,200,000	
Proceeds Of Disposition = $687,000	(687,000)
Ending Balance With No Remaining Assets In Class	$ 113,000
Terminal Loss	(113,000)
January 1, 2021, UCC	Nil

Note 4 The property taxes on the vacant land are not deductible. They can be added to the cost of the land if the land was acquired for the purpose of earning either business or property income and may be deducted to the extent of any net income earned on the land.

Summary Of The Results (Not Required)
The maximum 2020 CCA and January 1, 2021, UCC balances can be summarized as follows:

Class	Maximum CCA	UCC
Class 1 - Main Class	$ 40,000	$ 960,000
Class 1 - Separate Class	47,250	477,750
Class 8	930,000	3,570,000
Class 10	Nil	Nil
Total	$1,017,250	

In addition, there was a taxable capital gain on the sale of the Class 8 assets of $75,000 and a terminal loss in Class 10 of $113,000.

Solution to Self Study Problem Six - 11

Part I

A. As covered in this Chapter 6, ITA 12(1)(l) requires inclusion of business income from a partnership. As explained in more detail in Chapter 18, "Partnerships", each partner's share of partnership profits is considered personal income of each partner. The profit is calculated as though the partnership was an individual resident of Canada. Once determined, it is allocated as per the partnership agreement, with the allocated amount being included in the individual tax returns of each partner.

B. The basic rules of ITA 249.1(1) require that, in general, a partnership with members who are individuals use a December 31 fiscal year end. While ITA 249.1(4) allows a partnership to elect a fiscal year end other than December 31, this election requires complex adjustments for Additional Business Income that may or may not be worthwhile.

C. This question requires an analysis of whether the arrangement with the seamstresses is one of employment. This material is discussed in Chapter 3, which covers employment income. Detailed guidance can be found in the CRA Guide titled "Employee Or Self-Employed?" (RC4110).

The general approach to the employee vs. self-employed question is to determine the intent of the parties to the arrangement. While not conclusive, the first question that will be examined in making this determination is whether the business and the workers intended to have an employee/employer relationship or, alternatively, have the work done by the individuals as self-employed contractors. While there is not sufficient information to make this determination given the information in the problem, the partners should be advised that intent should be determined and supported by the appropriate actions (e.g., have the workers register for GST if they wish to treat them as self-employed contractors).

In the absence of information on intent, other factors can be considered as follows:

Control   It appears that Montpetit does not exercise a large degree of control over the seamstresses. They are free to work when they choose and may provide their services to different payers at the same time. The seamstresses can choose to accept or refuse work from Montpetit.

Ownership Of Tools And Equipment   The seamstresses provide the tools and equipment required for the work and the work is done in their homes, not in space provided by Montpetit.

Ability To Subcontract Or Hire Assistants   It appears that Montpetit does not exercise control over who does the work as long as the quality is satisfactory.

Financial Risk   Since the work is done for a set fee and the fabric and accessories are provided, there is no financial risk for seamstresses.

Responsibility For Investment And Management   There is not enough information for this factor to be considered.

Opportunity For Profit   Since the work is done for a set fee, a seamstress cannot increase her proceeds and hence the profit from a gown. Since the fabric and accessories are supplied and there would appear to be no other material expenditures needed for a gown, there is no opportunity to decrease expenses and increase profit on a gown. As a result, it does not appear that a profit could arise.

In addition to these factors, the work is for a specific gown, not general sewing as part of an ongoing relationship.

On balance, the seamstress contracts for the creation of designer gowns are likely contracts for service (self-employment contracts). Given this, source deductions would not be required.

Part II

A. The $2,400 legal fees would be allocated to Class 14.1. The rate for this class is 5 percent and it is eligible for the AccII provisions. For the current year, the partnership could deduct CCA of $180 [(5%)(1.5)($2,400)].

B. The sewing machines are capital expenditures and cannot be deducted in the current year. However, a deduction will be available for CCA on these amounts. The sewing accessories can be deducted in the first year as they will be used and replaced in the same year.

C. While this point is not covered in the Chapter, because of its non-arm's length nature, interest paid to partners cannot be deducted in the determination of partnership income (see Chapter 18 on partnerships). Rather it will be treated as a drawing by the partners.

The $10,000 contributions are of a capital nature and are not deductible in the calculation of personal Taxable Income.

D. The designer clothes held on consignment at year end are inventory of the partnership and are not deductible as cost of sales. The inventory will be valued either at lower of cost and market or, alternatively, market. The cost is given as $95,000 ($50,000 + $45,000) and the retail price is given as $260,000. It is likely that the net realizable value will be less than the full retail value, but the value cannot be determined with the information given.

E. The $15,000 payment for a limited term distribution right is a capital cost that cannot be currently deducted. However, it would be allocated to Class 14 (limited life intangibles) where it will be available for the deduction of CCA.

F. The payment of the annual membership is not deductible. The Crepe Suzette Diner expenses for entertainment of clients would be deductible, but they are subject to a 50 percent limitation, which means $750 [(50%)($1,500)] of these costs would be allowed as a business expense. The personal usage is not deductible.

Solution to Self Study Problem Six - 12

Christine's minimum net business income can be calculated as follows:

Design Power
Statement of Income and Expenses
For The Seven Month Period Ended December 31, 2020

Revenues		
Revenue collected	$22,000	
Revenue billed	4,000	
Work-In-Progress (Note 1)	1,500	$27,500
Expenses		
Capital cost allowance (Note 2)	($ 6,446)	
Work space in home expenses		
[(20%)($6,400)]	(1,280)	
Legal and business licence fees	(1,000)	
Meals and entertainment [(50%)($500)]	(250)	
Automobile expenses (Note 3)	(1,960)	
Office and computer supplies	(650)	
Printing subcontract fees	(1,800)	(13,386)
Net Business Income		$14,114

Note 1   ITA 34, which provided for the use of the billed basis of revenue recognition by some professionals, is being phased out. However, this is not relevant in this problem as visual designers were never eligible for the use of this provision.

Note 2   CCA amounts are calculated as follows:

	Class 8 Furniture	Class 10 Car	Class 50 Computer
Additions	$2,000	$18,000	$5,000
AccII Adjustment (50% Of Additions)	1,000	9,000	2,500
CCA Base	$3,000	$27,000	$7,500
CCA Rate	20%	30%	55%
CCA For Full Year	$600	$8,100	$4,125
Non-Business Car Usage (30%)	N/A	(2,430)	N/A
Balance	$600	$5,670	$4,125
Short Fiscal Period Factor	214/365	214/365	214/365
Deductible Amount	$352	$3,324	$2,418

Class 12 (Software) rate is 100%, but Class 12 is still under the (old) half-year rule. As a result, the CCA for Class 12 is:

Class 12 CCA = ($1,200)(1/2)(100%)(214/365) = $352

The non-business usage of the car is 30 percent. CCA is also restricted by the fact that Christine's taxation year only contains 214 days. Given these factors, the total maximum CCA is $6,446 ($352 + $3,324 + $2,418 + $352). Note that the CCA calculation is based on the portion of the year since the inception of the business, not the portion of the year since the assets were acquired.

Note 3   As the interest amount is well below the prescribed limit, the amount is eligible for deduction, limited only by the amount of business usage. Also note that no portion of the down payment is deductible.

The deduction for automobile costs can be calculated as follows:

Gasoline And Oil	1,100
Licence And Registration	200
Insurance	800
Interest On Car Loan	700
Potential Automobile Cost Deduction	$ 2,800
Business Usage	70%
Deductible Amount	$ 1,960

Solution to Self Study Problem Six - 13

Carla's minimum net business income can be calculated as follows:

Carla Jensen
Statement Of Business Income
For The Year Ending December 31, 2020

Revenues		
Billable Hours (Given)	$ 116,000	
January 1, 2020		
Unbilled Work In Process (Note 1)	17,400	
December 31, 2020		
Unbilled Work In Process (Note 1)	(14,000)	$119,400
Expenses		
Building Operating Costs	($ 24,500)	
Vehicle Operating Costs (Note 2)	(7,200)	
Payments To Assistants	(13,500)	
Miscellaneous Office Costs	(3,750)	
Business Meals [(50%)($4,200)]	(2,100)	
CCA (Note 3)	(36,633)	
Terminal Loss For Class 10 (Note 4)	(4,955)	(92,638)
Net Business Income		$ 26,762

Note 1 As Carla is a professional accountant she is eligible for the use of the billed basis of recognition. The problem requires the minimum business income, so we can assume she makes the ITA 34 election to use the billed basis.

However, as noted in the text, this provision is being phased out over five years at the rate of 20 percent per year. This means that only $17,400 [(60 percent of $29,000)] of the ending 2019 balance could be deferred in that year. This amount will have to be brought back into net business income in 2020.

For 2020, only $14,000 [(40%)($35,000)] of the ending 2020 balance can be deferred. The amount collected has no effect on the calculation of income under the accrual method.

Note 2 The car leasing costs would be wholly deductible as the monthly lease charge and the manufacturer's list price are within the prescribed limits.

Note 3 The total CCA deductible would be as follows (calculations shown separately):

Class 1	$13,560
Class 8	17,700
Class 12	363
Class 14.1	3,525
Class 50	1,485
Total CCA	$36,633

Class 1 As the building is used 100 percent for non-residential purposes, it is eligible for the enhanced rate of 6 percent. This means that the maximum CCA would be:

Class 1 [($226,000)(6%)]	$ 13,560

Class 8 The required calculations are as follows:

Opening Balance		$ 46,500
Additions	$34,000	
Disposal - Lesser Of:		
• Proceeds = $6,000		
• Cost = $18,000	(6,000)	28,000
AccII Adjustment		14,000
CCA Base		$88,500
Rate		20%
Class 8 CCA		$ 17,700

Class 12 The CCA on the applications software would be calculated as follows:

Class 12 [(1/2)($725)(100%)]	$363

Class 14.1 The CCA on the client list would be calculated as follows:

Class 14.1 [(150%)($47,000)(5%)]	$3,525

Class 50 The CCA on the new computer would be calculated as follows:

Class 50 [(150%)($1,800)(55%)]	$1,485

Note 4 As the only vehicle used by the business was disposed of during the year, there is no CCA for Class 10. However, as there is a balance left in the class, there would be a terminal loss calculated as follows:

UCC Of The Class At The Beginning Of The Year	$17,255
Deduct: Dispositions During The Year - Lesser Of:	
• Capital Cost = $20,300	
• Proceeds Of Disposition = $12,300	(12,300)
Ending Balance With No Remaining Assets = Terminal Loss	$ 4,955

Solution to Self Study Problem Six - 14

Part A - No Election

If the ITA 22 election is not made, the tax consequences for Gail Gates would be as follows:

Add: 2019 Reserve For Doubtful Debts	$15,000
2020 Income Inclusion	$15,000

While Gail has an allowable capital loss of $7,000 [(1/2)($263,000 - $249,000)], she will not be able to deduct this amount as she has had no capital gains in the previous three years and does not expect to have any in the current or subsequent years.

If the ITA 22 election is not made, the tax consequences to Mandy Portals would be as follows:

Proceeds Of Disposition (Amount Collected)	$ 251,000
Adjusted Cost Base	(249,000)
Capital Gain	$ 2,000
Inclusion Rate	1/2
2020 Income Inclusion	$ 1,000

Part A - Election
If the ITA 22 election is made, the tax consequences for Gail would be as follows:

Add: 2019 Reserve For Doubtful Debts	$15,000
Deduct: Business Loss ($263,000 - $249,000)	(14,000)
2020 Income Inclusion	$ 1,000

If the ITA 22 election is made, the tax consequences to Mandy would be as follows:

Add: Face Value - Price Paid ($263,000 - $249,000)	$14,000
Deduct: Actual Write-Offs ($263,000 - $251,000)	(12,000)
2020 Income Inclusion	$ 2,000

Part B
For Gail Gates, the ITA 22 election is clearly desirable, converting a $15,000 income inclusion into a $1,000 inclusion.

For Mandy Portals, the fact that actual collections ($251,000) exceed the estimated value of the accounts receivable on the date of the sale ($249,000) means that the ITA 22 election would not be desirable. It would double her income inclusion from $1,000 to $2,000.

Solution to Self Study Problem Six - 15

Net Employment Income
The required calculations here are as follows:

Salary	$123,000
Additions	
Commissions	11,500
Car Allowance [($800)(12)]	9,600
Stock Option Benefit [($28 - $23)(500)]	2,500
Deductions	
RPP Contributions	(6,300)
Car Operating Costs [($9,300)(31,000 ÷ 46,000)]	(6,267)
Car CCA [($30,000)(30%)(150%)(31,000 ÷ 46,000)]	(9,098)
Travel [($8,500 + $4,500 + (1/2)($2,000)]	(14,000)
Client Meals And Entertainment (See Notes)	Nil
Parking	Nil
Net Employment Income	$ 110,935

Notes:
- The fact the initial option price is below market value does not change the calculation of the employment income inclusion. However, there will be no deduction under ITA 110(1)(d) in the determination of Taxable Income.
- The car allowance must be included in income as it is not based on kilometres of use.
- The base for the CCA on the car is limited to $30,000.
- Travel and client promotion costs of $18,300 [($8,500 + $4,500 + (1/2)($2,000 + $8,600)] could be deducted under ITA 8(1)(f). However, this deduction is limited to his commission income of $11,500. He is better off deducting the travel costs of $14,000 [$8,500 + $4,500 + (1/2)($2,000)] using ITA 8(1)(h). As discussed in the text, he cannot use both of the provisions in the same year.

Net Business Income

The required calculations for net business income are as follows:

Net Business Income Before CCA (Given)	$189,000
Class 1 CCA [(4%)($472,200)]	(18,888)
Class 8 CCA [(20%)($143,300)]	(28,660)
Class 50 CCA [(55%)($12,500)]	(6,875)
Net Business Income	$134,577

Net Income For Tax Purposes And Taxable Income

Since there is no stock option benefit deduction, the required calculation here is as follows:

Net Employment Income	$110,935
Net Business Income	134,577
Deductible CPP ($2,898 - $2,732)	(166)
Net Income For Tax Purposes And Taxable Income	$245,346

Tax Payable

The required calculations are as follows:

Tax On First $214,368		$49,645
Tax On Next $30,978 ($245,346 - $214,368) At 33 Percent		10,223
Tax Before Credits		$59,868
Tax Credits:		
Basic Personal Amount (Andrew)	($12,298)	
Common-Law Partner Including Infirm Amount		
($12,298 + $2,273 - $4,500)	(10,071)	
Canada Caregiver - Bart	(7,276)	
Transfer Of John's Disability Credit	(8,576)	
EI Premiums	(856)	
CPP Contributions	(2,732)	
Canada Employment	(1,245)	
Transfer Of Tuition - Lesser Of:		
• Absolute Limit Of $5,000		
• Actual Tuition Of $17,000	(5,000)	
Medical Expenses (Note)	(17,419)	
Total Credit Base	($65,473)	
Rate	15%	(9,821)
Federal Tax Payable		$50,047

Note The medical expense credit base would be calculated as follows:

Medical Expenses For Andrew, John, And Carl		
($2,300 + $12,600 + $400)		$15,300
Reduced By The Lesser Of:		
• [(3%)($245,512)] = $7,365		
• 2020 Threshold Amount = $2,397		(2,397)
Balance Before Dependants 18 And Over		$12,903
Bart's Medical Expenses	$4,600	
Reduced By The Lesser Of:		
• $2,397		
• [(3%)($2,800)] = $84	(84)	4,516
Total Medical Expense Claim		$ 17,419

Solution to Self Study Problem Six - 16

Net Employment Income

The Net Employment Income component of Net Income For Tax Purposes would be calculated as follows:

Salary	$ 89,000
Additions	
Commissions	12,000
Automobile Benefit (Note 1)	1,140
Travel Allowance (Note 2)	Nil
Art Course Tuition Benefit (Note 3)	600
Near Cash Gift (Note 4)	400
Stock Option Benefit [(1,500)($61 - $52)]	13,500
Deductions	
RPP Contributions	(3,750)
Union Dues	(430)
Net Employment Income	$112,460

Note 1 The automobile benefit would be calculated as follows:

Standby Charge [(2/3)($459)(11)(8,500 ÷ 18,337)]	$ 1,560
Operating Cost Benefit - Lesser Of:	
• [($0.28)(8,500)] = $2,380	
• ($1,560 ÷ 2) = $780	780
Total Benefit Before Repayment	$ 2,340
Repayment	(1,200)
Automobile Benefit	$ 1,140

Note 2 As the travel allowance appears to be reasonable given his actual costs, it does not have to be included in Mr. Bowles' income and it is more advantageous for him not to do so. Correspondingly, he cannot deduct the travel costs incurred.

Note 3 Tuition for the marketing course would appear to be employment related and, as a consequence, would not be included in Mr. Bowles' employment income.

Note 4 While the non-cash gift for years of service does not have to be included in income, the $400 gift certificate (i.e., a near cash gift), must be included.

Net Business Income

The Net Business Income component of Net Income For Tax Purposes would be calculated as follows:

Amounts Billed		$50,250
Deductions:		
Office Rent (12 Months At $500)	($ 6,000)	
CCA (Note 5)	(7,967)	
Part Time Assistant	(5,725)	
Office Supplies	(347)	
Monthly Telephone Service	(312)	
Cell Phone Charges	(211)	
Meals And Entertainment [(1/2)($3,150)]	(1,575)	(22,137)
Net Business Income		$ 28,113

Note 5 Maximum CCA would be calculated as follows:

Class 13 [(150%)($12,000 ÷ 5*)]	$3,600
Class 8 [(150%)(20%)($10,000)]	3,000
Class 50 [(150%)(55%)($1,150)]	949
Class 12 [(1/2)(100%)($836)] (No AccII Adjustment)	418
Total	$7,967

*With respect to the Class 13 amount, this is a straight-line class and it is subject to the half year rules. While the term of the lease is only three years, the deductible amount is the lesser of the capital cost divided by the term of the lease and one-fifth of the capital cost. In this case, the deduction is limited to one-half of one-fifth of the capital cost.

Net Income For Tax Purposes And Taxable Income

Mr. Bowles has Net Income For Tax Purposes and Taxable Income as follows:

Net Employment Income	$ 112,460
Net Business Income	28,113
Deductible CPP Contribution ($2,898 - $2,732)	(166)
Net Income For Tax Purposes	$ 140,407
Stock Option Deduction [($13,500)(1/2)]	(6,750)
Taxable Income	$ 133,657

Federal Tax Payable

The required calculations are as follows:

Tax On First $97,069		$ 17,230
Tax On Next $36,588 ($133,657 - $97,069) At 26 Percent		9,513
Tax Before Credits		$ 26,743
Tax Credits:		
Basic Personal Amount	($ 13,229)	
Spouse ($13,229 - $3,450)	(9,779)	
EI Premiums	(856)	
CPP Contributions	(2,732)	
Canada Employment	(1,245)	
Tuition Credit - Mr. Bowles (Note 6)	(600)	
Transfer Of Tuition - Lesser Of:		
• $5,000		
• $9,800	(5,000)	
Medical Expenses (Note 7)	(10,093)	
Total Credit Base	($ 43,534)	
Rate	15%	(6,530)
Charitable Donations		
[(15%)($200) + (29%)($1,425 - $200)]		(385)
Political Contributions [(3/4)($275)]		(206)
Federal Tax Payable Before Refundable Credits		$ 19,622

Note 6 As Mr. Bowles included the reimbursement of the art course in his employment income as a taxable benefit, he can claim the tuition fee credit.

Note 7 The amount of medical expenses that can be included is calculated as follows:

Medical Expenses For Martin, Sally, And Marie ($2,500 + $1,850 + $1,600)		$ 5,950
Lesser Of:		
• [(3%)($133,823)] = $4,015		
• 2020 Threshold Amount = $2,397		(2,397)
Balance Before Dependants 18 And Over		$ 3,553
Ellen's Medical Expenses	$ 6,540	
Reduced By The Lesser Of:		
• $2,397		
• [(3%)(Nil)] = Nil	Nil	6,540
Total Medical Expense Claim		$10,093

Chapter 7 Learning Objectives

After completing Chapter 7, you should be able to:

1. Explain the nature of property income (paragraph [P hereafter] 7-1 to 7-5).
2. Describe the rules applicable to the deductibility of interest payments and be able to apply these rules to various types of borrowing (P 7-6 to 7-28).
3. Apply the provisions relating to the treatment of discount and premium on long term issued debt (P 7-29 to 7-37).
4. Calculate the taxable amount of interest income for both individuals and corporations (P 7-38 to 7-45).
5. Explain the tax treatment of discounts and premiums on long term debt holdings (P 7-46 and 7-47).

6. Apply the provisions related to accrued interest at the time of transfer of debt obligations (P 7-48 to 7-50).
7. Describe tax procedures for royalties and payments based on production or use (P 7-51 to 7-53).
8. Calculate net rental income (P 7-54 to 7-65).
9. Apply the gross up and tax credit procedures to determine the tax consequences of receiving eligible and non-eligible dividend income (P 7-66 to 7-95).
10. Compare the after tax returns from various types of investments (P 7-96 to 7-97).

11. Discuss the provisions relating to investments in income trusts (P 7-98 to 7-111).
12. Discuss the provisions relating to investments in mutual funds (P 7-112 to 7-122).
13. Explain the general treatment of stock dividends and capital dividends (P 7-123 to 7-128).
14. Explain the general tax treatment of withholdings on foreign source business and non-business income (P 7-129 to 7-132).
15. Explain the general treatment of shareholder benefits (P 7-133 to 7-135).
16. Explain the general treatment of the dividend tax credit and foreign income tax credit (P 7-136 to 7-139).

How to Work Through Chapter 7

We recommend the following approach in dealing with the material in this chapter:

Property Income - General Concept
-   Read paragraph 7-1 to 7-5 (in the textbook).

Interest As A Deduction, Including IT Folio S3-F6-C1
-   Read paragraph 7-6 to 7-28.
-   Do Self Study Problem Seven-1, which is available on MyLab, and check the solution in this Study Guide.

Discount And Premium On Long Term Issued Debt

- Read paragraph 7-29 to 7-35.
- Do Exercise Seven-1 (in the textbook) and check the solution in this Study Guide.
- Read paragraph 7-36 to 7-37.
- Do Exercise Seven-2 and check the solution in this Study Guide.

Interest Income - General Provisions

- Read paragraph 7-38 to 7-45.
- Do Exercise Seven-3 and check the solution in this Study Guide.

Discount And Premium On Long Term Debt Holdings

- Read paragraph 7-46 to 7-47.

Accrued Interest At Transfer

- Read paragraph 7-48 to 7-50.
- Do Exercise Seven-4 and check the solution in this Study Guide.

Payments Based On Production Or Use (Royalties)

- Read paragraph 7-51 to 7-53.

Rental Income

- Read paragraph 7-54 to 7-65.
- Do Exercise Seven-5 and check the solution in this Study Guide.
- Do Self Study Problem Seven-2 and check the solution in this Study Guide.

Eligible And Non-Eligible Cash Dividends Received

- Read paragraph 7-66 to 7-85.
- Do Exercise Seven-6 and check the solution in this Study Guide.
- Read paragraph 7-86 to 7-95.
- Do Exercise Seven-7 and check the solution in this Study Guide.

Comparison Of Investment Returns

- Read paragraph 7-96 to 7-97.
- Do Self Study Problems Seven-3 to Seven-6 and check the solutions in this Study Guide.

Income Trusts

- Read paragraph 7-98 to 7-111.
- Do Exercise Seven-8 and check the solution in this Study Guide.

Mutual Funds

- Read paragraph 7-112 to 7-122.
- Do Exercise Seven-9 and check the solution in this Study Guide.
- Do Self Study Problem Seven-7 and check the solution in this Study Guide.

Stock Dividends And Capital Dividends

- Read paragraph 7-123 to 7-128.
- Do Exercise Seven-10 and check the solution in this Study Guide.

Foreign Source Income

- Read paragraph 7-129 to 7-132.
- Do Exercise Seven-11 and check the solution in this Study Guide.

Shareholder Benefits

- Read paragraph 7-133 to 7-135.

Tax Credits Revisited - Dividend And Foreign Tax Credits

- Read paragraph 7-136 to 7-139.
- Do Self Study Problems Seven-8 and Seven- 9 and check the solutions in this Study Guide.

To Complete This Chapter

- If you would like more practice in problem solving, do the Supplementary Self Study Problems for the chapter. These problems and solutions are available on MyLab.
- Review the Key Terms Used In This Chapter in the textbook at the end of Chapter 7. Consult the Glossary for the meaning of any key terms you do not know.
- Test yourself with the Chapter 7 Glossary Flashcards available on MyLab.
- Ensure you have achieved the Chapter 7 Learning Objectives listed in this Study Guide.
- As a review, we recommend you view the PowerPoint presentation for Chapter 7 that is on MyLab.

Practice Examination

- Write the Practice Examination for Chapter 7 that is on MyLab. Mark your examination using the Practice Examination Solution that is also on MyLab.

Solutions to Chapter 7 Exercises

Exercise Seven - 1 Solution

Tax Consequences   The tax consequences would be as follows:

Annual Deduction - 2020 Through 2022 [($1,000,000)(4%)]	$ 40,000
Maturity Amount	$1,000,000
Proceeds Of Sale	(985,000)
2022 Loss	$ 15,000

The bonds are sold for more than 97 percent of their maturity amount. In addition, the four-thirds test is met since the effective interest rate of 4.6 percent is less than four-thirds of the coupon rate [(4%)(4/3) = 5.3%]. As a result, this loss would be fully deductible. This gives a total deduction of $135,000 over the three year period [(3)($40,000) + $15,000].

Accounting Consequences   The accounting consequences would be as follows:

Annual Interest Payment [($1,000,000)(4%)]	$40,000
Discount Amortization [($1,000,000 - $985,000) ÷ 3]	5,000
Annual Interest Expense - 2020 Through 2022	$45,000

Payment of the maturity amount in 2022 would have no tax consequences. Note that the total for the three year period would be the same $135,000 [(3)($45,000)] that was deducted for tax purposes.

Exercise Seven - 2 Solution

The tax consequences under each of the three assumptions would be as follows:

Money Lender   In this case, there would be an income inclusion of $400,000 ($1,400,000- $1,000,000) in the current year. The interest deduction for the year would be $180,000 [(18%)($1,000,000)].

No Deliberate Premium   In this case, the premium would have no immediate tax consequences and there would be no tax consequences when the bonds mature. The interest deduction for the year would be $180,000 [(18%)($1,000,000)]. Given that the bonds are paid off for less than the proceeds from their issuance, this result provides the issuer of the bonds with a tax free capital receipt of $400,000.

Deliberate Premium In this case, the premium would be amortized at the rate of $40,000 per year ($400,000 ÷ 10). This means the interest deduction for the year would be $140,000 ($180,000- $40,000).

Exercise Seven - 3 Solution

The total interest to be recorded on the instrument is $28,800 [($60,000)(8%)(6 years)]. It will be allocated as follows:

Year	Interest Paid	Interest Reported
2020	Nil	Nil
2021	Nil	$ 4,800
2022	Nil	4,800
2023	$15,600	6,000
2024	Nil	3,600
2025	Nil	4,800
2026	13,200	4,800
Total	$28,800	$28,800

2020 As no anniversary date occurred and no interest was received during 2020, no interest will have to be included in Ms. Dumont's 2020 tax return.

2021 The first anniversary date occurs on September 30 and this requires the recognition of $4,800 [(8%)($60,000)] of interest.

2022 The second anniversary date occurs and this requires the recognition of an additional $4,800 of interest.

2023 An additional $4,800 will have to be recognized because of the third anniversary date. Also during this year, a payment of $15,600 [($4,800)(3.25)] is received. Of this total, $14,400 [(3)($4,800)] has been recognized because of the three anniversary dates. This will require the recognition of an additional $1,200 ($15,600 - $14,400) in 2023, bringing the total for the year to $6,000 ($4,800 + $1,200).

2024 The anniversary date will require recognition of $4,800. However, only $3,600 of this amount will be included as $1,200 was received and recognized in 2023.

2025 $4,800 will be recognized on the anniversary date.

2026 Payment of $13,200 [(2.75)($4,800)] will be received. As $8,400 ($3,600 + $4,800) of the amount received has been recorded on the previous two anniversary dates, the total for 2026 will be $4,800 ($13,200 - $8,400).

Exercise Seven - 4 Solution

Mr. Lay will include the full $6,000 received in income. However, he can deduct the interest that was accrued on the bonds at the time of purchase of $1,989 [($3,000)(120/181)]. The net amount that will be included in his tax return is $4,011 ($6,000 - $1,989).

Exercise Seven - 5 Solution

The maximum CCA for Class 1 would be calculated as follows:

Capital Cost ($185,000 - $42,000)	$ 143,000
Improvements	35,000
Total Additions	$ 178,000
Accelerated Investment Incentive (AccII) Multiplier	150%
Adjusted CCA Base	$ 267,000
Rate	4%
Maximum CCA	$ 10,680

The required rental income calculation would be as follows:

Rental Revenues	$ 7,200
Rental Expenses Other Than CCA	(5,100)
Rental Income Before CCA	$2,100
CCA (Maximum)	(2,100)
Net Rental Income	Nil

As CCA cannot be used to create a net rental loss, the actual deduction is limited to $2,100, the rental income before CCA. Also note that the maximum available CCA is not limited by the fact the property was purchased in September as the calendar year is considered the fiscal year for property income purposes for individuals.

Exercise Seven - 6 Solution

The Tax Payable by Ms. Holt would be calculated as follows:

Eligible Dividends Received	$15,000
Gross Up At 38 Percent	5,700
Taxable Dividends	$20,700
Combined Federal/Provincial Tax Rate (29% + 14.5%)	43.5%
Tax Before Dividend Tax Credit	$ 9,005
Dividend Tax Credit [(6/11 + 30%)($5,700)]	(4,819))
Federal And Provincial Tax Payable	$ 4,186

The after tax retention is $10,814 ($15,000 - $4,186). Note that to calculate this amount, the taxes are deducted from the dividends received and not the grossed up taxable dividends.

Exercise Seven - 7 Solution

The Tax Payable by Mr. Johns would be calculated as follows:

Non-Eligible Dividends Received	$ 17,000
Gross Up At 15 Percent	2,550
Taxable Dividends	$19,550
Combined Federal/Provincial Tax Rate (29% + 12%)	41%
Tax Before Dividend Tax Credit	$ 8,016
Dividend Tax Credit [(9/13 + 30%)($2,550)]	(2,530)
Federal And Provincial Tax Payable	$ 5,486

The after tax retention is $11,514 ($17,000 - $5,486). Note that to calculate this amount, the taxes are deducted from the dividends received and not the grossed up taxable dividends.

Exercise Seven - 8 Solution

John will include an additional $7,000 [(2,000)($5.00 - $1.50)] in his Net Income For Tax Purposes. His adjusted cost base will be increased by the $10,000 [(2,000)($5.00)] reinvestment of the distribution and reduced by the $3,000 [(2,000)($1.50)] return of capital.

The reinvestment of the $10,000 distribution will result in the acquisition of an additional 175.44 ($10,000 ÷ $57) units. The adjusted cost base calculations are as follows:

	Amount	Number Of Units
Original Investment	$110,000	2,000.00
Reinvestment Of Distribution	10,000	175.44
Tax Free Return Of Capital	(3,000)	N/A
Adjusted Cost Base/Number Of Units	$ 117,000	2,175.44

This will result in an average cost of $53.78 ($117,000 ÷ 2,175.44) per unit.

Exercise Seven - 9 Solution

Given the purchase price per unit is $13, the reinvestment will result in Ms. Tiompkins receiving 80.77 ($1,050 ÷ $13) additional units. This will leave her holding 3,580.77 units with an adjusted cost base of $40,425 ($39,375 + $1,050). Her adjusted cost base per unit after the reinvestment is $11.29 ($40,425 ÷ 3,580.77).

Exercise Seven - 10 Solution

The required calculations would be as follows:

Original Shares Held	200,000
Stock Dividend Percentage	10%
New Shares Acquired	20,000
Per Share Addition To Paid Up Capital	$ 15
Eligible Stock Dividend Received	$300,000
Gross Up At 38 Percent	114,000
Taxable Eligible Dividend	$414,000

There would be a federal dividend tax credit of $62,182 [(6/11)($114,000)]. The $300,000 stock dividend would be added to the $2,400,000 [($12)(10%)(2,000,000)] original cost of his shares and the adjusted cost base per share would be calculated as follows:

$$[(\$2,400,000 + \$300,000) \div (200,000 + 20,000)] = \$12.27$$

Note that his percentage of ownership remains at 10 percent (220,000 ÷ 2,200,000).

Exercise Seven - 11 Solution

The federal Tax Payable on the amount received assuming it is foreign non-business income or business income would be calculated as follows:

	Non-Business Income	Business Income
Amount Received	$22,500	$22,500
Foreign Tax Withheld	7,500	7,500
Inclusion For Foreign Income	$30,000	$30,000
Deduction Of Excess Withholding		
[$7,500 - (15%)($30,000)]	(3,000)	N/A
Increase In Taxable Income	$ 27,000	$30,000
Rate	29%	29%
Tax Payable Before Credit	$ 7,830	$ 8,700
Foreign Tax Credit [(15%)($30,000)]	(4,500)	
Foreign Tax Credit (Amount Withheld)		(7,500)
Federal Tax Payable	$ 3,330	$ 1,200

Note that the total tax cost if the foreign income is business income is $8,700 ($7,500 + $1,200). This is the same amount that would have been paid by Norah on the receipt of $30,000 of Canadian source business income [(29%)($30,000) = $8,700]. This compares to a tax cost of $10,830 ($7,500 + $3,330) in the non-business income case. This reflects the fact that the $3,000 deduction of the excess foreign tax withholding is not as valuable as the $3,000 credit against Tax Payable that was received in the business income case.

Solution to Self Study Problem Seven - 1

Case A

The interest would be deductible as the direct use of the borrowed funds was to acquire the Bee Ltd. shares.

Case B

Since the proceeds exceed the borrowings, Ms. Burns has complete flexibility with respect to linking. She could allocate all of the $225,000 to property B or alternatively, $50,000 to property A, with the other $175,000 going to property B. Any other allocation totaling $225,000 would be acceptable.

Case C

When the value of the replacement property is less than the amount borrowed, the taxpayer must use a pro-rata allocation of the borrowed money. In this case, the result would be an allocation of $71,053 [($60,000 ÷ $190,000)($225,000)] to property A and an allocation of $153,947 [($130,000 ÷ $190,000)($225,000)] to property B.

Case D

Under ITA 20.1 (the disappearing source rules), the $145,000 balance will be deemed to be used to produce income. Therefore, he can continue to deduct the interest.

Solution to Self Study Problem Seven - 2

2019

The maximum CCA for 2019 would be calculated as follows:

	Class 1	Class 8
Addition	$ 690,000	$ 43,000
AccII Adjustment	345,000	21,500
CCA Base	$1,035,000	$ 64,500
Maximum CCA:		
[(4%)($1,035,000)]	(41,400)	
[(20%)($64,500)]		(12,900)
AccII Adjustment Reversal	(345,000)	(21,500)
January 1, 2020, UCC	$ 648,600	$ 30,100

Net Rental Income for 2019 would be calculated as follows:

Rental Revenue	$81,000
Expenses Other Than CCA	(23,400)
Income Before CCA	$ 57,600
Class 1 CCA	(41,400)
Class 8 CCA	(12,900)
Net Rental Income	$ 3,300

Note that when an individual uses assets to produce property income (e.g., rental income), the full calendar year is considered to be the taxation year of the individual. This means that the short fiscal period rules are not applicable to Mr. Thorne.

2020

The results of the Class 8 disposition would be calculated as follows:

January 1, 2020, UCC	$30,100
Disposition - Lesser Of:	
• Cost = $43,000	
• Proceeds Of Disposition = $31,000	(31,000)
Negative Balance At Year End	($ 900)
Recapture Of CCA	900
January 1, 2021, UCC - Class 8	Nil

The recapture of CCA will be added to the Class 8 UCC, leaving a January 1, 2021, balance of nil.

The maximum CCA for 2020 would be $25,944 [(4%)($648,600)]. As this is less than net rental income before the deduction of CCA, this full amount can be deducted. Net rental income for 2020 would be calculated as follows:

Rental Revenue	$54,500
Recapture Of CCA	900
Expenses Other Than CCA	(29,400)
Income Before CCA	$26,000
CCA	(25,944)
Net Rental Income	$ 56

The January 1, 2021, UCC of the Class 1 building would be calculated as follows:

January 1, 2020, UCC	$648,600
2020 CCA Deducted	(25,944)
January 1, 2021, UCC - Class 1	$622,656

Solution to Self Study Problem Seven - 3

Part A - Bonds (Interest)

The after tax returns on the bonds would be calculated as follows:

	Sarah	Sally	Suzanne
Interest [(4.5%)($15,000)]	$675	$675	$675
Federal/Provincial Tax Payable			
Sarah (15% + 5% = 20%)	(135)		
Sally (26% + 11% = 37%)		(250)	
Suzanne (33% + 16% = 49%)			(331)
After Tax Return - Interest	$540	$425	$344

Part B - Preferred Stock (Dividends)

The after tax returns resulting from an investment in the preferred stock begins with the calculation of the federal and provincial Tax Payable:

	Sarah (20%)	Sally (37%)	Suzanne (49%)
Dividends [(5.6%)($15,000)]	$ 840	$ 840	$ 840
Gross Up Of 38 Percent	319	319	319
Taxable Dividend	$1,159	$1,159	$1,159
Combined Rate (See Part A)	20%	37%	49%
Tax Before Dividend Tax Credit	$ 232	$ 429	$ 568
Dividend Tax Credit			
[(6/11 + 27%)($319)]	(260)	(260)	(260)
Tax Payable (Tax Savings)	($ 28)	$ 169	$ 308

Based on the preceding calculations of federal and provincial Tax Payable, the after tax returns on the preferred shares are calculated as follows:

	Sarah (20%)	Sally (37%)	Suzanne (49%)
Dividends [(5.6%)($15,000)]	$840	$840	$840
Tax Savings (Tax Payable)	28	(169)	(308)
After Tax Return - Dividends	$868	$671	$532

Comparison

A comparison of the after tax rates of return can be made as follows:

	Sarah (20%)	Sally (37%)	Suzanne (49%)
After Tax Dividends	$868	$671	$532
After Tax Interest	(540)	(425)	(344)
Advantage Of Preferred Stock	$328	$246	$188

Recommendation

For each of the sisters, the preferred stock offers the superior after tax return. Note, however, that the advantage of the dividends declines as the taxpayer's tax rate increases. In addition, there is a somewhat higher level of risk associated with preferred shares.

Solution to Self Study Problem Seven - 4

In the following solution, note that the after tax return amount does not include the original investment. Some students add $600,000 to the after tax return, which is not correct.

Guaranteed Investment Certificate

The required calculations for this investment are as follows:

Interest Received [($600,000)(4.5%)]	$27,000
Combined Federal/Provincial Tax Rate (29% + 12%)	41%
Tax Payable	$11,070
Interest Received	$27,000
Tax Payable	(11,070)
After Tax Return - Guaranteed Investment Certificate	$15,930

Preferred Shares

The required calculations for this investment are as follows:

Dividends Received [($600,000)(5.25%)]	$31,500
Gross Up of 38 Percent	11,970
Taxable Income	$43,470
Combined Federal/Provincial Tax Rate (29% + 12%)	41%
Tax Payable Before Dividend Tax Credit	$17,823
Federal/Provincial Dividend Tax Credit	
[($11,970)(6/11 + 28%)]	(9,881)
Total Tax Payable	$ 7,942
Dividends Received (Before Gross Up)	$31,500
Tax Payable	(7,942)
After Tax Return - Preferred Shares	$23,558

High Tech Shares

The required calculations for this investment are as follows:

Proceeds Of Disposition	$675,000
Adjusted Cost Base	(600,000)
Capital Gain	$ 75,000
Inclusion Rate	1/2
Taxable Capital Gain	$ 37,500
Combined Federal/Provincial Tax Rate (29% + 12%)	41%
Tax Payable	$ 15,375
Capital Gain Realized (100%)	$ 75,000
Tax Payable	(15,375)
After Tax Return - High Tech Shares	$ 59,625

Solution to Self Study Problem Seven - 5

The major considerations in deciding between the three alternative investment strategies are the after tax return and the certainty of the related cash flows.

Guaranteed Investment Certificate As long as the certificate is purchased from a financial institution that is guaranteed by the Federal government, there is virtually no risk that the principal or interest could be lost. Your combined federal and provincial tax rate for interest is 44 percent (29% + 15%). This means that the $100,000 investment would provide an after tax amount calculated as follows:

Interest [($100,000)(5.5%)]	$5,500
Federal/Provincial Tax Payable [($5,500)(33% + 18%)]	(2,805)
After Tax Cash Flow - Guaranteed Investment Certificate	$2,695

Common Stock Purchase   If you invest the $100,000 in common stock, you will be exposing yourself to a greater risk and uncertainty of cash flows than the guaranteed investment certificate alternative. There is no guarantee that the stock will pay a dividend of $5,000 during the year. There is the possibility that more or less than $5,000 will be paid. In addition, the estimated market price of at least $106,000 on December 31, 2020, is not certain. The price on that date could be higher or lower.

Assuming that the stock does pay $5,000 in dividends and you sell the shares for $106,000 on December 31, 2020, your after tax return on the investment is as follows:

Dividends Received	$5,000
Gross Up [(38%)($5,000)]	1,900
Taxable Dividends	$6,900
Taxable Capital Gain [(1/2)($106,000 - $100,000)]	3,000
Taxable Income	$9,900
Combined Tax Rate (33% + 18%)	51%
Tax Payable Before Dividend Tax Credit	$5,049
Dividend Tax Credit [($1,900)(6/11 + 27%)]	(1,549)
Tax Payable	$3,500
Dividends Received	$5,000
Capital Gain (100%)	6,000
Tax Payable	(3,500)
After Tax Cash Flow - Common Stock Purchase	$7,500

Rental Property   If you invest the $100,000 in real estate, you will be choosing the highest risk alternative. Rental properties can require significant personal involvement if there are problems with the tenant or repairs become necessary. The transaction costs (e.g., real estate commissions and legal fees), would be much higher on this investment than on either of the other two. In addition, the real estate investment is the least liquid of the three alternatives and you might encounter difficulties in the disposition of this investment. The estimated net proceeds of $175,000 on December 31, 2020, is not certain. The net proceeds could be higher or lower.

Assuming that the property has the anticipated revenues and expenses and you net $175,000 when you sell the property on December 31, 2020, your after tax return on the investment is as follows:

Gross Rents	$13,200
Expenses	(9,600)
CCA (Property Sold Prior To Year End)	Nil
Net Rental Income	$ 3,600

In addition to this net rental income, you anticipate a capital gain of $10,000 ($175,000 - $165,000), of which one-half, or $5,000, would be included in your income. Based on these figures, the Tax Payable would be calculated as follows:

Net Rental Income	$3,600
Taxable Capital Gain	5,000
Taxable Income	$8,600
Tax Rate (33% + 18%)	51%
Tax Payable	$4,386

The total after tax cash flow would be as follows:

Net Rental Income	$ 3,600
Capital Gain (Cash Flow is 100% Of Gain)	10,000
Tax Payable	(4,386)
After Tax Cash Flow - Rental Property	$ 9,214

Conclusion   Based purely on after tax returns, it would appear that you should acquire the rental property. However, as previously indicated, this alternative involves the most risk and uncertainty.

In choosing between the guaranteed investment certificate and the shares of Norton Ltd., the after tax cash flows from the shares are considerably higher. However, the return on the shares is made up of dividends and a potential capital gain, both of which are more uncertain than the interest on the guaranteed investment certificate. Given this, the possibility of greater than anticipated dividends and/or capital gains must be weighed against the additional risk of lower than anticipated returns.

Other factors that may influence your decision are as follows:

- The funds are locked into the investment certificate and can only be withdrawn prior to maturity at a severe interest penalty, if at all.

- The investment in common stock would give you more flexibility if you should require some of the funds before the end of the year. All or some portion of the stockholding could be sold during the year.

- Any dividends or rent that is paid will be available for your use as at the payment date. The interest will not be available to you until maturity.

Solution to Self Study Problem Seven - 6

Ms. Smursch's minimum Net Income For Tax Purposes would be calculated as follows:

Income From A Business Or Profession:		
Billable Hours (Given)	$345,000	
December 31, 2019, Unbilled		
Work-In-Progress (Note 1)	13,800	
December 31, 2020, Unbilled		
Work-In-Progress (Note 2)	(5,600)	
Office Supplies And Office Expenses	(23,000)	
Rent	(60,000)	
Meals And Entertainment [(1/2)($18,000)]	(9,000)	
Convention Expenses (Note 3)	(2,400)	$258,800
Property Income:		
Income From Income Trust [($3.50 - $1.50)(2,500)]		5,000
Taxable Capital Gain (Note 4)		8,417
Minimum Net Income For Tax Purposes		$272,217

Note 1   As Sarah is a professional accountant she is eligible to use the billed basis of recognition. However, as noted in the text, this provision is being phased out over five years at the rate of 20 percent per year. This means that for 2019, she was only able to defer $13,800, 60 percent of her $23,000 unbilled work-in-progress. This amount will have to be taken into income in 2020.

Note 2   With respect to the December 31 unbilled work-in-progress, she can defer only $5,600, 40 percent of the December 31 balance of $14,000.

Note 3   Unless the scope of Ms. Smursch's business is likely to extend to this activity in the Middle East, the costs of the Beirut convention cannot be deducted.

Note 4   The adjusted cost base of the Realty Income Trust units would be calculated as follows:

Original Cost [(2,500)($43.00])	$ 107,500
Reinvestment Of Distribution [(2,500)($3.50)]	8,750
Tax Free Return Of Capital [(2,500)($1.50)]	(3,750)
Adjusted Cost Base	$112,500

The taxable capital gain on the disposition of all the units would be calculated as follows:

Proceeds Of Disposition	$129,333
Adjusted Cost Base	(112,500)
Capital Gain	$ 16,833
Inclusion Rate	1/2
Taxable Capital Gain	$ 8,417

The distribution reinvestment resulted in 194.44 additional shares ($8,750 ÷ $45). However, this number is irrelevant as all of the units were sold.

Solution to Self Study Problem Seven - 7

Note To Instructors   This problem is somewhat unrealistic in that, under the Canada/ U.K. tax treaty, it is unlikely that there would be any amounts withheld on interest payments between the two countries. Note that this problem does not contain enough information to do a complete calculation of the foreign tax credit, which is not covered until Chapter 11. We have assumed that the credit is equal to the maximum 15 percent of the amount withheld.

Taxable Income And Tax Payable
The amount of taxable income and tax payable resulting from the investments would be calculated as follows:

Interest On Term Deposit [(7%)(£200,000)($1.70)]	$23,800	
Excess Withholding (See Note)	(2,380)	$21,420
B&B Trust Distribution [($1.50)(8,000)]	$12,000	
Return Of Capital [($0.50)(8,000)]	(4,000)	8,000
Liberty Inc. Dividends [($1.60)(2,000)]	$3,200	
Dividend Gross Up [(38%)(3,200)]	1,216	4,416
Temple Capital Gain [($0.40)(2,500)]	$1,000	
Non-Taxable One-Half	(500)	500
Temple Eligible Dividends [($1.00)(2,500)]	$2,500	
Dividend Gross Up [(38%)($2,500)]	950	3,450
Temple Interest [($1.00)(2,500)]		2,500
Taxable Income		$40,286
Tax Rate (29% + 16%)		45%
Tax Before Credits		$18,129
Dividend Tax Credit [($1,216 + $950)(6/11 + 30%)]		(1,831)
Foreign Tax Credit - Note [(15%)(7%)(£200,000)($1.70)]		(3,570)
Tax Payable		$12,728

Note - Foreign Source Property Income As required, 100 percent of the foreign interest is included in Net Income For Tax Purposes. However, for individuals, the credit against Tax Payable that is provided under ITA 126(1) is limited to a maximum of 15 percent of the foreign source non-business income and the excess withholding is deducted. With the withholding rate at 25 percent, this deduction would be equal to $2,380 [(25% - 15%)(7%)(£200,000)($1.70)].

Adjusted Cost Base - B&B Trust

The reinvestment of the $12,000 [($1.50)(8,000)] distribution at $52 per unit would acquire an additional 230.77 units. After recognizing these changes, the adjusted cost base per unit would be as follows:

$$\$30.13 \ [(\$240,000 + \$12,000 - \$4,000) \div (8,000 + 230.77)]$$

Adjusted Cost Base - Temple Small Cap

The reinvestment of the $6,000 [($2.40)(2,500)] distribution at $38 per unit would acquire an additional 157.89 units. After recognizing these changes, the adjusted cost base per unit would be as follows:

$$\$39.88 \ [(\$100,000 + \$6,000) \div (2,500 + 157.89)]$$

Solution to Self Study Problem Seven - 8

Employment Income

Jeremy's net employment income would be calculated as follows:

Gross Wages	$74,000
RPP Contributions	(5,600)
Union Dues	(896)
Net Employment Income	$67,504

Property Income
Jeremy's property income would be calculated as follows:

Eligible Dividends Received	$ 8,600
Gross Up Of Eligible Dividends (38%)	3,268
Non-Eligible Dividends Received	6,400
Gross Up Of Non-Eligible Dividends (15%)	960
Foreign Dividends Before Withholding ($13,600 ÷ 85%)	16,000
Interest	3,420
Property Income	$38,648

Net Business Income
Jeremy's net business income would be calculated as follows:

Net Cash Flow	$ 187,000
Principal Payments On Car Loan ($14,400 - $5,100)	9,300
Non-Deductible Interest [($5,100 - (365)($10 Daily Maximum)]	1,450
December 31 Receivables	26,700
January 1 Billed Receivables	(23,200)
December 31 Work In Process (Note 1)	31,300
January 1 Work In Process	(28,900)
December 31 Accounts Payable	(14,200)
January 1 Accounts Payable	15,600
Subtotal	$205,050
CCA ($26,150 + $9,253 + $13,500) (Note 2)	(48,903)
Car Operating Costs (Already Deducted)	Nil
Net Business Income	$ 156,147

Note 1 Since Jeremy is a management consultant, he was not able to use the billed basis of income recognition. This means that he is not eligible for the transitional provision related to the billed basis and must include 100 percent of his unbilled work in progress in his income.

Note 2 The CCA would be calculated as follows:

Class 1 CCA

January 1, 2020, UCC	$342,837
Additions (Improvements)	62,000
AccII Adjustment [(50%)($62,000)]	31,000
Base For CCA	$435,837
Rate	6%
CCA	$ 26,150

As the building was acquired new and was used 100 percent for non-residential purposes, it is eligible for the 6 percent CCA rate. The fact that it was the only building owned by the business would result in it automatically being allocated to a separate class, but it must remain in a separate Class 1 to continue to qualify for the 6 percent rate.

Class 8 CCA

January 1, 2020, UCC	$10,564
Additions	47,000
Disposals - Lesser Of:	
• Proceeds Of Disposition = $23,200	
• Capital Cost = $25,000	(23,200)
AccII Adjustments [(50%)($47,000 - $23,200)]	11,900
Base For CCA	$46,264
Rate	20%
CCA	$ 9,253

Class 10.1 CCA

As the cost of the car exceeds $30,000, the addition to Class 10.1 is limited to this value. The maximum deduction for 2020 would be $13,500 [(150%)(30%)($30,000)].

Net Income For Tax Purposes And Taxable Income

There are no Taxable Income deductions available. As a consequence, Taxable Income is equal to Net Income For Tax Purposes.

Net Employment Income	$ 67,504
Property Income	38,648
Net Business Income	156,147
Pension Income	32,500
Deductible CPP ($2,898 - $2,732)	(166)
Net Income For Tax Purposes And Taxable Income	$294,633

Tax Payable

Tax Payable would be calculated as follows:

Tax On First $214,368		$49,645
Tax On Next $80,265 ($294,633 - $214,368) At 33 Percent		26,487
Tax Before Credits		$76,132
Tax Credits:		
Basic Personal Amount (Jeremy)	($12,298)	
Spouse ($12,298 - $8,400)	(3,898)	
Canada Caregiver - Sarah	(7,276)	
Jeremy's Age Credit [$7,637 - (15%)($294,633 - $38,508)	Nil	
Jeremy's Pension Credit	(2,000)	
EI	(856)	
CPP	(2,732)	
Canada Employment	(1,245)	
Transfer Of Spouse's Age Credit		
[$7,637 - (15%)($8,400 - $38,508)	(7,637)	
Transfer Of Spouse's Pension Credit	(2,000)	
Transfer Of Sarah's Disability Credit	(8,576)	
Transfer Of Samantha's Tuition Credit (Note 5)	(5,000)	
Medical Expenses (Note 6)	(14,503)	
Total Credit Base	($68,021)	
Rate	15%	(10,203)
Charitable Donations (Note 7)		(756)
Dividend Tax Credit On:		
Eligible Dividends [(6/11)($3,268)]		(1,783)
Non-Eligible Dividends [(9/13)($960)]		(665)
Foreign Tax Credit - Amount Withheld [(15%)($16,000)]		(2,400)
Federal Tax Payable		$60,325

Note 5 Samantha's child support received is not included in her Net Income For Tax Purposes. Given this, Samantha has Net Income For Tax Purposes of nil and would qualify as a dependant of Jeremy's. Even though she lives with Jeremy, he cannot claim the Canada caregiver tax credit for her or her children as they are not mentally or physically infirm.

The maximum transfer of the tuition credit would be the lesser of:

- The actual tuition of $16,400.
- The absolute maximum of $5,000.

Note 6 The claim for medical expenses is determined as follows:

Medical Expenses Of Jeremy And Sandra ($4,000 + $1,700)		$ 5,700
Reduced By The Lesser Of:		
• [(3%)($294,633)] = $8,839		
• 2020 Threshold Amount = $2,397		(2,397)
Balance Before Dependants 18 And Over		$ 3,303
Sarah's Medical Expenses	$9,400	
Reduced By The Lesser Of:		
• $2,397		
• [(3%)(Nil)] = Nil	Nil	9,400
Samantha's Medical Expenses	$1,800	
Reduced By The Lesser Of:		
• $2,397		
• [(3%)(Nil)] = Nil	Nil	1,800
Total Medical Expense Claim		$14,503

Note 7 Jeremy's charitable donations tax credit would be calculated as follows:

15 Percent Of $200	$ 30
33 Percent Of The Lesser Of:	
($2,400 - $200) = $2,200	
$294,633 - $214,368 = $80,265	726
29 Percent Of [($2,400 - ($200 + $2,200)]	Nil
Total Credit	$756

Solution to Self Study Problem Seven - 9

Net Business Income
Derek's Net Business Income is calculated as follows:

Accounting Net Income		$211,000
Additions:		
Amortization Expense	$18,000	
Meals And Entertainment (Note 1)	5,750	
Automobile Operating Costs - Personal (Note 2)	1,350	25,100
		$236,100
Deductions:		
Capital Cost Allowance		
Automobile (Note 3)	($ 9,703)	
Furniture And Fixtures (Note 4)	(11,100)	
Building [(6%)($450,000)] (Note 5)	(27,000)	(47,803)
Net Business Income For Tax Purposes		$188,297

Note 1 As the business deducted 100 percent of the meals and entertainment costs, the non-deductible one-half of this amount needs to be added back to arrive at Net Business Income For Tax Purposes.

Note 2 As the business deducted 100 percent of the automobile operating costs, the portion related to Derek's personal use must be added back. This amount would be $1,350 [($4,800)(9,000 ÷ 32,000)].

Note 3 The addition to UCC for the car would be limited to $30,000, and it would be allocated to a separate Class 10.1. Maximum CCA for 2020 would be $13,500 [(150%)(30%)($30,000)]. However, the business can only deduct $9,703 [($13,500)(23,000 ÷ 32,000)].

Note 4 CCA for Class 8 would be calculated as follows:

UCC January 1, 2020	$42,000
Additions	12,000
Disposals - Lesser Of:	
Proceeds Of Disposition = $3,000	
Capital Cost = $10,000	(3,000)
AccII Adjustment [(50%)($12,000 - $3,000)]	4,500
Base For CCA	$55,500
Rate	20%
Class 8 CCA	$11,100

Note 5 As the building was acquired new and was used 100 percent for non-residential purposes, it is eligible for the 6 percent CCA rate. The fact that it was the only building owned by the business would result in it automatically being allocated to a separate class, but it must remain in a separate Class 1 to continue to qualify for the 6 percent rate.

Property Income

Derek's property income is calculated as follows:

Eligible Dividends On Breax	$ 8,000
Gross Up On Eligible Dividends [(38%)($8,000)]	3,040
Realco Income Trust Units [(5,000)($1.50)]	7,500
Debt Securities (Note 6)	12,000
Foreign Term Deposit (Note 7)	15,000
Total Property Income	$45,540

Note 6 Derek would have to recognize $8,000 [(8%)($100,000)] in interest on the July 1, 2020, anniversary of the debt security. In addition, because a $12,000 payment is received on December 31, 2020, he would have to recognize an additional $4,000 ($12,000, less the $8,000 recognized on the anniversary date).

Note 7 As non-business income is involved, the tax credit will be limited to $3,000 [(15%)($20,000)]. The remaining $5,000 ($8,000- $3,000) can be deducted against the interest. This leaves an inclusion of $15,000 ($20,000- $5,000).

Capital Gain

The adjusted cost base of the Breax shares that were sold was $52 ($130,000 ÷ 2,500). Given this, the capital gain on the Breax common shares would be calculated as follows:

Proceeds [($65)(1,000)]	$65,000
Adjusted Cost Base [($52)(1,000)]	(52,000)
Capital Gain	$13,000
Inclusion Rate	1/2
Taxable Capital Gain	$ 6,500

Net Income For Tax Purposes And Taxable Income

There are no Taxable Income deductions available. As a consequence, Taxable Income is equal to Net Income For Tax Purposes.

Net Business Income	$188,297
Total Property Income	45,540
Taxable Capital Gain	6,500
Net Income For Tax Purposes And Taxable Income	$240,337

Tax Payable

Tax Payable would be calculated as follows:

Tax On First $214,368		$ 49,645
Tax On Next $25,969 ($240,337 - $214,368) At 33 Percent		8,570
Tax Before Credits		$ 58,215
Tax Credits:		
Basic Personal Amount (Derek)	($12,298)	
Spouse ($12,298 - $9,500)	(2,798)	
Canada Caregiver For A Child	(2,273)	
Disability Transferred From Brad	(8,576)	
Disability Supplement For Brad (Note 8)	Nil	
First Time Home Buyers	(5,000)	
Transfer Of Bill's Tuition Credit (Note 9)	(5,000)	
Medical Expenses (Note 10)	(18,603)	
Total Credit Base	($54,548)	
Rate	15%	(8,182)
Dividend Tax Credit On Eligible Dividends [(6/11)($3,040)]		(1,658)
Foreign Tax Credit [(15%)($20,000)]		(3,000)
Federal Tax Payable		$ 45,375

Note 8   Since Brad's medical expenses claimed for the medical expense tax credit total more than $7,933 ($5,003 + $2,930), Derek cannot claim the disability supplement for him.

Note 9   As Bill's income is below the basic credit amount of $13,229, he cannot use any of his available tuition credit. Given this, the maximum transfer is the lesser of:

- The actual tuition of $8,500.
- The absolute maximum of $5,000.

Note 10   The base for the medical expense tax credit is calculated as follows:

Medical Expenses Of Derek, Emily, Brad And Barbara ($1,400 + $1,600 + $11,400 + $2,300)		$16,700
Lesser Of:		
• [(3%)($240,337)] = $7,210		
• 2020 Threshold Amount = $2,397		(2,397)
Balance Before Dependants 18 And Over		$14,303
Bill's Medical Expenses	$ 4,600	
Reduced By The Lesser Of:		
• $2,397		
• [(3%)($10,000)] = $300	(300)	4,300
Medical Expense Tax Credit Base		$18,603

Chapter 8 Learning Objectives

After completing Chapter 8, you should be able to:

1. Explain the economic basis for treating capital gains more favourably than other types of income (paragraph [P hereafter] 8-1 to 8-10).
2. Apply the general rules for the determination of gains and losses on the disposition of capital assets (P 8-11 to 8-36).
3. Calculate capital gains and losses on dispositions of identical properties (P 8-37 to 8-38).
4. Determine the tax consequences associated with partial dispositions of capital assets (P 8-39).
5. Calculate capital gains and losses on dispositions of capital assets with warranties attached (P 8-40 to P 8-41).

6. Apply the rules related to capital gains reserves (P 8-42 to 8-61).
7. Determine the tax consequences of a bad debt arising on a debt from the sale of capital assets (P 8-62 and 8-63).
8. Apply the special rule for sales of real property (P 8-64 to 8-71).
9. Apply the basic rules related to the reduction of taxation of capital gains arising from the disposition of a principal residence (P 8-72 to 8-81).
10. Describe the approaches available on the disposition of farm property that is also a principal residence (P 8-82 to 8-86).

11. Determine the tax consequences that result from dispositions of personal use property (P 8-87 to 8-91).
12. Determine the tax consequences that result from dispositions of listed personal property (P 8-92 to 8-94).
13. Determine the tax consequences that result from foreign currency transactions (P 8-95 to 8-106).
14. Determine the tax consequences that result from dispositions of options (P 8-107 to 8-112).
15. Determine the amount of capital gain or loss resulting from a change in the use of a capital asset (P 8-113 to 8-121).

16. Describe the principal residence elections that are available when there is a change in use (P 8-122 to 8-130).
17. Describe how an individual deals with the CCA on automobiles where the amount of employment or business usage changes over time. (P 8-131).
18. Explain the basic requirements for deemed dispositions on departures from Canada (P 8-132 to 8-133).
19. Apply the deferral provisions for capital gains arising on the disposition of small business investments (P 8-134 to 8-136).
20. Apply the deferral provisions for capital gains arising on voluntary and involuntary dispositions of property that is subsequently replaced (P 8-137 to 8-149).

21. Apply the deferral provisions for recapture arising on voluntary and involuntary dispositions of capital property that is subsequently replaced (P 8-150 to 8-165).
22. Explain the role of capital gains and losses in tax planning (P 8-166 to 8-168).

How to Work Through Chapter 8

We recommend the following approach in dealing with the material in this chapter:

Economic Background And General Rules For Capital Gains Taxation
- Read paragraph 8-1 to 8-30 (in the textbook).
- Do Exercises Eight-1 and Eight-2 (in the textbook) and check the solutions in this Study Guide.
- Read paragraph 8-31 to 8-36.

Identical Properties
- Read paragraph 8-37 to 8-38.
- Do Exercise Eight-3 and check the solution in this Study Guide.
- Do Self Study Problem Eight-1 which is available on MyLab and check the solution in this Study Guide.

Partial Dispositions And Warranties On Capital Assets
- Read paragraph 8-39 to 8-41.
- Do Exercise Eight-4 and check the solution in this Study Guide.
- Do Self Study Problem Eight-2 and check the solution in this Study Guide.

Capital Gains Reserves
- Read paragraph 8-42 to 8-61.
- Do Exercise Eight-5 and check the solution in this Study Guide.
- Do Self Study Problems Eight-3 and Eight-4 and check the solutions in this Study Guide.

Bad Debts On Sales Of Capital Property
- Read paragraph 8-62 to 8-63.
- Do Exercise Eight-6 and check the solution in this Study Guide.
- Do Self Study Problems Eight-5 and Eight-6 and check the solutions in this Study Guide.

Special Rule For Sales Of Real Property
- Read paragraph 8-64 to 8-71.
- Do Exercise Eight-7 and check the solution in this Study Guide.

Principal Residence
- Read paragraph 8-72 to 8-81.
- Do Exercises Eight-8 and Eight-9 and check the solutions in this Study Guide.
- Do Self Study Problem Eight-7 and check the solution in this Study Guide.
- Read paragraph 8-82 to 8-86.

Personal Use And Listed Personal Property
- Read paragraph 8-87 to 8-94.
- Do Exercise Eight-10 and check the solution in this Study Guide.
- Do Self Study Problem Eight-8 and check the solution in this Study Guide.

Gains And Losses On Foreign Currency
- Read paragraph 8-95 to 8-106.
- Do Exercise Eight-11 and check the solution in this Study Guide.
- Do Self Study Problem Eight-9 and check the solution in this Study Guide.

Options
- Read paragraph 8-107 to 8-112.

Deemed Dispositions - Change In Use Including Principal Residences
- Read paragraph 8-113 to 8-121.
- Do Exercise Eight-12 and check the solution in this Study Guide.
- Read paragraph 8-122 to 8-128.

- Do Exercise Eight-13 and check the solution in this Study Guide.
- Read paragraph 8-129 to 8-130.
- Do Exercise Eight-14 and check the solution in this Study Guide.
- Do Self Study Problems Eight-10 and Eight-11 and check the solutions in this Study Guide.
- Read paragraph 8-131.

Deemed Dispositions - Departures From Canada
- Read paragraph 8-132 to 8-133.
- Do Exercises Eight-15 and Eight-16 and check the solutions in this Study Guide.
- Do Self Study Problem Eight-12 and check the solution in this Study Guide.

Deferral Provisions On Small Business Investments
- Read paragraph 8-134 to 8-136.
- Do Exercise Eight-17 and check the solution in this Study Guide.
- Do Self Study Problem Eight-13 and check the solution in this Study Guide.

Deferral Provisions On Replacement Property For Capital Gains And CCA
- Read paragraph 8-137 to 8-153.
- Do Exercise Eight-18 and check the solution in this Study Guide.

Replacement Property - Combined Use Of Deferral Elections
- Read paragraph 8-154 to 8-165.
- Do Exercise Eight-19 and check the solution in this Study Guide.

Capital Gains And Tax Planning
- Read paragraph 8-166 to 8-168.
- Do Self Study Problems Eight-14 to Eight-18 and check the solutions in this Study Guide.

To Complete This Chapter
- If you would like more practice in problem solving, do the Supplementary Self Study Problems for the chapter. These problems and solutions are available on MyLab.
- Review the Key Terms Used In This Chapter in the textbook at the end of Chapter 8. Consult the Glossary for the meaning of any key terms you do not know.
- Test yourself with the Chapter 8 Glossary Flashcards available on MyLab.
- Ensure you have achieved the Chapter 8 Learning Objectives listed in this Study Guide.
- As a review, we recommend you view the PowerPoint presentation for Chapter 8 that is on MyLab.

Practice Examination
Write the Practice Examination for Chapter 8 that is on MyLab. Mark your examination using the Practice Examination Solution that is also on MyLab.

Solutions to Chapter 8 Exercises

Exercise Eight - 1 Solution
The capital cost of this Class 1 asset would be $3,500,000 ($5,600,000 - $600,000 - $1,500,000). As it is used 100 percent for non-residential purposes and is in a separate Class 1, the maximum CCA for 2020 would be $315,000 [(150%)($3,500,000)(6%)].

Exercise Eight - 2 Solution

Proceeds Of Disposition [(1,000)($14.50)]	$14,500
Adjusted Cost Base [(1,000)($23.00)]	(23,000)
Total Capital Loss	($ 8,500)
Disallowed Portion [(600)($23 - $14.50)]	5,100
Adjusted Capital Loss	($ 3,400)
Inclusion Rate	1/2
Allowable Capital Loss	($ 1,700)

The adjusted cost base of the acquired shares would be calculated as follows:

Purchase Price [(600)($13.75)]	$ 8,250
Disallowed Loss [(600)($23 - $14.50)]	5,100
Adjusted Cost Base	$13,350

Exercise Eight - 3 Solution

The relevant average cost calculations are as follows:

Acquisition Date Or Sale Date	Shares Purchased (Sold)	Cost Per Share	Total Cost	Average Cost/Share
January 15, 2019	650	$23.50	$15,275	
March 12, 2019	345	24.25	8,366	
Subtotal	995		$23,641	$23.76
September 15, 2019	(210)	$23.76	(4,990)	
Subtotal	785		$18,651	
February 14, 2020	875	$26.75	23,406	
Subtotal	1,660		$42,057	$25.34
October 1, 2020	(340)	$25.34	(8,616)	
End Of Year Balances	1,320		$33,441	

Ms. Montrose's taxable capital gain for 2019 is calculated as follows:

Proceeds Of Disposition [($25.50)(210)]	$5,355
Adjusted Cost Base [($23.76)(210)]	(4,990)
Capital Gain	$ 365
Inclusion Rate	1/2
Taxable Capital Gain	$ 183

Ms. Montrose's taxable capital gain for 2020 is calculated as follows:

Proceeds Of Disposition [($29.50)(340)]	$10,030
Adjusted Cost Base [($25.34)(340)]	(8,616)
Capital Gain	$ 1,414
Inclusion Rate	1/2
Taxable Capital Gain	$ 707

Exercise Eight - 4 Solution

For 2019, there will be a taxable capital gain of $27,500 [(1/2)($292,000 - $237,000)]. For 2020, there will be an allowable capital loss of $2,400 [(1/2)($4,800)]. This allowable capital loss will only be deductible in the determination of 2020 Net Income For Tax Purposes, to the extent that there are 2020 taxable capital gains. Any undeducted loss is subject to the carry over provisions described in Chapter 11. This would include carrying the loss back to apply against the 2019 taxable capital gain.

Exercise Eight - 5 Solution

Mr. Goodson's capital gain on this transaction is $71,800 ($382,000 - $293,000 - $17,200) and the uncollected proceeds are $300,000 ($382,000 - $82,000). Given this, the maximum reserve for 2019 is $56,387, the lesser of:

- [($71,800)($300,000 ÷ $382,000)] $56,387 (Reserve)
- [($71,800)(20%)(4 - 0)] $57,440 (Reserve)

His taxable capital gain for 2019 is $7,707 [(1/2)($71,800 - $56,387)].

At the end of 2020, the uncollected proceeds are $240,000 ($300,000 - $60,000). Based on this, the capital gain to be recognized for 2020 would be as follows:

2019 Reserve Added To Income	$56,387
2020 Reserve - Lesser Of:	
• [($71,800)($240,000 ÷ $382,000)] = $45,110	
• [($71,800)(20%)(4 - 1)] = $43,080	(43,080)
2020 Capital Gain	$13,307

His taxable capital gain for 2020 is $6,654 [(1/2)($13,307)].

Exercise Eight - 6 Solution

For 2019, there will be an allowable capital loss of $7,500 [(1/2)($110,000 - $125,000)]. For 2020, there will be an allowable capital loss of $17,500 [(1/2)(Nil - $35,000)]. The total allowable capital loss of $25,000 ($7,500 + $17,500) over the two years is equivalent to the allowable capital loss that would have resulted if the property had been sold for cash of $75,000. The capital loss would equal $50,000 ($125,000 - $75,000) and the allowable capital loss would be $25,000 [(1/2)($50,000)].

These allowable capital losses will only be deductible against taxable capital gains. However, they can be carried over to other years in which the taxpayer has taxable capital gains and deducted in the determination of Taxable Income. (See Chapter 11.)

Exercise Eight - 7 Solution

A comparison of the tax effects for Part 1 and Part 2 is as follows:

(See Following Explanations)	Part 1	Part 2
Building - Fair Market Value	$500,000	
Building - Deemed Proceeds		$615,000
UCC	(615,000)	(615,000)
Terminal Loss	($115,000)	Nil

(See Following Explanations)	Part 1	Part 2
Land - Fair Market Value	$750,000	
Land - Deemed Proceeds		
($1,250,000 - $615,000)		$635,000
Adjusted Cost Base	(425,000)	(425,000)
Capital Gain	$325,000	$210,000
Inclusion Rate	1/2	1/2
Taxable Capital Gain	$162,500	$105,000
Terminal Loss	(115,000)	Nil
Net Income Inclusion	$ 47,500	$105,000

Part 1 Explanation In the absence of the special rule, there would be a taxable capital gain of $162,500 on the land. This would be reduced by the $115,000 ($615,000 - $500,000) terminal loss on the building, resulting in a net income inclusion of $47,500.

Part 2 Explanation ITA 13(21.1)(a) modifies the results in such situations by deeming the proceeds of disposition for the building to be:

The Lesser Of:

- The FMV of the land and building $1,250,000
  Reduced By The Lesser Of:
  - The ACB of the land = $425,000
  - The FMV of the land = $750,000   (425,000)   <u>$825,000</u>

- The Greater Of:
  - The FMV of the building = $500,000
  - The Lesser Of:
    The cost of the building = $930,000
    The UCC of the building = $615,000   <u>$615,000</u>

With the building proceeds at $615,000, the terminal loss is eliminated. The $635,000 deemed proceeds for the land result in a capital gain of $210,000. In effect, this eliminates the terminal loss of $115,000 by reducing the capital gain by the same amount (from $325,000 to $210,000) and increases the net income inclusion by one-half of this amount or $57,500 ($105,000 - $47,500).

Exercise Eight - 8 Solution

There would be no tax consequences due to the sales. There would be a capital gain on the first sale of $20,500 ($109,500 - $89,000). This gain could be eliminated by designating the first property as his principal residence for the six years 2011 through 2016. The gain reduction would be calculated as follows:

$$\left(\$20,500 \times \frac{(6 + 0)^*}{6} \right) = \underline{\$20,500} \quad (\textbf{Reduction,} \text{ Not Gain})$$

*Although the gain reduction formula includes a +1 in the numerator, the numerator cannot exceed the denominator as the gain reduction cannot be larger than the total capital gain.

The $26,000 ($178,000 - $152,000) capital gain on the second home could be eliminated by designating the second property as his principal residence for the years 2017 through 2020 and adding the plus one in the numerator. The gain reduction would be calculated as follows:

$$\left(\$26,000 \times \frac{(4 + 1)}{5} \right) = \underline{\$26,000} \quad (\textbf{Reduction,} \text{ Not Gain})$$

Exercise Eight - 9 Solution

The total gain on the two properties can be calculated as follows:

	City Home (12 Years)	Cottage (9 Years)
Sales Price	$198,000	$143,500
Adjusted Cost Base	(126,000)	(85,000)
Total Capital Gain	$ 72,000	$ 58,500

In this example, the years 2012 through 2020 could be allocated to either property. This raises the question of which property should be designated the principal residence during these years. If both properties had been owned for the same length of time, you would simply allocate the number of years owned, less 1 year, to the property with the larger gain. However, that is not the case here. Given the different ownership periods, the optimum solution requires the calculation of annual increases in value for each property.

The annual calculations are as follows:

Annual Gain - City Home ($72,000 ÷ 12)	$6,000
Annual Gain - Cottage ($58,500 ÷ 9)	$6,500

Given these values, the years 2012 through 2020 (1 year less than owned) should be allocated to the cottage. When these 8 years are combined with the plus 1 in the numerator of the reduction formula, the $58,500 gain on the cottage will be completely eliminated. This leaves the years 2009 through 2012 for the Ottawa house, resulting in the following gain reduction:

$$\left(\$72,000 \times \frac{(4 + 1)}{12} \right) = \underline{\$30,000} \quad \textbf{(Reduction,} \text{ Not Gain)}$$

This will leave a total capital gain on the sale of the two properties of $42,000 ($58,500 - $58,500 + $72,000 - $30,000).

Exercise Eight - 10 Solution

The results would be as follows:

	Personal Use Property	Listed Personal Property
Gain On Sailboat ($68,000 - $43,000)	$25,000	
Gain On Oil Painting ($25,000 - $1,000)		$24,000
Loss On Personal Automobile	Nil	
Loss On Necklace ($18,000 - $46,000)		(28,000)
Capital Gain	$25,000	Nil
Inclusion Rate	1/2	N/A
Net Taxable Capital Gain	$12,500	Nil

The only tax consequence of these dispositions is a taxable capital gain of $12,500 [(1/2)($25,000)]. The gain on the oil painting is completely eliminated by the loss on the necklace. As this loss on the necklace is greater than the gain on the painting, there is a listed personal property loss carry over of $2,000 [(1/2)($28,000 - $24,000)].

Exercise Eight - 11 Solution

In 2019, as a result of his share purchase, Mr. Pratt will have an exchange gain of $612 [(450)(TT$68)(C$0.23 - C$0.21)]. As this qualifies as an ITA 39(2) foreign currency capital gain, he will only include $206 [(1/2)($612 - $200)] of this in his Net Income For Tax Purposes.

In 2020, there will be a capital gain on the sale of $1,170 {[(450)(TT$96)(C$0.19)] - [(450)(TT$68)(C$0.23)]}. None of this gain qualifies under ITA 39(2), so there would be no $200 exclusion. Mr. Pratt's 2020 Net Income For Tax Purposes will include $585 [(1/2)($1,170)] of this gain.

Exercise Eight - 12 Solution

The change in use will trigger capital gains on the land and building as follows:

	Land	Building
Proceeds Of Disposition	$120,000	$111,000
Adjusted Cost Base	(20,000)	(23,000)
Capital Gain	$100,000	$ 88,000
Inclusion Rate	1/2	1/2
Taxable Capital Gain	$ 50,000	$ 44,000

For capital gains purposes, the new capital cost will be $111,000 for the building and $120,000 for the land.

As the change is from personal to business use and the fair market value is greater than the cost, the new UCC for the building will be its cost, plus one-half of the difference between the fair market value and the cost. The relevant CCA calculation is as follows:

Original Cost	$23,000
Bump Up [(1/2)($111,000 - $23,000)]	44,000
Cost For CCA Purposes = UCC	$67,000
One-Half Net Additions	(33,500)
CCA Base	$33,500
Rate	4%
2020 CCA	$ 1,340

Note that for individuals, the calendar year is considered the fiscal year for property income purposes. As a consequence, there is no adjustment for a short fiscal period in the year of acquisition. Also note that, the half-year rule is generally not applicable to non-arm's length transfers if the transferor used the property as a depreciable property prior to the transfer. The cottage was not previously used as a depreciable property and, as a result, the half-year provisions are applicable.

Exercise Eight - 13 Solution

No ITA 45(3) Election The maximum CCA for 2019 would be $7,500 [($375,000)(4%)(1/2)]. Deducting this amount would result in a 2019 net rental income of $2,300 ($9,800 - $7,500).

The maximum CCA for 2019 would be $4,200 [($210,000)(4%)(1/2)]. This would result in a net rental income for 2019 of $4,800 ($21,600 - $12,600 - $4,200).

When the property is sold in 2020, she would have a taxable capital gain of $67,500 [($345,000 - $210,000)(1/2)]. In addition, there would be recapture of CCA of $4,200, the amount of CCA taken in 2019 for a total income inclusion of $71,700 ($67,500 + $4,200).

ITA 45(2) Election If she did not take CCA in 2019, her net rental income would be $9,000 ($21,600 - $12,600), $4,200 higher than when no ITA 45(2) election is made. However, she could then elect under ITA 45(2) and this means that the property could continue to be designated as her principal residence in 2020. Given this, the capital gain could be eliminated by the principal residence deduction. This is clearly a better alternative as shown in the following table:

	No Election	ITA 45(2) Election
2019 Income	$ 4,800	$9,000
2020 Income	71,700	Nil
Total	$76,500	$9,000

Exercise Eight - 14 Solution

No ITA 45(3) Election The maximum CCA for 2019 would be $22,500 [($375,000)(4%)(1.5)]. However, as the deduction of CCA cannot be used to create a rental loss, the deduction is limited to $9,800, the net rental income before deducting CCA. This would result in a 2019 net rental income of nil ($9,800 - $9,800).

Because he has deducted CCA for this year, he cannot treat the property as his principal residence and, when he moves in on January 1, 2020, the change in use will create a deemed disposition/ re-acquisition at the fair market value of $450,000. This will result in a taxable capital gain of

$37,500 [($450,000 - $375,000)(1/2)]. There would also be recapture of the $9,800 of CCA taken in 2019.

When he sells the property at the end of the year for $510,000, there will be an additional taxable capital gain of $30,000 [($510,000 - $450,000)(1/2)]. However, as he lived in the condominium during 2020, this gain would be eliminated through the use of the principal residence exemption. This would leave a 2020 income inclusion of $45,000 ($37,500 + $7,500 + $30,000 - $30,000).

ITA 45(3) Election   If he does not take CCA in 2019, his net rental income will be $9,800. However, if he makes the ITA 45(3) election, the unit can be designated as his principal residence for both 2019 and 2020. This means that there will be no additional income in 2020. This is clearly a better alternative as shown in the following table:

	No Election	**ITA 45(3) Election**
2019 Income	$ 2,300	$9,800
2020 Income	45,000	Nil
Total	$ 47,300	$9,800

Exercise Eight - 15 Solution
There would be a deemed disposition on his departure, leaving him liable for the taxes on a $55,000 [(1/2)($1,030,000 - $920,000)] taxable capital gain.

Exercise Eight - 16 Solution
As real property is exempt from the deemed disposition provision contained in ITA 128.1(4)(b), there would be no tax consequences with respect to the rental property at the time of Ms. Twain's departure. However, real property is Taxable Canadian Property and, as a consequence, as explained in Chapter 1, she would be liable for Canadian taxes on both recapture and capital gains resulting from a subsequent sale of the property, even after she becomes a non-resident.

Exercise Eight - 17 Solution
The capital gain would be calculated as follows:

Proceeds Of Disposition	$1,350,000
Adjusted Cost Base	(750,000)
Capital Gain	$ 600,000

As the lesser of the proceeds of disposition and the cost of the replacement shares is the $1,200,000 cost of the replacement shares, the maximum deferral would be $533,333 [($600,000)($1,200,000 ÷ $1,350,000)].

The adjusted cost base of the new shares would be calculated as follows:

Initial Cost	$1,200,000
Deferred Capital Gain	(533,333)
Adjusted Cost Base	$ 666,667

Exercise Eight - 18 Solution
The Company would have to record recapture of $750,000 ($650,000 - $1,400,000) for 2019. This is reversed during 2020 by electing under ITA 13(4). Since the replacement cost of the new

building exceeds the normal recapture of CCA, the amended recapture of CCA is nil. Using the ITA 13(4) formula, the amended 2019 recapture of CCA would be calculated as follows:

UCC Balance		$650,000
Deduction:		
Lesser Of:		
• Proceeds Of Disposition = $1,400,000		
• Capital Cost = $1,500,000	$1,400,000	
Reduced By The Lesser Of:		
• Normal Recapture = $750,000		
• Replacement Cost = $2,350,000	(750,000)	(650,000)
Recapture Of CCA (Amended)		Nil

The result is that the UCC of the replacement building would be limited to $1,600,000 ($2,350,000 - $750,000). This also reflects the economic substance of the replacement transaction ($650,000 + $2,350,000 - $1,400,000 = $1,600,000).

Exercise Eight - 19 Solution
As the replacement did not occur until 2020, Hadfeld's 2019 tax return will include a capital gain of $225,000 ($950,000 - $725,000), of which one-half or $112,500 is taxable, and recapture of $101,850 ($725,000 - $623,150).

Since the cost of the replacement property exceeded the proceeds of disposition for the old property, these amounts can be reversed in 2020 through a 2019 amended return. The deemed capital cost and UCC of the new building are as follows:

Actual Capital Cost	$980,000
Capital Gain Deferred By Election ($950,000 - $725,000)	(225,000)
Deemed Capital Cost	$755,000
Recapture Deferred By Election ($725,000 - $623,150)	(101,850)
2020 UCC	$653,150

Each of these amounts are $30,000 more than the old capital cost and UCC. This reflects the $30,000 ($980,000 - $950,000) over and above the insurance proceeds that the Company spent on replacing the building.

Solution to Self Study Problem Eight - 1

Part A
The total cost of the 1,222 shares remaining on December 31, 2020 would be $17,077. This is calculated in the following table:

Acquisition Or Sale Date	Shares Purchased (Sold)	Cost Per Share	Total Cost	Average Cost/Share
March 2014	650	$11.00	$ 7,150	
September, 2015	922	13.00	11,986	
May, 2017	480	17.00	8,160	
Subtotal	2,052		$27,296	$13.30
November, 2017 Sale	(610)	$13.30	(8,113)	
July, 2020	240	18.00	4,320	
Subtotal	1,682		$23,503	$13.97
October, 2020	(460)	$13.97	(6,426)	
December 31, 2020 Balances	1,222		$17,077	

Part B
The average cost of the shares sold during July, 2020 would be calculated as follows:

April, 2019 Purchase [(2,200)($12)]	$26,400
December, 2019 Purchase [(1,450)($17)]	24,650
Total Cost	$51,050
Average Cost ($51,050 ÷ 3,650)	$ 13.99

Given this average cost, the taxable capital gain on the July, 2020 sale of shares would be calculated as follows:

Proceeds [(2,840)($22)]	$62,480.00
Cost [(2,840)($13.99)]	(39,731.60)
Capital Gain	$22,748.40
Inclusion Rate	1/2
Taxable Capital Gain	$11,374.20

Solution to Self Study Problem Eight - 2

No recognition can be given to the warranty at the time the land is sold. This means that a taxable capital gain of $600,000 [(1/2)($2,600,000 - $1,400,000)] will result from this sale. However, since no reduction in the capital gain can be made to reflect potential outlays under the warranty, the subsequent outlays that are required under the warranty agreement will be treated as a capital loss. Thus, the $1,040,000 payment that is required in 2020 will result in a $520,000 [(1/2)($1,040,000)] allowable capital loss.

This allowable capital loss must first be deducted against taxable capital gains that occur in 2020. If such gains are not sufficient to absorb the loss, some or all of the $520,000 can be carried back to 2019 to be applied against the gain that was recognized when the sale occurred.

Any loss that is not carried back can be carried forward indefinitely and applied against future capital gains. (Loss carry overs are covered in Chapter 11.)

Solution to Self Study Problem Eight - 3

The capital gain on the two tracts of land would be calculated as follows:

	Tract A	**Tract B**
Proceeds Of Disposition	$127,000	$106,000
Adjusted Cost Base	(71,000)	(87,000)
Capital Gain	$ 56,000	$ 19,000

2020 Solution
At the end of 2020, the proceeds not due for Tract A is $110,000 ($127,000 - $17,000). The corresponding figure for Tract B is $74,000 ($106,000 - $32,000).

The minimum taxable capital gain to be included in Ms. Helm's income for 2020 would be calculated as follows:

	Tract A	Tract B
Total Capital Gain	$56,000	$19,000
Maximum Reserve For 2020:		
Tract A - Lesser Of:		
[($56,000)($110,000 ÷ $127,000)] = $48,504		
[($56,000)(20%)(4)] = $44,800	(44,800)	
Tract B - Lesser Of:		
[($19,000)($74,000 ÷ $106,000)] = $13,264		
[($19,000)(20%)(4)] = $15,200		(13,264)
Subtotal	$11,200	$ 5,736
Inclusion Rate	1/2	1/2
2020 Inclusion	$ 5,600	$ 2,868

2021 Solution

At the end of 2021, the proceeds not due for Tract A is $85,000 ($110,000 - $25,000). The proceeds not due for Tract B are not changed from 2020.

The minimum taxable capital gain to be included in Ms. Helm's income for 2021 would be calculated as follows:

	Tract A	Tract B
2020 Reserve Added Back	$44,800	$13,264
2021 Reserve:		
Tract A - Lesser Of:		
[($56,000)($85,000 ÷ $127,000)] = $37,480		
[($56,000)(20%)(3)] = $33,600	(33,600)	
Tract B - Lesser Of:		
[($19,000)($74,000 ÷ $106,000)] = $13,264		
[($19,000)(20%)(3)] = $11,400		(11,400)
Subtotal	$11,200	$ 1,864
Inclusion Rate	1/2	1/2
2021 Inclusion	$ 5,600	$ 932

Solution to Self Study Problem Eight - 4

Capital Gain And Recapture

The immediate tax consequences of the sale can be calculated as follows:

	Land	Building	Total Gain
Proceeds Of Disposition	$300,000	$1,200,000	
Adjusted Cost Base/Capital Cost	(250,000)	(950,000)	
Capital Gain	$ 50,000	$ 250,000	$300,000

	Building
Opening UCC Balance Of Class 1	$790,742
Lesser Of:	
• Proceeds Of Disposition = $1,200,000	
• Capital Cost = $950,000	(950,000)
Negative Ending Balance = Recapture Of CCA	($ 159,258)

Part A - Down Payment = 10 Percent
2020 Results
The $159,258 of recapture must be included in income in this year.

With a down payment of $150,000 [(10%)($1,500,000)], interest must be accrued on the out-standing balance of $1,350,000 ($1,500,000 - $150,000). At 6 percent, the amount would be $81,000.

With respect to the capital gains, under ITA 40(1)(a)(iii), the amount that can be deducted as a capital gains reserve is equal to the lesser of:

- [(Capital Gain)(Proceeds Not Yet Due ÷ Total Proceeds)]
- [(Capital Gain)(20%)(4 - Number Of Preceding Years Ending After Disposition)]

While the gains on the land and building must be calculated separately, there is no reason to separate them for the purposes of determining the available reserve. This is based on the fact that, in the absence of some reason to apply it differently, the 10 percent down payment would apply equally to each component of the sale.

With a down payment of $150,000, the available reserve would be the lesser of:

- [($300,000)($1,350,000 ÷ $1,500,000)] = $270,000
- [($300,000)(20%)(4 - 0)] = $240,000

Using the lesser figure of $240,000, the taxable capital gain to be included in Net Income For Tax Purposes would be $30,000 [(1/2)($300,000 - $240,000). The total inclusion in Net Income For Tax Purposes for 2020 would be as follows:

Recapture	$ 159,258
Interest	81,000
Taxable Capital Gain	30,000
Total For 2020	$270,258

2021 Results
For this year, the reserve would be the lesser of:

- [($300,000)($1,350,000 ÷ $1,500,000)] = $270,000
- [($300,000)(20%)(4 - 1)] = $180,000

Based on this, the total inclusion in Net Income For Tax Purposes for 2021 would be as follows:

2020 Reserve Added To Income	$240,000
2021 Reserve	(180,000)
Net Capital Gain	$ 60,000
Inclusion Rate	1/2
Net Taxable Capital Gain	$ 30,000
Interest (Same As 2020)	81,000
Total For 2021	$111,000

2022 Results
For this year, the reserve would be the lesser of:

- [($300,000)(Nil ÷ $1,500,000)] = Nil
- [($300,000)(20%)(4 - 2)] = $120,000

Based on this, the total inclusion in Net Income For Tax Purposes for 2022 would be as follows:

2021 Reserve Added To Income	$180,000
2022 Reserve	Nil
Net Capital Gain	$180,000
Inclusion Rate	1/2
Net Taxable Capital Gain	$ 90,000
Interest	Nil
Total For 2022	$ 90,000

Part B - Down Payment = 30 Percent

2020 Results

While the down payment is changed in this case, the amount of recapture would be the same as in Part A. However, the interest would be reduced to $63,000 [(6%)($1,500,000 - $450,000)].

With the down payment of $450,000 [(30%)($1,500,000)], the available reserve would be the lesser of:

- [($300,000)($1,050,000 ÷ $1,500,000)] = $210,000
- [($300,000)(20%)(4 - 0)] = $240,000

Using the lesser figure of $210,000, the taxable capital gain to be included in Net Income For Tax Purposes would be $45,000 [(1/2)($300,000 - $210,000)].

The total inclusion in Net Income For Tax Purposes for 2020 would be as follows:

Recapture	$159,258
Interest	63,000
Taxable Capital Gain	45,000
Total For 2020	$267,258

2021 Results

For this year, the reserve would be the lesser of:

- [($300,000)($1,050,000 ÷ $1,500,000)] = $210,000
- [($300,000)(20%)(4 - 1)] = $180,000

Based on this, the total inclusion in Net Income For Tax Purposes for 2021 would be as follows:

2020 Reserve Added To Income	$210,000
2021 Reserve	(180,000)
Net Capital Gain	$ 30,000
Inclusion Rate	1/2
Net Taxable Capital Gain	$ 15,000
Interest (Same As 2020)	63,000
Total For 2021	$ 78,000

2022 Results

For this year, the results are the same as in Part A. The reserve would be the lesser of:

- [($300,000)(Nil ÷ $1,500,000)] = Nil
- [($300,000)(20%)(4 - 2)] = $120,000

Based on this, the total inclusion in Net Income For Tax Purposes for 2022 would be as follows:

2021 Reserve Added To Income	$180,000
2022 Reserve	Nil
Net Capital Gain	$180,000
Inclusion Rate	1/2
Net Taxable Capital Gain	$ 90,000
Interest	Nil
Total For 2022	$ 90,000

Solution to Self Study Problem Eight - 5

For 2019, Mrs. Simpkins would have a capital gain of $10,000 ($25,000 - $15,000), of which one-half is taxable, resulting in a taxable capital gain of $5,000. While this could have been reduced through the use of reserves, Mrs. Simpkins chose not to do so.

In 2020, the inability to collect the note payment would result in a capital loss of $10,000 (Nil - $10,000). The $5,000 allowable amount of this loss must first be applied against any taxable capital gains that are realized in 2020. If such gains are not sufficient to absorb the loss, all or part of the $5,000 can be carried back and applied against the taxable capital gain that was recognized in 2019 (assuming there were no 2019 allowable capital losses net against it).

Any loss that is not carried back can be carried forward indefinitely and applied against future capital gains. (Loss carry overs are covered in Chapter 11.)

Solution to Self Study Problem Eight - 6

Capital Gains Reserve
With respect to the capital gains, under ITA 40(1)(a)(iii), the amount that can be deducted as a capital gains reserve is equal to the lesser of:

- [(Capital Gain)(Proceeds Not Yet Due ÷ Total Proceeds)]
- [(Capital Gain)(20%)(4 - Number Of Preceding Years Ending After Disposition)]

2020 Results
The only tax consequence in this year is the capital gain that occurs on the sale. The gain, along with the maximum deductible reserve, would be calculated as follows:

Proceeds Of Disposition	$6,680,000
Adjusted Cost Base	(2,160,000)
Capital Gain	$4,520,000
Reserve - Lesser Of:	
• [($4,520,000)($4,500,000 ÷ $6,680,000)] = $3,044,910	
• [($4,520,000)(20%)(4 - 0)] = $3,616,000	(3,044,910)
Capital Gain	$1,475,090
Inclusion Rate	1/2
Taxable Capital Gain	$ 737,545

As no provision can be made for the estimated cost of the warranty, the total Net Income For Tax Purposes inclusion for 2020 would be $737,545.

2021 Results

For this year, the reserve would be the lesser of:

- [($4,520,000)($3,000,000 ÷ $6,680,000)] = $2,029,940
- [($4,520,000)(20%)(4 - 1)] = $2,712,000

Based on this, the total inclusion in Net Income For Tax Purposes for 2021 would be as follows:

2020 Reserve Added To Income	$3,044,910
2021 Reserve	(2,029,940)
Capital Gain	$1,014,970
Inclusion Rate	1/2
Taxable Capital Gain	$ 507,485
Interest [(4%)($4,500,000)]	180,000
Total	$ 687,485

2022 Results

For this year, the reserve would be the lesser of:

- [($4,520,000)($1,500,000 ÷ $6,680,000)] = $1,014,970
- [($4,520,000)(20%)(4 - 2)] = $1,808,000

He will have a capital gain consisting of the addition of the 2021 reserve in income and the deduction of a new reserve for 2022. He will also have a capital loss due to the $1,000,000 payment to the developer. As this payment is required by a warranty on a capital asset, it is a capital loss.

Based on this, the total inclusion in Net Income For Tax Purposes for 2022 would be as follows:

2021 Reserve Added To Income	$2,029,940
2022 Reserve	(1,014,970)
Capital Gain	$1,014,970
Capital Loss Warranty Payment [(50)($20,000)]	(1,000,000)
Net Capital Gain	$ 14,970
Inclusion Rate	1/2
Net Taxable Capital Gain	$ 7,485
Interest [(4%)($3,000,000)]	120,000
Total	$ 127,485

2023 Results

With the bankruptcy of the developer, no interest will be collected in 2023 and the balance of the loan must be written off as a bad debt, resulting in a capital loss of $1,500,000 [(Nil - ($4,500,000 - $3,000,000)].

Lawrence will include the 2022 reserve of $1,014,970 in income. Since the loan was to be paid off in 2023, there would have been no new reserve to be deducted, regardless of the bankruptcy.

The capital loss can be deducted to the extent of the capital gain of $1,014,970. The remaining allowable capital loss of $242,515 [(1/2)($1,500,000 - $1,014,970)] can only be deducted in 2023 to the extent of taxable capital gains in that year. However, it can be carried back to be applied to the capital gains that were recognized in previous years.

Summary (Not Required)

The results can be summarized as follows:

Year	Interest	Net Taxable Gain (Allowable Loss)
2020	Nil	$ 737,545
2021	$ 180,000	507,485
2022	120,000	7,485
2023	Nil	(242,515)
Totals	$ 300,000	$1,010,000

The amount of the taxable capital gain can be verified as follows:

Initial Capital Gain	$4,520,000
Warranty Payment	(1,000,000)
Bad Debt	(1,500,000)
Capital Gain	$2,020,000
Inclusion Rate	1/2
Taxable Capital Gain	$1,010,000

Solution to Self Study Problem Eight - 7

The gains on the two properties can be calculated as follows:

	Country Home	Condominium
Proceeds Of Disposition	$1,200,000	$900,000
Adjusted Cost Base	(850,000)	(625,000)
Real Estate Commissions		
[(5%)($1,200,000)]	(60,000)	
[(5%)($900,000)]		(45,000)
Total Capital Gain	$ 290,000	$230,000

The annual gain was $18,125 ($290,000 ÷ 16) on the country home and $28,750 ($230,000 ÷ 8) on the condominium. This would indicate that the maximum number of years should be allocated to the condominium. However, because of the plus 1 in the reduction formula, one year can be left off.

Based on this analysis, the seven years 2014 through 2020 should allocated to the condominium, with the nine years 2005 through 2013 being allocated to the country home. The required calculations would be as follows:

	Country Home	Condominium
Total Capital Gain	$290,000	$230,000
Exemption:		
Country Home		
[$290,000][(9 + 1) ÷ 16]	(181,250)	
Condominium		
[$230,000][(7 + 1) ÷ 8]		(230,000)
Capital Gain	$108,750	Nil
Inclusion Rate	1/2	N/A
Taxable Capital Gain	$ 54,375	Nil

This gives a total taxable capital gain on the two properties of $54,375.

Solution to Self Study Problem Eight - 8

Classification Of Property

All of the items sold are personal use property. However, if they can be classified as "listed personal property", their tax treatment will be different. Under ITA 54, listed personal property consists of the following items.

    (i)   print, etching, drawing, painting, sculpture, or other similar work of art,

    (ii) jewelry,

    (iii) rare folio, rare manuscript, or rare book,

    (iv) stamp, or

    (v) coin.

The Paul Borduas painting, as well as the Hemingway first edition clearly fall into the listed personal property classification. The Bentley and the Chris Craft clearly do not.

The classification of the fountain pen collection is not clear. The issue is whether a pen can be considered jewelry (and not a writing implement) as there are fountain pens that cost as much as $100,000 and are made from precious metals and stones.

The dictionary definition of jewel includes "a precious possession". However, the definition of jewelry is more narrow, referring to "ornaments for personal adornment". Whether something that is displayed on one's desk would be considered personal adornment would be debatable, but the fact that Mr. Howard always "wears" the pens prominently would favour the jewelry classification.

In the solution which follows, we have classified the pens as jewelry. However, we recognize that this classification could be subject to challenge.

Effect On Net Income For Tax Purposes

The overall amount to be included in Net Income For Tax Purposes can be calculated as follows:

Personal Use Property (Note 1)		
Gain On Antique Boat ($62,000 - $45,000)	$17,000	
Loss On Bentley	Nil	$17,000
Listed Personal Property		
Gain On First Edition ($31,000 - $12,000)	$19,000	
Gain On Painting ($132,000 - $128,000)	4,000	
Total Listed Personal Property Gains	$23,000	
Loss On Pens (Note 2)	(23,000)	Nil
Net Capital Gains		$17,000
Inclusion Rate		1/2
Addition To Net Income For Tax Purposes		$ 8,500

Note 1   Unless an item of personal use property can be classified as listed personal property, losses on its disposition cannot be deducted. However, gains on such property are taxable, without regard to the classification.

Note 2   The total loss on the pen collection is $29,000 ($13,000 - $42,000). However, the current year deduction is limited to the $23,000 in gains on listed personal property. The remaining $6,000 ($29,000 - $23,000) can be carried back 3 years and forward 7 years to be applied against gains on listed personal property that have occurred in previous years or may occur in subsequent years.

Solution to Self Study Problem Eight - 9

The taxable capital gain on the sale of securities would be calculated as follows:

Proceeds Of Disposition [(3,500)(€33.50)($1.49)]	$174,703
Adjusted Cost Base [(3,500)(€30.00)($1.46)]	(153,300)
Capital Gain On Sale Of Securities	$ 21,403
Inclusion Rate	1/2
Taxable Capital Gain	$ 10,702

The taxable capital gain on the foreign exchange conversion would be calculated as follows:

Proceeds Of Conversion [(€117,250)($1.52)]	$178,220
Adjusted Cost Base Of Currency [(€117,250)($1.49)]	(174,703)
Capital Gain On Foreign Exchange	$ 3,517
ITA 39(1.1) Reduction Of Capital Gain	(200)
Net Capital Gain	$ 3,317
Inclusion Rate	1/2
Taxable Capital Gain	$ 1,659

Ms. Laval's minimum Net Income For Tax Purposes inclusion would be a total taxable capital gain of $12,361 ($10,702 + $1,659).

Because Ms. Laval is an individual, the ITA 39(1.1) deduction of $200 reduces the capital gain on the foreign exchange conversion.

Solution to Self Study Problem Eight - 10

2018 Results

During 2018, 100 percent of the property was used for income producing purposes. The CCA for the year would be calculated as follows:

Capital Cost ($645,000 - $120,000)	$525,000
One-Half Net Additions*	(262,500)
CCA Base	$262,500
Maximum CCA [(4%)($262,500)]	(10,500)
One-Half Net Additions	262,500
UCC - January 1, 2019	$514,500

*As the acquisition was made prior to November 21, 2018, the AccII provisions are not available and half-year rule is applicable.

There are no additional tax consequences during this year.

2019 Results

On January 1, 2019, there would be a deemed disposition/acquisition of 25 percent of the depreciable property. The transaction would be measured using the building's fair market value of $460,000 ($560,000 - $100,000). Given this, the maximum CCA on the remaining 75 percent would be calculated as follows:

Opening UCC	$ 514,500
Deemed Disposition - Lesser Of:	
• Capital Cost [(25%)($525,000)] = $131,250	
• Deemed Proceeds [(25%)($460,000)] = $115,000	(115,000)
CCA Base	$ 399,500
Maximum CCA [(4%)($399,500)]	(15,980)
UCC - January 1, 2020	$ 383,520

While the value of the building has declined from $525,000 ($645,000 - $120,000) to $460,000 ($560,000 - $100,000), no loss can be recognized. As there is still an asset in the Class, a terminal loss cannot be recognized. In addition, we would remind you that you cannot have a capital loss on a depreciable asset disposition.

The allowable capital loss on the land of $2,500 [(25%)(1/2)($120,000 - $100,000)] can be deducted against the taxable capital gains on dispositions from her portfolio. Since her income from other sources is so high, she will deduct maximum CCA regardless of how the business is doing.

The cost to Laci of the 25 percent of the property that is being used for personal purposes would be $115,000 [(25%)($460,000)] allocated to the building and $25,000 [(25%)($100,000)] allocated to the land.

2020 Results

On January 1, 2020, there would be a deemed acquisition of 25 percent of the depreciable property. The capital cost of the building acquisition would be $140,000 [(25%)($690,000 - $130,000)]. However, as the change is from personal use to business use and the fair market value of the building is greater than its cost, the UCC will be limited to her cost plus one-half of the difference between fair market value and cost or $127,500 [$115,000 + (1/2)($140,000 - $115,000)].

Maximum CCA for would be calculated as follows:

Opening UCC	$383,520
Deemed Acquisition	
[$115,000 + (1/2)($140,000 - $115,000)]	127,500
One-Half Net Additions [(1/2)($127,500)]*	(63,750)
CCA Base	$447,270
Maximum CCA [(4%)($447,270)]	(17,891)
One-Half Net Additions	63,750
UCC - January 1, 2021	$493,129

*As noted in the text, the AccII provisions cannot be used for acquisitions of assets that were previously owned by the purchaser. This means that the half-year rule is still applicable.

As a result of the deemed disposition, Laci would have a taxable capital gain on both the land and the building. They would be calculated as follows:

	Land	Building
Proceeds Of Disposition		
[(25%)($130,000)]	$32,500	
[(25%)($560,000)]		$140,000
Adjusted Cost Base [(25%)($100,000)]	(25,000)	
Capital Cost [(25%)($460,000)]		(115,000)
Capital Gains	$ 7,500	$ 25,000
Inclusion Rate	1/2	1/2
Taxable Capital Gains	$ 3,750	$ 12,500

Even though Laci has a home other than the apartment, she could eliminate these gains by making use of the +1 year in the principal residence exemption formula. Assuming she did that, she would have to allow for the designated year in the exemption formula when she sells her home.

Solution to Self Study Problem Eight - 11

2018 Results

During 2018, 80 percent of the property is used for income producing purposes. Based on this the maximum CCA that can be deducted for this year is calculated as follows:

Capital Cost [(80%)($500,000)]	$400,000
One-Half Net Additions*	(200,000)
CCA Base	$200,000
Maximum CCA [(4%)($200,000)]	(8,000)
One-Half Net Additions	200,000
UCC - January 1, 2019	$392,000

*As the property was acquired prior to November 21, 2018, the AccII provisions are not available. Given this, the half-year rule is applicable.

There are no additional tax consequences during this year.

2019 Results - Business To Personal Use

On January 1, 2019, there would be a deemed disposition/acquisition of 20 percent of the total property. This would result in a taxable capital gain on the land calculated as follows:

Proceeds Of Disposition [(20%)($230,000)]	$46,000
Adjusted Cost Base [(20%)($225,000)]	(45,000)
Capital Gain	$ 1,000
Inclusion Rate	1/2
Taxable Capital Gain On Land	$ 500

There would also be taxable capital gain on the building, calculated as follows:

Proceeds Of Disposition [(20%)($585,000)	$117,000
Adjusted Cost Base [(20%)($500,000)]	(100,000)
Capital Gain	$ 17,000
Inclusion Rate	1/2
Taxable Capital Gain	$ 8,500

The maximum CCA for 2019 would be calculated as follows:

Opening UCC	$392,000
Disposition: Lesser Of:	
Capital Cost [(20%)($500,000)] = $100,000	
Proceeds Of Disposition	
[(20%)($585,000) = $117,000	(100,000)
CCA Base	$292,000
Maximum CCA [(4%)($292,000)]	(11,680)
UCC - January 1, 2020	$280,320

2020 Results - Personal To Business Use

On January 1, 2020, there would be a deemed disposition/acquisition of 40 percent of the total property. This would result in a taxable capital gain on the land, calculated as follows:

Proceeds Of Disposition [(40%)($245,000)]		$98,000
Adjusted Cost Base:		
[(20%)($225,000)]	($45,000)	
[(20%)($230,000)]	(46,000)	(91,000)
Capital Gain		$ 7,000
Inclusion Rate		1/2
Taxable Capital Gain On Land		$ 3,500

There would also be a taxable capital gain on the building, calculated as follows:

Proceeds Of Disposition [(40%)($630,000)]		$252,000
Adjusted Cost Base:		
[(20%)($500,000)]	($100,000)	
[(20%)($585,000)]	(117,000)	(217,000)
Capital Gain		$ 35,000
Inclusion Rate		1/2
Taxable Capital Gain		$ 17,500

With respect to maximum CCA, this change in use involves a deemed disposition/acquisition from personal use to business use. In addition, the fair market value of the building is greater than her cost. Given this, the UCC will be limited to her cost plus one-half of the difference between fair market value and cost. As calculated in the preceding table, the increase in value is $35,000, with one-half of this amount being $17,500.

Maximum CCA for would be calculated as follows:

Opening UCC		$280,320
Deemed Acquisition Cost		
[(20%)($500,000)]	$100,000	
[(20%)($585,000)]	117,000	
Bump Up	17,500	234,500
One-Half Net Additions [(1/2)($234,500)]*		(117,250)
CCA Base		$397,570
Maximum CCA [(4%)($397,570)]		(15,903)
One-Half Net Additions		117,250
UCC - January 1, 2021		$498,917

*Because the acquired asset was previously owned, the AccII provisions are not applicable and the half-year rule must be applied.

Note To Students

In the Required we have asked you to ignore the principal residence exemption as the focus of the problem is on change in use. The textbook states that if there is non-residential use of a principal residence, the CRA will not apply the partial disposition rules so long as the income use is ancillary to the main use as a principal residence, there is no structural change to the property, and no CCA is claimed.

CCA was claimed on the 20 percent that went from business to principal residence back to business and the textbook does not specifically cover the effect of this CCA issue or a property where the principal residence portion is originally a small percentage of the total, on the principal residence exemption.

The fact that the business had claimed CCA on the 20 percent portion that was subsequently added to the personal portion when the business use dropped from 80 percent to 60 percent would not cause any adjustment to the principal residence. From a tax policy point of view, a change from personal use to business use is a concern since the personal use disposition results in capital gains with the added cost potentially being fully deductible as CCA. This is the reason why the change of use rules only allow half the increase in value to be added to cost. This issue does not arise, however when the property is converted from an income use to a personal use.

If the principal residence exemption was considered, when the 40 percent principal residence portion is changed to business use in 2020, that event would cause a disposition of a principal residence which would then be eligible for the principal residence exemption. As a result, there would be no net capital gain for 2020.

Solution to Self Study Problem Eight - 12

Mr. Lange's taxable capital gain on deemed dispositions resulting from his departure from Canada would be calculated as follows:

Vacant land	N/A
Automobile	N/A
Coin Collection ($11,000 - $5,000)	$ 6,000
Enbridge Shares ($38,000 - $24,000)	14,000
BCE Shares ($35,000 - $42,000)	(7,000)
Royal Bank Shares ($23,000 - $15,000)	8,000
Nal Enterprises Ltd. Shares ($153,000 - $26,000)	127,000
Capital Gain	$148,000
Inclusion Rate	1/2
Taxable Capital Gain On Departure	$ 74,000

The vacant land is exempt from the deemed disposition rules that are applicable to individuals leaving Canada. However, as it is taxable Canadian property, a later sale of this land will attract Canadian income taxes, even though Mr. Lange is no longer a Canadian resident.

The loss on the automobile is not deductible as the vehicle is a personal use property.

Solution to Self Study Problem Eight - 13

First Sale

Since Ms. Tosh has held the Tech Ltd. common shares for more than 185 days, it is a qualifying disposition. Since the Small Oil common shares were purchased immediately, they can be designated as replacement shares.

Preferred shares cannot be designated as replacement shares. As a result, the Small Bank Inc. shares do not qualify as replacement shares.

The capital gain on the Tech Ltd. disposition is $700,000 ($4,200,000 - $3,500,000). As the cost of replacement shares is only $3,800,000, the permitted deferral is limited as per the following calculation:

$$[(\$700,000)(\$3,800,000 \div \$4,200,000)] = \$633,333 \text{ Deferral}$$

Given this, the adjusted cost base of the Small Oil shares would be calculated as follows:

Unadjusted Cost	$3,800,000
Deferral Amount	(633,333)
Adjusted Cost Base Of Small Oil Shares	$3,166,667

Second Sale

Since Ms. Tosh has held the Future Inc. common shares for more than 185 days, it is a qualifying disposition. Since the eligible small business corporation common shares were purchased in the current year, they can be designated as replacement shares.

The capital gain on the disposition of Future Inc. shares is $1,800,000 ($5,600,000 - $3,800,000). Of the $5,600,000 in proceeds, only $5,200,000 ($2,400,000 + $2,800,000) was invested in replacement shares. This means that the permitted deferral will be limited as per the following calculation:

$$[(\$1,800,000)(\$5,200,000 \div \$5,600,000)] = \$1,671,429 \text{ Deferral}$$

Using this information, the adjusted cost base of the newly acquired shares would be calculated as follows:

	Sombra Shares	Ziff Shares
Purchase Price	$2,400,000	$2,800,000
Deferral:		
[($1,671,429)($2,400,000 ÷ $5,200,000)]	(771,429)	
[($1,671,429)($2,800,000 ÷ $5,200,000)]		(900,000)
Adjusted Cost Base	$1,628,571	$1,900,000

Net Taxable Capital Gain

If Ms. Tosh does not purchase any other replacements shares within 120 days of December 31, 2020, the two sales would result in a taxable capital gain, calculated as follows:

	Total Gain	Deferral	Net Gain
Tech Ltd. Shares	$ 700,000	$ 633,333	$ 66,667
Future Inc. Shares	1,800,000	1,671,429	128,571
Totals	$2,500,000	$2,304,762	$195,238
Inclusion Rate			1/2
Net Taxable Capital Gain			$ 97,619

Tax Advice

Less than all of the proceeds from the 2020 sales were invested in new qualifying small business corporations. The shortfall totaled $800,000, $400,000 ($4,200,000 - $3,800,000) on the first sale and $400,000 ($5,600,000 - $5,200,000) on the second sale. If she invests in her brother's company within 120 days of December 31, 2020, she can designate up to $800,000 of this amount as replacement shares, allowing her to to defer of the capital gains on the two sales of shares.

If she wants to invest in her brother's company after the 120 days has passed, she should review her other investments to determine if she can use the deferral provisions on small business investments to her advantage to obtain the $1,000,000.

There is the question of whether Ms. Tosh should invest in her brother's new company, but that would involve an analysis that goes beyond the scope of the material in the text.

Solution to Self Study Problem Eight - 14

2020 Results
The insurance proceeds would create recaptured CCA, calculated as follows:

Opening UCC Balance	$368,000
Disposition - Lesser Of:	
• Cost = $500,000	
• Proceeds Of Disposition = $490,000	(490,000)
Negative Closing Balance = Recapture	($ 122,000)
Recapture	122,000
January 1, 2021 UCC	Nil

The $122,000 in recapture would be taken into 2020 income and added back to the UCC to create a UCC balance of nil.

2021 Results
Using ITA 13(4), Trail Resources Ltd. would file an amended return for the 2020 taxation year. The revised recapture would be calculated as follows:

January 1, 2020 UCC Balance		$368,000
Deduction:		
Lesser Of:		
• Proceeds Of Disposition = $490,000		
• Capital Cost = $500,000	$490,000	
Reduced By The Lesser Of:		
• Normal Recapture = $122,000		
• Replacement Cost = $650,000	(122,000)	(368,000)
Recapture Of 2020 CCA (Amended)		Nil

The new nil figure for the recapture on the disposition of the old building will replace the old figure of $122,000 that was included in the original 2020 return.

The UCC of the new building will be adjusted for this change as follows:

Cost Of New Building	$650,000
Reversal Of Recapture - ITA 13(4) Election	(122,000)
UCC	$528,000

Given this, the required maximum CCA for 2021 and the January 1, 2022 UCC balance would be calculated as follows:

Opening UCC - Class 1	Nil
Addition Of UCC Of New Building	$528,000
AccII Adjustment	264,000
Base For CCA	$792,000
Maximum CCA [($792,000)(6%)]	(47,520)
AccII Adjustment Reversal	(264,000)
January 1, 2022 UCC	$480,480

The reasonableness of the CCA base calculation can be verified by noting that the $528,000 is equal to the initial UCC of $368,000, plus the cost of the new building of $650,000, less the insurance proceeds of $490,000. The AccII provisions are applied to the addition to Class 1.

Solution to Self Study Problem Eight - 15

Part A

The 2020 tax consequences would be as follows:

Land The Company would have a taxable capital gain on the Land calculated as follows:

Proceeds Of Disposition	$1,100,000
Adjusted Cost Base	(350,000)
Capital Gain	$ 750,000
Inclusion Rate	1/2
Taxable Capital Gain	$ 375,000

Building The Company would have a taxable capital gain and recapture calculated as follows:

Proceeds Of Disposition	$2,300,000
Capital Cost	(2,100,000)
Capital Gain	$ 200,000
Inclusion Rate	1/2
Taxable Capital Gain	$ 100,000

Opening UCC	$ 850,000
Deduct Disposition - Lesser Of:	
Capital Cost = $2,100,000	
Proceeds Of Disposition = $2,300,000	(2,100,000)
Negative Closing UCC Balance = Recapture	($1,250,000)
Recapture (Included In Income)	1,250,000
UCC - January 1, 2021	Nil

Equipment The Company would have recapture calculated as follows:

Opening UCC	$165,000
Deduct Disposition - Lesser Of:	
Capital Cost = $450,000	
Proceeds Of Disposition = $320,000	(320,000)
Negative Closing UCC Balance = Recapture	($155,000)
Recapture (Included In Income)	155,000
UCC - January 1, 2021	Nil

Part B

Land With respect to the Land, the capital gain resulting from the use of the ITA 44(1) election would be the lesser of:

- $750,000 (regular capital gain); and
- $500,000 (the excess of the $1,100,000 proceeds of disposition for the old land over the $600,000 cost of the replacement land).

The taxable amount would be $250,000 [(1/2)($500,000)] and this would be included in the revised 2020 Net Income For Tax Purposes. The original gain of $375,000 would be eliminated in the revised return.

If the ITA 44(1) election is used in 2021, the deemed adjusted cost base of the replacement land would be calculated as follows:

Actual Cost	$600,000
Capital Gain Reversed By Election ($750,000 - $500,000)	(250,000)
Deemed Adjusted Cost Base Of Replacement Land	$350,000

Note that the deemed adjusted cost base of the replacement land has been reduced to the adjusted cost base of the old land.

Building   If the ITA 44(1) election is used in 2021, the amended 2020 capital gain would be nil, the lesser of:

- $200,000 (regular capital gain); and
- Nil (reflecting the fact that there was no excess of the $2,300,000 proceeds of disposition for the old building over the $2,500,000 cost of the replacement building).

Using this election will reduce the deemed capital cost for the building as follows:

Actual Cost	$2,500,000
Capital Gain Reversed By Election	(200,000)
Deemed Capital Cost Of Replacement Building	$2,300,000

If the ITA 13(4) election is used in 2021, the amended 2020 recapture would be calculated as follows:

January 1, 2020 UCC Balance		$850,000
Deduction:		
Lesser Of:		
• Proceeds Of Disposition = $2,300,000		
• Capital Cost = $2,100,000	($2,100,000)	
Reduced By The Lesser Of:		
• Normal Recapture = $1,250,000		
• Replacement Cost = $2,500,000	1,250,000	(850,000)
Recapture Of 2020 CCA (Amended)		Nil

If both elections are used in 2021, the UCC of the replacement building is calculated as follows:

Deemed Capital Cost	$2,300,000
Recapture Reversed By Election	(1,250,000)
UCC - Replacement Building	$1,050,000

Note that the $1,050,000 UCC for the new building is equal to the UCC of the old building ($850,000), plus the additional $200,000 ($2,500,000 - $2,300,000) in funds required for its replacement.

These new nil figures for the capital gain and the recapture on the disposition of the old building will replace the old figures of $100,000 and $1,250,000 that were included in the original 2020 return.

Equipment   As this is a voluntary disposition, the ITA 13(4) and 44(1) elections can only be used on real property (land and buildings). They cannot be used on the equipment and, as a consequence, the $155,000 in recapture will not be altered in the amended return. As the elections cannot be used, both the capital cost and the UCC of the new equipment will be $520,000.

Part C

The Election   The ITA 44(6) election applies when there is a disposition involving a combination of part land and part building. If, for either of the assets, the proceeds of disposition exceed the adjusted cost base, the election allows the transfer of all or part of that excess to the other asset.

As will be demonstrated in this problem, this can provide some relief when ITA 44(1) and ITA 13(4) fail to eliminate all of the capital gains arising on one part of the disposition of the old property. ITA 44(1) fully eliminated the capital gain on the building. However, a $500,000 capital gain remained on the land. This would suggest that it could be advantageous to transfer some of the proceeds of disposition from the land to the building.

The excess of the proceeds of disposition of the old land over the cost of the replacement land was $500,000 ($1,100,000 - $600,000). This is the maximum available transfer from the land to the building. However, the excess of the cost of the replacement building over the old building's proceeds of disposition is only $200,000 ($2,500,000 - $2,300,000). If a transfer in excess of this amount is made, any reduction in the capital gain on the land will be matched by an increased capital gain on the building.

Applying ITA 44(6) in an optimal manner will result in the following adjusted proceeds of disposition:

	Land	**Building**
Actual Proceeds Of Disposition	$1,100,000	$2,300,000
Optimal Transfer Land To Building	(200,000)	200,000
Adjusted Proceeds Of Disposition	$ 900,000	$2,500,000

Application To Land   If both ITA 44(1) and ITA 44(6) are applied, the resulting capital gain on the land will be calculated as the lesser of:

- $550,000 ($900,000 - $350,000); and
- $300,000 (the excess of the $900,000 adjusted proceeds of disposition for the old land over the $600,000 cost of the replacement land).

This is a reduction of $200,000 ($500,000 - $300,000) from the amount that was calculated when only ITA 44(1) was applied. However, the adjusted cost base of the land would be unchanged by the use of ITA 44(6):

Actual Cost	$600,000
Capital Gain Reversed By Election ($550,000 - $300,000)	(250,000)
Deemed Adjusted Cost Base Of Replacement Land	$350,000

Application To Building   With the proceeds of disposition transfer limited to $200,000, the capital gain on the building is still nil. Specifically, the gain will be the lesser of:

- $400,000 ($2,500,000 - $2,100,000); and
- Nil (reflecting the fact that there was no excess of the $2,500,000 adjusted proceeds of disposition for the old building over the $2,500,000 cost of the replacement building).

However, the capital cost and UCC of the building will be reduced by the application of ITA 44(6):

Actual Cost	$2,500,000
Capital Gain Reversed By The Two Elections	(400,000)
Deemed Capital Cost	$2,100,000
Recapture Reversed By Election	(1,250,000)
UCC - Replacement Building	$ 850,000

Note that the UCC for the new building is equal to the UCC of the old building.

Comparison The table which follows compares the results of using only ITA 44(1) and ITA 13(4) with the results that arise when the ITA 44(6) election is also used.

	No ITA 44(6)	With ITA 44(6)
Capital Gains		
Land	$ 500,000	$ 300,000
Building	Nil	Nil
Replacement Property		
Adjusted Cost Base Of Land	$ 350,000	$ 350,000
Capital Cost Of Building	2,300,000	2,100,000
UCC	1,050,000	850,000

As you can see in the table, the use of ITA 44(6) has reduced the capital gain on the land by $200,000. However, it has done so at the cost of reducing the capital cost and UCC of the replacement building. There is a tax cost associated with this trade off in that only one-half of the capital gain would have been taxed in the current year, whereas the future CCA that has been lost would be fully deductible.

Solution to Self Study Problem Eight - 16

Part A

The proceeds of disposition were greater than the relevant capital costs for all the destroyed and expropriated assets. As a result, with respect to Net Income For Tax Purposes, the 2020 tax effects related to the involuntary dispositions would be as follows:

	Old Land	Old Building	Old Contents
Proceeds Of Disposition	$723,000	$4,800,000	$1,256,000
Adjusted Cost Base/Capital Cost	(256,000)	(3,700,000)	(972,000)
Capital Gains	$467,000	$1,100,000	$ 284,000
Inclusion Rate	1/2	1/2	1/2
Taxable Capital Gains	$233,500	$ 550,000	$ 142,000

		Old Building	Old Contents
Opening UCC		$1,856,000	$ 72,000
Capital Cost (Less Than Proceeds)		(3,700,000)	(972,000)
Closing UCC		($1,844,000)	($900,000)
Recapture Of CCA		1,844,000	900,000
UCC - January 1, 2021		Nil	Nil

The increase in Net Income For Tax Purposes totals $3,669,500 ($233,500 + $550,000 + $142,000 + $1,844,000 + $900,000).

Part B - Land

As the land, building and contents were replaced before the end of the second taxation year following the involuntary dispositions, Fraser can use both ITA 44(1) and ITA 13(4) to modify these results. These changes will be implemented through an amended return.

With respect to the land, the capital gain resulting from the use of the ITA 44(1) election would be the lesser of:

- $467,000 (regular capital gain); and
- $223,000 (the excess of the $723,000 proceeds of disposition for the old land over the $500,000 cost of the new land).

The taxable amount of this capital gain will be $111,500 [(1/2)($223,000)]. The original gain of $467,000 would be eliminated in the revised return.

Part B - Building

With respect to the building, the capital gain resulting from the use of the ITA 44(1) election would be nil, the lesser of:

- $1,100,000 (regular capital gain); and
- Nil (reflecting the fact that there was no excess of the $4,800,000 proceeds of disposition for the old building over the $5,700,000 cost of the replacement building).

Under ITA 13(4), the revised recapture would be calculated as follows:

January 1, 2020 UCC Balance		$1,856,000
Deduction:		
Lesser Of:		
• Proceeds Of Disposition = $4,800,000		
• Capital Cost = $3,700,000	($3,700,000)	
Reduced By The Lesser Of:		
• Normal Recapture = $1,844,000		
• Replacement Cost = $5,700,000	1,844,000	(1,856,000)
Recapture Of 2020 CCA (Amended)		Nil

These new nil figures for the capital gain and recapture on the building disposition will replace the old figures of $1,100,000 and $1,844,000 that were included in the original 2020 return.

Part B - Building Contents

If this was a voluntary disposition, the building contents would not be "former business property" and would not qualify for either the ITA 13(4) election or the ITA 44(1) election. However, as this is an involuntary disposition, both elections are available.

Under ITA 44(1), the revised capital gain would be $23,000, the lesser of:

- $284,000 (regular capital gain); and
- $23,000 (the excess of the $1,256,000 proceeds of disposition for the old building contents over the $1,233,000 cost of the replacement contents)

The taxable amount of the gain will be $11,500 [(1/2)($23,000)].

Under ITA 13(4), the revised recapture would be reduced from $900,000 to nil. The calculation is as follows:

January 1, 2020 UCC Balance		$72,000
Deduction:		
Lesser Of:		
• Proceeds Of Disposition = $1,256,000		
• Capital Cost = $972,000	($972,000)	
Reduced By The Lesser Of:		
• Normal Recapture = $900,000		
• Replacement Cost = $1,233,000	900,000	(72,000)
Recapture Of 2020 CCA (Amended)		Nil

These new figures for the capital gain and recapture on the contents disposition will replace the old figures of $284,000 and $900,000 that were included in the original 2020 return.

Comparison - Part A and Part B

As shown in the table which follows, the disposition of the land, building and contents resulted in an increase in 2020 Net Income For Tax Purposes of $3,669,500. When the two elections are used, the amended 2020 return will show a Net Income For Tax Purposes of only $123,000. This is a savings of $3,546,500 ($3,669,500 - $123,000).

	Part A As Reported	Part B With Elections
Land - Taxable Capital Gain	$ 233,500	$111,500
Building - Taxable Capital Gain	550,000	Nil
Contents - Taxable Capital Gain	142,000	11,500
Building - Recaptured CCA	1,844,000	Nil
Contents - Recaptured CCA	900,000	Nil
Total Increase	$3,669,500	$123,000

Part C

Assuming Fraser decides to use the elections under ITA 44(1) and ITA 13(4), the deemed cost and UCC of the replacement properties would be as follows:

	Land	Building	Contents
Actual Cost Of Replacement Property	$500,000	$5,700,000	$1,233,000
Capital Gain Reversed By Election			
Land ($467,000 - $223,000)	(244,000)		
Building ($1,100,000 - Nil)		(1,100,000)	
Contents ($284,000 - $23,000)			(261,000)
Deemed Cost Of Replacement Property	$256,000	$4,600,000	$ 972,000

	Building	Contents
Deemed Capital Cost Of Replacement Property	$4,600,000	$972,000
Recaptured CCA Reversed By Election		
Building ($1,844,000 - Nil)	(1,844,000)	
Contents ($900,000 - Nil)		(900,000)
UCC - Replacement Property	$2,756,000	$ 72,000

The deemed adjusted cost base of the replacement land has been reduced to the adjusted cost base of the old land.

The $4,600,000 deemed capital cost of the replacement building is equal to the $3,700,000 capital cost of the old building, plus the additional $900,000 ($5,700,000 - $4,800,000) in funds paid by Fraser in excess of the insurance proceeds.

In a similar fashion, the UCC for the new building is equal to the UCC of the old building ($1,856,000), plus the additional $900,000 ($5,700,000 - $4,800,000) in funds paid by Fraser in excess of the insurance proceeds.

The deemed capital cost of the new Class 8 assets is equal to the $972,000 capital cost of the old assets.

In a similar fashion, the UCC for the new Class 8 assets is equal to the $72,000 UCC of the old Class 8 assets. Since the $1,233,000 cost of the replacement assets is less than the $1,256,000 in insurance proceeds, there is no increase in the UCC.

Part D - Optimal Transfer

The ITA 44(6) election applies when there is a disposition involving a combination of part land and part building. If, for either of the assets, the proceeds of disposition exceed the adjusted cost base, the election allows the transfer of all or part of that excess to the other asset.

As will be demonstrated in this problem, this can provide some relief when ITA 44(1) and ITA 13(4) fail to eliminate all of the capital gains arising on one part of the disposition of the old property. ITA 44(1) fully eliminated the capital gain on the building. However, a $223,000 capital gain remained on the land. This would suggest that it could be advantageous to transfer some of the proceeds of disposition from the land to the building.

The excess of the proceeds of disposition of the old land over the cost of the replacement land was $223,000 ($723,000 - $500,000). This is the maximum transfer needed from the land to the building. Since the excess of the cost of the replacement building over the old building's proceeds of disposition is $900,000 ($5,700,000 - $4,800,000), this transfer can be made with creating a capital gain on the building.

Applying ITA 44(6) will result in the following adjusted proceeds of disposition:

	Land	Building
Actual Proceeds Of Disposition	$723,000	$4,800,000
Transfer Needed - Land To Building	(223,000)	223,000
Adjusted Proceeds Of Disposition	$500,000	$5,023,000

Part D - Application To Land

If both the ITA 44(1) and the ITA 44(6) elections are used, the capital gain on the land will be nil, calculated as the lesser of:

- $244,000 ($500,000 - $256,000); and
- Nil (the excess of the $500,000 adjusted proceeds of disposition for the old land over the $500,000 cost of the new land).

Given this result, the adjusted cost base of the replacement property will be calculated as follows:

Actual Cost	$500,000
Capital Gain Reversed By The Two Elections	(244,000)
Deemed Adjusted Cost Base Of Replacement Land	$256,000

Note that this is equal to the adjusted cost base of the old land.

Part D - Application To The Building

With the proceeds of disposition transfer limited to $223,000, the capital gain on the building is still nil. Specifically, the gain will be the lesser of:

- $1,323,000 ($5,023,000 - $3,700,000); and
- Nil (there is still no excess of the $5,023,000 proceeds of disposition over the replacement cost of $5,700,000).

The deemed capital cost and UCC for the building would be calculated as follows:

Actual Cost	$5,700,000
Capital Gain Reversed By The Two Elections	(1,323,000)
Deemed Capital Cost	$4,377,000
Recapture Reversed By ITA 13(4)	(1,844,000)
UCC - Replacement Building	$2,533,000

Part D - Comparison

The table which follows compares the results of using only ITA 44(1) and ITA 13(4) with the results that arise when the ITA 44(6) election is also used.

	No ITA 44(6)	With ITA 44(6)	Difference
Capital Gains			
Land	$ 223,000	Nil	($223,000)
Building	Nil	Nil	
Replacement Property			
Adjusted Cost Base Of Land	$ 256,000	$ 256,000	Nil
Capital Cost Of Building	4,600,000	4,377,000	(223,000)
UCC	2,756,000	2,533,000	(223,000)

Note that this election is not made without a cost. Had the $223,000 been left as a capital gain, tax would have applied on only one-half of the total. While we have eliminated this $111,500 in income, we have given up future CCA for the full amount of the $223,000. In other words, we have given up $223,000 in future deductions in return for eliminating $111,500 of income in 2020.

Solution to Self Study Problem Eight - 17

Employment Income

Paul's commission income of $62,500 is large enough not to limit the deduction of his employment related expenses. The required calculations would be as follows:

Salary	$ 85,000
Additions:	
Commissions	62,500
Stock Option Benefit [(1,500)($19 - $15)]	6,000
Expense Allowance [(12)($2,500)]	30,000
Deductions:	
RPP Contributions	(4,100)
Professional Association Dues	(1,500)
Work Space In The Home Expenses (Note 1)	(2,290)
Automobile Costs	
CCA (Note 2)	(3,960)
Operating Costs [(80%)($6,100)]	(4,880)
Hotel Costs	(11,500)
Airline And Other Transportation	(9,200)
Client Meals And Entertainment [(1/2)($10,400)]	(5,200)
Net Employment Income	$140,870

Note 1 As Paul has commission income, he can deduct 20 percent of all of the costs except the mortgage interest. This will provide a deduction of $2,290 [(20%)($3,400 + $7,200 + $850)].

Note 2 The 2020 CCA would be based on a UCC calculated as though 100 percent of the available CCA had been taken in 2019. The 100 percent CCA for 2019 would be $13,500 [(150%)(30%)($30,000)]. Using this figure, the deductible 2020 CCA would be $3,960 [(80%)(30%)($30,000 - $13,500)]. Note that the original base for CCA is limited to the Class 10.1 maximum of $30,000.

Property Income

The required calculations here would be as follows:

Non-Eligible Dividends	$ 5,400
Gross Up On Non-Eligible Dividends [(15%)($5,400)]	810
Net Rental Income (Note 3)	9,500
Net Property Income	$15,710

Note 3   As the change in use is from personal to business, the base for calculating CCA would be as follows:

Cost Of Building ($250,000 - $75,000)		$175,000
Fair Market Value At Change In Use		
($375,000 - $100,000)	$275,000	
Cost	(175,000)	
Increase In Value (Bump Up)	$100,000	
Inclusion Factor	1/2	50,000
Cost For UCC And CCA Purposes		$225,000
One-Half Net Additions [(1/2)(($225,000)]		(112,500)
CCA Base		$112,500
Rate For Class 1		4%
CCA		$ 4,500

Using this CCA figure, net rental income would be $9,500 ($14,000 - $4,500). Note that, since the change in use involved a transfer from a non-arm's length person, the AccII provisions are not applicable.

Net Taxable Capital Gains

The required calculations here would be as follows:

Stock Option Shares [(1,500)($22 - $19)]		$ 4,500
Sale Of Paintings (Note 4)		Nil
Land Sale		
Total Gain ($350,000 - $100,000)	$250,000	
Reserve For Land Sale (Note 5)	(178,571)	71,429
Change In Use:		
Cottage - Land ($100,000 - $75,000)	$ 25,000	
Cottage - Building ($275,000 - $175,000)	100,000	125,000
Net Capital Gains		$200,929
Inclusion Rate		1/2
Net Taxable Capital Gains		$ 100,465

Note 4   The paintings would be listed personal property, which means that losses are only deductible to the extent of gains on listed personal property. While there was a gain on one painting of $5,000 ($15,000 - $10,000), there was a loss on the second painting of $6,000 ($10,000 - $4,000). This loss can be used to eliminate the gain on the first painting. However, the remaining $1,000 ($6,000 - $5,000) cannot be deducted in the current year. It can be carried back 3 years and forward 7 years to be applied against listed personal property gains in those years.

Note 5   The total proceeds of disposition for the land would be $350,000 [$100,000 + (5)($50,000)]. Given this, the gain on the land would be $250,000 ($350,000 - $100,000). The maximum reserve would be $178,571, the lesser of:

- $178,571 [($250,000)($250,000 ÷ $350,000)]
- $200,000 [($250,000)(20%)(4 - 0)]

Net And Taxable Income

The required calculations here would be as follows:

Net Employment Income	$140,870
Net Property Income	15,710
Net Taxable Capital Gains	100,465
Net Income For Tax Purposes	**$256,879**
Stock Option Deduction [(1/2)($6,000)]	(3,000)
Taxable Income	**$253,879**

Federal Tax Payable

The required calculations here would be as follows:

Tax On First $214,368		$49,645
Tax On Next $39,511 ($253,879 - $214,368) At 33 Percent		13,039
Tax Before Credits		$62,684
Tax Credits:		
Basic Personal Amount	($12,298)	
Spouse ($12,298 - $8,400)	(3,898)	
Canada Caregiver For Child - May	(2,273)	
Transfer Of May's Disability	(8,576)	
Disability Supplement	(5,003)	
Transfer Of Tuition Credit (Note 6)	(5,000)	
Medical Expenses (Note 7)	(14,403)	
EI	(856)	
CPP	(2,732)	
Canada Employment	(1,245)	
Total Credit Base	($56,284	
Rate	15%	(8,443)
Subtotal		$54,241
Charitable Donations Credit (Note 8)		(360)
Non-Eligible Dividend Tax Credit [(9/13)($810)]		(561)
Federal Tax Payable		$53,320

Note 6 The transfer of Virginia's tuition credit would be $5,000, the lesser of:

- $5,000
- $9,350

Note 7 The base for the medical expense tax credit would be calculated as follows:

Total Medical Expenses		$16,800
Lesser Of:		
• [(3%)($256,879)] = $7,706		
• 2020 Threshold Amount = $2,397		(2,397)
Medical Expense Tax Credit Base		$14,403

Note 8 The charitable donations tax credit would be calculated as follows:

15 Percent Of $200		$ 30
33 Percent Of The Lesser Of:		
$1,200 - $200 = $1,000		
$253,879 - $214,368 = $39,511		330
29 Percent Of Nil ($1,200 - $1,200)		Nil
Total Credit		$360

Solution to Self Study Problem Eight - 18

Employment Income

Lorenzo's commission income of $43,000 is large enough not to limit the deduction of his employment related expenses. The required calculations here would be as follows:

Salary	$ 136,000
Additions	
Commissions	43,000
One-Half Total Bonus (Note 1)	11,000
Expense Allowance [(12)($2,500)]	30,000
Stock Option Benefit [(500)($108 - $92)]	8,000
Deductions	
RPP Contributions	(4,200)
Professional Association Dues	(1,500)
Automobile Costs	
CCA (Note 2)	(3,960)
Operating Costs [(80%)($6,300)]	(5,040)
Hotel Costs	(9,700)
Airline And Other Transportation	(5,400)
Client Meals And Entertainment [(1/2)($9,300)]	(4,650)
Workspace In Home Expenses (Note 3)	(978)
Net Employment Income	$ 192,572

Note 1 As the bonus is paid more than 180 days after the employer's year end, the employer will not be able to deduct the accrual in 2020. This, however, does not change Lorenzo's tax position. He will not have to include one-half of the bonus in income until it is paid in 2021.

Note 2 The 2020 CCA would be based on a UCC calculated as though 100 percent of the available CCA had been taken in 2019. The 100 percent CCA of the Class 10.1 vehicle for 2019 would be $13,500 [(150%)(30%)($30,000 maximum)]. Using this figure, the deductible 2020 CCA would be $3,960 [(80%)(30%)($30,000 - $13,500)].

Note 3 As Lorenzo has commission income, he can deduct 12 percent of all of the costs except the mortgage interest. This will provide a deduction of $978 [(12%)($1,250 + $1,300 + $5,600)].

Property Income

The required calculations here would be as follows:

Net Rental Income (Note 4)	$ 2,610
Income Trust Distribution [(500)($2.40)]	1,200
Eligible Dividends	4,200
Gross Up On Eligible Dividends [(38%)($4,200)]	1,596
Total Property Income	$ 9,606

Note 4 As the change in use is from personal to business, the base for calculating CCA would be as follows:

Cost Of Building ($105,000 - $42,000)		$ 63,000
Fair Market Value At Change In Use		
($350,000 - $100,000)	$250,000	
Cost	(63,000)	
Increase In Value (Bump Up)	$187,000	
Inclusion Factor	1/2	93,500
Cost For UCC And CCA Purposes		$156,500
One-Half Net Additions [(1/2)($156,500)]		(78,250)
CCA Base		$ 78,250
Rate For Class 1		4%
CCA		$ 3,130

Using this CCA figure, net rental income would be $2,610 ($5,740 - $3,130). Note that, as the change in use involves a non-arm's length transfer, the AccII provisions are not applicable.

Net Taxable Capital Gains

The required calculations here would be as follows:

Stock Option Shares [(500)($115 - $108)]		$ 3,500
Sculpture (Note 5)		38,000
Change In Use:		
Cottage - Land ($100,000 - $42,000)	$ 58,000	
Cottage - Building ($250,000 - $63,000)	187,000	245,000
Real Property Income Trust (Note 6)		2,161
Land Sale ($180,000 - $78,000)	$102,000	
Reserve For Land Sale (Note 7)	(71,400)	30,600
Net Capital Gains		$319,261
Inclusion Rate		1/2
Net Taxable Capital Gains		$159,631

Note 5 As the actual adjusted cost base of this personal use property is less than $1,000, its deemed adjusted cost base is $1,000 (the floor). This results in a gain of $38,000 ($39,000 - $1,000).

Note 6 The $1,200 income trust distribution was used to acquired 20.51 additional units ($1,200 ÷ $58.50). Using this figure, the capital gain calculation would be:

Proceeds Of Disposition [(520.51)($60.25)]	$31,361
Adjusted Cost Base [(500)($56) + $1,200)]	(29,200)
Capital Gain	$ 2,161

Note 7 The gain on the land would be $102,000 ($180,000 - $78,000). The maximum reserve would be $71,400, the lesser of:

- $71,400 [($102,000)($126,000 ÷ $180,000)]
- $81,600 [($102,000)(20%)(4 - 0)]

Net And Taxable Income

The required calculations here would be as follows:

Net Employment Income	$192,572
Property Income	9,606
Net Taxable Capital Gains	159,631
Deductible CPP ($2,898 - $2,732)	(166)
Net Income For Tax Purposes	$361,643
Stock Option Deduction [(1/2)($8,000)]	(4,000)
Taxable Income	$ 357,643

Federal Tax Payable

The required calculations here would be as follows:

Tax On First $214,368		$49,645
Tax On Next $143,275 ($357,643 - $214,368) At 33 Percent		47,281
Tax Before Credits		$96,926
Tax Credits:		
Basic Personal Amount	($12,298)	
Spouse ($12,298 - $6,300)	(5,998)	
Canada Caregiver For Child - Anita	(2,273)	
Transfer Of Anita's Disability	(8,576)	
Disability Supplement	(5,003)	
Transfer Of Tuition - Lesser Of:		
• Absolute Limit Of $5,000		
• Actual Tuition Of $9,300	(5,000)	
Medical Expenses (Note 8)	(15,228)	
EI	(856)	
CPP	(2,732)	
Canada Employment	(1,245)	
Total Credit Base	($59,209)	
Rate	15%	(8,881)
Subtotal		$88,045
Charitable Donations Credit (Note 9)		(756)
Dividend Tax Credit [(6/11)($1,596)]		(871)
Federal Tax Payable		$86,418

Note 8 The base for the medical expense tax credit would be calculated as follows:

Total Medical Expenses	$ 17,625
Lesser Of:	
• [(3%)($361,643)] = $10,849	
• 2020 Threshold Amount = $2,397	(2,397)
Medical Expense Tax Credit Base	$15,228

Note 9 The charitable donations tax credit would be calculated as follows:

15 Percent Of $200	$ 30
33 Percent Of The Lesser Of:	
$2,200 ($2,400 - $200)	
$143,275 ($357,643 - $214,368)	726
29 Percent Of Nil ($2,200 - $2,200)	Nil
Total Credit	$756

CHAPTER 9

Chapter 9 Learning Objectives

After completing Chapter 9, you should be able to:

1. Identify the major other sources of income that are listed under Subdivision d of the *Income Tax Act* (paragraph [P hereafter] 9-1 to 9-19).
2. Identify the income inclusions from deferred income plans (P 9-20 and 9-21).
3. Apply the rules related to education assistance payments, social assistance, workers' compensation payments, and the universal child care benefit (P 9-22 to 9-27).
4. Determine the deductible amount of CPP contributions on self-employed income (P 9-28 to 9-31).
5. Determine the deductible amount of moving expenses for an individual (P 9-32 to 9-45).

6. Determine the deductible amount of child care expenses (P 9-46 to 9-57).
7. Apply the provisions related to the disability supports deduction (P 9-58 to 9-66).
8. Apply the provisions related to EI benefits and repayments (P 9-67 and 9-68).
9. Explain the general rules for pension income splitting (P 9-69 to 9-77).
10. Explain the tax treatment of child support and spousal support payments and receipts (P 9-78 to 9-87).

11. Determine the taxable portion of annuity payments received (P 9-88 to 9-96).
12. Describe the major features of Tax Free Savings Accounts (P 9-97 to 9-101).
13. Explain the provisions associated with Registered Education Savings Plans, Canada Education Savings Grants, and Canada Learning Bonds (P 9-102 to 9-129).
14. Compare the major features of TFSAs, RRSPs, and RESPs (P 9-130 to 9-138).
15. Describe the major features of Registered Disability Savings Plans (P 9-139 to 9-141).

16. Determine the tax consequences of non-arm's length transfers of property at values other than fair market value (P 9-142 to 9-159).
17. Describe the special rollover provisions applicable to inter vivos transfers of capital property to a spouse (P 9-160 to 9-167).
18. Determine the tax consequences of non-arm's length transfers of depreciable property (P 9-168 to 9-172).
19. Describe the special rollover provisions applicable to inter vivos transfers of farm or fishing property to a child (P 9-173 to 9-176).
20. Explain the basic requirements for deemed dispositions on death and any rollovers available at that time (P 9-177 to 9-186).

21. Apply the income attribution rules to inter vivos transfers of capital property to a spouse and to related individuals who are under the age of 18 (P 9-187 to 9-205).

22. Describe the income attribution rules applicable to transfers to other related parties (P 9-206 to 9-209).
23. Describe some of the anti-avoidance provisions that relate to the income attribution rules (P 9-210 and 9-211).
24. Describe some of the tax planning techniques that are available to mitigate the income attribution rules (P 9-212).

How to Work Through Chapter 9

We recommend the following approach in dealing with the material in this Chapter:

Coverage And Organization Of Chapter 9
- Read paragraph 9-1 to 9-10 (in the textbook).

Inclusions - Pension Benefits, Retiring Allowances, And Death Benefits
- Read paragraph 9-11 to 9-19.

Inclusions - Deferred Income Plans, Scholarships, Social Assistance Payments, Universal Child Care Benefits
- Read paragraph 9-20 to 9-27.

Deductions - CPP Contributions On Self-Employed Earnings
- Read paragraph 9-28 to 9-31.

Deductions - Moving Expenses
- Read paragraph 9-32 to 9-45.
- Do Exercise Nine-1 (in the textbook) and check the solution in this Study Guide.
- Do Self Study Problem Nine-1, which is available on MyLab, and check the solution in this Study Guide.

Deductions - Child Care Expenses
- Read paragraph 9-46 to 9-57.
- Do Exercise Nine-2 and check the solution in this Study Guide.
- Do Self Study Problems Nine-2 and Nine-3 and check the solutions in this Study Guide.

Deductions - Disability Supports Deduction
- Read paragraph 9-58 to 9-66.
- Do Exercise Nine-3 and check the solution in this Study Guide.

Related Inclusions/Deductions - Employment Insurance Benefits
- Read paragraph 9-67 and 9-68.

Related Inclusions/Deductions - Pension Income Splitting
- Read paragraph 9-69 to 9-77.
- Do Exercise Nine-4 and check the solution in this Study Guide.
- Do Self Study Problems Nine-4 and Nine-5 and check the solutions in this Study Guide.

Related Inclusions/Deductions - Spousal And Child Support
- Read paragraph 9-78 to 9-87.
- Do Exercise Nine-5 and check the solution in this Study Guide.

Related Inclusions/Deductions - Annuity Payments Received
- Read paragraph 9-88 to 9-96.
- Do Exercise Nine-6 and check the solution in this Study Guide.

Tax Free Savings Accounts (TFSAs)
- Read paragraph 9-97 to 9-101.

Registered Education Savings Plans (RESPs), Canada Education Savings Grants
- Read paragraph 9-102 to 9-110.
- Do Exercise Nine-7 and check the solution in this Study Guide.
- Read paragraph 9-111 to 9-129.
- Do Self Study Problem Nine-6 and check the solution in this Study Guide.

Comparison of TFSAs, RRSPs, And RESPs
- Read paragraph 9-130 to 9-138.

Registered Disability Savings Plans (RDSPs)
- Read paragraph 9-139 to 9-141.

Non-Arm's Length Transfers Of Property - Inadequate Considerations (ITA 69)
- Read paragraph 9-142 to 9-156.
- Do Exercise Nine-8 and check the solution in this Study Guide.
- Read paragraph 9-157 to 9-159.
- Do Exercise Nine-9 and check the solution in this Study Guide.
- Do Self Study Problem Nine-7 and check the solution in this Study Guide.

Inter Vivos Transfers To A Spouse
- Read paragraph 9-160 to 9-167.
- Do Exercise Nine-10 and check the solution in this Study Guide.

Non-Arm's Length Transfers Of Depreciable Assets
- Read paragraph 9-168 to 9-172.
- Do Exercises Nine-11 and Nine-12 and check the solutions in this Study Guide.
- Do Self Study Problem Nine-8 and check the solution in this Study Guide.

Inter Vivos Transfer Of Farm Or Fishing Property To A Child
- Read paragraph 9-173 to 9-176.
- Do Exercise Nine-13 and check the solution in this Study Guide.

Deemed Dispositions - On Death
- Read paragraph 9-177 to 9-185.
- Do Exercise Nine-14 and check the solution in this Study Guide.
- Read paragraph 9-186.
- Do Self Study Problem Nine-9 and check the solution in this Study Guide.

Income Attribution
- Read paragraph 9-187 to 9-205.
- Do Exercises Nine-15 to Nine-17 and check the solutions in this Study Guide.
- Read paragraph 9-206 to 9-209.
- Do Self Study Problems Nine-10 and Nine-11 and check the solutions in this Study Guide.

Anti-Avoidance Provisions And Tax Planning
- Read paragraph 9-210 to 9-212.
- Do Self Study Problems Nine-12 and Nine-13 and check the solutions in this Study Guide.

To Complete This Chapter
- If you would like more practice in problem solving, do the Supplementary Self Study Problems for the chapter. These are available on MyLab.
- Review the Key Terms Used In This Chapter in the textbook at the end of Chapter 9. Consult the Glossary for the meaning of any key terms you do not know.
- Test yourself with the Chapter 9 Glossary Flashcards available on MyLab.
- Ensure you have achieved the Chapter 9 Learning Objectives listed in this Study Guide.

- As a review, we recommend you view the PowerPoint presentation for Chapter 9 that is on MyLab.

Practice Examination
- Write the Practice Examination for Chapter 9 that is on MyLab. Mark your examination using the Practice Examination Solution that is also on MyLab.

Solutions to Chapter 9 Exercises

Exercise Nine - 1 Solution
Ms. Chevlak cannot deduct the $1,300 house hunting trip. However, this amount can be reimbursed by her employer without creating a taxable benefit. Given these facts, the employer should reimburse this amount directly, with the balance of $4,700 being paid as a general moving allowance. The amount that can be deducted in 2020 against this general allowance, as well as the amount to be carried forward, would be calculated as follows:

Allowance Paid By Employer ($6,000 - $1,300)	$4,700
Moving Costs	(6,400)
Lease Penalty	(1,200)
Available Deduction	($2,900)
Income At New Location = Maximum Deduction	2,000
Carry Forward	($ 900)

The maximum moving expense deduction is limited to $2,000, the income at the new location. The remaining $900 can be carried forward and deducted against income earned at the new location in a subsequent year.

If a $6,000 moving allowance had been paid, the full amount would have been included in employment income with the same deductions of $7,600 ($6,400 + $1,200). After the $2,000 in income, this would have left $400 in income rather than a future deduction of $900. The $1,300 difference is the cost of the house hunting trip.

Exercise Nine - 2 Solution
The deduction will have to be made by the lower income spouse, Mr. Sampras. The deduction will be the least of the following amounts:

- The actual costs of $10,500.
- Annual Child Care Expense Amount of $18,000 [(1)($8,000) + (2)($5,000)].
- 2/3 of Mr. Sampras' earned income, an amount of $13,000 [(2/3)($14,000 + $5,500)].

The least of these three amounts is $10,500.

Exercise Nine - 3 Solution
As Jose is not eligible for the disability tax credit, he will deduct the cost of full time attendant care under ITA 64. When combined with the other disability support costs and the reimbursement, the qualifying costs total $36,000 ($23,000 + $18,000 - $5,000). As this is less than his income from employment, he will be able to deduct the full amount of these costs as his disability supports deduction.

Exercise Nine - 4 Solution
In the absence of pension income splitting John would not pay any taxes for 2020. Joanna's Net Income For Tax Purposes before any OAS clawback would be $92,400 ($85,000 + $7,400). There would be an OAS clawback of $2,002 [(15%)($92,400 - $79,054), leaving Joanna with a Net and Taxable Income of $90,398 ($92,400 - $2,002). Based on this figure, her 2020 Amount Owing would be calculated as follows:

Tax Of First $48,535		$ 7,280
Tax On Next $41,863 ($90,398 - $48,535) At 20.5%		8,582
Total Before Credits		$15,862
Basic Personal	($13,229)	
Credits:		
Spousal ($13,229 - $7,400)	(5,829)	
Age [$7,637 - (15%)($90,177 - $38,508)]	Nil	
Pension	(2,000)	
Spouse's Age	(7,637)	
Total	($28,695)	
Rate	15%	(4,304)
Federal Tax Payable		$11,558
OAS Clawback		2,002
Total Amount Owing - Joanna Only		$13,560

If maximum pension splitting is used, it will give both Joanna and John Net and Taxable Income of $49,900 [($85,000)(1/2) + $7,400]. Since this is below the income threshold, there will be no clawback of OAS for Joanna or John. Based on these figures, the Amount Owing for both Joanna and John would be the same and is calculated as follows:

Tax On First $48,535		$ 7,280
Tax On Next $1,365 ($49,900 - $48,535) At 20.5%		280
Total Before Credits		$ 7,560
Credits:		
Basic Personal	($13,229)	
Age [$7,637 - (15%)($49,900 - $38,508)]	(5,928)	
Pension	(2,000)	
Total	($ 21,157)	
Rate	15%	(3,174)
Federal Tax Payable		$4,386
OAS Clawback		Nil
Total Amount Owing For Each		$ 4,386

With pension income splitting , the total amount owing by Joanna and John would be $8,772 [(2)($4,386)]. This is an improvement of $4,788 over the $13,560 that Joanna would have paid without income splitting . Further savings would be available at the provincial level.

Exercise Nine - 5 Solution
The total required child support is $9,000 [(6 Months)($1,500)] and Sandra's $12,000 [(3)($1,500 + $2,500)] in payments will be allocated to this requirement first. This means that $9,000 of her payment will not be deductible to her or taxable to Jerry. The remaining $3,000 ($12,000 - $9,000) will be considered a payment toward spousal support and will be deductible to Sandra and taxable to Jerry.

Exercise Nine - 6 Solution
A total of $63,492 [(4)($15,873)] in payments will be received from this annuity. The $15,873 will be included in his annual tax return. However, because the annuity was purchased with after tax funds, he is eligible for a deduction equal to:

$$\left[\frac{\$55,000}{\$63,492}\right] [\$15,873] = \underline{\$13,750} \text{ Deduction}$$

As a result, Mr. Hollock's Net Income For Tax Purposes will increase by $2,123 ($15,873 - $13,750) each year.

Exercise Nine - 7 Solution

For 2019, the contributions to Jeanine's RESP total $1,700 ($500 + $1,200). This is within the $2,500 limit for contributions eligible for CESGs. This means that the 2019 CESG would be calculated as follows:

First $500 At 40 Percent	$200
Remaining $1,200 ($1,700 - $500) At 20 Percent	240
Total CESG For 2019	$440

For 2020, the contributions to Jeanine's RESP total $3,900 ($1,500 + $2,400). The CESG room is limited to $3,300 [(2)($2,500) - $1,700 from the previous year]. This means that $600 ($3,900 - $3,300) of the total contributions will not be eligible for CESGs. Given this, the 2020 CESG would be calculated as follows:

First $500 At 40 Percent	$200
Remaining $2,800 ($3,300 - $500) At 20 Percent	560
Total CESG For 2020	$760

If it is expected that annual contributions to Jeanine's RESP will be less than $2,500 in the future, this would suggest that Jeanine's father should limit his 2020 contribution to $900 and defer the extra $600 to the following year. In that year, it would be eligible for the CESG.

Exercise Nine - 8 Solution

Mr. Lipky's proceeds of disposition will be the amount received of $95,000, resulting in a capital loss of $5,000 ($95,000 - $100,000). His brother's adjusted cost base will be the fair market value of the land, or $75,000, and he will have no gain or loss on his sale at $75,000. In this case, the application of the ITA 69 rules has resulted in the potential loss of $20,000 ($95,000 - $75,000) not being available to either Carl Lipky or his brother.

Exercise Nine - 9 Solution

Under ITA 69(1.2), the proceeds of disposition in this case will be the greater of the $33,000 actual proceeds and the $211,000 fair market value of the property without considering the lease. The greater amount would be $211,000, resulting in a taxable capital gain for Mr. Bates of $89,000 [(1/2)($211,000 - $33,000)]. The adjusted cost base to the corporation would be the actual transfer price of $33,000. This would lead to double taxation on a subsequent sale of the property on the difference between $211,000 and $33,000.

Exercise Nine - 10 Solution

ITA 73(1) Applies   If Mr. Schwartz does not elect out of ITA 73(1), the results are as follows:

- His deemed proceeds of disposition will be equal to the $225,000 adjusted cost base of the land. Given this, there will be no tax consequences as a result of this transfer.
- The adjusted cost base to his spouse will be deemed to be $225,000, despite the fact that she paid $300,000 for the land.

Elect Out Of ITA 73(1)   If Mr. Schwartz elects out of ITA 73(1):

- The adjusted cost base of the land to his spouse will be $300,000, the amount she paid.

- He will have to include a taxable capital gain in his Net Income For Tax Purposes calculated as follows:

Proceeds Of Disposition	$300,000
Adjusted Cost Base	(225,000)
Capital Gain	$ 75,000
Inclusion Rate	1/2
Taxable Capital Gain	$ 37,500

Exercise Nine - 11 Solution

ITA 73(1) Applies   If Ms. Sharp does not elect out of ITA 73(1), the results will be as follows:

- The deemed proceeds to Ms. Sharp will be the $110,000 UCC value, resulting in no tax consequences for her at the time of transfer.
- For CCA and recapture purposes the spouse will receive the property at $110,000.
- Despite the fact that her spouse paid $225,000, he would retain her $175,000 capital cost, with the difference between $175,000 and the $110,000 UCC balance considered to be deemed CCA.

Elect Out Of ITA 73(1)   If Ms. Sharp elects out of ITA 73(1):

- For capital gains purposes, the capital cost for Ms. Sharp's spouse would be $225,000. However, for CCA and recapture purposes, ITA 13(7)(e) would deem the spouse's capital cost to be $200,000 [($175,000 + (1/2)($225,000 - $175,000)].
- She will include the following amounts in her Net Income For Tax Purposes:

Proceeds Of Disposition	$ 225,000
Capital Cost	(175,000)
Capital Gain	$ 50,000
Inclusion Rate	1/2
Taxable Capital Gain	$ 25,000

UCC	$ 110,000
Deduct Lesser Of:	
Proceeds Of Disposition = $225,000	
Capital Cost = $175,000	(175,000)
Negative Ending Balance = Recapture Of CCA	($ 65,000)

Exercise Nine - 12 Solution

Ms. Lee   The tax consequence for Ms. Lee is as follows:

UCC For Ms. Lee	$ 37,200
Deduct Lesser Of:	
Proceeds Of Disposition = $40,000	
Capital Cost = $53,000	(40,000)
Negative Ending Balance = Recapture Of CCA	($ 2,800)

Ms. Lee's Father   As this was a non-arm's length transfer at a value below the transferor's capital cost, ITA 13(7)(e) will deem the father's capital cost to be equal to Ms. Lee's capital cost of $53,000. The $13,000 difference between this value and the $40,000 he paid for the asset is treated as deemed CCA, resulting in a UCC value of $40,000. When he later sells the asset for $44,000, the result will be as follows:

UCC For Ms. Lee's Father	$40,000
Deduct Lesser Of:	
Proceeds Of Disposition = $44,000	
Deemed Capital Cost = $53,000	(44,000)
Negative Ending Balance = Recapture Of CCA	($ 4,000)

Exercise Nine - 13 Solution

With respect to the land, the $280,000 paid is between the $250,000 adjusted cost base floor and the $325,000 fair market value ceiling. Therefore, the proceeds of disposition would be $280,000, resulting in a taxable capital gain for Mr. Nobel of $15,000 [(1/2)($280,000 - $250,000)]. The $280,000 would also be the adjusted cost base for his daughter.

With respect to the barn, as there was no consideration given, the transfer would take place at the UCC floor of $85,000. There would be no tax consequences for Mr. Nobel. With respect to his daughter, she would assume a UCC value of $85,000 but would retain the original capital cost of $115,000. The $30,000 difference would be considered deemed CCA.

Exercise Nine - 14 Solution

With respect to truck A, it would be transferred to her husband at its UCC value of $25,500 [(1/2)($51,000)]. No income would be included in Ms. Lardner's final tax return and, while the UCC value for the truck in Michel's hands would be the $25,500 transfer value, it would retain its original capital cost of $42,000 with the difference between the two values being treated as deemed CCA.

Truck B would be transferred to Melinda at its fair market value of $33,000. This means that the proceeds of disposition for the two trucks would be $58,500 ($25,500 + $33,000). This would result in recapture of $7,500 ($51,000 - $58,500) being included in Ms. Lardner's final tax return. The $33,000 transfer price would be the UCC value to Melinda. Since Ms. Lardner's original capital cost exceeds the $33,000 fair market value, Melinda would retain Ms. Lardner's $42,000 capital cost with the difference between the two values being treated as deemed CCA.

Exercise Nine - 15 Solution

> **NOTE**   You may find it helpful to review Exercises Nine-10 and Nine-11 before completing this Exercise as many students find the rules related to the ITA 73(1) rollovers difficult to understand.

ITA 73(1) provides for a tax free rollover of capital property to a spouse. The tax consequences for Mr. and Mrs. Moreau for the two years can be outlined as follows:

- 2019 for Mr. Moreau - none.
- 2019 for Mrs. Moreau - none.
- 2020 for Mr. Moreau - none.
- 2020 for Mrs. Moreau - total income of $12,950. She would have taxable dividends of $3,450 and the taxable capital gain of $9,500 [(1/2)($42,000 - $23,000)] attributed to her.

Exercise Nine - 16 Solution

There is no provision for a tax free transfer of shares to a child. The tax consequences for Norah and Nicki Moreau for the two years can be outlined as follows:

- 2019 for Nicki - none.
- 2019 for Norah - a taxable capital gain of $7,000 [(1/2)($37,000 - $23,000)].
- 2020 for Nicki - a taxable capital gain of $2,500 [(1/2)($42,000 - $37,000)].
- 2020 for Norah - taxable dividends of $3,450 attributed to her.

Exercise Nine - 17 Solution

Since Mr. Bronski does not elect out of ITA 73(1) by including a gain on his tax return at the time of the transfer, the income attribution rules will apply. Even if he did elect out of ITA 73(1), the rules would still apply as the loan does not bear interest at the prescribed rate.

There will be no tax consequences for either Mr. or Mrs. Bronski in 2019. Because the transfer is a tax free rollover, the adjusted cost base of the bonds to Mrs. Bronski will be $115,000. All of the 2020 interest income of $6,100 will be attributed to Mr. Bronski. In addition to the interest of $6,100, there would be a taxable capital gain of $7,000 [(1/2)($129,000 - $115,000)], which would also be attributed to Mr. Bronski. The total addition to Mr. Bronski's income for 2020 is $13,100 ($6,100 + $7,000). There will be no tax consequences for Mrs. Bronski in 2020.

Solution to Self Study Problem Nine - 1

Costs for food and lodging at or near an old or new residence are limited to a maximum period of 15 days. Note that the 9 days spent traveling to Vancouver are not included in the 15 day total. Since the daily costs for her Montreal stay are higher than those for her Vancouver stay, she claims the 15 day maximum at the Montreal rate.

The deductible moving expenses can be calculated as follows:

House Hunting Trip Hotel And Food (Not Deductible)		Nil
Real Estate Commission - Montreal Home		$27,500
Legal Fees - Montreal Home		800
Other Montreal Home Costs (Not Deductible)		Nil
Storage Costs		2,200
Moving Company Charges		10,200
Hotel In Montreal (15 Nights At $350)		5,250
Food - Maximum (15 Days At $51 Flat Rate)		765
Expenses Of Travel To Vancouver:		
Gas (Using Simplified Method)	Nil	
Simplified Mileage Rate		
[(4,558 @ $0.58)	$2,644	
Hotel (9 Nights - Total)	1,575	
Food (9 Days At $51 Simplified Rate)	459	4,678
Vancouver Hotel		Nil
Moving Expense Deductions Available		$51,393

Moving costs can only be deducted against "income earned at the new work location". This raises the question as to whether the general moving allowance, compensation for house loss, and payment for higher housing costs would fall into this category. It would be our view that since these amounts were paid by the Vancouver office subsequent to Michelle commencing work at that location, they would qualify. Based on this view, the total employment income at the new work location would be as follows:

Salary At New Location (One Month @ $15,000)	$15,000
General Moving Allowance	20,000
Compensation For Loss On Montreal Residence (Note 1)	30,000
Payment For Higher Housing Costs (Note 2)	10,000
Total Employment Income At New Location	$75,000

Note 1 Under ITA 6(20), one-half of any housing loss reimbursement in excess of $15,000 must be included in income. As the total reimbursement was $75,000 ($625,000 - $550,000), the inclusion would be $30,000 [(1/2)($75,000 - $15,000)].

Note 2 Any amounts paid to compensate an employee for higher housing costs must be included in income in full.

As the deductible costs are less than the income at the new location, they are fully deductible in Michelle's 2020 tax return. There would be no carry forward of moving costs

Solution to Self Study Problem Nine - 2

Mrs. Fortin

Generally, the spouse with the lower income must claim the deduction for child care expenses. However, under certain circumstances, for example if this spouse is hospitalized, the spouse with the higher income can claim the deduction for the period of hospitalization. Thus Mrs. Fortin can claim the least of the following:

	Case A	Case B
Actual Payments [($400)(48)]	$19,200	$19,200
2/3 Of Earned Income [(2/3)($84,000)]	$56,000	$56,000
Annual Expense Limit:		
Case A [(2)($8,000)]	$16,000	
Case B [(2)($8,000) + (1)($5,000)]		$21,000
Periodic Expense Limit:		
Case A [(2)($200)(6 weeks)]	$ 2,400	
Case B {[(2)($200)(6 weeks)] + [(1)($125)(6 weeks)]}		$ 3,150

In Case A, the least of these figures is $2,400, the Periodic Expense Limit. In Case B, the least of the figures is $3,150, also the Periodic Expense Limit.

Mr. Fortin

The calculations for Mr. Fortin are as follows:

	Case A	Case B
Actual Payments	$19,200	$ 19,200
2/3 Of Earned Income [(2/3)($8,000)]	$ 5,333	$ 5,333
Annual Expense Limit:		
Case A [(2)($8,000)]	$16,000	
Case B [(2)($8,000) + (1)($5,000)]		$21,000

The lowest figure in both cases is $5,333, two-thirds of Mr. Fortin's earned income. Mr. Fortin's deduction for the current year will be reduced by the amount claimed by Mrs. Fortin. Mr. Fortin's deduction for the current year is $2,933 ($5,333 - $2,400) in Case A and $2,183 ($5,333 - $3,150) in Case B.

Solution to Self Study Problem Nine - 3

The deductible actual costs are as follows:

Actual Costs Excluding Camp Costs (48 weeks At $260)	$12,480
Periodic Cost Limit For Camp Weeks	
[($125)(1)(4 weeks) + ($200)(1)(4 weeks) + ($275)(1)(4 weeks)]	2,400
Deductible Actual Costs	$14,880

Generally, the common-law partner with the lower income must claim the deduction for child care expenses. In this case, that would be Sue Brendal. However, under certain circumstances, the common-law partner with the higher income can claim a deduction that is subject to a weekly limitation.

One of these circumstances is when the lower income common-law partner is in attendance on a full time basis at a designated educational institution. This means that for the five week period that Sue is attending the accounting course, Maureen can deduct limited child care expenses.

The relevant calculations for determining the deductible costs for each individual are as follows:

	Maureen	Sue
Actual Costs And Limited Camp Costs	$ 14,880	$ 14,880
Annual Expense Limit [($5,000)(1) + ($8,000)(1) + ($11,000)(1)]	$ 24,000	$ 24,000
2/3 Of Earned Income [(2/3)($216,000)] [(2/3)($24,000)]	$ 144,000	$ 16,000
Periodic Expense Limit [($125)(1)(5 weeks) + ($200)(1)(5 weeks) + ($275)(1)(5 weeks)]	$ 3,000	N/A

The least of these amounts for Maureen is $3,000. You should note that there is no requirement that actual payments be allocated on the basis of the time that Sue was attending the accounting course.

The lowest figure for Sue is $14,880, the actual child care costs. Sue's deduction for the current year of $11,880 ($14,880 - $3,000) has been reduced by the amount claimed by Maureen.

As Maureen is the higher income common-law partner, her three week stay in the hospital has no effect on the child care expense calculations.

Solution to Self Study Problem Nine - 4

Net And Taxable Income

John's Income	No Split	With Split
Pension Receipt	$64,000	$64,000
Net Rental Income	23,000	23,000
Pension Income To Fatima	N/A	(32,000)
Net And Taxable Income	$ 87,000	$55,000

Fatima's Income	No Split	With Split
Interest Income	$ 8,400	$ 8,400
Pension Income From John	N/A	32,000
Net And Taxable Income	$ 8,400	$40,400

Federal Tax Payable With No Pension Income Splitting

Fatima   Fatima's federal Tax Payable with no pension income splitting would be calculated as follows:

Tax Before Credits [(15%)($8,400)]	$1,260
Basic Personal Credit [(15%)($13,229)]	(1,984)
Federal Tax Payable - Fatima	Nil

John Without pension income splitting, John's Tax Payable would be calculated as follows:

Tax Of First $48,535		$ 7,280
Tax On Next $38,465 ($87,000 - $48,535) At 20.5%		7,885
Total Before Credits		$15,165
Credits:		
Basic Personal	($13,229)	
Spousal ($13,229 - $8,400)	(4,829)	
Pension	(2,000)	
Total	($ 20,058)	
Rate	15%	(3,009)
Federal Tax Payable - John		$12,156

Federal Tax Payable With Pension Income Splitting

Fatima When pension income splitting is used, Fatima's Tax Payable would be as follows:

Tax Before Credits [(15%)($40,400)]		$6,060
Credits:		
Basic Personal	($13,229)	
Pension	(2,000)	
Total	($15,229)	
Rate	15%	(2,284)
Federal Tax Payable - Fatima		$3,776

John With pension income splitting, John's Tax Payable would be calculated as follows:

Tax On First $48,535		$7,280
Tax On Next $6,465 ($55,000 - $48,535) At 20.5%		1,325
Tax Before Credits		$8,605
Credits:		
Basic Personal	($13,229)	
Spousal	Nil	
Pension	(2,000)	
Total	($15,229)	
Rate	15%	(2,284)
Federal Tax Payable - John		$6,321

Comparison

Federal Tax Payable Without Income Splitting (John Only)	$12,156
Federal Tax Payable With Income Splitting ($3,776 + $6,321)	(10,097)
Savings With Pension Income Splitting	$ 2,059

Solution to Self Study Problem Nine - 5

Part A - Net And Taxable Income

Martin's Income	Scenario 1	Scenario 2
Pension Receipt	$124,000	$124,000
Pension Income To Sally	N/A	(62,000)
OAS	N/A	7,400
Net Income Before OAS Clawback	$124,000	$ 69,400
OAS Clawback (Notes 1 and 2)	N/A	N/A
Net And Taxable Income - Martin	$124,000	$ 69,400

Sally's Income	Scenario 1	Scenario 2
OAS	$ 7,400	$ 7,400
Interest Earned	43,000	43,000
Pension Income From Martin	N/A	62,000
Net Income Before OAS Clawback	$50,400	$ 112,400
OAS Clawback (Note 3)	Nil	(5,002)
Net And Taxable Income - Sally	$50,400	$107,398

Note 1 As Martin did not apply for OAS in Scenario 1, there can be no clawback.

Note 2 In Scenario 2, Martin's Net Income is less than the clawback income threshold of $79,054, so there is no clawback

Note 3 With pension income splitting , the OAS clawback for Sally would be $5,002 [(15%)($112,400 - $79,054)].

Part B - Scenario 1

Without pension income splitting, Martin's Amount Owing would be calculated as follows:

Tax On First $97,069		$17,230
Tax On Next $26,931 ($124,000 - $97,069) At 26%		7,002
Tax Before Credits		$24,232
Credits:		
Basic Personal	($13,229)	
Age [$7,637 - (15%)($124,000 - $38,508)	Nil	
Pension	(2,000)	
Total	($ 15,229)	
Rate	15%	(2,284)
Federal Tax Payable		$21,948
OAS Clawback		N/A
Total Amount Owing - Martin		$21,948

Without pension income splitting, Sally's Amount Owing would be calculated as follows:

Tax On First $48,535		$7,280
Tax On Next $1,865 ($50,400 - $48,535) At 20.5%		382
Tax Before Credits		$7,662
Credits:		
Basic Personal	($13,229)	
Age [$7,637 - (15%)($50,400 - $38,508)	(5,853)	
Disability	(8,576)	
Total	($ 27,658)	
Rate	15%	(4,149)
Total Amount Owing (No Clawback) - Sally		$3,513

Part B - Scenario 2

With pension income splitting and the OAS payments, Martin's Amount Owing would be calculated as follows:

Tax On First $48,535		$ 7,280
Tax On Next $20,865 ($69,400 - $48,535) At 20.5%		4,277
Tax Before Credits		$11,557
Credits:		
Basic Personal	($13,229)	
Age [$7,637 - (15%)($69,400 - $38,508)]	(3,003)	
Pension	(2,000)	
Total	($ 18,232)	
Rate	15%	(2,735)
Total Amount Owing (No Clawback) - Martin		$ 8,822

With pension income splitting, Sally's Amount Owing would be calculated as follows:

Tax On First $97,069		$ 17,230
Tax On Next $10,329 ($107,398 - $97,069) At 26%		2,686
Tax Before Credits		$19,916
Credits:		
Basic Personal	($13,229)	
Age [$7,637 - (15%)($107,398 - $38,508)]	Nil	
Disability	(8,576)	
Pension	(2,000)	
Total	($ 23,805)	
Rate	15%	(3,571)
Federal Tax Payable		$16,345
OAS Clawback		5,002
Total Amount Owing - Sally		$21,347

Part B - Comparison Of After Tax Income

This amount would be calculated as follows:

Amount Owing - Scenario 1 ($21,948 + $3,513)		$25,461
Amount Owing - Scenario 2 ($8,822 + $21,347)	($30,169)	
OAS Benefits Received - Scenario 2	7,400	(22,769)
Cash Advantage - Scenario 2		$ 2,292

This problem illustrates the complexity associated with pension income splitting. Although Scenario 2 served to make the incomes more equal, it had several negative side effects (e.g., the clawback of a large part of Sally's OAS, as well as the elimination of her age credit.) However, there is a definite cash advantage to Scenario 2.

The result would be improved if pension income splitting were limited to an amount that would give Martin a Net Income of the OAS clawback income threshold, as that would reduce Sally's OAS clawback without clawing back his OAS. However, that may not be the best solution. Finding the optimum solution is not an intuitive process, especially if there are other factors such as medical costs, and would require the use of tax software

Solution to Self Study Problem Nine - 6

Part A - Net Income For Tax Purposes

The minimum Net Income For Tax Purposes that can be reported by Mr. Masters is calculated as follows:

Wages From Summer Employment		5,400
Moving Costs To Pelican Lake (Note 1)		(350)
Scholarship Received	$3,500	
Exempt Portion Of Scholarship (100%)	(3,500)	Nil
Moving Costs To Winnipeg (Note 1)		Nil
Eligible Dividends Received		2,000
Gross Up Of Dividends (38 Percent)		760
Child Support Received (Note 2)		Nil
Inheritance (Not Taxable)		Nil
TFSA Contributions (Note 3)		Nil
TFSA Withdrawal (Note 3)		Nil
Net Income For Tax Purposes		$ 7,810

Note 1 The cost of the move to Pelican Lake is deductible against the income that was earned there as it is more than 40 kilometres from Winnipeg. Since there was no addition to his Net Income For Tax Purposes due to his scholarship, he cannot deduct the cost of the move back to Winnipeg.

Note 2 While spousal support is taxable to the recipient and deductible to the payor, child support is not taxable to the recipient or deductible to the payor.

Note 3 TFSA contributions and withdrawals have no tax consequences since the total $20,000 contributed is less than the maximum contribution allowable. There is also no income attribution as a result of the TFSA contribution by Mr. Masters' wife.

Part B - Registered Education Savings Plan

Payments into an RESP are not deductible. However, no tax liability is created by the amounts earned on the assets held in the plan. Rather, the earnings of these assets will be taxed in the hands of the recipient (presumably Mr. Masters' son) when the funds are withdrawn. However, to be eligible to receive these payments, the child must be in full time or part time attendance at an institution that would qualify the child for the education tax credit.

Mr. Masters must obtain information regarding the contribution room available for the Canada Education Savings Grant (CESG). Since his parents have been contributing to the RESP, it is not possible to determine how much CESG his son has available without more information.

Given his wife's profession, it is likely the family income is far too high to qualify for the Canada Learning Bonds program. As a result, that program would have no impact on any advice related to Mr. Masters' son's RESP.

Solution to Self Study Problem Nine - 7

Part A - Case 1 - Sale To Arm's Length Party
The result for Martin would be as follows:

Proceeds Of Disposition	$500,000
Adjusted Cost Base	(360,000)
Capital Gain	$140,000
Inclusion Rate	1/2
Taxable Capital Gain	$ 70,000

With respect to the subsequent sale by the arm's length purchaser, the results for that individual would be as follows:

Proceeds Of Disposition	$500,000
Adjusted Cost Base	(500,000)
Capital Gain	Nil

Part A - Case 2 - Sale To Sister
The result for Martin would be as follows:

Deemed Proceeds Of Disposition - ITA 69(1)(b)	$500,000
Adjusted Cost Base	(360,000)
Capital Gain	$140,000
Inclusion Rate	1/2
Taxable Capital Gain	$ 70,000

With respect to the subsequent sale by Martin's sister, the results for her would be as follows:

Proceeds Of Disposition (Actual)	$500,000
Adjusted Cost Base	(360,000)
Capital Gain	$140,000
Inclusion Rate	1/2
Taxable Capital Gain	$ 70,000

Note that in this case the $140,000 capital gain is subject to double taxation.

Part A - Case 3 - Gift To Son
The result for Martin would be as follows:

Deemed Proceeds Of Disposition - ITA 69(1)(b)	$500,000
Adjusted Cost Base	(360,000)
Capital Gain	$140,000
Inclusion Rate	1/2
Taxable Capital Gain	$ 70,000

With respect to the subsequent sale by Martin's son, the results for him would be as follows:

Proceeds Of Disposition	$500,000
Adjusted Cost Base (Actual)	(500,000)
Capital Gain	Nil

The fact that his son is younger than 18 years of age does not affect the results.

Part A - Case 4 - Sale To Mother

The result for Martin would be as follows:

Proceeds Of Disposition (Actual)	$600,000
Adjusted Cost Base	(360,000)
Capital Gain	$240,000
Inclusion Rate	1/2
Taxable Capital Gain	$120,000

With respect to the subsequent sale by Martin's mother, the results for her would be as follows:

Proceeds Of Disposition (Actual)	$500,000
Adjusted Cost Base - ITA 69(1)(a)	(500,000)
Capital Gain	Nil

Despite the fact that Martin had to record the actual proceeds of $600,000, his mother's adjusted cost base will be the fair market value of $500,000, resulting in double taxation of the $100,000 excess of the original sale price over the asset's fair market value. This means that she did not have a $100,000 capital loss to economically offset (for the family unit) the effect of his capital gain.

Part B

In Case 2, the sale was for $360,000, less than the $500,000 fair market value of the asset. Martin might agree to do this in an attempt to transfer the $140,000 gain to his sister. This could be motivated by the fact that she is in a lower tax bracket. It could also reflect the fact that she has unused capital losses that she would like to be able to use.

In Case 4, the sale was for $600,000, more than the $500,000 fair market value of the asset. The motivation here could be that his mother has capital gains that she would like to offset with a capital loss resulting from her re-selling the asset for $500,000 and/or Martin has unused capital losses greater than $140,000 that he would like to be able to use.

Solution to Self Study Problem Nine - 8

Scenario 1 - FMV > Transferor's Capital Cost

The results of the disposition for Martin can be calculated as follows:

UCC Balance	$36,000
Lesser Of:	
Proceeds Of Disposition = $87,000	
Capital Cost = $52,000	(52,000)
Negative Ending UCC Balance = Recapture Of CCA	($16,000)

Proceeds Of Disposition	$87,000
Capital Cost	(52,000)
Capital Gain	$35,000
Inclusion Rate	1/2
Taxable Capital Gain	$17,500

Martin's Net Income For Tax Purposes will increase by $33,500 ($16,000 + $17,500).

For his sister, her capital cost for capital gains purposes will be the transfer price of $87,000. However, because the fair market value of the asset exceeded its original capital cost, ITA 13(7)(e) will limit the value used for CCA and recapture calculations to the following amount:

$$[\$52,000 + (1/2)(\$87,000 - \$52,000)] = \$69,500$$

Scenario 2 - FMV < Transferor's Capital Cost

The results of this disposition for Marion can be calculated as follows:

UCC Balance	$105,000
Lesser Of:	
Proceeds Of Disposition = $142,000	
Capital Cost = $212,000	(142,000)
Negative Ending UCC Balance = Recapture Of CCA	($ 37,000)

Marion's Net Income For Tax Purposes will increase by $37,000.

In this case, where the fair market value of the asset is less than its capital cost, ITA 13(7)(e) deems the transferee's capital cost of the transferred asset to be equal to the transferor's capital cost, an amount of $212,000. This capital cost will be used for purposes of determining any capital gain and/or recapture on a future disposition.

The $70,000 ($212,000 - $142,000) difference between this value and the transfer price will be considered deemed CCA. The resulting UCC balance of $142,000 will be used by Marion's brother for calculating future CCA.

Solution to Self Study Problem Nine - 9

Note To Student   Part B of this problem requires knowledge of ITA 13(21.1) as there is a capital gain on the land and a terminal loss on the building. This provision is covered in detail in Chapter 8.

Case A(1)

Assuming that the transfer was to Margarette's spouse, the land would have been transferred at its cost and the building would have been transferred at its UCC. As a consequence, there would have been no tax effects to be included in Margarette's final return.

For CCA purposes, the building would have been transferred at Margarette's UCC of $363,000. Given this, maximum CCA would be $14,520 [(4%)($363,000)] for 2020 leaving a UCC of $348,480. Since the acquisition of the building is a non-arm's length transaction, it was used and continues to be used to produce income and was owned for more than one year by Margarette, the half year rule does not apply to Gianni.

Note, however, that after the transfer, Gianni would have retained the building's old capital cost of $473,000. Using this figure for the building, the tax effects that would occur at the time of the 2021 sale of the property would be as follows:

	Land	Building
Proceeds Of Disposition	$160,000	$525,000
Adjusted Cost Base/Capital Cost	(150,000)	(473,000)
Capital Gain	$ 10,000	$ 52,000
Inclusion Rate	1/2	1/2
Taxable Capital Gain	$ 5,000	$ 26,000
UCC		$348,480
Deduct Disposition - Lesser Of:		
• Capital Cost = $473,000		
• Proceeds Of Disposition = $525,000		(473,000)
Negative Closing UCC Balance = Recaptured CCA		($ 124,520)

A total of $155,520 ($5,000 + $26,000 + $124,520) would be added to the 2021 Net Income For Tax Purposes of Gianni. With the death of Margarette, there can be no income or capital gains attributed to her from Gianni.

Case A(2)

As the transfer was to her daughter, Ciara, the deemed proceeds will be recorded at fair market value for the land and building. Based on this, the following calculations show the tax effects that will be included in Margarette's final return:

	Land	Building
Deemed Proceeds	$ 175,000	$ 571,000
Adjusted Cost Base/Capital Cost	(150,000)	(473,000)
Capital Gain	$ 25,000	$ 98,000
Inclusion Rate	1/2	1/2
Taxable Capital Gain	$ 12,500	$ 49,000
UCC		$363,000
Deduct Disposition - Lesser Of:		
• Capital Cost = $473,000		
• Deemed Proceeds = $571,000		(473,000)
Negative Closing UCC Balance = Recaptured CCA		($ 110,000)

A total of $171,500 ($12,500 + $49,000 + $110,000) would be added to Margarette's 2020 Net Income For Tax Purposes.

With respect to Ciara's tax records, the land will have a tax cost of $175,000 and the building will be a Class 1 asset with a tax cost equal to Margarette's deemed proceeds of $571,000.

Maximum 2020 CCA is $22,840 [($571,000)(4%)], leaving a UCC of $548,160 ($571,000 - $22,840). Since the acquisition of the building is a non-arm's length transaction, it was used and continues to be used to produce income, and was owned for more than one year by Margarette, the half year rule does not apply to Ciara. In addition, ITA 13(7)(e), which requires the calculation of a limited UCC balance, is not applicable to transfers at death.

Since there cannot be a capital loss on depreciable property and the building is the only asset in the class, the 2021 tax effects associated with the sale of the building would be calculated as follows:

	Land	Building
Proceeds Of Disposition	$ 160,000	$525,000
Adjusted Cost Base	(175,000)	
Capital Cost Limited To Proceeds		($525,000)
Capital Gain (Loss)	($ 15,000)	Nil
Inclusion Rate	1/2	N/A
Allowable Capital Loss	($ 7,500)	Nil
UCC		$ 548,160
Deduct Disposition - Lesser Of:		
• Capital Cost = $571,000		
• Proceeds Of Disposition = $525,000		(525,000)
Positive Closing UCC Balance = Terminal Loss		$ 23,160

A total of $30,660 ($23,160 + $7,500) would be deducted from the 2021 Net Income For Tax Purposes of Ciara as the problem indicates that she has sufficient income and taxable capital gains.

Comparison Case A(1) And A(2)

The overall tax consequences in the two cases are as shown in the following table:

	Case A(1) Gianni	Case A(2) Margarette	Case A(2) Ciara
2020	Nil	$171,500	Nil
2020 - CCA Taken	($ 14,520)		($22,840)
2021	155,520		(30,660)
Net Income For Tax Purposes (Loss)	$141,000	$171,500	($ 53,500)

There is a difference in the Case A(1) and Case A(2) results of $23,000 [$141,000 - ($171,500 - $53,500)]. This reflects the fact that, in Case A(2), a portion of the amount that was taxed as a capital gain (50 percent) in Margarette's final return was deducted by Ciara as CCA and a terminal loss (100 percent).

This can be shown in the following calculation:

Actual Sale Price Of Building For Ciara	$525,000
Fair Market Value (Deemed Proceeds) At Death	(571,000)
Amount Deducted By Ciara As CCA And Terminal Loss*	($ 46,000)
Portion Taxed As Capital Gain In Final Return [(1/2)($46,000)]	23,000
Difference	($ 23,000)

*$23,160 + $22,840 = $46,000

Part B

If the proceeds of the sale of the property by Ciara were allocated $300,000 to the land and $385,000 to the building, the tax effects associated with the sale of the building would be initially calculated as follows.

	Land	Building
Proceeds Of Disposition	$300,000	$ 385,000
Adjusted Cost Base	(175,000)	
Capital Cost Limited To Proceeds		(385,000)
Capital Gain	$125,000	Nil
Inclusion Rate	1/2	1/2
Taxable Capital Gain	$ 62,500	Nil

	Building
UCC	$ 548,160
Deduct Disposition - Lesser Of: • Capital Cost = $571,000 • Proceeds Of Disposition= $385,000	(385,000)
Positive Closing UCC Balance = Terminal Loss	$ 163,160

Since there is a capital gain on the land and a terminal loss on the building, ITA 13(21.1)(a) requires the deemed proceeds of disposition for the building to be determined as follows:

The Lesser Of:

- The FMV of the land and building $685,000
  Reduced By The Lesser Of:
  - The ACB of the land = $175,000
  - The FMV of the land = $300,000   (175,000) $510,000

- The Greater Of:
  - The FMV of the building = $385,000
  - The Lesser Of:
    The cost of the building = $571,000
    The UCC of the building = $548,160 $548,160

The proceeds that would be allocated to the building would be $510,000, leaving $175,000 ($685,000 - $510,000) to be allocated to the land. The net result is that the terminal loss would be reduced by $125,000 (the amount of the potential capital gain) to $38,160 ($510,000 - $548,160) and the capital gain would be nil ($175,000 - $175,000).

Solution to Self Study Problem Nine - 10

Alonso
At Transfer
As Alonso did not elect out of the ITA 73(1) spousal rollover, no income will result from the transfer to his spouse, Alice. However, there is no rollover for the transfer of public company shares to a related minor. This means there will be a taxable capital gain on the transfer of 10,000 shares to his son as follows:

Deemed Proceeds Of Disposition [($17.00)(10,000)]	$170,000
Adjusted Cost Base [($12.50)(10,000)]	(125,000)
Capital Gain	$ 45,000
Inclusion Rate	1/2
Taxable Capital Gain	$ 22,500

Dividends
As all of the shares were given to a spouse and a related minor, 100 percent of the dividends would be attributed back to Alonso. His increase in Net Income For Tax Purposes due to the dividends would be $16,560 [(15,000)(138%)($0.80)].

Sale Of Shares
As there is no attribution of capital gains when shares are transferred to a related minor, the sale of shares by Alonso's son would have no effect on Alonso's 2020 Net Income For Tax Purposes. However, the gain on the sale of shares by his spouse would be attributed back to Alonso. The amount is calculated as follows:

Proceeds Of Disposition [($16.00)(5,000)]	$80,000
Adjusted Cost Base [($12.50)(5,000)]	(62,500)
Capital Gain	$ 17,500
Inclusion Rate	1/2
Taxable Capital Gain	$ 8,750

Alice

None of these transactions would have any effect on Alice's 2020 Income For Tax Purposes.

Alonso Jr.

When Alonso Jr. sells his Lisgar Inc. shares, he will have an allowable capital loss calculated as follows:

Proceeds Of Disposition [($16.00)(10,000)]	$160,000
Adjusted Cost Base [($17.00)(10,000)]	(170,000)
Capital Loss	($ 10,000)
Inclusion Rate	1/2
Allowable Capital Loss	($ 5,000)

This loss can only be deducted in 2020 to the extent that Alonso Jr. has taxable capital gains during 2020. As a result, the sale will not affect Net Income For Tax Purposes unless he has taxable capital gains.

Solution to Self Study Problem Nine - 11

Note

As the farm would be considered qualified farm property, any capital gains arising from a disposition could be eligible for the lifetime capital gains deduction. If Long Consulting Ltd. is a qualified small business corporation, capital gains on the disposition of these shares could also be eligible for the lifetime capital gains deduction. As this deduction is not discussed until Chapter 11, the problem specifies that these possibilities should be ignored.

Long Consulting Ltd.

1. Gift To Spouse - ITA 73(1) Applies

ITA 73(1) permits transfers of a capital property to a spouse at its tax value (adjusted cost base or UCC). This means that the shares in Long Consulting Ltd. could be gifted to Mr. Long with no immediate tax consequences.

The tax basis for these shares for the spouse would remain at the adjusted cost base of $210,000.

Any dividends paid on the shares would be attributed to Mrs. Long.

If Mr. Long subsequently sells these shares for $525,000 ($50,000 more than the $475,000 fair market value at the time of the gift), the resulting taxable capital gain of $157,500, as calculated in the following table, would also be attributed to Mrs. Long.

Proceeds (Fair Market Value)	$525,000
Adjusted Cost Base	(210,000)
Capital Gain	$315,000
Inclusion Rate	1/2
Taxable Capital Gain	$ 157,500

2. Gift To Spouse - Elect Out Of ITA 73(1)

As an alternative, Mrs. Long could elect out of the provisions of ITA 73(1). Under ITA 69, the gift would be recorded as a disposition at the $475,000 fair market value. Mrs. Long would have an immediate taxable capital gain of $132,500 [(1/2)($475,000 - $210,000)] and Mr. Long's adjusted cost base would be $475,000. However, since the transfer is a gift, and Mr. Long does not use his own funds to purchase the shares, income attribution would apply to any dividends received by Mr. Long. In addition, if the property were subsequently sold by Mr. Long for $525,000, the resulting taxable capital gain of $25,000 [(1/2)(525,000 - $475,000)] would be attributed back to Mrs. Long.

3 And 4. Gift To Children
Under ITA 69, a gift to a related party is deemed to be a transfer at fair market value. Given this, a taxable capital gain of $132,500 [(1/2)($475,000 - $210,000) would result from a transfer to either child.

The adjusted cost base to the children would be the fair market value of $475,000.

Under the general income attribution rules, the dividend income paid on the shares given to Mary, who is under 18, would be attributed back to Mrs. Long. The problem specifies that the tax on split income should be ignored. However, as is discussed in Chapter 11, this dividend income would be subject to the tax on split income and, because of this, it would be exempt from the general income attribution rules.

As Barry is over 18, the gift would not result in attribution of dividends.

There is no attribution of capital gains on assets transferred to children, without regard to their age. This means that, if the property was later sold for $525,000, the resulting taxable capital gain of $25,000 would be taxed in the hands of the child who received the gift.

Rental Property

1. Gift To Spouse - ITA 73(1) Applies
Here again, ITA 73(1) would permit a transfer to Mr. Long at tax values with no immediate tax consequences.

The tax cost of the building to Mr. Long would be the UCC of $125,000. However, Mr. Long would retain the capital cost of $190,000. With respect to the land, its adjusted cost base would be $100,000. This was Mrs. Long's tax cost and the current fair market value of the land.

As the transfer is a gift, income attribution rules would apply. This means that any net rental income would be attributed to Mrs. Long.

If Mr. Long were to later sell the building for $325,000 ($50,000 more than its fair market value at the time of the gift), the following amounts would be attributed to Mrs. Long:

Capital Cost	$190,000
UCC	(125,000)
Recaptured CCA	$ 65,000
Proceeds Of Disposition	$325,000
Adjusted Cost Base	(190,000)
Capital Gain	$135,000
Inclusion Rate	1/2
Taxable Capital Gain	$ 67,500

Since we are assuming the value of the land on which the building was situated has not changed, the sale of the land by Mr. Long would have no tax consequences for Mrs. Long. As you are asked to assume that no CCA is taken between the date of the gift and the date the property is sold, there would be no recapture of CCA resulting from the sale.

2. Gift To Spouse - Elect Out Of ITA 73(1)
Mrs. Long could also elect out of the provisions of ITA 73(1) and transfer the rental property at its fair market value. However, if she does, she would immediately be taxed on the recapture

of $65,000, as well as the taxable capital gain of $42,500 [(1/2)($275,000 - $190,000)]. There would be no tax consequences related to the land as its tax cost is equal to its fair market value.

In this case, the cost of the building to Mr. Long for capital gains purposes would be $275,000. For CCA and recapture purposes, the value would be limited to $232,500 [$190,000 + (1/2)($275,000 - $190,000)]. His cost for the land would be $100,000.

Electing out of ITA 73(1) would not change the fact that the transfer is a gift to a spouse and, as a consequence, future rental income would be attributed to Mrs. Long.

If Mr. Long subsequently sells the building for $325,000, the additional taxable capital gain of $25,000 [(1/2)($325,000 - $275,000)] would also be attributed back to Mrs. Long. As we are assuming the value of the land remains at $100,000 and that no CCA is taken prior to the sale, there are no tax consequences associated with its sale.

3 And 4.   Gift To Children

There is no exemption from the general rules of ITA 69 for transfers of depreciable property to children. As a consequence, Mrs. Long would be subject to taxation based on a disposition of the property at its fair market value of $275,000. This would result in immediate taxation on a $42,500 [(1/2)($275,000 - $190,000)] taxable capital gain, as well as on recapture of $65,000 ($190,000 - $125,000). There would be no tax consequences related to the land as its tax cost is equal to its fair market value.

The cost of the building to either of the children for capital gains purposes would be $275,000. The cost for the land would be $100,000. For CCA and recapture purposes, the value would be limited to $232,500 [$190,000 + (1/2)($275,000 - $190,000)].

If this property were given to Mary, the income attribution rules of ITA 74.1 would apply to any amount of property income subsequently earned. This would mean that until Mary reached 18 years of age, any property income from the rental property would be attributed to Mrs. Long. Alternatively, if the property were gifted to her son, Barry, all subsequent income would be taxed in his hands.

There is no attribution of capital gains on gifts to related children under 18. There would be no attribution of capital gains on a gift to either child. This means that if the property were later sold for $325,000 ($275,000 + $50,000), the $25,000 taxable capital gain would be taxed in the hands of the child who received the gift. As noted in the discussion of the alternative gift recipients, there would be no recapture of CCA resulting from the sale.

Dynamics Inc.

1.   Gift To Spouse - ITA 73(1) Applies

As with the other properties, these shares could be given to Mr. Long and, under the provisions of ITA 73(1), no immediate tax consequences would arise.

The tax basis for Mr. Long would be unchanged at $212,000.

Any dividend income on the shares would be attributed to Mrs. Long.

If Mr. Long were to subsequently sell the shares for $434,000 ($50,000 more that their $384,000 fair market value at the time of the gift), the income attribution rules of ITA 74.1 would require that the following taxable capital gain be attributed to the income of Mrs. Long:

Proceeds Of Disposition	$434,000
Adjusted Cost Base	(212,000)
Capital Gain	$222,000
Inclusion Rate	1/2
Taxable Capital Gain	$ 111,000

2.   *Gift To Spouse - Elect Out Of ITA 73(1)*

Mrs. Long could elect out of ITA 73(1) by recording the $86,000 [(1/2)($384,000 - $212,000)] taxable capital gain at the time of the transfer to her spouse.

In this case the adjusted cost base to Mr. Long would be $384,000.

However, as long as the property was transferred as a gift, attribution would apply to both dividend income received by Mr. Long and to any further capital gains realized on a subsequent sale. If the property was subsequently sold for $434,000, Mr. Long would have a taxable capital gain of $25,000 [(1/2)($434,000 - $384,000)] that would be attributed back to Mrs. Long.

3 And 4.   *Gift To Children*

In the case of a transfer to either of her children, ITA 69 would require that the gift be treated as a deemed disposition with the proceeds at the fair market value of $384,000. This would result in an immediate taxable capital gain of $86,000 [(1/2)($384,000 - $212,000)].

The tax base to the children would be the fair market value of $384,000.

A transfer to Mary would result in the application of the income attribution rules of ITA 74.1. This would mean that subsequent dividend income on these shares would be allocated to Mrs. Long until Mary reaches 18 years of age. If the shares were transferred to Barry, there would be no attribution of dividends.

There is no attribution of capital gains on assets transferred to children, without regard to their age. This means that, if the property were later sold for $434,000, the resulting taxable capital gain of $25,000 [(1/2)($434,000 - $384,000)] would be taxed in the hands of the child who received the gift.

Farm Land

1.   *Gift To Spouse - ITA 73(1) Applies*

As with all of the other properties, Mrs. Long could make a tax free transfer of the farm land to her husband under ITA 73(1).

The adjusted cost base to Mr. Long would remain unchanged at $80,000.

As farm income is considered to be business income rather than property income, there would be no attribution of any farm income that arises while Mr. Long is holding the property.

In the event of a subsequent sale of the farm land for $225,000 ($50,000 more than the fair market value at the time of transfer), the following taxable capital gain would be attributed to Mrs. Long under ITA 74.1:

Proceeds Of Disposition	$225,000
Adjusted Cost Base	(80,000)
Capital Gain	$145,000
Inclusion Rate	1/2
Taxable Capital Gain	$ 72,500

2.   *Gift To Spouse - Elect Out Of ITA 73(1)*

Alternatively, Mrs. Long could elect out of ITA 73(1) and transfer the property at its fair market value of $175,000. This would result in an immediate taxable capital gain of $47,500 [(1/2)($175,000 - $80,000)].

In this case the adjusted cost base to Mr. Long would be $175,000.

A noted, farm income is business income and this would not be attributed to Mrs. Long

As the transfer was a gift, the income attribution rules would apply to subsequent capital gains on the property. If Mr. Long sells the property for $225,000, the resulting $25,000 [(1/2)($225,000 - $175,000)] taxable capital gain would be attributed back to Mrs. Long.

3 And 4.   Gift To Children

ITA 73(3) permits the inter vivos transfer of farm property used by the taxpayer or her family to a child on a tax free basis. The deemed proceeds would be Mrs. Long's adjusted cost base, which means that Mrs. Long would incur no taxation at the time of the gift to either child.

The adjusted cost base to either child would be the same $80,000 that was deemed to be the proceeds of the disposition.

As noted in our discussion of the transfer of this property to Mr. Long, because farm income is business income rather than property income, there will be no attribution of farm income in the case of a transfer to either child.

On most transfers to related minors, there is no attribution of capital gains. This is a reflection of the fact that, unlike the rules for transfers to a spouse, there is no general rollover provision for transfers to related minors on a tax free basis. However, when a transfer is made to a related minor under the provisions of ITA 73(3) and the transfer value is below fair market value, ITA 75.1 requires that any subsequent gain resulting from a disposition by the transferee before they reach age 18 be attributed back to the transferor.

This means that, if the farm property is transferred to Mary and she sells the property for $225,000 before she reaches age 18, a taxable capital gain of $72,500 [(1/2)($225,000 - $80,000)] will be attributed to Mrs. Long. If the transfer was to Barry, this capital gain would not be attributed to Mrs. Long and would be taxed in his hands.

Solution to Self Study Problem Nine - 12

Net Employment Income

Carolyn's employment income would be calculated as follows:

Salary [(10 Months)($5,000)]	$50,000
RPP Contributions (Note 1)	(2,600)
Automobile (Note 2)	6,047
Travel Allowance (Note 3)	Nil
Moving Cost Allowance	10,000
Housing Loss Reimbursement (Note 4)	Nil
Housing Cost Allowance (Note 5)	7,500
Net Employment Income	$70,947

Note 1   While Carolyn's RPP contributions can be deducted, the matching contribution by her employer does not create a taxable benefit.

Note 2   The automobile benefit would be calculated as follows:

Standby Charge [(2%)($42,000)(9)(8,000 ÷ 15,003*)]	$4,031
Operating Cost Benefit - Lesser Of:	
• [(1/2)($4,031)] = $2,016	
• [(8,000)($0.28)] = $2,240	2,016
Total Benefit	$6,047

* [(9)(1,667)]

Note 3 As the allowance appears to be reasonable, it does not have to be included in income. Given this, Carolyn cannot deduct her actual costs.

Note 4 As the housing loss reimbursement is less than $15,000, it does not have to be included in income.

Note 5 Assistance with higher housing costs related to a required move must be included in an employee's income.

Property Income

Carolyn's property income is calculated as follows:

Eligible Dividends Received	$ 5,800
Gross Up At 38 Percent	2,204
Recapture On Rental Property (Note 6)	20,000
Total Property Income	$28,004

Note 6 The fair market value of the rental building when it is bequeathed to Carolyn is $270,000 ($320,000 - $50,000). While this would be the UCC value that Carolyn would use to calculate CCA, because the fair market value of the property at the time of transfer is less than its capital cost, Carolyn must use her mother's capital cost of $300,000 ($400,000 - $100,000).

Carolyn's proceeds from the sale of the building is $290,000 ($340,000 - $50,000) and, when she subtracts the lesser of the capital cost ($300,000) and the proceeds ($290,000) from the $270,000 UCC, the result is recapture of $20,000 ($270,000 - $290,000).

Taxable Capital Gains

Carolyn's only capital gains will arise on the sale of the shares that were gifted to her by her father. Note that her adjusted cost base for these shares will be their fair market value at the time of the gift.

Proceeds Of Disposition	$74,000
Adjusted Cost Base	(62,000)
Capital Gain	$12,000
Inclusion Rate	1/2
Taxable Capital Gain	$ 6,000

Other Income And Deductions

Carolyn's other income and other deductions amount is calculated as follows:

Spousal Support (Note 7)	$ 500
Moving Costs (Note 8)	(27,950)
Child Care Cost (Note 9)	(7,300)
Total Other Income And Deductions	($34,750)

Note 7 When the full amount of support is not paid, the first payments are deemed to be for child support. Given the total payments of $12,500 and the required child support of $12,000 [(12)($1,000)], Carolyn will include only $500 in her Net Income For Tax Purposes.

Note 8 Costs for food and lodging at or near an old or new residence are limited to a maximum period of 15 days. Carolyn has a total of 23 eligible days: 14 days in Lethbridge and 9 days in Edmonton. Note that the 2 days spent traveling to Edmonton are not included in the 15 day total. As the hotel in Edmonton is the more expensive, she will deduct all 9 days spent there. Carolyn's deductible moving costs can be calculated as follows:

Selling Cost Of Lethbridge Property	$12,500
Legal Fees - Sale Of Lethbridge Property	600
Legal Fees - Purchase Of Edmonton Property	450
Storage Costs - February 15 Through March 10	1,400
Cost Of Moving Belongings	7,250
Lodging In Lethbridge And Edmonton	
(9 @ $200 + 6 @$175)	2,850
Simplified Meal Cost [(3)($51)(15 + 2 Days)]	2,601
Simplified Milage [($.59)(506)]	299
Total Deductible Moving Costs	$27,950

As this amount is less than her income at her new job, she will be able to deduct the full amount of these expenses.

Note 9 Carolyn's deductible care costs would be the least of three amounts:

Actual Costs Plus Deductible Camp Costs		
Edmonton Cost [(38)(($175)]	$6,650	
Camp [(2)($200 + $125)]	650	$ 7,300
Annual Limit ($8,000 + $5,000)		$13,000
Two-Thirds Earned Income		
[(2/3)($70,947 + $2,600 RPP)]		$49,031

The least of these three amounts is the actual cost of $7,300.

Net Income For Tax Purposes

Carolyn's Net Income For Tax Purposes would be determined as follows:

Net Employment Income	$70,947
Property Income	28,004
Taxable Capital Gains	6,000
Other Income And Deductions	(34,750)
Deductible CPP Contributions ($2,898 - $2,732)	(166)
Net Income For Tax Purposes	$70,035

Taxable Income

As Carolyn has no Division C deductions, her Taxable Income would be equal to her Net Income For Tax Purposes.

Tax Payable

Carolyn's Tax Payable would be determined as follows:

Tax On First $48,535		$ 7,280
Tax On Next $21,500 ($70,035 - $48,535) At 20.5 Percent		4,408
Tax Before Credits		$11,688
Tax Credits:		
Basic Personal	($13,229)	
Eligible Dependant	(13,229)	
EI Premiums	(856)	
CPP Contributions	(2,732)	
Canada Employment	(1,245)	
Medical Expenses (Note 10)	(5,499)	
Total Credit Base	($ 36,790)	
Rate	15%	(5,519)
Dividend Tax Credit [(6/11)($2,204)]		(1,202)
Charitable Donations (Note 11)		
[(15%)($200) + (29%)($600 - $200)]		(146)
Federal Tax Payable		$ 4,821

Note 10 The medical expenses eligible for the credit are as follows:

Total Medical Costs		$7,600
Lesser Of:		
• $2,101 [(3%)($70,035)]		
• 2020 Threshold Amount = $2,397		(2,101)
Medical Expense Tax Credit Base		$5,499

Note 11 As none of her income is taxed at 33 percent, this rate will not be applicable to the calculation of the charitable donations tax credit.

Solution to Self Study Problem Nine - 13

Part A - Net Income For Tax Purposes And Taxable Income For Mr. Winded

The Net Income For Tax Purposes for Mr. Winded would be calculated as follows:

Net Employment Income		
Salary [($84,000)(2/12)]	$14,000	
Standby Charge [(2/3)($360)(2)]	480	
Operating Cost Benefit [(90%)(3,000)($0.28)]		
(Alternate calculation not available)	756	
Taxable Portion Of Gift ($700 - $500)	200	
Stock Option Benefit [(1,500)($11 - $8)]	4,500	
RPP Contributions	(500)	$ 19,436
Net Business Income (Note 1)		13,395
Property Income		
Interest Income	$ 3,478	
Eligible Dividends Received	1,700	
Eligible Dividends Attributed From Mrs. Winded	1,400	
Gross Up [(38%)($1,700 + $1,400)]	1,178	
Non-Eligible Dividends Received From Sail	800	
Gross Up [(15%)($800)]	120	
Net Rental Income (Note 2)	Nil	8,676

Net Taxable Capital Gains

TCG On Sale Of Celebrate Ltd. Shares			
[(1/2)(1,000)($17 – $11)]			$ 3,000
Attributed TCG On Sale Of Preferred Shares			
[(1/2)(($31,000 - $27,000)]			2,000
TCG On Listed Personal Property			
Stamps ($5,000 – $8,000)	($3,000)		
Rare Book ($4,200 – $1,000)	3,200		
Painting ($1,000 – $1,000)	Nil		
	$ 200		
Inclusion Rate	1/2	100	
Loss On Furniture (PUP) Of $3,800			
($4,800 - $1,000 Floor) Not Deductible		Nil	
TCG On Sale Of Sail Shares			
[(1/2)($48,000 – $12,000)]		18,000	
TCG On Sale Of CNR Shares (Note 3)		1,230	
ACL On Sale Of BCE Shares (Note 4)		(400)	
TCG On Sale Of Cottage (Note 5)		50,000	73,930

Other Income And Deductions

Old Age Security	$ 5,350	
CPP Receipts	9,600	
Pension Income From Celebrate Ltd. Pension Plan	44,000	
RRIF Withdrawal	8,000	
Moving Expenses (Note 6)	(23,000)	
Pension Income Transferred To Spouse		
[(1/2)($44,000 + $8,000)]	(26,000)	17,950

Net Income Before Clawback	$133,387
OAS Clawback - Lesser Of:	
• Amount Received = $5,350	
• $8,511 [(15%)($135,797 - $79,054)]	(5,350)
Net Income For Tax Purposes - Mr. Winded	$128,037

Note 1 Net Business Income would be calculated as follows:

Revenues		$38,000
Expenses:		
Supplies		(16,000)
Advertising		(1,000)
Home Office Costs (See Following Calculation)		(3,060)
CCA		
Class 50 [(55%)(1.5)($3,800)]	($3,135)	
Class 8		
{[20%][$2,400 + (1/2)($1,600)]}	(960)	
Class 12 [(100%)($450)]*	(450)	(4,545)
Net Business Income		$13,395

*As the two hand tools cost a total of $450, each must have cost less than $500. As a result, the first year one-half rule is not applicable.

The deductible home office costs can be calculated as follows:

Mortgage Interest	$ 4,000
Utilities	3,600
Property Taxes	4,500
Insurance	1,400
Maintenance	1,800
Total	$15,300
Floor Space Used	20%
Deductible Amount	$ 3,060

Note 2   Net Rental Income would be calculated as follows:

	Property A	Property B	Total
Rental Revenues	$ 98,000	$62,000	$160,000
Operating Expenses	(104,000)	(54,000)	(158,000)
Income (Loss) Before CCA	($ 6,000)	$ 8,000	$ 2,000
Class 8 CCA*			(2,000)
Net Rental Income			Nil

*Maximum CCA on Class 8 would have been $5,600 [(20%)($12,000 + $16,000)]. However, the actual deduction is limited to the amount that would reduce the Net Rental Income to nil. Note that the CCA was claimed on Class 8 in order to preserve the Class 1 UCC balances. This will result in a lower amount of recapture when the buildings are sold. The Class 8 assets would likely have little or no proceeds of disposition when they are disposed of. This means that recapture on these assets would be unlikely.

Note 3 - The taxable capital gain on the sale of CNR shares would be calculated as follows:

Proceeds Of Disposition [($67.00)(300)]	$20,100
Adjusted Cost Base [($58.80*)(300)]	(17,640)
Capital Gain	$ 2,460
Inclusion Rate	1/2
Taxable Capital Gain	$ 1,230

*The average cost of these shares would be calculated as follows:

	Shares	Total	Per Share
May 1, 2016, Purchase At $52	200	$ 10,400	
May 1, 2017, Purchase At $46	300	13,800	
Balance	500	$ 24,200	$48.40
May 1, 2018, Sale At Cost Of $48.40			
($24,200 ÷ 500)	(400)	(19,360)	
Balance	100	$ 4,840	$48.40
May 1, 2019, Purchase At $64	200	12,800	
Balance	300	$ 17,640	$ 58.80

Note 4 The allowable capital loss on the sale of BCE shares would be calculated as follows:

Proceeds Of Disposition [(1,000)($36)]	$36,000
Adjusted Cost Base [(1,000)($38)]	(38,000)
Capital Loss	($ 2,000)
Capital Loss Per Share ($2,000 ÷ 1,000)	$2 Loss/Share

As 600 of the shares were reacquired within 30 days of the sale, with respect to these 600 shares, the capital loss is considered a superficial loss and is disallowed. This will leave an allowable capital loss of $400 [(1/2)($2)(400)]. The remaining capital loss of $1,200 [($2)(600)] will be added to the adjusted cost base of the 600 reacquired shares.

Note 5 The taxable capital gain on the sale of the cottage would be calculated as follows:

	Winnipeg Home	Lake Winnipeg Cottage
Proceeds Of Disposition	$ 313,000	$290,000
Selling Costs	(13,000)	(10,000)
Adjusted Cost Base	(140,000)	(80,000)
Capital Gain	$ 160,000	$200,000
Exempt Portion		
Home [($160,000)(9+1)] ÷ 10]	(160,000)	
Cottage [($200,000)(7+ 1)] ÷ 16]		(100,000)
Capital Gain	Nil	$ 100,000
Inclusion Rate		1/2
Taxable Capital Gain	Nil	$ 50,000

*The costs of selling a previously occupied residence that was ordinarily inhabited can be deducted as part of moving expenses. There is no restriction on claiming the selling costs to both reduce the capital gain on the old residence and also to increase moving expenses.

The annual gain on the two properties is as follows:

- Winnipeg Home ($160,000 ÷ 10) = $16,000
- Lake Winnipeg Cottage ($200,000 ÷ 16) = $12,500

Given this, maximum available years should be allocated to the Winnipeg property. These would be the nine years 2011 through 2020. This would leave the seven years 2005 through 2011 for the cottage.

Note 6 As there is no income in the Vancouver location during 2019, the moving expenses incurred in that year will have to be deducted in 2020. None of the costs of the house hunting trip are deductible. The eligible moving expenses that were incurred in 2019 and 2020 are as follows:

Legal Fees - Purchase Of New Home	$ 4,800
January Air Fare	1,200
Selling Costs - Sale Of Old Home	13,000
Transport Of Household Effects	4,000
Total Available Moving Expenses	$23,000

These expenses can only be deducted to the extent of employment and business income earned during 2020. As these two amounts total $35,241 ($19,436 + $15,805), the full amount of eligible expenses can be deducted.

Part A - Taxable Income For Mr. Winded

Taxable Income for Mr. Winded would be calculated as follows:

Net Income For Tax Purposes	$128,037
Stock Option Deduction [($4,500)(1/2)]	(2,250)
Taxable Income - Mr. Winded	$125,787

Part A - Net Income For Tax Purposes And Taxable Income For Mrs. Winded

Mrs. Winded has no Taxable Income deductions. This means that her Taxable Income is equal to her Net Income For Tax Purposes, which would be calculated as follows:

Old Age Security	$ 7,400
Canada Pension Plan	3,100
Transferred Pension Income	26,000
Dividends (Attributed Back To Mr. Winded)	Nil
Net Income For Tax Purposes = Taxable Income - Mrs. Winded	$36,500

Part B - Federal Balance Owing (Tax Payable) For Mrs. Winded

While the medical expenses can be claimed by either spouse, they are claimed on Mrs. Winded's return as she has the lower Net Income For Tax Purposes. This results in a lesser reduction of the medical expenses claimed in the computation of the credit. She does have sufficient Tax Payable to fully utilize the credit.

Mrs. Winded's federal Tax Payable would be calculated as follows:

Tax Before Credits [(15%)($36,500)]		$5,475
Tax Credits:		
Basic	($13,229)	
Age (Note 7)	(7,637)	
Disability	(8,576)	
Pension Amount	(2,000)	
Medical Expenses (Note 8)	(2,455)	
Total Credit Base	$33,897	
Rate	15%	(5,085)
Federal Tax Payable		$ 390

Note 7 Rachel's income is below the income threshold for the age credit. This means the full age amount is available to her.

Note 8 The base for the medical expense credit is calculated as follows:

Total Medical Expenses ($150 + $4,600 - $1,200)	$3,550
Reduced By The Lesser Of:	
• [(3%)($36,500)] = $1,095	
• 2020 Threshold Amount = $2,397	(1,095)
Base For Medical Expense Credit	$2,455

Part B - Federal Tax Payable For Mr. Winded

As Mrs. Winded has fully utilized her credits, there are none to be transferred to Mr. Winded. The Federal Balance Owing for Mr. Winded would be calculated as follows:

Tax On First $97,069		$ 17,230
Tax On Next $28,718 ($125,787 - $97,069) At 26 Percent		7,467
Tax Before Credits		$24,697
Tax Credits:		
Basic	($13,229)	
Spousal (Income Exceeds $15,502)	Nil	
Age (Income Exceeds $89,421)	Nil	
Pension Amount	(2,000)	
CPP	(700)	
EI	(200)	
Canada Employment	(1,245)	
Total Credit Base	($ 17,374)	
Rate	15%	(2,606)
Charitable Donations (Note 9) P		
[(15%)($200) + (29%)($3,700 - $200)]		(1,045)
Dividend Tax Credits		
Eligible Dividends [(6/11)($1,178)]		(643)
Sail Ltd. Dividends [(9/13)($120)]		(83)
Federal Tax Payable		$20,320
OAS Repayment		5,350
Total Balance Owing		$25,670

Note 9   As none of his income is taxed at 33 percent, this rate will not be applicable to the calculation of the charitable donations tax credit.

Chapter 10 Learning Objectives

After completing Chapter 10, you should be able to:

1. Explain the general procedures used to provide tax deferral on retirement saving (paragraph [P hereafter] 10-1 to 10-16).
2. Describe the difference between a defined benefit pension plan and a defined contribution (a.k.a. money purchase) pension plan (P 10-17 to 10-19).
3. Describe the basic operation of RRSPs (P 10-20 to 10-37).
4. Understand the terms RRSP Deduction Limit, Unused RRSP Deduction Room, and RRSP Dollar Limit (P 10-38 to 10-45).
5. Calculate Earned Income for RRSP purposes (P 10-46 to 10-48).

6. Explain the concepts underlying Pension Adjustments (PAs) (P 10-49 to 10-60).
7. Explain the concepts underlying Past Service Pension Adjustments (PSPAs) (P 10-61 to 10-66).
8. Explain the concepts underlying Pension Adjustment Reversals (PARs) (P 10-67 to 10-71).
9. Calculate an individual's maximum RRSP deduction and Unused RRSP Deduction Room (P 10-72).
10. Apply the tax treatment for undeducted RRSP contributions (P 10-73 and 10-74).

11. Determine whether an individual has made "excess" contributions to an RRSP and identify associated tax planning issues, including the use of TFSAs (P 10-75 to 10-82).
12. Recall the tax treatment of RRSP and RRIF administration fees (P 10-83).
13. Apply the provisions relating to RRSP withdrawals and voluntary conversions of RRSPs (P 10-84 to 10-91).
14. Apply the provisions relating to RRSP terminations due to the age limitation (P 10-92 to 10-93).
15. Apply the provisions associated with spousal RRSPs and identify associated tax planning issues (P 10-94 to 10-102).

16. Describe and apply the provisions of the Home Buyers' Plan (P 10-103 to 10-113).
17. Describe and apply the provisions of the Lifelong Learning Plan (P 10-114 to 10-122).
18. Apply the RRSP provisions relating to departure from Canada and death of the registrant (P 10-123 to 10-138).
19. Explain the general provisions associated with Registered Pension Plans (RPPs) (P 10-139 to 10-157).
20. Describe, in general terms, Pooled Registered Pension Plans (PRPPs) and Target Benefit Plans (P 10-158 to 10-161).

21. Describe how an expanded CPP program could help the retirement savings problem (P 10-162 to 10-167).
22. Describe the basic operation of RRIFs and the role that RRIFs play in tax planning for retirement (P 10-168 to 10-186).
23. Explain the general rules for Deferred Profit Sharing Plans (P 10-187 to 10-192).

24. Describe, in general terms, Profit Sharing Plans (P 10-193 to 10-196).
25. Describe the tax free transfers that can be made between various types of plans (P 10-197 and 10-198).

26. Apply the special rules associated with RRSP contributions and retiring allowances (P 10-199 and 10-200).
27. Explain the general provisions related to Retirement Compensation Arrangements (P 10-201 to 10-210).
28. Describe Salary Deferral Arrangements (P 10-211 to 10-218).

How to Work Through Chapter 10

We recommend the following approach in dealing with the material in this Chapter:

Planning For Retirement

- Read paragraph 10-1 to 10-19 (in the textbook).

Registered Retirement Savings Plans (RRSPs)

- Read paragraph 10-20 to 10-36.
- Do Exercise Ten-1 (in the textbook) and check the solution in this Study Guide.
- Read paragraph 10-37.

RRSP Deduction Limit

- Read paragraph 10-38 to 10-48.
- Do Exercises Ten-2 and Ten-3 and check the solutions in this Study Guide.

Pension Adjustments (PAs)

- Read paragraph 10-49 to 10-51.
- Do Exercise Ten-4 and check the solution in this Study Guide.
- Read paragraph 10-52 to 10-59.
- Do Exercise Ten-5 and check the solution in this Study Guide.
- Read paragraph 10-60.

Past Service Pension Adjustments (PSPAs) And Pension Adjustment Reversals

- Read paragraph 10-61 to 10-71.
- Do Self Study Problem Ten-1, which is available on MyLab, and check the solution in this Study Guide.

Examples Of RRSP Deduction Calculations

- Read paragraph 10-72.
- Do Exercises Ten-6 and Ten-7 and check the solutions in this Study Guide.

Undeducted And Excess RRSP Contributions, Including Tax Planning For

- Read paragraph 10-73 to 10-78.
- Do Exercise Ten-8 and check the solution in this Study Guide.
- Read paragraph 10-79 to 10-82.
- Do Self Study Problem Ten-2 to Ten-5 and check the solutions in this Study Guide.

RRSP And RRIF Administration Fees

- Read paragraph 10-83.

RRSP Withdrawals, Voluntary Conversions, And Involuntary Termination (Age)

- Read paragraph 10-84 to 10-93.

Spousal RRSP

- Read paragraph 10-94 to 10-102.
- Do Exercise Ten-9 and check the solution in this Study Guide.

Home Buyers' Plan (HBP) And Lifelong Learning Plan (LLP)

- Read paragraph 10-103 to 10-113.
- Do Exercise Ten-10 and check the solution in this Study Guide.
- Read paragraph 10-114 to 10-122.
- Do Exercise Ten-11 and check the solution in this Study Guide.

RRSPs - Departure From Canada And Death Of The RRSP Registrant

- Read paragraph 10-123 to 10-138.
- Do Self Study Problem Ten-6 and check the solution in this Study Guide.

Registered Pension Plans (RPPs)

- Read paragraph 10-139 to 10-157.

Pooled Registered Pension Plans, Target Benefit Plans, And Expanded CPP

- Read paragraph 10-158 to 10-167.

Registered Retirement Income Funds (RRIFs) - General Rules

- Read paragraph 10-168 to 10-178.
- Do Exercise Ten-12 and check the solution in this Study Guide.

RRIFs - Death Of The RRIF Registrant And Evaluation Of RRIFs

- Read paragraph 10-179 to 10-186.

Deferred Profit Sharing Plans And Profit Sharing Plans

- Read paragraph 10-187 to 10-196.

Transfers Between Plans And Retiring Allowances

- Read paragraph 10-197 to 10-200.
- Do Exercise Ten-13 and check the solution in this Study Guide.
- Do Self Study Problem Ten-7 and check the solution in this Study Guide.

Retirement Compensation Arrangements, Salary Deferral Arrangements, And Individual Pension Plans

- Read paragraph 10-201 to 10-221.
- Do Self Study Problems Ten-8 and Ten-9 and check the solutions in this Study Guide.

To Complete This Chapter

- If you would like more practice in problem solving, do the Supplementary Self Study Problems for the chapter. These problems and solutions are available on MyLab.

- Review the Key Terms Used In This Chapter in the textbook at the end of Chapter 10. Consult the Glossary for the meaning of any key terms you do not know.
- Test yourself with the Chapter 10 Glossary Flashcards available on MyLab.
- Ensure you have achieved the Chapter 10 Learning Objectives listed in this Study Guide.
- As a review, we recommend you view the PowerPoint presentation for Chapter 10 that is on MyLab.

Practice Examination

- Write the Practice Examination for Chapter 10 that is on MyLab. Mark your examination using the Practice Examination Solution that is also on MyLab.

Solutions to Chapter 10 Exercises

Exercise Ten - 1 Solution

Invested Inside RRSP

Deductible Contribution	$20,000
Dividends Received [(5)(5%)($20,000)]	5,000
Balance After Five Years	$25,000
Tax On Withdrawal [(40%)($25,000)]	(10,000)
Available For Vacation	$15,000

Invested Inside TFSA

Initial Investment [($20,000)(1 - .40)]	$12,000
Tax Free Dividends [(5)(5%)($12,000)]	3,000
Available For Vacation	$15,000

Invested Outside RRSP And TFSA

Initial Investment [($20,000)(1 - .40)]	$20,000
After Tax Dividends [(5)(5%)($12,000)(1 - .22)]	2,340
Available For Vacation	$14,340

Investing outside the RRSP or TFSA is the worst alternative by $660 ($15,000 - $14,340).

Exercise Ten - 2 Solution
His Earned Income for RRSP purposes would be $70,500 ($56,000 + $2,500 + $12,000).

Exercise Ten - 3 Solution
Her Earned Income for RRSP purposes would be $54,500 ($82,000 + $3,000 - $12,500 - $18,000).

Exercise Ten - 4 Solution
The basic mechanism here is the Pension Adjustment (PA). Individuals who belong to an RPP or a DPSP have their RRSP Deduction Limit reduced by the amount of their PA for the previous year. PAs are designed to reflect the amount of contributions or benefits that have been accumulated in employer sponsored RPPs and DPSPs.

Exercise Ten - 5 Solution
The Pension Adjustment will be $6,400 ($2,300 + $1,800 + $2,300).

Exercise Ten - 6 Solution

The required calculations would be as follows:

Unused Deduction Room - End Of 2019	$ 4,800
Lesser Of:	
• 2020 RRSP Dollar Limit = $27,230	
• 18% Of 2019 Earned Income Of $38,000 = $6,840	6,840
2020 RRSP Deduction Limit	$11,640
RRSP Deduction Is Least Of:	
• RRSP Deduction Limit = $11,640	
• Available Contributions = $6,000	
• Amount Mr. Haslich Chooses To Deduct = $4,500	(4,500)
Unused RRSP Deduction Room - End Of 2020	$ 7,140

Assuming Mr. Haslich deducted only $4,500, he would have $1,500 ($6,000 - $4,500) in undeducted contributions that can be carried forward and deducted in a subsequent year.

If Mr. Haslich wanted to deduct his maximum RRSP deduction of $11,640, he would have to contribute an additional $5,640 ($11,640 - $6,000).

Exercise Ten - 7 Solution

The required calculations would be as follows:

Unused Deduction Room - End Of 2019	$10,750
Lesser Of:	
• 2020 RRSP Dollar Limit = $27,230	
• 18% Of 2019 Earned Income Of $66,530* = $11,975	11,975
Less 2019 PA	(4,800)
2020 RRSP Deduction Limit	$ 17,925
RRSP Deduction Is Lesser Of:	
• RRSP Deduction Limit = $17,925	
• Available Contributions = $19,760 ($6,560 + $13,200)	(17,925)
Unused RRSP Deduction Room - End Of 2020	Nil

*Earned Income = $6,530 - $18,000 + $75,600 + $2,400 (RPP)

Mr. Black's maximum RRSP deduction is $17,925. While he has no Unused RRSP Deduction Room, he has $1,835 ($19,760 - $17,925) in undeducted contributions that can be carried forward and deducted in a subsequent year in which there is sufficient RRSP deduction room.

Exercise Ten - 8 Solution

In 2018 and 2019, 18 percent of Ms. Brownell's $160,000 in earned income is more than the RRSP dollar limit for those years. Her 2020 Earned Income is not relevant in this Exercise as it will not be used until 2021. Given this, the calculation of the excess amount of contributions is as follows:

2019 Contribution (July 1)	$27,350
2019 Addition To Deduction Room = RRSP Dollar Limit	(26,230)
Excess Contributions For 2019 (Less Than $2,000)	$ 1,120
2020 Contribution (May 1)	30,000
2020 Addition To Deduction Room = RRSP Dollar Limit	(27,230)
Permitted $2,000 Cushion	(2,000)
Excess Contributions Subject To Penalty	$ 2,620

As the excess contribution for 2019 was less than $2,000, there is no penalty for that year. There will be a 2020 penalty of $210 [(1%)($2,620)(8 months)]. The fact that there is no RRSP deduction is not relevant to the penalty.

Exercise Ten - 9 Solution
As a spousal contribution was made in 2019, one of the two years prior to 2020, income attribution will apply. However, it will only apply to the extent of the $5,000 contribution made by Mrs. Garveau. This means that $5,000 of the withdrawal will be taxed in the hands of Mrs. Garveau, with the remaining $4,000 taxed in the hands of Mr. Garveau.

Exercise Ten - 10 Solution
Ms. DeBoo will have to repay $867 [(1/15)($18,000 - $5,000)] during 2020. Note that the voluntary payment that was made during 2019 did not reduce the fraction of the remaining balance that must be paid in 2020.

Exercise Ten - 11 Solution
There are no tax consequences associated with the withdrawal of $5,000. He is not enrolled in a qualifying education program in either 2019 or 2020 and, as a consequence, his repayment period begins in 2020. As he makes the required payments of $500 ($5,000 ÷ 10) within 60 days of the end of each of the years 2020 through 2028, there are no tax consequences associated with his repayments.

Exercise Ten - 12 Solution
He has no required minimum withdrawal for 2020, the year the RRIF is established. His minimum withdrawal for 2021 will be $27,500 [$660,000 ÷ (90 - 66)].

Exercise Ten - 13 Solution
It would appear that Mr. Bartoli began working for his employer in 1976. Given this, he can rollover a total of $59,500 [($2,000)(20 Years Before 1996) + ($1,500)(13 Years Before 1989)] to his RRSP. The remainder of the retiring allowance will be taxed in 2020.

Solution to Self Study Problem Ten - 1

Case 1
The required 2020 PA would be calculated as follows:

Employer's Contribution To DPSP	$2,500
Employer's Contribution To RPP	1,000
Fredia's Contribution To RPP	1,000
PA	$4,500

Case 2
The required 2020 PA would be calculated as follows:

$$[(1.25\%)(9)(\$71,000)] = \$7,988$$

Note that the contributions made during 2020 have no influence on the PA for a defined benefit RPP.

Case 3
The required PSPA would be calculated as follows:

2018 Amount [(1.1%)(9)($38,000)]	$3,762
2019 Amount [(1.1%)(9)($42,000)]	4,158
2020 PSPA	$7,920

In addition to the PSPA calculated above, there would be a 2020 PA of $5,049 [(1.1%)(9)($51,000)].

Case 4
The required PAR would be calculated as follows:

2018 PA	$ 5,200
2019 PA	5,400
2020 PAR	$10,600

Case 5
The required PSPA would be calculated as follows:

2018 Amount [(1.5% - 1.3%)(9)($58,000)]	$1,044
2019 Amount [(1.5% - 1.3%)(9)($62,000)]	1,116
2020 PSPA	$2,160

There would also be a 2020 PA. However, this cannot be calculated as the problem does not provide the 2020 pensionable earnings.

Solution to Self Study Problem Ten - 2

Part A - Maximum RRSP Deduction
Deeta's maximum 2020 RRSP deduction would be calculated as follows:

Unused Deduction Room - January 1, 2019	$35,000
2019 Addition	Nil
2020 Addition (Based On 2019 Earned Income Of Nil)	Nil
Maximum 2020 RRSP Deduction	$35,000

Part B - Excess RRSP Contributions
At the beginning of 2019, Deeta's undeducted contributions of $37,000 are equal to her $35,000 unused deduction room, plus the permitted $2,000 cushion. As she withdraws $25,000 and made no further contributions during 2019, there are no excess contributions during the 2019 taxation year.

The excess contributions for 2020 would be calculated as follows:

Undeducted Contributions	
January 1, 2020 ($37,000 - $25,000)	$12,000
Additional Contribution On May 2, 2020	40,000
Total Undeducted Contributions	$52,000
Unused Deduction Room	(35,000)
Permitted Cushion	(2,000)
Excess Contributions Subject To Penalty	$15,000
Penalty Rate	1%
Monthly Penalty	$ 150
Months (May To December)	8
Total Penalty For 2020	$ 1,200

Part C - Advice On Tax Planning
As the preceding calculation demonstrates, Deeta's excess contributions are attracting a significant penalty, based on a monthly charge of 1 percent of the excess amount.

As her Earned Income for 2020 will be $61,000, the addition to her 2021 deduction room will be $10,980. As her December 31, 2020, excess contributions are $15,000, she will need to withdraw $4,020 ($15,000 - $10,980) in order to avoid having an additional penalty in 2021. If the excess contributions are withdrawn from the RRSP prior to the end of the year following the year in which an assessment is received for the year in which the contribution is made, an offsetting deduction is available. If, however, any excess is not withdrawn within this specified time frame, it will be included in income and taxed on withdrawal, even though it was never deducted from income. Deeta should withdraw the $4,020 immediately to stop the assessment of the penalty.

Since she has never had a TFSA, she should open one. The withdrawn funds should be contributed to her TFSA, along with any other excess funds up to her TFSA contribution room. For 2020, the maximum total contributions are $69,500 and, while TFSA contributions are not deductible, earnings accumulate on a tax free basis. In addition, withdrawals can be made without tax consequences.

Whether Deeta should withdraw the $2,000 cushion as well depends on future expectations. As there is no time limit on using contributions that are in the plan, it would make sense to simply leave the $2,000 in place, provided that she expects to have earned income in some future year.

In the future, she should ensure that she continues to contribute to her RRSP and TFSA, but should limit the amounts to the maximum permitted contribution.

Solution to Self Study Problem Ten - 3

Mr. Barnes' 2019 Earned Income for RRSP purposes would be calculated as follows:

Salary	$55,000
Taxable Benefits	1,150
Union Dues	(175)
Net Employment Income	$55,975
Business Income	4,150
Rental Loss	(11,875)
Spousal Support Received	2,400
Earned Income	$50,650

Note that CPP and EI contributions do not reduce Earned Income for RRSP purposes.

Since Mr. Barnes has no undeducted RRSP contributions, his maximum deductible RRSP contribution for 2020 is equal to his RRSP Deduction Limit.

This is calculated for Part A (not a member of RPP or DPSP) and Part B (member of RPP) as follows:

	Part A	Part B
Unused Deduction Room - End Of 2019	Nil	Nil
Annual Addition - Lesser Of:		
• 2020 RRSP Dollar Limit = $27,230		
• 18% of 2019 Earned Income Of $50,650 = $9,117	9,117	9,117
Less 2019 PA	N/A	(4,200)
Maximum Deductible RRSP Contribution	$9,117	$4,917

Solution to Self Study Problem Ten - 4

The annual addition for 2020 would be the lesser of $27,230 and 18 percent of Earned Income for 2019. The latter amount would be calculated as follows:

Salary	$86,200
Taxable Benefits	5,600
RPP Contributions (Note 1)	Nil
Union Dues	(450)
Net Employment Income (RRSP Figure)	$91,350
Business Loss	(4,500)
Rental Income	6,700
Common-Law Partner Support Paid	(12,000)
Eligible Dividends (Note 2)	Nil
Interest (Note 2)	Nil
2019 Earned Income	$81,550
Rate	18%
Annual Addition (Less Than $27,230)	$14,679

Note 1   While Ms. Storm's RPP contribution would be deducted in determining Net Income For Tax Purposes, it is not deducted in calculating employment income for RRSP Earned Income purposes.

Note 2   Neither the eligible dividends nor the interest are part of RRSP Earned Income.

Ms. Storm's maximum deductible RRSP contribution would be calculated as follows:

Opening Unused RRSP Deduction Room	$17,000
Annual Addition	14,679
2019 Pension Adjustment [(2)($2,500)]	(5,000)
RRSP Deduction Limit For 2020	$26,679
Undeducted Contributions From Prior Years	(8,000)
Maximum Deductible Contribution For 2020	$18,679

Solution to Self Study Problem Ten - 5

Part A

For purposes of determining her maximum 2020 RRSP contribution, 2019 Earned Income would be calculated as follows:

Net Employment Income*		
Salary	$150,000	
Automobile Benefit	6,500	
Employee Stock Option Benefit	3,000	
Benefit On Interest Free Loan	1,500	
Deductible Employment Expenses	(3,400)	$157,600
Net Business Income		14,600
Royalty Income (Own Invention)		6,600
Net Rental Loss		(10,000)
Spousal Support Received		24,000
Earned Income		$192,800

*Note that, in calculating Earned Income for RRSP purposes, no deduction is made from net employment income for contributions made to an RPP.

A listing of the items that are not included in the calculation of Earned Income is as follows:

- Registered Pension Plan Contributions
- Interest Income
- Taxable Capital Gains
- Eligible Dividends

Part B

The calculation of Sherly's maximum deductible RRSP contribution for 2020 is as follows:

2018 RRSP Dollar Limit	$26,230
2019 RRSP Dollar Limit	26,500
Opening Unused RRSP Deduction Room	$52,730
Annual Addition - Lesser Of:	
• 2020 RRSP Dollar Limit = $27,230	
• 18 Percent Of 2019 Earned Income	
[(18%)($192,800)] = $34,704	27,230
2019 PA	(15,000)
Maximum Deductible RRSP Contribution For 2020	$64,960

Solution to Self Study Problem Ten - 6

Part A

Mr. Sabatini's minimum net employment income would be calculated as follows:

Salary	$ 58,000
Commissions	74,000
Registered Pension Plan Contributions	(3,500)
Net Disability Benefits (Note 1)	3,950
Life Insurance Premium Taxable Benefit	
[(50%)($3,000)]	1,500
Automobile Benefit (Note 2)	6,671
Stock Option Benefit	
[($23.50 - $12.50)(1,000 Shares)]	11,000
Golf And Country Club Costs (Note 3)	(3,400)
Net Employment Income	$148,221

Note 1 As Mr. Sabatini's employer has made contributions to the sickness and accident plan, the benefit of $4,500 is taxable. This is reduced by the payments of $550 [($100)(12 - 1/2)] that were made by Mr. Sabatini during the year, leaving a net benefit of $3,950.

Note 2 With respect to the standby charge, Mr. Sabatini's employment-related usage is over 50 percent of the total and, as a consequence, he can reduce his standby charge to the extent of personal usage that is less than 1,667 kilometres per month. Also note that, as the car was not available during November, his standby charge would be based on 335 days of availability. This would be rounded to 11 months (335/30). Given this, the standby charge would be as follows:

$$[(\$68,000)(11 \text{ Months})(2\%)(7,000/18,337)] = \$5,711$$

As Mr. Sabatini's employment-related use was over 50 percent of the total use, he can base his operating cost benefit on one-half of the standby charge. Given this, the benefit would be the lesser of:

- [($0.28)(7,000)] = $1,960; and
- [(1/2)($5,711)] = $2,856

Using the lesser figure of $1,960, the total benefit would be calculated as follows:

Standby Charge	$5,711
Operating Cost Benefit	1,960
Payment To Employer	(1,000)
Total Automobile Benefit	$6,671

Note 3   Only 50 percent of the $6,800 country club entertainment costs can be deducted by Mr. Sabatini. The $5,000 membership fee would not be a taxable benefit and would not be deductible by his employer.

Other Notes

- The travel costs that the corporation reimbursed to Mr. Sabatini have no tax effect.
- The CPP and EI contributions are not deductible. They can be used to create credits against Tax Payable.
- Income taxes withheld are not deductible.
- Donations to a registered charity will create a credit against Tax Payable, but cannot be deducted in the determination of net employment income.
- Parking fees related to Mr. Sabatini's normal employment location are not deductible.
- Although he cannot deduct his share of the life insurance premiums, the life insurance proceeds will not be taxable.

- The use of frequent flyer points earned on employment-related travel does not normally create a taxable benefit.

- The discounts on merchandise provided by the employer are not a taxable benefit.

Part B

Mr. Sabatini's 2019 Earned Income and maximum deductible 2020 RRSP contribution would be calculated as follows:

2019 Earned Income From Employment (Given)	$116,000
2019 Business Loss	(12,500)
2019 Rental Income	7,500
2019 Earned Income	$111,000

Unused Deduction Room - End Of 2019	Nil
Annual Addition - Lesser Of:	
• 2020 RRSP Dollar Limit = $27,230	
• 18% of 2019 Earned Income Of $111,000 = $19,980	$19,980
Less 2019 PA	(6,800)
2020 RRSP Deduction Limit	$13,180

RRSP Deduction For 2020	$ 2,600

While Mr. Sabatini has deduction room of $13,180, only the $2,600 contribution to his wife's plan can be deducted. His $10,000 contribution to his own RRSP is not relevant as it was deducted in the previous year.

Part C

Since the RRSP has no beneficiary specified, an amount equal to the fair market value of all the property held in the RRSP at the time of death will have to be reported on Mr. Sabatini's return for 2021, the year of death.

Part D

Since Mr. Sabatini's wife is the sole beneficiary, she can choose to transfer all the assets in the RRSP to an RRSP in her name. If this is done, there will be no tax consequences for either his wife or Mr. Sabatini's final return. This would likely be the most tax advantageous arrangement for dealing with Mr. Sabatini's RRSP.

Note that there are also provisions that allow RRSPs to be transferred to a financially dependent child on a basis that shifts the tax burden to the child. Given Mr. Sabatini is receiving child support for an 8 year son, this approach might also be tax advantageous.

Solution to Self Study Problem Ten - 7

Part A

Ms. Wheeler's net employment income for 2019 would be $20,800, her gross salary of $22,000 reduced by her RPP contributions of $1,200.

Part B

The annual addition for 2020 would be the lesser of $27,230 and 18 percent of Earned Income for 2019. The latter amount would be calculated as follows:

Net Employment Income (Part A)	$20,800
Add Back RPP Contributions	1,200
Spousal Support Received [(6)($1,200)]	7,200
Net Business Loss	(2,500)
Earned Income	$26,700
Percent	18%
Annual Addition (Less than $27,230)	$ 4,806

Ms. Wheeler's maximum deductible RRSP contribution would be calculated as follows:

Opening Unused Deduction Room	Nil
Annual Addition	$4,806
Less 2019 PA ($1,200 + $1,200)	(2,400)
Maximum Deductible RRSP Contribution	$2,406

Part C

As Ms. Wheeler has made no contributions prior to 2020, she has no undeducted contributions. In addition, she has interest income and dividends that are subject to current Tax Payable. Given this, as well as the fact that her lump sum payment of $80,000 and $50,000 inheritance leaves her with cash in excess of her needs, she should contribute the maximum deductible amount of $2,406 for 2020.

While she could deduct the $2,406 in 2020, it would be advantageous to defer this deduction until 2021 when she expects to be in a higher tax bracket. At the federal level, the tax savings will be $626 [(26%)($2,406)] in 2021, as compared to $361 [(15%)($2,406)] in 2020.

Given her available funds, Ms. Wheeler should be advised to consider contributing the maximum allowable amount to a Tax Free Savings Account, as well as over contributing up to $2,000 to her RRSP. Although she would not be able to deduct these contributions, they would enjoy the benefit of having any income earned while in the plan compounded on a tax free basis. An over contribution to her RRSP would be deductible in a future year with sufficient RRSP deduction room.

All of these contributions should be made as soon as possible in order to maximize the tax free earnings that will accrue inside of her RRSP and/or TFSA.

Solution to Self Study Problem Ten - 8

Part A

Jeff's Net Income For Tax Purposes would be calculated as follows:

Income Under ITA 3(a):		
Net Employment Income	$59,000	
Interest	2,300	
Eligible Dividends	1,400	
Gross Up [(38%)($1,400)]	532	
Royalties	5,000	
Spousal Support Received	12,000	
Child Support Received (Non-Taxable)	Nil	$ 80,232
Income Under ITA 3(b):		
Taxable Capital Gains	$62,000	
Allowable Capital Losses	(6,000)	56,000
Balance From ITA 3(a) And (b)		$136,232
Subdivision e Deductions		
Spousal Support Paid	($24,000)	
Child Care Costs	(5,000)	(29,000)
Balance From ITA 3(c)		$107,232
Deductions Under ITA 3(d):		
Net Rental Loss		(27,200)
Net Income For Tax Purposes		$ 80,032

The capital loss carry forward would affect his Taxable Income only.

Part B

Jeff's 2019 Earned Income would be calculated as follows:

Net Employment Income	$59,000
Add Back RPP Contributions	1,500
Royalties (Taxpayer's Own Work)	5,000
Spousal Support Received	12,000
Spousal Support Paid	(24,000)
Net Rental Loss	(27,200)
Earned Income	$26,300

Given this, his maximum 2020 contribution would be calculated as follows:

Unused Deduction Room - End Of 2019	$18,000
Annual Addition - Lesser Of:	
• 2020 RRSP Dollar Limit = $27,230	
• 18% of 2019 Earned Income Of $26,300 = $4,734	4,734
Less 2019 PA ($1,500 + $1,500 + $1,000)	(4,000)
2020 RRSP Deduction Limit	$18,734
Allowable Excess Amount	2,000
Non-Penalty Contribution Limit	$20,734
Undeducted Contributions From Previous Years	(20,000)
Maximum RRSP Contribution	$ 734

If Jeff contributes this amount of $734, his deduction will be equal to $18,734 and he will carry forward undeducted RRSP contributions of $2,000 ($20,000 + $734 - $18,734).

Part C

With the additional $175,000 of business income, Jeff's earned income would be calculated as follows:

Net Employment Income	$ 59,000
Add Back RPP Contributions	1,500
Royalties	5,000
Spousal Support Received	12,000
Spousal Support Paid	(24,000)
Net Rental Loss	(27,200)
Net Business Income	175,000
Earned Income	$201,300

Given this, his maximum 2020 contribution would be calculated as follows:

Unused Deduction Room - End of 2019	$18,000
Annual Addition - Lesser Of:	
• 2020 RRSP Dollar Limit = $27,230	
• 18% of 2019 Earned Income Of $201,300 = $36,234	27,230
Less 2019 PA ($1,500 + $1,500 + $1,000)	(4,000)
2020 RRSP Deduction Limit	$41,230
Allowable Excess Amount	2,000
Non-Penalty Contribution Limit	$43,230
Undeducted Contributions From Previous Years	(20,000)
Maximum RRSP Contribution	$23,230

If Jeff contributes the amount of $23,230, his deduction will be equal to $41,230 and he will carry forward undeducted RRSP contributions of $2,000 ($20,000 + $23,230 - $41,230).

Solution to Self Study Problem Ten - 9

General Tax Planning Goals

The most desirable solution would be to find benefits that would be fully deductible to the company and free of taxation for Mr. Jones. The only items that fall into this category would be:

- payments for private health care plans;
- payments for disability insurance;
- discounts on company merchandise; and
- annual non-cash gifts with a value of $500 or less.

Discounts on industrial engines are not likely to be of any value to Mr. Jones. However, Mr. Jones should arrange to have the company provide private health care coverage, including a dental plan. The company could also pay the premiums on a disability insurance plan without it becoming a taxable benefit to Mr. Jones at the time of payment (benefits received would be taxable). Finally, an annual non-cash gift with a value of $500 or less would be deductible to the company and received tax free by Mr. Jones.

Use Of RPP, DPSP, RRSP, And Retiring Allowance

In terms of tax deferral, Mr. Jones should be included in the company's Registered Pension Plan (RPP). Once he is admitted to the plan, both he and the company should make the maximum contributions that are permitted under the terms of the plan. The limiting factor here is that these contributions cannot result in a Pension Adjustment that is in excess of the lesser of 18 percent of Mr. Jones' compensation for the year or the money purchase limit for the year under consideration ($27,830 for 2020).

While there is no indication that the company has such an arrangement, a Deferred Profit Sharing Plan (DPSP) might also be useful. Whether or not Mr. Jones would be able to use such an arrangement would depend on the total employee/employer contributions to the company's RPP. Contributions to a DPSP are included in the calculation of Mr. Jones' Pension Adjustment and, when combined with the RPP contributions, the total is subject to the limitation described in the preceding paragraph.

Housing Loan

The company could provide a loan to Mr. Jones to purchase his new residence. A low interest or interest free loan will result in imputed interest being added to Mr. Jones' Taxable Income without an offsetting deduction. Note, however, that the prescribed rate for this purpose is at the low rate of 2 percent. At this rate, even if the loan is interest free, the taxable benefit associated with such loans is fairly small and could make a large interest free loan desirable. On the $100,000 he requires to buy a residence, the benefit on an interest free loan would only be $2,000 [(2%)(100,000)].

As there is an intent to compensate, arrangements would have to be made for forgiving the loan after Mr. Jones retires. While such forgiveness would be taxable to Mr. Jones, he expects to be in a lower tax bracket after retiring, resulting in an absolute tax savings.

Company Car

The company could provide Mr. Jones with an automobile. In this case, Mr. Jones will be assessed for a personal benefit of a standby charge (24 percent per year of the capital cost or two-thirds of the lease payments, if he is not eligible for a reduction) and for operating costs (one-half of the standby charge or $0.28 per kilometre of personal use). Whether or not this will be desirable depends on an analysis of how Mr. Jones would actually use the car. In some cases, especially if the car has a list price of more than $30,000, the taxable benefit may exceed the actual benefit, making this an undesirable form of compensation.

Recreational Facilities

The company could pay the dues for any recreational facilities that Mr. Jones might wish to use. While these amounts will not be treated as a taxable benefit to Mr. Jones, the payments will not be deductible to the company. Given that the company is subject to a marginal tax rate that is lower than Mr. Jones' combined rate, it is unlikely the company would agree to do this.

Moving Costs

The company could provide assistance with the costs that will be incurred by Mr. Jones in moving to Hamilton. With respect to costs that Mr. Jones would be permitted to deduct, it makes little difference whether the company pays the costs or simply pays an equivalent amount in salary and lets Mr. Jones pay the costs and deduct them. However, certain types of moving costs that would not be deductible by Mr. Jones can be paid by the company without creating a taxable benefit. An example of this would be compensation for a loss on a personal residence owned by Mr. Jones if a loss exists on his house in Windsor. (See Chapter 9.)

Bonus And/Or Stock Options

If Martin Manufacturing has a year end after July 6, it can declare a bonus in the third year, but not pay it until the following calendar year. This will defer Mr. Jones' taxation of the bonus by one year without deferring Martin's deduction.

As an incentive, the company could grant Mr. Jones options to purchase its stock. This would have no tax cost to the company. The timing of the tax cost of the options for Mr. Jones could be delayed until after retirement.

Services As A Self-Employed Contractor Or Through A Corporation

Since Mr. Jones has been operating as a consultant, it may be possible to structure the project so that he will be considered an independent contractor rather than an employee. This would considerably increase the amount and type of expenditures that would be deductible by him and also create an opportunity to income split with his wife, if she could assist him in the project in some way. Her assistance would have to have a business purpose (supernatural phenomena expertise would have questionable value) and any payments to her would have to be reasonable in the circumstances.

In considering this alternative it should be kept in mind that, if Mr. Jones is not an employee, some of the possibilities that have been previously discussed would no longer be feasible. For example, unless Mr. Jones is an employee, it would not be possible for him to be a member of the company's RPP.

Another possibility would be for Mr. Jones to provide his services through a corporation. However, this would probably not be helpful. Given his relationship with Martin Manufacturing Company, any corporation would likely be viewed as a personal services business and taxed at full corporate rates. (Personal services corporations are covered in Chapter 12, "Taxable Income And Tax Payable For Corporations".)

Solution to Self Study Problem Ten - 10

Part A - RRSP Contribution

In order to calculate the maximum deductible RRSP contribution, net employment income and net rental income must first be calculated.

Net Employment Income

The calculations required for 2019 (to be used in the RRSP Earned Income calculation) and 2020 would be as follows:

	2019	2020
Gross Salary	$47,000	$53,000
Commissions	6,200	7,800
RPP Contributions	(1,800)	(1,950)
Work Space In Home Costs (Note 1)	(1,001)	(1,073)
Net Employment Income	$50,399	$57,777

Note 1 As an employee, Kerri cannot deduct either the listed mortgage interest or CCA on this office space. Because she has commission income, Kerri can deduct all of the other listed costs. Given this, the 2019 and 2020 deductions are as follows:

	2019	2020
Utilities And Maintenance	$1,850	$2,040
Insurance	625	715
Property Taxes	4,200	4,400
Total	$6,675	$7,155
Percentage Used	15%	15%
Deductible Amount	$1,001	$1,073

Net Rental Income

The calculations required for 2019 and 2020 would be as follows:

	2019	2020
Rents	$ 8,400	$13,800
Expenses Other Than CCA	(10,300)	(11,100)
Income (Loss) Before CCA	($ 1,900)	$ 2,700
CCA (Note 2)	N/A	(2,700)
Net Rental Income	($ 1,900)	Nil

Note 2 As CCA cannot be used to increase or create a rental loss, no deduction can be made in 2019. For 2020, the maximum available CCA deduction is $10,400 [(4%) ($340,000 - $80,000)]. However, the actual deduction is limited to the $2,700 of rental income prior to the deduction of CCA. The first year one-half rule is not applicable as this is the second year the property is owned. The fact that no CCA was deducted in the first year is not relevant.

RRSP Calculations

Determining the appropriate amount here requires the calculation of Earned Income for 2019. The calculation is as follows:

2019 Net Employment Income	$50,399
2019 RPP Contributions Deducted	1,800
Spousal Support Received [(12)($500)]	6,000
2019 Net Rental Loss	(1,900)
2019 Earned Income	$56,299

Using this figure, Ms. Sosteric's maximum 2020 deduction, along with the additional contribution required to make this deduction, would be calculated as follows:

Opening Unused Deduction Room	$ 6,200
Annual Addition - Lesser Of:	
• 2020 RRSP Dollar Limit = $27,230	
• 18% Of 2019 Earned Income Of $56,299 = $10,134	10,134
Less 2019 PA (Employee And Employer RPP Contributions)	(3,600)
Maximum RRSP Deduction	$12,734
Undeducted Contributions In Plan	(5,800)
Required Additional Contribution	$ 6,934

Part B - Net Income For Tax Purposes And Taxable Income

Other Required Information

While we can use several of the figures from Part A to calculate Net Income For Tax Purposes, two other items must be calculated before we can complete this figure.

Taxable Capital Gain And Dividends - Employer's Shares

The tax consequences related to buying, holding, and selling her employer's shares are as follows:

Proceeds Of Disposition [(5,000)($14.75)]	$73,750
Adjusted Cost Base [(5,000)($12.00)]	(60,000)
Capital Gain	$13,750
Inclusion Rate	1/2
Taxable Capital Gain	$ 6,875

Eligible Dividends [(5,000)($0.60)]	$ 3,000

Child Care Costs

Kerri's deductible child care costs are the least of three amounts:

Actual Costs The actual costs were given as $8,600.

Annual Limit The annual limit is $13,000 ($8,000 for Barry and $5,000 for Kim).

Income Limit   For this purpose, Ms. Sosteric's "earned income" is her gross employment income of $60,800 ($53,000 + $7,800). Two-thirds of this amount is $40,533.

The least of these figures is the actual costs of $8,600.

As Ms. Sosteric has no deductions applicable to the determination of Taxable Income, her Taxable Income is equal to her Net Income For Tax Purposes, which is as follow:

Net Employment Income (Part A)	$57,777
Net Rental Income (Part A)	Nil
RRSP Deduction (Part A)	(12,734)
Spousal Support Received	6,000
Taxable Capital Gains	6,875
Eligible Dividends [(5,000)($0.60)]	3,000
Gross Up [(38%)($3,000)]	1,140
Child Care Costs	(8,600)
Deductible CPP ($2,898 - $2,732)	(166)
Net Income For Tax Purposes And Taxable Income	$53,292

Part B - Tax Payable

The required calculations for her Tax Payable are as follows:

Tax On First $48,535		$7,280
Tax On Next $4,757 ($53,292 - $48,535) At 20.5 Percent		975
Tax Before Credits		$8,255
Tax Credits:		
Basic Personal Amount	($13,229)	
Eligible Dependant - Either Child	(13,229)	
EI Premiums	(856)	
CPP Contributions	(2,732)	
Canada Employment	(1,245)	
Medical Expenses (Note 3)	(1,021)	
Total Credit Base	($32,312)	
Rate	15%	(4,847)
Dividend Tax Credit [(6/11)($1,140)]		(622)
Federal Tax Payable		$2,786

Note 3   The base for Ms. Sosteric's medical expense tax credit would be calculated as follows:

Eligible Expenses	$2,620
Reduced By The Lesser Of:	
• [(3%)($53,292)] = $1,599	
• 2020 Threshold Amount = $2,397	(1,599)
Base For Credit	$1,021

Solution to Self Study Problem Ten - 11

Part A - Spousal RRSP Contribution

As noted in the problem, we are to assume that Ahmed's 2019 Earned Income is equal to his 2020 Earned Income. In order to calculate the 2020 Earned Income, we need to calculate both net employment income and net rental income. These are the only components of Mr. Sidi's Earned Income.

Net Employment Income

Even though Ahmed is no longer an employee, he has employment income related to the exercise of his stock option shares. The calculations are as follows:

Exercise Date Value [(5,000)($21)]	$105,000
Option Price [(5,000)($15)]	(75,000)
Employment Income Inclusion	$ 30,000

There will be a deduction in the determination of Taxable Income equal to one-half of this inclusion or $15,000.

Net Rental Income

The required calculations here are as follows:

Revenues ($34,000 + $42,000 + $26,000)	$102,000
Recapture On Property A (Note 1)	138,000
Expenses Other Than CCA	
($29,000 + $37,000 + $23,000)	(89,000)
CCA (Note 1)	(38,240)
Net Rental Income	$112,760

Note 1 CCA on the rental properties would be calculated as follows:

	Property A	Property B	Property C
UCC On January 1	$422,000	$571,000	$385,000
Dispositions - Capital Cost	(560,000)	N/A	N/A
Subtotal	($ 138,000)	$571,000	$385,000
Recapture	138,000	N/A	N/A
Balance Subject To CCA	Nil	$571,000	$385,000
Rate N/A	4%	4%	4%
CCA	Nil	$ 22,840	$ 15,400

The total 2020 CCA would be $38,240 ($22,840 + $15,400).

RRSP Deduction

Since we are assuming that Ahmed's 2019 Earned Income is equal to his 2020 Earned Income, the required figure is calculated as follows:

Employment Income	$ 30,000
Net Rental Income	112,760
2019 Earned Income (Assumed To Be Equal To 2020)	$142,760

The maximum deductible spousal RRSP contribution for 2020 would be the lesser of $25,697 [(18%)($142,760)] and the 2020 RRSP Dollar Limit of $27,230. Using the lesser figure, the maximum deductible contribution would be $25,697.

Part B - Net Income For Tax Purposes

While the employment income and rental income figures from Part A are components of Net Income For Tax Purposes, other figures are needed to complete this Part B calculation.

Taxable Capital Gains

There will be a taxable capital gain on the sale of the shares, calculated as follows:

Proceeds Of Disposition [(5,000)($23)]	$115,000
Adjusted Cost Base [(5,000)($21)]	(105,000)
Capital Gain	$ 10,000
Inclusion Rate	1/2
Taxable Capital Gain	$ 5,000

In addition, there will be a capital gain on the sale of Property A, calculated as follows:

	Land	Building
Proceeds Of Disposition	$340,000	$620,000
Adjusted Cost Base/Capital Cost	(100,000)	(560,000)
Capital Gain	$240,000	$ 60,000

The total capital gain is $300,000 ($240,000 + $60,000). However, as the total proceeds were not collected in the year of sale, he can reduce his income inclusion through the use of a reserve.

Total Capital Gain ($240,000 + $60,000)	$300,000
Reserve - Lesser Of:	
• [($300,000)($864,000 ÷ $960,000)] = $270,000	
• [($300,000)(20%)(4 - 0)] = $240,000	(240,000)
Capital Gain	$ 60,000
Inclusion Rate	1/2
Taxable Capital Gain For 2020	$ 30,000

Minimum RRIF Withdrawal

A registrant can irrevocably elect to base the minimum RRIF withdrawal calculation on the age of his spouse rather than his own age. If the spouse is younger, this will minimize the required withdrawal. Adrianna is aged 66, which is five years younger than Ahmed.

For individuals under the age of 71, the minimum RRIF withdrawal is calculated by dividing the fair market value of the assets in the plan at the beginning of the year by the number 90, less the registrant's age, or the spouse's age if elected.

The minimum RRIF withdrawal would be $52,083 [$1,250,000 ÷ (90 - 66)].

Pension Income Splitting

The election to split CPP benefits is provided for in the Canada Pension Plan regulations and results in an actual split of the payments. The ITA 60.03 legislation allows certain other types of pension income to be split. Both payments of RPPs and withdrawals from RRIFs qualify for this split, which is implemented solely on the tax returns. The total qualifying pension income for Ahmed is $138,083 ($86,000 + $52,083), one-half of which is $69,042.

Net Income For Tax Purposes

Based on the preceding calculations and the Other Information provided in the problem, Ahmed's minimum Net Income For Tax Purposes can be calculated as follows:

Employment Income - Part A	$ 30,000
Net Rental Income - Part A	112,760
Spousal RRSP Deduction - Part A	(25,697)
RPP Receipts (Pension Split)	86,000
CPP Receipts After Election To Split With Wife	5,500
Taxable Capital Gain - Option Shares	5,000
Taxable Capital Gain - Rental Property	30,000
Minimum RRIF Withdrawal (Pension Split)	52,083
Interest From Canadian Sources	18,000
Eligible Dividends Received	2,200
Gross Up [(38%)($2,200)]	836
Foreign Source Interest (100 Percent)	3,000
Net Income For Tax Purposes Before Pension Split	$319,682
Income Allocated To Wife [(1/2)($86,000 + $52,083)]	(69,042)
Net Income For Tax Purposes	$250,640

Part B - Taxable Income

Ahmed's Taxable Income would be calculated as follows:

Net Income For Tax Purposes	$250,640
Stock Option Deduction - Part A	(15,000)
Taxable Income	$235,640

Part B - Tax Payable

As the problem requires the minimum Tax Payable, Ahmed has claimed the credits for his son, the medical expenses, and charitable donations. These could have been claimed by Adrianna. The required calculations are as follows:

Tax On First $214,368			$49,645
Tax On Next $21,272 ($235,640 - $214,368) At 33 Percent			7,020
Tax Before Credits			$56,665
Tax Credits:			
Basic Personal Amount	($12,298)		
Spousal (Note 2)	Nil		
Age (Net Income Too High)	Nil		
Canada Caregiver - Son	(7,276)		
Canada Employment	(1,245)		
Pension Income	(2,000)		
Transfer Of Disability From Son	(8,576)		
Medical Expenses (Note 3)	(13,003)		
Total Credit Base	($44,398)		
Rate	15%		(6,660)
Charitable Donations (Note 4)			(1,284)
Dividend Tax Credit On Eligible Dividends [(6/11)($836)]			(456)
Foreign Tax Credit (Amount Withheld)			(300)
Federal Tax Payable			$47,965

Note 2   While Adrianna has only $7,400 of OAS and the $5,500 in CPP benefits in her name, the added amounts resulting from the pension income splitting of more than $69,000 will be more than enough to eliminate the spousal tax credit. This additional income will use up all of her other tax credits (age and pension), preventing any transfers to Ahmed.

Note 3   The base for the medical expense tax credit is calculated as follows:

Ahmed And Adrianna ($2,500 + $3,100)		$ 5,600
Lesser Of:		
• [(3%)($250,640)] = $7,519		
• 2020 Threshold Amount = $2,397		(2,397)
Subtotal		$ 3,203
Son's Medical Expenses	$9,800	
Reduced By The Lesser Of:		
• $2,397		
• [(3%)(Nil)] = Nil	Nil	9,800
Allowable Amount Of Medical Expenses		$13,003

Note 4   Ahmed's charitable donations tax credit would be calculated as follows:

15 Percent Of $200		$ 30
33 Percent Of The Lesser Of:		
($4,000 - $200) = $3,800		
($235,640 - $214,368) = $21,272		1,254
Total Credit		$1,284

Part C - Pension Income Splitting

Given Ahmed's high Taxable Income, even after pension splitting more than $21,000 is being taxed at the maximum 33 percent federal rate. Despite splitting the maximum amount of pension income, none of Adrianna's income is taxed at higher than 20.5 percent federally.

As a result, maximum pension income splitting appears to be advantageous if only federal tax rates are considered.

What should also be considered is the effect of the pension income splitting on the OAS clawback for Adrianna and the effect of provincial income taxes on both Ahmed and Adrianna. The effect of the OAS clawback and provincial taxes could make it more advantageous to reduce the amount of income splitting so that Adrianna's Net Income For Tax Purposes is below the OAS clawback income threshold.

While the ability to claim more medical expenses could be a factor in some pension income splitting analyses, it would have very little influence in this case given the high levels of Net Income involved.

Chapter 11 Learning Objectives

After completing Chapter 11, you should be able to:

1. Recall the specified deductions from Net Income For Tax Purposes in the calculation of Taxable Income (paragraph [P hereafter] 11-1 to 11-7).
2. Apply the rules related to lump sum payments (P 11-8 to 11-13).
3. Recall the general rules for the treatment of losses and loss carry overs (P 11-14 to 11-29).
4. Explain the treatment of losses on personal use property (P 11-30).
5. Apply the loss carry over provisions applicable to losses on listed personal property (P 11-31 to 11-35).

6. Apply the loss carry over provisions applicable to non-capital losses (P 11-36 to 11-40).
7. Apply the loss carry over provisions applicable to net capital losses (P 11-41 to 11-44).
8. Apply the rules for the conversion of a net capital loss carry over to a non-capital loss carry over (P 11-45 to 11-49).
9. Explain the special rules for net capital losses that are applicable to deceased taxpayers (P 11-50 to 11-54).
10. Explain the special features associated with Allowable Business Investment Losses (P 11-55 to 11-62).

11. Apply the loss carry over provisions applicable to regular and restricted farm losses (P 11-63 to 11-67).
12. Apply the provisions of the lifetime capital gains deduction (P 11-68 to 11-97).
13. Describe the importance of the ordering of deductions and losses in computing Net Income For Tax Purposes and Taxable Income (P 11-98 to 11-103).
14. Describe Basic Federal Tax Payable (P 11-104 to 11-109).
15. Identify amounts that may be taxed as split income (P 11-110 to 11-124).

16. Determine the applicability of the Tax On Split Income (TOSI) (P 11-125 to 11-131).
17. Describe those items that will be Excluded Amounts with respect to the TOSI (P 11-132 to 11-142).
18 Calculate the amount of the TOSI (P 11-143 to 11-147).
19. Apply the provisions for the transfer of dividends to a spouse or common-law partner (P 11-148).
20. Calculate the charitable donations tax credit for donations of various types of property (P 11-149 to 11-174).

21. Calculate foreign business and non-business income tax credits (P 11-175 to 11-186).
22. Apply the provisions associated with the alternative minimum tax (P 11-187 to 11-200).
23. Review a personal tax return completed using the ProFile T1 tax preparation software program.

How to Work Through Chapter 11

We recommend the following approach in dealing with the material in this Chapter:

Taxable Income Introduction And Overview
- Read paragraph 11-1 to 11-7 (in the textbook).

Lump Sum Payments
- Read paragraph 11-8 to 11-13.

Loss Carry Over Provisions, Listed Personal Property Losses
- Read paragraph 11-14 to 11-35.
- Do Exercise Eleven-1 (in the textbook) and check the solution in this Study Guide.

Non-Capital Losses
- Read paragraph 11-36 to 11-38.
- Do Exercise Eleven-2 and check the solution in this Study Guide.
- Read paragraph 11-39 to 11-40.

Net Capital Losses (Including Special Rules At Death)
- Read paragraph 11-41 to 11-49.
- Do Exercise Eleven-3 and check the solution in this Study Guide.
- Read paragraph 11-50 to 11-54.
- Do Exercise Eleven-4 and check the solution in this Study Guide.

Allowable Business Investment Losses (ABILs)
- Read paragraph 11-55 to 11-62.
- Do Exercise Eleven-5 and check the solution in this Study Guide.
- Do Self Study Problem Eleven-1, which is available on MyLab, and check the solution in this Study Guide.

Farm Losses
- Read paragraph 11-63 to 11-67.
- Do Exercise Eleven-6 and check the solution in this Study Guide.
- Do Self Study Problem Eleven-2 and check the solution in this Study Guide.

Lifetime Capital Gains Deduction
- Read paragraph 11-68 to 11-85.
- Do Exercise Eleven-7 and check the solution in this Study Guide.
- Read paragraph 11-86 to 11-93.
- Do Exercise Eleven-8 and check the solution in this Study Guide.
- Do Self Study Problem Eleven-3 and check the solution in this Study Guide.

Ordering Of Deductions And Losses
- Read paragraph 11-94 to 11-103.
- Do Exercise Eleven-9 and check the solution in this Study Guide.

Tax Payable Overview And Tax On Split Income (TOSI)
- Read paragraph 11-104 to 11-147.
- Do Exercise Eleven-10 and check the solution in this Study Guide.
- Do Self Study Problem Eleven-4 and check the solution in this Study Guide.

Transfer Of Dividends To A Spouse Or Common-Law Partner
- Read paragraph 11-148.
- Do Exercise Eleven-11 and check the solution in this Study Guide.
- Do Self Study Problems Eleven-5 and Eleven-6 and check the solutions in this Study Guide.

Charitable Donations Credit - Gifts Of Capital Property
- Read paragraph 11-149 to 11-166.
- Do Exercise Eleven-12 and check the solution in this Study Guide.
- Read paragraph 11-167.
- Do Exercise Eleven-13 and check the solution in this Study Guide.
- Read paragraph 11-168 to 11-174.

Foreign Tax Credits Revisited
- Read paragraph 11-175 to 11-186.
- Do Exercise Eleven-14 and check the solution in this Study Guide.

Alternative Minimum Tax (AMT)
- Read paragraph 11-187 to 11-200.
- Do Exercise Eleven-15 and check the solution in this Study Guide.

Comprehensive Tax Payable And Sample Personal Tax Return For Chapter 11
- Read paragraph 11-201.
- Do Self Study Problems Eleven-7 to Eleven-11 and check the solutions in this Study Guide.
- Read the Sample Personal Tax Return For Chapter 11 found in this Chapter of this Study Guide. The complete tax returns are available on MyLab in two formats, a T1 ProFile return file and a .PDF file.

Tax Software Self Study Problem
- Do Tax Software Self Study Problem - Chapter 11 using the ProFile T1 Software. The Self Study Case is found in this Chapter of this Study Guide. The complete tax return is available on MyLab.

To Complete This Chapter
- If you would like more practice in problem solving, do the Supplementary Self Study Problems for the chapter. These are available on MyLab.
- Review the Key Terms Used In This Chapter in the textbook at the end of Chapter 11.
- Consult the Glossary for the meaning of any key terms you do not know.
- Test yourself with the Chapter 11 Glossary Flashcards on MyLab.
- Ensure you have achieved the Chapter 11 Learning Objectives listed in this Study Guide.
- As a review, we recommend you view the PowerPoint presentation for Chapter 11 that is on MyLab.

Practice Examination
Write the Practice Examination for Chapter 11 that is onMyLab. Mark your examination using the Practice Examination Solution that is also on MyLab.

Sample Personal Tax Return For Chapter 11

The following example contains a T1 individual income tax return completed using the ProFile T1 Personal Income Tax Program for 2019 tax returns from Intuit Canada. As software for 2020 is not yet available, this example contains 2019 rates and credits.

The updated 2020 filing version of the ProFile software will be available in January 2021. Non-filing versions will be available prior to that date, but include a number of 2020 draft forms that have not yet been updated. On installation, the program defaults to check for updates, so non-filing versions may be installed automatically. In January 2021, after the first 2020 filing version is released, the updated 2020 version of this sample return will be available on MyLab at:

http://www.pearsonmylabandmastering.com

This example was introduced in Chapter 4 and is expanded in Chapter 11 to contain other components of Taxable Income and Tax Payable. For comparison purposes, you might find it useful to review the Chapter 4 version of this example before proceeding with this version.

In the following example, the relevant T1 schedule or ProFile form name is provided in square brackets to indicate where the information is input.

Sample Problem Data

DISCLAIMER: All characters appearing in this example are fictitious. Any resemblance to real persons, living or dead, is purely coincidental.

George Pilot (SIN 527-000-145) is a married, semi-retired air force pilot living in Banff, Alberta. His wife, Deborah (SIN 130-692-544), was mauled by a grizzly bear while hiking three years ago. The attack left her blind and limited her mobility. [Schedule 2 - Yes to disability amount. Check appropriate box on the Info form on Deborah's return under Filing. Press F5 on the info tab to move to and from the spouse's info.]

They have been your clients for many years. George was born on February 24, 1968, and Deborah was born on April 10, 1972. They are both Canadian citizens.

After some discussion with George and Deborah, you confirm that they have never owned any foreign property. They both authorize the CRA to provide information to Elections Canada and authorize you to e-file their returns. They are currently living at 69 BBB Street in Banff, Alberta T9Z 0C0. Their home phone number is (403) 111-1111.

George and Deborah have three children who are all in good health:

- Bryan (SIN 527-000-947) was born on March 12, 2012, and had no income during the year.

- Janice (SIN 527-000-269) was born on June 6, 2006, and is in high school. She had income from babysitting totaling $400 during 2019.

- Willa (SIN 527-000-228) was born on January 22, 2000, and is attending university in Edmonton. Willa had net income of $3,300 during 2019.

George has a passion for flying and was hired in February to fly fire bombers June 1 to September 30 for the provincial forest service fire control squad located in Banff.

George informs you that on February 12, 2019, he received $2 million from his mother's estate. Using some of these funds, George bought a house in Banff. The remainder of the funds were invested with his stockbroker, $$$$ Inc.

Deborah, a voice teacher, adapted to her blindness quickly and required no outside help to take care of the family last year or for the first eight months of 2019. She decided to move temporarily to Edmonton with Willa to attend the music program at the University of Alberta.

During 2019, Deborah made a $50,000 loan to her brother, Andrew, who used the funds to expand his business. On December 31, 2019, Andrew paid her $6,500, which included a principal payment of $5,000 and all interest accrued to that date in the amount of $1,500. Since the CRA administrative policy is not to require the preparation of a T5 ("Statement of Investment Income") for transactions between individuals, no T5 has been prepared. Include the interest income on Deborah's tax return on the form titled "Other Income" for line 12100, which can be accessed by right clicking that line. Also in 2019, Deborah provided teaching services, specifically private voice lessons, earning a gross total of $3,200. No expenses have been claimed. If you right click on line 13700 of her T1 you will see a reference to the T2125 (Statement of Business and Professional Activities) that you must complete. The self-employment form will also be generated once you have completed the T2125.

George brings you the following receipts and documents:

1. A T4, T4A, and a T5 (included in this example). A statement from his bank stating that he paid $7,382 in interest on the mortgage on his house during 2019. (See Items 17 and 23.)

2. A T2202A "Tuition And Enrollment Certificate" for himself from Athabasca University. It showed he was a part time student for six months and paid $591 in tuition for 2019. [T2202]

3. Two charitable donation receipts. One in George's name for $1,000 from the Canadian Wildlife Federation dated April 10, 2019. A second receipt in Deborah's name for $100 from the Canadian National Institute for the Blind (CNIB) dated December 3, 2019. [Donations]

4. A statement from the Banff Dental Clinic that George paid a total of $1,650 during 2019. This consisted of $850 for himself on November 24, and $200 each for Deborah, Bryan, Willa, and Janice on December 15. [Medical]

5. An invoice from the CNIB in Deborah's name for $375 dated December 26, 2019, for computer peripherals designed exclusively for a person who is blind to use a computer. She had obtained a prescription from her doctor specifying her need for this equipment. [Medical]

6. George spent $14,700 during 2019 on various permanent modifications to the house. His goal for these changes was to allow Deborah to be more mobile inside and outside the house (e.g., outside ramps and railings in the halls and stairways) and to reduce the risk of harm to her (a walk-in bathtub). George has detailed invoices for the renovations. Since Deborah's mobility impairment is not severe, these expenditures do not qualify as allowable medical expenses. [Schedule 12]

7. An agreement of purchase and sale for a house at 69 BBB St. in Banff. The purchase price was $800,000 and the invoice for legal fees totaled $1,200. The deal closed March 31, 2019, and George paid the purchase price of the house in cash. George and his family had been living in a rented townhouse for the last five years. Prior to that George had owned a house, but it went to his ex-wife in the divorce settlement. Deborah has never owned a principal residence. [Other Credits for the Home Buyers' Credit.]

8. An instalment statement for 2019 that showed that George had paid the CRA instalments of $1,500 on September 14 and December 14 ($3,000 in total). These were the instalments requested by the CRA for the year due to his self-employed income in the previous year. [Other Credits]

9. A T2202A "Tuition And Enrollment Certificate" for Deborah from the University of Alberta. It showed she was a full time student for four months and paid $2,600 in tuition for 2019. [Schedule 2]

10. A T2202A "Tuition And Enrollment Certificate" for Willa from the University of Alberta. It showed she was a full time student for eight months and paid $6,200 in tuition for 2019. She had signed the certificate authorizing the maximum transfer of her tuition amount to her father. [Dependant]

11. His 2018 Notice of Assessment that shows that his 2019 RRSP Deduction Limit is $13,979. He has no undeducted RRSP contributions from previous years. [RRSP]

12. A contribution receipt to a spousal RRSP (George contributed to Deborah's RRSP) for $2,000 from $$$$ Inc. dated February 20, 2020. [RRSP]

13. A receipt for $2,000 from George's 40 year old sister, Shirley Burns (SIN 527-000-582), for child care. She took care of Bryan after school during 2019 while Deborah was in Edmonton. [Input on Dependants, flows to T778]

14. A receipt for Janice, an accomplished trombone player, from the Peak Music Camp in Whistler, B.C. The receipt for $1,600 was for two weeks of intensive music instruction at the

camp. This fee also included $400 in accommodations and $325 for meals. [Input on Dependants, flows to T778]

15. A receipt for $2,148 dated April 1, 2019, from the Mountain Moving Company. The invoice describes the charges as fees for packing, moving, and delivering George's household effects and furniture from his former rented home at 123 CCC Avenue in Calgary (the "old home") to his newly purchased home in Banff (the "new home") a distance of 125 kilometres. The distance between the old home and George's place of employment at Alberta Fire and Brimstone Control was 130 kilometres whereas the distance between the new home and the place of employment is only 5 kilometres.

16. In July 2019, George asked you how much he could contribute to TFSAs for himself and Deborah. By accessing their accounts through the CRA's online Represent A Client service, you informed him that he could contribute $25,000 for both himself and Deborah. George brings in TFSA statements for himself and Deborah that shows he made the maximum contribution to each TFSA on October 20, 2019. It also shows that Deborah withdrew $3,000 from her TFSA on December 15, 2019.

17. George's new stockbroker, Mr. Ace Securities at $$$$ Inc., convinces him to take out a mortgage on his new home in order to invest the funds in various stocks. George assumes a $500,000 mortgage as of June 1, 2019. On that date, the funds from his mortgage are transferred to $$$$ Inc. into a trading (i.e., non-registered) account. The $7,382 mortgage interest on the bank statement relates to this mortgage. The stockbroker assures George that the funds will remain fully invested in the trading account. Investment income such as interest and taxable dividends was formerly included on Schedule 4, which no longer exists. This information together with the deduction of carrying charges is now included on the "worksheet for the return."

18. George's capital gain transaction summary statement for 2019 issued from $$$$ Inc. lists the details of 33 separate share sale transactions. The separate details of each transaction would be required to be entered in Schedule 3. The ProFile software requires that the form S3 Details be completed to record each transaction, which is then automatically entered into Schedule 3. Assume for this purpose that the details are combined into one transaction to be entered in S3 Details as follows:

Code 3a for Mutual Funds/Shares

Date of disposition: 12/12

Proceeds of disposition: $100,000

Adjusted Cost Base (ACB): $94,000

Outlays and Expenses: $1,928.00

19. On January 8, 2019, George sold his 1971 Ford Mustang for $50,000. The car was driven only on sunny Sunday afternoons. Its original price in 2002 was $6,000, and George reconditioned it over the years at a cost of $12,000. [S3 Details]

20. At the beginning of 2019, George has a net capital loss carry forward of $2,580 [(1/2)($5,160)] from 2017. [Loss Net Cap]

21. During 2019, he paid $6,000 in spousal support to his ex-wife, Marilyn (SIN 527-000-103), pursuant to a written agreement. [Support payments]

22. George owns a commercial property at 999 JJJ Avenue, Edmonton, Alberta T9Z 0C0. The property was 10 years old when he purchased it on February 15, 2017, for $600,000, of which $160,000 was allocated to the land. Shortly after George purchased the building, the major tenant went bankrupt and he had rental losses for 2017 and 2018. No capital additions were made since the building's acquisition. The financial information for the property, for the year ended December 31, 2019, is as follows [Rental, T776, T776 Asset and T776 CCA will be completed]:

Rental income	$46,700
Mortgage interest	$19,500
Maintenance and repairs	5,100
Management and administration fees	8,200
Legal fees	1,000
Property taxes	11,750
Total expenses	$45,550
Net Income before amortization	$ 1,150

23. In Calgary in prior years, George gave the occasional private flying lesson and found it very rewarding. After moving to Banff, he began to pursue private pilot training in earnest beginning April 1 through his business, Pilot's Flying School. A portion of his new house is used exclusively for various training activities such as one-to-one ground instruction. He also writes and reviews practice pilot exams. George's fiscal year end for the business is December 31.

The business area of the house occupies 420 square feet of the 2,100 square foot house. George does not intend to claim any CCA on the house. At your request he provides the following costs related to the house during the period April 1, 2019, through December 31, 2019 [T2125, T2125 Asset and T2125 CCA]:

Utilities	$1,500
Repairs And Maintenance	4,325
Home Insurance	700
Mortgage Interest	7,382
Property Taxes	2,600

24. On April 15, 2019, George purchased a laptop computer and various software that will be used solely for his business activities. The laptop cost $1,900 and the software costs totaled $800. Prior to this, George had not been using a computer for business purposes. [T2125]

25. George provides the following other information for Pilot's Flying School, for the fiscal period ended December 31, 2019:

Lesson and training fees received	$40,200
Plane rental fees	9,600
Business meals with clients	3,250
Licences and fees	1,650
Office expenses	550
Accounting fees	300

Completed Tax Returns And Related Notes

There are three sample tax returns available on MyLab in two versions, a T1 ProFile return file and a .PDF file. Notes to the returns are in a separate .PDF file.

A. A single return assuming George does not elect to split his pension income and Deborah does not file a tax return.

B. A coupled return assuming George elects to split his pension income with Deborah and she files a tax return as well.

Notes To The Chapter 11 Return - No Pension Splitting
Only George Is Filing A Return
General Notes

- Inheritances are not taxable.

- Willa's tuition fees total more than $5,000. As a result, her transfer to George is limited to the $5,000 maximum. Only Willa can claim the unused credits in the future. Willa should file a return in order to receive the GST credit and to help her keep track of her tuition credit carry forward.

- Since Willa is over 17 years of age, her medical expenses are reduced by 3 percent of her Net Income For Tax Purposes.

- George is not eligible for the refundable medical expense supplement or the Canada Workers Benefit as his income is too high. Given 3 percent of his Net Income is greater than the medical expense threshold, the only allowable medical expenses are those of Willa.

- In the ProFile tax file there is a memo attached to the line "Total medical expenses- line 330" (green highlight) that says "Net Income too high, do not claim medical expenses except for Willa so carry forward is optimized". Since they were paid in November and December, they could be claimed in the following year if the 12 month limit is used.

- Deborah has interest income of $1,500 and professional fees of $3,200. As a result, the spousal credit base is decreased by this amount on Schedule 2. Note that the principal repayment of $5,000 is not income. Deborah's disability credit has been transferred to George, as well as all of her tuition tax credit since it totals less than $5,000.

- As a resident of Alberta George qualifies for the refundable Climate Action Incentive payment for 2019. This refundable credit is available to individuals who are residents of Ontario, Manitoba, Saskatchewan, and Alberta in 2019. The maximum credit for a family of four in Alberta is $888.

- George's 2019 CPP contribution of $790.50 is calculated as 5.1 percent of insurable earnings, which are equal to his employment income of $19,000 minus a basic exemption of $3,500. There are two components to the CPP contribution rate of 5.1 percent. The first is a basic contribution rate of 4.95 percent and the second an additional amount of 0.15 percent referred to as an enhancement. The enhancement represents an effort by the Federal government to provide increased CPP retirement pension benefits. The basic 4.95 percent or $767.25 is treated as a non-refundable tax credit and the enhanced portion of $23.25 is allowed as a deduction (new line 22215).

Item Specific Notes

- (Item 3) For couples, the CRA's administrative practices permit either spouse to claim some or all of the donations made by the couple. George should claim both donations as combining them is advantageous given the 15 percent rate on the first $200 of donations.

- (Item 5) Both ITA 118.2 and Income Tax Folio S1-F1-C1 clearly state that medical expenses can only be deducted by the individual who paid for them. However, in the T1 Guide, this rule is contradicted for couples. According to this Guide, either spouse can claim the medical expense credit, without regard to who actually paid for the expenses. This administrative position is used in practice. As a result, George is claiming the amount Deborah paid for the computer peripherals.

- (Item 6) George's receipts for the expenses eligible for the Home Accessibility Credit total more than the $10,000 maximum for the year on the "other credits" form. As a result the maximum credit of $1,500 [(15%)($10,000)] is available.

- (Item 7) The Home Buyers' Tax Credit of $750 [(15%)($5,000)] is available since George had been living in a rented town house for five years and neither he nor Deborah had another principal residence.

- (Items 13 and 14) Since Deborah was in full time attendance at the University of Alberta, George can deduct child care costs of up to $4,000 [(2)($125)(16 weeks)]. The $2,000 paid to Shirley Burns is totally deductible. The deduction for child care costs is limited to $125 per week for overnight camp fees. This results in maximum deductible child care costs of $2,250.

- (Item 15) Form T1M, Claim For Moving Expenses should be filled out to calculate the deductible moving expenses. George cannot deduct the legal fees related to the purchase of his new home because he had been living in a rented townhouse in Calgary. On Form T1M, since the "Simplified Method" box is checked, the program calculates the allowable deduction for mileage using the 2019 Alberta rate.

- (Item 17) The house was purchased for cash and the mortgage was obtained for investment purposes only. As a result all of the interest is deductible on the "other deductions" form. Note that Schedule 4 no longer exists. In order that all of the interest remains deductible in the future, George should ensure that the $500,000 from the mortgage remain invested and is not used for personal purposes.

- (Item 20) George has claimed his net capital loss carry forward of $2,580 as his total taxable capital gains were well in excess of this amount.

- (Item 22) Since the rental property has been showing a loss since its acquisition, no CCA could have been taken prior to 2019. As a result, the beginning of the year UCC of the building will be George's original allocation of $440,000 ($600,000- $160,000 land cost). The CCA for 2019 is limited to $1,150, the amount that reduces his rental income to nil.

T2125 (Items 24 to 26)

- The Industry Code must be chosen from the list near the top right corner of the T2125. The appropriate choice is 611690, "All Other Schools And Instruction".

- Expenses for income tax purposes are applied against the source of income to which they relate. Since the mortgage interest of $7,382 is sourced to investment income no part of it can be sourced to the professional income of the flying school as a business use of home expense. The interest expense is included on the "other deductions" form of the ProFile software. In years prior to 2019 Schedule 4 was used, but beginning in 2019 Schedule 4 no longer exists.

- There are three CCA rules that affect the amount of CCA that can be claimed for 2019 with respect to the laptop and software. The three rules are (1) the short fiscal period rule (ITR 1100(3)), (2) the regular half year rule (ITR 1100(2)), and (3) the accelerated investment incentive rules (ITR 1104(4)). The laptop falls into Class 50 (55 percent) and the software into Class 12 (100 percent). The fiscal period of the business in its first year is short, beginning April 1, 2019, and ending December 31, 2019 (275 days). This results in a prorated CCA amount that is automatically calculated by ProFile. In the T2125 Statement of Business or Professional Activities for the flying school business make sure to enter April 1, 2019, as the start of the fiscal period.

- The regular half year rule applies to depreciable property that is not eligible for the Accelerated Investment Incentive (AII). Most depreciable property acquired in arm's length transactions between November 21, 2019, and December 31, 2023, is eligible for a first year accelerated CCA claim rather than a reduced claim under the historical half year rule. Since Class 12 property is eligible for a 100 percent rate the government opted to exclude such property from the new AII rules. As a result the laptop is eligible for the AII whereas the software is not but instead is subject to the half year rule.

Tax Planning Points

- If he has sufficient funds, George should contribute the maximum deductible for 2019 of $16,669 [see RRSP Limit form] to a spousal RRSP as soon as possible. Since George is already getting a pension and Deborah appears to have little income, a spousal RRSP would offer more opportunity for future income splitting. Although the pension income splitting legislation allows for some flexibility, the maximum split is 50 percent. With a spousal RRSP, Deborah can be taxed on 100 percent of the funds from her RRSP.

- George should consider opening RESPs for Bryan and Janice if he has not already done so. How much he should contribute will depend on many factors (see the text), but it is probably advisable that he contribute enough to take advantage of the Canada Education Savings Plan each year if he has sufficient funds.

- Deborah has created some RRSP contribution room with her professional income. George should consider whether Deborah should contribute to her own RRSP. Funds for George's RRSP and the RESPs should probably have priority given George's higher tax bracket and the Canada Education Savings Plan, though with his inheritance there should be sufficient funds to contribute to all the plans.

- Since TFSA contributions are not deductible and withdrawals are not taxable, the TFSAs will not have an effect on any of the tax returns. George should try to contribute the maximum to both his and Deborah's TFSA on an ongoing basis if he has sufficient funds. He should replace Deborah's withdrawal as soon as possible as it was withdrawn in the preceding calendar year. As long as there are other funds available where related income would be taxable, it would be advisable not to make withdrawals from the TFSAs in order to take advantage of the tax free earnings.

- George should consider a TFSA for Willa. If her income is earned income for RRSP purposes, he should also consider contributing to an RRSP in Willa's name.

Notes To The Chapter 11 Returns - With Pension Splitting
Both Are Filing Returns With Pension Income Splitting
The notes to the return with no pension income splitting are also relevant in this scenario.

In creating Deborah's tax return, the following forms and schedules were filled in:

- T2202 - Tuition slips
- T2125 - Statement of Business or Professional Activities
- T1032 - Joint Election To Split Income (originated from George's return)

Neither Deborah or George should claim the medical expenses, other than George claiming the medical expenses for Willa. Although 3 percent of Deborah's Net Income is less than the threshold, which would enable her to make a claim where George cannot, the tuition fee credit is calculated before consideration of medical expenses, so the claim for medical expenses has no effect on her Tax Payable and does not save her any taxes.

To test this, click Yes that Deborah should claim the medical expenses. What you will find is that her total non-refundable tax credits are greater than her Tax Payable because her tuition tax credit does not change. This means that the medical expense credit would be wasted. Since they were paid in November and December, they could be claimed in the following year if the 12 month limit is used.

Willa's medical expenses could have been claimed by Deborah, but since it will make no difference to her federal Tax Payable, it is more advantageous to have George claim Willa's medical expenses.

In addition, although we do not cover provincial tax rules in the text, if you examine Deborah's Alberta tax credits [AB428], you will see that she does not utilize all of her non-refundable Alberta tax credits, even if she does not claim any medical expenses. Claiming Willa's medical credit will decrease George's Alberta and federal Tax Payable.

Since the couple has elected to split the pension income, the withholdings on the pension income must also be split.

The tax savings can be determined by utilizing the "Optimize – split-pension income" function, which is accessed from the pension transferors' (George) tax return. In this case the optimum pension transfer is $12,066.04, which produces the following results:

Combined Refund – No Pension Splitting	$ 923.95
Combined Refund – With Pension Splitting	2,904.38
Tax Savings	$1,980.43

T1032Opt

Optimize - Split-pension income

Calculation of the elected split-pension amount

		Zero transfer	Suggested transfer
Elected split-pension amount		0.00	12,066.04
Total payable (line 43500)	George - Chapter 11 NO SPLIT	8,964.05	6,983.62
	Deborah		
	Combined	8,964.05	6,983.62
Balance owing / refund	George - Chapter 11 NO SPLIT	(923.95)	(1,755.23)
	Deborah		(1,149.15)
	Combined	(923.95)	(2,904.38)
Combined net benefit (cost)			1,980.43

		Calculator			
		Scenario #1	Scenario #2	Scenario #3	Scenario #4
Elected split-pension amount		21,000.00	15,000.00		
Total payable (line 43500)	George - Chapter 11 NO SPLIT	7,198.51	7,262.36		
	Deborah	77.10			
	Combined	7,275.61	7,262.36		
Balance owing / refund	George - Chapter 11 NO SPLIT	(689.49)	(1,197.07)		
	Deborah	(1,922.90)	(1,428.57)		
	Combined	(2,612.39)	(2,625.64)		
Combined net benefit (cost)		1,688.44	1,701.69		

Summary of the elected split-pension amount

We have determined that transferring **$12,066.04** to Deborah's return will result in the lowest combined total payable. If you elect to transfer the suggested amount, the refund of $923.95 is increased to $2,904.38. This represents an overall savings of **$1,980.43**.

Maximum split-pension amount (from line F of your T1032)	21,000.00	F
This amount will appear on line G on your T1032. Elected split-pension amount	12,066.04	G

Impact of electing a split-pension amount on your combined total payable

Tax Software Self Study Problem - Chapter 11

This Problem is an expansion of the Tax Software Self Study Problem - Chapter 4.

Note   The following problem contains the 2019 updated version of the problem that was revised following the release of the 2019 Intuit ProFile software in January 2020.

DISCLAIMER: All characters appearing in this problem are fictitious. Any resemblance to real persons, living or dead, is purely coincidental.

Ms. Eleanor Victoria's husband died two years ago. After her husband died, she moved from her house in Prince George, B.C., to a rented house in Victoria, B.C.

Ms. Victoria's widowed mother, Marjorie Vancouver, lives with Ms. Victoria and takes care of the house, Ms. Victoria's younger daughter, Amy, and all of the household cooking. In addition to OAS benefits, Marjorie has a very small income from her deceased husband's life insurance policy. She has never filed a tax return and she is not infirm.

Diane Victoria, Eleanor's older daughter, is studying psychology at McGill University in Montreal. Her field is addiction research with a special emphasis on gambling. She does volunteer work at a gambling addiction treatment centre in Montreal in the summers. As Eleanor has paid for her tuition and living costs, Diane has agreed that the maximum tuition amount should be transferred to her mother.

Diane has decided not to file a tax return this year as she knows she does not owe any taxes. Her income was earned driving for a client of the addiction treatment centre who had lost his licence after being charged with impaired driving.

Late in December 2018, Eleanor was notified that she had inherited $500,000 from an aunt. Eleanor loves her work and though she plans to travel more, she has no plans to retire.

Information concerning Ms. Victoria for 2019 is given on the following pages.

Required:

A. With the objective of minimizing Ms. Victoria's Tax Payable, prepare the 2019 income tax return of Eleanor Victoria using the ProFile tax software program. List any assumptions you have made, and any notes and tax planning issues you feel should be discussed with Ms. Victoria. Ignore HST implications in your solution by assuming that Ms. Victoria does not qualify for the GST/HST rebate.

B. Calculate the maximum deductible contribution Ms. Victoria can make to her RRSP for the 2019 taxation year. What advice would you give Ms. Victoria concerning the various deferred savings plans available to her given the funds from her inheritance?

Personal Information

Title	Ms.
First Name	Eleanor
Last Name	Victoria
SIN	527-000-087
Date of birth (Y/M/D)	1972-05-15
Marital Status	Widowed
Canadian citizen?	Yes
Provide information to Elections Canada?	Yes
Own foreign property of more than $100,000 Canadian?	No

Taxpayer's Address

111 VVV Street Victoria, B.C. V4H 3W4
Phone number (250) 111-1111

Dependants

Dependants	Child 1	Child 2	Mother
First Name	Diane	Amy	Marjorie
Last Name	Victoria	Victoria	Vancouver
SIN	527-000-293	None	527-000-483
Date of birth (Y/M/D)	1999-05-14	2007-10-11	1947-05-21
Net income	$2,300	Nil	$8,000

T4	Box	Amount
Issuer - 1750 Canada Inc.		
Employment income	14	60,201.80
Employee's CPP contributions	16	2,748.90
Employee's EI premiums	18	860.22
RPP contributions	20	2,406.16
Pension adjustment	52	7,829.00
Income tax deducted	22	6,408.00
Employment commissions	42	0
Union dues	44	748.59
Charitable donations	46	175.00

Eleanor has a signed T2200 from her employer specifying her work requires her to have an office in the home. She meets the conditions required to deduct work space in the home expenses. Of the 1,800 square feet in the house, her office, waiting area, and storage space totals 310 square feet. She doesn't qualify for the GST rebate.

During 2019 she paid the following:

Rent for the year (No GST charged)	$30,000
Utilities (hydro and gas) for the year	2,500
Cleaning services (No GST charged)	1,200
Insurance for household effects (No GST charged)	400
Car insurance (No GST charged)	700

T2202A - (Diane)	Box	Amount
Tuition fees - for Diane Victoria (daughter)	A	7,000
Number of months in school - part time	B	2
Number of months in school - full time	C	8

Eleanor and her family had the following medical expenses, all of which Eleanor paid for:

Patient	(Y/M/D)	Medical Expenses	Description	Am't
Eleanor	2019-08-15	Grace Hospital	Ambulance charge	392
Eleanor	2019-08-18	Paramed Home Health	Nursing care	1,350
Marjorie	2019-05-20	Dr. Zhang (Optometrist)	Contact lenses	110
Marjorie	2019-07-06	Pharmacy	Prescription	75
Diane	2019-09-01	Dr. Glassman	Physiotherapist	100
Amy	2019-05-11	Walk Right Foot Clinic	Orthotics	450
Amy	2019-01-23	Dr. Tamo	Dental Fees	1,120

Donor	Charitable Donation Receipts	Am't
Eleanor	Heart and Stroke (annual donation)	375
Eleanor	Terry Fox Foundation (annual donation)	50
Diane	Addiction Research Council of Canada (annual donation)	100

T3	Box	Amount
Issuer - Global Strategy Financial		
Foreign country - United States		
Capital gains (Foreign)	21	982.22
Foreign non-business income	25	310.94

T4A	Box	Amount
Issuer - 3601 Canada Inc. (Survivor benefit from husband)		
Pension	16	22,249.44
Income tax deducted	22	3,510.78

T4A(P)	Box	Amount
Survivor benefit	15	4,823.28
Income tax deducted	22	Nil

T5	Box	Slip 1	Slip 2
Issuer		Scotiabank	Bank of Montreal
Actual amount of eligible dividends	24		1,603.00
Taxable amount of eligible dividends	25		2,212.14
Interest from Canadian sources	13	509.45	

RRSP information	(Y/M/D)	Amount
Issuer of receipt - Scotiabank	2020-02-10	2,620.00
Earned income for 2018		38,873.00
Pension adjustment for 2018		4,376.00
Unused deduction room at the end of 2018		1,666.00

Child	Child Care Expenses	No. of weeks	Amount
Amy	Croft Computer Camp (14 days overnight)	2	1,000
Amy	Y Day Camp (July)	3	400

Eleanor did not sell her house in Prince George when she moved to Victoria as it was her intention to move back into it within three years. It has been rented on a month-to-month lease since November 2017. She claimed a rental loss of $4,250 in 2018.

Real Estate Rental	Amount
Address - 222 PPP Street, Prince George, B.C. V4H 3W4	
Gross rents (12 months for 2018)	15,600.00
Property taxes	2,190.00
Insurance	1,093.27
Interest on mortgage	5,377.58
Payment on principal	3,688.95
Plumbing repairs	290.94
Snow plow annual contract	300.00
Lawyer's fees for new lease	172.54
Hydro (during vacancy)	288.34
Building purchased October 1, 2016 for $168,900 - UCC beginning of year	168,900.00
Washer/dryer purchased May 9, 2018 for $921 - UCC beginning of year	921.00
Stove and refrigerator purchased August 17, 2019	1,500.00

Solutions to Chapter 11 Exercises

Exercise Eleven - 1 Solution

Mr. Smothers will have a listed personal property loss carry forward from 2019 of $5,500 [(1/2)($89,000 - $100,000)]. This can only be applied against the 2020 taxable gain on listed personal property of $2,000 [(1/2)($5,000 - $1,000)]. Based on this, his Net and Taxable Income would be calculated as follows:

Income Under ITA 3(a)	$62,000
Income Under ITA 3(b) ($2,000 - $2,000)	Nil
Net Income For Tax Purposes And Taxable Income	$62,000

In this case, the listed personal property loss carry forward of $3,500 ($5,500 - $2,000) can only be applied against taxable capital gains on listed personal property.

If the sale had been of shares, Mr. Smothers would have had a regular net capital loss carry forward of $5,500 from 2019. His Net and Taxable Income would be calculated as follows:

Income Under ITA 3(a)	$62,000
Income Under ITA 3(b)	2,000
Net Income For Tax Purposes ($2,000 Higher)	$64,000
Loss Carry Forward (Limited To Taxable Capital Gains)	(2,000)
Taxable Income (Same)	$62,000

In this case, the $3,500 net capital loss carry forward can be applied against any taxable capital gains.

Exercise Eleven - 2 Solution

The required calculation is as follows:

Amount E ($58,000 + $2,200)	$60,200
Amount F ($35,000 + $13,000)	(48,000)
Amount D	(2,200)
Non-Capital Loss	$10,000

Note that this is the excess of the business loss of $58,000, over the $48,000 in positive sources of income for the year. The additional farm loss of $2,200 would be allocated to a separate loss balance. It is included in the E component and then deducted in the D component. Since it is less than $2,500, the farm loss is not restricted and is fully deductible against any type of income.

Exercise Eleven - 3 Solution

If Laura makes no effort to minimize the net capital loss carry forward, her Net Income For Tax Purposes and Taxable Income would be calculated as follows:

Net Taxable Capital Gain	$40,000
Rental Loss	(30,000)
Net Income For Tax Purposes	$10,000
Net Capital Loss Carry Forward (Taxable Income To Nil)	(10,000)
Taxable Income	Nil

This approach results in a net capital loss carry forward of $5,000 and a non-capital loss carry over of nil.

Alternatively, if she chooses to completely eliminate the net capital loss carry forward, the non-capital loss would be calculated as follows:

Amount E ($30,000 + $15,000)	$45,000
Amount F - Income Under ITA 3(c)	(40,000)
Non-Capital Loss Carry Over	$ 5,000

While Taxable Income remains unchanged at nil, the net capital loss carry forward has been reduced from $5,000 to nil, with the non-capital loss carry forward increased from nil to $5,000.

Exercise Eleven - 4 Solution

If Derek were alive, his 2020 taxable capital gain would limit the use of his net capital loss carry forward in 2020. This limitation does not apply in the year of death. To maximize tax savings, his final return should have a Taxable Income of $13,229, the 2020 basic personal amount. This means that $10,571 ($23,800 - $13,229) of the net capital loss carry forward should be deducted. This can be applied against any type of income in 2020. The $9,429 ($20,000 - $10,571) can be carried back to 2019 in an amended return and applied against any type of income in that year.

Exercise Eleven - 5 Solution

The Allowable Business Investment Loss for the year would be calculated as follows:

Actual Loss On Disposition	$50,000
Disallowed By Lifetime Capital Gains Deduction Use	(26,000)
Business Investment Loss	$24,000
Inclusion Rate	1/2
Allowable Business Investment Loss	$12,000

All of the $12,000 can be deducted against Mr. Latvik's employment income. With respect to the disallowed $26,000, it becomes an ordinary capital loss, of which $18,000 can be deducted against the current year's capital gains on the publicly traded securities. This leaves a net capital loss carry over of $4,000 [(1/2)($26,000 - $18,000)].

Exercise Eleven - 6 Solution

It appears that Ms. Bodkin's farming activities are a subordinate source of income. Given this, the deduction of the 2019 loss would be limited to $17,500 [$2,500 + (1/2)($32,500 - $2,500)]. The remaining $18,500 ($36,000 - $17,500) is a restricted farm loss carry forward.

In 2020, $3,500 of this carry forward can be deducted against the 2020 farm income. This leaves a restricted farm loss carry forward of $15,000 ($18,500 - $3,500). Ms. Bodkin's 2020 Net Income For Tax Purposes is $88,500 ($85,000 + $3,500) and her 2020 Taxable Income is $85,000 ($85,000 + $3,500 - $3,500).

Exercise Eleven - 7 Solution

The annual gains limit is **$26,000** ($42,000 - $16,000). This is calculated using the ITA 110.6 formula of A - B where:

The A component of the formula would be equal to **$42,000,** the lesser of:

- $74,000 ($114,000 + $42,000 - $82,000); and
- $42,000.

The B component would be **$16,000,** the sum of:

- $13,000*; and
- $3,000.

    *The amount by which $45,000 exceeds $32,000 ($114,000 - $82,000 + $42,000 - $42,000).

Note that the net taxable capital gain on non-qualified property was $32,000 ($114,000 - $82,000). The mechanics of the B component of the formula are such that the first $32,000 of the $45,000 net capital loss deduction was charged against these gains and did not erode the annual gains limit. Only the remaining $13,000 ($45,000 - $32,000) served to reduce the annual gains limit.

To make maximum use of her lifetime capital gains deduction, it would be advisable for Ms. Slovena to deduct only $32,000 of the net capital loss carry forward. If she did this, the B component would be $3,000 and her annual gains limit would increase to $39,000 [$42,000 - (Nil + $3,000)]. Although she would have used $13,000 ($39,000 - $26,000) more of her lifetime capital gains deduction, her tax liability for 2020 would not change and she would have a net capital loss carry forward of $13,000 ($45,000 - $32,000) that could be applied against any type of capital gain for an unlimited period of time.

Exercise Eleven - 8 Solution

His maximum lifetime capital gains deduction is $223,500, the least of the following:

Available Deduction His remaining deduction would be $423,692 ($441,692 - $5,000 - $13,000).

Annual Gains Limit In the absence of capital gains on non-qualified property in any of the years under consideration, the simplified version of this calculation can be used. Given this, this limit would be calculated as follows:

Qualified Gain [(1/2)($510,000)]	$255,000
Net Capital Loss Deducted [(1/2)($63,000)]	(31,500)
Annual Gains Limit	$223,500

Cumulative Gains Limit In the absence of capital gains on non-qualified property in 2013 and 2015, the annual gains limits for 2013 and 2015 would simply be the amount of the taxable capital gains on shares in a qualified small business corporation in those years. Given this, the required calculation would be as follows:

Sum Of Annual Gains Limits	
($5,000 + $13,000 + $223,500)	$241,500
Previous Years' Capital Gains Deduction ($5,000 + $13,000)	(18,000)
Cumulative Net Investment Loss	Nil
Cumulative Gains Limit	$223,500

Exercise Eleven - 9 Solution

Alan's Net Income For Tax Purposes would be calculated as follows:

Income Under ITA 3(a):		
Business Income	$12,000	
Employment Income	56,000	
Farming Income	3,500	$71,500
Income Under ITA 3(b):		
Taxable Capital Gains		9,000
Net Income For Tax Purposes		$80,500

Alan's Taxable Income is as follows:

Net Income For Tax Purposes	$80,500
Loss Carry Forwards:	
Restricted Farm Losses (Limited to farming income)	(3,500)
Net Capital Losses (Limited to taxable capital gains)	(9,000)
Non-Capital Losses (All)	(36,000)
Taxable Income	$32,000

Loss Carry Forwards

• Restricted farm loss carry forward ($8,000 - $3,500)	$ 4,500
• Net capital loss carry forward ($20,000 - $9,000)	$11,000
• Non-capital loss carry forward	Nil

Exercise Eleven - 10 Solution

The regular Tax Payable would be calculated as follows:

Income Sources:	
Taxable Non-Eligible Dividends [(115%)($15,000)]	$ 17,250
Contract Income	15,200
Taxable Eligible Dividends [(138%)($8,600)]	11,868
Deduction For Split Income - Taxable Non-Eligible Dividends	(17,250)
Net Income For Tax Purposes = Taxable Income	$ 27,068
Rate	15%
Tax Payable Before Credits	$ 4,060
Basic Personal Credit [(15%)($13,229)]	(1,984)
Dividend Tax Credit - Eligible Dividends [(6/11)(38%)($8,600)]	(1,783)
Regular Tax Payable	$ 293

The Tax Payable on Split Income would be calculated as follows:

Split Income - Taxable Non-Eligible Dividends	$ 17,250
Rate	33%
Tax Payable Before Dividend Tax Credit	$ 5,693
Dividend Tax Credit [(9/13)(15%)($15,000)]	(1,558)
Tax Payable On Split Income	$ 4,135

The total Tax Payable would be $4,428 ($293 + $4,135).

Exercise Eleven - 11 Solution

Without the transfer, Mr. Ho's wife would have income of $11,730 [(138%)($8,500)], $1,499 less than the base for the spousal credit of $13,229. This would result in a small spousal credit of $225 [(15%)($1,499)]. With the transfer, he would be eligible for the full $1,984, an increase of $1,759 [($1,984 - $225). Given this, the analysis of his position at the federal level is as follows:

Additional Taxes On Dividends [(33%)(138%)($8,500)]	$3,871
Increase In Spousal Tax Credit	(1,759)
Dividend Tax Credit [(6/11)(38%)($8,500)]	(1,762)
Tax Increase (Decrease)	$ 350

As the result of the transfer is a tax increase, the election would not be desirable. With or without the election Mrs. Ho will have no Tax Payable.

Exercise Eleven - 12 Solution

With the gift being made at $85,000, Ms. Felder will have a taxable capital gain of $11,500 [(1/2)($85,000 - $62,000)], plus recapture of $34,000 ($62,000 - $28,000), for a total Net Income For Tax Purposes of $45,500. Given this, her maximum credit base would be calculated as follows:

75% Of Net Income For Tax Purposes [(75%)($45,500)]	$34,125
25% Of Taxable Capital Gain [(25%)($11,500)]	2,875
25% Of Recaptured CCA [(25%)($34,000)]	8,500
Charitable Donations Credit Base Limit	
(Equals Income From Donation)	$45,500

Note that, because Ms. Felder's Taxable Income is less than $214,368, the 33 percent tax rate is not relevant in calculating the charitable donations tax credit. This base results in a potential credit of $13,167 [(15%)($200) + (29%)($45,500 - $200)]. While this amount could be used, she does not have sufficient Tax Payable to utilize the whole potential credit. Her federal Tax Payable for the year would be calculated as follows:

Tax Before Credits [(15%)($45,500)]	$6,825
Basic Personal Credit	(1,984)
Federal Tax Payable Before Donations Credit	$4,841

In order to reduce her Tax Payable to nil, Ms. Felder should use a sufficient amount of her charitable donations credit base to produce a tax credit of $4,841. To arrive at the credit base that will result in this tax credit, the following equation must be solved for X:

$4,841 = [(15%)($200)] + [(29%)(X - $200)
$4,841 - $30 + $58 = [(29%)(X)]

Solving this equation for X provides a value of $16,790, which equals the amount of her donation that produces the $4,841 [(15%)($200) + (29%)($16,790 - $200)] credit that will reduce her federal Tax Payable to nil. This leaves a carry forward of $68,210 ($85,000 - $16,790).

Exercise Eleven - 13 Solution

As a donation of publicly traded shares is involved, there will be no recognized capital gain on the sale. This means that Mr. Radeem's Taxable Income for 2020 will consist of his employment income of $90,000. The limit for the base of Mr. Radeem's charitable donations tax credit would be $67,500 [(75%)($90,000)]. If he were to use this amount, his 2020 charitable donations tax credit would be $19,547 [(15%)($200) + (29%)($67,500 - $200)]. Note that, because Mr. Radeem's Taxable Income is less than $214,368, the 33 percent tax rate is not relevant in calculating the charitable donations tax credit.

As it would exceed his Tax Payable after other tax credits, Mr. Radeem will not want to deduct the maximum available charitable donations tax credit. Given this, he needs to determine the amount of the credit that will reduce his Tax Payable to nil. This is determined as follows:

Tax On First $48,535	$ 7,280
Tax On Next $41,465 ($90,000 - $48,535) At 20.5 Percent	8,500
Tax Before Credits	$15,780
Tax Credits (Given)	(4,000)
Federal Tax Payable Before Donations Credit	$11,780

In order to reduce his Tax Payable to nil, Mr. Radeem should use a sufficient amount of his charitable donations credit base to produce a tax credit of $11,780. To arrive at the credit base that will result in this tax credit, the following equation must be solved for X:

$11,780 = [(15%)($200)] + [(29%)(X - $200)
$11,780 - $30 + $58 = [(29%)(X)]

Solving this equation for X provides a value of $40,717, which equals the amount of his donation that will produce the $11,780 [(15%)($200) + (29%)($40,717 - $200)] credit that will reduce his federal Tax Payable to nil. This leaves a carry forward of $69,283 ($110,000 - $40,717).

Exercise Eleven - 14 Solution

Ms. Cheung's Net Income For Tax Purposes and Taxable Income would be calculated as follows:

Net Rental Income	$44,000
Net Taxable Capital Gains	2,500
Foreign Non-Business Income	3,500
Net Income For Tax Purposes	$50,000
Net Capital Loss Carry Forward	(1,000)
Adjusted Division B Income	$49,000
Non-Capital Loss Carry Forward	(4,000)
Taxable Income	$45,000

Ms. Cheung's credit for foreign tax paid would be the lesser of the foreign tax withheld of $385 [(11%)($3,500)] and an amount determined by the following formula:

$$\left[\frac{\text{Foreign Non-Business Income}}{\text{Adjusted Division B Income}}\right][\text{Tax Otherwise Payable}]$$

In this formula, the Adjusted Division B Income would be $49,000 (as shown in the preceding table). Note that, because the non-capital loss is not deducted here, this is not the same as her Taxable Income of $43,500.

Ms. Cheung's Tax Otherwise Payable would be calculated as follows (note that the foreign tax credit is not subtracted in this calculation):

Tax Before Credits [(15%)($45,000)]	$6,750
Basic Personal Credit	(1,984)
Tax Otherwise Payable	$4,766

Using this information, the formula amount would be $340 [($3,500 ÷ $49,000)($4,766)]. As this is less than the $385 withheld, this would be the foreign tax credit. Based on this, Ms. Cheung's actual federal Tax Payable would be calculated as follows:

Tax Before Credits [(15%)($45,000]	$6,750
Basic Personal Credit	(1,984)
Foreign Tax Credit	(340)
Federal Tax Payable	$4,426

Exercise Eleven - 15 Solution

Mr. Blouson's regular Tax Payable would be calculated as follows:

Tax On First $48,535	$ 7,280
Tax On Next $36,465 ($85,000 - $48,535) At 20.5%	7,475
Total	$14,755
Basic Personal Credit	(1,984)
Dividend Tax Credit [(6/11)(38%)($20,000)]	(4,145)
Regular Federal Tax Payable	$ 8,626

For alternative minimum tax purposes, his adjusted taxable income would be calculated as follows:

Regular Taxable Income	$85,000
30 Percent Of Capital Gains [(30%)(2)($22,500)]	13,500
Dividend Gross Up [(38%)($20,000)]	(7,600)
Adjusted Taxable Income	$90,900

Calculation of the alternative minimum tax would be as follows:

Adjusted Taxable Income	$90,900
Basic Exemption	(40,000)
Amount Subject To Tax	$50,900
Rate	15%
Minimum Tax Before Credit	$ 7,635
Basic Personal Credit	(1,984)
Alternative Minimum Tax	$ 5,651

Mr. Blouson would not pay the alternative minimum tax as it is less than the regular Tax Payable. Note that the $50,000 RRSP deduction does not affect the alternative minimum tax calculation.

Solution to Self Study Problem Eleven - 1

The calculation of Miss Atwater's Taxable Income for 2019 would be as follows:

Net Rental Income	$34,200
Interest Income	4,000
Net Income For Tax Purposes And Taxable Income	$38,200

The corresponding calculation for 2020 is as follows:

Net Rental Income	$ 35,200	
Interest Income	4,200	$39,400
Allowable Business Investment Loss		
[(1/2)($170,000)]		(85,000)
Net Income For Tax Purposes And Taxable Income		Nil

There is a deemed disposition of the shares for proceeds of nil due to the bankruptcy of the company. As the capital loss relates to the shares of a small business corporation, it is a Business Investment Loss. This means that, in contrast to other types of capital losses, the allowable portion can be deducted against any source of income. The total Allowable Business Investment Loss (ABIL) that is available for deduction in 2020 is $85,000 [(1/2)($170,000)].

As the ABIL was recognized in 2020, it must first be used to reduce that year's income to nil. Note that, because of this rule, she cannot deduct a smaller amount in order to have sufficient income to absorb her basic personal tax credit. This will use up $39,400 of the $85,000 total and leave a balance of $45,600 to be carried over to other years.

In carrying this amount back to 2019, the optimum solution would leave $12,069 of Taxable Income so that Miss Atwater can take advantage of her basic personal tax credit. Note that the calculation of the optimum carry back uses the basic personal amount of the carry back year, not the current year.

This means that she needs a loss carry back deduction of $26,131 ($38,200 - $12,069) in 2019. This deduction will leave a Taxable Income of $12,069. As planned, the federal taxes on this amount will be eliminated by the basic personal credit.

A carry back of $26,131 to 2019 leaves a carry forward balance of $19,469 ($45,600 - $26,131) to be used in future years.

The undeducted Allowable Business Investment Loss can be deducted against other sources of income in the 10 (not 20) year carry forward period. If it has not been utilized within the 10 years, it then becomes a net capital loss carry forward, deductible for an unlimited number of future periods, but only against net taxable capital gains.

Solution to Self Study Problem Eleven - 2

2017 Analysis
The required information can be calculated as follows:

ITA 3(a)		
Business Income	$19,800	
Taxable Dividends [(138%)($1,870)]	2,581	$22,381
ITA 3(b)		
Taxable Capital Gains [(1/2)($1,320)]	$ 660	
Allowable Capital Losses [(1/2)($4,620)]	(2,310)	Nil
ITA 3(c)		$22,381
ITA 3(d)		
Farm Loss (See Note)		(6,750)
Net Income For Tax Purposes And Taxable Income		$15,631

Note   Dale's farm losses are restricted as follows:

Total Farm Loss		$11,000
Deductible Amount:		
First $2,500	($2,500)	
One-Half Of $8,500 ($11,000 - $2,500)	(4,250)	(6,750)
Restricted Farm Loss Carry Forward		$ 4,250

As noted in the problem, none of the losses can be carried back before 2017. This would leave the following carry forward balances at the end of 2017:

- Restricted Farm Loss Carry Forward $4,250
- Net Capital Loss Carry Forward ($2,310 - $660) $1,650

2018 Analysis
The required information can be calculated as follows:

ITA 3(a)		
Farm Income	$ 2,200	
Taxable Dividends [(138%)($2,351)]	3,244	$ 5,444
ITA 3(b)		
Taxable Capital Gains [(1/2)($2,200)]	$ 1,100	
Allowable Capital Losses	Nil	1,100
ITA 3(c)		$ 6,544
ITA 3(d)		
Business Loss		(15,400)
Net Income For Tax Purposes		Nil
2017 Net Capital Loss Carry Forward		($ 1,100)
Taxable Income (Loss)		Nil

Since there are taxable capital gains this year, and the problem states that Dale would like to deduct the maximum amount of his net capital loss carry forwards, the net capital loss carry forward of $1,100 is added to the balance of the non-capital loss.

The non-capital loss carry over is calculated as follows:

Business Loss	$15,400
2017 Net Capital Loss Deducted	1,100
ITA 3(c) Income	(6,544)
Non-Capital Loss Carry Over For 2018	$ 9,956

The entire non-capital loss carry over could be carried back to 2017, but since Dale requires $15,400 in Taxable Income to fully utilize his tax credits, the maximum carry back to 2017 is $231, calculated as follows:

2017 Taxable Income (As Reported)	$15,631
Non-Capital Loss Carry Back From 2018	(231)
2017 Amended Taxable Income (Minimum)	$15,400

This carry back leaves Dale with his required $15,400 in Taxable Income. There would be the following carry forward balances at the end of 2018:

- Restricted Farm Loss Carry Forward (Unchanged) $4,250
- Net Capital Loss Carry Forward ($1,650 - $1,100)] $ 550
- Non-Capital Loss Carry Forward ($9,956 - $231) $9,725

2019 Analysis

The required information can be calculated as follows:

ITA 3(a)		
Business Income	$33,000	
Farm Income	3,465	
Taxable Dividends [(138%)($3,160)]	4,361	$40,826
ITA 3(b)		
Taxable Capital Gains [(1/2)($4,400)]	$ 2,200	
Allowable Capital Losses	Nil	2,200
Net Income For Tax Purposes		$43,026
Restricted Farm Loss Carry Forward (Equal To Farm Income)		(3,465)
Net Capital Loss Carry Forward (Less Than $2,200)		(550)
Non-Capital Loss Carry Forward (All)		(9,725)
Taxable Income		$29,286

There would be the following carry forward balance at the end of 2019:

- Restricted Farm Loss Carry Forward ($4,250 - $3,465) $ 785

2020 Analysis

The required information can be calculated as follows:

ITA 3(a)		
Taxable Dividends [(138%)($5,140)]		$ 7,093
ITA 3(b)		
Taxable Capital Gains [(1/2)($4,950)]	$ 2,475	
Allowable Capital Losses [(1/2)($15,950)]	(7,975)	Nil
ITA 3(c)		$ 7,093
ITA 3(d)		
Business Loss	($20,900)	
Farm Loss	(2,200)	(23,100)
Net Income For Tax Purposes And Taxable Income		Nil

The available non-capital loss can be calculated as follows:

Business Loss	$20,900	
Farm Loss (Unrestricted)	2,200	$23,100
ITA 3(c) Income		(7,093)
Non-Capital Loss Carry Over For 2020		$16,007

Although technically the farm loss is accounted for separately from the non-capital loss, since the farm loss is less than $2,500 it is treated as an unrestricted farm loss and can be applied against all types of income. ITA 31 states that any loss allowed under that provision is considered an unrestricted loss from a farming business for the year for the purposes of calculating the non-capital loss carryover. As a result, the preceding loss carry over of $16,007 is available for carry back to 2019 to be applied against any type of income.

With respect to the net capital loss of $5,500 ($7,975- $2,475), there are $1,650 ($2,200 - $550) in taxable capital gains left in 2019 as the basis for a carry back. This means that $1,650 of the 2020 net capital loss can be carried back, leaving $3,850 ($5,500- $1,650) to be carried forward as a net capital loss balance.

If both the $16,007 non-capital loss and the $1,650 net capital loss were carried back to 2019, the result would be a Taxable Income of $11,629 ($29,286 - $16,007 - $1,650), less than the $15,400 that is required to fully utilize Dale's available tax credits. As the net capital loss can only be deducted to the extent of taxable capital gains, it would be advisable to claim the full amount of this loss carry back. Based on this view, the non-capital loss deduction will be limited to $12,236 ($29,286 - $15,400 - $1,650), an amount that will provide for full use of Dale's 2019 tax credits:

2019 Taxable Income (As Reported)	$29,286
Non-Capital Loss Carry Back From 2020	(12,236)
Net Capital Loss Carry Back From 2020	(1,650)
2019 Amended Taxable Income	$15,400

These carry backs leave Dale with his required $15,400 in 2019 Taxable Income. There would be the following carry forward balances at the end of 2020:

- Restricted Farm Loss Carry Forward (Unchanged) $ 785
- Net Capital Loss Carry Forward ($5,500 - $1,650)] $3,850
- Non-Capital Loss Carry Forward (Nil + $16,007 - $12,236) $3,771

Solution to Self Study Problem Eleven - 3

To the extent that there has been use of the lifetime capital gains deduction in previous years, Business Investment Losses (BILs) are disallowed. When they are disallowed, they become ordinary capital losses that must be deducted against the current year's taxable capital gains. Given this, the non-disallowed portion of the BIL would be calculated as follows:

2020 BIL Realized ($55,000 - $228,000 - $1,000)	$174,000
BIL Disallowed By Previous Use Of ITA 110.6 ($38,000 + $21,000)	(59,000)
Remaining Business Investment Loss	$115,000
Inclusion Rate	1/2
Allowable Business Investment Loss	$ 57,500

Using this analysis, Mr. Barkin's minimum Net Income For Tax Purposes and Taxable Income would be calculated as follows:

Net Employment Income		$115,000
Allowable Business Investment Loss		(57,500)
Net Taxable Capital Gains:		
Taxable Capital Gain		
[(1/2)($328,000 - $153,000 - $2,000)]	$86,500	
Allowable Capital Loss (Disallowed ABIL)		
[(1/2)($59,000)]	(29,500)	57,000
Net Income For Tax Purposes		$114,500
Lifetime Capital Gains Deduction (Note 1)		Nil
Net Capital Loss Carry Forward Deducted (Note 2)		(13,700)
Taxable Income		$100,800

Note 1 As the only capital gains during 2020 are on qualified property, the simplified formula for the annual gains limit can be used. Given this, the lifetime capital gains deduction is nil, the least of:

Amount Available [(1/2)($883,384)]*	$441,692412,192
Amount Used [(1/2)($38,000 + $21,000)]	(29,500)
Amount Available	$403,956

*This is the 2020 limit for gains on dispositions of shares of a qualified small business corporation. For gains on qualified farm or fishing property, the 2020 limit would be $1,000,000.

Taxable Capital Gain On Qualified Property	$86,500
Allowable Capital Loss Deducted (Disallowed ABIL)	(29,500)
ABIL Realized	(57,500)
Annual Gains Limit Prior To Loss Carry Forward	Nil
Net Capital Loss Deducted	(13,700)
Annual Gains Limit	Nil
Sum Of Annual Gains Limits ($19,000 + $10,500 + Nil)	$29,500
Amounts Deducted In Previous Years ($19,000 + $10,500)	(29,500)
CNIL	(4,800)
Cumulative Gains Limit	Nil

Note 2 Even without the deduction of the net capital loss carry forward, the annual gains limit was nil, preventing the deduction of any amount for the lifetime capital gains deduction. Given this, it is appropriate to deduct the net capital loss carry forward.

Solution to Self Study Problem Eleven - 4

CASE A

As Marty is actively engaged in the business on a regular, continuous, and substantial basis, the corporation is an Excluded Business. Given this, Marty's dividends will not be classified as Split Income.

While Miranda is not actively engaged in the business, she is over 24 years of age and owns at least 10 percent of both the number of voting rights and the fair market value of the corporation's outstanding shares. In addition, the company is not a professional corporation, less than 90 percent of its business involves performing services, and substantially all of its income is not from a related business. Given this, she would meet the Excluded Shares test and the dividends she received will not be classified as Split Income.

CASE B

As Jerome is actively engaged in the business on a regular, continuous, and substantial basis, the corporation is an Excluded Business from his point of view. Given this, Jerome's dividends will not be classified as Split Income.

While Jeff has not been active in the business in either 2019 or 2020, he worked full time in the business for more than the required five years (2013 through 2018). Given this, the corporation is an Excluded Business and Jeff's dividends will not be classified as Split Income.

CASE C

As Charles is actively engaged in the business on a regular, continuous, and substantial basis, the corporation is an Excluded Business. Given this, Charles' dividends will not be classified as Split Income.

As Clifford has never been actively involved in Clill, it is not an Excluded Business from his point of view. However, Clifford is over 24 years of age and owns more than 10 percent of the number of voting rights and the fair market value of the Clill shares. In addition, Clill is not a professional corporation, less than 90 percent of its business involves performing services, and substantially all of its income is not from a related business. Given this, Clifford's shares would be Excluded Shares and the dividends he received would not be classified as Split Income.

Solution to Self Study Problem Eleven - 5

Part A - Taxable Income

Mr. and Mrs. Hanson's Taxable Income would be calculated as follows:

	Mr. Hanson	Mrs. Hanson
Old Age Security Benefits	$ 7,400	$ 7,400
RRIF Income	50,000	Nil
Registered Pension Plan Receipts	25,380	1,680
Dividends Received	800	180
Gross Up On Dividends (38 Percent)	304	68
Interest On Government Bonds	500	4,359
Net Taxable Capital Gain	Nil	Nil
Net Income Before Clawback	$84,384	$13,687
Social Benefits Repayment (See Note)	(800)	Nil
Net Income For Tax Purposes And Taxable Income	$83,584	$13,687

Note Mrs. Hanson would not have to repay any of her OAS benefits as her Net Income is well below the threshold income of $79,054. Mr. Hanson's social benefits repayment would be the lesser of:

- $7,400, and
- [(15%)($84,384 - $79,054)] = $800.

Part A - Tax Credits

Mr. Hanson cannot take the spousal credit because Mrs. Hanson's Net Income is more than the $13,229 base for this credit. Mrs. Hanson cannot transfer her dividends under ITA 82(3) as the transfer would leave her with Net Income of $13,439 ($13,687 - $180 - $68). This would still be more than the $13,229 base for the spousal credit and, as a consequence, no spousal tax credit would be created. Given these considerations, the amount that can be transferred from Mrs. Hanson to Mr. Hanson is calculated as follows:

Age	$7,637
Pension (On RPP Only)	1,680
Reduced By Mrs. Hanson's Taxable Income In Excess	
Of Her Basic Personal Tax Credit($13,439 - $13,229)	(210)
Credit Base Transferred To Spouse	$9,107

Mr. Hanson's maximum tax credits would be as follows:

Basic Personal Amount	$13,229
Age $7,637 - [(15%)($83,584 - $38,508)]	876
Pension	2,000
Transfers From Mrs. Hanson (See Preceding)	9,107
Total Base	$25,212
Rate	15%
Total	$ 3,782
Dividend Tax Credit [(6/11)($304)]	166
Charitable Donations	
[(15%)($200) + (29%)($600 + $200 - $200)]	204
Total Credits	$ 4,152

Charitable donations can be claimed by either spouse, as long as the total donations are less than 75 percent of the claiming spouse's Net Income For Tax Purposes. As Mrs. Hanson has no Tax Payable, Mr. Hanson will claim her charitable donations. It is usually advantageous for one spouse to claim all the charitable donations if they total more than $200, as the low rate of credit is only applied once. Note that as none of Mr. Hanson's Taxable Income is taxed at the 33 percent federal tax rate, that rate is not relevant to the calculation of his charitable donations tax credit.

Part A - Loss Carry Overs

Mrs. Hanson's net capital loss of $175 [(1/2)($725 - $375)] can be carried back three years and forward indefinitely to be claimed against taxable capital gains.

Part B - Pension Income Splitting

The optimum use of pension income splitting would accomplish the following objectives:

- it would permit Mrs. Hanson to claim her dividend tax credit,
- it would permit Mrs. Hanson to fully utilize her pension income tax credit,
- it would eliminate Mr. Hanson's OAS clawback, and
- it would enable both Mr. and Mrs. Hanson to be in the same 20.5 percent tax bracket.

Solution to Self Study Problem Eleven - 6

Part A

Mr. and Mrs. Dalton's Taxable Income would be calculated as follows:

	Mr. Dalton	Mrs. Dalton
Old Age Security Benefits	$ 7,400	$ 7,400
Registered Pension Plan Receipts	Nil	62,000
RRIF Income	1,640	12,420
Interest On Government Bonds	1,420	2,580
Eligible Dividends Received	3,420	460
Gross Up On Dividends (38 Percent)	1,300	175
Net Income Before Clawback	$15,180	$85,035
Social Benefits Repayment (Note 1)	Nil	(897)
Net Income For Tax Purposes And Taxable Income Before Any Transfer Of Dividends	$15,180	$84,138

Note 1 Mr. Dalton would not have to repay any of his OAS benefits as his Net Income is well below the threshold income of $79,054. Mrs. Dalton's social benefits repayment would be the lesser of:

- $7,400, and
- [(15%)($85,035 - $79,054)] = $897.

Mr. Dalton's Tax Payable would be calculated as follows:

Federal Tax Before Credits [(15%)($15,180)]		$2,277
Tax Credits		
Basic Personal	($13,229)	
Other (Transferred To Mrs. Dalton)	Nil	
Total Base	($13,229)	
Rate	15%	(1,984)
Dividend Tax Credit [(6/11)($1,300)]		(709)
Federal Tax Payable		Nil

The transfer to Mrs. Dalton would be calculated as follows:

Credits Available For Transfer:		
Age		$ 7,637
Pension (Limited To RRIF Receipts)		1,640
Disability		8,576
Total Available		$ 17,853
Reduced By Excess Of:		
Mr. Dalton's Net Income	($15,180)	
Over Basic Personal Credit Amount	13,229	(1,951)
Available For Transfer To Mrs. Dalton		$15,902

The amount owing for Mrs. Dalton would be calculated as follows:

Tax On First $48,535	$ 7,280	
Tax On Next $35,603 ($84,138- $48,535) At 20.5 Percent	7,299	$14,579
Tax Credits		
Basic Personal	($13,229)	
Spousal Including Extra Infirm Amount		
($13,229 + $2,273 - $15,180)	322	
Additional Caregiver Amount (Note 2)	(6,954)	
Age {$7,637 - [(15%)($84,138 - $38,508)]}	(793)	
Pension	(2,000)	
Transfer From Spouse (Preceding Calculation)	(15,902)	
Credit Base	($39,200)	
Rate	15%	(5,880)
Charitable Donations		
[(15%)($200) +(29%)($350 + $960 - $200)] (Note 3)		(352)
Dividend Tax Credit [(6/11)($175)]		(95)
Federal Tax Payable		$ 8,252
OAS Clawback (Note 1)		897
Amount Owing - Mrs. Dalton		$ 9,149

Note 2 Mr. Dalton's income was below the Canada caregiver income threshold of $17,085. In the absence of the spousal credit, the Canada caregiver amount would have been $7,276. Given this, the additional Canada caregiver amount would be $6,954 ($7,276 - 322).

Note 3 Charitable donations can be claimed by either spouse, as long as the total donations are less than 75 percent of the claiming spouse's Net Income For Tax Purposes. As Mr. Dalton has no Tax Payable, Mrs. Dalton will claim his charitable donations. It is usually advantageous for one spouse to claim all the charitable donations if they total more than $200, as the low rate of credit is only applied once. Note that as none of Mrs. Dalton's Taxable Income is taxed at the 33 percent federal tax rate, that rate is not relevant to the calculation of her charitable donations tax credit.

Part B - Eligibility For Transfer

If Mr. Dalton transfers his dividends to Mrs. Dalton under ITA 82(3), the transfer would leave Mr. Dalton with a Net Income of $10,460 ($15,180 - $3,420 - $1,300). Based on this, her spousal credit would be $756 [(15%)($13,229 + $2,273 - $10,460)], an increase from the pre-transfer credit of $322. Given this, the transfer is permitted.

Part C

If all of Mr. Dalton's dividends are transferred to Mrs. Dalton, their new Taxable Income figures would be calculated as follows:

	Mr. Dalton	Mrs. Dalton
Net Income Before Clawback As Per Part A	$15,180	$85,035
Dividend Transfer	(3,420)	3,420
Gross Up Transfer	(1,300)	1,300
Net Income After Dividend Transfer Before Clawback	$10,460	$89,755
Social Benefits Repayment (Note 4)	Nil	(1,605)
Net Income For Tax Purposes And Taxable Income	$10,460	$88,150

Note 4   Mr. Dalton would not have to repay any of his OAS benefits as his Net Income is well below the threshold income of $79,054. Mrs. Dalton's social benefits repayment would be the lesser of:

- $7,400, and
- [(15%)($89,755- $79,054)] = $1,605.

As Mr. Dalton's revised income figure is below the basic personal credit of $13,229, his Tax Payable would continue to be nil. The transfer to Mrs. Dalton would be calculated as follows:

Credits Available For Transfer:		
Age		$ 7,637
Pension (Limited To RRIF Receipts)		1,640
Disability		8,576
Total Available		$17,853
Reduced By Excess Of:		
Mr. Dalton's Net Income	($10,460)	
Over Basic Personal Credit Amount	13,229	(Nil)
Available For Transfer		$17,853

With respect to Mrs. Dalton, her amount owing would be calculated as follows:

Tax On First $48,535	$7,280	
Tax On Next $39,615 ($88,150 - $48,535) At 20.5%	8,121	$15,401
Tax Credits		
Basic Personal	($13,229)	
Spousal Including Infirm Amount		
($13,229 +$2,273 - $10,460)	(5,042)	
Additional Caregiver Amount (Note 5)	(2,234)	
Age {$7,637- [(15%)($88,150 - $38,508)]}	191	
Pension	(2,000)	
Transfer From Spouse (Preceding Calculation)	(17,853)	
Credit Base	($40,549)	
Rate	15%	(6,082)
Charitable Donations [(15%)($200) +		
(29%)($350 + $960 - $200)]		(352)
Dividend Tax Credit [(6/11)($175 + $1,300)]		(805)
Federal Tax Payable		$ 8,162
OAS Clawback (Note 4)		1,605
Amount Owing - Mrs. Dalton		$ 9,767

Note 5   As was the case before the transfer of dividends, Mr. Dalton's income is below the Canada caregiver income threshold of $17,085. In the absence of the spousal credit, the Canada caregiver amount would have been $7,276. Given this, the additional Canada caregiver amount would be $2,234 ($7,276 - $5,042).

Conclusion

The use of the ITA 82(3) dividend transfer has decreased Mrs. Dalton's federal Tax Payable by $90 ($8,252- $8,162). However, it has increased her OAS clawback by $708 ($1,605 - $897). Since the net effect is an increase in the amount owing of $618 ($9,767- $9,149), the dividend transfer should not be done.

Solution to Self Study Problem Eleven - 7

The regular Tax Payable calculations would be as follows:

	Walter	Wendel	Winston
Employment And Business Income	$ 52,100	$42,300	$ 41,300
Eligible Dividends Received	82,300	Nil	12,300
Dividend Gross Up (38 Percent)	31,274	Nil	4,674
RRSP Deduction	Nil	(27,000)	Nil
Taxable Capital Gains	36,400	Nil	226,550
Net Income For Tax Purposes	$202,074	$15,300	$284,824
Lifetime Capital Gains Deduction	(36,400)	Nil	(221,500)
Taxable Income	$165,674	$15,300	$ 63,324
Federal Tax (Note 2)	$ 35,523	$ 2,295	$ 10,312
Basic Personal Credit	(1,951)	(1,984)	(1,984)
Dividend Tax Credit (6/11 of Gross Up)	(17,059)	Nil	(2,549)
Regular Federal Tax Payable	$ 16,513	$ 311	$ 5,779

Note 1 Walter's Basic Personal Amount would be calculated as follows:

$13,229 - [($931][($165,674 - $150,473) ÷ $63,895] = $13,008

Walter's credit would be $1,951 [(15%)($13,008)]

Note 2 The federal tax payable, before the dividend tax credit, is as follows:

	Taxable Income	Federal Tax Calculations	Federal Tax
Walter	$165,674	$31,115 + (29%)($15,201)	$35,523
Wendel	$ 15,300	(15%)($15,300)	$ 2,295
Winston	$ 63,324	$7,280 + (20.5%)($14,789)	$10,312

The alternative minimum tax (AMT) calculations would be as follows:

	Walter	Wendel	Winston
Regular Taxable Income	$165,674	$15,300	$ 63,324
30% Of Capital Gains (Note 3)	21,840	Nil	135,930
Dividend Gross Up	(31,274)	Nil	(4,674)
Adjusted Taxable Income	$156,240	$15,300	$194,580
AMT Exemption	(40,000)	(40,000)	(40,000)
AMT Base	$116,240	$ Nil	$154,580
Rate	15%	15%	15%
Federal AMT Before Credit	$ 17,436	$ Nil	$ 23,187
Basic Personal Credit	(1,951)	(1,984)	(1,984)
Federal AMT	$ 15,485	Nil	$ 21,203
Regular Federal Tax Payable	(16,513)		(5,779)
Additional Tax Required (Note 4)	Nil	Nil	$ 15,424

Note 3 The 30 percent capital gain inclusion can be calculated by taking 30 percent of double the taxable capital gain.

Note 4 The excess AMT over regular tax payable for Winston can be carried forward for seven years and applied against any future excess of regular Tax Payable over the alternative minimum tax.

Solution to Self Study Problem Eleven - 8

Part A - Net Income For Tax Purposes

Ms. Worthmore's minimum Taxable Income is calculated as follows:

Employment Income		
Gross Salary - Intra Graphics	$73,532	
Gross Salary - Lindworth Inc.	2,500	
RPP Contributions	(1,233)	$74,799
Income From Property		
Eligible Dividend Attribution (Note One)	$ 182	
Gross Up [(38%)($182)]	69	
Non-Eligible Dividends From Lindworth	4,325	
Gross Up [(15%)($4,325)]	649	5,225
Taxable Capital Gains		
Attribution From Husband (Note Two)	$ 1,144	
Transfer To Jayne (Note Three)	122	
Lackmere Shares (Note Four)	394	
Agricultural Land (Note Five)	9,000	10,660
Other Income And Deductions		
Spousal Support Payments [($225)(12)]	($ 2,700)	
RRSP Deduction (Note Six)	(6,849)	(9,549)
Deductible CPP ($2,898 - $2,732)		(166)
Net Income For Tax Purposes		$80,969

Note One There would be income attribution for the $182 [($3.50)(52)] in dividends received by Mr. Dalton on the shares received as a gift.

Note Two In the case of transfers to a spouse, unless an election is made not to have Section 73 apply, the property is transferred at the adjusted cost base of the transferor. There is no recognition of capital gains at the time of transfer. However, when Mr. Dalton sells the shares on August 31, 2020, there would be attribution of taxable capital gains in the amount of $1,144 [($56 - $12)(52)(1/2)].

Note Three In the case of a gift to a minor child, it is treated as a deemed disposition at fair market value. This results in a taxable capital gain at the time of transfer in the amount of $122 [($27 - $18)(27)(1/2)].

Note Four The taxable capital gain on the Lackmere Ltd. shares would be computed using the average value for the shares. The average value would be calculated as follows:

122 Shares At $92	$11,224
178 Shares At $71	12,638
Total Cost	$23,862
Average Cost ($23,862 ÷ 300 Shares)	$ 79.54

Based on this, the gain would be calculated as follows:

Proceeds Of Disposition [(122)($86)]	$10,492
Adjusted Cost Base [(122)($79.54)]	(9,704)
Capital Gain	$ 788
Inclusion Rate	1/2
Taxable Capital Gain	$ 394

Note Five   When there is a non-arm's length transfer of property for consideration of less than fair market value, ITA 69 deems that, for the transferor, the transfer takes place at fair market value. Given this, the taxable capital gain would be calculated as follows:

Deemed Proceeds Of Disposition (FMV)	$28,000
Adjusted Cost Base	(10,000)
Capital Gain	$18,000
Inclusion Rate	1/2
Taxable Capital Gain	$ 9,000

Note Six   Ms. Worthmore's 2019 Earned Income (assumed to be equal to the 2020 figure) is as follows:

Gross Salary - Intra	$73,532
Gross Salary - Lindworth	2,500
Spousal Support Paid And Deducted [(12)($225)]	(2,700)
Earned Income	$73,332

Ms. Worthmore's maximum deductible 2020 RRSP contribution is calculated as follows:

Unused Deduction Room - End of 2019	Nil
Lesser Of:	
• 2020 RRSP Dollar Limit = $27,230	
• [(18%)($73,332)] = $13,200	$13,200
Less 2019 PA	(6,351)
Maximum Deductible RRSP Contribution	$ 6,849

This means the excess contribution of $651 ($7,500 - $6,849) can be carried forward and deducted in future years.

Part B - Taxable Income

As Ms. Worthmore has no deductions from her Net Income For Tax Purposes, her 2020 Taxable Income would be $80,969, the same amount as her 2020 Net Income For Tax Purposes

Part C - Tax Payable

Ms. Worthmore's federal Tax Payable can be calculated as follows:

Tax On First $48,535		$ 7,280
Tax On Next $32,343 ($80,969 - $48,535) At 20.5 Percent		6,649
Gross Federal Tax Payable		$13,929
Basic Personal Amount	($13,229)	
Spousal $13,229 - $1,065	(12,164)	
CPP Contribution	(2,732)	
EI Premiums	(856)	
Canada Employment	(1,245)	
Transfer Of Spouse's Tuition Credit - Lesser of:		
• Absolute Limit Of $5,000		
• Tuition Paid Of $2,300	(2,300)	
Medical Expenses (Note Seven)	(10,709)	
Credit Base	($43,235)	
Rate	15%	(6,485)
Eligible Dividend Tax Credit [(6/11)($69)]		(38)
Non-Eligible Dividend Tax Credit [(9/13)($649)]		(449)
Charitable Donations (Note Eight)		
[(15%)($200) + (29%)($342 - $200)]		(71)
Political Contributions [(3/4)($100)]		(75)
Federal Tax Payable		$ 6,811

Note Seven   Ms. Worthmore can claim all of the medical expenses of her husband and daughters, Joyce and June, without taking into consideration June's income, as she is under 18 years of age. Allowable medical expenses are as follows:

John Dalton, Joyce, And June Medical Expenses	
($1,056 + $2,200 + $9,850)	$13,106
Threshold - Lesser Of:	
[(3%)($80,969)] = $2,429	
2020 Limit Of $2,397	(2,397)
Allowable Medical Expenses	$10,709

Note Eight   As none of her income is taxed at 33 percent, this rate will not be applicable to the calculation of the charitable donations tax credit.

Solution to Self Study Problem Eleven - 9

Taxable Income

Mr. Slater's Net Income For Tax Purposes And Taxable Income would be calculated as follows:

Employment Income - Salary		$ 35,000
Proprietorship Income ($28,300 - $2,300 - Note One)		26,000
Property Income:		
Interest On Savings Account	$ 4,450	
Interest On Loans To Friends	12,000	
Eligible Canadian Dividends	44,000	
Gross Up [($44,000)(38%)]	16,720	
Dividends From U.S. Corporations		
(Before Withholding, No Gross Up)	10,000	87,170
Taxable Capital Gain [(1/2)($111,500 - $23,000)]		44,250
CPP Benefits		5,100
Old Age Security Benefits (Note Three)		7,400
Restricted Farm Loss (Note Two)		(5,750)
Net Income Before OAS Repayment		$199,170
OAS Repayment (Note Three) - Lesser Of:		
• $7,400		
• $18,017 [(15%)($199,170 - $79,054)]		(7,400)
Net Income For Tax Purposes And Taxable Income		$191,770

Note One   The drawings from the proprietorship have no effect on the Taxable Income of Mr. Slater. Funds invested are capital and not deductible. The proprietorship income of $28,300 is reduced by the interest of $2,300 on the proprietorship bank loan.

Note Two   Since Mr. Slater's farming operation is a subordinate source of income, his farm loss would be restricted as follows:

Farm Revenues	$36,000
Farm Expenses	(45,000)
Total Farm Loss	($ 9,000)
Deductible Portion [$2,500 + (1/2)($9,000 - $2,500)]	5,750
Restricted Farm Loss Carry Over	($ 3,250)

The $3,250 restricted farm loss carry over could be carried back to the preceding three years and forward for 20 years to be deducted against farming income.

Note Three   Even though Mr. Slater did not receive the $7,400, it must be included in income and deducted because he has received an information return that includes the amount.

Tax Payable

Mr. Slater's federal Tax Payable would be calculated as follows:

Tax On First $150,473		$31,115
Tax On Next $41,297 ($191,770 - $150,473) At 29 Percent		11,976
Gross Federal Tax		$43,091
Tax Credits:		
Basic Personal Amount (Note Four)	($12,627)	
Spousal, Including Extra Amount For Infirmity ($12,630 + $2,273)	(14,903)	
Mr. Slater's Age {$7,637 - [(15%)($191,770 - $38,508)]}	Nil	
Spouse's Disability	(8,576)	
Canada Employment	(1,245)	
Credit Base	($37,351)	
Rate	15%	(5,603)
Charitable Donations (Note Five) [(15%)($200) + (29%)($2,700 - $200)]		(755)
Subtotal = Tax Otherwise Payable For Foreign Tax Credit		$36,733
Dividend Tax Credit [(6/11)($16,720)]		(9,120)
Foreign Tax Credit (Note Six)		(1,500)
Federal Political Contributions Tax Credit (Note Seven)		(350)
OAS Clawback		7,400
OAS Withheld		(7,400)
Federal Tax Payable		$25,763

Note Four   The Basic Personal Amount would be calculated as follows:

$13,229 - [$931][($191,770 - $150,473) ÷ $63,895] = $12,627

Note Five   As none of his income is taxed at 33 percent, this rate will not be applicable to the calculation of the charitable donations tax credit.

Note Six   The federal foreign tax credit will be the lesser of the foreign tax actually paid of $1,500 and an amount determined by the following formula:

$$\left[\frac{\text{Foreign Non}-\text{Business Income}}{\text{Adjusted Division B Income}} \right] [\text{Tax Otherwise Payable}]$$

The Tax Otherwise Payable is equal to federal Tax Payable before the dividend tax credit and political contributions tax credit is deducted (the Subtotal in the preceding table). This amount would be $1,915 [($10,000 ÷ $191,770)($36,733)], leaving the actual taxes of $1,500 as the lesser amount.

Note Seven   The political contributions tax credit can be calculated as follows:

3/4 Of First $400	$300
1/2 Of The Next $100	50
Total Credit	$350

Other Notes

- The gambling income would not be taxable as Mr. Slater's activity is not extensive enough to be considered a business given his winnings and funds lost in gambling.
- Inheritances are capital receipts and do not constitute Taxable Income.
- The life insurance premiums are not deductible.
- The mortgage payments on his personal residence are not deductible.

Solution to Self Study Problem Eleven - 10

Deemed Dispositions Immediately Before Death

Immediately before the time of Mrs. Steele's death, there is a deemed disposition of all of her capital property. If the beneficiary is a spouse, the deemed proceeds of disposition will, in general, be equal to the tax cost of the property (ACB or UCC). If Andrea's representatives choose to do so, they can elect out of this rollover and record the transfer at fair market value. For the transfers to her daughter, the deemed proceeds of disposition must be equal to fair market value.

Principal Residence To Daughter

The bequest of the family home to her daughter would result in a capital gain of $134,600 ($544,000 - $409,400). As it appears to have been Mrs. Steele's principal residence, the application of the principal residence exemption formula to this amount would result in a deduction of the maximum amount of $134,600.

Other Properties At Death

Under ITA 70(6), property may be transferred at death to a spouse on the basis of adjusted cost base or its UCC. This means that the Rolston Inc. shares, the painting, and the assets of the boutique can be transferred to Mr. Steele with no tax effects in Mrs. Steele's final return. The adjusted cost base and UCC of these properties to Mr. Steele will be the same amounts that applied to Mrs. Steele, prior to her death.

Although the AGF Industries shares would also be eligible for a tax free rollover, it would not be advantageous to do so as there is an unrealized capital loss on these shares. It would be preferable for the legal representative of Mrs. Steele to elect in the final return to have the AGF Industries shares transferred to Mr. Steele at fair market value in order to utilize the capital loss. Electing out of ITA 70(6) is implemented in the final tax return and does not require the filing of a form.

There is no rollover available for the rental property as that is being transferred to her daughter. There is a taxable capital gain for the rental property on both the building and the land and recaptured CCA on the building.

The allowable capital loss resulting from the election on the shares and the taxable capital gains and recaptured CCA on the deemed disposition of the rental property can be calculated as follows:

	AGF Shares	Land	Building
Fair Market Value	$ 7,900	$164,000	$235,000
Adjusted Cost Base/Capital Cost	(10,600)	(92,000)	(183,000)
Capital Gain (Loss)	($ 2,700)	$ 72,000	$ 52,000
Inclusion Rate	1/2	1/2	1/2
Taxable Capital Gain (Loss)	($ 1,350)	$ 36,000	$ 26,000

	Building
Capital Cost	$183,000
UCC	(144,800)
Recapture Of CCA	$ 38,200

Mortgage Interest - Attribution

With respect to the mortgage interest received by Mr. Steele, it was earned on mortgages given to him by Mrs. Steele and, as a consequence, it would be attributed to her up until her death on June 3, 2020. This means that $886 [(154/365)($2,100)] of the $2,100 would be included in her income. As attribution from a spouse ceases when the transferor spouse dies, the remaining $1,214 ($2,100 - $886) would be included in Mr. Steele's income. When this is combined with his $425 boutique salary, his total income for the year is $1,639. His income for the whole year, not just prior to Mrs. Steele's death, will decrease the spousal credit available on Mrs. Steele's final return.

Net Income For Tax Purposes And Taxable Income

Mrs. Steele's minimum Taxable Income (ignoring CPP) would be calculated as follows:

Business Income		$ 55,200
Property Income:		
Eligible Dividends Received	$ 1,090	
Gross Up [(38%)($1,090)]	414	
Interest	2,025	
Attributed Mortgage Interest (Note One)	886	
Rent Revenues	41,200	
Rental Expenses (Note Two)	(24,650)	
Recaptured CCA On Rental Property	38,200	59,165
Net Taxable Capital Gains:		
Taxable Capital Gains On Rental Property		
($26,000 + $36,000)	$62,000	
Allowable Capital Loss On AGF Industries Shares	(1,350)	60,650
Net Income		$175,015
Net Capital Loss Carry Forward (Note Three)		(76,500)
Taxable Income		$ 98,515

Note One Income attribution would cease with Ms. Steele's death on June 3, 154 days into 2020. Given this, the amount of mortgage interest attribution would be $886 [(2,100)(154/365)].

Note Two As there was a deemed disposition of the rental property immediately before the time of Mrs. Steele's death, no CCA can be taken for 2020.

Note Three In the year of death, any capital losses and capital loss carry forwards can be deducted against any type of income, not just capital gains, as long as the lifetime capital gains deduction has not been claimed. As a result, although she has net taxable capital gains of only $60,650, she can deduct her total net capital loss carry forward of $76,500.

Tax Payable

Mrs. Steele's minimum federal Tax Payable would be calculated as follows:

Tax On First $97,069		$17,230
Tax On Remaining $1,446 ($98,515 - $97,069) At 26 Percent		376
Gross Federal Tax		$17,606
Basic Personal Amount	($13,229)	
Spousal ($13,229 - $1,639)	(11,590)	
Credit Base	($24,819)	
Rate	15%	(3,723)
Dividend Tax Credit [(6/11)(38%)($1,090)]		(226)
Federal Tax Payable		$13,657

Solution to Self Study Problem Eleven - 11

Part A - Taxable Income

Daniel Tong's employment income would be calculated as follows:

Inclusions:		
Salary	$78,000	
2019 Bonus (Cash Basis)	6,000	
Home Office Allowance	2,400	
Standby Charge - No Reduction [($5,200)(2/3)]	3,467	
Automobile Operating Benefit [(14,000 km)($0.28)]	3,920	
Group Term Life Insurance Premium	650	
Dental Insurance	Nil	
Stock Option Benefit [(2,500)($15 - $12)]	7,500	$101,937
Deductions:		
Company Pension Contributions	($ 3,900)	
Home Office [(30/300)($2,100 + $750)]	(285)	
Office Supplies	(230)	(4,415)
Net Employment Income		$ 97,522

Notes

- In general, the only home office costs that can be deducted are utilities and maintenance. In the case of employees with commission income, a pro rata share of insurance and property taxes would also be deductible. However, it does not appear that Mr. Tong has any commission income.
- As the only capital costs that are deductible by an employee are those related to an automobile, aircraft, or musical instrument, the cost of the computer and peripherals are not deductible.
- The use of employment-related frequent flyer points is not considered a taxable benefit by the CRA.

Mr. Tong's Net Income For Tax Purposes and Taxable Income would be calculated as follows:

Net Employment Income (See Preceding)		$ 97,522
Business Income - Sale Of Automobile		
[$14,500 - ($2,500 + $8,100)]		3,900
Property Income:		
Portus Dividends Received	$4,500	
Gross Up [(38%)($4,500)]	1,710	
Less Interest Expense	(1,200)	5,010
Spousal RRSP Withdrawal (Attributed To Mr. Tong)		1,000
Net Taxable Capital Gain:		
Taxable Capital Gain On Portus Shares (Note 1)	$3,581	
Allowable Capital Loss On Global Shares (Note 2)	Nil	3,581
RRSP Contribution (Note 3)		(10,200)
Deductible CPP ($2,898 - $2,732)		(166)
Net Income For Tax Purposes		$100,647
Stock Option Benefit [(1/2)($7,500)]		(3,750)
Net Capital Loss Carry Forward (Note 4)		(3,581)
Taxable Income		$ 93,316

Note 1 For shares acquired through the exercise of stock options, the adjusted cost base is the fair market value of the shares at the time of exercise. Based on this, the average cost of his Portus Ltd. shares is calculated as follows:

2,500 Shares At $15	$37,500
250 Shares At $18	4,500
Total Adjusted Cost Base	$42,000

Based on this total, the average cost per share is $15.27 ($42,000 ÷ 2,750). Using this figure, the taxable capital gain would be calculated as follows:

Proceeds [(1,250)($21)]	$26,250
Adjusted Cost Base [(1,250)($15.27)]	(19,088)
Capital Gain	$ 7,162
Inclusion Rate	1/2
Taxable Capital Gain	$ 3,581

Note 2 The $2,400 loss ($8,600 - $11,000) is deemed to be superficial, as Mr. Tong repurchased more than 800 Global shares within 30 days of the original disposition. This means that the loss will be disallowed. However, it will be added to the adjusted cost base of the replacement shares, giving a total adjusted cost base of $8,200 ($5,800 + $2,400).

Note 3 Mr. Tong's 2020 RRSP deduction room would be calculated as follows:

Lesser Of:	
2020 RRSP Limit = $27,230	
18% Of $61,500 = $11,070	$11,070
2019 Pension Adjustment	Nil
Total 2020 Deduction Room	$11,070

While he has $11,070 in deduction room, his actual deduction is limited to $10,200, his $2,200 in undeducted contributions from the beginning of the year, plus his $8,000 contribution to his wife's RRSP.

Note 4 Mr. Tong has a net capital loss balance of $11,500 ($2,500 + $6,000 + $3,000). However, the amount that can be deducted is limited to the 2020 taxable capital gain, or $3,581. This will leave a net capital loss balance of $7,919 ($11,500 - $3,581).

Part B - Tax Payable

Mr. Tong's minimum federal Tax Payable is calculated as follows:

Tax On First $48,535		$ 7,280
Tax On Next $44,781 ($93,316 - $48,535) At 20.5 Percent		9,180
Gross Federal Tax		$16,460
Basic Personal Amount	($13,229)	
Spousal	(13,229)	
CPP	(2,732)	
EI	(856)	
Canada Employment	(1,245)	
Transfer Of Tuition (Note 5)	(5,000)	
Credit Base	($36,291)	
Rate	15%	(5,444)
Dividend Tax Credit [(6/11)(38%)($4,500)]		(933)
Federal Tax Payable		$10,083

Note 5   Marion's federal Tax Payable is nil as the scholarship is not taxable income.

Interest Income	$ 3,000
Scholarship ($10,000 - $10,000)	Nil
Taxable Income	$ 3,000
Basic Personal Amount	(13,229)
Federal Tax Payable	Nil

As Marion is unable to use any of her tuition credit, the transfer is the lesser of:

- The absolute limit of $5,000
- The actual tuition cost of $7,150

Given this, the maximum transfer is $5,000. However, the $2,150 ($7,150 - $5,000) excess can be carried forward indefinitely to be used against Marion's future Tax Payable.

Part B - Carry Forwards

- From Note 4, there is a net capital loss of $7,919 available for carry forward to subsequent years.

- From Note 5, Marion has a $2,150 tuition amount available for carry forward to subsequent years.

Solution to Tax Software Self Study Problem - Chapter 11

The complete 2019 tax return is available on the MyLab in two versions, a T1 ProFile return file and a .PDF file.

For more information on how to use the ProFile tax program, refer to the Chapter 4 sample tax return in this Study Guide.

Notes To Tax Return

- Diane transfers the $5,000 maximum tuition amount to Eleanor and carries forward the remaining $2,000 [$7,000- $5,000]. The carry forward can only be used by Diane.

- Eleanor cannot claim the charitable donation made by Diane, but Diane can carry it forward for up to five years.

- Since Amy is under 18 and wholly dependent, Eleanor claimed the eligible dependant credit for Amy.

- Note that, because Marjorie is not infirm, Eleanor can claim no credit for her.

- Since Diane and Marjorie are over 17 years of age, their medical expenses are reduced by 3 percent of their Net Income For Tax Purposes. This means that none of Marjorie's medical expenses can be claimed by Eleanor.

- In calculating work space in the home costs, the household insurance is not deductible as the T4 information shows she has no commission income. The car insurance is not relevant as there is no information that Eleanor uses her car for employment-related purposes.

- The Croft Computer Camp was an overnight camp, which means that the deductible costs are limited to $125 per week, a total of $250 [(2)($125)]. In contrast, there is no limit on the costs of day camps. This provides for the deduction of the entire $400 cost of the Y Day Camp.

- Since Eleanor is currently renting out her house, but plans to move back into it, no CCA is taken on the Class 1 building to preserve her principal residence status. Since she had a rental loss in the previous year, and the cost is equal to the UCC, no CCA has been taken on the building nor on the washer/dryer. Her CCA on the Class 8 assets would not affect her principal residence election and should be taken. The payments on principal are not deductible.

  There are two potential relevant CCA rules that affect the amount of CCA that can be claimed for 2019 with respect to (1) the washer/dryer and (2) the stove and refrigerator. The two rules are (1) the regular half-year rule (ITR 1100(2)) and (2) the Accelerated Investment Incentive (AII) rules (ITR 1104(4). The appliances fall into Class 8 (20 percent). The regular half-year rule generally applies to depreciable property that is not eligible for the AII. Most depreciable property acquired in arm's length transactions between November 21, 2018, and December 31, 2023, is eligible for a first year accelerated CCA claim rather than a reduced claim under the historical half-year rule. Since the washer/dryer was acquired prior to November 21, 2018 (May 9, 2018), it is not eligible for the AII increased first year CCA, and since 2019 is the second year of ownership, the half-year rule does not apply. The stove and refrigerator, however, were acquired after November 20, 2018 (August 17, 2019) and are eligible for enhanced CCA under the AII rules. The CCA would be calculated as [(20%)($921) + (20%)(1.5)(1,500)], which equals $634.20.

  Given her inheritance, she should have more than sufficient funds to pay her income taxes without taking CCA on her rental property. As a result, she should preserve her ability to claim the principal residence gain reduction by not taking CCA on the house.

Tax Planning Points

- Since Marjorie is taking care of Amy and is over 18 years old, Eleanor could pay her for child care costs and deduct them. Given Marjorie's low income, it is probable that Eleanor is already providing some funds to her. The amount should be calculated on a basis that is no more than the going rate per hour for similar services for the time when Amy is home and Eleanor is not. As long as Marjorie's income remains below the basic personal credit plus the age credit, it would not result in any income tax liability for Marjorie. Since she is over 80 years old, there would be no CPP liability.

- Although she is not required to file, Marjorie should file a tax return, otherwise she will not be eligible for the GST credit. If Eleanor pays her for child care in the future, filing a tax return could also reduce the probability that Eleanor will be asked for proof of payment.

- Although she is not required to file, Diane should file a tax return, otherwise she will not be eligible for the GST credit and she will not benefit from the RRSP deduction room created during the year. Filing a tax return will also make her tuition tax credit and charitable donation tax credit easier to keep track of for carry forward purposes.

- With the inflow of funds from the inheritance, Eleanor should review her debt outstanding and pay off any balances that have non-deductible interest, such as credit card balances. Although it is not exactly a tax planning point, Eleanor should compare the after tax cost of the interest she is paying on her rental property mortgage with the after tax yields that she can obtain on her investments to determine whether she should pay off her mortgage.

Part B

The maximum deductible RRSP contribution that Eleanor can make for 2020 is calculated as $4,440 by the program on the form "RRSPLimit". To access the form, press <F4> and type "rrsplimit" in the form box.

Note that if Eleanor chooses to deduct CCA on her rental building and reduce her net rental income to nil, her maximum deductible RRSP contribution will be reduced by $1,000 [(18%)($5,553)]. This is another reason she should not take CCA on the rental building.

Given her inheritance, Eleanor should contribute the maximum deductible RRSP contribution as early in 2020 as possible.

Eleanor should open an RESP for Amy if she has not already done so. How much she should contribute will depend on many factors (see the text), but she should request that her accountant create a contribution schedule that will maximize Canada Education Savings Plan contributions and optimize RESP contributions.

Eleanor should open TFSAs for herself, Diane, and possibly Marjorie and determine how much she should contribute to each. This would involve many investment and budgeting factors, as well as her future financial plans. Since the contributions are not deductible and the withdrawals are not taxable, the TFSAs will not have an effect on any of the tax returns.

Given her inheritance she should also consider overcontributing up to $2,000 to her RRSP, which would allow her to take advantage of the tax free earnings in the RRSP without penalty. This would only be advantageous as long as she plans to have earned income for RRSP purposes sufficient to deduct the $2,000 in the future.

CHAPTER 12

Chapter 12 Learning Objectives

After completing Chapter 12, you should be able to:

1. Calculate a corporation's Net Income For Tax Purposes (paragraph [P hereafter] 12-1 to 12-4).
2. List the deductions that are available to corporations in calculating Taxable Income (P 12-5 to 12-9).
3. Apply the treatment for different types of dividends received, including the application of the stop loss rules (P 12-10 to 12-23).
4. Calculate the non-capital loss carry over for a corporation (P 12-24 to 12-30).
5. Determine the optimum ordering of the deductions available in calculating corporate Taxable Income (P 12-31 to 12-36).

6. Allocate corporate Taxable Income to specific provinces (P 12-37 to 12-44).
7. Apply the basic corporate tax rate and explain the effect of the federal tax abatement and the general rate reduction (P 12-45 to 12-51).
8. Calculate provincial Tax Payable for a corporation using a supplied schedule of rates and other data (P 12-52 to 12-62).
9. List the important non-revenue raising goals of the corporate tax system (P 12-63 and 12-64).
10. Explain the rules for determining which corporations and what amounts of income are eligible for the small business deduction (P 12-65 to 12-90).

11. Calculate the amount of the small business deduction (P 12-91 to 12-101).
12. Calculate the reduction in the small business deduction that is applicable to large CCPCs (P 12-102 to 12-120).
13. Identify personal services corporations and explain their tax treatment (P 12-121 to 12-127).
14. Identify professional corporations and management companies and explain their tax treatment (P 12-128 and 12-129).
15. Calculate the manufacturing and processing profits deduction for all types of corporations (P 12-130 to 12-146).

16. Calculate the general rate reduction that is available to all corporations and the specific application of the general rate reduction to CCPCs (P 12-147 to 12-160).
17. Calculate the foreign non-business (property) and business income tax credits for corporations and apply the rules that deal with any excess of foreign tax withheld over the foreign tax credit (P 12-161 to 12-173).
18. Describe the refundable journalism labour tax credit (P 12-174 to 12-177).

How to Work Through Chapter 12

We recommend the following approach in dealing with the material in this Chapter:

Note On Recent Developments
- Read the Note at the beginning of the Chapter (in the textbook).

Computation Of Net Income For Corporations
- Read paragraph 12-1 to 12-4.
- Do Exercise Twelve-1 (in the textbook) and check the solution in this Study Guide.
- Do Self Study Problem Twelve-1, which is available on MyLab, and check the solution in this Study Guide.

Deductions Available For Corporations In The Computation Of Taxable Income
- Read paragraph 12-5 to 12-9.

Dividends Received From Other Corporations
- Read paragraph 12-10 to 12-12.
- Do Exercise Twelve-2 and check the solution in this Study Guide.

Dividends Received - Other Situations Including Stop Loss Rules
- Read paragraph 12-13 to 12-22.
- Do Exercise Twelve-3 and check the solution in this Study Guide.
- Read paragraph 12-23.
- Do Self Study Problem Twelve-2 and check the solution in this Study Guide.

Non-Capital Loss Carry Over For A Corporation
- Read paragraph 12-24 to 12-30.
- Do Exercises Twelve-4 and Twelve-5 and check the solutions in this Study Guide.

Ordering Of Taxable Income Deductions
- Read paragraph 12-31 to 12-36.
- Do Self Study Problems Twelve-3 and Twelve-4 and check the solutions in this Study Guide.

Geographical Allocation Of Income To Permanent Establishments
- Read paragraph 12-37 to 12-44.
- Do Self Study Problem Twelve-5 and check the solution in this Study Guide.

Federal Tax Payable For Corporations
- Read paragraph 12-45 to 12-51.
- Do Exercise Twelve-6 and check the solution in this Study Guide.

Provincial Tax Payable For Corporations
- Read paragraph 12-52 to 12-62.

Other Goals Of The Corporate Tax System
- Read paragraph 12-63 to 12-64.

Small Business Deduction - Definitions And Calculation
- Read paragraph 12-65 to 12-101.
- Do Exercise Twelve-7 and check the solution in this Study Guide.

Elimination Of The Small Business Deduction For Large CCPCs
- Read paragraph 12-102 to 12-113.
- Do Exercise Twelve-8 and check the solution in this Study Guide.
- Read paragraph 12-114 to 12-117.
- Do Exercise Twelve-9 and check the solution in this Study Guide.

- Read paragraph 12-118 to 12-120.
- Do Exercise Twelve-10 and check the solution in this Study Guide.

Personal Services Corporations, Professional Corporations, And Management Companies
- Read paragraph 12-121 to 12-129.

Manufacturing And Processing Profits Deduction
- Read paragraph 12-130 to 12-146.
- Do Exercise Twelve-11 and check the solution in this Study Guide.

General Rate Reduction
- Read paragraph 12-147 to 12-154.
- Do Exercise Twelve-12 and check the solution in this Study Guide.
- Read paragraph 12-155 to 12-160.
- Do Exercise Twelve-13 and check the solution in this Study Guide.
- Do Self Study Problems Twelve-6 to Twelve-9 and check the solutions in this Study Guide.

Foreign Income Tax Credits For Corporations
- Read paragraph 12-161 to 12-173.
- Do Exercise Twelve-14 and check the solution in this Study Guide.
- Do Self Study Problem Twelve-10 and check the solution in this Study Guide.

Refundable Journalism Labour Tax Credit
- Read paragraph 12-174 to 12-177.

To Complete This Chapter
- If you would like more practice in problem solving, do the Supplementary Self Study Problems for the chapter. These problems and solutions are available on MyLab.
- Review the Key Terms Used In This Chapter in the textbook at the end of Chapter 12. Consult the Glossary for the meaning of any key terms you do not know.
- Test yourself with the Chapter 12 Glossary Flashcards available on MyLab.
- Ensure you have achieved the Chapter 12 Learning Objectives listed in this Study Guide.
- As a review, we recommend you view the PowerPoint presentation for Chapter 12 that is on MyLab.

Practice Examination
- Write the Practice Examination for Chapter 12 that is on MyLab. Mark your examination using the Practice Examination Solution that is on MyLab.

Solutions to Chapter 12 Exercises

Exercise Twelve - 1 Solution

Item 1   You would add the accounting loss of $5,600 ($48,300 - $53,900). You would also add the recapture of CCA of $13,700 ($34,600 - $48,300), for a total addition of $19,300.

Item 2   As goodwill is not amortized for accounting purposes and there was no impairment during the year, no adjustment of the accounting figures is required. However, when the goodwill is added to Class 14.1, it would be subject to the half year rule and amortization at a rate of 5 percent per year. This means that you would subtract of CCA $13,500 [($180,000)(1.5)(5%)].

Item 3   You would add the charitable donations of $15,000.

Item 4   You would deduct the premium amortization of $4,500.

Exercise Twelve - 2 Solution

Net Income For Tax Purposes	$263,000
Dividends Received	(14,200)
Charitable Donations	(8,600)
Non-Capital Loss Carry Forward (All)	(82,000)
Net Capital Loss Carry Forward*	(14,250)
Taxable Income	$143,950

*While there is a net capital loss of $18,000 available, the actual deduction is limited to the current year's taxable capital gains of $14,250. The remaining net capital loss carry forward is $3,750 ($18,000 - $14,250).

Exercise Twelve - 3 Solution
Although Loren has held the shares for more than 365 days, it owns more than 5 percent of the shares. As a result, this transaction would be subject to the stop loss rules. The deductible loss would be calculated as follows:

Proceeds Of Disposition [($21.15)(1,000)]	$21,150
Adjusted Cost Base [($25.30)(1,000)]	(25,300)
Total Loss	($ 4,150)
Disallowed Portion [($2.16)(1,000)]	2,160
Capital Loss	($ 1,990)
Inclusion Rate	1/2
Allowable Capital Loss	($ 995)

Exercise Twelve - 4 Solution
Hacker's Net Income For Tax Purposes would be nil, the business and property income of $63,500, less the allowable business investment loss of $75,750 [(1/2)($151,500)].

The net capital loss carry over balance at the end of the year would be $7,650 [(1/2)($23,100 - $38,400)].

The non-capital loss carry over would be calculated as follows:

Amount E (The ABIL)	$75,750
Amount F - ITA 3(c) Income	(63,500)
Non-Capital Loss At End Of Year	$12,250

Exercise Twelve - 5 Solution
The non-capital loss balance at the end of the year would be calculated as follows:

Amount E:	
Net Business Loss	$273,000
ABIL	5,250
Dividends Received And Deducted	48,000
Net Capital Loss Carry Forward Deducted (Limited To Net Taxable Capital Gains For The Year)	13,500
Total For Amount E	$339,750

Amount F - ITA 3(c) Income:

Interest	($27,200)	
Dividends	(48,000)	
Net Taxable Capital Gains		
[(1/2)($111,000 - $84,000)]	(13,500)	(88,700)
Non-Capital Loss At End Of Year		$251,050

Net Capital Loss Carry Forward ($19,000 - $13,500)		$ 5,500

Exercise Twelve - 6 Solution

The percentage of Taxable Income earned in each province would be calculated as follows:

	Gross Revenues		Wages And Salaries	
	Amount	**Percent**	**Amount**	**Percent**
Ontario	$1,303,000	44.6%	$ 52,000	31.5%
Manitoba	896,000	30.7%	94,000	57.0%
Not Related To A Province	724,000	24.7%	19,000	11.5%
Total	$2,923,000	100.0%	$165,000	100.0%

The average of the two percentages applicable for income not related to a province is 18.1 percent, leaving an average for income related to a province of 81.9 percent. Given this, federal Tax Payable can be calculated as follows:

Base Amount Of Part I Tax [(38%)($226,000)]	$85,880
Federal Tax Abatement [(10%)(81.9%)($226,000)]	(18,509)
General Rate Reduction [(13%)($226,000)]	(29,380)
Federal Tax Payable	$ 37,991

Exercise Twelve - 7 Solution

As a CCPC throughout the year and with no associated companies, Kartoom is eligible for the full amount of the $500,000 annual business limit. The amount eligible for the small business deduction will be the least of:

Active Business Income	**$425,000**
Adjusted Taxable Income (See following calculation)	**$292,857**
Annual Business Limit	**$500,000**

Net Income For Tax Purposes	$570,000
Dividends Received	(85,000)
Non-Capital Loss Carry Forward	(160,000)
Taxable Income	$325,000
100/28 Times Foreign Non-Business Tax Credit	
[(100/28)(15%)($60,000)]	(32,143)
Adjusted Taxable Income	$292,857

The least of these figures is the adjusted Taxable Income of $292,857.

Exercise Twelve - 8 Solution

The B component of the ITA 125(5.1) reduction formula is $2,925 [(.00225)($11,300,000 - $10,000,000)]. Given this, the required reduction would be calculated as follows:

$$[(\$500,000)(\$2,925 \div \$11,250)] = \underline{\$130,000} \text{ Reduction}$$

This reduction leaves the annual business limit at $370,000 ($500,000 - $130,000).

The foreign non-business income tax credit is equal to $5,400 [(15%)($36,000)]. The small business deduction for Largely Small Inc. is equal to 19 percent of the least of:

• Active Business Income ($1,233,000 - $36,000)		$1,197,000
• Taxable Income ($1,233,000 - $914,000)	$319,000	
Less 100/28 Times Non-Business Income FTC		
Of $5,400	(19,286)	$ 299,714
• Reduced Annual Business Limit ($500,000 - $130,000)		$ 370,000

The small business deduction is equal to $56,946 [(19%)($299,714)]. The foreign non-business income is less than $50,000, so the calculation of the passive income grind is not required.

Exercise Twelve - 9 Solution

The required reduction in the annual business limit would be calculated as follows:

$$[(\$300,000/\$500,000)][(5)(\$105,000 - \$50,000)] = \underline{\$165,000} \text{ Reduction}$$

This reduction would leave the company's annual business limit at $135,000 ($300,000 - $165,000).

• Active Business Income	$350,000
• Taxable Income	$475,000
• Reduced Annual Business Limit	$135,000

The small business deduction is equal to $25,650 [(19%)($135,000)].

Exercise Twelve - 10 Solution

Case 1 The B component of the TCEC reduction formula is $7,875 [(.00225)($13,500,000 - $10,000,000)]. Given this, the required reduction would be calculated as follows:

$$[(\$350,000)(\$7,875 \div \$11,250)] = \underline{\$245,000} \text{ Reduction}$$

The calculation of the AAII grind would be calculated as follows:

$$[(\$350,000/\$500,000)][(5)(\$72,000 - \$50,000)] = \underline{\$77,000} \text{ Reduction}$$

The greater of these reductions is the TCEC grind amount of $245,000. This leaves an annual business limit of $105,000 ($350,000 - $245,000). Using this, the 2020 small business deduction for Reduco would be 19 percent of the least of:

• Active Business Income	$450,000
• Taxable Income ($540,000 - $60,000)	$480,000
• Reduced Annual Business Limit	$105,000

The small business deduction in this Case 1 is equal to $19,950 [(19%)($105,000)].

Case 2 The B component of the TCEC reduction formula is $2,250 [(.00225)($11,000,000 - $10,000,000)]. Given this, the required reduction would be calculated as follows:

$$[(\$350,000)(\$2,250 \div \$11,250)] = \underline{\$70,000} \text{ \textbf{Reduction}}$$

The AAII reduction would be the same $77,000 that was determined in Case 1. This would also be the greater of the two reductions, resulting in an annual business limit of $273,000 ($350,000 - $77,000). Given this, the small business deduction for Reduco is equal to 19 percent of the least of:

- Active Business Income $450,000
- Taxable Income ($540,000 - $60,000) $480,000
- Reduced Annual Business Limit $273,000

The small business deduction in this Case 2 is equal to $51,870 [(19%)($273,000)].

Exercise Twelve - 11 Solution

The small business deduction for Marion Manufacturing would be equal to 19 percent of the least of:

• Canadian Active Business Income (M&P Profits)		$411,000
• Taxable Income ($462,000 - $310,000)	$152,000	
Less 4 Times Business Income FTC Of $3,150	(12,600)	$139,400
• Annual Business Limit		$500,000

Based on this, the small business deduction would be $26,486 [(19%)($139,400)].

The M&P deduction would be equal to 13 percent of the lesser of:

• M&P Profits	$411,000	
Less Amount Eligible For Small Business Deduction	(139,400)	$271,600
• Taxable Income ($462,000 - $310,000)	$152,000	
Less:		
Amount Eligible For Small Business Deduction	(139,400)	
4 Times Business FTC Of $3,150	(12,600)	
Aggregate Investment Income (Taxable Capital Gain)	(30,000)	$ Nil

The M&P profits deduction would be equal to nil.

It would have been possible to increase the small business deduction to the full $411,000 of active business income by increasing Taxable Income to $423,600 ($411,000 + $12,600 FTC adjustment that will be deducted). This could be accomplished by limiting the deduction for charitable donations to $38,400 ($462,000 - $423,600). The remaining unclaimed donations of $271,600 ($310,000 - $38,400) could be carried forward for up to five years.

Although this increases Taxable Income and the total Tax Payable for the year, there could still be an ultimate tax savings with this approach, as the small business deduction cannot be carried forward, while charitable donations can be. As the Exercise states that Marion expects large increases in income in the future, this approach would be advantageous if Marion's expectations turn out to be correct.

Exercise Twelve - 12 Solution

The federal Tax Payable for Marchand Inc. would be calculated as follows:

Base Amount Of Part I Tax [(38%)($320,000)]	$121,600
Federal Tax Abatement [(10%)($320,000)]	(32,000)
M&P Deduction [(13%)($180,000)]	(23,400)
General Rate Reduction [(13%)($320,000 - $180,000)]	(18,200)
Federal Tax Payable	$ 48,000

As you would expect, the overall tax rate is equal to 15 percent ($48,000 ÷ $320,000).

Exercise Twelve - 13 Solution

The federal Tax Payable for Redux Ltd. would be calculated as follows:

Base Amount Of Part I Tax [(38%)($200,000)]	$76,000
Federal Tax Abatement [(10%)($200,000)]	(20,000)
Small Business Deduction (Note One)	(26,600)
M&P Deduction (Note Two)	(650)
General Rate Reduction (Note Three)	(7,150)
Federal Tax Payable	$21,600

Note One The small business deduction would be equal to $26,600, 19 percent of $140,000, the least of:

Active Business Income	200,000
Taxable Income	200,000
Business Limit	140,000

Note Two The M&P deduction would be equal to $650, 13 percent of $5,000, the lesser of:

• M&P Profits	$145,000	
Amount Eligible For Small Business Deduction	(140,000)	$ 5,000
• Taxable Income	$200,000	
Amount Eligible For Small Business Deduction	(140,000)	$60,000

Note Three The general rate reduction would be calculated as follows:

Taxable Income	$200,000
Amount Eligible For The SBD	(140,000)
Amount Eligible For The M&P Deduction	(5,000)
Full Rate Taxable Income	$ 55,000
Rate	13%
General Rate Reduction	$ 7,150

Exercise Twelve - 14 Solution

The Taxable Income figure would be calculated as follows:

Net Income For Tax Purposes	$146,000
Dividends Received	(30,000)
Non-Capital Loss Carry Forward	(75,000)
Net Capital Loss Carry Forward	(25,000)
Taxable Income	$ 16,000

Starting with this figure, the required calculation of Part I Tax Payable would be as follows:

Base Amount Of Part I Tax [(38%)($16,000)]	$6,080
Federal Tax Abatement [(88%)(10%)($16,000)]	(1,408)
General Rate Reduction [(13%)($16,000)]	(2,080)
Foreign Business Income Tax Credit (See Note)	(879)
Part I Tax Payable	$1,713

Note The foreign business income tax credit would be $879, the least of:

- The amount withheld — $3,000

- $\left[\dfrac{\$20,000}{\$146,000 - \$30,000 - \$25,000}\right][\$6,080 - \$2,080]$ — $ 879

- $6,080 - $2,080 — $4,000

The unused foreign business tax amount of $2,121 ($3,000 - $879) can be carried back 3 years and forward for 10 years. In calculating the allowable tax credit for such carry overs, these unused amounts will be added to the foreign tax paid factor in the calculation of the foreign business income tax credit.

Solution to Self Study Problem Twelve - 1

1. The required adjustments would be:

    - Add: Amortization expense of $254,000.
    - Deduct: CCA of $223,000.

2. The required adjustment would be:

    - Deduct: Premium amortization of $2,000.

3. The capital gain on this sale is $40,000 ($120,000 - $80,000). Because $48,000 ($120,000 - $72,000) of the proceeds are outstanding at the end of the current year, a reserve can be deducted. The reserve will be the lesser of:

    - $16,000 [($40,000)($48,000 ÷ $120,000)]
    - $32,000 [($40,000)(20%)(4 - 0)]

    The deduction of the lesser value of $16,000 will leave a capital gain of $24,000 ($40,000 - $16,000). Based on this, the required adjustments are:

    - Deduct: Accounting gain of $67,000 ($120,000 - $53,000).
    - Add: Taxable capital gain of $12,000[(1/2)($24,000)].

    There is no recapture on this disposition as the company still owns Class 44 assets, and there is a positive balance in the class at the end of the year.

4. The required adjustments would be:

    - Add: Membership fees of $8,000.
    - Add: Non-deductible entertainment expenses of $6,000[(50%)($12,000)].

5. The required adjustment would be:

    - Add: Charitable donations of $11,000.

6. The required adjustments would be:

    - Add: Accounting loss of $16,000 ($23,000 - $39,000).
    - Add: Recapture of $23,000 (Nil - $23,000).

Solution to Self Study Problem Twelve - 2

1. The adjustments here would be as follows:

   - Add the donation of $45,000.
   - Deduct the accounting gain of $7,000 ($45,000 - $38,000).
   - Add the taxable capital gain of $1,500 [(1/2)($45,000 - $42,000)].
   - Add the recapture of $5,500 ($42,000 - $36,500).

2. The adjustments here would be as follows:

   - Add the amortization expense of $32,450.
   - Deduct the CCA of $27,650.

3. The adjustment here would be as follows:

   - Add the increase in the warranty liability of $2,010 ($10,470 - $8,460).

4. Since item 1 created a taxable capital gain of $1,500, the adjustments here would be as follows:

   - Add the accounting loss of $550 ($12,870 - $12,320).
   - Deduct the allowable capital loss of $275 [(1/2)($12,870 - $12,320)].

5. The adjustment here would be as follows:

   - Add the $2,600 in bond discount amortization.

6. The adjustments here would be as follows:

   - Add the accounting loss of $14,810 ($107,000 - $92,190).
   - Deduct the terminal loss of $9,580 ($92,190 - $101,770).

Solution to Self Study Problem Twelve - 3

The required calculation of Net Income For Tax Purposes and Taxable Income is as follows:

ITA 3(a) Dividends		$ 22,300
ITA 3(b) Taxable Capital Gains	$15,600	
Allowable Capital Losses	(3,450)	12,150
ITA 3(c)		$ 34,450
ITA 3(d) Business Loss		(126,000)
Net Income For Tax Purposes		Nil
Dividends Received		($ 22,300)
Net Capital Loss Carry Forward		
(Limited To Net Taxable Capital Gains)		(12,150)
Charitable Donations		Nil
Taxable Income		Nil

The carry forward balances available at the end of the year are as follows:

Net Capital Loss Carry Forward

Beginning Balance	$ 42,300
Used During Year	(12,150)
Net Capital Loss Carry Forward	$ 30,150

Charitable Donations Carry Forward

Beginning Balance	$3,500
Added During Year	2,600
Used During Year	Nil
Unused Charitable Donations	$6,100

Non-Capital Loss

Balance Under E	
Dividends	$ 22,300
Business Loss	126,000
Net Capital Loss Carry Forward Deducted	12,150
Subtotal	$160,450
Balance Under F - Income Under ITA 3(c)	(34,450)
Non-Capital Loss	$126,000

Non-Capital Loss Carry Forward

Balance From Previous Years	$ 33,500
Added During Year	126,000
Used During Year	Nil
Non-Capital Loss Carry Forward	$159,500

As per the policy of the company, this solution minimizes the net capital loss carry forward. In the absence of this policy, an alternative solution could minimize the non-capital loss balance.

Solution to Self Study Problem Twelve - 4

2017 Analysis

Net And Taxable Income

Net Income For Tax Purposes and Taxable Income would be calculated as follows:

Business Income	$ 95,000
Dividends	12,000
Net Income For Tax Purposes	**$107,000**
Dividends	(12,000)
Charitable Donations	(21,400)
Taxable Income	**$ 73,600**

There would be a current year net capital loss of $5,000 [(1/2)($10,000)].

Loss Carry Forward

At the end of 2017, there would be a net capital loss carry forward of $5,000 [(1/2)($10,000)].

2018 Analysis

Net And Taxable Income

Both Net Income For Tax Purposes and Taxable Income would be nil, as shown in the following calculation:

Business Loss	($205,000)
Dividends	42,000
Net Income For Tax Purposes	**Nil**
Dividends	(42,000)
Taxable Income	**Nil**

This would leave a non-capital loss balance of $205,000, calculated as follows:

Amount E ($205,000 + $42,000)	$ 247,000
Income Under ITA 3(c) - Dividends	(42,000)
Non-Capital Loss for 2018	$205,000

There would also be a current year net capital loss of $7,000 [(1/2)($14,000)].

Carry Back And 2017 Amended Return

Of the total non-capital loss of $205,000, $73,600, can be carried back to 2017, resulting in the following amended return for that year:

Taxable Income As Previously Reported	$ 73,600
Non-Capital Loss Carry Back From 2018	(73,600)
Amended 2017 Taxable Income	Nil

Carry Forwards

After the carry back, the following carry forward balances would be available at the end of 2018:

• Charitable Donations	$ 4,600
• Non-Capital Loss Carry Forward ($205,000 - $73,600)	$131,400
• Net Capital Loss Carry Forward ($5,000 + $7,000)	$ 12,000

2019 Analysis

Net And Taxable Income

Net Income For Tax Purposes and Taxable Income would be calculated as follows:

Business Income	$ 69,500
Taxable Capital Gains [(1/2)($9,000)]	4,500
Dividends	28,000
Net Income For Tax Purposes	**$102,000**
Dividends	(28,000)
Charitable Donations	(8,000)
Taxable Income Before Carry Forwards	$ 66,000
Net Capital Loss Carry Forward	
(Limited To Taxable Capital Gains)	(4,500)
Charitable Donations Carry Forward (All)	(4,600)
Non-Capital Loss Carry Forward (Note)	(56,900)
Taxable Income	**Nil**

Note The amount of the non-capital loss carry forward that was deducted was the amount required to reduce the 2019 Taxable Income to nil.

While the various balances carried forward from 2018 could be used in any order that Linden chooses, it is the policy of the company to minimize its net capital loss balance. Also, since the charitable donations can only be carried forward for five years, it is more advantageous to deduct the charitable donations rather than more of the non-capital loss carry forward as the non-capital loss carry forward has a 20 year carry forward period.

Loss Carry Forwards

After the preceding allocation of losses, the following balances remain:

• Non-Capital Loss Carry Forward ($131,400 - $56,900)	$74,500
• Net Capital Loss Carry Forward ($12,000 - $4,500)	$ 7,500

2020 Analysis

Net And Taxable Income

Net Income For Tax Purposes and Taxable Income would be calculated as follows:

Business Income	$ 90,000
Taxable Capital Gains [(1/2)($10,000)]	5,000
Dividends	32,000
Net Income For Tax Purposes	**$ 127,000**
Dividends	(32,000)
Charitable Donations	(22,000)
Taxable Income Before Carry Forwards	$ 73,000
Net Capital Loss Carry Forward	
(Limited To Taxable Capital Gains)	(5,000)
Non-Capital Loss Carry Forward	
(Amount That Reduces Taxable Income To Nil)	(68,000)
Taxable Income	**Nil**

Loss Carry Forwards

After the preceding allocation of losses, the following balances remain:

- Non-Capital Loss Carry Forward ($74,500 - $68,000) $6,500
- Net Capital Loss Carry Forward ($7,500 - $5,000) $2,500

Solution to Self Study Problem Twelve - 5

The allocation to each of these provinces and the United States would be based on the following calculations:

Province	Salaries And Wages Amount	Salaries And Wages Percent	Gross Revenues Amount	Gross Revenues Percent
Manitoba	$ 369,750	15%	$1,252,000	20%
Ontario	616,250	25%	1,565,000	25%
Quebec	986,000	40%	2,191,000	35%
United States	493,000	20%	1,252,000	20%
Total	$2,465,000	100%	$6,260,000	100%

The province by province average of the two percentages, calculated above, would be used to allocate the total Taxable Income of $1,467,000 as follows:

Province	Wages	Revenues	Average	Taxable Income
Manitoba	15%	20%	17.5%	$ 256,725
Ontario	25%	25%	25.0%	366,750
Quebec	40%	35%	37.5%	550,125
United States	20%	20%	20.0%	293,400
Total	100%	100%	100.0%	$1,467,000

Solution to Self Study Problem Twelve - 6

Jordu's Part I tax payable for the year would be calculated as follows:

Base Amount Of Part I Tax [(38%)($1,265,000)]	480,700
Federal Tax Abatement [(10%)(95.5%)($1,265,000)] (Note One)	(120,808)
Foreign Business Tax Credit	
(Assumed To Be Equal To Taxes Withheld)	(19,500)
Small Business Deduction (Note Two)	(8,326)
General Rate Reduction (Note Three)	(158,753)
Part I Tax Payable	$ 173,313

Note One The federal tax abatement must be reduced because of the foreign business income. The percentage would be calculated as follows:

• Canadian Gross Revenues As A Percentage Of Total (28% + 63%)	91%
• Canadian Wages And Salaries As Percentage Of Total	100%

Using these figures, the average percent would be 95.5 percent.

Note Two Since Jordu and its associated companies have combined Taxable Capital Employed in Canada for 2019 that was greater than $10 million, its small business deduction is reduced. The B component of the ITA 125(5.1) reduction formula is $7,306 [(.00225)($13,246,900 - $10,000,000)]. In addition, because of Jordu's association with other companies, the A component of the formula would be reduced to $125,000 ($500,000 ÷ 4). Given these considerations, the reduction would be calculated as follows:

$$[(\$125,000)(\$7,306 \div \$11,250)] = \$81,178$$

Using this information, Jordu's small business deduction is equal to 19 percent of the least of:

• Canadian Active Business Income ($1,265,000 - $130,000)		$1,135,000
• Taxable Income	$1,265,000	
Less: Foreign Tax Credit Adjusted [(4)($19,500)]	(78,000)	$1,187,000
• Reduced Annual Business Limit ($125,000 - $81,178)		$ 43,822

The small business deduction would be $8,326 [(19%)($43,822)].

Note Three The general rate reduction would be calculated as follows:

Taxable Income	$1,265,000
Amount Eligible For Small Business Deduction	(43,822)
Full Rate Taxable Income	$1,221,178
Rate	(13%)
General Rate Reduction	$ 158,753

Solution to Self Study Problem Twelve - 7

The Taxable Income and Tax Payable for the Serendipity Shop Corp. for the year would be calculated as follows:

Net Income For Tax Purposes		$240,000
Deductions:		
Dividends	($20,000)	
Donations	(48,000)	(68,000)
Taxable Income		$172,000
Base Amount Of Part I Tax [(38%)($172,000)]		$ 65,360
Federal Tax Abatement [(10%)($172,000)]		(17,200)
Small Business Deduction (Note)		(25,650)
General Rate Reduction [(13%)($172,000 - $135,000)]		(4,810)
Part I Federal Tax Payable		$ 17,700

Note The small business deduction is based on the least of the following:

Active business income	$220,000
Taxable Income	172,000
Allocated annual business limit	135,000

The small business deduction is equal to $25,650 [(19%)($135,000)].

Solution to Self Study Problem Twelve - 8

Part A - Net Income For Tax Purposes
The minimum Net Income For Tax Purposes for Borscan Inc. would be calculated as follows:

Accounting Income Before Taxes		$1,275,000
Additions:		
Taxable Capital Gain - Building		
[(1/2)($625,000 - $500,000 - $100,000)]	$ 12,500	
Taxable Capital Gain - Land ($100,000 - $100,000)	Nil	
Recaptured CCA ($500,000 - $350,000)	150,000	
Amortization Expense	255,000	
Interest And Penalties - Late Payment	500	
Charitable Donations	13,500	431,500
		$1,706,500
Deductions:		
Capital Cost Allowance	($287,000)	
Gain On Expropriated Building		
(From Income Statement)	(25,000)	(312,000)
Net Income For Tax Purposes		$1,394,500

Part B - Taxable Income
The minimum Taxable Income for Borscan Inc. would be calculated as follows:

Net Income For Tax Purposes	$1,394,500
Dividends Received	(25,000)
Charitable Donations	(13,500)
Net Capital Loss Carry Forward (Note)	(12,500)
Non-Capital Loss Carry Forward	(35,000)
Taxable Income	$1,308,500

Note The net capital loss carry forward can be used only to the extent of the taxable capital gain for the year, resulting in a deduction of $12,500. This leaves a remaining net capital loss carry forward of $17,500 ($30,000 - $12,500).

Part C - Tax Payable

The minimum federal Tax Payable for Borscan Inc. is as follows:

Base Amount Of Part I Tax [(38%)($1,308,500)]	$ 497,230
Federal Tax Abatement [(10%)($1,308,500)]	(130,850)
General Rate Reduction [(13%)($1,308,500)]	(170,105)
Federal Tax Payable	$ 196,275

Solution to Self Study Problem Twelve - 9

Part A - Net Income

Net Income For Tax Purposes for Industrial Tools Ltd. would be calculated as follows:

Accounting Income Before Taxes		$2,305,000
Additions:		
Taxable Capital Gain On Building (Note)	$ 37,500	
Taxable Capital Gain On Land		
($200,000 - $200,000)	Nil	
Recaptured CCA ($875,000 - $625,000)	250,000	
Charitable Donations	28,000	
Interest And Penalties	2,500	
Warranty Reserve	20,000	
Amortization Expense	478,000	816,000
		$3,121,000
Deductions:		
Accounting Gain On Building (Given)	($225,000)	
CCA	(523,000)	(748,000)
Net Income For Tax Purposes		$2,373,000

Note The taxable capital gain on the building would be calculated as follows:

Proceeds Of Disposition ($1,150,000 - $200,000)	$950,000
Adjusted Cost Base ($1,075,000 - $200,000)	(875,000)
Capital Gain	$ 75,000
Inclusion Rate	1/2
Taxable Capital Gain	$ 37,500

As its value has not changed, there is no capital gain on the land.

Part B - Taxable Income

Taxable Income for Industrial Tools Ltd. would be calculated as follows:

Net Income For Tax Purposes	$ 2,373,000
Dividends Received	(42,000)
Charitable Donations	(28,000)
Net Capital Loss Carry Forward (Note)	(37,500)
Taxable Income	$ 2,265,500

Note The net capital loss carry forward can be used only to the extent of the taxable capital gain for the year, resulting in a deduction of $37,500. This leaves a remaining net capital loss carry forward of $52,500 ($90,000 - $37,500).

Part C - Tax Payable

Federal Tax Payable for Industrial Tools Ltd. would be calculated as follows:

Base Amount Of Part I Tax [(38%)($2,265,500)]	$ 860,890
Federal Tax Abatement [(10%)($2,265,500)]	(226,550)
General Rate Reduction [(13%)($2,265,500)]	(294,515)
Federal Part I Tax Payable	$ 339,825

Solution to Self Study Problem Twelve - 10

Note to Instructor As the ART is not covered until Chapter 13, this problem does not require the calculation of the ART. However, given the capital loss carry forward applied during the year, it would be nil.

Part A - Net Income For Tax Purposes

The calculation of Mamora's Net Income For Tax Purposes would be as follows:

Accounting Net Income Before Taxes			$1,115,050
Additions, Including Relevant Problem Part:			
1	Amortization Expense	$405,525	
2	Taxable Capital Gain On Building (Note 1)	25,000	
2	Taxable Capital Gain On Building Land (Note 1)	12,500	
3	Taxable Capital Gain On Vacant Land (Note 2)	15,918	
2	Recapture On Building (Note 3)	250,000	
2	Accounting Loss On Vehicles (Given)	63,000	
6	Foreign Tax Withheld	2,700	
7	Articles Of Incorporation Amendment Costs	21,000	
8	Bond Discount Amortization	4,600	
8	Donations To Registered Charities	12,500	
8	Interest On Late Income Tax Instalments	1,400	
8	Interest On Late Municipal Taxes	Nil	
9	Non-Deductible Meals And Entertainment		
	(50% of $42,000)	21,000	
9	Golf Club Membership Fees	23,000	858,143
			$1,973,193
Deductions:			
2	Accounting Gain On Building (Given)	($175,000)	
2	Capital Cost Allowance (Note 3)	(628,575)	
2	Terminal Loss (Note 3)	(20,000)	
3	Accounting Gain On Vacant Land (Given)	(75,000)	
4	Landscaping	(53,000)	(951,575)
	Net Income For Tax Purposes		$1,021,618

Note 1   While the accounting gain on the building of $175,000 is calculated on the combined value of the land and building, separate tax figures are required for each asset. The taxable capital gains on the building and land are calculated as follows:

Proceeds Of Disposition ($1,725,000 - $375,000)	$1,350,000
Capital Cost ($1,650,000 - $350,000)	(1,300,000)
Capital Gain	$ 50,000
Inclusion Rate	1/2
Taxable Capital Gain - Building	$ 25,000

Proceeds Of Disposition	$ 375,000
Capital Cost	(350,000)
Capital Gain	$ 25,000
Inclusion Rate	1/2
Taxable Capital Gain - Land	$ 12,500

Note 2   There is a capital gain and accounting gain on the vacant land of $75,000 ($695,000 - $620,000). However, as not all of the proceeds of disposition were received in 2020, a reserve can be deducted for tax purposes. The reserve will be the lesser of the following two amounts:

- [($75,000)($400,000 ÷ $695,000)] =$43,165
- [($75,000)(20%)(4 - 0)] = $60,000

Deducting the lesser amount leaves a capital gain of $31,835 ($75,000 - $43,165) and a taxable capital gain of $15,918 [(1/2)($31,835)].

Note 3   Maximum CCA and other related inclusions and deductions are found in the tables that follow. Note that the new building was added to a separate class in order to qualify for the enhanced CCA rate of 10 percent for M&P buildings. This resulted in recapture on the old building that was disposed of.

Class 1 - Old Building

January 1, 2020, Class 1 Balance	$1,050,000
Disposition - Lesser Of:	
• Proceeds = $1,350,000 ($1,725,000 - $375,000)	
• Capital Cost = $1,300,000 ($1,650,000 - $350,000)	(1,300,000)
Negative Ending UCC Balance	($ 250,000)
Recapture	250,000
January 1, 2021, UCC Balance	Nil

Class 1 - New Building

New Class 1 Addition ($2,100,000 - $400,000)	$1,700,000
AccII Adjustment	850,000
Balance	$2,550,000
CCA [(10%)($2,550,000)]	(255,000)
AccII Adjustment Reversal	(850,000)
January 1, 2021, UCC Balance	$1,445,000

Class 8

January 1, 2020, Class 8 Balance	$1,460,000
Additions	150,000
AccII Adjustment	(75,000)
CCA Base	($1,685,000)
CCA [(20%)($1,685,000)]	(337,000)
AccII Adjustment Reversal	(75,000)
January 1, 2021, UCC Balance	1,273,000

Class 10

January 1, 2020, Class 10 Balance	$142,000
Disposition - Lesser Of:	
• Proceeds = $122,000	
• Capital Cost = $285,000	(122,000)
Positive Ending Balance With No Assets Left In Class	($ 20,000)
Terminal Loss	(20,000)
January 1, 2021, UCC Balance	Nil

Class 13

January 1, 2020, Class 13 Balance	$175,000
2020 CCA:	
2015 Expenditures ($250,000 ÷ 10 Years)	(25,000)
2019 Expenditures ($60,000 ÷ 6 Years)	(10,000)
January 1, 2021, UCC Balance	140,000

Class 14.1

January 1, 2020, Class 14.1 Balance	Nil
2020 Additions	$21,000
AccII Adjustment	10,500
CCA Base	$31,500
CCA [(5%)($31,500)]	(1,575)
AccII Adjustment Reversal	(10,500)
January 1, 2021, UCC Balance	$19,425

The cost of amending the articles of incorporation does not qualify for the $3,000 deduction under ITA 20(1)(b) as the costs were not incurred for incorporation.

Summary Of CCA And UCC Results

Class	Maximum CCA	UCC
Class 1 - Old (Recapture = $250,000)	Nil	Nil
Class 1 - New	$255,000	$1,445,000
Class 8	337,000	1,273,000
Class 10 (Terminal Loss = $20,000)	Nil	Nil
Class 13 ($25,000 + $10,000)	35,000	140,000
Class 14.1	1,575	19,425
Total	$628,575	

Part B - Taxable Income

Mamora's Taxable Income would be calculated as follows:

Net Income For Tax Purposes	$1,021,618
13 Dividends From Taxable Canadian Corporations	(22,000)
8 Contributions To Registered Charities	(12,500)
11 Net Capital Loss Carry Forward (Note 4)	(53,418)
11 Non-Capital Loss Carry Forward (All)	(95,000)
Taxable Income	$ 838,700

Note 4 Mamora's Net Income For Tax Purposes contained net taxable capital gains calculated as follows:

Taxable Capital Gain On Building (Note 1)	$25,000
Taxable Capital Gain On Building Land (Note 1)	12,500
Taxable Capital Gain On Vacant Land (Note 2)	15,918
Total Taxable Capital Gains	$53,418

While there is a net capital loss carry forward of $210,000, the amount to be used is limited to the $53,418 in net taxable capital gains for the year.

Part B - Loss Carry Forwards

At the end of 2020, there would be a net capital loss carry forward of $156,582 ($210,000 - $53,418). There is no remaining non-capital loss carry forward.

Part C - Federal Tax Payable

Mamora's federal Tax Payable would be calculated as follows:

Base Amount Of Part I Tax [(38%)($838,700)]	$318,706
Federal Tax Abatement [(10%)(88%)($838,700)]	(73,806)
Small Business Deduction (Note 5)	(33,250)
M&P Deduction (Note 6)	(32,500)
General Rate Reduction (Note 7)	(53,781)
Foreign Business Tax Credit (Given)	(2,700)
Part I Tax Payable	$122,669

Note 5 The amount eligible for the small business deduction would be the least of the following amounts:

Canadian Source Active Business Income (Given)	**$976,380**
Taxable Income	$838,700
Less: 4 Times The Foreign Business Tax Credit [(4)($2,700)]	(10,800)
Adjusted Taxable Income	**$ 827,900**
Annual Business Limit (Given)	$ 175,000

The least of these figures is $175,000, resulting in a small business deduction of $33,250 [(19%)($175,000)].

Note 6 The base for the M&P deduction would be the lesser of:

M&P Profits (Given)	$425,000
Less: Amount Eligible For The Small Business Deduction	(175,000)
Balance	$250,000

Taxable Income	$838,700
Less:	
Amount Eligible For The Small Business Deduction	(175,000)
4 Times The Foreign Business Tax Credit [(4)($2,700)]	(10,800)
Aggregate Investment Income ($53,418 - $53,418)	Nil
Adjusted Taxable Income	$652,900

The lesser of these two figures is $250,000, resulting in an M&P deduction of $32,500 [(13%)($250,000)]. The Aggregate Investment Income is reduced to nil by the application of the net capital loss carry forward.

Note 7 The general rate reduction would be calculated as follows:

Taxable Income	$838,700
Amount Eligible For The Small Business Deduction	(175,000)
Amount Eligible For The M&P Deduction	(250,000)
Full Rate Taxable Income	$413,700
Rate	13%
General Rate Reduction	$ 53,781

Chapter 13 Learning Objectives

After completing Chapter 13, you should be able to:

1. Explain the goal of integration in the design of the Canadian corporate tax system (paragraph [P hereafter] 13-1 to 13-5).
2. Calculate after tax income retained from eligible and non-eligible dividends received (P 13-6 to 13-14).
3. Demonstrate how the dividend gross up and tax credit procedures work to implement integration with respect to business income (P 13-15 to 13-22).
4. List the components of Aggregate Investment Income as it is defined in ITA 129(4) and describe the basic concept of refundable taxes (P 13-23 to 13-38).
5. Calculate the additional refundable tax (ART) on the investment income of a CCPC (P 13-39 to 13-47).

6. Calculate the Part I refundable tax on the investment income of a CCPC (P 13-48 to 13-66).
7. Apply the provisions related to the Part IV refundable tax on private corporations, including those related to dividends from a connected corporation (P 13-67 to 13-94).
8. Explain and apply the eligible dividend designation calculations relevant to CCPCs and their GRIP (P 13-95 to 13-104).
9. Explain and apply the eligible dividend designation calculations relevant to non-CCPCs and their LRIP (P 13-105 to 13-108).
10. Describe and calculate the Part III.1 tax on excessive eligible dividend designations (EEDD) (P 13-109 to 13-117).

11. Apply the transitional provision to the balance in the Refundable Dividend Tax On Hand (RDTOH) account (P 13-118 to 13-127).
12. Calculate the Part I refundable tax (P 13-128 to 13-139).
13. Calculate the balance in the Eligible and Non-Eligible (RDTOH) accounts (P 13-140 to 13-148).
14. Calculate the dividend refund on the payment of eligible and non-eligible dividends (P 13-149 to 13-152).
15. Describe the economic impact of the change in RDTOH rules (P 13-153 to 13-170).

16. Use a logical approach to deal with comprehensive calculations of corporate Taxable Income and Tax Payable (P 13-171 to 13-172).
17. Review a simple corporate tax return completed using the ProFile T2 tax preparation software program.

How to Work Through Chapter 13

We recommend the following approach in dealing with the material in this Chapter:

Note On Current Developments
- Read the Note at the beginning of the Chapter (in the textbook).

Integration
- Read paragraph 13-1 to 13-20.
- Do Exercises Thirteen-1 and Thirteen-2 (in the textbook) and check the solutions in this Study Guide.
- Do Self Study Problem Thirteen-1, which is available on MyLab, and check the solution in this Study Guide.
- Read paragraph 13-21 to 13-22.

Refundable Tax On Aggregate Investment Income
- Read paragraph 13-23 to 13-38.

Additional Refundable Tax On Investment Income (ART)
- Read paragraph 13-39 to 13-42.
- Do Exercise Thirteen-3 and check the solution in this Study Guide.
- Read paragraph 13-43 to 13-53.

Refundable Portion Of Part I Tax
- Read paragraph 13-54 to 13-66.
- Do Exercise Thirteen-4 and check the solution in this Study Guide.

Refundable Part IV Tax On Dividends Received
- Read paragraph 13-67 to 13-92.
- Do Exercise Thirteen-5 and check the solution in this Study Guide.
- Read paragraph 13-93 and 13-94.

Designation Of Eligible Dividends
- Read paragraph 13-95 to 13-98.

CCPCs And Their GRIP
- Read paragraph 13-99 to 13-104.
- Do Exercise Thirteen-6 and check the solution in this Study Guide.

Non-CCPCs And Their LRIP
- Read paragraph 13-105 to 13-108.

Part III.1 Tax On Excessive Eligible Dividend Designations (EEDDs)
- Read paragraph 13-109 to 13-117.

Refundable Dividend Tax On Hand (RDTOH)
- Read paragraph 13-118 to 13-139.
- Do Exercise Thirteen-7 and check the solution in this Study Guide.

Eligible And Non-Eligible RDTOH Balances Defined
- Read paragraph 13-140 to 13-152.
- Do Exercise Thirteen-8 and check the solution in this Study Guide.
- Do Self Study Problems Thirteen-2 to Thirteen-5 and check the solutions in this Study Guide.

Economic Impact Of Changes
- Read paragraph 13-153 to 13-158.

Example Of RDTOH Calculations
- Read paragraph 13-159 to 13-170

Working Through Large Corporate Problems
- Read paragraph 13-171 and 13-172.
- Do Self Study Problems Thirteen-6 to Thirteen-8 and check the solutions in this Study Guide.

Sample Corporate Tax Return
- Read the Sample Corporate Tax Return found on in this Study Guide. The complete tax return is available on MyLab in two formats, a T2 ProFile return file and a .PDF file.

To Complete This Chapter
- If you would like more practice in problem solving, do the Supplementary Self Study Problems for the chapter. These problems and solutions are available on MyLab.
- Review the Key Terms Used In This Chapter in the textbook at the end of Chapter 13. Consult the Glossary for the meaning of any key terms you do not know.
- Test yourself with the Chapter 13 Glossary Flashcards available on MyLab.
- Ensure you have achieved the Chapter 13 Learning Objectives listed in this Study Guide.
- As a review, we recommend you view the PowerPoint presentation for Chapter 13 that is on MyLab.

Practice Examination
- Write the Practice Examination for Chapter 13 that is on MyLab. Mark your examination using the Practice Examination Solution that is on MyLab.

Sample Corporate Tax Return

Note The following simplified example contains the 2019 updated version of the T2 corporate income tax return completed using the 2019 Profile T2 corporate tax preparation program from Intuit Canada released in January 2020. The updated version of this problem will be available on MyLab at:

http://www.pearsonmylabandmastering.com

As this example is designed to illustrate corporate tax return calculations, limited GIFI (General Index of Financial Information) data has been included. The relevant T2 schedule or form name is provided in square brackets to make it easier for users to find where the information is input. Note that capital dividends are covered in detail in Chapter 14.

Sample Files On MyLab
To View The Tax Return Files
The complete sample tax return is available on MyLab in two versions, a T2 ProFile return file and a .PDF file.

To view the ProFile return file (with a .GT2 extension), you must have the ProFile program installed. For information on how to obtain the program for free, see MyLab.

To view the .PDF files, you must have the Adobe Reader program installed. This program can be installed for free from the Adobe website (www.adobe.com).

Sample Problem Data

Note: The government's Crown Copyright does not permit us to use fake Business Numbers in software examples. To reduce the number of ProFile's error messages because of this, we have used NR (for not registered) in the Business Number field.

On the ProFile schedule titled "Info", the Filing question "Complete return from GIFI?" is answered Yes by default. Click the No box and you can ignore the GIFI requirements.

MetroFaux Inc. is a Canadian controlled private corporation based in Saskatoon that manufactures metal and composite office furniture. Its head office is located at 123 ABC Avenue, Saskatoon, SK S7G 1A1, phone number (306)111-1111. The signing officer and contact person is the President of the company, Jack Saskatoon. MetroFaux Inc. was incorporated on August 28, 1977.

Most of its income is earned from active business in Canada. The company has no associated corporations. Although the company has a sophisticated website, it is only for information purposes. It has no income from a web page or website. [Schedule 88 is not applicable.]

As at December 31, 2018, the following information applied to MetroFaux Inc:

Taxable Capital Employed In Canada [Info]	$1,590,000
RDTOH [T2, line 460]	Nil
Dividends Declared And Paid During 2018	Nil
GRIP Balance [Schedule 53]	276,000

During the taxation year ending December 31, 2019, the condensed before tax Income Statement of MetroFaux Inc. was prepared in accordance with International Financial Reporting Standards (IFRS). In condensed form it is as follows:

MetroFaux Inc.
Condensed Income Statement
Year Ending December 31, 2019

Sales	$3,980,000	
Gain On Building Sale	160,000	$4,140,000
Amortization Expense	$ 607,000	
Other Expenses Excluding Taxes	1,773,000	2,380,000
Accounting Income Before Taxes		$1,760,000

Preliminary GIFI Procedures

On the ProFile schedule titled "Info", the Filing question "Complete return from GIFI?" is answered Yes by default. Click the No box. Ignore the GIFI requirements except as follows:

- On GIFI Schedule 125 (Income Statement), input the total sales as "Trade sales of goods and services" (Code 8000) and the Gain On Building Sale as "Realized gains / losses on disposal of assets" (Code 8210) from the drop down menu under Revenues. Input the Amortization Expense as "Amortization of tangible assets" (Code 8670) and the Other Expenses as "Other expenses" (Code 9270) from the drop down menu under Operating Expenses.

- On GIFI Schedule 100 (Balance Sheet), input the Net Income figure as "Cash and deposits" (Code 1000) in order to make the total assets equal to the total liabilities and equity.

Although this will not properly complete the GIFI statements, it will eliminate the warning messages that would otherwise be generated when the Net Income figure and Amortization Expense are input on Schedule 1. These GIFI entries will have no effect on the calculations in the tax return. To prevent audit warnings, S141, "Notes Checklist", has to be completed. Assume there are no notes to the financial statements and answer "No" to any other relevant questions.

Other Information:

1. Expenses include interest and penalties of $2,300 resulting from late income tax instalments and a failure to file the 2018 tax return within the prescribed time period. [Schedule 1]

2. Expenses include a deduction for charitable donations to the Cancer Research Society in the amount of $15,000. [Schedule 2]

3. Revenues include eligible dividends of $36,000 from Canadian Tax Save Inc., a taxable Canadian corporation. MetroFaux Inc. has no association with Canadian Tax Save Inc. and considers the dividends portfolio dividends. [Schedule 3. Note that under the GRIP/LRIP double column, "Column F deduction type" = s. 112 and $36,000 must be placed in the "Indicate eligible dividends" column.]

4. The company paid $100,000 in taxable eligible dividends during 2019. [Schedule 3]

5. The company has available a non-capital loss carry over from the previous year of $56,000 [S4Supp]. The net capital loss carry forward from 2016 is $22,500 (1/2 of $45,000). [Schedule 4 - note 100 percent figures are used for the capital loss]

6. During 2019, the company earned $97,000 of interest income on bonds purchased in 2018 that mature in 2022. [Schedule 7]

7. Amortization expense on the Income Statement amounts to $607,000. The opening UCC balance was $905,000 for Class 8, $800,000 for Class 10, and $429,000 for Class 53. The only fixed asset acquisition was $100,000 in Class 53 manufacturing equipment on May 1, 2019. There were no dispositions in Classes 8 or 10. [Schedule 8 flows to Schedule 1]

8. The Gain On Building Sale resulted from the sale of a building for proceeds of $792,000 of which $120,000 was allocated to the land. The building at 456 DEF Street, Regina, Saskatchewan S7G 1A1, was acquired on August 28, 2009, for $764,000, of which $100,000 was allocated to the land. The sales office of the company had been located in this building and the sales office has subsequently moved to leased space in Saskatoon. As the company leases all of its other buildings and equipment, the building was the only asset in Class 1. The Undepreciated Capital Cost of this class prior to the disposition of the building was $514,000. [Schedules 1, 6 and 8]

9. Information related to Canadian manufacturing and processing activities for the year is as follows: [Schedule 27]

Cost of capital [(10% of $6,000,000) + ($200,000 in rental costs)]	$ 800,000
Portion of capital used in M&P activities	500,000
Cost of labour	1,000,000
Portion of labour used in M&P activities	760,000

10. All of the common shares of MetroFaux Inc. are held by the president, Jack Saskatoon (SIN 527-000-582). [Schedule 50]

11. The beginning balance in the company's capital dividend account is nil [CDA]. Note that capital dividends are covered in detail in Chapter 14.

12. The company paid one federal income tax instalment of $212,000 on September 1, 2018 [TaxPaid].

Completed Tax Return

The complete sample tax return is available on MyLab in two versions, a T2 ProFile return file and a .PDF file.

Notes On Sample Corporate Tax Return

Loss Carry Forwards

The losses of prior taxation years deducted in the calculation of Taxable Income consist of the non-capital loss of $56,000 and a $14,000 net capital loss. As calculated on Schedule 4, the net capital loss carry forward deduction is limited by the $28,000 capital gain for the year and leaves a capital loss carry forward of $17,000. Note Schedule 4 uses the 100 percent amounts. There is no non-capital loss carry forward remaining.

Building Sale

The $160,000 Gain On Building Sale is deducted on Schedule 1 as the tax effects of the disposition are included in Net Income For Tax Purposes. As calculated on Schedule 6, the taxable capital gain on the building sale is $14,000 [(1/2)($792,000 - $764,000)].

As calculated on Schedule 8, the recapture of CCA on the building is equal to $150,000 ($664,000 - $514,000). This is shown as an addition on Schedule 1, separate from the CCA.

Aggregate Investment Income

As calculated on Schedule 7, Part 1, the aggregate investment income of $97,000 consists of:

- the taxable capital gains of $14,000, less
- the $14,000 net capital loss carry forward claimed, plus
- net property income of $133,000 (dividends received of $36,000 plus interest income of $97,000), less
- taxable dividends deductible of $36,000.

This figure is used in calculating the refundable portion of Part I tax.

Active Business Income

As calculated on Schedule 7, Part 6, income eligible for the small business deduction of $1,505,800 is Net Income For Tax Purposes of $1,652,800 less the sum of

- The taxable capital gains of $14,000, plus
- Net property income of $133,000 (eligible dividends of $36,000 plus interest on five year bonds of $97,000)

This amount is used in both the small business deduction calculation of Schedule 7 and the T2 together with the calculation of the M&P tax credit in Schedule 27.

M&P Labour

As the grossed up M&P Labour of $1,013,333 [(100/75)($760,000)] is greater than the $1,000,000 Cost of Labour, M&P Labour in the Schedule 27, Part 7 calculation is limited to $1,000,000.

As mentioned in the text, although the effect of the federal M&P deduction has been negated by the general rate reduction, there are still provincial M&P tax reductions available. In this example, MetroFaux Inc. is eligible for the Saskatchewan M&P tax reduction. (See Schedule 404.) You will note that the federal amount upon which the M&P credit is based of $828,647 as shown in Schedule 27 is different than the amount of $728,647 used to calculate the Saskatchewan M&P credit as shown in the provincial form S404. The $100,000 difference is attributable to the fact that starting January 1, 2018, Saskatchewan increased the small business limit by an additional $100,000 from $500,000 to $600,000.

CCA – Class 53 & Schedule 8

Most depreciable property acquired in arm's length transactions between November 21, 2019, and December 31, 2023, are eligible for a first year accelerated CCA claim rather than a reduced claim under the historical half year rule. The corporation acquired Class 53 manufacturing depreciable property May 1, 2019, for $100,000. This acquisition qualifies for the Accelerated Investment Incentive (AII). Column 4 of Schedule 8 requires identifying and including any qualifying depreciable property. Once identified, most qualifying property is eligible for CCA equal to three times the CCA that would have been determined under the regular half year rules. Class 53, however, is given special treatment, the result of which is to ensure that 100 percent of the cost can be claimed as CCA in the year of acquisition. In this case CCA for Class 53 is calculated as [(50%)($429,000) + (50%)(2.0)($100,000)], which equals $314,500.

Capital Dividend Account

The balance in the Capital Dividend Account is $14,000 [(1/2)($692,000 - $664,000)]. A tax free capital dividend of $14,000 could have been paid if form T2054 had been filed. (See Chapter 14.)

Adjusted Aggregate Investment Income (AAII) & The New Passive Investment Rules (ITA 125(5.1))

The above rules, with the exception of GRIP, become effective for corporate taxation years that begin after December 31, 2018. In our case the fiscal year is January 1, 2019, to December 31, 2019, therefore all of these rules apply in this case.

The new passive investment rules limit the amount that can be claimed for the small business deduction grinding down and reducing the current year, small business limit of $500,000 based on the AAII of the corporation for its immediately preceding year, which in this case would be the year ending December 31, 2018. The reduction begins when the AAII exceeds $50,000 and is eliminated altogether when AAII reaches $150,000. As we do not have that information, no adjustment has been made to the 2019 T2 corporate tax return.

AAII starts with Aggregate Investment Income (AII) and makes certain adjustments. Both AII and AAII are found in Schedule 7 in Parts 1 and 2, respectively. While AII includes all taxable capital gains, AAII excludes taxable capital gains from "active assets," which are typically property actually used in a business that generates active business income. Our objective is not to explain the legislation, which can be found in the textbook, but rather to point out this new information, which is now contained within the ProFile and other tax software. In this case you will note that we have left the taxable capital gain line 705 blank. The reason is that the taxable capital gains relate to the sale of land and building that were used in the business and are therefore active assets. The interest on five year bonds, however, is another matter and is included. The 2019 AAII of $97,000 only becomes relevant for the 2020 taxation year of the company. The 2020 impact would be to reduce the small business limit of $500,000 in 2020 by $235,000 to $265,000. The reduction is calculated as [(500,000/500,000)(5)(97,000 - 50,000)].

GRIP, Dividend Refunds & Eligible And Non-Eligible RDTOH

Schedule 53 is used to determine the GRIP for the year. It begins with an opening balance of $276,000 and makes adjustments based upon the income received including the receipt of eligible dividends.

The T2 corporate tax return includes the calculations for the opening RDTOH balance (Lines 460, 465, & 480). The corporation is subject to a new set of RDTOH rules for its 2019 taxation year that divides the RDTOH into two new accounts referred to as eligible RDTOH or ERDTOH (line 530) and non-eligible RDTOH or NERDTOH (line 545). We refer you to the textbook for the details, but the general rule is that the designation and payment of eligible dividends will not trigger a dividend refund unless the corporation has an ERDTOH account at year end. In this case the corporation paid a taxable eligible dividend of $100,000, which would normally entitle it to a dividend refund of $38,333 (see line 530 AA). However, since the ERDTOH is only $13,800 (Line 530 BB), the dividend refund is restricted to $13,800 (see line 530 CC).

There is also a transitional rule that allows the conversion of splitting of RDTOH in the year before the new rules apply (December 31, 2018, in our case) based upon the GRIP balance on that same date. You will see this between lines 480 and 520 at "H" ($276,000) and "I" ($105,800). If, for example, the RDTOH at December 31, 2018, had been $120,000 the ERDTOH would have been $105,800 with the balance of $14,200 representing the NERD-TOH opening balances. In our case there was no opening RDTOH and therefore the GRIP adjustment had no effect.

Solutions to Chapter 13 Exercises

Exercise Thirteen - 1 Solution
If she incorporates, the corporation will pay taxes of $15,000 [(15%)($100,000)], leaving $85,000 to be distributed as dividends. Her individual Tax Payable on these non-eligible dividends would be calculated as follows:

Non-Eligible Dividends Received	$ 85,000
Gross Up [(15%)($85,000)]	12,750
Grossed Up Dividends	$ 97,750
Personal Tax Rate	45%
Tax Before Credit	$ 43,988
Dividend Tax Credit [(9/13 + 30%)($12,750)]	(12,652)
Tax Payable On Dividends	$ 31,336

The net after tax retention would be $53,664 ($85,000 - $31,336). This compares to $55,000 [($100,000)(1 - .45)] retained if a corporation is not used. Clearly the use of a corporation is not desirable in this situation. This result reflects the fact that the corporate tax rate is above the 13.04 percent required for integration and the provincial dividend tax credit is below the 30.8 percent required for integration.

Exercise Thirteen - 2 Solution
If he incorporates, the corporation will pay taxes of $30,000 [(30%)($100,000)], leaving $70,000 to be distributed as dividends. His individual Tax Payable on these eligible dividends would be calculated as follows:

Eligible Dividends Received	$ 70,000
Gross Up [(38%)($70,000)]	26,600
Grossed Up Dividends	$ 96,600
Personal Tax Rate	42%
Tax Before Credit	$ 40,572
Dividend Tax Credit [(6/11 + 28%)($26,600)]	(21,957)
Tax Payable On Dividends	$ 18,615

The net after tax retention would be $51,385 ($70,000 - $18,615). This compares to $58,000 [($100,000)(1 - .42)] retained if a corporation is not used. Clearly the use of a corporation is not desirable in this situation. While the corporate tax rate of 30 percent is greater than the required 27.54 percent, the real problem here is the fact that the provincial dividend tax credit of 28 percent is significantly below the required 45.5 percent.

Exercise Thirteen - 3 Solution
Zircon's Taxable Income would be calculated as follows:

Net Income For Tax Purposes	$281,000
Dividends From Taxable Canadian Corporations	(22,000)
Net Capital Loss Carry Forward	(26,000)
Non-Capital Loss Carry Forward	(23,000)
Taxable Income	$210,000

Zircon's amount eligible for the small business deduction of $198,000 is the least of active business income of $198,000, Taxable Income of $210,000, and the annual business limit of $500,000.

Given these calculations, Zircon's additional refundable tax on investment income would be calculated using the lesser of:

Aggregate Investment Income		
Taxable Capital Gains	$ 46,000	
Net Capital Loss Deducted	(26,000)	
Interest Income	15,000	$35,000
Taxable Income	$ 210,000	
Amount Eligible For SBD	(198,000)	$12,000

The additional refundable tax on investment income would be $1,280 [(10-2/3%)($12,000)]. Note that the Taxable Income limit is $23,000 ($35,000 - $12,000) less than the Aggregate Investment Income. This difference is the result of the deduction of the $23,000 non-capital loss carry forward.

Exercise Thirteen - 4 Solution

If Ms. Nicastro receives the income directly, she will retain $49,000 [($100,000)(1 - .51)]. Alternatively, if the investments are transferred to a corporation, the results would be as follows:

Corporate Investment Income	$100,000
Corporate Tax At 52 Percent	(52,000)
After Tax Income	$ 48,000
Dividend Refund [($48,000 ÷ .61667) - $48,000]	29,837
Non-Eligible Dividends Paid To Ms. Nicastro	$ 77,837
Non-Eligible Dividends Received	$ 77,837
Gross Up Of 15 Percent	11,676
Personal Taxable Income	$ 89,513
Personal Tax Rate	51%
Tax Payable Before Dividend Tax Credit	$ 45,652
Dividend Tax Credit [(9/13 + 30%)($11,676)]	(11,586)
Personal Tax Payable With Corporation	$ 34,066
Non-Eligible Dividends Received	$ 77,837
Personal Tax Payable	(34,066)
After Tax Cash Retained With Corporation	$ 43,771

There would be no tax deferral with the corporation as the corporate taxes of $52,000 are $1,000 more than the $51,000 she would pay on direct receipt of the income. In addition, the use of a corporation would reduce the after tax funds retained by $5,229 ($43,771 vs. $49,000). There is clearly a disadvantage resulting from the use of a corporation.

Exercise Thirteen - 5 Solution

The amount of Part IV Tax Payable would be calculated as follows:

Tax On Portfolio Investments [(38 - 1/3%)($14,000)]	$5,367
Tax On Emerald Inc. Dividends	Nil
Tax On Ruby Inc. Dividends [(30%)($15,000)]	4,500
Part IV Tax Payable	$9,867

Exercise Thirteen - 6 Solution

Since Taxable Income is greater than Aggregate Investment Income (comparison used in D in the following table), the 2020 ending balance in GRIP will be calculated as follows:

C - GRIP Balance At End Of 2019		$ 35,000
D - Taxable Income	$960,000	
Income Eligible For SBD ($42,750 ÷ 19%)	(225,000)	
Aggregate Investment Income		
($65,000 + $23,000 - $14,000)	(74,000)	
Adjusted Taxable Income	$661,000	
Rate	72%	475,920
E - Eligible Dividends Received		85,000
G - Eligible Dividends Designated in 2019		(25,000)
GRIP At End Of 2020		$570,920

The eligible dividends paid during 2020 will be deducted from the GRIP in 2021.

Note that, in this Exercise, there is no ADJUSTED Aggregate Investment Income grind to the annual business limit for the small business deduction. This is because the 2020 grind would be based on the 2019 ADJUSTED Aggregate Investment Income, which is less than $50,000.

Exercise Thirteen - 7 Solution

The refundable amount of Debut Inc.'s Part I tax would be the least of the following three figures:

Foreign Non-Business Income (100 Percent)		$ 15,000
Taxable Capital Gains [(1/2)($38,250)]		19,125
Net Rental Income		6,500
Interest Income		9,200
Net Capital Loss Carry Forward Deducted		(9,000)
Aggregate Investment Income Under ITA 129(4)		$40,825
Rate		30-2/3%
Amount Before Foreign Income Adjustment		$ 12,520
Deduct Excess Of:		
Foreign Non-Business Tax Credit	($ 750)	
Over 8 Percent Of Foreign Non-Business		
Income [(8%)($15,000)]	1,200	Nil
Amount Under ITA 129(4)(a)(i)		$ 12,520

Taxable Income ($121,825 - $22,000 - $9,000)		$ 90,825
Deduct:		
Amount Eligible For The Small Business Deduction ($9,500 ÷ 19%)	(50,000)
[(100 ÷ 38-2/3)($750)] Foreign Non-Business Tax Credit	(1,940)
Adjusted Taxable Income		$ 38,885
Rate		30-2/3%
Amount Under ITA 129(4)(a)(ii)		$ 11,925

Amount Under ITA 129(4)(a)(iii) = Part I Tax Payable (Given)	$ 19,536

The least of these three amounts is $11,925, and this would be the refundable portion of Part I tax for the year.

Exercise Thirteen - 8 Solution

Dividend Refund On Eligible Dividends   The dividend refund on eligible dividends would be $76,667, the lesser of:

- $76,667 (38-1/3% of the $200,000 of eligible dividends paid in 2020)

- $134,167 (the balance in the Eligible RDTOH on December 31, 2020)

Dividend Refund On Non-Eligible Dividends   Component 1 of the dividend refund on non-eligible dividends would be $95,833, the lesser of:

- $153,333 (38-1/3% of the $400,000 of non-eligible dividends paid in 2020)

- $95,833 (the balance in the Non-Eligible RDTOH on December 31, 2020)

With respect to Component 2, 38-1/3 percent of the $400,000 of non-eligible dividends paid during 2020 exceeds the balance in the Non-Eligible RDTOH by $57,500 ($153,333 - $95,833). Given this, Component 2 would be equal to the lesser of:

- the excess of $57,500; and
- $57,500 ($134,167 - $76,667), the balance left in the Eligible RDTOH after the refund on eligible dividends paid.

Solution to Self Study Problem Thirteen - 1

The required calculations would be as follows:

Corporate Taxes

Income For The Year	$50,000
Corporate Taxes (17%)	(8,500)
Income Available For Dividends	$41,500

Personal Taxes On Dividends

Dividend Income	$41,500
Gross Up (15%)	6,225)
Taxable Dividends	$47,725

Tax Payable Before Dividend Tax Credit [(33% + 16%)($47,725)]	$23,385
Dividend Tax Credit [(9/13 + 4/13)($6,225)]	(6,225)
Personal Tax Payable	$ 17,160

Total Taxes On Corporate Flow Through

Corporate Taxes	$ 8,500
Personal Taxes	17,160)
Total Taxes	$25,660

Total Taxes On Income Earned Directly

Income For The Year	$50,000
Combined Federal/Provincial Tax Rate (33% + 16%)	49%)
Personal Tax Payable	$24,500

While the provincial dividend tax credit is at the rate required for perfect integration, the combined corporate federal/provincial tax rate is above the 13.04 percent that is required to achieve this goal. The result is that taxes on $50,000 of income flowed through a corporation is $1,160 ($25,660 - $24,500) higher than the taxes on the same $50,000 of income received directly.

Solution to Self Study Problem Thirteen - 2

Dividend Refund On Eligible Dividends The refund on eligible dividends would be the lesser of:

- $115,000 (38-1/3 percent of the $300,000 of eligible dividends paid in 2020)

- $201,250 (the balance in the Eligible RDTOH on December 31, 2020)

Dividend Refund On Non-Eligible Dividends Component 1 of the refund on non-eligible dividends would be the lesser of:

- $230,000 (38-1/3 percent of the $600,000 of non-eligible dividends paid in 2020)

- $143,750 (the balance in the Non-Eligible RDTOH on December 31, 2020)

Component 2 would be equal to $86,250, the excess of $230,000, 38-1/3 percent of the $600,000 of non-eligible dividends paid during 2020, over $143,750, the balance in the Non-Eligible RDTOH on December 31, 2020. Note that this component of the refund will have to be taken out of the corporation's Eligible RDTOH.

The total refund resulting from the payment of non-eligible dividends is $230,000 ($143,750 + $86,250). Note that $230,000 is equal to 38-1/3 percent of the $600,000 in non-eligible dividends paid.

You should also be aware that the combined refund of $345,000 ($115,000 + $230,000) is equal to the combined balances ($201,250 + $143,750) in the two RDTOH accounts.

Solution to Self Study Problem Thirteen - 3

Part A - Required Balances For FOL
For FOL, the only refundable taxes paid in 2020 would be on the $7,000 of Canadian interest income. This amount would be added to the Non-Eligible RDTOH for this corporation. Given this, the December 31, 2020, Non-Eligible RDTOH balance for FOL would be as follows:

Opening Non-Eligible RDTOH	$2,000
Refundable Portion Of Part I Tax [(30-2/3%)($7,000)]*	2,147
December 31, 2020, Non-Eligible RDTOH	$4,147

*While the full calculation of the refundable portion of Part I tax would require selecting the least of the amounts described in ITA 129(4)(a)(i), (ii), and (iii), the problem asks you to assume that refundable portion of Part I tax is equal to 30-2/3 percent of Aggregate Investment Income.

Based on this information, FOL's 2020 dividend refund would be $4,147, the lesser of:

- $28,750 [(38-1/3%)($75,000)]; and
- $4,147, the balance in the Non-Eligible RDTOH.

Part B - Required Balances For SHI

For 2020, SHI would pay Part IV tax as follows:

Part IV Tax Payable On Eligible Dividends From Royal Bank [(38-1/3%)($8,000)]	$3,067
Part IV Tax Payable SHI's Share Of FOL's Dividend Refund On Payment Of Non-Eligible Dividends (100%) - Part B	4,147
Part IV Tax Payable	$7,214

SHI's Part I refundable taxes would be as follows:

Interest Income	$12,000
Taxable Capital Gain [(1/2)($47,250)]	23,625
Aggregate Investment Income	$35,625
Rate	30-2/3%
Refundable Portion Of SHI's Part I Tax Payable	$10,925

The December 31, 2020, balances in SHI's RDTOH accounts would be as follows:

Opening Eligible RDTOH	Nil
Part IV Tax On Royal Bank Eligible Dividends	$3,067
December 31, 2020, Eligible RDTOH	$3,067

Opening Non-Eligible RDTOH	$10,000
Part IV Tax On FOL's Non-Eligible Dividends	4,147
Part I Refundable Tax On Aggregate Investment Income	10,925
December 31, 2020, Non-Eligible RDTOH	$25,072

Part C - SHI's Dividend Refund

The amount of dividends that can be designated as eligible is limited by the corporation's GRIP. The balance in this account is $8,000, the initial balance of nil, plus the $8,000 in eligible dividends received from Royal Bank. This means that the maximum amount of dividends that can be designated as eligible is $8,000 and the dividend refund on these dividends would be $3,067, the lesser of:

- $3,067 [(38-1/3%)($8,000)]; and
- $3,067, the balance in SHI's Eligible RDTOH.

With $8,000 of the dividends paid designated as eligible, the remaining $42,000 ($50,000 - $8,000) would be non-eligible. The dividend refund on these dividends would be $16,100, the lesser of:

- $16,100 [(38-1/3%)($42,000)]; and
- $25,072, the balance in SHI's Non-Eligible RDTOH.

SHI's total dividend refund would be as follows:

Dividend Refund On Eligible Dividends	$ 3,067
Dividend Refund On Non-Eligible Dividends	16,100)
Total Dividend Refund	$19,167

Solution to Self Study Problem Thirteen - 4

Note To Students The assumed Tax Payable of $23,960 cannot be verified based on the information in the problem. It is, however, a reasonable figure given the information that is available.

Part A - Part IV Tax Payable
The Part IV Tax Payable for Insal Ltd. would be calculated as follows:

Dividend Refund Received By Dorne Inc.	$8,400
Insal's Percentage Of Ownership	45%
Part IV Tax Payable On Dorne's Non-Eligible Dividends	$3,780
Part IV Tax Payable On Enbridge's Eligible Dividends	
[(38-1/3%)($6,200)]	2,377
Part IV Tax Payable	$6,157

Part B - Part I Refundable Tax Paid
The refundable portion of the Part I tax would be the least of the following amounts:

Taxable Capital Gain [(1/2)($24,600)]	$ 12,300
Net Rental Income	4,200
Aggregate Investment Income	$ 16,500
Rate	30-2/3%
ITA 129(4)(a)(i)	$ 5,060

Taxable Income	$ 123,400
Amount Eligible For Small Business Deduction	
(See Note)	(45,000)
Total	$ 78,400
Rate	30-2/3%
ITA 129(4)(a)(ii)	$ 24,043

ITA 129(4)(a)(iii) Part I Tax Payable - Given	$ 23,960

Note As the problem indicates that Insal's Tax Payable was reduced by a small business deduction of $8,550, the amount eligible for this deduction must have been $45,000 ($8,550 ÷ 19%).

The refundable portion of Part I tax is equal to $5,060, which is the least of the preceding three amounts.

Part C - Eligible RDTOH
The December 31, 2021, Eligible RDTOH balance would be as follows:

Opening Eligible RDTOH	$ Nil
Part IV Taxes Paid On Enbridge's Eligible Dividends	2,377
December 31, 2021, Eligible RDTOH	$2,377

As none of the dividends paid by Dorne were designated as eligible, the Part IV tax paid on these dividends cannot be added to Insal's Eligible RDTOH. While the $6,200 of eligible dividends received from Enbridge can be added to Insal's GRIP, the non-eligible dividends received from Dorne cannot be.

Part C - Non-Eligible RDTOH

Insal's December 31, 2021, Non-Eligible RDTOH would be calculated as follows:

Opening Non-Eligible RDTOH	$ 4,150
Part IV Tax Payable On Dorne's Non-Eligible Dividends	3,780
Refundable Part I Tax	5,060
December 31, 2021, Non-Eligible RDTOH	$12,990

Part D - Dividend Refund

The maximum amount of dividends that can be designated as eligible is limited by Insal's GRIP. We know that the initial 2021 balance here was nil and that the $6,200 of eligible dividends received from Enbridge would be added. There is also the possibility that a further amount would be added as a result of some of the corporation's income not being eligible for the small business deduction. (This amount cannot be determined based on the information in the problem.)

However, given Insal's policy of designating dividends as eligible only when a dividend refund is available, a further addition to the GRIP would not be relevant in this problem. This is because a dividend refund will only be available for the balance in the Eligible RDTOH, an amount of $2,377. Based on this, the eligible dividend designation will be for $6,200, the amount of the eligible dividends received. The refund on these dividends will be $2,377 [($6,200)(38-1/3%)].

The remaining dividends of $12,050 ($18,250 - $6,200) will be non-eligible.

The refund on these non-eligible dividends would be $4,619, the lesser of:

- $4,619 [(38-1/3%)($12,050)]; and
- $12,990, the balance in the Non-Eligible RDTOH.

The total dividend refund would be as follows:

Dividend Refund On Eligible Dividends	$2,377
Dividend Refund On Non-Eligible Dividends	4,619
Total Dividend Refund	$6,996

Solution to Self Study Problem Thirteen - 5

Part A - Part I Tax Payable

The required calculations to determine Part I federal Tax Payable are as follows:

Net Income For Tax Purposes	$473,900
Dividends ($108,000 + $56,000)	(164,000)
Taxable Income	$309,900
Base Amount Of Part I Tax [(38%)($309,900)]	$117,762
Federal Tax Abatement [(10%)($309,900)]	(30,990)
Small Business Deduction (Note One)	(41,097)
Additional Refundable Tax On Investment Income (Note Two)	9,984
General Rate Reduction (Note Three)	Nil
Part I Federal Tax Payable	$ 55,659

Note One The small business deduction is 19 percent of the least of the following three amounts:

1.	Active Business Income	$216,300
2.	Taxable Income (no foreign tax credit adjustment)	$309,900
3.	Allocated Annual Business Limit ($500,000 - $200,000)	$300,000

The lowest of these figures is the active business income of $216,300 and this gives a small business deduction of $41,097 [(19%)($216,300)].

Note Two The aggregate investment income of $93,600 is calculated as follows:

Interest On Government Bonds	$36,300
Taxable Capital Gains	57,300
Aggregate Investment Income	$93,600

The ITA 123.3 refundable tax (ART) is 10-2/3 percent of the lesser of:

1.	Aggregate Investment Income		$93,600
2.	Taxable Income	$309,900	
	Deduct: Amount Eligible For The SBD	(216,300)	$93,600

The ITA 123.3 tax on Aggregate Investment Income is $9,984 [(10-2/3%)($93,600)].

Note Three The general rate reduction would be calculated as follows:

Taxable Income	$309,900
Amount Eligible For The Small Business Deduction	(216,300)
Aggregate Investment Income (Note Two)	(93,600)
Full Rate Taxable Income	Nil
Rate	13%
General Rate Reduction	Nil

Part B - Refundable Part I Tax Payable

The refundable portion of Part I Tax Payable would be the least of:

- Amount Under ITA 129(4)(a)(i) [(30-2/3%)($93,600)] $28,704
- Amount Under ITA 129(4)(a)(ii) [(30-2/3%)($309,900 - $216,300)] $28,704
- Amount Under ITA 129(4)(a)(iii) Part I Tax Payable (Part A) $55,659

The Part I refundable Tax Payable would be $28,704.

Part C - Part IV Tax Payable

The required calculation of the Part IV Tax Payable is as follows:

Part IV Tax On Portfolio Investments [($56,000)(38-1/3%)]	$21,467
Part IV Tax On Subsidiary Dividends*	Nil
Total Part IV Tax	$21,467

*The subsidiary is a connected corporation. As it did not receive a dividend refund as a result of paying the dividends, Part IV tax is not applicable.

Part D - GRIP Balance

Since Taxable Income is greater than Aggregate Investment Income, the December 31, 2020, GRIP balance would be calculated as follows:

GRIP Balance At End Of 2019		$ 59,000
Taxable Income	$309,900	
Income Eligible For SBD	(216,300)	
Aggregate Investment Income	(93,600)	
Adjusted Taxable Income	Nil	
Rate	72%	Nil
Eligible Dividends Received		56,000
Eligible Dividends Designated in 2019		Nil
GRIP Balance At End Of 2020		$115,000

Part E - RDTOH Balances - December 31, 2020

The December 31, 2020, balance in the Eligible RDTOH would be as follows:

Opening Balance	$	Nil
Part IV Tax On Portfolio Investments		21,467
Eligible RDTOH - December 31, 2020		$21,467

The December 31, 2020, balance in the Non-Eligible RDTOH would be as follows:

Opening Balance	$	Nil
Part I Refundable Tax		28,704
Non-Eligible RDTOH - December 31, 2020		$28,704

Part F - Dividend Refunds

The corporation's GRIP balance at the end of 2020 is $115,000. As this is greater than the $32,400 of dividends paid in the year, all of these dividends can be designated as eligible.

The Eligible RDTOH of $21,467 is sufficient to support a full dividend refund on $56,000 ($21,467 ÷ 38-1/3%). This is also greater than the $32,400 of eligible dividends paid and means that the dividend refund on eligible dividends paid in 2020 would be equal to $12,420 [(38-1/3%)($32,400)].

No dividend refund would be claimed for 2020 on non-eligible dividends because no non-eligible dividends were paid in 2020.

Part G - Total Federal Tax Payable

The required calculation to determine federal Tax Payable is as follows:

Part I Tax (Part A)	$55,659
Part IV Tax (Part C)	21,467
Dividend Refund (Part F)	(12,420)
Federal Tax Payable	$64,706

Part H - RDTOH Balances - January 1, 2021

The January 1, 2021, balance in the Eligible RDTOH would be as follows:

Eligible RDTOH - December 31, 2020	$21,467
Dividend Refund On 2020 Eligible Dividends Paid	(12,420)
Eligible RDTOH - January 1, 2021	$ 9,047

The January 1, 2021, balance in the Non-Eligible RDTOH would be as follows:

Non-Eligible RDTOH - December 31, 2020	$28,704
Dividend Refund On 2020 Non-Eligible Dividends Paid	Nil
Non-Eligible RDTOH - January 1, 2021	$28,704

Solution to Self Study Problem Thirteen - 6

Part A - Part I Tax Payable

The Part I Tax Payable is calculated as follows:

Base Amount Of Part I Tax [(38%)($503,500)]	$ 191,330
Federal Tax Abatement [(10%)(72.95%)($503,500)]	(36,730)
Small Business Deduction [(19%)($200,000 Which Was Given)]	(38,000)
Additional Refundable Tax On Investment Income (Note One)	11,781
General Rate Reduction (Note Three)	(25,097)
Foreign Non-Business Income Tax Credit (Given)	(8,250)
Foreign Business Income Tax Credit (Given)	(34,300)
Part I Tax Payable	$ 60,734

Note One The aggregate investment income of $110,450 is calculated as follows:

Interest On Loan To Subsidiary	$ 43,250
Foreign Investment Income	55,000
Taxable Capital Gains	24,500
Net Capital Losses Claimed	(12,300)
Aggregate Investment Income (Note Two)	$ 110,450

The ITA 123.3 refundable tax (ART) is 10-2/3 percent of the lesser of:

1.	Aggregate Investment Income	$ 110,450

2.	Taxable Income	$503,500	
	Deduct: Amount Eligible For The SBD	(200,000)	$ 303,500

The ITA 123.3 tax on aggregate investment income is $11,781 [(10-2/3%)($110,450)].

Note Two The definition contained in ITA 129(4.1) excludes income from property that is incidental to carrying on an active business and, as a consequence, we have left out the $5,050 of term deposit interest. With respect to the interest on the loan to the subsidiary, if the subsidiary had deducted the $43,250 in computing active business income eligible for the small business deduction, ITA 129(6) would have deemed this interest to be active business income rather than investment income. However, the problem notes that the subsidiary was not involved in the production of active business income and, as a consequence, the interest from the subsidiary is included in the above calculation of aggregate investment income.

Note Three The general rate reduction is based on the amount of Taxable Income that is not subject to other types of favourable tax treatment. The reduction would be calculated as follows:

Taxable Income	$ 503,500
Amount Eligible For The Small Business Deduction (Given)	(200,000)
Aggregate Investment Income (Note One)	(110,450)
Full Rate Taxable Income	$ 193,050)
Rate	13%
General Rate Reduction	$ 25,097

Part B - Refundable Portion Of Part I Tax Payable

The refundable portion of Part I tax would be the least of the following three amounts:

Aggregate Investment Income (See Note One)		$ 110,450
Rate		30-2/3%
Total		$ 33,871
Deduct Excess Of:		
Foreign Non-Business Tax Credit	($8,250)	
Over 8% Of Foreign Non-Business Income [(8%)($55,000)]	4,400	(3,850)
Amount Under ITA 129(4)(a)(i)		$ 30,021

Taxable Income	$ 503,500
Deduct:	
Amount Eligible For The Small Business Deduction	(200,000)
[(100 ÷ 38-2/3)($8,250)] Foreign Non-Business Tax Credit	(21,336)
[(4)($34,300)] Foreign Business Tax Credit	(137,200)
Total	$ 144,964
Rate	30-2/3%
Amount Under ITA 129(4)(a)(ii)	$ 44,456

Amount Under ITA 129(4)(a)(iii) = Part I Tax Payable (Part A)	$ 60,734

The least of these three amounts is $30,021, the amount calculated under ITA 129(4)(a)(i).

Part C - Part IV Tax Payable

The Part IV Tax Payable would be calculated as follows:

On Eligible Portfolio Dividends Received [(38-1/3%)($19,600)]	$ 7,513
Share Of Dividend Refund Included In Non-Eligible Dividends From Subsidiary [(75%)($12,750)]	9,563
Part IV Tax Payable	$17,076

Part D - GRIP Balance

Since Taxable Income is greater than Aggregate Investment Income, the December 31, 2020, GRIP balance would be calculated as follows:

GRIP Balance At End Of 2019		$ Nil
Taxable Income	$503,500	
Income Eligible For SBD	(200,000)	
Aggregate Investment Income	(110,450)	
Adjusted Taxable Income	$193,050	
Rate	72%	138,996
Eligible Dividends Received		19,600
Eligible Dividends Designated in 2019		Nil
GRIP Balance At End Of 2020		$158,596

Part E - RDTOH Balances

The December 31, 2020, balance in the Eligible RDTOH would be as follows:

Opening Balance	$ Nil
Part IV Tax On Eligible Dividends - Portfolio Investments	7,513
Eligible RDTOH - December 31, 2020	$7,513

The December 31, 2020, balance in the Non-Eligible RDTOH would be as follows:

Opening Balance ($23,500 - $9,600)	$13,900
Part I Refundable Tax	30,021
Part IV Tax On Non-Eligible Subsidiary Dividends	9,563
Non-Eligible RDTOH - December 31, 2020	$53,484

Part F - Dividend Refund

Dividend refunds are calculated on the basis of dividends paid, not dividends declared. The relevant total here is $109,000 [$25,000 + (3)($28,000)].

As the corporation's GRIP balance is larger than this total, the corporation's policy would require that the full amount of the dividend be designated as eligible. The Eligible RDTOH of $7,513 is sufficient to support a full dividend refund on $19,600 ($7,513 ÷ 38-1/3%). If $109,000 of dividends paid are designated eligible, the refund on these eligible dividends would be $7,513, the lesser of:

- $41,783 [(38-1/3%)($109,000)]; and
- $7,513, the balance in the Eligible RDTOH.

The Non-Eligible RDTOH of $53,484 is sufficient to support a full dividend refund on $139,523 ($53,484 ÷ 38-1/3%). If all of the dividends paid are designated eligible, no dividend refund could be claimed on non-eligible dividends because no non-eligible dividends were paid in 2020.

Part G - Total Federal Tax Payable

The required calculation to determine federal Tax Payable is as follows:

Part I Tax (Part A)	$60,734
Part IV Tax (Part C)	17,076
Dividend Refund (Part F)	(7,513)
Federal Tax Payable	$70,297

Part H - Advice On Dividend Policy

The change in tax rules for years after 2018 affects the dividend refund available on the payment of eligible dividends. Sinzer's dividend policy to maximize eligible dividends, which was beneficial to you personally before 2020 now limits the dividend refund that can be claimed by your corporation. I suggest you change the policy to paying the maximum amount of eligible dividends on which a dividend refund would be available. That will increase the taxes paid by you personally on the total dividends received, but will give you an increase in the dividend refund at the corporate level.

The Eligible RDTOH of $7,513 would all be refunded on the payment of $19,600 in eligible dividends [(38-1/3%)($19,600) = $7,513]. This is equal to the eligible dividends received during 2020. The remaining $89,400 would be non-eligible dividends, which would enable Sinzer to claim a dividend refund of $34,270 [(38-1/3%)($89,400)] because it is less than the balance in the Non-Eligible RDTOH.

The increase in the personal tax rate going from eligible to non-eligible dividends is about 8 percentage points on average. Using that estimate means that it will cost you personally $7,152 [(8%)($89,400)] in taxes to receive a dividend refund of $34,270 in your corporation. As you are the sole shareholder, you will benefit from the dividend refund.

Solution to Self Study Problem Thirteen - 7

Part A - Net And Taxable Income

The calculation of Acme Imports' Net Income For Tax Purposes and Taxable Income would be as follows:

Accounting Income Before Taxes		$232,300
Additions:		
Amortization Expense	$29,500	
Charitable Donations	25,000	
Taxable Capital Gain On Sale Of Equipment [(1/2)($84,500 - $62,000)]	11,250	
Golf Club Membership	2,800	
50 Percent Of Business Meals And Entertainment	3,360	
Share Issue Costs [(80%)($950)]	760	
Costs Of Supplementary Letters Patent	7,000	
Interest On Mortgage For The Land	12,300	91,970
Deductions:		
CCA (Note One)	($53,050)	
Gain On Sale Of Equipment ($84,500 - $27,500)	(57,000)	(110,050)
Net Income For Tax Purposes		**$214,220**
Charitable Donations		(25,000)
Dividends From Sarco Ltd.		(24,000)
Taxable Income		**$165,220**

Note One   The maximum CCA on the Class 8 equipment would be calculated as follows:

Opening UCC	$256,000
Disposition - Lesser Of:	
Proceeds Of Disposition = $84,500	
Capital Cost = $62,000	(62,000)
CCA Base	$194,000
Rate	20%
CCA - Class 8	$ 38,800

The customer list, as well as the cost of the supplementary letters patent, would be added to Class 14.1. The maximum CCA for this class would be as follows:

Opening UCC	Nil
Additions ($183,000 + $7,000)	$ 190,000
AccII Adjustment [(1/2)($190,000)]	95,000
CCA Base	$ 285,000
Rate	5%
CCA - Class 14.1	$ 14,250

Based on this, the maximum total CCA would be $53,050 ($38,800 + $14,250).

Several of the items in this problem need further comment. These are as follows:

- **Item 4**   With respect to the costs of issuing shares, such amounts have to be deducted over at least five years at a maximum rate of 20 percent per year.

- **Item 6**   Only 50 percent of the $6,720 in charges at the local golf and country club are deductible.

- **Item 7**   The cars provided to the principal shareholder and to the manager of the company will result in their being assessed for a substantial taxable benefit. However, the costs are fully deductible to the company.

- **Item 10**   The fees paid to the site consultant are deductible as indicated in ITA 20(1)(dd). ITA 18(3.1) disallows the deduction of interest on financing related to land during construction. The $12,300 interest on the $244,000 mortgage on the land would be capitalized and is not deductible.

Part B - Active Business Income

The active business income of Acme is as follows:

Net Income For Tax Purposes		$ 214,220
Dividends		(24,000)
Aggregate Investment Income:		
Interest Revenue	($ 10,000)	
Taxable Capital Gain	(11,250)	(21,250)
Active Business Income		$ 168,970

Part C - Federal Tax Payable

The calculation of Acme Ltd.'s federal Tax Payable would be as follows:

Base Amount Of Part I Tax [(38%)($165,220)]	$62,784
Federal Tax Abatement [(10%)($165,220)]	(16,522)
Small Business Deduction (Note Two)	(31,392)
Additional Refundable Tax On Investment Income (Note Three)	Nil
General Rate Reduction (Note Four)	Nil
Part I Tax Payable	$ 14,870
Part IV Tax Payable (Note Five)	3,000
Dividend Refund (No Dividends Declared)	Nil
Federal Tax Payable	$ 17,870

Note Two   As Acme and Sarco's combined ADJUSTED Aggregate Investment Income exceeds $50,000, there will be a grind of the annual business limit. The amount of the grind is as follows:

$$[(\$500,000/\$500,000)][(5)(\$110,000 - \$50,000)] = \$300,000$$

Applying this grind, the small business deduction is 19 percent of the least of the following three amounts:

1.	Active Business Income (Part B)	$168,970
2.	Taxable Income (no foreign tax credit adjustment)	$165,220
3.	Reduced Annual Business Limit ($500,000 - $300,000)	$200,000

This gives a small business deduction of $31,392 [(19%)($165,220)].

Note Three   The ITA 123.3 refundable tax (ART) is 10-2/3 percent of the lesser of:

1.	Aggregate Investment Income (Part B)		$21,250
2.	Taxable Income	$165,220	
	Deduct: Amount Eligible For The SBD	(165,220)	Nil

Since the income eligible for the small business deduction is equal to Taxable Income, there is no ITA 123.3 tax on investment income payable.

Note Four   The general rate reduction would be nil, calculated as follows:

Taxable Income	$165,220
Amount Eligible For The Small Business Deduction	(165,220)
Aggregate Investment Income (Part B)	(21,250)
Full Rate Taxable Income	Nil
Rate	13%
General Rate Reduction	Nil

Note Five   The Part IV Tax on Sarco's non-eligible dividend would be as follows:

Sarco's Dividend Refund	$5,000
Acme's Ownership Percentage	60%
Acme's Share Of Refund = Part IV Tax Payable	$3,000

Part D - RDTOH Balances

The amount of refundable Part I tax will be the least of the following three amounts. In this problem, the calculation of these amounts is greatly simplified by the absence of foreign non-business income. The calculations are as follows:

ITA 129(4)(a)(i) $6,517 - This amount would be 30-2/3 percent of Aggregate Investment Income of $21,250 ($10,000 + $11,250).

ITA 129(4)(a)(ii)   Nil - This amount would be 30-2/3 percent of Taxable Income, reduced by the amount of income that is eligible for the small business deduction [(30-2/3%) ($165,220 - $165,220)].

ITA 129(4)(a)(iii) $14,870 - This amount would be the Part I Tax Payable.

The least of these amounts is nil, so there would be no refundable portion of Part I tax.

At the beginning of 2020, both the Eligible RDTOH and the Non-Eligible RDTOH were nil. As there is no addition to the Eligible RDTOH for the year, the December 31, 2020, balance in the Eligible RDTOH is nil.

The December 31, 2020, balance in the Non-Eligible RDTOH would be as follows:

Opening Non-Eligible RDTOH	$ Nil
Part IV Tax Payable On Sarco's Non-Eligible Dividend	3,000
Non-Eligible RDTOH - December 31, 2020	$3,000

The December 31, 2020, GRIP would be as follows:

GRIP Balance At End Of 2019		Nil
Taxable Income	$165,220	
Income Eligible For SBD	(165,220)	
Aggregate Investment Income	(21,250)	
Adjusted Taxable Income	$ Nil	
Rate	72%	Nil
Eligible Dividends Received		Nil
Eligible Dividends Designated in 2019		Nil
GRIP Balance At End Of 2020		Nil

Solution to Self Study Problem Thirteen - 8

Part A - Net And Taxable Income

Brasco's minimum Net Income For Tax Purposes and Taxable Income would be calculated as follows:

Active Business Income (Given)		$ 171,000
Net Taxable Capital Gains (Given)		36,000
Canadian Source Interest Income		2,200
Eligible Portfolio Dividends		15,800
Foreign Source Investment Income (Gross Amount)		4,500
Non-Eligible Dividends From Subsidiary		37,800
Net Income For Tax Purposes		**$ 267,300**
Dividends Received:		
Portfolio	($ 15,800)	
Subsidiary	(37,800)	(53,600)
Charitable Donations		(11,900)
Non-Capital Loss Carry Forward Deducted		(25,800)
Net Capital Loss Carry Forward Deducted (Note One)		(36,000)
Taxable Income		**$140,000**

Note One Note that the net capital loss carry forward is limited to the taxable capital gains. This will leave a net capital loss carry forward of $28,500 ($64,500 - $36,000) for subsequent periods.

Part B - Part I Tax Payable (FTC = Amount Withheld)

Assuming the foreign non-business tax credit is equal to the amount withheld, Brasco's Tax Payable would be calculated as follows:

Base Amount Of Part I Tax [(38%)($140,000)]	$ 53,200
Federal Tax Abatement [(10%)($140,000)]	(14,000)
Small Business Deduction (Note Two)	(23,750)
Additional Refundable Tax On Investment Income (Note Three)	715
General Rate Reduction (Note Four)	(1,079)
Foreign Non-Business Tax Credit (Given As Amount Withheld)	(675)
Part I Tax Payable	$ 14,411

Note Two The small business deduction is 19 percent of the least of the following three amounts:

1.	Active Business Income (Given)	$171,000

2.	Taxable Income	$140,000	
	Deduct:		
	[(100/28)($675)] Foreign Non-Business Tax Credit	(2,411)	$137,589

3.	Allocated Annual Business Limit (Given)	$125,000

The lowest of these figures is the allocated annual limit of $125,000, and this gives a small business deduction of $23,750 [(19%)($125,000)].

Note Three The aggregate investment income of $6,700 is calculated as follows:

Taxable Capital Gains	$ 36,000
Net Capital Loss Carry Forward Deducted	(36,000)
Canadian Interest	2,200
Foreign Investment Income	4,500
Aggregate Investment Income	$ 6,700

The ITA 123.3 refundable tax (ART) is 10-2/3 percent of the lesser of:

1.	Aggregate Investment Income		$ 6,700
2.	Taxable Income	$140,000	
	Deduct: Amount Eligible For The SBD	(125,000)	$15,000

The ITA 123.3 tax on aggregate investment income is $715 [(10-2/3%)($6,700)].

Note Four The general rate reduction is based on the amount of Taxable Income that is not subject to other types of favourable tax treatment. The reduction would be calculated as follows:

Taxable Income	$ 140,000
Amount Eligible For The Small Business Deduction (Note Two)	(125,000)
Aggregate Investment Income (Note Three)	(6,700)
Full Rate Taxable Income	$ 8,300
Rate	13%
General Rate Reduction	$ 1,079

Part C - Refundable Part I Tax Payable

The refundable portion of Part I tax will be the least of the following three amounts:

Aggregate Investment Income (Note Three)		$ 6,700
Rate		30-2/3%
		$ 2,055
Deduct Excess Of:		
Foreign Non-Business Tax Credit	($675)	
Over 8% Of Foreign Non-Business Income		
[(8%)($4,500)]	360	(315)
Amount Under ITA 129(4)(a)(i)		$ 1,740

Taxable Income		$ 140,000
Deduct:		
Amount Eligible For The Small Business Deduction		(125,000)
[(100 ÷ 38-2/3)($675)] Foreign Non-Business Tax Credit		(1,746)
Adjusted Taxable Income		$ 13,254
Rate		30-2/3%
Amount Under ITA 129(4)(a)(ii)		$ 4,065

Amount Under ITA 129(4)(a)(iii) = Part I Tax Payable	$ 14,411

The least of these three amounts would be $1,740, the amount calculated under ITA 129(4)(a)(i).

Part D - Part IV Tax Payable

The calculation of Part IV Tax Payable would be as follows:

Part IV Tax On Masco's Non-Eligible Dividends [(60%)($24,1520)]	$14,490
Part IV Tax On Eligible Dividends From Portfolio Investments	
[(38-1/3%)($15,800)]	6,057
Part IV Tax Payable	$20,547

Part E - GRIP Balance

The 2020 ending balance in GRIP will be calculated as follows:

GRIP Balance At Beginning Of 2020		$ 126,000
Taxable Income	$140,000	
Income Eligible For SBD	(125,000)	
Aggregate Investment Income	(6,700)	
Adjusted Taxable Income	$ 8,300	
Rate	72%	5,976
Eligible Dividends Received		15,800
Eligible Dividends Designated in 2019		Nil
GRIP Balance At End Of 2020		$ 147,776

Any eligible dividends paid during 2020 will be deducted from the GRIP in 2021.

Part F - RDTOH Balances

The December 31, 2020, Eligible RDTOH balances would be as follows:

Opening Balance	$ 7,000
Part IV Tax On Eligible Dividends - Portfolio Investments	6,057
Eligible RDTOH - December 31, 2020	$13,057

The December 31, 2020, balance in the Non-Eligible RDTOH would be as follows:

Opening Balance	$ Nil
Part I Refundable Tax	1,740
Part IV Tax On Masco's Non-Eligible Dividends	14,490
Non-Eligible RDTOH - December 31, 2020	$ 16,230

Part G - Dividend Refund

Brasco paid $39,000 in dividends, creating a potential refund of $14,950 [(38-1/3%)($39,000)]. Given Brasco's GRIP balance of $147,776, the entire $39,000 dividend could be designated as eligible. However, the Eligible RDTOH balance is only $13,057. Given this, the maximum designation on which a full refund would be available would be $34,062 ($13,057 ÷ 38-1/3%).

If $34,062 of the dividends paid are designated eligible, the dividend refund on these eligible dividends would be $13,057, the lesser of:

- $13,057 [(38-1/3%)($34,062)]; and
- $13,057, the balance in the Eligible RDTOH.

This would leave $4,938 ($39,000 - $34,062) as non-eligible dividends. The dividend refund on these non-eligible dividends would be $1,893, the lesser of:

- $1,893 [(38-1/3%)($4,938)]; and
- $16,230, the balance in the Non-Eligible RDTOH.

Based on this, the total dividend refund would be as follows:

Dividend Refund On Eligible Dividends	$ 13,057
Dividend Refund On Non-Eligible Dividends	1,893
Total Dividend Refund	$ 14,950

Part H - Foreign Tax Credit

If you cannot assume that the foreign tax credit is equal to the amount withheld, the actual foreign tax credit is a complex calculation in this situation. The use of foreign taxes paid as credits against Canadian Tax Payable is limited by a formula that includes the "tax otherwise payable". In the case of foreign taxes paid on non-business income, the "tax otherwise payable" in the formula includes the ART that is assessed under ITA 123.3 and the general rate reduction. This creates a problem in that the calculation of the ART and the general rate reduction include the amount eligible for the small business deduction [ITA 123.3(b)]. In turn, the determination of the amount eligible for the small business deduction requires the use of the foreign tax credits for foreign taxes paid on non-business and business income [ITA 125(1)(b)(i) and (ii)].

To solve this circular calculation, for the purpose of calculating the small business deduction, the foreign tax credit for taxes paid on non-business income is calculated using a "tax otherwise payable" figure that does not include the ART under ITA 123.3 or the general rate reduction. This means that in situations where foreign non-business income, the small business deduction, and the ART are involved, the following procedures should be used:

1. Calculate the foreign non-business tax credit using a "tax otherwise payable" that excludes both the ART and the general rate reduction. This initial version of the foreign non-business tax credit will be used only for determining the small business deduction, with the actual credit available calculated after the ART and the general rate reduction have been determined.

2. Calculate the amount eligible for the small business deduction using the number determined in step 1.

3. Calculate the ART and the general rate reduction using the amount eligible for the small business deduction determined in step 2.

4. Calculate the actual foreign non-business tax credit using a "tax otherwise payable" figure that includes the ART and the general rate reduction.

The initial version of the foreign non-business tax credit (Step 1) will be the lesser of the actual tax paid of $675, and an amount determined by the following formula:

$$\left(\frac{\text{Foreign Non-Business Income}}{\text{Adjusted Net Income}}\right)(\text{Part I Tax Otherwise Payable Excluding The ART And GRR})$$

$$= \left(\frac{\$4,500}{\$267,300 - \$53,600 - \$36,000}\right)(\$53,200 - \$14,000)$$

$$= \$993$$

Part I tax otherwise payable in the preceding formula does not include the ART under ITA 123.3 or the general rate reduction. Adjusted Net Income in the formula is Net Income For Tax Purposes minus deductible dividends and the net capital loss carry forward claimed in the current year. In this case, the actual tax paid of $675 will be the credit. This means that the previously calculated small business deduction will be unchanged (Note 2, Step 2) and, in turn, the ART (Note 3, Step 3) and general rate reduction (Note 4, Step 3) will be unchanged.

We can now calculate the actual foreign non-business tax credit, which takes into consideration the ART and the general rate reduction (Step 4). It is the lesser of the actual taxes paid of $675 and an amount determined by the following formula:

$$\left(\frac{\text{Foreign Non-Business Income}}{\text{Adjusted Net Income}}\right)(\text{Part I Tax Otherwise Payable Including The ART And GRR})$$

$$= \left(\frac{\$4,500}{\$267,300 - \$53,600 - \$36,000}\right)(\$53,200 - \$14,000 + \$715 - \$1,079)$$

$$= \$983$$

In this calculation, the actual taxes paid of $675 will again be the credit.

CHAPTER 14

Chapter 14 Learning Objectives

After completing Chapter 14, you should be able to:

1. Explain the need for, and the tax implications of, a deemed year end when there has been an acquisition of control (paragraph [P hereafter] 14-1 to 14-13).
2. Apply the provisions related to charitable donations and loss carry forwards when there has been an acquisition of control (P 14-14 to 14-21).
3. Explain the treatment of unrecognized losses at a deemed year end resulting from an acquisition of control (P 14-22 to 14-34).
4. Apply the associated companies rules (P 14-35 to 14-52).
5. Apply the general rules applicable to investment tax credits and SR&ED expenditures by CCPCs (P 14-53 to 14-65).

6. Apply the provisions related to refundable investment tax credits (P 14-66 to 14-70).
7. Apply the carry over rules for investment tax credits, as well as describe the influence of an acquisition of control on their availability (P 14-71 to 14-75).
8. Explain the relationship between tax basis Shareholders' Equity and Shareholders' Equity as presented under GAAP (P 14-76 to 14-78).
9. Explain the concept of, and calculate the amount of, Paid Up Capital (P 14-79 to 14-82).
10. Identify and explain the major components of Tax Basis Retained Earnings (P 14-83 to 14-91).

11. Explain the objectives of, and list the major components of, the capital dividend account (P 14-92 to 14-95).
12. List the various types of dividends used to distribute corporate surplus (P 14-96 to 14-100).
13. Apply the procedures related to the declaration and payment of cash dividends (P 14-101 to 14-104).
14. Apply the procedures related to the declaration and payment of stock dividends (P 14-105 to 14-107).
15. Apply the procedures related to the declaration and payment of dividends in kind (P 14-108 to 14-110).

16. Apply the procedures related to the declaration and payment of capital dividends (P 14-111 to 14-115).
17. Explain and apply the procedures related to ITA 84(1) deemed dividends when there has been an increase in PUC (P 14-116 to 14-121).
18. Explain and apply the procedures related to ITA 84(2) deemed dividends on winding up (P 14-122 to 14-126).
19. Explain and apply the procedures related to ITA 84(3) deemed dividends on redemption, acquisition, or cancellation of shares (P 14-127 to 14-130).
20. Explain and apply the procedures related to ITA 84(4) and 84(4.1) deemed dividends (P 14-131 to 14-136).

How to Work Through Chapter 14

We recommend the following approach in dealing with the material in this chapter:

Acquisition Of Control Rules, Including Effect On Loss Carry Forwards
- Read paragraph 14-1 to 14-21 (in the textbook).
- Do Exercise Fourteen-1 (in the textbook) and check the solution in this Study Guide.
- Read paragraph 14-22 to 14-24.
- Do Exercise Fourteen-2 and check the solution in this Study Guide.
- Read paragraph 14-25 to 14-34.
- Do Exercise Fourteen-3 and check the solution in this Study Guide.
- Do Self Study Problems Fourteen-1 and Fourteen-2, which are available on MyLab, and check the solutions in this Study Guide.

Associated Companies
- Read paragraph 14-35 to 14-52.
- Do Exercise Fourteen-4 and check the solution in this Study Guide.
- Do Self Study Problems Fourteen-3 and Fourteen-4 and check the solutions in this Study Guide.

Investment Tax Credits And SR&ED Expenditures By CCPCs
- Read paragraph 14-53 to 14-62.
- Do Exercise Fourteen-5 and check the solution in this Study Guide.
- Read paragraph 14-63 to 14-65.
- Do Exercise Fourteen-6 and check the solution in this Study Guide.

Refundable Investment Tax Credits
- Read paragraph 14-66 to 14-71.
- Do Exercise Fourteen-7 and check the solution in this Study Guide.
- Do Self Study Problem Fourteen-5 and check the solution in this Study Guide.
- Read paragraph 14-72 to 14-75.

Shareholders' Equity Under GAAP
- Read paragraph 14-76 to 14-78.

Paid Up Capital
- Read paragraph 14-79 to 14-82.
- Do Exercise Fourteen-8 and check the solution in this Study Guide.

Tax Basis Retained Earnings
- Read paragraph 14-83 to 14-91.

Capital Dividend Account
- Read paragraph 14-92 to 14-95.
- Do Exercise Fourteen-9 and check the solution in this Study Guide.
- Do Self Study Problems Fourteen-6 and Fourteen-7 and check the solutions in this Study Guide.

Distributions Of Corporate Surplus Through Cash, Stock, And In Kind Dividends
- Read paragraph 14-96 to 14-107.
- Do Exercise Fourteen-10 and check the solution in this Study Guide.
- Read paragraph 14-108 to 14-110.
- Do Exercise Fourteen-11 and check the solution in this Study Guide.

Capital Dividends
- Read paragraph 14-111 to 14-115.

ITA 84(1) Deemed Dividends - Increase In PUC
- Read paragraph 14-116 to 14-120.
- Do Exercise Fourteen-12 and check the solution in this Study Guide.
- Read paragraph 14-121.

ITA 84(2) Deemed Dividends - On Winding-Up
- Read paragraph 14-122 to 14-126.
- Do Exercise Fourteen-13 and check the solution in this Study Guide.

ITA 84(3) Deemed Dividends - Redemption, Acquisition, Or Cancellation Of Shares
- Read paragraph 14-127 to 14-130.
- Do Exercise Fourteen-14 and check the solution in this Study Guide.

ITA 84(4) And ITA 84(4.1) Deemed Dividends
- Read paragraph 14-131 to 14-136.
- Do Exercise Fourteen-15 and check the solution in this Study Guide.
- Do Self Study Problem Fourteen-8 and check the solution in this Study Guide.

To Complete This Chapter
- If you would like more practice in problem solving, do the Supplementary Self Study Problems for the chapter. These problems and solutions are available on MyLab.
- Review the Key Terms Used In This Chapter in the textbook at the end of Chapter 14. Consult the Glossary for the meaning of any key terms you do not know.
- Test yourself with the Chapter 14 Glossary Flashcards available on MyLab.
- Ensure you have achieved the Chapter 14 Learning Objectives listed in this Study Guide.
- As a review, we recommend you view the PowerPoint presentation for Chapter 14 that is on MyLab.

Practice Examination
- Write the Practice Examination for Chapter 14 that is on MyLab. Mark your examination using the Practice Examination Solution that is on MyLab.

Solutions to Chapter 14 Exercises

Exercise Fourteen - 1 Solution
No Acquisition Of Control   Net Income For Tax Purposes for 2020 is $289,000 ($42,000 + $247,000) and, if there was no acquisition of control, the total $135,000 non-capital loss carry forward could be deducted. This would result in a 2020 Taxable Income of $154,000 ($289,000 - $135,000).

Acquisition Of Control   If there was an acquisition of control on January 1, 2020, Net Income For Tax Purposes would still be $289,000. However, in this case, the non-capital loss carry forward could only be used to the extent of the pen business income of $42,000. This means that Taxable Income would be $247,000 ($289,000 - $42,000) with a non-capital loss carry forward of $93,000 ($135,000 - $42,000).

Exercise Fourteen - 2 Solution
The tax consequences of the acquisition of control procedures are as follows:

Land   As the fair market of the land is less than its adjusted cost base, ITA 111(4)(c) will require that it be written down to its fair market value of $215,000. This will result in an allowable capital loss of $39,000 [($293,000 - $215,000) ÷ 2].

Class 8 Assets As the fair market value of this property is less than its UCC, ITA 111(5.1) requires that it be written down to its fair market value. The $92,000 ($276,000 - $184,000) write-down will be treated as CCA to be deducted in the deemed taxation year. For capital gains purposes, the property will retain its original capital cost of $416,000.

Exercise Fourteen - 3 Solution

It would clearly be desirable to elect to have a deemed disposition of the non-depreciable assets. This could be achieved by electing to have a deemed disposition of the non-depreciable assets for $650,000. This would result in a $75,000 taxable capital gain [(1/2)($650,000 - $500,000)] on the deemed disposition. This will leave $35,000 ($110,000 - $75,000) of the net capital loss carry forward.

This $35,000 could be eliminated by electing to have a deemed disposition of the depreciable property at an elected value of $470,000. This election would produce the required taxable capital gain of $35,000 [(1/2)($470,000 - $400,000)].

The election would also produce recapture of $50,000 ($400,000 - $350,000). As this is $5,000 ($50,000 - $45,000) greater than the operating loss, this would result in Taxable Income and Tax Payable. However, the ability to use the remaining $35,000 net capital loss carry forward is probably worth the cost of the Tax Payable on the extra $5,000 of income. In addition, the election would result in increased future CCA based on a new capital cost, for CCA purposes only, of $435,000 [$400,000 + (1/2)($470,000 - $400,000)].

Exercise Fourteen - 4 Solution

Top And Middle Top and Middle are associated under ITA 256(1)(a) as Top controls Middle.

Top And Bottom Top and Bottom are associated under ITA 256(1)(b) as they are both controlled by the same person, Mr. Top. He controls Top directly. In addition, he controls Bottom through a combination of direct ownership, indirect ownership, and deemed ownership. His majority interest would be calculated as follows:

Direct Interest in Bottom	5%
Indirect Interest Through Top Company [(100%)(10%)]	10%
Indirect Interest Through Control Of Middle Company	35%
Deemed Interest Through Son - ITA 256(1.3)	15%
Deemed Interest Through Options - ITA 256(1.4)	10%
Controlling Interest	75%

Middle And Bottom Middle and Bottom are associated under ITA 256(1)(b) as they are both controlled by the same person, Mr. Top. Mr. Top controls Middle indirectly through Top. He controls Bottom through a combination of direct and indirect control, as described in the discussion of Top and Bottom.

Exercise Fourteen - 5 Solution

With respect to the $125,000 in apprentice salaries, the investment tax credit is available on an annual salary maximum of $20,000 per apprentice. As a result, there will be a $10,000 [(5)(10%) ($20,000)] credit against 2020 federal Tax Payable. This $10,000 credit will be added to income in 2021.

With respect to the $3,000,000 in capital expenditures, there will be a 2020 credit against federal Tax Payable of $300,000 [(10%)($3,000,000)]. The $300,000 credit will not influence the calculation of 2020 CCA. This amount will be $900,000 [(20%)(1.5)($3,000,000)].

In 2021, the $300,000 credit will be deducted from the January 1, 2021, UCC, leaving a balance of $1,800,000 ($3,000,000 - $900,000 - $300,000). Given this, 2021 CCA will be $360,000 [(20%)($1,800,000)].

Exercise Fourteen - 6 Solution

For 2020, the A value in the reduction formula would be $2,500,000 ($12,500,000 - $10,000,000). Based on this, the amount that would be available for the enhanced 35 percent credit would be calculated as follows:

$$[\$3,000,000][(\$40,000,000 - \$2,500,000) \div \$40,000,000] = \$2,812,500$$

Exercise Fourteen - 7 Solution

As Sci-Tech has Taxable Income of less than $500,000 in the previous year, and its Taxable Capital Employed In Canada is less than $10 million, it is a qualifying company and its annual expenditure limit is not reduced from the maximum value of $3,000,000.

Given the $3,000,000 annual expenditure limit for the 35 percent rate, the total amount of investment tax credits available can be calculated as follows:

Qualified Property [(10%)($123,000)]	$ 12,300
SR&ED Current Expenditures [(35%)($1,200,000)]	420,000
Total Available Amount	$432,300

The refund available would be as follows:

Qualified Property [(40%)($12,300)]	$ 4,920
SR&ED Current Expenditures [(100%)($420,000)]	420,000
Total Refund Available	$424,920

The non-refunded investment tax credit of $7,380 ($432,300 - $424,920) can be carried forward 20 years to be applied against Tax Payable. There was no Tax Payable in the last three years so it cannot be carried back.

The cost of the qualified property will be reduced in the following year by the refundable investment tax credit of $4,920. The $420,000 tax credit on current SR&ED expenditures will be added to income in the following taxation year.

Exercise Fourteen - 8 Solution

The adjusted cost base of the shares would be determined as follows:

	Number of Shares	Cost/Share	Total Cost
First Purchase	2,400	$1.10	$2,640
Second Purchase	3,850	$1.82	7,007
Totals	6,250		$9,647

The adjusted cost base for all of the investor's shares is $9,647. The adjusted cost base per share would be $1.54 ($9,647 ÷ 6,250).

The PUC for the investor's shares would be calculated as follows:

	Number of Shares	PUC/Share	Total PUC
First Sale	100,000	$1.10	$110,000
Second Sale	50,000	$1.35	67,500
Third Sale	30,000	$1.82	54,600
Total PUC Of Outstanding Shares	180,000		$232,100

Number Of Shares (From First Table)	6,250
PUC Per Share [$232,100 ÷ 180,000 Shares]	$ 1.29
PUC For Investor's Shares	$8,063

Exercise Fourteen - 9 Solution

The balance in the capital dividend account as at December 31, 2020, would be as follows:

2018 Capital Gain On Land [(1/2)($22,000)]	$ 11,000
2019 Capital Dividend Received	8,200
2020 Sale Of Goodwill [(1/2)($43,000 - Nil)]	21,500
2020 Capital Dividend Paid	(16,000)
Balance - End Of 2020	$24,700

Exercise Fourteen - 10 Solution

The required calculations are as follows:

Fair Market Value Per Share	$ 25.00
New Shares Received [(5%)(1,000)]	50
Non-Eligible Dividend Received	$1,250.00
Gross Up [(15%)($1,250.00)]	187.50
Taxable Dividend	$ 1,437.50
Dividend Tax Credit [(9/13)(15%)($1,250)]	$ 129.81

Jean's Net Income For Tax Purposes would be increased by the taxable dividend of $1,437.50. His federal Tax Payable would be decreased by the dividend tax credit of $129.81.

	Number of Shares	ACB/Share	Total ACB
Pre-Dividend Shares	1,000	$18	$18,000
Stock Dividend Addition	50	$25	1,250
Totals	1,050		$19,250

The per share adjusted cost base of Jean's shares would be $18.33 ($19,250 ÷ 1,050).

Exercise Fourteen - 11 Solution

The required calculations for the corporation are as follows:

Proceeds Of Disposition [($51)(150,000)]	$ 7,650,000
Adjusted Cost Base [($42)(150,000)]	(6,300,000)
Capital Gain	$ 1,350,000
Inclusion Rate	1/2
Taxable Capital Gain	$ 675,000

The calculations for Sandrine are as follows:

Dividend Received [(15%)($51)(150,000)]	$ 1,147,500
Gross Up [(15%)($1,147,500)]	172,125
Taxable Dividend	$1,319,625
Dividend Tax Credit [(9/13)(15%)($1,147,500)]	$ 119,163

Cloutier Ltd.'s Net Income For Tax Purposes would be increased by the $675,000 taxable capital gain. Sandrine's Net Income For Tax Purposes would be increased by the taxable dividend of $1,319,625. Her federal Tax Payable would be decreased by the dividend tax credit of $119,163.

Exercise Fourteen - 12 Solution

This transaction will result in an ITA 84(1) deemed dividend for all shareholders, calculated as follows:

PUC Of New Shares [(40,000)($12.70)]	$508,000
Increase In Net Assets	(450,000)
ITA 84(1) Deemed Dividend	$ 58,000

This would be allocated to all 166,000 (126,000 + 40,000) shares outstanding, on the basis of $0.35 per share. This would be a taxable dividend, subject to either the eligible or non-eligible dividend gross up and tax credit procedures. The $0.35 per share dividend would also be added to the adjusted cost base of all 166,000 shares.

With the addition of $0.35 resulting from the ITA 84(1) deemed dividend to the original issue price of $10.50, the adjusted cost base of these shares is now $10.85 per share. Mr. Uni's sale of 5,000 shares at $13.42 per share would result in a taxable capital gain calculated as follows:

Proceeds Of Disposition [($13.42)(5,000)]	$ 67,100
Adjusted Cost Base [($10.85)(5,000)]	(54,250)
Capital Gain	$12,850
Inclusion Rate	1/2
Taxable Capital Gain	$ 6,425

Exercise Fourteen - 13 Solution

The analysis of the $2,350,000 distribution would be as follows:

Cash Distributed	$2,350,000
PUC Of Shares	(250,000)
ITA 84(2) Deemed Dividend	$2,100,000
ITA 83(2) Capital Dividend	(340,000)
ITA 88(2)(b) Taxable Dividend	$1,760,000

To the extent the company has a balance in its GRIP account, some amount of the $1,760,000 dividend could be designated as eligible. Any remainder will be taxed as a non-eligible dividend.

The wind-up results in a disposition of the shares. The tax consequences of this disposition are as follows:

Cash Distributed	$2,350,000
ITA 84(2) Deemed Dividend	(2,100,000)
ITA 54 Proceeds Of Disposition	$ 250,000
Adjusted Cost Base	(250,000)
Capital Gain	Nil

As shown by the preceding calculation, there would be no capital gain on the disposition.

Exercise Fourteen - 14 Solution

The redemption transaction would have no tax consequences for Ms. Tandy. The tax consequences to Jesuiah Tandy resulting from the redemption of his shares would be as follows:

Proceeds Of Redemption [(15,000)($11.75)]	$176,250
PUC [(15,000)($8.25)]	(123,750)
ITA 84(3) Deemed Dividend	$ 52,500
Gross Up Of 15 Percent	7,875
Taxable Dividend	$ 60,375
Dividend Tax Credit [(9/13)(15%)($52,500)]	$ 5,452
Proceeds Of Redemption [(15,000)($11.75)]	$176,250
ITA 84(3) Deemed Dividend	(52,500)
ITA 54 Proceeds Of Disposition	$123,750
Adjusted Cost Base [(15,000)($7.90)]	(118,500)
Capital Gain (PUC - ACB)	$ 5,250
Inclusion Rate	1/2
Taxable Capital Gain	$ 2,625

Both the taxable dividend and the taxable capital gain would increase Jesuiah's Net Income For Tax Purposes by a total of $63,000 ($60,375 + $2,625). The federal dividend tax credit would decrease federal Tax Payable by $5,452.

Exercise Fourteen - 15 Solution

To the extent of the $225,000 PUC reduction, the dividend will be treated as a tax free distribution. The tax consequences will be a reduction in the PUC of these shares to $225,000 ($450,000 - $225,000), as well as an adjusted cost base reduction to $400,000 ($625,000 - $225,000). The $105,000 ($330,000 - $225,000) excess of the distribution over the PUC reduction will be an ITA 84(4) deemed dividend, subject to either the eligible or non-eligible dividend gross up and tax credit procedures. As it will be taxed as a dividend, this part of the distribution will not be subtracted from the adjusted cost base of the shares.

Solution to Self Study Problem Fourteen - 1

Part A - Non-Capital And Net Capital Losses

Net Business Loss The net business loss for the period to March 31, 2020, would be as follows:

Loss As Per March 31, 2020, Income Statement	($23,000)
Required Accounts Receivable Adjustment ($45,000 - $33,000)	(12,000)
Building Election - Recaptured CCA ($285,000 - $270,000)	15,000
Fixtures And Equipment - Deemed CCA ($95,000 - $90,000)	(5,000)
Vehicles Election - Recaptured CCA ($87,000 - $80,000)	7,000
Net Business Loss For Period Ending March 31, 2020	($18,000)

Net And Taxable Income Net Income For Tax Purposes and Taxable Income for the period ending March 31, 2020, calculated as per the ITA 3 rules, would be as follows:

ITA 3(a) - Non-Capital Income (Positive Amounts Only)		Nil
ITA 3(b) - Net Taxable Capital Gains (Losses):		
Elections Under ITA 111(4)(e):		
Gain On Land [(1/2)($420,000 - $275,000)]	$72,500	
Gain On Building [(1/2)($320,000 - $285,000)]	17,500	
Required Write-Down - ITA 111(4)(c) And (d)		
Loss On Temporary Investments		
[(1/2)($53,000 - $23,000)]	(15,000)	75,000
ITA 3(c) - Total		$75,000
ITA 3(d) - Business Loss For The Period		(18,000)
Net Income For Tax Purposes		$ 57,000
Net Capital Loss Carry Forward		
(Limited To Amount Included Under ITA 3(b))		(75,000)
Taxable Income		Nil

Lost Net Capital Loss   The net capital loss that would be lost would be calculated as follows:

From 2018 [(1/2)($68,000)]	$34,000
From 2019 [(1/2)($85,000)]	42,500
Net Capital Loss Balance At March 31, 2020	$76,500
Amount Deducted In 2020	(75,000)
Net Capital Loss Lost On Acquisition of Control	$ 1,500

Non-Capital Loss Carry Forward   The non-capital loss carry forward would be calculated as follows:

Net Business Loss For Period	$ 18,000
Net Capital Loss Deducted	75,000
Subtotal	$ 93,000
Income Under ITA 3(c)	(75,000)
Non-Capital Loss For The Period Ending March 31, 2020	$ 18,000
Non-Capital Loss Carry Forward From 2018	63,500
Non-Capital Loss Carry Forward From 2019	78,500
Non-Capital Loss Carry Forward At March 31, 2020	$ 160,000

Part B - Loss Carry Forward In 2020

The April 1 to December 31, 2020, Net Income For Tax Purposes would be $78,000 ($123,000 - $45,000). Note that there is no restriction against deducting the current year loss on bread operations against other sources of income. However, none of the non-capital loss carry forward of $160,000 can be used as these losses can only be applied against income in the bread operations. This leaves the 2020 Taxable Income equal to the Net Income For Tax Purposes of $78,000. The non-capital loss carry forward at December 31, 2020, is unchanged at $160,000.

Part C - Loss Carry Forward In 2021

The $40,000 loss on the figurines must be deducted from the profits of the bread operations to produce a Net Income For Tax Purposes of $171,000 ($211,000 - $40,000). As this income is entirely from bread operations, all of the $160,000 non-capital loss carry forward can be deducted, leaving a Taxable Income of $11,000. There is no remaining non-capital loss carry forward at December 31, 2021.

Solution to Self Study Problem Fourteen - 2

Part A

As a result of the acquisition of control, LF will have a deemed taxation year end on April 30, 2020. This results in a short January 1, 2020, through April 30, 2020, taxation year for LF. The effects of this include:

- An additional year will be counted toward the expiry of the non-capital losses.
- If CCA is to be taken, it will have to be calculated for a short fiscal period.
- All of the usual year end procedures (timing of bonuses, inclusion of reserves, etc.) will have to be carried out.
- For the first year after the acquisition of control, LF can choose a new fiscal year end, on any date up to 53 weeks after the deemed year end.

Other implications are as follows:

- Any net capital loss balance that remains cannot be used after the deemed year end.
- Any non-capital loss balance that is carried forward can only be used against profits earned in the same or a similar line of business.
- The manufacturing equipment, because its fair market value is less than its UCC, will have to be written down to the $285,000 UCC value. The $90,000 ($375,000 - $285,000) amount of the write-down will be treated as deemed CCA.

Part B

The land, Class 1 assets, and Class 8 assets all have fair market values in excess of their tax values. If the deemed disposition election is made and the fair market value of these assets is used as the elected value, the results would be as follows:

Asset	Recapture	Capital Gain
Land ($925,000 - $450,000)	N/A	$475,000
Class 1 ($650,000 - $515,000)	$135,000	Nil
Class 8 ($15,000 - $10,000)	5,000	Nil
Total Income	$140,000	$475,000

Part C

If the companies believe that they will be able to generate sufficient income to use the non-capital loss carry forward in future periods, they will not want to make elections that will result in any unneeded pre-acquisition income. If the elections are made, the losses will increase the adjusted cost base or UCC balance of the assets the elections are made on. In the case of the land, the increased cost will not be of benefit until the land is sold. In the case of the depreciable assets, the increased UCC will only be deductible at the applicable rates of 4 or 20 percent. Alternatively, a non-capital loss carry forward can be deducted in full, as soon as the companies have sufficient appropriate income to absorb it.

The situation with net capital losses is different. If such losses are not used during the short fiscal period prior to the acquisition of control, they will be lost forever. Given this, it would be appropriate to make an election that would absorb the $65,000 net capital loss from 2018. This will require a capital gain of $130,000 [(2)($65,000)], which can be created by electing a deemed disposition on the land at a value of $580,000. This election will create a taxable capital gain of $65,000 [(1/2)($580,000 - $450,000)].

Given the required write-down of the manufacturing equipment, the Net Business Loss would be calculated as follows:

Operating Loss To April 30, 2020 (Given)	($ 55,000)
Deemed CCA On Class 53 ($375,000 - $285,000)	(90,000)
Net Business Loss For The Period Ending April 30, 2020	($ 145,000)

Using this figure, along with the results of the election on the land, Net and Taxable Income would be calculated as follows:

ITA 3(a) Non-Capital Income (Positive Amounts Only)		Nil
ITA 3(b) Net Taxable Capital Gains		
Election Under ITA 111(4)(e) On Land		$ 65,000
ITA 3(c) Total		$ 65,000
ITA 3(d) Net Business Loss For The Period		(145,000)
Net Income For Tax Purposes		Nil
Net Capital Loss Carry Forward (See Following)		($ 65,000)
Taxable Income		Nil

The non-capital loss carry forward at April 30, 2020, would be calculated as follows:

Net Business Loss For The Period	$ 145,000
Net Capital Loss Deducted	65,000
Subtotal	$ 210,000
Income Under ITA 3(c)	(65,000)
Non-Capital Loss For The Period Ending April 30, 2020	$ 145,000
Carry Forward From 2018	180,000
Carry Forward From 2019	140,000
Non-Capital Loss Carry Forward	$ 465,000

The net capital loss balance from 2018 would be eliminated by the $65,000 carry forward deduction, leaving a balance of nil to be carried forward.

Part D

If there is uncertainty with respect to the ability of OLC and LF to generate income in the same or a similar line of business in amounts sufficient to absorb the non-capital loss carry forward, additional elections should be made to absorb as much of this balance as possible. This would require elections on all of the assets with capital gains or recapture. Under this approach Net Business Income would be calculated as follows:

Operating Loss To April 30, 2020 (Given)	($ 55,000)
Deemed CCA On Class 53 ($375,000 - $285,000)	(90,000)
Class 1 - Recaptured CCA	135,000
Class 8 - Recaptured CCA	5,000
Net Business Loss For The Period Ending April 30, 2020	($ 5,000)

The resulting Net and Taxable Income amounts would be calculated as follows:

ITA 3(a) - Non-Capital Income (Positive Amounts Only)	Nil
ITA 3(b) - Net Taxable Capital Gains (Losses):	
Capital Gain On Land [(1/2)($925,000 - $450,000)]	$ 237,500
ITA 3(c) - Total	$ 237,500
ITA 3(d) - Business Loss For The Period	(5,000)
Net Income For Tax Purposes	$ 232,500
Net Capital Loss Carry Forward (All)	(65,000)
Subtotal	$ 167,500
Non-Capital Loss Carry Forward	
(Maximum Needed To Reduce Income To Nil)	(167,500)
Taxable Income	Nil

Under this Part D approach, the non-capital loss carry forward at April 30, 2020, would be calculated as follows:

Net Business Loss For The Period	$ 5,000
Net Capital Loss Deducted	65,000
Subtotal	$ 70,000
Income Under ITA 3(c)	(237,500)
Non-Capital Loss For The Period Ending April 30, 2020	Nil
Carry Forward From 2018	$ 180,000
Carry Forward From 2019	140,000
Non-Capital Loss Carry Forward Deducted	
For The Period Ending April 30, 2020	(167,500)
Non-Capital Loss Carry Forward	$ 152,500

As in Part C, the net capital loss from 2018 is eliminated by the $65,000 loss carry forward deduction.

Solution to Self Study Problem Fourteen - 3

Part A

By virtue of ITA 251(2)(a), John Fleming and Eric Flame are related by the fact that they are married to persons who are connected by a blood relationship (their wives). In addition, under ITA 256(1.5) a person who owns shares in two or more corporations shall be, as a shareholder of one of the corporations, deemed to be related to himself as a shareholder of the other corporation(s).

Given this, Fleming Ltd. and Lartch Inc. are associated under ITA 256(1)(d). John Fleming controls Fleming Ltd., is a member of a related group (John Fleming and Eric Flame) that controls Lartch Inc., and owns more than 25 percent of the voting shares of Lartch Inc.

In a similar fashion, Flame Ltd. is associated with Lartch Inc. under ITA 256(1)(d), as Eric Flame controls Flame Ltd., is a member of a related group (John Fleming and Eric Flame) that controls Lartch Inc., and owns more than 25 percent of Lartch Inc.

Based on these associations, Fleming Ltd. and Flame Ltd. are associated under ITA 256(2), as they are both associated with a third corporation, Lartch Inc. If it were desirable, Lartch Inc. could make the appropriate election under ITA 256(2) to be deemed not to be associated with Fleming Ltd. and Flame Ltd., which would allow Fleming Ltd. and Flame Ltd. to avoid association. However, the annual business limit for Lartch Inc. would be reduced to nil.

Part B

Mr. and Mrs. Cuso are a group with respect to both Male Ltd. and Female Inc. [ITA 256(1.2)(a) - two or more persons holding shares in the same corporation]. As a group, they control both Male Ltd. and Female Inc. Therefore, the two companies are associated under ITA 256 (1)(b). The fact that Mr. and Mrs. Cuso are related is not relevant.

Part C

Ms. Jones and Miss Lange are a group that controls Alliance Ltd. However, they do not control Breaker Inc., as Mrs. Kelly (not a member of the group that controls Alliance Ltd.) owns 50 percent of the shares. Therefore, Alliance Ltd. and Breaker Inc. are not associated.

Part D

While they are not related, Mr. Martin and Mr. Oakley constitute a group [ITA 256(1.2)(a)] with respect to both Martin Inc. and Oakley Ltd. As both Martin Inc. and Oakley Ltd. are controlled by the same group, the two companies are associated under ITA 256(1)(b).

Part E

The two companies are related, but not associated. While Lily and James are related, they are not a group with respect to the two companies and there is no cross-ownership of shares.

Solution to Self Study Problem Fourteen - 4

Case 1

As a group, Mr. Jones and Mr. Twitty control both Jones Ltd. and Twitty Inc. As a consequence, these two companies would be associated under ITA 256(1)(b).

Case 2

Ms. Wynette controls Wynette Enterprises Ltd. and is related to each member of the group that controls Lynn Inc. In addition, Ms. Wynette has the necessary 25 percent plus cross-ownership in Lynn Inc. As a consequence, Wynette Enterprises Ltd. and Lynn Inc. are associated under ITA 256(1)(d).

Case 3

A group, consisting of Mr. Travis and Mr. Cash, has control of both Cowboys Ltd. and Horses Inc. Therefore, Cowboys Ltd. and Horses Inc. are associated under ITA 256(1)(b).

Case 4

As Randy's Boots Inc. controls Hill Inc., those two companies are associated under ITA 256(1)(a).

As Mr. Nelson owns 80 percent of the shares of Willie's Hits Ltd., he controls that company. This gives him control over the 20 percent of Hill Inc. shares that are owned by Willie's Hits.

However, Mr. Nelson does not control Randy's Boots, and this means that his indirect interest in Hill Inc. through Randy's Boots of 24 percent [(30%)(80%)] is the product of the two ownership percentages.

As a result, his overall interest in Hill Inc. is only 44 percent (20% + 24%), which is not sufficient to give him control over Hill. Therefore, Willie's Hits Ltd. and Hill Inc. are not associated and Willie's Hits Ltd. and Randy's Boots Inc. are not associated.

Case 5

Ms. Parton controls Alpha Company, is related to each member of the group (Ms. Parton and her spouse) that control Beta Company, and has cross-ownership of Beta Company in excess of 25 percent. This means that these two companies are associated under ITA 256(1)(d).

Her spouse controls Centra Company, is related to each member of the group (the spouse and Ms. Parton) that controls Beta Company, and has the necessary cross-ownership of at least

25 percent of Beta Company shares. This means that these two companies are also associated under ITA 256(1)(d).

As they are not controlled by the same individual or group, Alpha Company and Centra Company are not associated under ITA 256(1). However, as they are both associated with the same third corporation (Beta Company), Alpha and Centra would be associated under ITA 256(2). Note that ITA 256(2) allows Alpha and Centra to avoid association, provided Beta elects not to be associated with either company. This will mean, however, that Beta will have a business limit for the period of nil.

Case 6

For the purposes of determining associated companies, Ms. Gale is deemed to own the 30 percent interest in Norton Music Inc. that is held by her minor child [ITA 256(1.3)] and the 20 percent interest in Norton Music Inc. for which she holds an option [ITA 256(1.4)]. When this is combined with her own interest of 10 percent, she would be considered to control Norton Music Inc. As she controls both Kristal Enterprises Ltd. and Norton Music Inc., these companies are associated under ITA 256(1)(b).

Solution to Self Study Problem Fourteen - 5

Case A

Luxor's annual expenditure limit would be $2,887,500. This amount is calculated as follows:

$$[\$3,000,000][(\$40,000,000 - \$1,500,000) \div \$40,000,000]$$

Case B

Gargle's annual expenditure limit would be $2,827,500, calculated as follows:

$$[\$3,000,000][(\$40,000,000 - \$2,300,000) \div \$40,000,000]$$

As the eligible SR&ED current expenditures exceed this limit, some of the expenditures will only be eligible for the 15 percent rate:

Total Current SR&ED Expenditures	$ 3,200,000
Annual Expenditure Limit (Eligible For 35 Percent Rate)	(2,827,500)
Limited To 15 Percent Rate	$ 372,500

The total amount of investment tax credits available can be calculated as follows:

Qualified Property [(10%)($86,000)]	$ 8,600
SR&ED Current Expenditures:	
At 35 Percent Rate [(35%)($2,827,500)]	989,625
At 15 Percent Rate [(15%)($372,500)]	55,875
Total Available Amount	$1,054,100

Gargle is a qualifying corporation. The refund available would be as follows:

	Rate	ITC	Refund
Qualified Property	40%	$ 8,600	$ 3,440
SR&ED Current Expenditures	100%	989,625	989,625
SR&ED Current Expenditures	40%	55,875	22,350
Total Available		$1,054,100	$1,015,415

The non-refunded investment tax credit of $38,685 ($1,054,100 - $1,015,415) can be carried forward 20 years to be applied against Tax Payable. There was no Tax Payable in the last three years so it cannot be carried back.

The cost of the qualified property will be reduced in 2021 by the refundable investment tax credit of $3,440. The $1,011,975 ($989,625 + $22,350) refundable tax credit on current SR&ED expenditures will be added to income in 2021.

Case C

With respect to the $250,000 in apprentice salaries, the investment tax credit is available on an annual salary maximum of $20,000 per apprentice. As a result, there will be a $17,500 [(5)(10%)($15,000) + (5)(10%)($20,000 maximum)] credit against 2019 federal Tax Payable. This $17,500 credit will be added to income in 2020.

With respect to the $800,000 in capital expenditures, there will be a 2020 credit against federal Tax Payable of $80,000 [(10%)($800,000)].

The $80,000 credit will not influence the calculation of 2019 CCA. This amount will be $360,000 [(30%)(150%)($800,000)].

In 2020, the $80,000 credit will be deducted from the January 1, 2020, UCC, leaving a balance of $360,000 ($800,000 - $360,000 - $80,000). Given this, 2020 CCA will be $108,000 [(30%)($360,000)].

Solution to Self Study Problem Fourteen - 6

The December 31, 2019, balance in the capital dividend account is calculated as follows:

2008 Capital Gain [(1/2)($343,500 - $225,000)]	$ 59,250
2009 Life Insurance Proceeds	162,000
2011 Capital Loss [(1/2)($150,000 - $220,000)]	(35,000)
2013 Capital Dividend Received	26,000
2017 Net Capital Loss {[1/2][($80,000 - $50,000) - ($100,000 - $45,000)]}	(12,500)
Capital Dividends Paid [(3)($45,000)]	(135,000)
Balance December 31, 2019	$ 64,750

Solution to Self Study Problem Fourteen - 7

The December 31, 2019, balance in the capital dividend account is calculated as follows:

2008 Life Insurance Proceeds	$ 186,000
2010 Capital Dividend Received	26,300
2015 Capital Dividend Paid	(45,200)
2016 Capital Gain [(1/2)($226,100 - $184,300)]	20,900
2018 Capital Gain [(1/2)($93,400 - $48,600)]	22,400
2018 Capital Loss [(1/2)($108,300 - $112,600)]	(2,150)
2019 Capital Dividend Paid	(16,400)
Balance December 31, 2019	$ 191,850

Solution to Self Study Problem Fourteen - 8

Case 1
To the extent of the $163,000 PUC reduction, the liquidating dividend will be treated as a tax free distribution to Mr. Farnsworth. However, there will be tax consequences related to this distribution:

- The PUC of Mr. Farnsworth's shares will be reduced to $160,000 ($323,000 - $163,000).
- The ACB of Mr. Farnsworth's shares will be reduced to $299,000 ($462,000 - $163,000).

The $97,000 ($260,000 - $163,000) excess of the distribution over the PUC reduction will be an ITA 84(4) deemed dividend. For inclusion in Taxable Income, it will be grossed up to $111,550 [(115%)($97,000)]. It will generate a federal dividend tax credit of $10,073 [(9/13)(15%)($97,000)]. This deemed dividend part of the distribution will not be subtracted from the adjusted cost base of the shares.

Case 2
The tax consequences to Michelle Chawla resulting from the redemption of her shares would be as follows:

Proceeds Of Redemption [($20.80)(125,000)]	$ 2,600,000
PUC [($20)(125,000)]	(2,500,000)
ITA 84(3) Deemed Dividend	$ 100,000

Proceeds Of Redemption [($20.80)(125,000)]	$ 2,600,000
ITA 84(3) Deemed Dividend	(100,000)
ITA 54 Proceeds Of Disposition	$ 2,500,000
Adjusted Cost Base [($16.80)($125,000)]	(2,100,000)
Capital Gain	$ 400,000
Inclusion Rate	1/2
Taxable Capital Gain	$ 200,000

For purposes of determining Taxable Income, the ITA 84(3) dividend will be grossed up to $115,000 [(115%)($100,000)], resulting in a total increase in Taxable Income of $315,000 ($115,000 + $200,000). A federal dividend tax credit of $10,385 [(9/13)(15%)($100,000)] will result from this transaction.

Case 3
This transaction will result in an ITA 84(1) deemed dividend for all shareholders, calculated as follows:

PUC Of New Shares [(42,000)($24.10)]	$ 1,012,200
Increase In Net Assets (Liability Eliminated)	(900,000)
ITA 84(1) Deemed Dividend	$ 112,200

This would be allocated to all 275,000 (233,000 + 42,000) shares outstanding, on the basis of $0.408 per share ($112,200 ÷ 275,000).

Sue's share of the dividend would be $9,506 [(23,300)($0.408)]. For inclusion in her Taxable Income, this amount will be grossed up to $10,932 [(115%)($9,506)].

The deemed dividend will be added to the adjusted cost base of Sue's shares, resulting in a value of $22.908 ($22.50 + $0.408)] per share. A federal dividend tax credit of $987 [(9/13)(15%) ($9,506)] will result from this transaction.

The tax consequences of Sue selling her shares would be as follows:

Proceeds Of Disposition [(23,300)($24.85)]	$579,005
Adjusted Cost Base [(23,300)($22.908)]	(533,756)
Capital Gain	$ 45,249
Inclusion Rate	1/2
Taxable Capital Gain	$ 22,625

This will result in a total increase in Taxable Income of $33,557 ($22,625 + $10,932).

Case 4

The analysis of the $3,175,000 distribution would be as follows:

Cash Distributed	$3,175,000
PUC Of Shares	(400,000)
ITA 84(2) Deemed Dividend	$2,775,000
ITA 83(2) Capital Dividend	(427,000)
ITA 88(2)(b) Wind-Up Dividend	$2,348,000

The capital dividend would be distributed tax free. For inclusion in Taxable Income, the $2,348,000 dividend would be grossed up to $2,700,200 [(115%)($2,348,000)]. It would generate a federal dividend tax credit of $243,831 [(9/13)(15%)($2,348,000)].

The transaction would also result in an allowable capital loss calculated as follows:

Cash Distributed	$3,175,000
ITA 84(2) Deemed Dividend	(2,775,000)
ITA 54 Proceeds Of Disposition	$ 400,000
Adjusted Cost Base	(1,450,000)
Capital Loss	($1,050,000)
Inclusion Rate	1/2
Allowable Capital Loss	($ 525,000)

The allowable capital loss can be used in the current year, only to the extent of taxable capital gains realized in the current year.

CHAPTER 15

Chapter 15 Learning Objectives

After completing Chapter 15, you should be able to:

1. Explain how a corporation can be used to reduce taxes, defer taxes, and facilitate income splitting (paragraph [P hereafter] 15-1 to 15-9).
2. Describe other advantages and disadvantages of incorporation (P 15-10 and 15-11).
3. Use various personal and corporate tax rates in the calculation of after tax retention of earnings flowed through a corporation (P 15-12 to 15-24).
4. Calculate the amount of tax reduction and tax deferral that is available through the use of a public corporation (P 15-25 to 15-34).
5. Calculate the amount of tax reduction and tax deferral that is available through the use of a CCPC earning active business income (P 15-35 to 15-40).

6. Explain the advantages of bonusing down to the owner of a CCPC eligible for the small business deduction (P 15-41 to 15-45).
7. Calculate the amount of tax reduction and tax deferral that is available through the use of a CCPC earning investment income other than dividends (P 15-46 to 15-49).
8. Calculate the amount of tax reduction and tax deferral that is available through the use of a CCPC earning dividend income (P 15-50 to 15-54).
9. Summarize the tax reduction and tax deferral that is available through the use of various types of corporations earning different types of income (P 15-55 to 15-57).
10. Identify the effect of provincial taxes on the decision to incorporate (P 15-58 to 15-76).

11. Explain why large amounts of dividends can be received on a tax free basis by individuals with no other source of income (P 15-77 to 15-88).
12. Describe and calculate the benefits that can be achieved by using a corporation to implement income splitting (P 15-89 to 15-91).
13. Determine the tax consequences of various shareholder benefits, including loans (P 15-92 to 15-113).
14. Explain the principles of management compensation in the context of an owner-managed corporation (P 15-114 to 15-120).
15. Describe the basic trade-off between the payment of salary and the payment of dividends for the owner-manager (P 15-121 to 15-127).

16. Calculate the appropriate choice between salary and dividends, taking into consideration factors other than federal tax savings (P 15-128 to 15-151).
17. Optimize the salary/dividend mix when all tax credits are not utilized or there is a limited amount of cash in the corporation (P 15-152 to 15-168).
18. Summarize the various non-tax factors that must be taken into consideration in making salary vs. dividend decisions (P 15-169 and 15-170).

How to Work Through Chapter 15

We recommend the following approach in dealing with the material in this chapter:

The Decision To Incorporate - Tax Considerations
- Read paragraph 15-1 to 15-9 (in the textbook).

Other Advantages And Disadvantages Of Incorporation
- Read paragraph 15-10 to 15-11.
- Do Self Study Problems Fifteen-1 and Fifteen-2, which are available on MyLab, and check the solutions in this Study Guide.

Basic Example Data - Tax Reduction And Deferral
- Read paragraph 15-12 to 15-24.

Public Companies - Tax Reduction And Deferral
- Read paragraph 15-25 to 15-34.
- Do Exercise Fifteen-1 (in the textbook) and check the solution in this Study Guide.

CCPCs - Active Business Income - Tax Reduction And Deferral
- Read paragraph 15-35 to 15-40.
- Do Exercise Fifteen-2 and check the solution in this Study Guide.
- Read paragraph 15-41 to 15-45.

CCPCs - Non-Dividend Investment Income - Tax Reduction And Deferral
- Read paragraph 15-46 to 15-49.
- Do Exercise Fifteen-3 and check the solution in this Study Guide.
- Do Self Study Problem Fifteen-3 and check the solution in this Study Guide.

CCPCs - Dividend Income - Tax Reduction And Deferral
- Read paragraph 15-50 to 15-54.

Conclusions On Tax Reductions And Deferrals
- Read paragraph 15-55 to 15-57.
- Do Exercises Fifteen-4 and Fifteen-5 and check the solutions in this Study Guide.
- Do Self Study Problem Fifteen-4 and check the solution in this Study Guide.

Provincial Taxes And Integration
- Read paragraph 15-58 to 15-76.
- Do Self Study Problem Fifteen-5 and check the solution in this Study Guide.

Tax Free Dividend Calculations
- Read paragraph 15-77 to 15-88.

Income Splitting
- Read paragraph 15-89 to 15-91.
- Do Self Study Problem Fifteen-6 and check the solution in this Study Guide.

Shareholder Benefits Including Loans
- Read paragraph 15-92 to 15-113.
- Do Exercises Fifteen-6 to Fifteen-8 and check the solutions in this Study Guide.
- Do Self Study Problems Fifteen-7 and Fifteen-8 and check the solutions in this Study Guide.

Management Compensation - General Principles
- Read paragraph 15-114 to 15-120.

Salary Vs. Dividend Decisions For The Owner-Manager
- Read paragraph 15-121 to 15-151.
- Do Exercise Fifteen-9 and check the solution in this Study Guide.

Salary Vs. Dividends - Use Of Tax Credits
- Read paragraph 15-152 to 15-168.
- Do Exercises Fifteen-10 and Fifteen-11 and check the solutions in this Study Guide.

Salary Vs. Dividends - Conclusion
- Read paragraph 15-169 to 15-170.
- Do Self Study Problems Fifteen-9 to Fifteen-11 and check the solutions in this Study Guide.

To Complete This Chapter
- If you would like more practice in problem solving, do the Supplementary Self Study Problems for the chapter. These problems and solutions are available on MyLab.
- Review the Key Terms Used In This Chapter in the textbook at the end of Chapter 15. Consult the Glossary for the meaning of any key terms you do not know.
- Test yourself with the Chapter 15 Glossary Flashcards available on MyLab.
- Ensure you have achieved the Chapter 15 Learning Objectives listed in this Study Guide.
- As a review, we recommend you view the PowerPoint presentation for Chapter 15 that is on MyLab.

Practice Examination
- Write the Practice Examination for Chapter 15 that is on MyLab. Mark your examination using the Practice Examination Solution that is on MyLab.

Solutions to Chapter Fifteen Exercises

Exercise Fifteen - 1 Solution

As the new corporation would not be allocated any part of the annual business limit, all of the $100,000 would be taxed at full corporate rates:

Corporate Income	$100,000
Corporate Taxes [(26.5%)($100,000)]	(26,500)
Available For Eligible Dividends	$ 73,500
Eligible Dividends Received By Ms. Ashley	$ 73,500
Gross Up At 38 Percent	27,930
Taxable Dividends	$101,430
Ms. Ashley's Tax Rate	45%
Tax Payable Before Dividend Tax Credit	$ 45,644
Dividend Tax Credit [(6/11 + 47.1%)($27,930)]	(28,390)
Personal Tax Payable	$ 17,254
Eligible Dividends Received	$ 73,500
Tax Payable	(17,254)
After Tax Retention	$ 56,246

This Exercise uses a below average corporate tax rate and an above average provincial dividend tax credit, both of which are favourable to the use of a corporation. Even with these favourable rates, use of a corporation only improves the after tax retention by $1,246 ($56,246 - $55,000).

Exercise Fifteen - 2 Solution

Mr. Slater's combined tax rate on income earned by the unincorporated business is 49 percent (33% + 16%). If he incorporates, all of the $126,000 will be eligible for the small business deduction. This means it will be taxed at a corporate rate of 12 percent (38% - 10% - 19% + 3%). Mr. Slater's tax rate on non-eligible dividend income is 41.92 percent [(115%)(49%) - (9/13 + 27%)(15%)].

Using these tax rates, a comparison of the income retained with and without the use of a corporation is as follows:

	With Corporation	Without Corporation
Business Income	$126,000	$ 126,000
Tax Rate	12%	49%
Tax Payable	$ 15,120	$ 61,740
Business Income	$126,000	$126,000
Tax Payable	(15,120)	(61,740)
Maximum Non-Eligible Dividend Payable	$110,880	N/A
Personal Tax On Dividends [(41.92%)($110,880)]	(46,481)	N/A
After Tax Income Retained By Mr. Slater	$ 64,399	$ 64,260

There is clearly a significant amount of tax deferral with respect to income left in the corporation. His Tax Payable on direct receipt of the $126,000 of business income would be $61,740, far higher than the $15,120 that would be paid by the corporation. There would also be a small tax savings as the $64,399 in income retained using the corporation is $139 greater than the $64,260 in income retained without the use of the corporation.

Exercise Fifteen - 3 Solution

Mr. Slater's combined tax rate on interest income earned outside the corporation is 51 percent (33% + 18%). His tax on the direct receipt of $126,000 of interest income would be $64,260.

If he incorporates, the interest income will not be eligible for the small business deduction or the general rate reduction, and it will be subject to the ART. This means that, if the investments are transferred to a corporation, the interest will be taxed at a rate of 50-2/3 percent (38% - 10% + 10-2/3% + 12%). Mr. Slater's tax rate on non-eligible dividends received is 44.2 percent [(115%) (51%) - (9/13 + 27%)(15%)].

Using these tax rates, a comparison of the income retained with and without the use of a corporation is as follows:

	With Corporation	Without Corporation
Interest Income	$ 126,000	$ 126,000
Tax Rate	50-2/3%	51%
Tax Payable	$ 63,840	$ 64,260
Interest Income	$ 126,000	$126,000
Tax Payable	(63,840)	(64,260)
Net Corporate Income Before Dividend Refund	$ 62,160	N/A
Maximum Dividend Refund (See Note)	38,640	
Maximum Dividend Payable	$ 100,800	
Personal Tax On Dividends [(44.2%)($100,800)]	(44,554)	
After Tax Income Retained By Mr. Slater	$ 56,246	$ 61,740

The balance in the Non-Eligible RDTOH would as follows:

Non-Eligible RDTOH Balance [(30-2/3%)($126,000)]	$ 38,640

Note The refund is the lesser of 38-1/3 percent of dividends paid and the balance in the Non-Eligible RDTOH account. The available cash of $62,160 would support a dividend of $100,800 ($62,160 ÷ .61667), which includes a potential dividend refund of $38,640 [(38-1/3%)($100,800)]. In this case the two figures are both equal to $38,640.

With Mr. Slater's individual tax rate at 51 percent and the corporate tax rate at 50-2/3 percent, there is a very small amount of deferral. The amount would be $420 ($64,260 - $63,840), not enough to justify the tax cost associated with using a corporation.

The after tax retention results with a corporation are significantly worse than when the income is received directly. After tax retention is reduced from $61,740 to $56,246, a reduction of $5,494. There is clearly a tax cost as a result of transferring the investments to a corporation.

Exercise Fifteen - 4 Solution

Direct Receipt If the income is received directly, the total Tax Payable will be as follows:

Eligible Dividends Received	$46,000	
Gross Up At 38 Percent	17,480	$ 63,480
Non-Eligible Dividends Received	$87,000	
Gross Up At 15 Percent	13,050	100,050
Taxable Dividends		$163,530
Interest Income		32,000
Taxable Income		$195,530
Personal Tax Rate (33% + 18%)		51%
Tax Payable Before Dividend Tax Credit		$ 99,720
Dividend Tax Credit		
[(6/11 + 5/11)($17,480)]	($17,480)	
[(9/13 + 4/13)($13,050)]	(13,050)	(30,530)
Personal Tax Payable		$ 69,190

The after tax retention can be calculated as follows:

Cash Received ($46,000 + $87,000 + $32,000)	$165,000
Tax Payable	(69,190)
After Tax Retention - Direct Receipt	$ 95,810

Transfer To Corporation If the investments are transferred to a corporation, the tax rate on the interest income is 50-2/3 percent (38% - 10% + 10-2/3% + 12%). Given this, the corporate taxes will be as follows:

Part IV Tax On Eligible Dividends Received [(38-1/3%)($46,000)]	$17,633
Part IV Tax On Non-Eligible Dividends Received	
(100% Of The Dividend Refund Received The Subsidiary)	29,000
Tax On Interest Income [(50-2/3%)($32,000)]	16,213
Corporate Tax Payable Before Refund	$62,846

As this Tax Payable is smaller than the Tax Payable that would be paid on the direct receipt of income, overall the use of a corporation provides significant tax deferral (the deferral is only on the interest and non-eligible dividends). However, as the client needs all of the income produced by these investments, this advantage will not be used by him.

As this would be a new corporation, it would have no transitional RDTOH balance from 2019. Given this, the balance in the Eligible RDTOH would equal the Part IV tax on the eligible dividends received and would as follows:

Eligible RDTOH Balance [(38-1/3%)($46,000)]	$17,633

The balance in the Non-Eligible RDTOH would be as follows:

Part IV Tax On Non-Eligible Dividends Received	$29,000
Part I Addition [(30-2/3%)($32,000)]	9,813
Non-Eligible RDTOH Balance	$38,813

The cash available for paying dividends would be $102,154 ($165,000 - $62,846). This represents 61.667 percent of $165,654. Paying a dividend in this amount would result in a refund of $63,500 [(38-1/3%)($165,654)]. However, this exceeds the sum of the RDTOH balances. This means that the total refund would be limited to $56,446 ($17,633 + $38,813), with a total dividend of $158,600 ($102,154 + $56,446).

The eligible dividends received by the corporation will be added to the GRIP balance, leaving $46,000 in this account. This means that $46,000 in dividends could be designated as eligible for the enhanced dividend gross up and tax credit procedures. The remainder of the dividends paid of $112,600 ($158,600 - $46,000) would be non-eligible.

This would result in personal taxes as follows:

Eligible Dividends Received	$ 46,000	
Gross Up At 38 Percent	17,480	$ 63,480
Non-Eligible Dividends Received	$112,600	
Gross Up At 15 Percent	16,890	129,490
Taxable Dividends		$192,970
Personal Tax Rate		51%
Tax Payable Before Dividend Tax Credit		$ 98,415
Dividend Tax Credit		
[(6/11 + 5/11)($17,480)]	($ 17,480)	
[(9/13 + 4/13)($16,890)]	(16,890)	(34,370)
Personal Tax Payable		$ 64,045
Dividends Received ($46,000 + $112,600)		$158,600
Personal Tax Payable		(64,045)
After Tax Retention - With Corporation		$ 94,555

As this is less than the $95,810 that would be retained on direct receipt of income, there is no tax advantage in going to the trouble and expense of forming a corporation to hold the client's investments.

Exercise Fifteen - 5 Solution

The client's combined tax rate on direct receipt of income is 49 percent (33% + 16%). Based on this, the after tax amount retained on direct receipt of income can be calculated as follows:

Capital Gain	$ 92,000
Personal Taxes On Taxable Capital Gain [(49%)(1/2)($92,000)]	(22,540)
After Tax Retention - Direct Receipt	$69,460

If the investments are transferred to a CCPC, the aggregate investment income will be $46,000 [(1/2)($92,000)]. The applicable tax rate will be 50-2/3 percent (38% - 10% + 10-2/3% + 12%). As this rate is higher than the client's personal rate on income received directly, there would be no possible deferral of tax through the use of a corporation. However, even if the rate was more favourable, deferral is not an issue here as the client needs all of the income produced by these investments for her forthcoming bicycle trip.

Based on this corporate tax rate, the maximum distribution that can be made would be calculated as follows:

Available Cash	$92,000
Corporate Tax Payable [(50-2/3%)($46,000)]	(23,307)
Tax Free Capital Dividend [(1/2)($92,000)]	(46,000)
Available For Non-Eligible Dividend	$22,693
Dividend Refund (See Note)	14,107
Non-Eligible Dividend Received	$36,800

As this would be a new corporation, it would have no transitional RDTOH balance from 2019. Given this, the balance in the Non-Eligible RDTOH would as follows:

Non-Eligible RDTOH Balance [(30-2/3%)($46,000)]	$14,107

Note   The refund is the lesser of 38-1/3 percent of taxable dividends paid and the balance in the Non-Eligible RDTOH account. The available cash of $22,693 would support a dividend of $36,800 ($22,693 ÷ .61667 with a $1 rounding error), which includes a potential dividend refund of $14,107 [(38-1/3%)($36,800)]. In this case, the two figures are both equal to $14,107.

The client's tax rate on non-eligible dividend income is 41.35 percent [(115%)(49%) - (9/13 + 4/13)(15%)]. Based on this, the net after tax retention when a corporation is used would be as follows:

Tax Free Capital Dividend Received	$46,000
Non-Eligible Dividend Received	36,800
Tax Payable On Non-Eligible Dividend Received [(41.35%)($36,800)]	(15,217)
After Tax Retention - With Corporation	$67,583

As this is less than the $69,460 that would be retained on direct receipt of the income, there is no tax advantage in going to the trouble and expense of forming a corporation to hold the client's investments.

Exercise Fifteen - 6 Solution

It is likely that Ms. Rourke will have to include the $50,000 principal amount of the loan in her Net Income For Tax Purposes in 2020. She owns more than 10 percent of the shares, making her a specified employee. This means that she does not qualify for the exception under ITA 15(2.4)(a). While she is an employee, it is unlikely that this type of loan would be generally available to all employees and, as a consequence, it is likely that she received the loan because of her position as a shareholder. This means that she does not qualify for the acquisition of an automobile exception under ITA 15(2.4)(d). If the loan is included in income, she will be entitled to a $50,000 deduction under ITA 20(1)(j) when she repays the loan in 2024.

In the unlikely event that the loan is not included in income and ITA 15(2) does not apply, she will have to include imputed interest at the prescribed rate for the period of the loan. Her shareholder benefit for 2020 is $500 [(2% - Nil)($50,000)(6/12)]. The imputed interest rate and benefit will vary as the prescribed rate changes. Note, however, if imputed interest is assessed, some portion of the amount may be deductible as it relates to the acquisition of an automobile to be used in employment duties.

Exercise Fifteen - 7 Solution

If the loan is repaid on January 1, 2021, it will not be included in two consecutive Generic Inc. Balance Sheets. As a consequence, the principal amount will not have to be included in Ms. Fisk's income. However, as it is an interest free loan, she will be assessed with a taxable benefit on the loan. The amount would be $1,890 [($162,000)(2% - Nil)(7/12)].

If the loan is not repaid until December 31, 2021, it will appear in two consecutive Generic Inc. Balance Sheets. This means the $162,000 in principal will have to be included in Ms. Fisk's income for the taxation year ending December 31, 2020. However, there will be no imputed interest benefit based on the loan's low rate of interest. In addition, when the loan is repaid, the payment can be deducted from Ms. Fisk's Net Income For Tax Purposes for the taxation year ending December 31, 2021.

Exercise Fifteen - 8 Solution

Mr. Hasid will repay 25 percent of the loan, or $30,750, on October 31, 2021. This will leave an outstanding balance of $92,250 ($123,000 - $30,750) until October 31, 2022.

If Granted As Employee   Provided Mr. Hasid receives the loan in his capacity as an employee of Hasid Ltd., the loan is one of the exceptions listed under ITA 15(2). This means that the principal amount will not have to be included in income. However, as the loan is interest free, a taxable benefit will arise. It will be calculated by applying the prescribed rate of 2 percent to the principal of the loan for all periods that it is outstanding.

The amount for 2020 would be $410 [($123,000)(2% - Nil)(2/12)] and $2,358 {[($123,000)(2% - Nil)(10/12)] + [($92,250)(2% - Nil)(2/12)]} for 2021. The taxable benefit calculations for 2022 to 2024 would be calculated in a similar fashion.

If Granted As Shareholder   If Mr. Hasid cannot claim that he received the loan in his capacity as an employee of Hasid Ltd., $92,250 will be included in his income for 2020. The remaining $30,750 would not be included in income as it will have been repaid before Hasid Ltd.'s second year end. However, this balance will attract an interest benefit of $102.50 [($30,750)(2% - Nil)(2/12)] in 2020, and $512.50 [($30,750)(2% - Nil)(10/12)] in 2021.

As the remaining balance is repaid in 2022 through 2024, the payments can be deducted under ITA 20(1)(j) in the year they are repaid.

Exercise Fifteen - 9 Solution
(1) Salary Compensation
If the full $550,000 is paid out as salary, it will be deductible and will reduce the company's Taxable Income to nil. This means that no corporate taxes will be paid. This salary payment will result in Ms. Broad having Taxable Income of $550,000. Given this, her Tax Payable will be calculated as follows:

Tax On First $214,368 (Given)	$ 75,000
Tax On Remaining	
$335,632 ($550,000 - $214,368) At 51%	171,172
Tax Payable Before Credits	$246,172
Personal Tax Credits (Given)	(5,000)
Total Tax Payable	$241,172

Based on the preceding Tax Payable, Ms. Broad's after tax retention would be $308,828 ($550,000 - $241,172), ignoring CPP contributions and the Canada employment credit.

(2) Dividend Compensation
As dividends are not deductible for tax purposes, corporate taxes will have to be paid prior to the payment of any dividends. While the $50,000 of income in excess of the annual business limit of $500,000 would not get the small business deduction, it would be eligible for the general rate reduction of 13 percent. Given this, the corporate rate on this income would be 29 percent (38% - 10% - 13% + 14%). On income eligible for the small business deduction, the rate would be 12 percent (38% - 10% - 19% + 3%). Using these rates, corporate taxes would be calculated as follows:

Income Not Eligible For SBD [(29%)($50,000)]	$14,500
Income Eligible For SBD [(12%)($500,000)]	60,000
Corporate Tax Payable	$74,500

After payment of these taxes, the maximum dividend that could be paid would be $475,500 ($550,000 - $74,500). The fact that the corporation's Taxable Income was in excess of the annual business limit of $500,000 will create an addition to the GRIP of $36,000 [(72%)($550,000 - $500,000)]. Given this, $36,000 of the dividend can be designated as eligible, leaving a non-eligible dividend of $439,500 ($475,500 - $36,000). The grossed up taxable dividends would be calculated as follows:

Total Eligible And Non-Eligible Dividends Received	$475,500
Gross Up:	
Eligible Dividends [(38%)($36,000)]	13,680
Non-Eligible Dividends [(15%)($439,500)]	65,925
Taxable Dividends	$555,105

Personal taxes on this dividend would be calculated as follows:

Tax On First $214,368 (Given)	$ 75,000
Federal Tax On Remaining	
$340,737 ($555,105 - $214,368) At 51%	173,776
Taxes Payable Before Credits	$248,776
Personal Tax Credits (Given)	(5,000)
Dividend Tax Credit:	
Eligible Dividends [(6/11 + 30%)($13,680)]	(11,566)
Non-Eligible Dividends [(9/13 + 30%)($65,925)]	(65,418)
Personal Tax Payable	$166,792

The after tax retention would be equal to $308,708 ($475,500 - $166,792). This is $120 more than the after tax retention in the salary option of $308,828.

Exercise Fifteen - 10 Solution

Required Salary Ms. Mortell's combined tax rate on additional salary is 45 percent (29% + 16%). In order to have $30,000 in after tax funds, she would have to receive salary of $54,545 [$30,000 ÷ (1 - .45)].

Required Dividend Ms. Mortell's tax rate on non-eligible dividends is 37.6 percent [(115%)(45%) - (9/13 + 25%)(15%)]. In order to have $30,000 in after tax funds, she would have to receive dividends of $48,077 [$30,000 ÷ (1 - .376)].

Tax Cost Of Salary The net tax cost of paying salary can be calculated as follows:

Personal Tax On Receipt Of Salary [(45%)($54,545)]	$24,545
Tax Savings To Corporation [(12%)($54,545)]	(6,545)
Net Tax Cost Of Salary Alternative	$18,000

Tax Cost Of Dividend As the dividend payment would not be deductible, its payment would not change corporate taxes. This means that the only tax cost would be the $18,077 [($48,077)(37.6%)] in personal taxes that Ms. Mortell would pay on the dividends received.

Conclusion As the tax cost associated with the payment of dividend is slightly larger, the salary alternative would be marginally preferable.

Exercise Fifteen - 11 Solution

Salary Alternative - As the available cash is less than Taxable Income, some corporate taxes will have to be paid since there is insufficient cash to pay a salary equivalent to Taxable Income. To determine the maximum salary that can be paid (X), it is necessary to solve the following equation:

$$X = \$18,500 - [(12\%)(\$21,500 - X)]$$
$$X - 0.12X = [\$18,500 - (12\%)(\$21,500)] = \$18,091$$

Corporate Cash Before Taxes		$18,500
Corporate Taxes [(12%)($21,500 - $18,091)]		(409)
Corporate Cash Available For Salary		$18,091
Salary Received		$18,091
Personal Tax Payable:		
Personal Tax On Salary [(25%)(18,091)]	($4,523)	
Personal Tax Credits (Given)	3,950	(573)
After Tax Cash Retained		$ 17,518

Dividend Alternative - After tax cash retained with the dividend alternative would be calculated as follows:

Corporate Cash Before Taxes	$18,500
Corporate Taxes [(12%)($21,500)]	(2,580)
Corporate Cash Available For Dividends	$15,920
Non-Eligible Dividend Received	$15,920
Individual Taxes*	Nil
After Tax Cash Retained	$15,920

*No taxes would be paid on this amount of dividends (see Paragraph 15-86 of the text).

Given these calculations, it is clear that the preferred approach is to pay the maximum salary. Note, however, some combination of dividends and salary may provide an even better result.

Solution to Self Study Problem Fifteen - 1

Part A - Goal Of Integration

The goal of integration is to ensure that the amount of after tax income that an individual receives from a given income source should be the same regardless of whether that income is earned directly or whether it is flowed through a corporation.

Part B - Tax Payable Without Corporation

Personal Tax Payable without the corporation would be calculated as follows:

	Business Income	Eligible Dividends
Income	$80,000	$ 96,000
Gross Up (38% Of $96,000)	N/A	36,480
Taxable Income	$80,000	$132,480
Tax Rate (33% + 18%)	51%	51%
Tax Payable Before Dividend Tax Credit	$40,800	$ 67,565
Dividend Tax Credit [(6/11 + 5/11)($36,480)]	N/A	(36,480)
Personal Tax Payable	$40,800	$ 31,085

The personal Tax Payable if the income is received directly totals $71,885 ($40,800 + $31,085).

Part C - Corporate Tax Payable

The portfolio dividends would result in Part IV tax of $36,800 [(38-1/3%)($96,000)]. However, this tax would be refunded on the payment of dividends. As a result, the portfolio dividends received of $96,000 would all be available for distribution.

The after tax corporate income available for distribution would be calculated as follows:

	Business Income	Dividends
Income	$80,000	$96,000
Part I Tax [(28% - 19% + 2%)($80,000)]	(8,800)	
Part IV Tax [(38-1/3%)($96,000)]		(36,800)
Available For Dividends	$71,200	$59,200
Dividend Refund [($59,200 ÷ .616667) - $59,200]	N/A	36,800
Total Distributable Income	$71,200	$96,000

The amount of the dividend refund would be limited by the balance in the RDTOH accounts. The balance here would reflect the Part IV taxes paid on the portfolio dividends, all of which would be allocated to the Eligible RDTOH. There would be no allocation to the Non-Eligible RDTOH.

At this point, Slater Ltd. has the cash to support a dividend of $167,200 ($71,200 + $96,000), including a refund of $36,800. As all of the $96,000 of portfolio dividends received were allocated to the company's GRIP account, this amount of dividends can be designated as eligible. The remaining dividends of $71,200 ($167,200 - $96,000) will be non-eligible.

The $36,800 refund would leave the balance in the company's Eligible RDTOH at nil.

Part C - Personal Tax Payable

Keith Slater's personal Tax Payable on receipt of the dividend distribution would be calculated as follows:

	Non-Eligible Dividends	Eligible Dividends
Eligible Dividends	N/A	$ 96,000
Gross Up At 38 Percent	N/A	36,480
After Tax ABI As Non-Eligible Dividends	$71,200	N/A
Gross Up At 15 Percent	10,680	N/A
Taxable Dividends	$81,880	$132,480
Tax Rate (33% + 18%)	51%	51%
Tax Payable Before Dividend Tax Credits	$41,759	$ 67,565
Dividend Tax Credits:		
Eligible Dividends [(6/11 + 5/11)($36,480)]	N/A	(36,480)
Non-Eligible Dividends [(9/13 + 4/13)($10,680)]	(10,680)	N/A
Personal Tax Payable	$31,079	$ 31,085

The corporate and personal Tax Payable if Slater Ltd. is used totals $70,964 ($8,800 + $31,079 + $31,085).

Part D - Comparison Of Results

Comparing the total Tax Payable under the two alternatives provides the following result:

Tax Payable - Without Corporation	$71,885
Tax Payable - With Corporation	(70,964)
Tax Savings With Corporation	$ 921

Flowing the income through Slater Ltd. results in a tax savings of $921. By calculating the tax burden on the active business income separately from the dividends, it is clear that there is perfect integration on the portfolio dividends. The Part IV tax paid at the corporate level is totally refunded, and the personal taxes paid on the dividends are the same with or without the corporation.

In this example, the Part I corporate rate of 11 percent on the active business income is lower than the 13.04 percent level that is required for perfect integration. In addition, the combined federal/provincial dividend tax credit is equal to the rate required for perfect integration. As a result, there is a tax savings of $921 when the income is flowed through the corporation.

Solution to Self Study Problem Fifteen - 2

Advantages Of Incorporation

Among the more commonly cited advantages of incorporation would be the following:

Tax Deferral   It would appear that, if he incorporates, all of the income earned by the corporation will be eligible for the small business deduction. As the corporate rate on this type of income is given as 11 percent, there would be tax deferral on income left within the corporation. As his marginal tax rate as an individual is in the 45 percent range, the amount of the deferral would be significant.

Tax Reduction   For CCPCs earning active business income, the tax rate required for perfect integration is 13.04 percent. As the relevant corporate rate in his province is 11 percent, this suggests that there would be a tax savings on income flowed through a corporation. However, the provincial dividend tax credit must also be considered. The required rate for perfect integration is 4/13 of the dividend gross up. If the rate in Gerald's province is below this, the savings resulting from the low corporate rate could be reduced or even eliminated.

Income Splitting   With a proper structuring of the ownership of the corporation, income can be channeled into the hands of other members of Mr. Copley's family. This can be in the form of either salary or dividends, and will be subject to what we would assume to be significantly lower rates of taxation. We would note, however, that the ability to use this technique may be limited by the application of the Tax On Split Income (TOSI).

Lifetime Capital Gains Deduction   For 2020, this provision allows for the deduction of up to $883,384 in capital gains. It is available on the disposition of shares in a qualified small business corporation. Properly structured, incorporation could permit all members of his family access to the lifetime capital gains deduction. To qualify, the corporation must be a Canadian controlled private corporation and have at least 90 percent of the fair market value of its assets being used in an active business in Canada. In addition, the shares:

- must not have been owned by anyone other than the taxpayer or a related party for at least 24 months preceding the disposition; and

- throughout this 24 month period, more than 50 percent of the fair market value of the corporation's assets must be used in an active business carried on primarily in Canada.

This deduction could represent a significant advantage of incorporating his business.

Employee Benefits   While Mr. Copley's organization may be somewhat small to make this feasible, the corporation can be used to establish various retirement programs, as well as group life and health insurance packages.

Estate Planning   A corporation can be useful in estate planning, particularly with respect to freezing the asset values in the estate (see Chapters 17 and 19).

Limited Liability   An investor in a corporation is, in general, not liable to the creditors for the debts of the corporation. In the case of large publicly traded corporations this is a very real and important consideration. However, in the case of a small owner-managed business such as Mr. Copley's, it is unlikely that creditors would extend significant sums without getting his personal guarantee for repayment.

However, limited liability could be important if his business is exposed to any type of product liability risk.

Liquidation Losses   If the business is unsuccessful and must be liquidated, the loss on corporate shares would be deductible as an allowable business investment loss. This means that one-half of the total amount could be deducted against any other income. However, it would require further analysis to ensure that this would involve a greater amount of deductions than would be the case if the business were liquidated in its present unincorporated form.

Disadvantages Of Incorporation

A list of the disadvantages associated with incorporation would include the following:

Administrative Costs   There will be higher legal, accounting, and other costs associated with meeting the various reporting requirements that are necessary for the start-up and maintenance of a corporation.

Losses   The losses of the corporation cannot be offset against other personal income that the shareholders might have. Further, allowable capital losses of corporations can only be deducted against the corporation's taxable capital gains.

Termination   If the corporation is terminated, there is no available rollover for transferring the assets back to Mr. Copley. Taxation will occur at fair market values. There is a further possibility of double taxation in that, while the corporation will be taxed on the disposition of its assets, the shareholder may be taxed on the same amounts when he disposes of his shares.

Higher Taxes   Under advantages we noted that there could be a tax reduction associated with a corporation earning income that is eligible for the small business deduction. On the other hand, if the corporation earns income that is not eligible for the small business deduction, there will be a significant extra payment of combined corporate and personal income tax when such income flows through the corporation in the form of dividends to its shareholders.

Winding Up Procedures   Because of its status as a separate legal entity, the procedures associated with winding up an incorporated business are significantly more complex than those associated with terminating an unincorporated enterprise.

Conclusions On Incorporation

In evaluating the preceding advantages and disadvantages, a recommendation that Mr. Copley incorporate his business seems to be appropriate. He does not appear to need all of the income produced by the business for personal living expenses and, as a consequence, the ability to defer income within the corporation is attractive. Further, his eligibility for the small business deduction could result in a reduction in taxes, even on amounts that are withdrawn from the corporation. Other advantages related to incorporating Mr. Copley's business are the opportunities that may be available to split income between the various members of his family and for estate planning, especially considering the lifetime capital gains deduction.

Solution to Self Study Problem Fifteen - 3

Part A - Direct Personal Investment

Mrs. Martin's marginal tax rate is 46 percent (29% + 17%). If Mrs. Martin invests the $200,000 as an individual, the after tax return can be calculated as follows:

Interest Income (All Taxable)	$14,000
Interest Received	$14,000
Personal Tax Payable At 46 Percent	(6,440)
After Tax Retention - Direct Receipt	$ 7,560

Part B - Investment Through Private Company

If Mrs. Martin invests the $200,000 through her private company, any dividends paid will be non-eligible. The after tax return would be as follows:

Interest Income	$14,000
Corporate Taxes At 52 Percent	(7,280)
Net Corporate Income Before Dividend Refund	$ 6,720
Maximum Dividend Refund (See Note)	4,177
Maximum Non-Eligible Dividend Payable	$10,897
Gross Up At 15 Percent	1,635
Taxable Dividend	$12,532
Personal Tax Rate	46%
Personal Tax Payable Before Dividend Tax Credit	$ 5,765
Dividend Tax Credit [(9/13 + 25%)($1,635)]	(1,541)
Personal Tax Payable	$ 4,224
Dividends Received	$10,897
Personal Tax Payable	(4,224)
After Tax Retention - With Corporation	$ 6,673

Note The Part I refundable taxes on the interest income would be $4,293 [(30-2/3%)($14,000)]. This full amount would be allocated to the Non-Eligible RDTOH balance.

The available corporate cash would support a dividend of $10,897 ($6,720 ÷ .61667), including a dividend refund of $4,177 [(38-1/3%)($10,897)]. As this refund is less than the balance in the Non-Eligible RDTOH, the refund would be limited to $4,177, for a total dividend of $10,897. The refund will leave a balance in the Non-Eligible RDTOH of $116 ($4,293 - $4,177).

As there is no balance in the new company's GRIP, all of the $10,897 dividend will be non-eligible.

The difference between the two alternatives is $887 ($7,560 - $6,673) in favour of direct personal investment.

Solution to Self Study Problem Fifteen - 4

Part A - Direct Personal Investment

Mr. Martin's marginal tax rate is 46 percent (29% + 17%). If Mr. Martin invests the $200,000 as an individual, the after tax return can be calculated as follows:

Eligible Dividends Received	$14,000
38 Percent Gross Up	5,320
Taxable Dividend	$19,320
Personal Tax Rate	46%
Personal Tax Payable Before Dividend Tax Credit	$ 8,887
Dividend Tax Credit [(6/11 + 25%)($5,320)]	(4,232)
Personal Tax Payable	$ 4,655
Dividends Received	$14,000
Personal Tax Payable	(4,655)
After Tax Retention - Direct Receipt	$ 9,345

Part B - Investment Through Private Company

If Mr. Martin invests the $200,000 through his private company, the eligible dividends received would be classified as portfolio dividends, subject to Part IV tax at 38-1/3 percent. There would also be an addition to the corporation's GRIP account of $14,000 (notice that eligible dividends are not multiplied by 72 percent for the GRIP addition). The after tax retention on the flow through the corporation would be as follows:

Eligible Dividends Received	$14,000
Part IV Tax At 38-1/3 Percent (Portfolio Dividends)	(5,367)
Earnings Retained By Corporation	$ 8,633
Refund When Dividends Paid (See Note)	5,367
Eligible Dividends Paid	$14,000

Note The available cash would support a dividend of $14,000 ($8,633 ÷ .61667), including a refund of $5,367 [(38-1/3%)($14,000)]. This refund is available as it is equal to the $5,367 balance in the RDTOH resulting from the payment of Part IV tax on the receipt of the dividends.

At this point, the corporation has paid no net amount of taxes and will be paying exactly the same amount of eligible dividends that it received. This will result in Mr. Martin paying exactly the same amount of taxes that he would have paid on direct receipt of the dividends. With the use of a corporation, the after tax retention would be identical to the after tax retention resulting from direct receipt of the dividends.

Solution to Self Study Problem Fifteen - 5

Approach 1 (Joins Partnership As Individual)

Cora's share of the partnership income would be $70,000 [(10%)($700,000)]. Cora's Tax Payable resulting from this approach would be calculated as follows:

Tax On First $48,535 At 23 Percent (15% + 8%)	$11,163
Tax On Next $21,465 ($70,000 - $48,535)	
At 32.5 Percent (20.5% + 12%)	6,976
Tax Payable Before Credits	$18,139
Personal Tax Credits - Given	(3,342)
Personal Tax Payable	$14,797
Business Income	$70,000
Personal Tax Payable	(14,797)
After Tax Retention - Alternative 1	$55,203

Approach 2 (All Dividends)

The total corporate taxes would be calculated as follows:

First $50,000 At 12 Percent	$ 6,000
Remaining $20,000 At 27 Percent	5,400
Corporate Tax Payable	$11,400

If all of the after tax income is paid out, the resulting dividend will be $58,600 ($70,000 - $11,400).

As $20,000 of the corporation's income was taxed at the general rate, there would be a GRIP balance of $14,400 [(72%)($20,000)]. This means that of the total dividend of $58,600, $14,400 could be designated as eligible, with the remaining $44,200 ($58,600 - $14,400) being non-eligible. Based on this, Cora's Taxable Income would be as follows:

Eligible Dividend	$14,400
Gross Up On Eligible Dividend At 38 Percent	5,472
Non-Eligible Dividend	44,200
Gross Up On Non-Eligible Dividend At 15 Percent	6,630
Total Taxable Income	$70,702

Based on this Taxable Income, her Tax Payable would be as follows:

Tax On First $48,535 At 23 Percent (15% + 8%)	$ 11,163
Tax On Remaining $22,167 ($70,702 - $48,535)	
At 32.5 Percent (20.5% + 12%)	7,204
Tax Payable Before Credits	$18,367
Personal Tax Credits - Given	(3,342)
Dividend Tax Credit = Gross Up ($5,472 + $6,630)	(12,102)
Personal Tax Payable	$ 2,923
Business Income	$70,000
Corporate Tax Payable	(11,400)
Personal Tax Payable	(2,923)
After Tax Retention - Alternative 2	$55,677

Approach 3 (Salary And Dividends)

With the payment of $20,000 in salaries to reduce corporate income to her $50,000 share of the small business deduction, corporate taxes would be $6,000 [(12%)($50,000)]. This would leave $44,000 ($70,000 - $20,000 - $6,000) for the payment of dividends.

Since no income was taxed at the general rate, the GRIP balance would be nil. This means that the total dividend of $44,000 would be non-eligible. Cora's Taxable Income would be calculated as follows:

Salary	$ 20,000
Non-Eligible Dividend	44,000
Gross Up On Non-Eligible Dividend At 15 Percent	6,600
Taxable Income	$70,600

Her Tax Payable would be calculated as follows:

Tax On First $48,535 At 23 Percent (15% + 8%)	$ 11,163
Tax On Next $22,065 ($70,600 - $48,535)	
At 32.5 Percent (20.5% + 12%)	7,171
Tax Payable Before Credits	$ 18,334
Personal Tax Credits - Given	(3,342)
Dividend Tax Credit = Gross Up	(6,600)
Personal Tax Payable	$ 8,392
Business Income	$ 70,000
Corporate Tax Payable After Salary [(12%)($70,000 - $20,000)]	(6,000)
Personal Tax Payable	(8,392)
After Tax Retention - Alternative 3	$ 55,608

Evaluation

The after tax amount retained for each of the three approaches is as follows:

Approach 1 (Joins Partnership As Individual)	$55,203
Approach 2 (All Dividends)	55,677
Approach 3 (Salary And Dividends)	55,608

If only after tax cash flows are considered, Approach 2 provides the highest value and would be the appropriate choice.

Other factors to consider:

- While Approach 2 provides the largest after tax retention, it does not take into consideration CPP contributions. If the effect of CPP were considered, she would pay two times the annual maximum in Approach 1, no CPP in Approach 2, and in Approach 3 both Cora and her corporation would pay less than the annual maximum. Paying CPP contributions would allow her to receive CPP payments in the future, but would incur a liability at the present time. Without going through the required calculations, it is likely that Approach 2 would be best if the required CPP contributions were considered.

- If the Canada employment credit were considered, it would only be applicable in Approach 3.

- If Cora wanted to participate in the Employment Insurance program on a voluntary basis, it would only be available to her in Approach 1 as a self-employed individual.

- If she wanted to contribute to an RRSP or deduct child care costs, she would need earned income. Dividends are not a component of earned income for either purpose. Earned income would be $70,000 in Approach 1 and $20,000 in Approach 3.

- Depending on the province, there could be additional payroll costs that her corporation would have to pay in Approach 3.

- The opportunity for income splitting may be easier with a corporation given that family members could buy shares that entitle them to share in the dividends. This, however, is likely to be limited by the application of the Tax On Split Income (TOSI). Income splitting through the partnership would be much more difficult given that, for the most part, the family members would have to be involved in partnership activity.

- Although an advantage of incorporation is the availability of the lifetime capital gains deduction, given the current situation, it is questionable whether her corporation could be sold for much of a gain given how important her personal services are to its value.

Solution to Self Study Problem Fifteen - 6

Part A - *Tax Payable With Corporation*

The business income of the corporation would be calculated as follows:

Management Fees		$82,900
Expenses:		
Mr. Ashley's Salary	($18,400)	
Office Salaries	(25,400)	
Office Rent	(8,180)	
CCA On Office And Dental Equipment	(5,700)	
Other Business Expenses	(2,170)	(59,850)
Business Income		$23,050
Rate On Active Business Income		11%
Tax Payable On Active Business Income		$ 2,536

Tax Payable on the dividends and investment income would be calculated as follows:

Interest Income	$ 21,600
Net Rental Income ($34,600 - $27,800)	6,800
Aggregate Investment Income	$ 28,400
Rate On Investment Income	51-2/3%
Part I Tax On Investment Income	$ 14,673
Part IV Tax On Dividends Received [(38-1/3%)($13,900)]	5,328
Tax Payable On Property Income	$ 20,001

The refundable portion of the Part I Tax Payable would be the least of the following amounts:

- $ 8,709 = 30-2/3% Of Aggregate Investment Income [(30-2/3%)($28,400)]

- $ 8,709 = 30-2/3% Of Taxable Income Less Amount Eligible For Small Business Deduction [(30-2/3%)($23,050 + $28,400 - $23,050)]

- $17,209 = Part I Tax Payable ($2,536 + $14,673)

The balances in the two RDTOH accounts would be as follows:

Non-Eligible RDTOH (Part I Refundable Tax)	$8,709

Eligible RDTOH (Part IV Tax Payable)	$5,328

The eligible dividends received by the corporation will be added to the GRIP balance, leaving $13,900 in this account (note that the amount received is added, not the amount received multiplied by 72 percent). This means that $13,900 in dividends could be designated as eligible for the enhanced dividend gross up and tax credit procedures.

Given the preceding calculations, the maximum eligible and non-eligible dividend that could be paid is as follows:

Business Income	$23,050
Taxes On Business Income	(2,536)
Interest Income	21,600
Net Rental Income	6,800
Taxes On Property Income	(20,001)
Eligible Dividends	13,900
Balance Before Refund	$42,813
Dividend Refund (See Note)	14,037
Available For Dividends	$56,850
Eligible Dividends (GRIP Balance)	(13,900)
Non-Eligible Dividends (Remainder)	$42,950

Note The available cash of $42,813 would support a dividend of $69,426 ($42,813 ÷ 0.61667), including a refund of $26,613 ([(38-1/3%)($69,426)]). However, the actual refund is the lesser of this figure and the $14,037 ($8,709 + $5,328) total of the two RDTOH accounts. Given this, the total dividend is limited to $56,850 ($42,813 + $14,037).

The refund will be deducted from the two RDTOH accounts, leaving each with a balance of nil.

With respect to the eligible dividends, $8,340 [(60%)($13,900)] would go to Mr. Ashley, and $5,560 [(40%)($13,900)] would go to Dr. Ashley. With respect to the non-eligible dividends, $25,770 [(60%)($42,950)] would go to Mr. Ashley, and $17,180 [40%)($42,950)] would go to Dr. Ashley. The resulting Tax Payable would be as follows:

	Dr. Ashley	Mr. Ashley
Salary	Nil	$18,400
Eligible Dividends ($13,900)	$ 5,560	8,340
Gross Up At 38 Percent	2,113	3,169
Non-Eligible Dividends ($42,950)	17,180	25,770
Gross Up At 15 Percent	2,577	3,866
Taxable Income	$ 27,430	$59,545
Tax Rate	47%	30%
Tax Payable Before Dividend Tax Credit	$12,892	$ 17,864
Dividend Tax Credits:		
Eligible Dividends [(6/11 + 25%)(Gross Up)]	(1,681)	(2,521)
Non-Eligible Dividends [(9/13 + 25%)(Gross Up)]	(2,428)	(3,643)
Tax Payable	$ 8,783	$ 11,700

This would leave after tax balances available to Dr. and Mr. Ashley as follows:

Ashley Management Services	Nil
Dr. Ashley ($5,560 + $17,180 - $8,783)	$ 13,957
Mr. Ashley ($18,400 + $8,340 + $25,770 - $11,700)	40,810
After Tax Retention - Dr. And Mr. Ashley	$54,767

Part B - Balances With No Corporation

If Dr. Ashley had received all of the amounts involved directly, her Tax Payable and net retention would be calculated as follows:

Business Income ($23,050 + $18,400 Salary To Husband)	$41,450
Interest Income	21,600
Rental Income (Net)	6,800
Eligible Dividends	13,900
Gross Up At 38 Percent	5,282
Taxable Income	$89,032
Tax Rate	47%
Tax Before Dividend Tax Credit	$41,845
Dividend Tax Credit [(6/11 + 25%)($5,282)]	(4,202)
Tax Payable	$ 37,643
Income Received ($41,450 + $21,600 + $6,800 + $13,900)	$ 83,750
Tax Payable	(37,643)
After Tax Retention - Dr. Ashley Only	$46,107

It is clear from these calculations that the use of the management company has had a positive effect on after tax retention of income. Without the corporation, Dr. Ashley would have ended up with only $46,107. This compares to a total of $54,767 for Mr. and Dr. Ashley when the corporation is used, an improvement of $8,660.

You should note, however, that Dr. Ashley could have paid a salary to her husband without using a corporation. This would have significantly improved the results in Part B.

The problem asked you to ignore personal tax credits, the Canada employment tax credit, CPP contributions, and GST. Personal tax credits would have made only a small difference, as Dr. Ashley would be able to claim the spousal credit in full if Mr. Ashley had no income.

While it is clear the Canada employment tax credit would favour paying Mr. Ashley a salary, the advantage or disadvantage of CPP contributions is less clear cut. Although GST is not covered in detail until Chapter 21, we noted in Chapter 12 that the GST/HST legislation has made management companies for GST exempt services such as dentistry less attractive.

Solution to Self Study Problem Fifteen - 7

Dwelling Loan

As such loans are available to all employees, Ms. Lord can claim that she has received the loan in her capacity as an employee. This means that the $200,000 principal does not have to be included in her 2020 Net Income For Tax Purposes. However, as the rate on the loan is below the prescribed rate, there will be a taxable benefit included in Ms. Lord's Net Income For Tax Purposes.

The amount to be accrued for 2020 is $1,000 [($200,000)(2% - 1%)(6/12)]. For 2021, the amount is $1,600 [($200,000 - $40,000)(2% - 1%)(12/12)], and for 2022, the amount is $1,200 [($200,000 - $80,000)(2% - 1%)(12/12)].

Automobile

As there are no bona fide arrangements for repaying the loan, the $25,000 principal amount must be included in Ms. Lord's 2020 Net Income For Tax Purposes. There will be no taxable interest benefit. However, when the loan is repaid, the $25,000 principal amount can be deducted in the determination of Net Income For Tax Purposes.

Other Loans

- **February 1, 2020**   As this loan is not repaid prior to August 31, 2021 (the second corporate year end), it has to be included in Ms. Lord's 2020 Net Income For Tax Purposes. In 2022, the year it is repaid, the $35,000 can be deducted from Ms. Lord's Net Income For Tax Purposes. As the loan is included in her income, there will be no benefit associated with the low interest rate. As this result would not be changed if the loan were interest free, paying interest on this loan was not good tax planning.

- **July 1, 2020**   As the loan is repaid prior to August 31, 2021 (the second corporate year end), it does not have to be included in Ms. Lord's 2020 Net Income For Tax Purposes. However, as it is interest free, there will be a taxable benefit for imputed interest. For 2020, the amount will be $250 [(2%)($25,000)(6/12)]. For 2021, the benefit will be $333 [(2%)($25,000)(8/12)].

- **December 10, 2020**   This loan is repaid prior to its inclusion in a second corporate Balance Sheet. As a consequence, it does not have to be included in income. In addition, as the interest rate of 2 percent on the loan is equal to the prescribed rate, there will be no imputed interest benefit.

Solution to Self Study Problem Fifteen - 8

Alternative Treatments

The tax consequences here will depend on whether the loan was given to Mr. Blaine in his capacity as an employee or, alternatively, in his capacity as a shareholder. Note that this loan would not qualify for a home relocation loan deduction as it can be assumed that the property that he is acquiring is not 40 kilometres closer to his work since the house seller is a neighbour and he bicycles to work.

Treatment As Shareholder Loan

If similar loans are not available to the other employees of Blaine Enterprises, it is likely that the CRA will take the view that Mr. Blaine received the loan in his capacity as a shareholder. If this is the case and the loan is included in the Balance Sheet of Blaine Enterprises at two consecutive year ends, the principal amount of the loan will have to be included in Mr. Blaine's Net Income For Tax Purposes in the year of the loan. In this situation, having the company grant the loan has basically the same tax consequences for Mr. Blaine as having the company pay a similar amount of salary. There are, however, several differences:

- When the loan is repaid, the repayment can be deducted under ITA 20(1)(j). In contrast, the receipt of salary cannot be reversed.

- Mr. Blaine's salary of $77,000 does not provide sufficient earned income to allow him to make maximum RRSP contributions. Paying salary would increase his earned income and allow him to make additional RRSP contributions.

- Salary would serve to reduce corporate Tax Payable. While the loan cannot be deducted by Blaine Enterprises in determining Net Income For Tax Purposes, salary payments can be.

Note that since Arthur is receiving a salary of $77,000, he is already eligible for the Canada employment tax credit and paying the maximum CPP contributions, so these factors are not relevant.

Treatment As Employee Loan

If similar loans are available to the other employees of Blaine Enterprises, Mr. Blaine can argue that he received the loan in his capacity as an employee. Provided there is a reasonable plan for repayment of the loan, he will not have to include the principal amount of the loan in his Net Income For Tax Purposes. However, he would be assessed a taxable benefit in the amount of imputed interest on the outstanding loan balance. The interest rate to be used in this calculation would be the prescribed rate (ITR 4301).

Evaluation

If he can claim that he received the loan in his capacity as an employee, the analysis will depend on the relationship between the prescribed rate and the rate that Mr. Blaine would have to pay if he financed his new home with a conventional mortgage. Generally, the prescribed rate tends to be several percentage points below the going rate for mortgages. Based on this, it would appear that if the loan principal can be kept out of his income, having his company provide the loan would be an effective form of tax planning for Mr. Blaine.

If Mr. Blaine is required to include the loan in income because he has received it as a shareholder, it should be determined whether Blaine Enterprises will require the $125,000 in the future. If the intention is to repay the funds, a loan will allow the deduction of the repayment and there will be no taxable benefit for interest. This analysis requires more information about the corporation to determine whether it is more advantageous to have the $125,000 included in Mr. Blaine's income as a shareholder loan or pay salary when both Mr. Blaine and Blaine Enterprises are considered.

Solution to Self Study Problem Fifteen - 9

Tax Reduction

Bonus Down

As salary payments can be deducted by the corporation, the entire $250,000 can be paid as salary since no taxes would be paid by the company on this amount. Mrs. Litvak's after tax retention would be as follows:

Salary Payment	$250,000
Personal Taxes On Salary [(52%)($250,000)]	(130,000)
After Tax Cash Retained After Bonus Down (2020)	$ 120,000

No Bonus Down

If Morcan Inc. does not pay the additional $250,000 in salary, an additional $67,500 [(27%)($250,000)] in corporate taxes would have to be paid. There would also be a $180,000 [(72%)($750,000 - $500,000)] addition to Morcan's GRIP account.

The after tax retention of funds in the corporation would be $182,500 ($250,000 - $67,500). If this amount is paid out as dividends in 2024, $180,000 (the balance in the GRIP account) could be designated as eligible, with the remaining $2,500 classified as non-eligible. Given this, the tax consequences of paying out these dividends would be as follows:

Eligible Dividends Received	$ 180,000
Gross Up At 38 Percent	68,400
Non-Eligible Dividends Received	2,500
Gross Up At 15 Percent	375
Taxable Dividend Paid In 2024	$ 251,275

Tax At 52 Percent [(52%)($251,275]	$ 130,663
Dividend Tax Credits:	
Eligible [(6/11 + 5/11)($68,400)] +	
Non-Eligible [(9/13 + 4/13)($375)]	(68,775)
Personal Tax Cost Of Dividends	$ 61,888

Dividends Received ($180,000 + $2,500)	$ 182,500
Personal Tax Cost	(61,888)
After Tax Cash Retained - No Bonus Down	$ 120,612

Conclusion

The difference in after tax retention between the two alternatives is only $612 ($120,612 - $120,000). While this is slightly in favour of bonusing down, the difference is not significant.

Tax Deferral

If Morcan Inc. pays the salary, there will be an immediate personal tax cost of $130,000. This is more than the $129,388 ($67,500 + $61,888) in taxes that would be paid if she did not bonus down and instead paid corporate taxes on the $250,000 with the remaining funds paid out as dividends in the future. However, Ms. Litvak has indicated that she does not need the additional income and, as a consequence, the payment of the personal taxes can be deferred until 2024. This means the current tax obligation would be limited to the $67,500 in corporate taxes and would constitute a significant tax deferral.

A potential problem with this is the question of whether the corporation can use the additional funds for business purposes. If not, and the funds were allocated to passive investments, the tax rate on investment income could be higher than the 52 percent rate that is applicable on amounts received directly by Ms. Litvak.

Conclusion

In terms of tax reduction, there is no significant advantage resulting from bonusing down. However, if the retained funds are not paid out as dividends until 2024, there is a significant tax deferral. This would favour not bonusing down. Note that this conclusion is dependent on how the funds will be used within the corporation.

Whether bonusing down will be advantageous will also depend on what use the funds can be put to directly by Mrs. Litvak. If, for example, she has not contributed fully to her RRSP and TFSA and/or her daughter's, bonusing down could be more advantageous.

An added consideration could be how Mrs. Litvak's father might react if she does not take his advice. This could have ramifications for her personally, but should not affect her tax situation.

Solution to Self Study Problem Fifteen - 10

Required Salary

Given Miss Morgan's personal tax rate of 51 percent (33% + 18%), a salary of $40,816 [$20,000 ÷ (1 - .51)] would be required to provide an additional $20,000 of after tax funds.

Tax Cost Of Salary Alternative

The net tax cost of this alternative would be calculated as follows:

Personal Taxes On Salary [(51%)($40,816)]	$20,816
Tax Savings To Corporation [(12%)($40,816)]	(4,898)
Net Tax Cost Of Salary Alternative	$15,918

Required Dividend

Miss Morgan's tax rate on non-eligible dividends would be as follows:

$$[(115\%)(51\%) - (9/13 + 25\%)(15\%)] = 44.52\%$$

This gives after tax retention of dividend income in the amount of 55.48 percent (1 - 44.52%). This means a dividend of $36,049 ($20,000 ˌ 55.48%) will be required to provide an additional $20,000 of after tax funds.

Tax Cost Of Dividend Alternative

The personal Tax Payable on the dividend would be calculated as follows:

Non-Eligible Dividends Received	$36,049
Gross Up At 15 Percent	5,407
Taxable Income	$41,456
Tax Rate (33% + 18%)	51%
Tax Payable Before Dividend Tax Credit	$21,143
Dividend Tax Credit [(9/13 + 25%)($5,407)]	(5,095)
Personal Tax Payable On Dividend Alternative	$16,048

Subtracting the Tax Payable of $16,048 from the dividends received of $36,049 gives $20,001 in after tax funds. (The extra $1 is a rounding issue).

As the dividend payment would not be deductible, its payment would not change corporate taxes. This means that the only tax cost would be the $16,048 in personal taxes that Miss Morgan would pay on the dividends received.

Conclusion

The salary alternative has a net tax cost that is $130 ($16,048 - $15,918) lower than the additional tax cost of paying dividends. Given this, the salary alternative would have a marginally lower tax cost.

Since Geraldine has already received a salary of $84,000, CPP contributions and the Canada employment credit are not relevant to this analysis as they would have already been accounted for and would not affect the conclusion.

Solution to Self Study Problem Fifteen - 11

Part A - Taxes And Salary

The combined federal/provincial tax rate applicable to Speelburg Films Ltd. would be 11 percent (38% - 10% - 19% + 2%).

As the corporation's Taxable Income exceeds the amount of cash available, the maximum amount of salary that can be paid (X) must be determined using the following simple equation:

$$X = \$49,000 - [(11\%)(\$123,000 - X)]$$

Solving this equation for X indicates that the maximum salary that can be paid is $39,854. This can be verified by the following calculation:

Corporate Taxable Income Before Salary	$123,000
Maximum Salary	(39,854)
Corporate Taxable Income After Salary	$ 83,146
Corporate Rate	11%
Corporate Tax Payable	$ 9,146

Payment of this amount of taxes will leave $39,854 ($49,000 - $9,146) available for payment of salary.

With this amount of salary, Mr. Lucas would have the following amount of after tax cash:

Salary Payment	$39,854
Rate (15% + 6%)	21%
Tax Before Credits	$ 8,369
Personal Tax Credits (Given)	(3,900)
Personal Tax Payable	$ 4,469
Salary Received	$39,854
Personal Tax Payable	(4,469)
After Tax Cash Retained (All Salary)	$35,385

Part B - All Dividends

As dividend payments are not deductible to the company, taxes of $13,530 [(11%)($123,000)] will have to be paid. This leaves a maximum of $35,470 ($49,000 - $13,530) to be used for the payment of non-eligible dividends. When this is paid, the after tax retention by Mr. Lucas will be as follows:

Non-Eligible Dividends Received	$35,470
Gross Up [(15%)($35,470)]	5,321
Taxable Dividends	$40,791
Personal Tax Rate (15% + 6%)	21%
Tax Payable Before Credits	$ 8,566
Personal Tax Credits (Given)	(3,900)
Dividend Tax Credit [(9/13 + 30%)($5,321)]	(5,280)
Tax Payable (Unused Credits = $614)	Nil

As there is no Tax Payable, Mr. Lucas will retain all of the $35,470 in dividends.

Part C - Possible Improvement

While the Tax Payable for Mr. Lucas is nil in Part B, subtracting personal and dividend tax credits from the tax balance gives a negative figure of $614. This means that the all dividend approach leaves unused tax credits. While not conclusive, this suggests that there may be a better solution than either all salary or all dividends.

Part D - Salary/Dividend Combination

To examine the possibility of an optimum solution using both salary and dividends, consider the result that occurs when $1,000 in salary is paid in lieu of some dividends. Because the deductible salary payment would reduce corporate taxes, dividends would only have to be decreased by $890 [($1,000)(1 - 0.11)]. The tax effects of this switch can be calculated as follows:

Increase In Salary		$ 1,000,000
Decrease In Dividend [($1,000)(1 - .11)]	(	890,000)
Decrease In Dividend Gross Up [(15%)($890.00)]	(	133,500)
Decrease In Mr. Lucas' Taxable Income	($	23,500)
Personal Tax Rate		21%
Decrease In Tax Payable Before Dividend Tax Credit	($	4,935)
Decrease In Dividend Tax Credit		
= Increase In Tax Payable [(9/13 + 30%)($133.50)]		132,473
Net Increase In Personal Tax Payable	$	127,538

The rate on a $1,000 increase in salary is 12.7538 percent ($127.538 ÷ $1,000). Applying this rate to the unused credits of $614 (see Part C) gives a required increase in salary of $4,814 ($614 ÷ 0.127538).

Payment of this amount of salary would result in corporate Tax Payable as follows:

Corporate Taxable Income Before Salary	$123,000
Salary	(4,814)
Corporate Taxable Income After Salary	$ 118,186
Corporate Rate	11%
Corporate Tax Payable	$ 13,000

Based on available cash of $49,000, the amount of dividend that could be paid is as follows:

Cash Available	$49,000
Corporate Tax Payable	(13,000)
Salary Payment	(4,814)
Available For Dividends	$31,186

After tax retention at the personal level would be calculated as follows:

Non-Eligible Dividends Received	$31,186
Gross Up [(15%)($31,186)]	4,678
Taxable Dividends	$35,864
Salary	4,814
Mr. Lucas' Taxable Income	$40,678
Personal Tax Rate (15% + 6%)	21%
Tax Payable Before Credits	$ 8,542
Personal Tax Credits (Given)	(3,900)
Dividend Tax Credit [(9/13 + 30%)($4,678)]	(4,642)
Tax Payable	Nil
Amounts Received ($31,186 + $4,814)	$36,000
Personal Tax Payable	Nil
After Tax Cash Retained (Salary And Dividends)	$36,000

The comparative results for the three alternatives are as follows:

All Salary	$35,385
All Dividends	$35,470
Salary/Dividend Combination	$36,000

The combination of salary and dividends will produce the maximum after tax cash retention for Mr. Lucas. It is a $615 ($36,000 - $35,385) improvement over the all salary solution and a $530 ($36,000 - $35,470) improvement over the all dividend solution.

Part E - Other Factors
Other factors that might be considered include:

- The Canada employment tax credit was ignored in the calculations as it is not a credit against provincial taxes. However, it would allow the first $1,245 of salary to be received with a nil federal tax cost.

- If the effect of CPP were considered, both Mr. Lucas and Speelburg Films Ltd. would pay CPP contributions if salary was paid. Paying CPP contributions would allow him to receive CPP payments in the future, but would require both a personal and a corporate cash outflow at the present time.
- If Speelburg Films Ltd. has benefits for employees, such as a private health services plan, this could make being an employee (by taking salary) more advantageous.
- Dividend payments are not Earned Income for purposes of making RRSP contributions or deducting child care costs.
- If Mr. Lucas has a CNIL balance, dividend payments will serve to reduce this constraint on the lifetime capital gains deduction.
- Mr. Lucas should consider declaring a bonus (a form of salary) to be paid after the end of the calendar year if he does not require the cash immediately. This would defer the personal taxes without affecting corporate taxes as long as the bonus was paid within 180 days of December 31.
- Though not relevant in this problem, some provinces have payroll taxes that could be incurred.

Chapter 16 Learning Objectives

After completing Chapter 16, you should be able to:

1. Describe the type of situation where ITA 85 is applicable (paragraph [P hereafter] 16-1 to 16-4).
2. Explain the general rules that are applicable to the transferor and the transferee under ITA 85 (P 16-5 to 16-11).
3. Describe the types of consideration that can be received by the transferor under ITA 85 (P 16-12 to 16-14).
4. Describe the procedures required for making the ITA 85 election (P 16-15 to 16-17).
5. Calculate the range of values that can be used in a transfer under the provisions of ITA 85 (P 16-18 to 16-30).

6. Apply the general rules applicable to all assets that determine the range of values that can be used in a transfer under the provisions of ITA 85 (P 16-31 to 16-36).
7. Apply the detailed rules for the transfer of accounts receivable, inventories, and non-depreciable capital property under ITA 85 (P 16-37 to 16-49).
8. Describe the rules related to the transfer of non-depreciable capital property, including disallowed capital losses on transfers to affiliated persons and the associated tax planning issues (P 16-50 to 16-61).
9. Apply the detailed rules for the transfer of depreciable assets under ITA 85 (P 16-62 to 16-69).
10. Describe the rules related to the disallowance of terminal losses arising on transfers of depreciable capital property to affiliated persons and associated tax planning issues (P 16-70 to 16-73).

11. Summarize the transfer price rules for all assets under ITA 85 (P 16-74).
12. Calculate the amount of the elected value that will be allocated to each component of the consideration received by the transferor under ITA 85 (P 16-75 and 16-76).
13. Calculate the amount of the elected value that will be allocated to each of the assets acquired by the transferee under ITA 85 (P 16-77 to 16-84).
14. Calculate the Paid Up Capital of the shares received by the transferor in an ITA 85 rollover (P 16-85 to 16-96).
15. Apply the ITA 85 rules to situations involving the incorporation of an unincorporated business (P 16-97 to 16-112).

16. Identify situations where the ITA 85 rules on gifts to related persons are applicable and make the appropriate adjustments that are required by these rules (P 16-113 to 16-127).
17. Identify situations where the ITA 85 rules on benefits to the transferor are applicable and make the appropriate adjustments that are required by these rules (P 16-128 to 16-131).
18. Identify situations where ITA 84.1 (dividend stripping rules) is applicable (P 16-132 to 16-139).

19. Apply the ITA 84.1 rules to situations involving dividend stripping (P 16-140 to 16-149).
20. Identify situations where ITA 55(2) (capital gains stripping rules) is applicable (P 16-150 to 16-154).
21. Apply the ITA 55(2) rules to situations involving capital gains stripping (P 16-155 to 16-167).

How to Work Through Chapter 16

We recommend the following approach in dealing with the material in this chapter:

Rollovers Under Section 85 - General Rules For The Transfer
- Read paragraph 16-1 to 16-26 (in the textbook).

Transfer Price Rules - Rules Applicable To All Assets
- Read paragraph 16-27 to 16-34.

Transfer Price Rules - Accounts Receivable
- Read paragraph 16-35 to 16-38.

Transfer Price Rules - Inventories And Non-Depreciable Capital Property
- Read paragraph 16-39 to 16-47.
- Do Exercise Sixteen-1 (in the textbook) and check the solution in this Study Guide.

Transfer Price Rules - Non-Depreciable Capital Property
- Read paragraph 16-48 to 16-59.

Transfer Price Rules - Depreciable Property
- Read paragraph 16-60 to 16-67.
- Do Exercise Sixteen-2 and check the solution in this Study Guide.

Transfer Price Rules - Depreciable Property And Disallowed Terminal Losses
- Read paragraph 16-68 to 16-71.

Transfer Price Rules - Eligible Capital Property
- Read paragraph 16-72.
- Do Self Study Problems Sixteen-1 and 2 and check the solutions in this Study Guide.

Allocation Of The Elected Value - Consideration Received By The Transferor
- Read paragraph 16-73 to 16-74.
- Do Exercise Sixteen-3 and check the solution in this Study Guide.

Allocation Of The Elected Value - Assets Acquired By The Corporation
- Read paragraph 16-75 to 16-82.

Paid Up Capital (PUC) Of Shares Issued - General Rules
- Read paragraph 16-83 to 16-85.

Paid Up Capital (PUC) Of Shares Issued - Paid Up Capital Reduction
- Read paragraph 16-86 to 16-90.

Paid Up Capital (PUC) Of Shares Issued - More Than One Class Of Shares
- Read paragraph 16-91 to 16-94.
- Do Exercise Sixteen-4 and check the solution in this Study Guide.
- Do Self Study Problem Sixteen-3 and check the solution in this Study Guide.

Comprehensive Example - Section 85 Rollovers
- Read paragraph 16-95 to 16-110.

- Do Exercise Sixteen-5 and check the solution in this Study Guide.
- Do Self Study Problems Sixteen-4, 5, 6, and 7 and check the solutions in this Study Guide.

Gift To Related Person - Section 85
- Read paragraph 16-111 to 16-125.
- Do Exercise Sixteen-6 and check the solution in this Study Guide.
- Do Self Study Problem Sixteen-8 and check the solution in this Study Guide.

Excess Consideration - Section 85
- Read paragraph 16-128 to 16-131.
- Do Exercise Sixteen-7 and check the solution in this Study Guide.
- Do Self Study Problem Sixteen-9 and check the solution in this Study Guide.

Dividend Stripping - ITA 84.1
- Read paragraph 16-132 to 16-149.
- Do Exercise Sixteen-8 and check the solution in this Study Guide.
- Do Self Study Problem Sixteen-10 and check the solution in this Study Guide.

Capital Gains Stripping - ITA 55(2)
- Read paragraph 16-150 to 16-167.
- Do Exercise Sixteen-9 and check the solution in this Study Guide.
- Do Self Study Problem Sixteen-11 and check the solution in this Study Guide.

To Complete This Chapter
- If you would like more practice in problem solving, do the Supplementary Self Study Problems for the chapter. These problems and solutions are available on MyLab.
- Review the Key Terms Used In This Chapter in the textbook at the end of Chapter 16.
- Consult the Glossary for the meaning of any key terms you do not know.
- Test yourself with the Chapter 16 Glossary Flashcards available on MyLab.
- Ensure you have achieved the Chapter 16 Learning Objectives listed in this Study Guide.
- As a review, we recommend you view the PowerPoint presentation for Chapter 16 that is on MyLab.

Practice Examination
- Write the Practice Examination for Chapter 16 that is on MyLab. Mark your examination using the Practice Examination Solution that is on MyLab.

Solutions to Chapter 16 Exercises

Exercise Sixteen - 1 Solution
Inventories The $125,000 amount is both the floor and the ceiling, making this the only possible elected value. The transfer would result in a loss of $15,000 ($140,000 - $125,000), an amount that would be fully deductible as a business loss (ITA 23).

Land The floor would be the boot of $150,000 and the ceiling would be the fair market value of $350,000. Electing the minimum amount would result in a taxable capital gain of $20,000 [($150,000 - $110,000)(1/2)].

Exercise Sixteen - 2 Solution

Class 1 Property The range would be from a floor of $250,000 (the boot) to a ceiling of $475,000 (fair market value). Election of the $250,000 floor value would result in recapture of $70,000 ($220,000 - $150,000) and a taxable capital gain of $15,000 [($250,000 - $220,000)(1/2)].

Class 10 Asset The range would be from a floor of $10,000 (the boot) to a ceiling of $12,000 (fair market value). Electing the minimum value of $10,000 would result in recapture of $2,000 ($10,000 - $8,000).

Exercise Sixteen - 3 Solution

The adjusted cost base amounts would be calculated as follows:

Elected Value	$62,000
ACB Of Note (Fair Market Value)	(51,000)
Available For Shares	$11,000
ACB Of Preferred Shares*	(11,000)
ACB Of Common Shares (Residual)	Nil

*Balance available as it is less than the fair market value of $53,000.

Exercise Sixteen - 4 Solution

The adjusted cost base amounts would be calculated as follows:

Elected Value	$114,000
ACB Of Note (Fair Market Value)	(83,000)
Available For Shares	$ 31,000
ACB Of Preferred Shares*	(31,000)
ACB Of Common Shares (Residual)	Nil

*Balance available as it is less than the fair market value of $97,000.

The total PUC reduction would be calculated as follows:

Increase In Legal Stated Capital ($97,000 + $54,000)		$151,000
Less The Excess Of:		
Total Elected Value	($114,000)	
Over The Total Non-Share Consideration	83,000	(31,000)
PUC Reduction		$120,000

Note that this reduction is equal to the deferred gain on the election ($234,000- $114,000). The PUC reduction would be allocated on the basis of fair market values as follows:

Preferred Shares [($120,000)($97,000 ÷ $151,000)]	$ 77,086
Common Shares [($120,000)($54,000 ÷ $151,000)]	42,914
Total PUC Reduction	$120,000

Subsequent to applying this reduction, the remaining PUC of the two classes of shares would be as follows:

	Preferred Shares	**Common Shares**
Legal Stated Capital	$ 97,000	$54,000
PUC Reduction (From Preceding)	(77,086)	(42,914)
Total PUC	$ 19,914	$ 11,086

Note that the sum of these two figures equals $31,000 ($19,914 + $11,086), the total adjusted cost base of the preferred and common shares, as well as the difference between the elected value of $114,000 and the total non-share consideration of $83,000.

Exercise Sixteen - 5 Solution

Part 1 The adjusted cost base of all of the consideration will total the elected value of $275,000. It will be allocated as follows:

Elected Value	$ 275,000
Non-Share Consideration ($83,000 + $17,000)	(100,000)
Adjusted Cost Base Of All Shares	$ 175,000
Adjusted Cost Base Of Preferred Shares (FMV)	(125,000)
Adjusted Cost Base Of Common Shares (Residual)	$ 50,000

Part 2 The PUC of the shares issued must be reduced as follows:

Increase In Legal Stated Capital ($125,000 + $925,000)		$1,050,000
Less The Excess Of:		
Elected Value	($275,000)	
Over The Non-Share Consideration	100,000	(175,000)
PUC Reduction		$ 875,000

This PUC reduction would be split between the preferred and common shares on the basis of their fair market values:

Preferred Shares [($125,000/$1,050,000)($875,000)]	$104,167
Common Shares [($925,000/$1,050,000)($875,000)]	770,833
Total PUC Reduction	$875,000

Subsequent to applying this reduction, the remaining PUC of the two classes of shares would be as follows:

	Preferred Shares	**Common Shares**
Legal Stated Capital	$125,000	$925,000
PUC Reduction (From Preceding)	(104,167)	(770,833)
Total PUC	$ 20,833	$ 154,167

Part 3 The tax consequences of the preferred shares redemption would be as follows:

Proceeds Of Redemption	$125,000
PUC Of The Preferred Shares	(20,833)
ITA 84(3) Deemed Dividend (Non-Eligible)	$104,167

Proceeds Of Redemption	$125,000
ITA 84(3) Deemed Dividend	(104,167)
ITA 54 Deemed Proceeds Of Disposition	$ 20,833
Adjusted Cost Base	(125,000)
Capital Loss	($104,167)
Inclusion Rate	1/2
Allowable Capital Loss - Disallowed	($ 52,084)

The grossed up non-eligible dividend of $119,792 [(115%)($104,167)] would qualify for a federal dividend tax credit of $10,817 [(9/13)(15%)($104,167)]. The allowable capital loss would be disallowed because the shareholder and the corporation are affiliated.

Exercise Sixteen - 6 Solution

Using the reassessed fair market value of $110,000, the calculation of the gift is as follows:

Fair Market Value Of Property Transferred (Reassessed Value)	$110,000
Less The Greater Of:	
• FMV Of Consideration Received = $65,000 ($50,000 + $15,000)	
• Elected Amount = $50,000	(65,000)
Excess = Gift To Daughter	$ 45,000

Given this gift, the tax consequences of the transfer for Ms. Bellows are as follows:

Deemed Elected Value = Deemed Proceeds Of Disposition ($50,000 + $45,000 Gift)	$95,000
Adjusted Cost Base	(50,000)
Capital Gain	$45,000
Inclusion Rate	1/2
Taxable Capital Gain	$22,500

The adjusted cost base of her preferred shares would be calculated as follows:

Elected Value (Original)	$ 50,000
Non-Share Consideration	(50,000)
Adjusted Cost Base Of Preferred Shares	Nil

As shown in the following calculation, there would be no PUC reduction for the preferred shares issued to Ms. Bellows:

Increase In Legal Stated Capital		$ 15,000
Less Excess, If Any, Of:		
Deemed Elected Value	($95,000)	
Over Non-Share Consideration	50,000	(45,000)
PUC Reduction		Nil
PUC Of Preferred Shares ($15,000 - Nil)		$ 15,000

The fair market value of the common shares issued to the daughter is $46,000 ($110,000 Reassessed Value + $1,000 - $50,000 - $15,000).

The sale of the shares for their fair market value would result in the following taxable capital gains:

	Preferred	Common
Proceeds (Fair Market Value)	$15,000	$46,000
Adjusted Cost Base	Nil	(1,000)
Capital Gain	$15,000	$45,000
Inclusion Rate	1/2	1/2
Taxable Capital Gain	$ 7,500	$22,500

If the property had simply been sold for its $110,000 post-reassessment fair market value, there would have been a $30,000 [(1/2)($110,000- $50,000) taxable capital gain. Using ITA 85, Ms. Bellows' total taxable capital gain on the transfer and sale of the preferred shares is also $30,000 ($22,500 + $7,500). However, because the common shares held by the daughter have increased in value by the $45,000 amount of the gift, with their adjusted cost base remaining at $1,000, there is an additional $22,500 taxable capital gain on the sale of her daughter's common shares. This reflects the fact that the $45,000 amount of the gift has been subject to double taxation.

Exercise Sixteen - 7 Solution

On the original transfer in 2019, Larry would have recognized a capital gain of $73,500 [(1/2) ($270,000- $123,000)]. Based on the original estimate of the fair market value of the assets transferred, there was no ITA 15(1) benefit.

With the lower value required by the reassessment, there is excess consideration and an ITA 15(1) benefit.

Fair Market Value Of Consideration	$270,000
Reassessed Value Of The Property	(217,000)
ITA 15(1) Shareholder Benefit	$ 53,000

With the value of the property transferred reassessed at $217,000, the elected value cannot exceed this amount. There would be a revised taxable capital gain, calculated as follows:

Elected Value Of Property After Reassessment	$ 217,000
Adjusted Cost Base	(123,000)
Capital Gain	$ 94,000
Inclusion Rate	1/2
Taxable Capital Gain On Property After Reassessment	$ 47,000

As a result of the reassessment, 2019 Net Income For Tax Purposes is increased from $73,500 to $100,000 ($47,000 + $53,000), an increase of $26,500 as shown in the following table:

Taxable Capital Gain After Reassessment	$ 47,000
Shareholder Benefit After Reassessment	53,000
Reversal Of Reported Taxable Capital Gain	(73,500)
Total Addition To Net Income For Tax Purposes	$26,500

The reason for this increase is that $53,000 of the capital gain, only one-half of which would be taxed, was converted to a 100 percent taxable shareholder benefit of $53,000. The ITA 15(1) benefit of $53,000 would be added to the adjusted cost base of the non-share consideration, resulting in the following adjusted cost base for the non-share consideration:

Elected Value	$ 217,000
ITA 15(1) Shareholder Benefit	53,000
Adjusted Cost Base Of Non-Share Consideration	$270,000

Both the adjusted cost base and the PUC of the preferred shares would be nil.

Exercise Sixteen - 8 Solution

Miss Cole (an individual) has sold shares of a subject corporation to a purchasing corporation, the purchasing corporation does not deal with Miss Cole at arm's length, and the two corporations are connected subsequent to the sale. As a consequence, ITA 84.1 is applicable. Given this, the tax consequences of this transaction to Miss Cole are as follows:

Increase In Legal Stated Capital		$ 317,000
Less Excess, If Any, Of:		
PUC And ACB Of Subject Shares	($125,000)	
Over The Non-Share Consideration	450,000	Nil
PUC Reduction		$ 317,000
PUC Of New Shares ($317,000 - $317,000)		Nil
Increase In Legal Stated Capital		$ 317,000
Non-Share Consideration		450,000
Total		$ 767,000
Less The Sum Of:		
PUC And ACB Of Subject Shares	($125,000)	
PUC Reduction	(317,000)	(442,000)
ITA 84.1 Deemed Dividend (Non-Eligible)		$ 325,000
Elected Proceeds Of Disposition For Subject Shares		$ 767,000
ITA 84.1 Deemed Dividend		(325,000)
Deemed Proceeds For Capital Gains Purposes		$ 442,000
ACB Of Subject Shares		(125,000)
Capital Gain		$ 317,000
Inclusion Rate		1/2
Taxable Capital Gain		$ 158,500
ACB Of New Shares ($767,000 - $450,000)		$ 317,000

The grossed up non-eligible dividend of $373,750 [(115%)($325,000)] would qualify for a federal dividend tax credit of $33,750 [(9/13)(15%)($325,000)]. In addition, there would be a taxable capital gain of $158,500 that would be eligible for the lifetime capital gains deduction. If Miss Cole claims the deduction, she may need to pay alternative minimum tax.

Economic Analysis Miss Cole is attempting to realize a capital gain of $642,000 ($767,000 - $125,000). However, her non-share consideration was $450,000, $325,000 more than the adjusted cost base of the Cole Inc. shares. ITA 84.1 acts to convert this from a capital gain to a deemed dividend. Note that the remaining $317,000 ($642,000 - $325,000) is allowed to flow through as a capital gain. This reflects the fact that Miss Cole did not attempt to take out the full $767,000 fair market value of the shares in the form of non-share consideration.

Exercise Sixteen - 9 Solution

A deductible dividend has been paid in conjunction with an arm's length sale of shares, and it would appear that the dividend payment served to eliminate the potential capital gain on the transaction. As a consequence, ITA 55 is applicable and the tax consequences of the transaction are as follows:

Dividends Received	$750,000
Dividends Attributable To Safe Income (Tax Free)	(225,000)
Amount Deemed By ITA 55(2)(a) To Not Be A Dividend And By ITA 55(2)(c) To Be A Capital Gain	$525,000
Capital Gain On Sale Of Shares ($90,000 - $75,000)	15,000
Total Capital Gain	$540,000
Inclusion Rate	1/2
Taxable Capital Gain	$270,000

The $225,000 of dividends paid from safe income will retain its status as a dividend and will be deducted in calculating Taxable Income, resulting in no tax cost.

Solution to Self Study Problem Sixteen - 1

Part A - No Election

The disposition of a business is a capital transaction and, in the absence of special provisions, any resulting gain or loss must be treated as a capital gain or loss. With respect to the Inventories, a special provision in ITA 23 indicates that, when such assets are sold as part of the disposition of a business, the sale is deemed to be in the ordinary course of carrying on business and any resulting gain or loss is considered business in nature. ITA 23 automatically applies in the disposition of a business and no election is required on the part of the vendor.

ITA 22 provides for a similar treatment of Accounts Receivable. However, a joint election by the vendor and purchaser is required before this business income treatment is applicable. In the absence of this election, losses on Accounts Receivable are treated as capital losses.

If the assets are transferred at fair market values, the Taxable Income resulting from the transfer can be calculated as follows:

Inventories - Business Income ($88,000 - $73,000)	$15,000
Furniture And Fixtures - Recaptured CCA ($45,000 - $38,000)	7,000
Capital Gain On Goodwill [(1/2)($150,000 - Nil)]	75,000
Taxable Income	$ 97,000

There is also an allowable capital loss of $3,000 [(1/2)($51,000 - $45,000)] on the disposition of the Accounts Receivable. However, it is a superficial loss in that the property is re-acquired within 30 days by an affiliated person (the new corporation would be affiliated with Ms. Flack). ITA 40(2)(g) deems such losses to be nil. This loss would be added to the tax cost of the Accounts Receivable on the corporation's books.

Part B - ITA 22 And ITA 85 Elections

The cash is not eligible to be transferred under ITA 85, but can be transferred to the corporation without a rollover. All of the other assets can be transferred at elected values under ITA 85. Under the provisions of this Section, the tax consequences would be as follows:

Accounts Receivable If the Accounts Receivable are transferred under ITA 85, the maximum value that can be elected is the fair market value of $45,000. This will result in a capital loss of $6,000 (allowable amount of $3,000). However, this loss will be disallowed under ITA 40(2)(g) because the transfer is to a corporation that will be controlled by Ms. Flack.

Inventories The Inventories can be transferred at an elected value of $73,000, resulting in no Taxable Income on the transfer.

Furniture And Fixtures The Furniture And Fixtures can be transferred at their UCC of $38,000, resulting in no Taxable Income on the transfer.

Goodwill The Goodwill can be transferred at a nominal value of $1, resulting in no significant Taxable Income on the transfer.

An alternative with respect to the Accounts Receivable would be to transfer these assets under the provisions of ITA 22. If Ms. Flack and her corporation were to make this joint election, the $6,000 loss resulting from transferring these assets to the corporation would be fully deductible as a business loss. As it is not a capital loss, it would not be disallowed and Ms. Flack would be able to deduct the full $6,000 against any other source of income in the year of transfer. As ITA 22 is a joint election, the corporation would have to include the $6,000 in income, but could then deduct actual bad debts as they occur. Using the ITA 22 election is the preferable approach to the transfer of these Accounts Receivable.

Solution to Self Study Problem Sixteen - 2

Part A - Assets To Be Transferred

Of the assets in the Balance Sheet, Cash is not among the eligible assets listed in ITA 85(1.1). This is of no consequence as the tax value of cash is always equal to its carrying value and can be transferred to the corporation without a rollover.

Accounts Receivable could be transferred under Section 85, but are usually transferred to the corporation under the provisions of ITA 22. ITA 22 is used for two reasons. First, it means that any loss on the transfer will be a fully deductible business loss, rather than a capital loss that will be disallowed on a transfer to a corporation controlled by the transferor under ITA 40(2)(g). In addition, the use of the ITA 22 joint election to make the transfer will permit the transferee corporation to deduct any additional bad debts as business losses, rather than capital losses, only one-half of which would be deductible.

There is a potential terminal loss on the transfer of the equipment as the fair market value of the equipment is less than the UCC of the class. Given this, ITA 13(21.2) indicates that ITA 85 does not apply and the proceeds of disposition are deemed to be the UCC amount thereby disallowing the terminal loss.

Part B - Minimum Transfer Values

The minimum transfer values for the assets to be included in the rollover would be as follows:

Inventories (Cost)	$261,000
Land (Adjusted Cost Base)	196,000
Building (UCC)	103,600
Equipment (UCC)	67,000
Goodwill (Nominal Value)	1

Note The Goodwill has been given a nominal elected value to ensure that it is specifically included in the transfer. A failure to do this could result in the Goodwill being assessed on the basis of a transfer at fair market value.

Part C - Tax Consequences

The tax consequences of the asset transfers with respect to both Ms. Speaks and Speaks Inc. can be described as follows:

Inventories The cost of the Inventories to Speaks Inc. would be the transfer price of $261,000. As this was the cost of the Inventories, there would be no tax consequence to Ms. Speaks.

Land The cost of the Land to Speaks Inc. would be the transfer price of $196,000. As this was the adjusted cost base of the Land, there would be no tax consequence to Ms. Speaks.

Building The capital cost of the Building to Speaks Inc. would be $155,500, and Speaks Inc. would be deemed to have taken CCA in the amount of $51,900. As the net value of the transfer is equal to UCC, there would be no tax consequence to Ms. Speaks.

Equipment The capital cost of the Equipment to Speaks Inc. would be $222,000, and Speaks Inc. would be deemed to have taken CCA in the amount of $155,000. As the net value of the transfer is equal to UCC, there would be no tax consequence to Ms. Speaks.

Goodwill The cost of the Goodwill to Speaks Inc. will be $1. In Ms. Speak's tax records, the proceeds of $1 will be subtracted from Class 14.1, leaving a negative balance in that Class. This amount will be treated as recapture and included in Ms. Speak's income. The $1 will also be added to Class 14.1, restoring the balance to nil. In the Speaks Inc.'s records, the $1 will be added to Class 14.1.

Solution to Self Study Problem Sixteen - 3

Approach 1

Immediate Tax Consequences The $230,000 elected value becomes the proceeds of disposition. As this amount is equal to the adjusted cost base of the land, there are no immediate tax consequences resulting from the transfer.

ACB Of The Land The ACB of the land to the corporation would be equal to the elected value of $230,000.

ACB Of Shares The ACB of the shares issued by the corporation would be calculated as follows:

Elected Value	$230,000
Fair Market Value Of Non-Share Consideration	Nil
ACB Of Shares	$230,000

PUC Of Shares   The required PUC reduction and resulting PUC would be calculated as follows:

Legal Stated Capital Of Shares		$ 660,000
Less Excess, If Any, Of:		
Elected Value	($230,000)	
Over The Non-Share Consideration	Nil	(230,000)
PUC Reduction		$ 430,000
PUC Of Shares ($660,000 - $430,000)		$ 230,000

Approach 2

Immediate Tax Consequences   The elected value of $500,000 becomes proceeds of disposition. As this value exceeds the $230,000 adjusted cost base of the land, there is a taxable capital gain of $135,000 [(1/2)($500,000 - $230,000).

ACB Of The Land   The ACB of the land to the corporation will be equal to the elected value of $500,000.

ACB Of Shares   The ACB of the shares issued by the corporation would be calculated as follows:

Elected Value	$500,000
Fair Market Value Of Non-Share Consideration	Nil
ACB Of Shares	$500,000

PUC Of Shares   The required PUC reduction and resulting PUC would be calculated as follows:

Legal Stated Capital Of Shares		$ 660,000
Less Excess, If Any, Of:		
Elected Value	($500,000)	
Over The Non-Share Consideration	Nil	(500,000)
PUC Reduction		$ 160,000
PUC Of Shares ($660,000 - $160,000)		$ 500,000

Approach 3

Immediate Tax Consequences   The elected value of $500,000 becomes proceeds of disposition. As this value exceeds the $230,000 adjusted cost base of the land, there is a taxable capital gain of $135,000 [(1/2)($500,000 - $230,000)].

ACB Of The Land   The ACB of the land to the corporation will be equal to the elected value of $500,000.

ACB Of Shares   The ACB of the shares issued by the corporation would be calculated as follows:

Elected Value	$500,000
Fair Market Value Of Non-Share Consideration	(500,000)
ACB Of Shares	Nil

PUC Of Shares   The required PUC reduction and resulting PUC would be calculated as follows:

Legal Stated Capital Of Shares		$160.000
Less Excess, If Any, Of:		
Elected Value	($500,000)	
Over The Non-Share Consideration	500,000	Nil
PUC Reduction		$160,000
PUC Of Shares ($160,000 - $160,000)		Nil

Solution to Self Study Problem Sixteen - 4

Part A - Adjusted Cost Base Of Consideration

The adjusted cost base for each item of consideration, under the three alternatives, would be calculated as follows:

	Alternative		
	One	**Two**	**Three**
Elected Transfer Price	$225,000	$225,000	$225,000
ACB - Boot	(150,000)	(175,000)	(210,000)
Available For Preferred And Common Shares	$ 75,000	$ 50,000	$ 15,000
ACB - Preferred Shares	(50,000)	(50,000)	N/A
ACB - Common Shares (Residual)	$ 25,000	N/A	$ 15,000

Part B - Legal Stated Capital And PUC

The legal stated capital for the two classes of shares would be as follows:

	Alternative		
	One	**Two**	**Three**
Preferred Shares	$ 50,000	$450,000	Nil
Common Shares	425,000	Nil	$415,000
Total Legal Stated Capital	$475,000	$450,000	$415,000

The required PUC reduction would be calculated as follows:

	Alternative		
	One	**Two**	**Three**
Increase In Legal Stated Capital - All Shares (A)	$475,000	$450,000	$415,000
Elected Amount	$225,000	$225,000	$225,000
Non-Share Consideration	(150,000)	(175,000)	(210,000)
Elected Amount, Less Boot (B)	$ 75,000	$ 50,000	$ 15,000
Required PUC Reduction (A - B)	$400,000	$400,000	$400,000

Alternative One   In Alternative One, the PUC reduction would have to be split between the two classes of shares on the basis of their relative fair market values. The relevant calculation would be as follows:

Preferred Shares:	[($400,000)($50,000 ÷ $475,000)] = $42,105
Common Shares:	[($400,000)($425,000 ÷ $475,000)] = $357,895

This would leave a PUC of $7,895 for the preferred shares ($50,000 - $42,105), and a PUC of $67,105 for the common shares ($425,000 - $357,895).

Alternative Two In Alternative Two, the entire PUC reduction of $400,000 would be allocated to the preferred shares, leaving a PUC of $50,000 ($450,000 - $400,000).

Alternative Three In Alternative Three, the entire PUC reduction of $400,000 would be allocated to the common shares, leaving a PUC of $15,000 ($415,000 - $400,000).

Solution to Self Study Problem Sixteen - 5

Part A - ACB Of The Shares
The adjusted cost base of the shares would be as follows:

Total Elected Value	$ 467,000
Non-Share Consideration ($122,000 + $128,000)	(250,000)
Adjusted Cost Base Preferred And Common Shares	$ 217,000
Allocated To Preferred Shares (FMV)	(150,000)
Adjusted Cost Base Of Common Shares (Residual)	$ 67,000

Part B - PUC Of The Shares
The legal stated capital of the preferred and common shares would be their respective fair market values of $150,000 and $326,000. The PUC reduction required under ITA 85(2.1) would be calculated as follows:

Increase In Legal Stated Capital ($150,000 + $326,000)		$476,000
Less Excess Of:		
Total Elected Value	($ 467,000)	
Over The Total Non-Share Consideration	250,000	(217,000)
Reduction In Paid Up Capital		$259,000

Note that this total reduction is equal to the deferred gain on the election ($726,000 - $467,000). The PUC reduction would be allocated on the basis of fair market values as follows:

Preferred Shares [($259,000)($150,000 ÷ $476,000)]	$ 81,618
Common Shares [($259,000)($326,000 ÷ $476,000)]	177,382
Total PUC Reduction	$259,000

Subsequent to applying this reduction, the remaining PUC of the two classes of shares would be as follows:

	Preferred Shares	Common Shares
Legal Stated Capital	$ 150,000	$326,000
PUC Reduction	(81,618)	(177,382)
PUC	$ 68,382	$ 148,618

Note that the combined PUC of the two classes of shares is $217,000 ($68,382 + $148,618). This is the same amount as the combined ACB of the two classes of shares ($150,000 + $67,000).

Part C - Tax Consequences Of Redemption

The tax consequences to Mr. Lardner, if the corporation redeemed both classes of shares at their respective fair market values, would be calculated as follows:

	Preferred Shares	Common Shares
Redemption Proceeds	$ 150,000	$ 326,000
PUC (See Preceding Calculations)	(68,382)	(148,618)
ITA 84(3) Deemed Dividend	$ 81,618	$ 177,382
Redemption Proceeds	$ 150,000	$ 326,000
ITA 84(3) Deemed Dividend	(81,618)	(177,382)
Deemed Proceeds Of Disposition	$ 68,382	$ 148,618
Adjusted Cost Base (Part A)	(150,000)	(67,000)
Capital Gain (Loss)	($ 81,618)	$ 81,618

Mr. Lardner would have a deemed non-eligible dividend of $259,000 ($81,618 + $177,382). The grossed up non-eligible dividend of $297,850[(115%)($259,000)] would qualify for a federal dividend tax credit of $26,896[(9/13)(15%)($259,000)]. He has a net capital gain of nil ($81,618 - $81,618).

Solution to Self Study Problem Sixteen - 6

Part A - Tax Consequences Of Transfer

With respect to the land, the $250,000 elected value will be both the proceeds of disposition to Mr. Bodin and the adjusted cost base to the corporation. As the elected value is equal to Mr. Bodin's adjusted cost base, there will be no tax consequences resulting from the transfer.

The elected value and proceeds of disposition for the building is $750,000, an amount that is less than its capital cost but more than its UCC. This will result in Mr. Bodin having to report recapture of $116,400 ($750,000- $633,600). The corporation's tax value will be $750,000. However, the corporation will retain the original capital cost of $1,100,000 ($1,350,000 - $250,000) for recapture and capital gains calculations. The $350,000 difference will be deemed to be CCA taken.

Part B - Adjusted Cost Base Of The Consideration

The adjusted cost base of all consideration received by Mr. Bodin will be the total elected value of $1,000,000 ($250,000 + $750,000). It will be allocated as follow:

Total Elected Value	$1,000,000
Total Non-Share Consideration	
($450,000 Assumed Mortgage + $400,000 New Debt)	(850,000)
Adjusted Cost Base Of Common Shares	$ 150,000

Part C - PUC Of The New Shares

The calculation of PUC would be as follows:

Increase In Legal Stated Capital (Fair Market Value)		$950,000
Less Excess Of:		
Elected Amount	($1,000,000)	
Over The Total Non-Share Consideration	850,000	(150,000)
Reduction In PUC		$800,000

The PUC of the common shares would be reduced to $150,000 ($950,000 - $800,000).

Part D - Sale Of Common Shares

The increase in Net Income For Tax Purposes from a sale of the shares for $950,000 would be as follows:

Proceeds Of Disposition	$950,000
Adjusted Cost Base	(150,000)
Capital Gain	$800,000
Inclusion Rate	1/2
Taxable Capital Gain	$400,000

As Taxable Income consequences are not required, the effect of the lifetime capital gains deduction has not been considered.

Part E - Redemption

The tax consequences of a redemption for $950,000 would be as follows:

Proceeds From Redemption	$950,000
PUC	(150,000)
ITA 84(3) Deemed Dividend (Non-Eligible)	$800,000

There would be no capital gain on this redemption as shown in the following calculation:

Redemption Proceeds	$950,000
ITA 84(3) Deemed Dividend	(800,000)
Deemed Proceeds Of Disposition	$150,000
Adjusted Cost Base	(150,000)
Capital Gain	Nil

The amount to be included in Net Income For Tax Purposes would be $920,000, the $800,000 deemed non-eligible dividend grossed up by 15 percent.

There would also be a federal dividend tax credit of $83,077 [(9/13)(15%)($800,000)]. However, as the problem only asks for the amounts to be included in Net Income For Tax Purposes, this is not a required part of the solution.

Solution to Self Study Problem Sixteen - 7

Part A - Assets To Be Transferred And Their Elected Values

Of the assets in Mr. Danforth's Balance Sheet accounts, Cash and Prepayments are not among the eligible assets listed in ITA 85(1.1). This is of no consequence as the tax value of these assets is generally equal to their carrying values.

The fair market value of the Accounts Receivable is $1,250 ($13,750 - $12,500) less than their face value, reflecting Mr. Danforth's estimate of accounts that will not be collected. While these Accounts Receivable could be transferred under Section 85, they are usually transferred under the provisions of ITA 22. ITA 22 is used for two reasons. First, it means that the $1,250 loss on the transfer will be a fully deductible business loss, rather than a capital loss that will be disallowed on a transfer to a corporation controlled by the transferor. In addition, the use of the ITA 22 joint election will permit the transferee corporation to deduct actual bad debts as they occur as business expenses, rather than as capital losses.

With respect to Inventories, their fair market value and their carrying value are equal. Given this, there is no reason to transfer them under the provisions of Section 85 and they should be sold to Danforth Inc. for their fair market value.

With respect to the Land, there is an unrealized capital loss which will be disallowed on a transfer to an affiliated person. This is the case, without regard to whether Mr. Danforth makes the transfer directly or under the provisions of ITA 85(1). Given this, there is no reason to use ITA 85(1) for this transfer and it should be sold to Danforth Inc. for its fair market value.

There is a potential terminal loss on the transfer of the equipment. Given this, ITA 13(21.2) indicates that ITA 85 does not apply and the proceeds of disposition are deemed to be the UCC amount thereby disallowing the terminal loss.

If we assume that Mr. Danforth chooses to make the ITA 22 election, the following assets will not be transferred under the provisions of ITA 85(1):

Cash (Not Eligible)	$ 2,500
Accounts Receivable (ITA 22 Election Used)	12,500
Inventories (Cost = FMV)	17,500
Prepayments (Cost = FMV)	7,500
Land (Disallowed Capital Loss)	77,500
Equipment (UCC)	20,000
Total	$137,500

In order to minimize capital gains arising on the transfer of proprietorship assets and liabilities to the corporation, the elected price should be the lower of the tax value or the fair market value. The appropriate elected values for the assets that will be transferred using ITA 85 are indicated in the schedule that follows:

	Tax Values	Fair Market Value	Elected Value
Temporary Investments	$27,500	$ 37,500	$27,500
Buildings	70,000	125,000	70,000
Goodwill (See Note)	Nil	117,500	1
Total Assets Transferred	$97,500	$280,000	$97,501

Note It is prudent to add at least a nominal elected value for goodwill. A failure to do so could result in the application of ITA 69, with the transfer assessed to the transferor at fair market value.

Part B - Maximum Non-Share Consideration

The liabilities that are assumed by the corporation are considered to be a part of the non-share consideration that is received by the transferor. The maximum amount of non-share consideration that can be received by Mr. Danforth on a tax free basis is $97,501. The non-share consideration would be made up of the corporation's assumption of the proprietorship's liabilities of $20,000, plus debt issued by the new corporation in the amount of $77,501.

Part C - Capital Gain On Sale Of Shares

The adjusted cost base of the shares would be nil, as per the following calculation:

Elected Value	$97,501
Non-Share Consideration Received	97,501
Adjusted Cost Base Of Shares	Nil

Given this, the taxable capital gain on the sale of the shares would be calculated as follows:

Proceeds Of Disposition	$208,000
Adjusted Cost Base Of Shares	Nil
Capital Gain	$208,000
Inclusion Rate	1/2
Taxable Capital Gain	$ 104,000

Since Danforth Inc. is a qualified small business corporation and Mr. Danforth has no CNIL, the taxable capital gain arising on the disposition of its shares would be eligible for the lifetime capital gains deduction. This means that he will be able to deduct an amount equal to the entire taxable capital gain in calculating his Taxable Income. However, use of his lifetime capital gains deduction to eliminate the taxable capital gain could result in a liability for alternative minimum tax.

Solution to Self Study Problem Sixteen - 8

Part A

The following table shows that the post-reassessment fair market value of the assets transferred to the corporation exceeds the fair market value of the consideration received:

Fair Market Value Of Assets Transferred ($1,578,000 + $430,000 - $350,000)	$1,658,000
Less The Greater Of:	
• Fair Market Value Of Consideration Received ($160,000 + $947,000 + $471,000) = $1,578,000	
• Elected Value = $1,107,000	(1,578,000)
Excess = Gift	$ 80,000

As Sarah Cheng is the only common shareholder of the new corporation, it is clear that Mr. Cheng has made a gift to his daughter. As a consequence, the amount of the gift must be added to the elected value in the rollover to arrive at a deemed proceeds of disposition. As the reassessment was on the non-depreciable capital asset land, the result will be a capital gain. This results in the following tax consequences for Mr. Cheng:

Deemed Elected Value = Deemed Proceeds Of Disposition ($1,107,000 + $80,000)	$1,187,000
Tax Values Of Assets Transferred	(1,107,000)
Capital Gain	$ 80,000
Inclusion Rate	1/2
Taxable Capital Gain	$ 40,000

The adjusted cost base of the preferred shares received by Mr. Cheng would be calculated as follows:

Elected Value (Original)	$1,107,000
Non-Share Consideration ($160,000 + $947,000)	(1,107,000)
Adjusted Cost Base Of Preferred Shares	Nil

The required PUC reduction and resulting PUC would be calculated as follows:

Increase In Legal Stated Capital		$471,000
Excess, If Any, Of:		
Deemed Elected Value		
($1,107,000 + $80,000)	($1,187,000)	
Over Non-Share Consideration	1,107,000	(80,000)
PUC Reduction		$391,000
PUC Of Preferred Shares ($471,000 - $391,000)		$ 80,000

Part B

The tax consequences to Mr. Cheng of having his shares redeemed would be as follows:

Proceeds Of Redemption	$471,000
PUC Of Shares	(80,000)
ITA 84(3) Deemed Dividend	$391,000
Proceeds Of Disposition	$471,000
ITA 84(3) Deemed Dividend	(391,000)
Adjusted Proceeds Of Disposition	$ 80,000
Adjusted Cost Base Of Shares	Nil
Capital Gain (Loss)	$ 80,000
Inclusion Rate	1/2
Taxable Capital Gain	$ 40,000

This non-eligible deemed dividend would be grossed up to $449,650[(115%)($391,000)] of Taxable Income and will generate a federal dividend tax credit of $ 40,604[(9/13)(15%)($391,000)].

Part C

The tax consequences of Sarah selling her shares would be as follows:

Proceeds Of Disposition	$90,000
Adjusted Cost Base Of Shares	(10,000)
Capital Gain	$80,000
Inclusion Rate	1/2
Taxable Capital Gain	$40,000

Economic Analysis (Not Required)

If Mr. Cheng had simply sold his business assets for their post reassessment fair market value, he would have had income as in the following calculation:

Fair Market Value After Reassessment ($1,578,000 + $80,000)	$1,658,000
Tax Values Of Assets	(1,107,000)
Income (Capital Gains And Recapture)	$ 551,000

Using the procedures in the problem, the results for Mr. Cheng are as follows:

Capital Gain At Transfer	$ 80,000
ITA 84(3) Deemed Dividend	391,000
Capital Gain On Redemption	80,000
Total	$551,000

While the composition of the income is different, the overall result is the same $551,000 that would have resulted from a simple sale of the listed business assets.

However, there is an impact on Sarah. The $80,000 gift added to the value of her shares with no corresponding increase in the adjusted cost base of the shares. As a result, when she sells the shares, there is a capital gain. In effect, the $80,000 amount of the gift will be subject to double taxation.

Overall, the procedures used in this situation resulted in Mr. Cheng being taxed on the same amount of income as would have been the case without the ITA 85(1) rollover. In addition, Sarah paid taxes on an additional capital gain of $80,000 ($40,000 taxable amount) that would not have occurred if Mr. Cheng had heeded the warnings of his accountant and used a valid fair market value for the land.

Solution to Self Study Problem Sixteen - 9

Part A

The original values used in the transfer resulted in a taxable capital gain of $162,500. Using these values did not indicate any excess consideration. However, with the reassessment value of $650,000 there is an excess, resulting in the following ITA 15(1) benefit:

Fair Market Value Of Consideration	$800,000
Reassessed Fair Market Value Of The Property	(650,000)
ITA 15(1) Shareholder Benefit	$ 150,000

With the value of the transferred property reassessed at $650,000, the elected value cannot exceed this amount. Based on this, there would be a revised taxable capital gain on the transfer, calculated as follows:

Elected Value Of Property After Reassessment	$650,000
Adjusted Cost Base	(475,000)
Capital Gain	$175,000
Inclusion Rate	1/2
Taxable Capital Gain On Property After Reassessment	$ 87,500

The net effect of the reassessment would be calculated as follows

Taxable Capital Gain After Reassessment	$ 87,500
Shareholder Benefit After Reassessment	150,000
Reversal Of Reported Taxable Capital Gain	(162,500)
Net Addition To Net Income For Tax Purposes	$ 75,000

The reason for this increase is that $75,000 ($162,500 - $87,500) of the original taxable capital gain was converted to a 100 percent taxable shareholder benefit of $150,000.

Part B

Because a $150,000 benefit will be included in Mel's income as a result of a property acquisition, ITA 52(1) requires that this amount be added to the adjusted cost base of the non-share consideration. Given this, the adjusted cost base of the non-share consideration would be as follows:

Revised Elected Value	$650,000
ITA 15(1) Shareholder Benefit	150,000
Adjusted Cost Base Of Non-Share Consideration	$800,000

Both the adjusted cost base and the PUC of the preferred shares issued is nil.

Solution to Self Study Problem Sixteen - 10

Part A - Tax Consequences Of Proposed Plan

Ms. Chadwick's plan involves the disposition of shares of a corporation resident in Canada to a corporation with which she does not deal at arm's length (Mr. Borque would be considered Ms. Chadwick's common-law partner.). Subsequent to the transaction, the two corporations are connected (Borque Inc. controls Norton Ltd.). Given these facts, the provisions of ITA 84.1 apply to this transaction.

The required calculations begin with the PUC reduction under ITA 84.1(1)(a):

Increase In Legal Stated Capital Of Borque Inc.		$1,590,000
Less The Excess, If Any, Of:		
Greater Of PUC And ACB Of Norton Ltd. Shares	($225,000)	
Over The Fair Market Value Of The Boot	875,000	Nil
PUC Reduction		$1,590,000
PUC After Reduction ($1,590,000 - $1,590,000)		Nil

The nil PUC reflects the fact that all of the PUC of the Norton Ltd. shares was taken out as non-share consideration.

The deemed non-eligible dividend under ITA 84.1(1)(b), and federal dividend tax credit, would be calculated as follows:

Increase In Legal Stated Capital Of Borque Inc.		$1,590,000
Fair Market Value Of Boot		875,000
Total		$2,465,000
PUC Of Norton Ltd. Shares	($ 225,000)	
PUC Reduction Under ITA 84.1(1)(a)	(1,590,000)	(1,815,000)
Deemed Dividend Under ITA 84.1(1)(b)		$ 650,000
Gross Up At 15 Percent		97,500
Taxable Non-Eligible Dividend		$ 747,500
Federal Dividend Tax Credit [(9/13)(15%)($650,000)]		$ 67,500

You will note that, because of the application of ITA 84.1, no capital gain eligible for the life-time capital gains deduction results from this transaction. This can be seen in the following calculation:

Proceeds Before Adjustment Of Norton Shares (Elected Amount)	$875,000
ITA 84.1(1)(b) Deemed Dividend	(650,000)
Adjusted Proceeds Of Disposition (ITA 54)	$225,000
Adjusted Cost Base Of Shares	(225,000)
Capital Gain	Nil

Part B - An Improved Solution

The approach suggested by Ms. Chadwick will not be successful in producing the required $650,000 capital gain. The reason that this approach cannot be successful is that Ms. Chadwick is trying to take out non-share consideration in excess of the $225,000 PUC and ACB of her Norton Ltd. shares. Fortunately, this situation can be corrected by reducing the amount of non-share consideration to $225,000. In conjunction with this reduction in the amount of non-share consideration, the PUC and fair market value of the retractable preferred shares will have to be increased to $2,240,000, so that the total fair market value of the consideration received by Ms. Chadwick equals $2,465,000, the fair market value of the Norton Ltd. shares given up in the transaction. Using this approach, the required PUC reduction under ITA 84.1(1)(b) would be as follows:

Increase In Legal Stated Capital Of Borque Inc.		$2,240,000
Less The Excess, If Any, Of:		
Greater Of PUC And ACB Of Norton Ltd. Shares	($225,000)	
Over The Fair Market Value Of The Boot	225,000	Nil
PUC Reduction		$2,240,000
PUC After Reduction ($2,240,000 - $2,240,000)		Nil

The deemed non-eligible dividend under ITA 84.1(1)(b) would be calculated as follows:

Increase In Legal Stated Capital Of Borque Inc.		$2,240,000
Fair Market Value Of Boot		225,000
Total		$2,465,000
PUC Of Norton Ltd. Shares	($ 225,000)	
PUC Reduction Under 84.1(1)(b)	(2,240,000)	(2,465,000)
Deemed Dividend Under ITA 84.1(1)(b)		Nil

Given the preceding, the capital gain resulting from this transaction is calculated as follows:

Proceeds Before Adjustment Of Norton Ltd. Shares (Elected Amount)	$875,000
ITA 84.1(1)(b) Deemed Dividend	Nil
Proceeds Of Disposition	$875,000
Adjusted Cost Base Of Norton Ltd. Shares	(225,000)
Capital Gain	$650,000

There would be no tax consequences using this approach, except for the possibility that the alternative minimum tax may be payable. While there would be a $650,000 capital gain, it could be completely eliminated by using Ms. Chadwick's lifetime capital gains deduction.

Part C - Sale Of Shares

As in the other Parts of this question, there is a sale of shares by an individual to a corporation with which the individual is not at arm's length. This means that ITA 84.1 is still applicable.

As no new Borque Inc. shares are issued, no PUC reduction is required.

The ITA 84.1(1)(b) deemed non-eligible dividend would be calculated as follows:

Increase In Legal Stated Capital Of Borque Inc.		Nil
Non-Share Consideration Of Shares Sold		
[(6,530 Shares)($2,465,000 ÷ 22,500)]		$715,398
Total		$715,398
PUC Of Norton Ltd. Shares [(6,530 Shares)($10)]	($65,300)	
PUC Reduction Under ITA 84.1(1)(a)	Nil	(65,300)
Deemed Dividend Under ITA 84.1(1)(b)		$650,098

The taxable non-eligible dividend of $747,613[(115%)($650,098)] would qualify for a federal dividend tax credit of $67,510[(9/13)(15%)($650,098)]. Given this deemed dividend, the sale of shares will not result in the desired capital gain. This can be seen in the following calculation:

Unadjusted Proceeds Of Disposition	
[(6,530 Shares)($2,465,000 ÷ 22,500)]	$715,398
Deemed Dividend Under ITA 84.1(1)(b)	(650,098)
Adjusted Proceeds Of Disposition	$ 65,300
Adjusted Cost Base Of Shares [(6,530 Shares)($10)]	(65,300)
Capital Gain	Nil

Solution to Self Study Problem Sixteen - 11

Part A

In the absence of ITA 55(2), the entire $2,000,000 dividend could be deducted in the determination of Lardley's Taxable Income. However, as a dividend has been paid in conjunction with a disposition of property to an arm's length party, ITA 55(2) is applicable. As a result, the following calculation is required for the dividend received by Lardley:

Dividends Received From Domas	$ 2,000,000
Dividend Attributable To Safe Income (Tax Free)	(565,000)
Amount Deemed By ITA 55(2)(a) To Not Be A Dividend	
And By ITA 55(2)(c) To Be A Capital Gain	$ 1,435,000
Inclusion Rate	1/2
Taxable Capital Gain	$ 717,500

As shown, $565,000 of the funds would be received by Lardley as a dividend from safe income and could be deducted under ITA 112, resulting in no tax cost. However, the remainder would be converted to deemed proceeds of disposition, resulting in a taxable capital gain of $717,500.

Part B

In the absence of ITA 55(2), the results for Lardley would be as follows:

Proceeds Of Redemption	$2,300,000
Paid Up Capital Of Preferred Shares	(300,000)
ITA 84(3) Deemed Dividend	$2,000,000
Proceeds Of Disposition	$2,300,000
ITA 84(3) Dividend	(2,000,000)
Adjusted Proceeds Of Disposition	$ 300,000
Adjusted Cost Base	(300,000)
Capital Gain	Nil

As the ITA 84(3) dividend can be deducted in the determination of Lardley's Taxable Income, the Company would have succeeded in disposing of the Domas shares without tax consequences.

However, as the redemption was in conjunction with a disposition of the property to an arm's length purchaser, ITA 55(2) alters this result. ITA 55(2)(a) would deem $1,435,000 ($2,000,000, less the Safe Income of $565,000) of the ITA 84(3) dividend to not be a dividend. ITA 55(2)(b) would then deem the $1,435,000 to be proceeds of disposition. The result would be a capital gain determined as follows:

Adjusted Proceeds Of Disposition	$ 300,000
Deemed Proceeds Of Disposition	1,435,000
Total Proceeds Of Disposition	$1,735,000
Adjusted Cost Base	(300,000)
Capital Gain	$1,435,000
Inclusion Rate	1/2
Taxable Capital Gain	$ 717,500

The overall result would be the same as in Part A. That is, a $565,000 tax free dividend and a taxable capital gain of $717,500.

Chapter 17 Learning Objectives

After completing Chapter 17, you should be able to:

1. Identify situations where the ITA 85.1 rollover provision is applicable (paragraph [P hereafter] 17-1 to 17-13).
2. Identify situations where the ITA 86 rollover provision is applicable (P 17-14).
3. Apply the ITA 86 rollover procedures to freeze an estate (P 17-15 to 17-16).
4. List the conditions that must be met in order to use the ITA 86 rollover provision (P 17-17 to 17-18).
5. Explain the procedures that are required in implementing an ITA 86 rollover (P 17-19 to 17-29).

6. Identify situations where the ITA 86(2) benefit rule is applicable and apply the required procedures to specific examples (P 17-30 to 17-40).
7. Describe the major tax planning considerations related to the use of ITA 86 (P 17-41 to 17-46).
8. Explain the nature of an ITA 87 amalgamation (P 17-47 to 17-50).
9. Describe the position of the amalgamated company subsequent to an ITA 87 amalgamation (P 17-51 to 17-55).
10. Describe the position of the shareholders of the amalgamated company subsequent to an ITA 87 amalgamation (P 17-56).

11. Identify the specific considerations involved in vertical amalgamations (P 17-57).
12. Explain the "asset bump-up" that is available under both ITA 87 and ITA 88(1) (P 17-58 to 17-61).
13. Explain both the non-tax considerations and tax planning considerations related to ITA 87 amalgamations (P 17-62 to 17-65).
14. Explain the nature of an ITA 88(1) winding-up of a 90 percent owned subsidiary (P 17-66 to 17-73).
15. Apply the procedures for recording the assets acquired by the parent company in an ITA 88(1) winding-up of a 90 percent owned subsidiary (P 17-74 to 17-84).

16. Apply the procedures required for the disposition of shares that occurs in the winding-up of a 90 percent owned subsidiary (P 17-85 and 17-86).
17. Compare the results of applying ITA 87 vs. the results of applying ITA 88(1) and any associated tax planning issues (P 17-87 to 17-93).
18. Apply the procedures required in an ITA 88(2) winding-up of a Canadian corporation (P 17-94 to 17-107).
19. Explain the procedures used under ITA 51 when there is a conversion of a corporation's preferred shares or debt securities (P 17-108 to 17-114).
20. Explain the basic alternatives for the sale of an incorporated business (P 17-115 to 17-116).

21. Explain the provisions relating to restrictive covenants (a.k.a. non-competition agreements) (P 17-117 to 17-120).
22. Describe the procedures used when the individual assets of a business are sold (P 17-121 to 17-123).
23. Describe the procedures used when the assets of a business are sold as a going concern (P 17-124 to 17-133).
24. Describe the procedures used when the shares of a business are sold (P 17-134 to 17-138).
25. Compare an offer to purchase the shares of a business and an offer to purchase its assets and determine the preferable alternative (P 17-139 to 17-153).

How to Work Through Chapter 17

We recommend the following approach in dealing with the material in this chapter:

Introduction
- Read paragraph 17-1 to 17-2 (in the textbook).

Share For Share Exchanges (ITA 85.1)
- Read paragraph 17-3 to 17-11.
- Do Exercise Seventeen-1 (in the textbook) and check the solution in this Study Guide.
- Read paragraph 17-12 to 17-13.
- Do Self Study Problems Seventeen-1 and Seventeen-2, which are available on MyLab, and check the solutions in this Study Guide.

Exchange Of Shares In A Reorganization (ITA 86)
- Read paragraph 17-14 to 17-29.
- Do Exercises Seventeen-2 to Seventeen-4 and check the solutions in this Study Guide.
- Do Self Study Problem Seventeen-3 and check the solution in this Study Guide.

Gift To Related Party - ITA 86(2) (Benefit Rule)
- Read paragraph 17-30 to 17-40.
- Do Exercise Seventeen-5 and check the solution in this Study Guide.

Using ITA 86 - Practical Considerations And Tax Planning Considerations
- Read paragraph 17-41 to 17-46.
- Do Self Study Problems Seventeen-4 and Seventeen-5 and check the solutions in this Study Guide.

Amalgamations (ITA 87)
- Read paragraph 17-47 to 17-65.
- Do Exercise Seventeen-6 and check the solution in this Study Guide.

Winding-Up Of A 90 Percent Owned Subsidiary
- Read paragraph 17-66 to 17-81.
- Do Exercise Seventeen-7 and check the solution in this Study Guide.
- Read paragraph 17-82 to 17-84.
- Do Exercise Seventeen-8 and check the solution in this Study Guide.
- Read paragraph 17-85 to 17-86.

Tax Planning Considerations - Amalgamation Vs. Winding-Up
- Read paragraph 17-87 to 17-93.
- Do Self Study Problem Seventeen-6 and check the solution in this Study Guide.

Winding-Up Of A Canadian Corporation
- Read paragraph 17-94 to 17-107.
- Do Exercise Seventeen-9 and check the solution in this Study Guide.
- Do Self Study Problem Seventeen-7 and check the solution in this Study Guide.

Convertible Properties
- Read paragraph 17-108 to 17-114.

Sale Of An Incorporated Business - Assets Vs. Shares
- Read paragraph 17-115 to 17-153.
- Do Self Study Problem Seventeen-8 and check the solution in this Study Guide.

To Complete This Chapter
- If you would like more practice in problem solving, do the Supplementary Self Study Problems for the chapter. These problems and solutions are available on MyLab.
- Review the Key Terms Used In This Chapter in the textbook at the end of Chapter 17.
- Consult the Glossary for the meaning of any key terms you do not know.
- Test yourself with the Chapter 17 Glossary Flashcards available on MyLab.
- Ensure you have achieved the Chapter 17 Learning Objectives listed in this Study Guide.
- As a review, we recommend you view the PowerPoint presentation for Chapter 17 that is on MyLab.

Practice Examination
- Write the Practice Examination for Chapter 17 that is on MyLab. Mark your examination using the Practice Examination Solution that is on MyLab.

Solutions to Chapter 17 Exercises

Exercise Seventeen - 1 Solution
This transaction involves a share for share exchange that meets the conditions of ITA 85.1. Unless Ms. Alee opts out of this rollover provision in her income tax return, the tax consequences of this transaction for Ms. Alee would be as follows:

- Ms. Alee would be deemed to have disposed of her Aayee Ltd. shares at a value equal to their adjusted cost base of $450,000. As a consequence, there would be no capital gain on the disposition.
- Ms. Alee would be deemed to have acquired her Global Outreach Inc. shares at a cost equal to the adjusted cost base of the Aayee Ltd. shares, or $450,000.
- The adjusted cost base of the Aayee Ltd. shares that have been acquired by Global Outreach Inc. would be deemed to be the lesser of their fair market value and their Paid Up Capital. In this case, the $450,000 PUC amount is the lower figure.
- The PUC of the Global Outreach Inc. shares that have been issued to Ms. Alee would be $450,000, the PUC of the Aayee Ltd. shares that were given up

Exercise Seventeen - 2 Solution
The required PUC reduction on the redeemable preferred shares would be calculated as follows:

Increase In Legal Stated Capital		$ 1,300,000
Less The Excess, If Any, Of:		
PUC Of Common Shares	($1,000,000)	
Over The Non-Share Consideration	1,000,000	Nil
PUC Reduction		$ 1,300,000

This means that the redeemable preferred shares would have a PUC of nil ($1,300,000 - $1,300,000).

The adjusted cost base of the redeemable preferred shares would be calculated as follows:

Adjusted Cost Base Of Common Shares	$ 1,000,000
Non-Share Consideration	(1,000,000)
Adjusted Cost Base Of Redeemable Preferred Shares	Nil

Because Sam took back cash equal to his PUC and ACB, there would be no ITA 84(3) deemed dividend and no capital gain or loss. These calculations would be as follows:

PUC Of New Shares	Nil
Plus Non-Share Consideration	$ 1,000,000
Proceeds Of Redemption Under ITA 84(5)(d)	$ 1,000,000
PUC Of Old Shares	(1,000,000)
ITA 84(3) Deemed Dividend	Nil
Adjusted Cost Base Of New Shares	Nil
Plus Non-Share Consideration	$ 1,000,000
Proceeds Of Disposition Under ITA 86(1)(c)	$ 1,000,000
ITA 84(3) Deemed Dividend	Nil
Adjusted Proceeds	$ 1,000,000
Adjusted Cost Base Of Old Shares	(1,000,000)
Capital Gain (Loss)	Nil

Exercise Seventeen - 3 Solution

The required PUC reduction on the redeemable preferred shares would be calculated as follows:

Increase In Legal Stated Capital		$ 1,300,000
Less The Excess, If Any, Of:		
PUC Of Common Shares	($ 1,000,000)	
Over The Non-Share Consideration	1,000,000	Nil
PUC Reduction		$ 1,300,000

This means that the redeemable preferred shares would have a PUC of nil ($1,300,000 - $1,300,000).

The adjusted cost base of the redeemable preferred shares would be calculated as follows:

Adjusted Cost Base Of Common Shares	$ 1,250,000
Non-Share Consideration	(1,000,000)
Adjusted Cost Base Of Redeemable Preferred Shares	$ 250,000

Because Sam took back cash equal to his PUC and less than his ACB, there would be no ITA 84(3) deemed dividend and no capital gain or loss. These calculations would be as follows:

PUC Of New Shares	Nil
Plus Non-Share Consideration	$ 1,000,000
Proceeds Of Redemption Under ITA 84(5)(d)	$ 1,000,000
PUC Of Old Shares	(1,000,000)
ITA 84(3) Deemed Dividend	Nil

Adjusted Cost Base Of New Shares	$ 250,000
Plus Non-Share Consideration	1,000,000
Proceeds Of Disposition Under ITA 86(1)(c)	$ 1,250,000
ITA 84(3) Deemed Dividend	Nil
Adjusted Proceeds	$ 1,250,000
Adjusted Cost Base Of Old Shares	(1,250,000)
Capital Gain (Loss)	Nil

Exercise Seventeen - 4 Solution

The required PUC reduction on the redeemable preferred shares would be calculated as follows:

Increase In Legal Stated Capital		$1,100,000
Less The Excess, If Any, Of:		
PUC Of Common Shares	($1,000,000)	
Over The Non-Share Consideration	1,200,000	Nil
PUC Reduction		$1,100,000

This means that the redeemable preferred shares would have a PUC of nil ($1,100,000 - $1,100,000).

The adjusted cost base of the redeemable preferred shares would be calculated as follows:

Adjusted Cost Base Of Common Shares	$ 1,250,000
Non-Share Consideration	(1,200,000)
Adjusted Cost Base Of Redeemable Preferred Shares	$ 50,000

Because the non-share consideration was greater than the PUC of the old shares, the resulting ITA 84(3) deemed dividend and the allowable capital loss would be calculated as follows:

PUC Of New Shares	Nil
Plus Non-Share Consideration	$ 1,200,000
Proceeds Of Redemption Under ITA 84(5)(d)	$ 1,200,000
PUC Of Old Shares	(1,000,000)
ITA 84(3) Deemed Dividend (Non-Eligible)	$ 200,000
Adjusted Cost Base Of New Shares	$ 50,000
Plus Non-Share Consideration	1,200,000
Proceeds Of Disposition Under ITA 86(1)(c)	$ 1,250,000
ITA 84(3) Deemed Dividend	(200,000)
Adjusted Proceeds	$ 1,050,000
Adjusted Cost Base Of Old Shares	(1,250,000)
Capital Gain (Loss)	($ 200,000)
Inclusion Rate	1/2
Allowable Capital Loss	($ 100,000)

The taxable amount of the non-eligible dividend would be $230,000 [(115%)($200,000)]. It would qualify for a federal dividend tax credit of $20,769 [(9/13)(15%)($200,000)].

Exercise Seventeen - 5 Solution

The amount of the gift can be calculated as follows:

Fair Market Value Of Shares [(80%)($1,600,000)]	$ 1,280,000
Consideration Received ($300,000 + $800,000)	(1,100,000)
Gift To Daughter	$ 180,000

As a gift is present in this transaction, ITA 86(2) is applicable.

The PUC reduction on the new shares would be calculated as follows:

Increase In Legal Stated Capital		$800,000
Less The Excess, If Any, Of:		
PUC Of Common Shares [(80%)($250,000)]	($200,000)	
Over The Non-Share Consideration	300,000	Nil
PUC Reduction		$800,000

This means that the redeemable preferred shares would have a PUC of nil ($800,000 - $800,000).

Under ITA 86(2)(e), the adjusted cost base of the redeemable preferred shares would be calculated as follows:

Adjusted Cost Base Of Common Shares		$200,000
Deduct:		
Non-Share Consideration	($300,000)	
Gift	(180,000)	(480,000)
Adjusted Cost Base Of Preferred Shares		Nil

Given the $180,000 gift, the ITA 84(3) deemed dividend and the taxable capital gain would be calculated as follows:

PUC Of New Preferred Shares	Nil
Plus Non-Share Consideration	$300,000
Proceeds Of Redemption Under ITA 84(5)(d)	$300,000
PUC Of Shares Given Up	(200,000)
ITA 84(3) Deemed Dividend (Non-Eligible)	$ 100,000

Proceeds Of Disposition Under ITA 86(2)(c) - Lesser Of:	
• Fair Market Value Of Shares Given Up = $1,280,000	
• Non-Share Consideration Plus Gift	
($300,000 + $180,000) = $480,000	$480,000
Less ITA 84(3) Deemed Dividend	(100,000)
Adjusted Proceeds	$380,000
Adjusted Cost Base Of Shares Given Up	(200,000)
Capital Gain	$180,000
Inclusion Rate	1/2
Taxable Capital Gain	$ 90,000

The taxable amount of the non-eligible dividend would be $115,000 [(115%)($100,000)]. It would qualify for a federal dividend tax credit of $10,385 [(9/13)(15%)($100,000)].

Her total gain is $280,000 ($100,000 + $180,000). In economic terms this reflects the $100,000 excess of the non-share consideration over the PUC and adjusted cost base of the old shares ($300,000 - $200,000) plus the $180,000 gift. Ms. Reviser would also have a deferred gain of $800,000, the excess of the $800,000 fair market value of the preferred shares over their PUC and adjusted cost base of nil.

The combination of the current and deferred gains is $1,080,000 ($800,000 + $280,000). This is the same amount of gain that would have occurred if Ms. Reviser had simply sold her shares for their fair market value of $1,280,000 ($1,280,000 - $200,000 = $1,080,000).

While this transaction has not changed Ms. Reviser's economic position, it has created an additional taxable amount for her daughter. Before this transaction, the fair market value of the daughter's holding was $320,000 [(20%)($1,600,000)]. This holding now has a value of $500,000. This is the $1,600,000 total value of Janrev Inc. prior to the transaction, less the cash of $300,000, less the fair market value of the preferred shares of $800,000. As there is no increase in her adjusted cost base, this extra $180,000 ($500,000 - $320,000) represents a deferred gain that will be taxed if her shares are redeemed or if she chooses to sell them.

Exercise Seventeen - 6 Solution

As Upton Inc. has a clear majority of the shares in Amalgo Inc., it would appear that they have acquired control of Downer Ltd. As the acquisition of control rules would be applicable, there would be a deemed year end for both companies that coincides with the amalgamated year end. The non-capital loss carry forward of Downer Ltd. will be flowed through to the amalgamated company, Amalgo Inc. However, because of the acquisition of control, the net capital loss carry forward cannot be used. In addition, the non-capital loss can only be applied against profits earned in the same business or a similar business.

Exercise Seventeen - 7 Solution

Subsequent to an ITA 88(1) winding-up, the parent company can deduct subsidiary losses in its first taxation year beginning after that date. This would be the year beginning on September 16, 2020.

Side's loss is deemed to occur in Park's taxation year that includes Side's year end. This would be the year ending September 15, 2020. This means that it will expire, after 20 taxation years, at the end of Park's taxation year ending September 15, 2040.

Exercise Seventeen - 8 Solution

Under ITA 88(1), a limited bump-up of non-depreciable capital assets is available. The basic limit would be calculated as follows:

Adjusted Cost Base Of Lorne Inc. Shares	$1,200,000
Tax Values Of Lorne Inc.'s Net Assets	
At Winding-Up ($500,000 - $75,000)	(425,000)
Dividends Paid By Lorne Since Acquisition	Nil
Excess	$ 775,000

However, this basic amount cannot exceed the difference between the fair market value of the non-depreciable capital assets at the time of the share acquisition and their tax cost at that time. This amount would be $130,000 ($270,000 - $140,000). The bump-up in the land value is limited to that amount, resulting in the following tax values for Lorne's assets at the time of the ITA 88(1) winding-up:

Cash	$ 120,000
Land ($140,000 + $130,000)	270,000
Depreciable Assets - At UCC	240,000
Total Assets	$630,000

Note that the remaining $645,000 ($775,000- $130,000) of the excess is lost as a result of this wind-up.

Exercise Seventeen - 9 Solution
Given the size of the proceeds, the balance in the combined RDTOH accounts will clearly be less than 38-1/3 percent of the dividends to be declared. Given this, the total distribution to shareholders will be $912,000 ($865,000 + $47,000).

The taxable dividend component of the total distribution to the shareholders is calculated as follows:

Total Distribution ($865,000 + $47,000)	$912,000
Paid Up Capital	(88,000)
ITA 84(2) Deemed Dividend On Winding-Up	$824,000
Capital Dividend Account (Election Required)	(26,000)
Non-Eligible Dividend Subject To Tax*	$798,000

*As the company's GRIP balance is nil, all of the dividends will be non-eligible.

The non-eligible dividend will be grossed up to $917,700 [(115%)($798,000)]. The shareholders will also have a federal dividend tax credit of $82,869 [(9/13)(15%)($798,000)].

As shown in the following calculation, the shareholders will not have a capital gain on the disposition of their shares:

Total Distribution To Shareholders	$912,000
ITA 84(2) Deemed Dividend	(824,000)
Deemed Proceeds Of Disposition	$ 88,000
Adjusted Cost Base Of Shares	(88,000)
Capital Gain	Nil

Solution to Self Study Problem Seventeen - 1

Part A - ITA 85.1 Applies
Jerry elected to transfer his business using ITA 85(1) at a value of $986,000. Given that he took back non-share consideration of $500,000, the adjusted cost base of his Jerry's Flowers common shares would be calculated as follows:

Elected Value	$986,000
Non-Share Consideration	(500,000)
Adjusted Cost Base Of Common Shares	$486,000

The PUC of these shares would be calculated as follows:

Increase in Legal Stated Capital		$1,840,000
Less Excess, If Any, Of:		
Elected Value	($986,000)	
Non-Share Consideration	500,000	(486,000)
PUC Reduction		$1,354,000
PUC Of Common Shares ($1,840,000 - $1,354,000)		$ 486,000

Using these values for the Jerry's Flowers shares, if Jerry does not opt out of ITA 85.1, the tax consequences would be as follows:

- Jerry would be deemed to have disposed of his Jerry's Flowers shares at a value equal to their adjusted cost base of $486,000. Given this, there would be no capital gain on the disposition.
- Jerry would be deemed to have acquired his Large Flowers Inc. shares at a cost equal to the $486,000 adjusted cost base of his Jerry's Flowers shares.
- The PUC of the Large Flowers Inc. shares that have been issued to Jerry would be $486,000, the PUC of the Jerry's Flowers shares that were given up.

Part A - Opting Out Of ITA 85.1

The total fair market value of the Large Flowers shares is $3,750,000. In order to opt out of ITA 85.1, he will have to include a taxable capital gain of $1,632,000 [(1/2)($3,750,000 - $486,000)] in his 2020 tax return. This has the advantage of absorbing his $800,000 net capital loss carry forward. However, it will result in his being required to pay taxes on the remaining $832,000 ($1,632,000 - $800,000). Because all of his shares are involved in the exchange, he has no choice as to the amount of the gain to be recognized.

Part B - ACB For Large Flowers Inc.

The adjusted cost base of the Jerry's Flowers shares in the hands of Large Flowers Inc. would be the lesser of their $3,750,000 fair market value and their PUC. In this case, the PUC amount of $486,000 is lower and will be the adjusted cost base amount.

Part C - Alternative Solutions

There are two possible solutions that would make full use of the $800,000 net capital loss carry forward and minimize the current payment of taxes.

Alternative One   Jerry could use ITA 85(1) to exchange the shares at an elected value of $2,086,000. If this value were elected, the resulting taxable capital gain would be equal to the required amount of $800,000 [(1/2)($2,086,000 - $486,000)]. Note that this would leave the adjusted cost base of the acquired shares at the elected value of $2,086,000. This compares to $486,000 if ITA 85.1 is used.

Alternative Two   Each share of Jerry's Flowers Ltd. has a fair market value of $3,750 ($3,750,000 ÷ 1,000) and an adjusted cost base of $486 ($486,000 ÷ 1,000). This means that each share that is sold to Large Flowers would generate a taxable capital gain of $1,632 [(1/2)($3,750 - $486)]. Given this, selling 490 of these shares to Large Flowers would result in a taxable capital gain of $799,680 [(490)($1,632)]. This would be eliminated by the application of the $800,000 net capital loss carry forward. The remaining 510 (1,000 - 490) shares of Jerry's Flowers could then be exchanged for Large Flowers Inc. shares on a tax free basis under either of ITA 85(1) or ITA 85.1.

Solution to Self Study Problem Seventeen - 2

Part A - ITA 85.1 Applies

Sarah elected to transfer her business using ITA 85(1) at a value of $842,000. Given that she took back non-share consideration of $360,000, the adjusted cost base of her Hartman shares would be calculated as follows:

Elected Value	$842,000
Non-Share Consideration	(360,000)
Adjusted Cost Base Of Common Shares	$482,000

The PUC of these shares would be calculated as follows:

Increase in Legal Stated Capital		$1,200,000
Less Excess, If Any, Of:		
Elected Value	($842,000)	
Non-Share Consideration	360,000	(482,000)
PUC Reduction		$ 718,000
PUC Of Common Shares ($1,200,000 - $718,000)		$ 482,000

Using these values for the Hartman shares, if Sarah does not opt out of ITA 85.1, the tax conse-quences would be as follows:

- Sarah would be deemed to have disposed of her Hartman shares at a value equal to their adjusted cost base of $482,000. Given this, there would be no capital gain on the disposition.

- Sarah would be deemed to have acquired her Grande Ltd. shares at a cost equal to the $482,000 adjusted cost base of her Hartman shares.

- The PUC of the Grande Ltd. shares that have been issued to Sarah would be $482,000, the PUC of the Hartman shares that were given up.

Part A - Opting Out Of ITA 85.1

Sarah can opt out of ITA 85.1 by including a $1,109,000 [(1/2)($2,700,000 - $482,000)] taxable capital gain in her income tax return. This may be desirable in that it will allow her to make use of her $625,000 net capital loss carry forward. However, the disadvantage of opting out of ITA 85.1 is that she will have to pay taxes on the net taxable capital gain of $484,000 ($1,109,000 - $625,000).

Because all of her shares are involved in the exchange, she has no choice as to the amount of the gain to be recognized.

Part B - ACB For Grande Ltd.

The adjusted cost base of the Hartman shares in the hands of Grande would be the lesser of their $2,700,000 fair market value and their PUC. In this case, the PUC amount of $482,000 is lower and will be the adjusted cost base amount.

Part C - Alternative Solutions

There are two possible solutions that would make full use of the $625,000 net capital loss carry forward and minimize the current payment of taxes.

Alternative One   Sarah could use ITA 85(1) to exchange the shares at an elected value of $1,732,000. If this value were elected, the resulting taxable capital gain would be equal to the required amount of $625,000 [(1/2)($1,732,000 - $482,000)]. Note that this would leave the adjusted cost base of the acquired shares at the elected value of $1,732,000. If ITA 85.1 were used, this value would be the $482,000 PUC of the shares.

Alternative Two   Each share of Hartman Inc. has a fair market value of $450 ($2,700,000 ÷ 6,000) and an adjusted cost base of $80.33 ($482,000 ÷ 6,000). This means that each share that is sold to Grande would generate a taxable capital gain of $184.84 [(1/2)($450 - $80.33)]. Given this, selling 3,382 of these shares to

Grande would result in a taxable capital gain of $625,128.88 [(3,382)($184.84)]. This would be largely eliminated by the application of the $625,000 net capital loss carry forward. The remaining 2,618 (6,000 - 3,382) shares of Hartman could then be exchanged for Grande Ltd. shares on a tax free basis under either of ITA 85(1) or ITA 85.1.

Solution to Self Study Problem Seventeen - 3

The fair market value of the business is $10,985,000, which is composed of tangible assets of $12,450,000 plus goodwill of $2,000,000 less the bank loan of $3,465,000.

To implement the ITA 86(1) rollover, the twins should each invest $10,000 in exchange for new common shares of BIL.

At this point, Ms. Boswick can exchange, on a tax free basis, her common shares for new preferred shares with a redemption value of $10,985,000. This would have no immediate tax consequences. The ACB and PUC of the new preferred shares would be calculated as follows:

Adjusted Cost Base Of Shares Given Up		$ 250,000
Non-Share Consideration		Nil
Adjusted Cost Base Of Preferred Shares		$ 250,000
Legal Stated Capital - Preferred Shares		$10,985,000
Less Excess, If Any, Of:		
PUC - Shares Given Up	($250,000)	
Non-Share Consideration	Nil	(250,000)
Required PUC Reduction		$10,735,000
PUC - Preferred Shares ($10,985,000 - $10,735,000)		$ 250,000

Ms. Boswick's preferred shares will not participate in the future growth of the company. This means that all of the future growth in Boswick Industries will accrue to the two children who are holding the common shares.

In order for Ms. Boswick to retain control, the preferred shares should be voting shares.

Subsequent to these transactions, the July 1, 2020, Balance Sheet would be as follows:

Boswick Industries Ltd.
Shareholders' Equity
As At July 1, 2020

Tangible Assets At Tax Values	
($12,450,000 + $10,000 + $10,000)	$12,470,000
Bank Loan	$ 3,465,000
Preferred Shares (Paid Up Capital)	250,000
Common Shares ($10,000 + $10,000)	20,000
Retained Earnings	8,735,000
Total	$12,470,000

Solution to Self Study Problem Seventeen - 4

Part A

Gift To Jack   This transaction involves a gift of $320,000 to Mr. Mark's son, Jack, calculated as follows:

Fair Market Value Of Common Shares Given Up	
[(80%)($2,400,000)]	$1,920,000
Fair Market Value Of Preferred Shares Received	(1,600,000)
Gift	$ 320,000

It is fair to assume that this amount is a gift to Jack, as he is the only remaining holder of common shares in Markit Ltd.

PUC Of New Preferred Shares   The PUC reduction required under ITA 86(2.1) would be calculated as follows:

Legal Stated Capital Of New Shares		$8,000
Deduct:		
PUC Of Old Shares	($8,000)	
Non-Share Consideration	Nil	(8,000)
PUC Reduction		Nil
PUC Of Preferred Shares ($8,000 - Nil)		$8,000

As the required PUC reduction is nil, the PUC of the new shares would be equal to the $8,000 PUC of the old shares.

Adjusted Cost Base Of New Preferred Shares   This amount would be calculated as follows:

Adjusted Cost Base Of Old Shares		$ 8,000
Deduct:		
Non-Share Consideration	$ Nil	
Gift	(320,000)	(320,000)
Adjusted Cost Base Of New Shares		Nil

Proceeds Of Redemption For Old Common Shares - ITA 84(5)(d)   For purposes of determining any ITA 84(3) deemed dividend on the redemption of the old shares, the proceeds of redemption would be as follows:

PUC Of New Preferred Shares	$8,000
Non-Share Consideration	Nil
Proceeds Of Redemption	$8,000

As this amount is equal to the old PUC, there is no ITA 84(3) deemed dividend on the transaction.

Proceeds Of Disposition For Old Common Shares - ITA 86(2)(c)   For purposes of determining any capital gain on the redemption of the old common shares, the proceeds of disposition would be the lesser of the $1,920,000 fair market value of the old common shares and the following amount:

Non-Share Consideration	$ Nil
Gift	320,000
Proceeds Of Disposition	$320,000

Using the lesser figure of $320,000, there would be a taxable capital gain on the transaction calculated as follows:

Proceeds Of Disposition	$320,000
ITA 84(3) Deemed Dividend	Nil
Adjusted Proceeds Of Disposition	$320,000
Adjusted Cost Base	(8,000)
Capital Gain	$312,000
Inclusion Rate	1/2
Taxable Capital Gain	$ 156,000

The total potential gain on Mr. Mark's shares is $1,912,000 ($1,920,000 - $8,000). Because there was a gift to his son, $312,000 of this amount must be recognized at the time of the rollover. The remaining $1,600,000 is deferred until the preferred shares are sold or redeemed. In the absence of the gift, all of this gain could have been deferred.

Part B

This transaction will not alter the total fair market value of the company and, as a consequence, the value of Jack's common shares will increase by the $320,000 amount of the gift. There will be no corresponding increase in the amount of the tax cost of these shares and, as a consequence, this value will be taxed when Jack sells the common shares. As this value has already been taxed in the hands of Mr. Mark, there will be double taxation on this amount.

Part C

If Mr. Mark's preferred shares were redeemed at their fair market value of $1,600,000, the tax consequences would be as follows:

Redemption Proceeds	$1,600,000
PUC	(8,000)
ITA 84(3) Deemed Dividend (Non-Eligible)	$1,592,000

Redemption Proceeds	$1,600,000
Deemed ITA 84(3) Dividend	(1,592,000)
Adjusted Proceeds Of Disposition	$ 8,000
Adjusted Cost Base	(Nil)
Capital Gain	$ 8,000
Inclusion Rate	1/2
Taxable Capital Gain	$ 4,000

The overall tax consequences of the redemption would be as follows:

Taxable Dividend [($1,592,000)(115%)]	$1,830,800
Taxable Capital Gain	4,000
Income Inclusion	$1,834,800

The deemed non-eligible dividend would qualify for a federal dividend tax credit of $165,323 [(9/13)(15%)($1,592,000)].

Note that Mr. Mark's dividends and capital gains from the rollover total $1,912,000 ($312,000 + $1,592,000 + $8,000). This is equal to the $1,912,000 [(80%)($2,400,000) - $8,000] capital gain that would have resulted from a sale of his shares at fair market value. From his point of view, the redemption result is less favourable in that part of the gain is in the form of more heavily taxed non-eligible dividends. In addition, if his son were to sell his shares, there would be additional income subject to tax of $320,000.

Solution to Self Study Problem Seventeen - 5

Approach One - No Gift

Part A

As the fair market value of the cash and preferred shares ($50,000 + $1,300,000) received by Ms. Platt is equal to the fair market value of the common shares she has given up ($1,350,000), no gift is involved.

Part B

The Paid Up Capital of the new shares would be reduced as follows:

Increase In Legal Stated Capital - New Shares		$90,000
Less The Excess, If Any, Of:		
PUC - Old Shares [(75%)($120,000)]	($90,000)	
Over Non-Share Consideration	50,000	(40,000)
Reduction In PUC - New Shares		$50,000

Given this reduction, the PUC of the new preferred shares would be as follows:

Increase In Legal Stated Capital - New Shares	$90,000
Reduction In PUC	(50,000)
PUC - New Shares	$40,000

Part C

The adjusted cost base of the preferred shares would be calculated as follows:

Adjusted Cost Base - Old Shares [(75%)($120,000)]	$90,000
Non-Share Consideration	(50,000)
Adjusted Cost Base - New Shares	$40,000

Part D

The proceeds of redemption would be calculated as follows:

PUC - New Shares	$40,000
Plus Non-Share Consideration	50,000
Proceeds Of Redemption [ITA 84(5)(d)]	$90,000

The proceeds of disposition would be calculated as follows:

Adjusted Cost Base - New Shares	$40,000
Plus Non-Share Consideration	50,000
Proceeds Of Disposition [ITA 86(1)(c)]	$90,000

Part E   Immediate Tax Consequences

As the ITA 84(5)(d) proceeds of redemption are equal to the PUC of the old shares, there is no ITA 84(3) deemed dividend. As the ITA 86(1)(c) proceeds of disposition are equal to the adjusted cost base of the old shares, there is no capital gain. This means there are no immediate tax consequences.

Part F   Tax Consequences Of Redemption Of New Shares

Redemption Proceeds	$1,300,000
PUC - New Shares	(40,000)
ITA 84(3) Deemed Dividend (Non-Eligible)	$1,260,000
Proceeds Of Disposition	$1,300,000
ITA 84(3) Deemed Dividend	(1,260,000)
Adjusted Proceeds Of Disposition	$ 40,000
Adjusted Cost Base - Preferred Shares	(40,000)
Capital Gain	Nil

The tax consequence would be an income inclusion of $1,449,000 [(115%)($1,260,000)], the grossed up value of the deemed non-eligible dividend. This would qualify for a federal dividend tax credit of $130,846 [(9/13)(15%)($1,260,000)].

Additional Analysis

While not a required part of the problem, you might wish to note that the $1,260,000 deemed dividend is the same amount of unadjusted income that would have been assessed to Ms. Platt if she had simply sold her shares ($1,350,000 - $90,000). However, it would have been more favourably taxed as a capital gain, rather than as a non-eligible dividend.

Approach Two - Gift

Part A

Under this approach, the fair market value of the cash and preferred shares received by Ms. Platt of $1,320,000 ($50,000 + $1,270,000) is less than the fair market value of the common shares she has given up ($1,350,000). As her son is in a residual equity position in PIL, there would appear to be a gift to him in the amount of $30,000 [$1,350,000 - ($50,000 + $1,270,000)]. Given this, ITA 86(2) is applicable.

Part B

The Paid Up Capital of the preferred shares would be reduced under ITA 86(2.1)(a) as follows:

Increase In Legal Stated Capital - New Shares		$1,270,000
Less The Excess, If Any, Of:		
PUC - Old Shares [(75%)($120,000)]	($90,000)	
Over Non-Share Consideration	50,000	(40,000)
Reduction In PUC - New Shares		$1,230,000
Increase In Legal Stated Capital - New Shares		$1,270,000
Reduction In PUC		(1,230,000)
PUC - New Shares		$ 40,000

Part C

The adjusted cost base of the preferred shares would be calculated as follows:

Adjusted Cost Base - Old Shares		$90,000
Deduct:		
Non-Share Consideration	($50,000)	
Gift	(30,000)	(80,000)
Adjusted Cost Base - New Shares		$10,000

Part D

The proceeds of redemption would be calculated as follows:

PUC - New Shares	$40,000
Non-Share Consideration	50,000
Proceeds Of Redemption [ITA 84(5)(d)]	$90,000

The proceeds of disposition would be calculated as follows:

Non-Share Consideration	$50,000
Gift	30,000
Proceeds Of Disposition [ITA 86(2)(c)]	$80,000

Part E   Immediate Tax Consequences

As the ITA 84(5)(d) proceeds of redemption are equal to the PUC of the old shares, there is no ITA 84(3) deemed dividend. However, the ITA 86(2)(c) proceeds of disposition are less than the adjusted cost base of the old shares, resulting in a capital loss of $10,000 ($80,000 - $90,000). This loss would be disallowed by ITA 86(2)(d).

Part F   Tax Consequences Of Redemption

Redemption Proceeds	$1,270,000
PUC - New Shares	(40,000)
ITA 84(3) Deemed Dividend (Non-Eligible)	$1,230,000
Proceeds Of Disposition	$1,270,000
ITA 84(3) Deemed Dividend	(1,230,000)
Adjusted Proceeds Of Disposition	$ 40,000
Adjusted Cost Base - New Shares	(10,000)
Capital Gain	$ 30,000
Inclusion Rate	1/2
Taxable Capital Gain	$ 15,000

The overall tax consequences of the redemption would be as follows:

Taxable Dividend [(115%)($1,230,000)]	$1,414,500
Taxable Capital Gain	15,000
Income Inclusion	$1,429,500

The deemed non-eligible dividend would qualify for a federal dividend tax credit of $127,731 [(9/13)(15%)($1,230,000)].

Additional Analysis

While this analysis is not required by the problem, you might note that the total unadjusted income accruing to Ms. Platt is $1,260,000 ($1,230,000 + $30,000). This is the same total that would have resulted from a sale of her shares [($1,350,000 - $90,000) = $1,260,000]. However, it is received in a less favourable form ($1,230,000 in non-eligible dividends as opposed to all capital gains on a sale of shares). In addition, the market value of her son's shares has increased by the $30,000 amount of the gift. Given that there is no corresponding increase in the adjusted cost base of his shares, this additional amount will be subject to tax if the shares are redeemed or sold.

Solution to Self Study Problem Seventeen - 6

Use Of Section 87

If ITA 87 is used, the tax consequences are as follows:

- The land will flow through to the amalgamated corporation at its adjusted cost base of $175,000. No capital gain or loss will be recorded.

- As the subsidiary is 100 percent owned, the ITA 88(1) bump-up provision is available. The bump-up will be the lesser of:

Adjusted Cost Base Of Lynn Shares		$390,000
Deduct:		
Lynn's Tax Value For Land -		
Original Cost	($175,000)	
Dividends Paid By Lynn	Nil	(175,000)
1st Value		$215,000
Value Of Land At Acquisition Of Lynn		$390,000
Adjusted Cost Base Of Land		(175,000)
2nd Value		$215,000

This will leave the adjusted cost base of the land at $390,000 ($175,000 + $215,000).

Use Of Section 88(1)

If ITA 88(1) is used, the tax consequences are as follows:

- Lynn will have proceeds of disposition equal to the adjusted cost base of the land of $175,000. No capital gain or loss will be recorded.

- Ricon Ltd. will have the same bump-up on the land as calculated under the ITA 87 approach. The adjusted cost base of the land will also be the same $390,000 that was calculated in the ITA 87 solution.

Conclusion

Both approaches result in a bump-up of $215,000 and an adjusted cost base for the land of $390,000. It does not appear to make any difference which of the two alternative approaches is used.

Solution to Self Study Problem Seventeen - 7

Part A - Funds Available For Distribution

The taxable capital gains and active business income (recapture) at the corporate level can be calculated as follows:

Asset	Taxable Capital Gains	Active Business Income
Inventories	Nil	Nil
Taxable Capital Gains:		
On Land [(1/2)($1,243,000 - $623,000)]	$310,000	Nil
On Building [(1/2)($1,173,000 - $775,000)]	199,000	
Recapture On Building ($775,000 - $586,000)		$189,000
Totals	$509,000	$189,000

As the active business income is less than the $500,000 annual business limit, there will be no addition to the General Rate Income Pool balance. The taxable capital gains are not eligible for addition to the GRIP balance.

Taxable Income will be $698,000 ($509,000 + $189,000). Tax Payable on this amount will be calculated as follows:

Federal Tax On Business Income [(38% - 10% - 19%)($189,000)]	$ 17,010
Federal Tax On Investment Income [(38% - 10% + 10-2/3%)($509,000)]	196,813
Part I Tax Payable	$213,823
Provincial Tax On Business Income [(3%)($189,000)]	5,670
Provincial Tax On Investment Income [(13%)($509,000)]	66,170
Total Corporate Tax Payable	$285,663

Non-Eligible RDTOH Balance

As Kruger's GRIP was nil, all of the opening RDTOH of $27,000 would be allocated to the Non-Eligible RDTOH.

The refundable portion of the Part I tax would be $156,093, the least of:

- 30-2/3 Percent Of Investment Income [(30-2/3%)($509,000)] $156,093
- 30-2/3 Percent Of Taxable Income, Less The Amount Eligible For The Small Business Deduction [(30-2/3%)($698,000 - $189,000)] $156,093
- Part I Tax Payable $213,823

This amount would be added to the Non-Eligible RDTOH. Based on this, the ending balance in this account would be calculated as follows:

Opening Non-Eligible RDTOH	$ 27,000
Refundable Portion Of Part I Tax	156,093
Ending Non-Eligible RDTOH	$183,093

The amount available for distribution to the shareholders, after the payment of taxes at the corporate level, can be calculated as follows:

Fair Market Values:	
Inventories	$ 35,000
Land	1,243,000
Building	1,173,000
Gross Proceeds	$2,451,000
Corporate Tax Payable	(285,663)
Dividend Refund (Note)	183,093
Funds Available For Distribution	$2,348,430

Note Technically, the dividend refund is the lesser of the $183,093 balance in the RDTOH account and 38-1/3 percent of taxable dividends paid. However, given the size of the distribution in this problem, it is clear that $183,093 will be the lower figure.

With respect to the capital dividend account, the final balance is calculated as follows:

Balance Before Dispositions	$215,000
Disposition Of Land	310,000
Disposition Of Building	199,000
Ending Balance	$724,000

Part B - Components Of Distribution

Assuming an election has been made to declare the maximum capital dividend, the taxable dividend component of the total distribution to the shareholders can be calculated as follows:

Distribution To Shareholders	$2,348,430
Paid Up Capital	(447,000)
ITA 84(2) Deemed Dividend	$1,901,430
Capital Dividend (Balance In Account)	(724,000)
Deemed Dividend Subject To Tax (Non-Eligible)	$ 1,177,430

As Kruger has no GRIP balance, all of this dividend will be non-eligible. The taxable amount will be $1,354,045 [(115%)($1,177,430)]. This dividend will qualify for a federal dividend tax credit of $122,272 [(9/13)(15%)($1,177,430)].

Part B - Capital Gain

With respect to capital gains, ITA 54 indicates that the proceeds of disposition for purposes of determining any capital gain on the disposition of shares does not include any amount paid out as ITA 84(2) dividends. Given the preceding calculation, the capital gain to the shareholders would be calculated as follows:

Actual Distribution To Shareholders	$2,348,430
ITA 84(2) Deemed Dividend	(1,901,430)
Deemed Proceeds Of Disposition	$ 447,000
Adjusted Cost Base For Shares	(447,000)
Capital Gain	Nil

Solution to Self Study Problem Seventeen - 8

Sale Of Assets

This calculation requires two steps. First, we must determine the after tax proceeds that will be available at the corporate level subsequent to the sale of the assets. Then, a second stage analysis is required to determine the amount that will be retained by Mr. Lange after he pays all of the taxes that are due on the proceeds that are distributed to him.

Cash Proceeds, Capital Gains, And Business Income

The direct sale of the assets would create the following amounts of cash, taxable capital gains, and business income:

Asset	Cash Proceeds	Taxable Capital Gains	Active Business Income
Accounts Receivable			
($91,000 - $83,000)	$ 91,000		$ 8,000
Inventories ($298,000 - $237,000)	298,000	Nil	61,000
Land [(1/2)($656,000 - $167,000)]	656,000	244,500	
Building:			
[(1/2)($652,000 - $582,000)]		35,000	
($582,000 - $176,000)	652,000		406,000
Goodwill	719,000	359,500	Nil
Totals For Purchased Assets	$ 2,416,000	$ 639,000	$475,000
Term Deposits	529,000	Nil	Nil
Totals	$ 2,945,000	$ 639,000	$475,000

Taxable Income And Tax Payable

Taxable Income will total $1,114,000 ($639,000 + $475,000). The Tax Payable on this amount would be calculated as follows:

Federal Tax On:	
Business Income [(38% - 10% - 19%)($475,000)]	$ 42,750
Investment Income [(38% - 10% + 10-2/3%)($639,000)]	247,080
Part I Tax Payable	$289,830
Provincial Tax On Business Income [(3%)($475,000)]	14,250
Provincial Tax On Investment Income [(14%)($639,000)]	89,460
Total Corporate Tax Payable	$393,540

Non-Eligible RDTOH Balance

There is no transitional balance in the RDTOH account. The only addition for 2019 would be the refundable portion of Part I tax. This amount would be the least of:

- 30-2/3 Percent Of Investment Income [(30-2/3%)($639,000)] $195,960

- 30-2/3 Percent Of Taxable Income, Less The Amount Eligible For The Small Business Deduction [(30-2/3%)($1,114,000 - $475,000)] $195,960

- Part I Tax Payable $289,830

The least of these items is the $195,960. This amount would be added to the Non-Eligible RDTOH and this would be the ending balance in that account.

Funds Available For Distribution

Based on the preceding figures, the amount of cash available for distribution would be calculated as follows:

Gross Proceeds For Assets	$2,945,000
Payment Of Liabilities	(355,000)
Tax Payable	(393,540)
Dividend Refund (Note)	195,960
Total Funds Available For Distribution	$2,392,420

Note Technically, the dividend refund is the lesser of the $195,960 balance in the Non-Eligible RDTOH account and 38-1/3 percent of taxable dividends paid. However, given the size of the distribution in this problem, it is clear that $195,960 will be the lower figure.

Capital Dividend Account

The balance in the capital dividend account would be calculated as follows:

Opening Balance	Nil
Non-Taxable One-Half Of Capital Gains (From Table Calculating Corporate Income On Asset Dispositions)	$639,000
Capital Dividend Account Balance	$639,000

Taxable Dividends Resulting From Distribution

Assuming an election has been made to declare the maximum capital dividend, the taxable dividend component of the total distribution to Mr. Lange can be calculated as follows:

Funds Available For Distribution	$2,392,420
Paid Up Capital	(135,000)
ITA 84(2) Deemed Dividend	$ 2,257,420
ITA 83(2) Capital Dividend (Balance In Account)	(639,000)
Non-Eligible Dividend	$1,618,420

There would be no capital gain on the disposition, as demonstrated in the following calculation:

Amount Distributed	$2,392,420
ITA 84(2) Deemed Dividend	(2,257,420)
Deemed Proceeds Of Disposition	$ 135,000
Adjusted Cost Base	(135,000)
Capital Gain	Nil

Personal Tax Payable

As there is no capital gain and the capital dividend is received tax free, the personal Tax Payable on the dividend subject to tax would be calculated as follows:

Non-Eligible Dividend	$1,618,420
15 Percent Gross Up	242,763
Taxable Amount Of Dividends	$1,861,183
Combined Rate (33% + 18%)	51%
Tax Before Dividend Tax Credit	$ 949,203
Dividend Tax Credit [(9/13 + 4/13)($242,763)]	(242,763)
Personal Tax Payable	$ 706,440

Sale Of Shares

The Tax Payable resulting from a sale of shares would be calculated as follows:

Proceeds From The Sale Of Shares	$2,380,000
Adjusted Cost Base	(135,000)
Capital Gain	$2,245,000
Inclusion Rate	1/2
Taxable Capital Gain	$1,122,500
Tax Rate (33% + 18%)	51%
Personal Tax Payable	$ 572,475

Note   This capital gain would not qualify for the lifetime capital gains deduction because shares of Alcove are not qualified small business corporation shares. The term deposits are not involved in producing active business income. As they clearly exceed 10 percent of the fair market value of the assets, Alcove shares are not qualified small business corporation shares.

Conclusion

Given the preceding calculations, the after tax, personal cash retention under both alternatives would be as follows:

	Asset Sale	Share Sale
Proceeds From Sale	$ 2,392,420	$2,380,000
Personal Tax Payable	(706,440)	(572,475)
After Tax Retention	$ 1,685,980	$ 1,807,525

As the after tax retention is $121,545 ($1,807,525 - $1,685,980) larger when shares are sold, this would be the preferable alternative. If the lifetime capital gains deduction were available, this alternative would have been even more favourable. We would note that this would not have been difficult to accomplish. All that would have been required was the sale of the term deposits and distribution of the proceeds prior to selling the shares.

CHAPTER 18

Chapter 18 Learning Objectives

1. Explain the basic approach of Canadian income tax legislation to the taxation of partnerships (paragraph [P hereafter] 18-1 to 18-7).
2. Define, for income tax purposes, a partnership arrangement (P 18-8 to 18-15).
3. List the various types of partnership arrangements that are used in Canada (P 18-16 to 18-23).
4. Describe the difference between partnership arrangements and such other forms of organization as co-ownership, joint ventures, and syndicates (P 18-24 to 18-36).
5. Explain the basic concepts that are involved in the determination of the partnership income, losses, and tax credits to be allocated to the partners (P 18-37 to 18-52).

6. Calculate the Net Business Income of the partnership (P 18-53 to 18-54).
7. Calculate the amount and type of partnership income other than business income that will be allocated to each partner under the terms of the partnership agreement (P 18-55 to 18-62).
8. Explain the concept of the adjusted cost base of a partnership interest (P 18-63 to 18-66).
9. Apply the procedures required to record the acquisition of a partnership interest (P 18-67 to 18-74).
10. Calculate the amount of the adjusted cost base of a partnership interest (P 18-75 to 18-88).

11. Apply the procedures required to record the disposition of a partnership interest because of a sale or withdrawal (P 18-89 to 18-90).
12. Define limited partner and limited partnership arrangement (P 18-91 to 18-93).
13. Apply the at-risk rules to limited partnership losses (P 18-94 to 18-102).
14. Define a Canadian partnership (P 18-103 to 18-106).
15. Apply the procedures related to transfers between a partnership and its partners when no rollover provision is used (P 18-107 to 18-109).
16. List and apply the common rollover provisions for transfers between a partnership and its partners (P 18-110 to 18-127).

How to Work Through Chapter 18

We recommend the following approach in dealing with the material in this chapter:

Introduction To Partnerships
*   Read paragraph 18-1 to 18-7 (in the textbook).

Partnerships Defined
*   Read paragraph 18-8 to 18-23.
*   Do Self Study Problem Eighteen-1 which is available on MyLab and check the solution in this Study Guide.

Co-Ownership, Joint Ventures, And Syndicates
- Read paragraph 18-24 to 18-36.
- Do Self Study Problem Eighteen-2 and check the solution in this Study Guide.

Determining Partnership Income, Losses, And Tax Credits
- Read paragraph 18-37 to 18-52.
- Do Exercise Eighteen-1(in the textbook) and check the solution in this Study Guide.
- Read paragraph 18-53 to 18-56.
- Do Exercise Eighteen-2 and check the solution in this Study Guide.
- Read paragraph 18-57 to 18-58.
- Do Exercise Eighteen-3 and check the solution in this Study Guide.

Allocations To Partners And Partner Expenses
- Read paragraph 18-59.
- Do Exercise Eighteen-4 and check the solution in this Study Guide.
- Read paragraph 18-60 to 18-62.
- Do Self Study Problems Eighteen-3 and Eighteen-4 and check the solutions in this Study Guide.

The Partnership Interest
- Read paragraph 18-63 to 18-74.
- Do Exercise Eighteen-5 and check the solution in this Study Guide.

Adjustments To The ACB Of A Partnership Interest
- Read paragraph 18-75 to 18-88.
- Do Exercise Eighteen-6 and check the solution in this Study Guide.
- Read paragraph 18-89 to 18-90.
- Do Self Study Problems Eighteen-5 and Eighteen-6 and check the solutions in this Study Guide.

Limited Partnerships And Limited Partners
- Read paragraph 18-91 to 18-102.
- Do Exercise Eighteen-7 and check the solution in this Study Guide.
- Do Self Study Problem Eighteen-7 and check the solution in this Study Guide.

Transfers Of Property To And From A Partnership - No Rollover
- Read paragraph 18-103 to 18-108.
- Do Exercise Eighteen-8 and check the solution in this Study Guide.
- Read paragraph 18-109.
- Do Exercise Eighteen-9 and check the solution in this Study Guide.

Common Partnership Rollovers
- Read paragraph 18-110 to 18-112.
- Do Exercise Eighteen-10 and check the solution in this Study Guide.
- Read paragraph 18-113 to 18-127.
- Do Self Study Problem Eighteen-8 and check the solution in this Study Guide.

To Complete This Chapter
- If you would like more practice in problem solving, do the Supplementary Self Study Problems for the chapter. These problems and solutions are available on MyLab.
- Review the Key Terms Used In This Chapter in the textbook at the end of Chapter 18. Consult the Glossary for the meaning of any key terms you do not know.
- Test yourself with the Chapter 18 Glossary Flashcards available on MyLab.
- Ensure you have achieved the Chapter 18 Learning Objectives listed in this Study Guide.
- As a review, we recommend you view the PowerPoint presentation for Chapter 18 that is on MyLab.

Practice Examination
- Write the Practice Examination for Chapter 18 that is on MyLab. Mark your examination using the Practice Examination Solution that is on MyLab.

Solutions to Chapter 18 Exercises

Exercise Eighteen - 1 Solution

The following amounts would be added to Mr. Peter's Net Income For Tax Purposes:

Business Income [(50%)($55,000)]	$27,500
Taxable Capital Gains [(50%)(1/2)($40,000)]	10,000
Eligible Dividends [(50%)($10,000)]	5,000
Gross Up [(38%)($5,000)]	1,900
Total Addition	$44,400

In addition, Mr. Peters would be eligible for a federal dividend tax credit of $1,036 [(6/11)($1,900)]. The drawings that he made during the year are not included in his 2020 Net Income For Tax Purposes.

Exercise Eighteen - 2 Solution

The JL Partnership's Net Business Income would be calculated as follows:

Accounting Net Income		$262,000
Add:		
Salary To J	$45,000	
Interest To L	22,000	
Amortization Expense	26,000	
Donations	2,500	95,500
Subtotal		$357,500
Deduct:		
Maximum CCA	($42,000)	
Accounting Gain On Sale Of Land	(24,000)	(66,000)
Net Business Income		$291,500
Priority Allocations For Salary And Interest		(67,000)
Residual To Be Split 60:40		$224,500

The allocation of this Net Business Income to the two partners would be as follows:

	Partner J	Partner L
Priority Allocation For Salary	$ 45,000	N/A
Priority Allocation For Interest	N/A	$ 22,000
Allocation Of Residual		
[(60%)($224,500)]	134,700	
[(40%)($224,500)]		89,800
Total Business Income Allocation	$ 179,700	$111,800

While not required, you might note that a taxable capital gain of $12,000 [(1/2)($24,000)] would be allocated to the partners on a 60:40 basis. With respect to the donations, the amount of the charitable donations of $2,500 would allocated on a 60:40 basis, leaving the individual partners to calculate the available credit.

Exercise Eighteen - 3 Solution

The ST Partnership's Net Business Income would be calculated as follows:

Accounting Net Income	$146,000
Amortization Expense = CCA	Nil
Eligible Dividends	(12,000)
Accounting Gain On Sale Of Land	(31,000)
Net Business Income	$103,000

The addition to Net Income For Tax Purposes for each of the two partners would be calculated as follows:

	Partner S	Partner T
Net Business Income [(50%)($103,000)]	$51,500	$51,500
Eligible Dividends [(50%)($12,000)]	6,000	6,000
Gross Up [(38%)($6,000)]	2,280	2,280
Taxable Capital Gain [(50%)(1/2)($31,000)]	7,750	7,750
Net Income For Tax Purposes Addition	$ 67,530	$ 67,530

While not required, you might note that each partner would be eligible for a federal dividend tax credit of $1,244 [(6/11)($2,280)].

Exercise Eighteen - 4 Solution
The tax credits that would be allocated to each of the partners would be calculated as follows:

Charitable Donations ($1,750 Each)	
[(15%)($200) + (29%)($1,750 - $200)]	$ 480
Political Contributions ($600 Each)	
[(3/4)($400)] + [(1/2)($200)]	400
Eligible Dividends ($2,100 Each)	
[(6/11)(38%)($2,100)]	435
Total Of Credits To Each Partner	$1,315

These amounts would serve to reduce the Tax Payable of each of the two partners for the year ending December 31, 2020.

Exercise Eighteen - 5 Solution
After the admission of Caitlan, Alan and Balan will each have a one-third interest in the partnership, down from the previous interest of one-half. They are each, in effect, selling one-third of their partnership interest [(1/2 - 1/3) ÷ 1/2]. The ACB of their distribution to Caitlan is $16,000 [(1/3)($48,000)], resulting in a capital gain of $24,000 ($40,000 - $16,000). The taxable capital gain is one-half of this amount or $12,000.

The partner capital account transactions and ending balances will be:

	Alan	Balan	Caitlin
Opening Capital Accounts	$48,000	$48,000	Nil
Adjustment For Caitlin's Admission	(16,000)	(16,000)	$32,000
Ending Capital Accounts (Accounting Values)	$32,000	$32,000	$32,000
ACB Of Partnership Interest	$32,000	$32,000	$80,000

Exercise Eighteen - 6 Solution

The ACB of Robert's partnership interest on December 31, 2020, and January 1, 2021, would be determined as follows:

Original Capital Contribution	$12,500
Additional Contribution	7,200
Drawing	(4,000)
ACB - December 31, 2020	$15,700
Adjustment For 2020 Income	
[(40%)($11,600 + $3,100 + $46,700)]	24,560
ACB - January 1, 2021	$40,260

Robert's inclusion in Net Income For Tax Purposes would be as follows:

Taxable Capital Gain [(40%)(1/2)($11,600)]	$ 2,320
Dividends Received [(40%)($3,100)]	1,240
Gross Up On Dividends [(40%)(38%)($3,100)]	471
Net Business Income [(40%)($46,700)]	18,680
Inclusion In 2020 Net Income For Tax Purposes	$ 22,711

Note that this $22,711 addition to Robert's Net Income For Tax Purposes is not the same amount as the $24,560 that was added to the ACB of Robert's partnership interest to reflect his share of 2020 partnership income. While not required by the problem, Robert can claim a federal dividend tax credit of $257 [(6/11)($471)].

Exercise Eighteen - 7 Solution

ACB Of Partnership Interest		$200,000
Share Of Partnership Income (Not Loss) For 2020		Nil
Subtotal		$200,000
Amounts Owed To The Partnership	($ 150,000)	
Other Amounts Intended To		
Reduce Investment Risk		
(General Partner Guarantee)	(50,000)	(200,000)
At-Risk Amount - December 31, 2020		Nil

As the at-risk amount is nil, none of the loss can be deducted in 2020. The limited partnership loss at the end of 2020 is 100 percent of the $75,000 loss allocation.

Exercise Eighteen - 8 Solution

Part A Charles is considered to have disposed of the land for $100,000, resulting in a $33,500 [(1/2)($100,000- $33,000)] taxable capital gain. LIU will be considered to have acquired the land for $100,000. Charles is considered to have made a capital contribution of $100,000 that will be added to the ACB of his partnership interest.

Part B Charles will have the same $33,500 taxable capital gain as in Part A and LIU will be considered to have acquired the land for $100,000. The capital contribution and the addition to the ACB of the partnership interest is equal to $75,000. This is the difference between the fair market value of the land transferred to LIU of $100,000 and the $25,000 in other consideration received by Charles on the property transfer.

Part C Charles will have the same $33,500 taxable capital gain as in Part A and LIU will be considered to have acquired the land for $100,000. No capital contribution is made. As Charles withdrew $12,000 ($112,000- $100,000) more from LIU than he transferred in, Charles will be considered to have made a net withdrawal. The ACB of his partnership interest will be reduced by $12,000.

Exercise Eighteen - 9 Solution

ITA 98(2) deems DG to have disposed of the share investments for the fair market value of $94,000, resulting in a $55,000 ($94,000- $39,000) capital gain. One-fifth of the capital gain, or $11,000, will be allocated to Darlene. One-half of this amount, or $5,500, will be a taxable capital gain that she will include in her income for 2020.

Darlene's adjusted cost base for the share investments is $18,800 [(20%)($94,000)].

The adjusted cost base of her partnership interest on December 31, 2020, and on January 1, 2021, is calculated as follows:

Partnership ACB Prior To Distribution	$30,000
Drawings [(20%)($94,000)]	(18,800)
Partnership ACB- December 31, 2020	$ 11,200
Allocated Capital Gain [(20%)($94,000- $39,000)]	11,000
Partnership ACB- January 1, 2021	$22,200

Exercise Eighteen - 10 Solution

Using the ITA 85(1) rollover provision, the property would be transferred at the $156,000 ACB of the land. Given this, the transfer would not result in any current income for Samantha. The cost of the land to the partnership would be the $156,000 elected value for the transfer. This same amount would be added to the adjusted cost base of Samantha's partnership interest.

Solution to Self Study Problem Eighteen - 1

The determination of the existence of a partnership is a mixed question of fact and law, based upon the intention of the parties that may be expressed clearly through a valid written partnership agreement or inferred from actions. In Canada, the relevant provincial partnership legislation is applicable to answering this question.

In this case, an analysis of the three elements of a partnership is as follows:

1. **Was the business carried on in common by two or more persons?**

    The details of the partnership agreement contain many of the necessary ingredients that the courts will look to in support of this element. Accordingly, it appears that this element has been met.

2. **Was a business carried on by the partnership?**

    A business has a beginning and an end. Ongoing profitable activity within the business may actually only occur between these two extremes, but the activity remains a business throughout the period. In other words, profitability is generally irrelevant to a finding that a business exists. In this case, the selling off of store property will likely occur as part of the wind-up process of the two stores. Accordingly, there are arguments that support the carrying on of a business.

3. **Was there a view to profit?**

    This element will be satisfied if there is a potential for profit even though one may never be realized. The facts clearly lead to a conclusion that there is no hope of profit. The additional fact that the partnership will be terminated once the property is sold and that losses are not only expected, but anticipated, speaks for itself. A tax motivation that predominates, such as this, will not invalidate a partnership as long as there is a profit potential and the other elements are met. This is not the case.

Conclusion: A partnership will not be created. As a result, no losses can be allocated to the investors. The losses belong to Wayout Ltd. only.

Solution to Self Study Problem Eighteen - 2

Part A - Partnership Results

As the original intention when the land was purchased was to develop and sell lots, the income from the sale of the lots would be reported as business income and not as a capital gain.

Using the provisions of ITA 97(2), Mr. Marrazzo could transfer the land to the partnership at its ACB of $400,000. There would be no effect on his Net Income For Tax Purposes in 2020. His partnership income inclusion for the two years would be calculated as follows:

2020 Addition To Net Income For Tax Purposes	Nil

The total net business income resulting from the 2021 sale of the property would be as follows:

Proceeds From Lot Sales	$4,400,000
Cost Of Land	(400,000)
Site Servicing Costs	(1,200,000)
Net Business Income	$2,800,000

Mr. Marrazzo's 2021 addition to his Net Income For Tax Purposes would be calculated as follows:

Priority Claim Of Accrued Gain ($1,300,000 - $400,000)	$ 900,000
Allocation Of Remaining Business Income [(50%)($2,800,000 - $900,000)]	950,000
2021 Addition To Net Income For Tax Purposes	$1,850,000

Part A - Joint Venture Results

No rollover under ITA 85(1) could take place because land inventory is not an eligible property. As a result, Mr. Marrazzo would recognize a 2020 gain on the transfer to Digger Inc. of $900,000 ($1,300,000 - $400,000). As previously noted, this gain would be treated as business income. His partnership income inclusion for the two years would be calculated as follows:

2020 Addition To Net Income For Tax Purposes	$ 900,000
Proceeds Of Disposition - Digger's Sale Of The Land	$4,400,000
Adjusted Cost Base Of Land	(1,300,000)
Site Servicing Costs	(1,200,000)
Net Business Income	$1,900,000
Mr. Marrazzo's Share	50%
2021 Addition To Net Income For Tax Purposes	$ 950,000

The addition to his Net Income For Tax Purposes over the two years is $1,850,000 ($900,000 + $950,000), the same total as in Part A.

Part A - Comparison

In total, Mr. Marrazzo will report the same increase in Net Income For Tax Purposes regardless of which form of organization is used. However, with the joint venture, he would have to report $900,000 of the income in 2020 and $950,000 in 2021. With the partnership, the entire $1,850,000 in income would be reported in 2021. Given that this approach provides significant tax deferral, the partnership approach appears preferable.

Part B - Adjusted Cost Base

The ACB of Mr. Marrazzo's partnership interest would be calculated as follows:

Capital Contribution - 2020	$ 400,000
Income Allocated To Mr. Marrazzo For 2020	Nil
ACB - December 31, 2021	$ 400,000
Income Allocated To Mr. Marrazzo For 2021 (Part A)	1,850,000
Mr. Marrazzo's ACB - January 1, 2022	$2,250,000

At this point, a winding-up of the partnership would have no tax consequences for Mr. Marrazzo.

The ACB of Digger Inc.'s partnership interest would be calculated as follows:

Capital Contribution - 2020	Nil
Income Allocated To Digger For 2020	Nil
Capital Contribution - 2021 = Servicing Costs	$ 1,200,000
ACB - December 31, 2021	$ 1,200,000
Income Allocated To Digger For 2021	
[(50%)($2,800,000 - $900,000) - See Part A]	950,000
Digger Inc.'s ACB - January 1, 2022	$ 2,150,000

Solution to Self Study Problem Eighteen - 3

Partnership Net Business Income

The Net Business Income of the partnership is calculated as follows:

Net Income As Per Income Statement		$ 192,100
Additions:		
Partners' Salaries [(2)($44,000)]	$88,000	
Amortization Deducted	12,500	
Charitable Donations	7,200	
Closing Accounts Receivable (Note One)	56,000	163,700
Deductions:		
Opening Accounts Receivable (Note One)	($ 27,000)	
Capital Gains On Securities (Note Two)	(14,000)	
Dividends Received (Note Three)	(48,000)	
CCA:		
Class 8 [(20%)($26,000)]	(5,200)	
Class 50 [(55%)(150%)($8,500)]	(7,013)	(101,213)
Net Business Income		$ 254,587

Note One The addition of closing accounts receivable and the deduction of the opening accounts receivable are required to adjust the cash based income figure to an accrual based income figure.

Note Two The total capital gain is deducted in the calculation of net business income. The taxable one-half of these gains is included on a flow through basis in the income of the individual partners.

Note Three The dividends received are deducted in the calculation of Net Business Income. They are flowed through as eligible dividends in the income of the individual partners.

Mr. Caldwell's Personal Income

Mr. Caldwell's Net Income For Tax Purposes would be calculated as follows:

Partnership Net Business Income	$254,587	
Mr. Caldwell's Share	50%	$ 127,294
Automobile Costs:		
CCA [($13,500)(30%)(75%)]		(3,038)
Operating Costs [($4,000)(75%)]		(3,000)
Net Business Income From Professional Practice		$121,256
Other Partnership Income:		
Taxable Capital Gains [(1/2)($14,000)]	$ 7,000	
Eligible Dividends Received	48,000	
Gross Up On Dividends [(38%)($48,000)]	18,240	
Subtotal	$ 73,240	
Mr. Caldwell's Share	50%	36,620
Net Income For Tax Purposes		$ 157,876

Mr. Caldwell's $3,600 [(50%)($7,200)] share of the charitable donations can be used as the basis for a credit against his personal Tax Payable. The amount of the credit would be $1,016 [(15%)($200) + (29%)($3,600- $200)] assuming this is his only charitable donation.

He is also entitled to a federal dividend tax credit of $4,975 [(50%)(6/11)($18,240)].

Solution to Self Study Problem Eighteen - 4

Part A - Income Inclusions
CCC has three sources of income. These are business income, property income (dividends), and taxable capital gains.

The calculation of the partnership's Net Business Income is as follows:

Net Income From Coffee Roasting		$ 37,200
Add:		
Salaries To Partners [(3)($2,400)]	$7,200	
Interest On Capital Contributions	2,000	
Personal Partner Expenses	1,100	
Charitable Donations	1,000	
Accounting Amortization	1,450	12,750
Deduct:		
CCA		(2,000)
Net Business Income		$ 47,950
Priority Allocations For Salaries And Interest ($7,200 + $2,000)		(9,200)
Residual To Be Allocated		$38,750

This amount would be allocated to the three partners as follows:

	Christine	Jennifer And Danny (Each)
Priority Allocation For Salaries	$2,400	$2,400
Priority Allocation For Interest	2,000	N/A
Allocation Of Residual On Equal Basis		
[(1/3)($38,750)]	12,917	12,917
Total Business Income Allocation	$17,317	$15,317

Other non-business income inclusions for each partner related to partnership activities would be as follows:

Eligible Dividends Received	$3,440
Gross Up [(38%)($3,440)]	1,307
Taxable Capital Gains [(1/2)($6,000)]	3,000
Total To Be Allocated	$ 7,747
Each Partner's Share	1/3
Non-Business Income Allocation	$ 2,582

This results in an addition to Net Income For Tax Purposes for Jennifer and Danny of $17,899 ($15,317 + $2,582). For Christine, the increase would include the $2,000 in interest and would equal $19,899 ($17,317 + $2,582).

Part B - Tax Credits

Charitable Donations   Each partner would be allocated $333 ($1,000 ÷ 3) in charitable donations. This would provide a federal tax credit of $69 [(15%)($200) + (29%)($133)] assuming this is their only charitable donation.

Dividends   Each of the partners would be eligible for a federal dividend tax credit of $238 [(1/3) (6/11)(38%)($3,440)].

Solution to Self Study Problem Eighteen - 5

Barry's Federal Tax Payable

The Net Business Income of the partnership would be calculated as follows:

Operating Income		$458,668
Additions:		
Amortization Expense	$ 17,466	
One-Half Meals And Entertainment		
[(1/2)($9,740)]	4,870	
Charitable Donations	8,658	
Opening Work In Progress		
[(60%)($65,464)]- See Note	39,278	70,272
Deductions:		
CCA	($ 23,562)	
Ending Work In Progress		
[(40%)($90,210)]- See Note	(36,084)	(59,646)
Net Business Income		$469,294

Note   As discussed in Chapter 6, the billed basis of revenue recognition is being phased out over a five year period beginning in 2019. Beginning in that year, the amount of unbilled work in process that can be deferred is reduced by 20 percent each year. This means that, in 2019, 80 percent of the unbilled work in process was deferred. This must be added back in this year. For 2020, 60 percent of unbilled work in process can be deferred.

Barry's Taxable Income and share of charitable donations for the year ending December 31, 2020, would be calculated as follows:

	Partnership	Share	Taxable Income
Partnership Business Income	$469,294	60%	$281,576
Taxable Capital Gain [(1/2)($18,660)]	9,330	Nil	Nil
Partnership Dividends Received	12,390	50%	6,195
38% Gross Up On Dividends Received	N/A		2,354
Taxable Income			$290,125
Charitable Donations	$8,658	50%	$4,329

Based on the preceding calculation, Barry's 2020 federal Tax Payable would be calculated as follows:

Tax On The First $214,378	$49,645
Tax On Additional	
$75,757 ($290,125- $214,369) At 33 Percent	25,000
Tax Payable Before Credits	$74,645
Basic Personal Credit [(15%)($13,229)]	(1,984))
Dividend Tax Credit [(6/11)($2,354)]	(1,284)
Charitable Donations Credit (See Note)	(1,393)
Federal Tax Payable	$69,904

Note The charitable donations tax credit would be calculated as follows:

$$[(15\%)(A)] + [(33\%)(B)] + [(29\%)(C)], \text{ where}$$

A = $200
B = The Lesser Of:
  • $4,329- $200 = $4,129
  • $290,125- $214,368 = $75,757
C = Nil [$4,329- ($200 + $4,129)]

The charitable donation credit would be equal to $1,393, calculated as [(15%)($200) + (33%)($4,129)].

Taxable Capital Gain From Sale Of Partnership Interest

The adjusted cost base of Barry's partnership interest on January 1, 2021, would be calculated as follows:

	Partnership	Share	ACB
Capital Contribution	N/A		$275,000
2019 Partnership Business Income	$372,466	60%	223,480
2019 Drawings	N/A		(114,000)
2020 Drawings	N/A		(142,000)
December 31, 2020			$242,480
2020 Partnership Business Income	$469,294	60%	281,576
2020 Capital Gain	9,330	Nil	Nil
2020 Partnership Dividends Received	12,390	50%	6,195
2020 Charitable Donations	(8,658)	50%	(4,329)
January 1, 2021, Adjusted Cost Base			$525,922

Given this calculation, the taxable capital gain on Barry's sale of the partnership interest would be calculated as follows:

Proceeds Of Disposition	$656,000
Adjusted Cost Base	(525,922)
Capital Gain	$ 130,078
Inclusion Rate	1/2
Taxable Capital Gain	$ 65,039

Solution to Self Study Problem Eighteen - 6

Part A - Adjusted Cost Base

The adjusted cost base of John Mathis' partnership interest would be calculated as follows

Initial Capital Contribution	$200,000
Additional Capital Contribution	75,000
Total Capital Contribution	$275,000
Drawings	(55,000))
Net Business Income [(1/3)($233,460)]	77,820
Capital Gains To Monroe and Mathis [(50%)($18,464)]	9,232
Dividends To Darin	Nil
Charitable Donations [(1/3)($8,460)]	(2,820)
Adjusted Cost Base- January 1, 2021	$304,232

Note Only the taxable one-half of the capital gain is included in the partner's income on the flow through of capital gains realized by a partnership. However, the remaining one-half is included in the assets of the partnership and, in the absence of a special provision to deal with this situation, the realization of this amount would be added to any capital gain realized on the disposition of the partnership interest. Given this, the full amount of John's share of realized capital gains is added to the partnership adjusted cost base.

Part B - Taxable Capital Gain On Disposition

Given the preceding calculation, the gain on the disposition of the partnership interest can be calculated as follows:

Proceeds Of Disposition		$320,000
Adjusted Cost Base:		
From Preceding Calculation	($304,232)	
Legal And Accounting Fees	(1,800)	(306,032)
Capital Gain		$ 13,968
Inclusion Rate		1/2
Taxable Capital Gain		$ 6,984

This amount would be included in John Mathis' Net Income For Tax Purposes for 2021 as a taxable capital gain. He would not include any partnership income for January as he was not allocated any of this income.

Part C - Effect On Other Partners

The fact that each partner paid $160,000 to John in return for one-half of his interest means that both Bob Darin and Matt Monroe would have a $160,000 increase in the adjusted cost base of their partnership interest.

Solution to Self Study Problem Eighteen - 7

Timing Of Income Inclusions For At-Risk Amounts vs. ACB

The addition of the share of the partnership income amounts to the at-risk balance as at December 31 is intended to ensure that this amount is taken into consideration in determining the amount that is actually at risk on that date. Notice, however, losses are not deducted at this time in the determination of the at-risk amount.

We would remind you that in calculating the adjusted cost base of the partnership interest, a partner's share of either a loss or a gain is not added until the first day of the following taxation year.

2020 Results

The required amounts would be calculated as follows:

ACB Of Partnership Interest- December 31, 2020	$ 50,000
Add: Share Of 2020 Partnership Income (Not Loss)	Nil
Subtotal	$ 50,000
Amounts Owed To The Partnership	(20,000)
At-Risk Amount- December 31, 2020	$ 30,000
Share of 2020 Loss [(10%)($400,000)]	($ 40,000)
At-Risk Amount- December 31, 2020	30,000
Limited Partnership Loss- December 31, 2020	($ 10,000)
Share of 2020 Loss [(10%)($400,000)]	($ 40,000)
Limited Partnership Loss- December 31, 2020	10,000
Deductible Loss For 2020	($ 30,000)

There is a limited partnership loss carry forward of $10,000 at the end of 2020.

2021 Results

ACB Of Partnership Interest- December 31, 2020	$50,000
Loss Deducted For 2020	(30,000)
ACB Of Partnership Interest- December 31, 2021	$20,000
Add: Share Of 2021 Partnership Income (Not Loss)	Nil
Subtotal	$20,000
Amounts Owed To The Partnership	Nil
At-Risk Amount- December 31, 2021	$20,000
Share of 2021 Loss [(10%)($70,000)]	($ 7,000)
Limited Partnership Loss Carry Forward	(10,000)
At-Risk Amount- December 31, 2021	20,000
Limited Partnership Loss- December 31, 2021	Nil
Share of 2021 Loss [(10%)($70,000)]	($ 7,000)
Limited Partnership Loss Carry Forward	(10,000)
Limited Partnership Loss- December 31, 2021	Nil
Deductible Loss For 2021	($ 17,000)

The $10,000 limited partnership loss carry forward from 2020 can be deducted as it is less than $13,000, the December 31, 2021, at-risk amount of $20,000 reduced by the allocated share of the 2021 partnership loss of $7,000. As a result, there is no limited partnership loss carry forward at the end of 2021.

2022 Results

ACB Of Partnership Interest- December 31, 2021	$20,000
Loss Deducted For 2021	(17,000)
ACB Of Partnership Interest- December 31, 2022	$ 3,000
Add: Share Of 2022 Partnership Income	Nil
Subtotal	$ 3,000
Amounts Owed To The Partnership	Nil
At-Risk Amount- December 31, 2022	$ 3,000

There is no limited partnership loss or deductible loss for 2022 and no limited partnership loss carry forward at the end of 2022.

Summary Of Results

The results are summarized in the following table:

	2020	2021	2022
ACB Of The Partnership Interest- December 31	$50,000	$20,000	$3,000
At-Risk Amount- December 31	30,000	20,000	3,000
Limited Partnership Loss	10,000	Nil	Nil
Deductible Loss	30,000	17,000	Nil
Limited Partnership Loss Carry Forward - December 31	10,000	Nil	Nil

Solution to Self Study Problem Eighteen - 8

Part A - Adjusted Cost Base Of Consideration

Cash   With all non-share consideration, the ACB is equal to its fair market value. In the case of cash, the fair market value is equal to the face value. Because there are differences in the ACB of the partnership interests, this cash will not be distributed equally. It will be distributed in a manner that will make the partnership interests equal. After the cash distribution, the total of the interests will be $912,000 ($1,634,000- $722,000). Dividing this by 3 gives individual interests of $304,000 ($912,000 ÷ 3). Based on this, the cash distribution would be as follows:

Porter ($382,000- $304,000)	$ 78,000
Quinn ($526,000- $304,000)	222,000
Roberts ($726,000- $304,000)	$422,000

Part A - Adjusted Cost Base Of Preferred Shares   With respect to the preferred shares received by each partner, ITA 85(3)(e) indicates that their ACB will be the lesser of:

- Their fair market value, which would be $180,000 for each of the three partners.
- The ACB of each partnership interest, reduced by the amount of non-share consideration received by the partner.

This latter value would be calculated as follows for each of the three partners:

	Porter	**Quinn**	**Roberts**
ACB (Equals Total Elected Value Of Corporate Assets Received)	$382,000	$526,000	$726,000
Cash Received	(78,000)	(222,000)	(422,000)
Balance	$304,000	$304,000	$304,000

For each of the three partners, the lower figure would be the fair market value of $180,000 and, as a consequence, this would be the ACB of their preferred shares.

Part A - Adjusted Cost Base Of Common Shares   Under ITA 85(3)(f), the ACB of the common shares received by each partner would be the ACB of their partnership interest less the sum of the value of the non-share consideration received and the value assigned to the preferred shares received. These amounts would be calculated as follows:

	Porter	**Quinn**	**Roberts**
ACB - Partnership Interest	$382,000	$526,000	$726,000
Cash Received	(78,000)	(222,000)	(422,000)
ACB - Preferred Shares	(180,000)	(180,000)	(180,000)
ACB - Common Shares	$ 124,000	$ 124,000	$ 124,000

Part B - Capital Gain Or Loss
As the non-share consideration had a value that was less than the value of the assets transferred, there will be no immediate gain or loss on this rollover. This can be demonstrated with the following calculation:

	Porter	**Quinn**	**Roberts**
Proceeds Of Disposition:			
Cash	$ 78,000	$222,000	$422,000
Preferred Shares	180,000	180,000	180,000
Common Shares	124,000	124,000	124,000
Total Proceeds	$382,000	$526,000	$726,000
ACB	(382,000)	(526,000)	(726,000)
Capital Gain (Loss)	Nil	Nil	Nil

From an economic point of view the gain is still present. The partners have simply deferred recording it for tax purposes by placing a value on the common shares of $372,000 [(3)($124,000)]. This is significantly below their current fair market value of $1,080,000. Note that the difference of $708,000 ($1,080,000- $372,000) is also the difference between the $2,342,000 fair market value of the total consideration given and the $1,634,000 value for the total ACB of the partnership interests.

CHAPTER 19

Chapter 19 Learning Objectives

After completing Chapter 19, you should be able to:

1. Explain the basic concepts of trusts (paragraph [P hereafter] 19-1 to 19-16).
2. Explain the difference between a trust and an estate, including the concept of a GRE (P 19-17 to 19-23).
3. Describe the procedures required to establish a trust (P 19-24 to 19-27).
4. Describe the procedures applicable to the filing of trust tax and information returns (P 19-28 to 19-29).
5. List the major non-tax reasons for using trusts (P 19-30 and 19-31).

6. Describe the different classifications of trusts (P 19-32 to 19-51).
7. Explain the basic model for the taxation of trusts (P 19-52 and 19-55).
8. Describe the rollovers available for contributions to a trust (P 19-56 to 19-68).
9. Describe the rollovers available to transfer assets to the capital beneficiaries of a trust (P 19-69 to 19-74).
10. Apply the deemed disposition rules after a trust has existed for 21 years and on the death of a settlor of an alter ego trust or survivor spouse of a qualifying spousal trust (P 19-75 to 19-78).

11. Calculate the Net Income For Tax Purposes and Taxable Income of a trust (P 19-79 to 19-92).
12. Describe the provisions relating to income allocations to beneficiaries (P 19-93 to 19-112).
13. Calculate the Tax Payable for testamentary and inter vivos trusts (P 19-113 to 19-121).
14. Explain how the income attribution rules may be applicable to trusts and describe any related tax planning considerations (P 19-122 to 19-127).
15. Explain the tax treatment of the purchase and sale of an interest in a trust (P 19-128 to 19-133).

16. Describe the major tax planning factors that should be considered when evaluating various types of trusts such as family, spousal, and alter ego (P 19-134 to 19-147).
17. List the non-tax and tax considerations that should be considered in estate planning (P 19-148 to 19-152).
18. Explain the objectives of an estate freeze (P 19-153 and 19-154).
19. Describe the estate freeze techniques that do not involve rollovers (P 19-155 to 19-162).
20. Describe the application of an ITA 86(1) share exchange to implement an estate freeze (P 19-163 to 19-171).
21. List the major considerations involved in choosing between a Section 85 and Section 86 rollover when implementing an estate freeze (P 19-172 to 19-174).

How to Work Through Chapter 19

We recommend the following approach in dealing with the material in this Chapter:

Introduction To Trusts And Estate Planning
- Read paragraph 19-1 to 19-7 (in the textbook).

Basic Concepts
- Read paragraph 19-8 to 19-23.

Establishing A Trust
- Read paragraph 19-24 to 19-27.
- Do Exercise Nineteen-1 (in the textbook) and check the solution in this Study Guide.

Returns And Payments - Trusts
- Read paragraph 19-28 to 19-29.

Non-Tax Reasons For Using Trusts
- Read paragraph 19-30 to 19-31.

Classification Of Trusts (Personal, Testamentary, And Inter Vivos)
- Read paragraph 19-32 to 19-51.

Taxation Of Trusts - The Basic Model
- Read paragraph 19-52 to 19-55.
- Do Exercise Nineteen-2 and check the solution in this Study Guide.

Rollovers To A Trust
- Read paragraph 19-56 to 19-64.
- Do Exercise Nineteen-3 and check the solution in this Study Guide.
- Read paragraph 19-65 to 19-68.
- Do Exercise Nineteen-4 and check the solution in this Study Guide.

Rollovers To Capital Beneficiaries
- Read paragraph 19-69 to 19-74.
- Do Self Study Problem Nineteen-1, which is available on MyLab, and check the solution in this Study Guide.

21 Year Deemed Disposition Rule And Other Deemed Dispositions
- Read paragraph 19-75 to 19-78.

Net Income For Tax Purposes And Taxable Income Of A Trust
- Read paragraph 19-79 to 19-92.
- Do Exercise Nineteen-5 and check the solution in this Study Guide.

Income Allocations To Beneficiaries
- Read paragraph 19-93 to 19-109.
- Do Exercise Nineteen-6 and check the solution in this Study Guide.

Allocation Of Business Income, CCA, Recapture of CCA, And Terminal Losses
- Read paragraph 19-110 and 19-111.
- Do Exercise Nineteen-7 and check the solution in this Study Guide.

Principal Residence Exemption
- Read paragraph 19-112.

Tax Payable Of Personal Trusts
- Read paragraph 19-113 to 19-121.
- Do Exercise Nineteen-8 and check the solution in this Study Guide.
- Do Self Study Problems Nineteen-2 to Nineteen-4 and check the solutions in this Study Guide.

Income Attribution - Trusts
- Read paragraph 19-122 to 19-124.
- Do Exercise Nineteen-9 and check the solution in this Study Guide.
- Do Self Study Problems Nineteen-5 and Nineteen-6 and check the solutions in this Study Guide.
- Read paragraph 19-125 to 19-127.

Purchase Or Sale Of An Interest In A Trust
- Read paragraph 19-128 to 19-133.
- Do Exercise Nineteen-10 and check the solution in this Study Guide.

Tax Planning Using Trusts (Family, Spousal, And Alter Ego Trusts)
- Read paragraph 19-134 to 19-142.
- Do Exercise Nineteen-11 and check the solution in this Study Guide.
- Read paragraph 19-143 to 19-147.

Estate Planning - Tax And Non-Tax Considerations
- Read paragraph 19-148 to 19-152.

Estate Freeze - Objectives And Techniques, Including ITA 86 Share Exchange
- Read paragraph 19-153 to 19-174.

SIFT Partnerships And Trusts
- Read paragraph 19-175.

To Complete This Chapter
- If you would like more practice in problem solving, do the Supplementary Self Study Problems for the chapter. These problems and solutions are available on MyLab.
- Review the Key Terms Used In This Chapter in the textbook at the end of Chapter 19. Consult the Glossary for the meaning of any key terms you do not know.
- Test yourself with the Chapter 19 Glossary Flashcards available on MyLab.
- Ensure you have achieved the Chapter 19 Learning Objectives listed in this Study Guide.
- As a review, we recommend you view the PowerPoint presentation for Chapter 19 that is on MyLab.

Practice Examination
- Write the Practice Examination for Chapter 19 that is on MyLab. Mark your examination using the Practice Exam Solution that is on MyLab.

Solutions to Chapter Nineteen Exercises

Exercise Nineteen - 1 Solution
Case A   While Mr. Black has transferred property, it is not clear that his intention was to create a trust. No trust would be created by his transfer.

Case B   Jane's "friends" cannot be considered to be an identifiable class. As a consequence, there is no certainty as to beneficiaries and no trust would be created by her transfer.

Case C   Robert's "children" would be an identifiable class. It would appear that a trust has been created.

Case D While Suzanne has signed the agreement, it does not appear that the property has been transferred. This means that no trust has been created.

Exercise Nineteen - 2 Solution

With respect to Joanne's transfer of her securities to the trust, the transaction would be deemed to take place at fair market value. This would result in a taxable capital gain to Joanne of $10,000 [(1/2)($220,000 - $200,000)]. There would be no tax consequences to Jocelyn or the trust as a result of this transfer.

As the trust distributed all of its income during the year, none of the interest would be taxed in the trust. All of the interest would be included in Jocelyn's income and, because she is an adult, there would be no income attribution to Joanne.

Under ITA 107(2), the transfer from the trust to Jocelyn on January 1, 2021, would take place at the trust's tax cost of $220,000. There would be no tax consequences for Joanne, Jocelyn, or the trust as a result of this transfer. However, as Jocelyn's adjusted cost base is $220,000, the sale at the fair market value of $230,000 would result in a taxable capital gain of $5,000 [(1/2)($230,000 - $220,000)].

Exercise Nineteen - 3 Solution

As there is a rollover available on transfers to a qualifying spousal trust, the accrued $30,000 gain ($90,000 - $60,000) will not be recognized until her husband or the spousal trust eventually disposes of the shares. The spousal trust acquires the shares (a non-depreciable capital asset) at Louise's adjusted cost base of $60,000, which will be her husband's adjusted cost base if the trust transfers the shares to him personally rather than selling them.

Exercise Nineteen - 4 Solution

In Scenarios 1, 2, and 3, the settlor has a taxable capital gain of $300 [(1/2)($1,600 - $1,000)] and the adjusted cost base to the trust is the fair market value of $1,600. In Scenarios 4 to 7, there is a tax free rollover. The results can be summarized as follows:

Scenario	Taxable Capital Gain (Settlor)	Adjusted Cost Base (Trust)
1. Inter vivos trust for adult child	$300	$1,600
2. Inter vivos trust for minor child	300	1,600
3. Testamentary trust for friend	300	1,600
4. Inter vivos qualifying spousal trust	Nil	1,000
5. Testamentary qualifying spousal trust	Nil	1,000
6. Joint spousal trust	Nil	1,000
7. Alter ego trust	Nil	1,000

Exercise Nineteen - 5 Solution

The required calculations are as follows:

Business Income	$220,000
Preferred Beneficiary Election	(50,000)
Distributions To Other Beneficiaries	(170,000)
Designation Under ITA 104(13.1)	
Amounts Deemed Not Paid	35,000
Net Income For Tax Purposes	$ 35,000
Business Loss Carry Forward	(35,000)
Taxable Income	Nil

The preferred beneficiary election would mean that the $50,000 would be taxed in the hands of the disabled beneficiary even though the funds are retained in the trust. Since this is an inter vivos trust, without the election the $50,000 would be taxed at the maximum rate in the trust. As the disabled beneficiary has no other source of income, the $50,000 would be subject to tax at lower rates than would be the case if it was taxed in the trust.

By designating $35,000 as amounts not paid, the trust can absorb the loss carry forward. As a result, the beneficiaries will not pay tax on this amount even though it has been distributed to them.

Exercise Nineteen - 6 Solution

The income allocation would be as follows:

	Received By Trust	Paid To Bryan	Retained By Trust
Eligible Dividends	$ 100,000	$ 60,000	$40,000
Non-Eligible Dividends From CCPC	30,000	30,000	Nil
Capital Gain	20,000	20,000	Nil
Totals	$ 150,000	$110,000	$40,000

The Net Income For Tax Purposes of the trust would be calculated as follows:

Eligible Dividends	$ 40,000
Gross Up Of Eligible Dividends At 38 Percent	15,200
Net Income For Tax Purposes - Trust	$ 55,200

The corresponding calculation for Bryan would be as follows:

Eligible Dividends	$ 60,000
Gross Up Of Eligible Dividends At 38 Percent	22,800
Non-Eligible Dividends From CCPC	30,000
Gross Up Of Non-Eligible Dividends At 15 Percent	4,500
Taxable Capital Gains [(1/2)($20,000)]	10,000
Net Income For Tax Purposes - Bryan	$127,300

Note that the non-taxable one-half of the capital gain would be received by Bryan on a tax free basis. Both the trust and Bryan will be able to deduct a federal dividend tax credit against federal Tax Payable. The TOSI is not applicable as Bryan is over 18 years of age and is actively engaged in the private corporation on a regular and continuous basis.

Exercise Nineteen - 7 Solution

If the property is sold in December 2020, no CCA can be deducted. This means that the total amount of property income to be distributed to Martin and taxed in his hands is $97,000 ($32,000 of rental income plus $65,000 of recapture). Given this distribution, the trust's Net Income For Tax Purposes will be nil.

Alternatively, if the rental property is not sold and all of the income is distributed to Martin, he will include $6,000 ($32,000 - $26,000) in his 2020 Net Income For Tax Purposes. The trust's 2020 Net Income For Tax Purposes will be nil.

Exercise Nineteen - 8 Solution

The Taxable Income in Parts A, B, and C is the same and would be calculated as follows:

Eligible Dividends Received	$100,000
Gross Up At 38 Percent	38,000
Taxable Income	$138,000

Part A   As all of its 2020 income has been distributed, there would be no Taxable Income or Tax Payable for the trust. This conclusion would not change if the trust were an inter vivos trust rather than a testamentary trust. The beneficiary's federal Tax Payable on the Taxable Income of $138,000 is calculated in the following table.

Part B   As none of the dividends are distributed by the trust to the beneficiary, there would be no Taxable Income or Tax Payable for the beneficiary. The trust's federal Tax Payable on the Taxable Income of $138,000 is calculated in the table that follows.

The federal Tax Payable for Parts A and B would be calculated as follows:

	Part A	Part B
Tax On First $97,069	$ 17,230	$ 17,230
Tax On Next $40,931 ($138,000 - $97,069) At 26 Percent	10,642	10,642
Total Tax Before Credits	$ 27,872	$ 27,872
Personal Tax Credit [(15%)($13,229)]	(1,984)	N/A
Federal Dividend Tax Credit [(6/11)($38,000)]	(20,727)	(20,727)
Federal Tax Payable	$ 5,161	$ 7,145

Notice that the difference between the Tax Payable in Part A and Part B is $1,984 ($7,294 - $7,145). This amount is equal to the basic personal tax credit.

Part C   Once again, with no distributions to the beneficiary, the trust's Taxable Income would be $138,000. There would be no Taxable Income or Tax Payable for the beneficiary. Based on this, the Tax Payable for the inter vivos trust would be calculated as follows:

Tax On $138,000 At 33 Percent	$45,540
Federal Dividend Tax Credit [(6/11)($38,000)]	(20,727)
Federal Tax Payable	$24,813

Comparison   As a comparison of these examples makes clear, if a trust has beneficiaries with no other sources of income, overall tax payments will be reduced by distributing eligible dividends to beneficiaries (Part A). While these examples do not illustrate this possibility, the conclusion would be the same if non-eligible dividends were involved. Note that the results in Part C would be the same for a testamentary trust that was not designated a graduated rate estate. In Parts B and C where the trust has paid the tax, the dividends would be distributed to the beneficiary on a tax free basis. However, in Part C, if the beneficiaries have a marginal federal tax rate that is less than 33 percent, there will be a tax cost in having the trust pay the tax.

Exercise Nineteen - 9 Solution

Income on the bonds is subject to the attribution rules to the extent that the income is allocated to Trevor's spouse, Carmen, and to their minor son, Mitch. This means that two-thirds of the interest will be attributed back to Trevor. With respect to the capital gain, the attribution rules do not apply on transfers to minors. This means that only Carmen's share of the gain will be attributed back to Trevor. The increase in Taxable Income for Trevor and the trust's beneficiaries are calculated as follows:

	Carmen	Mitch	Rhonda	Attributed To Trevor
Interest Income ($27,000 ÷ 3)	$9,000	$9,000	$ 9,000	
Interest Attribution To Trevor	(9,000)	(9,000)	Nil	$18,000
Taxable Capital Gain				
[(1/2)($6,000) ÷ 3]	1,000	1,000	1,000	
Capital Gain Attribution To Trevor	(1,000)	Nil	Nil	1,000
Increase In Taxable Income	Nil	$1,000	$10,000	$19,000

If Trevor had died on January 1 of the current year, there would be no income attribution for the year. Each of the beneficiaries would have Taxable Income of $10,000.

Exercise Nineteen - 10 Solution

With respect to Sam, he has acquired a capital interest for consideration of $190,000. This will be the adjusted cost base of the interest he has acquired.

With respect to Mehrdad, he has disposed of a capital asset for proceeds of disposition of $190,000. Since he did not purchase the interest in the trust, his adjusted cost base as usually determined would be nil. However, for this disposition, the adjusted cost base of the capital interest is the greater of nil and the cost amount as determined under ITA 108(1). The cost amount would be $125,000, one-half of the $250,000 tax cost of the assets in the trust. The result would be a taxable capital gain of $32,500 [(1/2)($190,000 - $125,000)].

The original cost of the securities of $120,000 is not relevant in these calculations as the father was taxed on the $130,000 ($250,000 - $120,000) capital gain in the year the securities were transferred.

Exercise Nineteen - 11 Solution

As Sarah's other income places her in the maximum federal tax bracket of 33 percent, her federal tax savings resulting from transferring the assets to the family trust would be $36,300 [($110,000)(33%)]. The federal tax that would be payable on the additional $55,000 received by Jerri is as follows:

Tax On First $48,535	$ 7,280
Tax On Additional $6,465 ($55,000 - $48,535) At 20.5 Percent	1,325
Tax Before Credit	$8,605
Personal Tax Credit	(1,984)
Tax Payable - Jerri	$6,621

The alternative minimum tax is not relevant for Jerri because the income is in the form of interest, not dividends. As Mark would be in a position to use all of his tax credits prior to receiving the additional $55,000 in income, they are not relevant to the determination of his marginal increase in taxes. The federal tax that would be payable on the additional $55,000 received by Mark is as follows:

Tax At 15.0 Percent ($48,535 - $48,000 = $535 @ 15.0%	$ 80
Tax At 20.5 Percent ($97,069 - $48,000 = $48,534 @ 20.5%)	$ 9,949
Tax At 26 Percent ($55,000 + $48,000 - $97,069 = $5,931 @ 26%)	1,542
Additional Tax Payable - Mark	$11,571

The total tax paid by the two children would be $18,192 ($6,621 + $11,571). This is $18,108 ($36,300 - $18,192) per year less than the amount that would be paid by Sarah without the trust. When combined with a reduction in provincial taxes, the total tax savings could be significantly larger. This should be more than enough to cover the costs of establishing and maintaining this trust.

One tax planning consideration would be to have the trust pay Mark's wife rather than Mark. Since she has no income, her federal tax payable would be the same as in Jerri's calculation. Although Mark would lose the spousal credit in this case, his wife would claim the basic personal credit herself. Despite the fact that having Mark's wife as the beneficiary would result in less taxes being paid, whether this would be advantageous for Mark (and his mother) would also depend on non-tax considerations such as the state of the marriage.

Solution to Self Study Problem Nineteen - 1

Case A

1. The settlor has deemed proceeds of disposition of the fair market value of $26,400 and will record a taxable capital gain of $1,550 [(1/2)($26,400 - $23,300)]. In addition, there will be recapture of CCA of $7,900 ($23,300 - $15,400).

2. The trust acquires the property at a deemed capital cost of $26,400. However, for purposes of calculating CCA and recapture, the ITA 13(7)(e) rules for non-arm's length transactions apply and the value will be $24,850 [$23,300 + (1/2)($26,400 - $23,300)].

Case B

1. The settlor has deemed proceeds of disposition of the fair market value of $15,200. This would result in the settlor having recapture of $2,800 ($15,200 - $12,400).

2. The asset would be recorded in the trust records at the settlor's capital cost of $19,500, with deemed CCA of $4,300, resulting in a UCC of $15,200.

3. When the asset is transferred to the capital beneficiary, the deemed proceeds to the trust will be the UCC at the date of distribution of $13,600, resulting in no gain or loss on the transfer. The beneficiary will be deemed to have acquired the property for the UCC amount of $13,600. However, the beneficiary will have a capital cost of $19,500 for subsequent recapture and capital gains calculation purposes.

Case C

1. Under the general ITA 70(6) rollover provision, the deemed proceeds to the decedent would be the property's cost of $18,200, resulting in no gain or loss on the transfer. As the deceased has net capital loss carry forwards, a better alternative would be to elect out of ITA 70(6) and transfer the property at its fair market value of $76,400. The loss carry forwards could then be used to eliminate taxation on the resulting taxable capital gain of $29,100 [(1/2)($76,400 - $18,200)].

2. Note that in the year of death, net capital loss carry forwards can be deducted against any type of income. If the decedent has other income against which the net capital loss carry forward can be deducted, it may not be advantageous to elect out of the rollover. More information on the spouse's current and future Taxable Income would be needed to optimize the use of the net capital loss carry forward.

3. Under the general ITA 70(6) rollover provision, the trust would record the property at the decedent's cost of $18,200. If the fair market value election is made, the spousal trust will have acquired the property at a deemed cost of $76,400. This higher value will serve to reduce any future gain on the property when it is sold.

Case D

1. The settlor has deemed proceeds of disposition of the fair market value of $123,200 and will record a taxable capital gain of $18,900 [(1/2)($123,200 - $85,400)].

2. The trust will record the property at a deemed cost equal to the fair market value of $123,200.

Case E

1. The settlor has deemed proceeds of disposition of the fair market value of $51,600 and will record a taxable capital gain of $4,200 [(1/2)($51,600 - $43,200)].

2. The asset would be recorded in the trust records at the fair market value of $51,600.

3. When the asset is transferred to the capital beneficiary, the deemed proceeds to the trust will be the carrying value of $51,600, resulting in no gain or loss on the transfer. The beneficiary will be deemed to have acquired the property at a cost of $51,600.

Case F

1. The deemed proceeds for the settlor would be the tax cost of $14,200, resulting in no gain or loss on the transfer.

2. The trust acquires the property at a deemed cost of $14,200.

Solution to Self Study Problem Nineteen - 2

Part A - Taxable Income For The GRE And Its Beneficiaries

The payments made by the GRE administrator will result in the following amounts of Taxable Income for the GRE and the two children:

	Daughter (30%)	Son (50%)	GRE (20%)
Eligible Dividends Received	$ 26,100	$ 43,500	$ 17,400
Gross Up Of 38 Percent	9,918	16,530	6,612
British Interest (Gross			
Amount Of $110,000)	33,000	55,000	22,000
Net Rental Income ($21,000)	6,300	10,500	4,200
Net And Taxable Income	$ 75,318	$125,530	$ 50,212
British Taxes Paid* ($16,500)	$ 4,950	$ 8,250	$ 3,300

*The net interest receipt of $93,500 equals 85 percent of $110,000 ($93,500 ÷ 85%). This means that the taxes withheld totaled $16,500 [(15%)($110,000)].

Part B - Federal Tax Payable For The GRE

Income that remains in a GRE is taxed using the same rates as would be applicable to an individual. However, the GRE would not be able to claim personal tax credits under ITA 118 to reduce the amount of Tax Payable.

The after tax income of the GRE can be distributed tax free to the beneficiaries of the GRE.

Federal Tax Payable for the GRE would be calculated as follows:

Federal Tax Payable:	
On First $48,535	$ 7,280
On Remaining $1,677 ($50,212 - $48,535) At 20.5 Percent	344
Federal Tax Payable Before Credits	$ 7,624
Federal Dividend Tax Credit [(6/11)($6,612)]	(3,607)
Foreign Tax Credit (See Note)	(3,300)
Federal Tax Payable	$ 717

Note The amount that can be deducted for the foreign tax credit is the lesser of the $3,300 of foreign taxes withheld and an amount determined by the following formula:

[(Foreign Non-Business Income ÷ Adjusted Net Income)(Tax Payable Before Credits)]

= [($22,000 ÷ $50,212)($7,624)]

= $3,340

As this amount is more than the actual foreign taxes of $3,300 allocated to the GRE, the actual foreign taxes paid would be the lesser amount, and would be the foreign tax credit.

Note that if the foreign taxes withheld had exceeded 15 percent of the gross amount of foreign income, the excess would have been deductible under ITA 20(11), rather than added to the amount of foreign tax withheld in the formula.

Solution to Self Study Problem Nineteen - 3

Parts A And B - Alternative One
The following tables assume that one-half of the dividend income will remain in the GRE. They provide the required information on Taxable Income and Tax Payable for the relevant taxation years:

Income Allocation	GRE	Rowena	Roger
Business Income	$ Nil	$ 12,000	$ 8,000
Interest	Nil	1,800	1,200
Non-Eligible Dividends Received	25,000	15,000	10,000
Dividend Gross Up (15%)	3,750	2,250	1,500
Net Rental Income (Note)	Nil	2,400	1,600
Net Income And Taxable Income	$28,750	$33,450	$22,300
Federal Income Tax At 15 Percent	$ 4,313	$ 5,018	$ 3,345
Basic Personal Credit	N/A	(1,984)	(1,984)
Federal Dividend Tax Credit			
[(9/13)(Gross Up)]	(2,596)	(1,558)	(1,038)
Federal Tax Payable (Total = $3,516)	$ 1,717	$ 1,476	$ 323

Note The $4,000 net rental income is calculated as the rent receipts of $12,000 less the operating expenses of $6,000 and CCA of $2,000. The CCA is claimed at the GRE level.

Parts A And B - Alternative Two

The following income allocation assumes that all of the GRE's income will be allocated to Rowena and Roger. This means that the Taxable Income and federal Tax Payable of the GRE will be nil. The calculations for Rowena and Roger for the year ending December 31, 2020, are as follows:

Income Allocation	Rowena	Roger
Business Income	$12,000	$ 8,000
Interest	1,800	1,200
Non-Eligible Dividends Received	30,000	20,000
Dividend Gross Up (15%)	4,500	3,000
Net Rental Income	2,400	1,600
Net And Taxable Income	$50,700	$33,800

	Rowena	Roger
Federal Income Tax:		
Roger: [(15%)($33,800)]		$ 5,070
Rowena: On First $48,535 At 15 Percent	$ 7,280	
Rowena: On Remaining $2,165		
($50,700 - $47,630) At 20.5 Percent	444	
Basic Personal Credit	(1,984)	(1,984)
Federal Dividend Tax Credit [(9/13)(Gross Up)]	(3,115)	(2,077)
Federal Tax Payable (Total = $3,634)	$ 2,625	$ 1,009

Part C - Comparison

The total federal Tax Payable in Alternative Two is $118 ($3,634 - $3,516) higher than the total in Alternative One. This difference reflects the fact that in Alternative Two, $2,165 of the total income was taxed at 20.5 percent, while in Alternative One, all of the income was taxed at 15 percent [(20.5% - 15%)($2,165)] = $119 ($1 rounding difference.)

Solution to Self Study Problem Nineteen - 4

Part A - Calculation Of Taxable Income

All amounts are allocated 45 percent to Jessica Jurgens, 40 percent to Joseph Jurgens, and 15 percent to the trust. The Taxable Income of the two beneficiaries and the trust would be calculated as follows:

	Jessica (45%)	Joseph (40%)	Trust (15%)
Interest On GICs	$ 56,700	$ 50,400	$ 18,900
Eligible Dividends Received	207,900	184,800	69,300
Gross Up Of 38 Percent	79,002	70,224	26,334
Taxable Capital Gain On Land			
[(1/2)($250,000 - $85,000)]	37,125	33,000	12,375
Taxable Capital Gain On Building			
[(1/2)($962,000 - $725,000)]	53,325	47,400	17,775
Net Rental Income (Note)	63,000	56,000	21,000
Net And Taxable Income	$497,052	$441,824	$165,684

Note The net rental income, including the recapture of CCA, can be calculated as follows:

Revenues From Rental Property		$ 125,000
Cash Expenses On Rental Property		(83,000)
Recapture Of CCA:		
Capital Cost Of The Building	$ 725,000	
UCC	(627,000)	98,000
Net Rental Income, Including Recapture		$ 140,000

Part B - Tax Payable For The Trust

The federal Tax Payable for the trust is as follows:

Federal Tax Before Credits [(33%)($165,684)]	$54,676
Federal Dividend Tax Credit [(6/11)($26,334)]	(14,364)
Federal Tax Payable	$40,312

As this trust is an inter vivos trust, all of its income is subject to federal tax at 33 percent [ITA 122(1)].

Solution to Self Study Problem Nineteen - 5

A. It is an inter vivos trust. In less technical terms, it could also be described as a family trust in that all of the beneficiaries are family members. In addition, it could be referred to as partially discretionary in that the trustee determines the timing of the income payments.

B. As the trust is an inter vivos trust, the year end will have to be December 31 of each year.

C. All of the income that is allocated to Mr. Dion will be subject to the income attribution rules. As a consequence, it will be included in the Net Income For Tax Purposes of Mrs. Dion. This includes interest, dividends, and capital gains earned by the trust.

As the twins are over the age of 17, the attribution rules will not apply to their share of the trust's income. This means that the income that is allocated to them will be reported as a part of their Net Income For Tax Purposes.

As all of the trust's income is either attributed back to Mrs. Dion or allocated to beneficiaries, the trust's Net Income For Tax Purposes will be nil.

D. The answer here will depend on the terms of the loan to the trust as the rules for non-arm's length loans apply. If it is an interest free loan, the results will be the same as in Part C. That is, the income allocated to Mr. Dion will be attributed back to Mrs. Dion, while the income allocated to the twins will be included in their Net Income For Tax Purposes. This would also be the result if the interest rate on the loan was less than the prescribed rate.

Alternatively, if the loan paid interest at the prescribed rate or higher, the income attribution rules would not apply and the trust income allocated to Mr. Dion would be taxed in his hands. Note that the loan would have to have bona fide repayment terms and the interest would have to be paid within 30 days of the end of each calendar year.

E. ITA 74.5(3) indicates that the income attribution rules do not apply to any income or loss from property that relates to the period throughout which the individuals are living separate and apart because of a breakdown of their marriage or common-law partnership. The attribution rules do not apply to income that accrues subsequent to a separation.

Solution to Self Study Problem Nineteen - 6

Part A - Trust For Daughter

The first trust created is a testamentary trust for the benefit of Mrs. Turner's daughter, Melanie. When there is a transfer of assets at death to any taxpayer other than a spouse or a spousal trust, there is a deemed disposition with proceeds equal to fair market value. Capital gains on all of the assets transferred would need to be realized along with recapture of CCA on the warehouse building.

The principal residence exemption could be used to eliminate the $165,000 [($120,000 - $20,000) + ($145,000 - $80,000)] capital gain on the principal residence. Melanie will not have a taxable benefit from use of the residence. However, since the trust pays for the upkeep and maintenance of the residence, the trust can deduct the costs and they are taxable as income to Melanie.

The capital gain and recapture on the disposition of the warehouse building would be included in Mrs. Turner's final tax return. The taxable capital gain on the warehouse land is $10,000 [(1/2) ($75,000 - $55,000)]. As the fair market value of the warehouse is equal to its capital cost, there is no capital gain on the warehouse building. However, there would be $40,000 ($85,000 - $45,000) of recaptured CCA. This amount would be included in Mrs. Turner's final tax return.

The trust will be deemed to acquire all of the assets at their fair market values. In the case of the warehouse land, the adjusted cost base will be the fair market value of $75,000. In the case of the warehouse building, the capital cost and the new UCC will be the fair market value of $85,000, which is equal to its original cost.

Part A - Trust For Husband

The second trust appears to be a qualifying spousal trust. Where there is a transfer at death to a qualifying spousal trust, the transfer is deemed to be a disposition with proceeds equal to the deceased taxpayer's tax cost. This would be the capital cost of the cottage and stock portfolio and, as a consequence of using this value, the transfer of assets to the trust will have no tax consequences for Mrs. Turner's final tax return.

The trust will be deemed to have acquired all of the assets at the same capital cost values that were used as proceeds of disposition by Mrs. Turner.

Part B - Death Of Husband

Unless Mr. West has remarried with great haste and can pass these assets on to a new spouse or qualifying spousal trust, his death will result in a deemed disposition of the trust's assets for proceeds equal to fair market value. In the case of the cottage, there is a capital gain of $170,000 [($200,000 - $40,000) + ($122,000 - $112,000)], one-half, or $85,000, of which is taxable. On the stock market portfolio there will be a taxable capital gain of $30,000 [(1/2)($280,000 - $220,000)].

Mr. West's death would have no effect on Mrs. Turner's final return or tax effect on Melanie. Of course, if Melanie is a beneficiary in Mr. West's will, his death will result in additional income and income tax for Melanie in the future, but this information is not in the problem.

Part C - Graduated Rate Estate

The principal advantage of a graduated rate estate is that any income that is not distributed is taxed at graduated rates, rather than at the maximum federal rate of 33 percent. As the problem does not state the marginal tax rates for either Mr. Turner or Melanie, we cannot determine whether or not this would be advantageous. If either of their marginal rates are above the minimum 15 percent rate, GRE status for the income producing properties could be advantageous.

Given Mr. West's short remaining life, any benefits from the GRE would be quite limited in his case.

CHAPTER 20

Chapter 20 Learning Objectives

After completing Chapter 20, you should be able to:

1. Describe the role of international tax treaties (paragraph [P hereafter] P 20-1 to 20-5).
2. Describe the liability for Part I tax of non-residents earning Canadian source income from business, employment, and the disposition of Taxable Canadian Property (P 20-6 to 20-30).
3. Describe the liability for Part XIII tax of non-residents earning Canadian source property income including income from interest, dividends, royalties, rents, and pensions (P 20-31 to 20-62).
4. Describe the deemed disposition/re-acquisition provisions related to immigration to Canada (P 20-63 to 20-65).
5. Describe the tax provisions related to emigration from Canada, including those related to elective dispositions and security for departure tax (P 20-66 to 20-79).

6. Describe the provisions available for unwinding a deemed disposition on departure from Canada (P 20-80 to 20-84).
7. Explain the rules applicable to short-term residents of Canada (P 20-85 to 20-87).
8. Describe the foreign investment reporting requirements of form T1135 (P 20-88 to 20-98).
9. Apply the appropriate tax treatment for Canadian residents of foreign source employment income, business income, and capital gains (P 20-99 to 20-107).
10. Describe the basic concepts behind the taxation of foreign source dividends received by resident individuals (P 20-108 to 20-120).

11. Describe the taxation of dividends received by resident corporations from non-affiliated corporations (P 20-121).
12. Identify foreign affiliates (P 20-122 to 20-125).
13. Describe the tax treatment of dividends received from non-controlled foreign affiliates, including identification of their various types of surplus balances (P 20-126 to 20-139).
14. Explain the concept of a controlled foreign affiliate (P 20-140 to 20-143).
15. Apply the rules associated with, and the appropriate tax treatment of, foreign property accrual income (FAPI) (P 20-144 to 20-151).
16. Describe the tax treatment of dividends paid from FAPI (P 20-152 to 20-153).

How to Work Through Chapter 20

We recommend the following approach in dealing with the material in this Chapter:

Subjects Covered In Chapter
- Read paragraph 20-1 to 20-5 (in the textbook).

Part I Tax On Non-Residents - Introduction
- Read paragraph 20-6 to 20-14.

Non-Residents Carrying On Business In Canada - Part I Tax
- Read paragraph 20-15 to 20-20.
- Do Exercise Twenty-1 and check the solution in this Study Guide.

Non-Residents Earning Employment Income In Canada - Part I Tax
- Read paragraph 20-21 to 20-25.
- Do Exercises Twenty-2 and Twenty-3 and check the solutions in this Study Guide.

Non-Residents Disposing Of Taxable Canadian Property - Part I Tax
- Read paragraph 20-26 to 20-30.
- Do Exercise Twenty-4 and check the solution in this Study Guide.
- Do Self Study Problem Twenty-1, which is available on MyLab, and check the solution in this Study Guide.

Part XIII Tax On Non-Residents - Introduction And Applicability
- Read paragraph 20-31 to 20-37.

Interest Income Earned By Non-Residents - Part XIII Tax
- Read paragraph 20-38 to 20-41.
- Do Exercise Twenty-5 and check the solution in this Study Guide.

Dividend, Royalty, And Rental Income Earned By Non-Residents - Part XIII Tax
- Read paragraph 20-42 to 20-52.
- Do Exercise Twenty-6 and check the solution in this Study Guide.

Pension And Other Benefits Earned By Non-Residents - Part XIII Tax
- Read paragraph 20-53 to 20-62.
- Do Self Study Problem Twenty-2 and check the solution in this Study Guide.

Entering Canada - Immigration
- Read paragraph 20-63 to 20-65.

Departing From Canada - Emigration
- Read paragraph 20-66.
- Do Exercises Twenty-7 and Twenty-8 and check the solutions in this Study Guide.
- Read paragraph 20-67 to 20-74.
- Do Exercise Twenty-9 and check the solution in this Study Guide.
- Read paragraph 20-75 to 20-79.
- Do Self Study Problem Twenty-3 and check the solution in this Study Guide.
- Read paragraph 20-80 to 20-87.
- Do Exercise Twenty-10 and check the solution in this Study Guide.

Foreign Source Income Of Canadian Residents - Introduction
- Read paragraph 20-88 to 20-90.

Foreign Source Income Of Canadian Residents - Reporting Requirements (T1135)
- Read paragraph 20-91 to 20-98.
- Do Exercise Twenty-11 and check the solution in this Study Guide.
- Do Self Study Problem Twenty-4 and check the solution in this Study Guide.

Foreign Source Employment Income Of Canadian Residents
- Read paragraph 20-99 to 20-100.
- Do Self Study Problem Twenty-5 and check the solution in this Study Guide.

Foreign Source Unincorporated Business Income Of Canadian Residents
- Read paragraph 20-101 to 20-103.
- Do Exercise Twenty-12 and check the solution in this Study Guide.

Foreign Source Interest Income And Capital Gains Of Canadian Residents
- Read paragraph 20-104 to 20-107.

Foreign Source Dividend Income Of Canadian Residents
- Including From Foreign Affiliates And FAPI
- Read paragraph 20-108 to 20-120.
- Do Self Study Problem Twenty-6 and check the solution in this Study Guide.
- Read paragraph 20-121 to 20-125.
- Do Exercise Twenty-13 and check the solution in this Study Guide.
- Read paragraph 20-126 to 20-151.
- Do Exercise Twenty-14 and check the solution in this Study Guide.
- Read paragraph 20-152 and 20-153.
- Do Exercise Twenty-15 and check the solution in this Study Guide.
- Do Self Study Problem Twenty-7 and check the solution in this Study Guide.

To Complete This Chapter
- If you would like more practice in problem solving, do the Supplementary Self Study Problems for the chapter. These problems and solutions are available on MyLab.
- Review the Key Terms Used In This Chapter in the textbook at the end of Chapter 20. Consult the Glossary for the meaning of any key terms you do not know.
- Test yourself with the Chapter 20 Glossary Flashcards available on MyLab.
- Ensure you have achieved the Chapter 20 Learning Objectives listed in this Study Guide.
- As a review, we recommend you view the PowerPoint presentation for Chapter 20 that is on MyLab.

Practice Examination
- Write the Practice Examination for Chapter 20 that is on MyLab. Mark your examination using the Practice Examination Solution that is on MyLab.

Solutions to Chapter 20 Exercises

Exercise Twenty - 1 Solution
Case 1   Jazzco is not carrying on business in Canada and would not be subject to Canadian taxes.

Case 2   Jazzco is carrying on business in Canada in a permanent establishment located in Toronto. Therefore, Jazzco is taxable in Canada under ITA 2(3) on the profits attributable to the Canadian factory.

Case 3   The tax treaty allows Canada to tax business income only if such income is attributable to a permanent establishment in Canada. The warehouse constitutes a fixed place of business regardless of whether it is owned or leased. However, since it appears to be used exclusively to maintain an inventory for delivery, under the Canada/U.S. tax treaty it would be an excluded facility and would not be considered to be a permanent establishment. Jazzco would not be taxable under ITA 2(3) on its Canadian profits. The fact that the employee acts on behalf of the non-resident employer would not alter the conclusion since the employee does not have the authority to conclude contracts.

Case 4   In this Case, because the employee has authority to conclude contracts on behalf of a non-resident enterprise, the employee is deemed to be a permanent establishment. This means that Jazzco is taxable in Canada under ITA 2(3) on its business profits attributable to the perma-nent establishment (i.e., the employee).

Case 5   Since the warehouse is not used exclusively for maintaining an inventory, the perma-nent establishment exception in the tax treaty would not apply with the result that profits attrib-utable to that warehouse would be taxable in Canada.

Exercise Twenty - 2 Solution
Dawn is an individual who has become a resident of another country but continues to receive remuneration from a resident Canadian taxpayer. Given that the tax treaty exempts her salary from taxation in Egypt, ITA 115(2) deems her to be employed in Canada and, as a consequence, she would be subject to Canadian taxes on her salary.

Exercise Twenty - 3 Solution
Case 1 The employment income is taxable in Canada. The Canada/U.S. tax treaty allows Canada to tax employment income earned in Canada unless either of two exceptions is applicable. The first exception is the $10,000 rule. This exception however does not apply since David earned $11,200 Canadian in 2020 [($2,800)(4 months)]. The second exception is the 183 day rule. Although David was in Canada for only 122 days during 2020 and therefore met the first part of the test, he failed the remaining part of the test since the employer was a Canadian resident and could deduct the payments.

Case 2 The employment income is not taxable in Canada. The 183 day rule exempts the income from Canadian taxation because the employer was not resident in Canada, did not have a permanent establishment in Canada, and could not deduct the payments for Canadian tax purposes.

Case 3 The employment income is taxable in Canada. The Canada/U.S. tax treaty would exempt the income from Canadian tax if the amount was less than $10,000 Canadian or if Sandra spent less than 183 days in Canada in any 12 month period beginning or ending in 2020. As she earned $50,000 Canadian and spent 238 days at her job in Canada, neither of these exceptions are applicable.

Exercise Twenty - 4 Solution
Case 1 Nancy is not taxable on the gain. As a non-resident, Nancy is only taxable in Canada on the disposition of Taxable Canadian Property. Shares of a resident public company are only Taxable Canadian Property if Nancy had owned more than 25 percent of the issued shares of any class of the company in the 60 months preceding the disposition.

Case 2 Joe is taxable on the gain. The condo is taxable Canadian property since it is real property (e.g., land and buildings) situated in Canada. The Canada/U.S. tax treaty gives Canada the right to tax such gains. The property is not exempt from Canadian tax as a principal residence since Joe did not acquire the condo for his own habitation.

Case 3 Joe would be taxable on the gain on the shares. Shares of an unlisted corporation are taxable Canadian property if at any time within the preceding 60 months more than 50 percent of the fair market value of the company is derived from Canadian real property. In addition, the Canada/U.S. tax treaty allows Canada to tax the gain on the disposition of shares if the corporation is resident in Canada and the value of the shares is derived principally from real property situated in Canada.

Case 4 Joe would not be taxable on the gain on the shares. The shares are taxable Canadian property because they represent shares of an unlisted non-resident corporation that, at some time in the 60 months preceding the disposition, derived more than 50 percent of their value from taxable Canadian property. However, the Canada/U.S. tax treaty does not list this as one of the items where Canada is allowed to tax U.S. residents.

Exercise Twenty - 5 Solution
Case 1 As Jason is at arm's length from the bank and the interest is not participating debt interest, he would not be subject to Part XIII tax.

Case 2 As Janice is at arm's length with the Canadian government and the interest is not participating debt interest, the interest would not be subject to Part XIII tax. Note that interest on Government of Canada bonds is fully exempt interest, but this fact does not affect the result in this case.

Case 3 As Julian is at arm's length from the bank and the interest is not participating debt interest, he would not have to withhold Part XIII tax.

Case 4 The Canada/U.S. tax treaty exempts U.S. residents from Part XIII tax. This means that Jasmine does not have to withhold Part XIII tax despite the fact that her brother is a non-arm's length party.

Exercise Twenty - 6 Solution

Case 1 Rentco appears to be carrying on business in Canada through a permanent establishment. As a result, no Part XIII tax is payable. However, Rentco would be subject to Part I tax on its income attributable to the permanent establishment in Saskatchewan.

Case 2 Jack would be subject to Part XIII tax of $10,500 [(25%)($42,000)]. This represents an effective tax rate of 37.5 percent on his net rental income of $28,000. Alternatively, Jack could elect under ITA 216 to be taxed under Part I on the net rental income of $28,000 ($42,000 - $14,000). Whether this is would be a good alternative depends on Jack's marginal tax rate. The break-even rate would be 37.5 percent ($10,500 ÷ $28,000). If his marginal rate is below this, taxation under Part I would be the better alternative. If his marginal rate exceeds 37.5 percent, taxation under Part XIII would be preferable.

Case 3 Jack would be subject to Part XIII tax on the gross rents received for the boats unless he would be considered to be carrying on a business. However, the Canada/U.S. tax treaty reduces the withholding tax to 10 percent of the gross rents received, or $800. Note that Jack would not be eligible to elect under ITA 216 to be taxed under Part I on the boat rents, since this election is generally restricted to real property.

Exercise Twenty - 7 Solution

There would be a deemed disposition on her departure, leaving her liable for the taxes on a $10,500 [(1/2)($49,000 - $28,000)] taxable capital gain.

Exercise Twenty - 8 Solution

As real property is exempt from the deemed disposition provision contained in ITA 128.1(4)(b), there would be no tax consequences with respect to the rental property at the time of Mr. Chrysler's departure. However, real property is Taxable Canadian Property and, as a consequence, he would be liable for Canadian taxes on both recapture and capital gains resulting from a subsequent sale of the property, even though he will be a non-resident.

Exercise Twenty - 9 Solution

With respect to the shares of the Canadian private company, there would be a required deemed disposition, resulting in a taxable capital gain of $57,500 [(1/2)($235,000 - $120,000)]. In the absence of an election on the rental property, this would be the only tax consequence resulting from her departure.

However, if Ms. Lopez elects under ITA 128.1(4)(d) to have a deemed disposition on her rental property, the results will be as follows:

Deemed Proceeds Of Disposition For Land	$ 30,000
Adjusted Cost Base	(60,000)
Capital Gain (Loss) On Land	($ 30,000)
UCC Of Building	$142,000
Lesser Of:	
Capital Cost = $160,000	
Deemed Proceeds Of Disposition = $100,000	(100,000)
Terminal Loss	$ 42,000

The net result would be as follows:

Taxable Capital Gain On Shares	$57,500
Allowable Capital Loss On Land [(1/2)($30,000)]	(15,000)
Terminal Loss On Building	(42,000)
Net Income Inclusion	$ 500

Exercise Twenty - 10 Solution

In the absence of ITA 128.1(4)(b)(iv), there would be a deemed disposition of both the U.K. shares and the Canadian shares at the time of Mr. Brookings' departure from Canada. As it appears that he has been in Canada for less than 60 months in the last 10 years, there will be no deemed disposition of the U.K. shares that he owned prior to his arrival in Canada. There will, however, be a deemed disposition of the Canadian shares acquired during his stay in Canada. This will result in a taxable capital gain of $8,500 [(1/2)($92,000 - $75,000)].

There will be no deemed disposition of the vacant Canadian land because real property is exempt from the deemed disposition requirement of ITA 128.1(4)(b). Note, however, that vacant land is Taxable Canadian Property. This means that any gain resulting from its disposition will be subject to Canadian taxes, without regard to whether the vendor is a Canadian resident.

Exercise Twenty - 11 Solution

The cost of Simon's foreign investments total £197,000 (£52,000 + £145,000), which put him over the $100,000 Canadian reporting limit [(£197,000)($1.70) = $334,900] for filing Form T1135 and over the $250,000 limit for the simplified method. He is required to report the following information on the T1135:

Funds Held Outside Canada
- The name of the bank that holds the funds - Bank of Scotland
- The country code for the country of residence of the bank (Scotland) - GBR (available from the CRA website)
- The maximum amount of funds held during the year - $88,400 [(£52,000)($1.70)]
- The funds held at year end - $69,700 [(£41,000)($1.70)]
- Income from the property - $1,700 [(£1,000)($1.70)]

Indebtedness Owed By A Non-Resident
- A description of the indebtedness - Interest free loan to brother-in-law
- The country code for the non-resident issuer's country of residence (Scotland) - GBR (available from the CRA website)
- The maximum cost amount during the year - $246,500 [(£145,000)($1.70)]
- The year end cost amount - $246,500 [(£145,000)($1.70)]
- The income or loss - Nil
- The gain or loss on disposition - N/A

Exercise Twenty - 12 Solution

The gross amount of the U.S. business income will be subject to tax in Canada. Jason's foreign business income tax credit is $1,800, the lesser of the $1,800 foreign tax withheld and $3,780 [($18,000 ÷ $100,000)($21,000)].

The required solution would be as follows:

Gross Foreign Business Income	$18,000
Canadian Tax Rate	44%
Canadian Tax Payable Before Credit	$ 7,920
Foreign Tax Credit = Foreign Tax Withheld	(1,800)
Net Canadian Tax Payable	$ 6,120
Foreign Tax Withheld	1,800
Total Taxes Payable	$ 7,920

Based on these figures, his after tax retention and overall tax rate on his foreign source income would be as follows:

After Tax Retention ($18,000 - $7,920)	$10,080
Overall Tax Rate ($7,920 ÷ $18,000)	44%

Exercise Twenty - 13 Solution

Forco 1 Canvest has the required 1 percent investment and, with its related subsidiary, has the required 10 percent investment. Forco 1 is a foreign affiliate.

Forco 2 Canvest has the required 1 percent investment. However, as it is not related to any of the other shareholders, the 10 percent test is not met. This means that Forco 2 is not a foreign affiliate.

Forco 3 Canvest has the required 1 percent investment and, with the controlling shareholder's spouse (a related person), has the required 10 percent investment. Forco 3 is a foreign affiliate.

Exercise Twenty - 14 Solution

Since Forco is a controlled foreign affiliate of Canco, Canco must accrue its proportionate share (100%) of Forco's investment income. The required calculations are as follows:

FAPI [ITA 91(1)]	$100,000
Deduct Lesser Of:	
• FAPI = $100,000	
• ITA 91(4) Deduction [(4)(18%)($100,000)]	(72,000)
Net Addition To Net Income For Tax Purposes	$ 28,000

Exercise Twenty - 15 Solution

Foreign Source Dividend – ITA 90(1)	$82,000
Deduct Lesser Of:	
• Previous FAPI After ITA 91(4) Deduction = $28,000	
• Dividend Received = $82,000	(28,000)
Net Addition To Net Income For Tax Purposes	$54,000

Note that the additions to Net Income For Tax Purposes for the two years total $82,000 ($28,000 + $54,000). This is equal to the $100,000 less the $18,000 in taxes paid in the foreign jurisdiction. Had there been any withholding taxes on the dividend, they would not have been eligible for a foreign tax credit.

While this is not a required part of the problem, you should note that Taxable Income and Tax Payable would be nil in this example. There would be a deduction under ITA 113(1)(b) equal to $54,000 [($18,000)(4 - 1)]. The resulting Taxable Income of nil reflects the fact that on Forco's income of $100,000, taxes at the usual Canadian rate of 25 percent have already been paid. This $25,000 [(25%)($100,000)] is made up of the $18,000 [(18%)($100,000)] paid by Forco in the foreign jurisdiction plus the $7,000 [(25%)($28,000)] of Canadian taxes on Canco's 2020 addition to Net Income For Tax Purposes.

Solution to Self Study Problem Twenty - 1

Case A

As Sharon is earning employment income in Canada, she would generally be taxable under ITA 2(3). With respect to the Canada/U.S. tax treaty provisions, while her income exceeds $10,000, her stay in Canada is less than 183 days. However, her employment income would be deductible by the payor Canadian corporation. This means that Sharon would be subject to Part I tax on her Canadian employment income.

Case B

As Mariah is earning employment income in Canada, she would generally be taxable under ITA 2(3). With respect to the Canada/U.S. tax treaty provisions, while her income exceeds $10,000, her stay in Canada is less than 183 days. In addition, the payor is not a Canadian entity that will be able to deduct these payments against Canadian taxes. Given this, Mariah would be exempt from Part I tax under the provisions of the Canada/U.S. tax treaty.

Case C

With respect to private companies incorporated in Canada if, within the preceding 60 month, more than 50 percent of their value is derived from Canadian real property, their shares are considered to be Taxable Canadian Property. This means that gains on the sale of such shares would be taxable under ITA 2(3). While the Canada/U.S. tax treaty serves to exempt gains on certain types of Taxable Canadian Property (generally, shares that during the last five years did not derive their value largely from Canadian real property), shares of Canadian incorporated private companies is not on this list. Therefore, Part I tax would be applicable on the gain.

Case D

Shares of unlisted companies are viewed as Taxable Canadian Property if, within the preceding 60 months, more than 50 percent of their value is derived from Canadian real property. This means that Rae's shares would be considered Taxable Canadian Property and the gain would be considered taxable under ITA 2(3). However, Rae's corporation is not a "Canadian" corporation, and this means that it is not on the Canada/U.S. tax treaty list of Taxable Canadian Property where gains accruing to U.S. residents are subject to Canadian tax. Therefore, Part I tax would not be applicable on the gain.

Case E

Under the Canada/U.S. tax treaty, Part I tax is applicable to a U.S. resident only when the business is carried on through a permanent establishment. While the U.S. firm in this Case is carrying on business, it is not through a permanent establishment. The treaty specifically exempts the warehouse as it is used exclusively for holding inventories. In addition, Martha Faulk could not be viewed as a permanent establishment as she does not have authority to conclude individual sales contracts. Part I tax would not be applicable in this case.

Case F

This Case differs from Case E in that the warehouse is used for more than holding inventories. This means that it is not an excluded facility under the Canada/U.S. treaty. Further, as Martha Faulk has the authority to conclude contracts, she, as a person, would be viewed as a permanent establishment. This means that Orex would be considered to be carrying on business in Canada through a permanent establishment. Therefore, Part I tax would be applicable.

Solution to Self Study Problem Twenty - 2

Case A
While the interest is being paid on participating debt, Martha is a resident of the U.S. The Canada/U.S. tax treaty exempts U.S. residents from Part XIII tax on all interest payments. Martha would not be subject to Part XIII tax and no Canadian tax would be payable.

Case B
As Brendan is not a resident of a country with which Canada has a tax treaty, he would be subject to Part XIII tax at a rate of 25 percent. This would require a payment of $23,500 [(25%)($94,000)]. Alternatively, he could elect to be taxed under Part I on his net income of $67,000 ($94,000 - $27,000). The Part XIII tax as a percent of his net rental income is 35.1 percent ($23,500 ÷ $67,000). If his personal tax rate in Canada is below this level, he would save taxes by electing to be taxed under Part I, rather than under Part XIII.

If the tax savings from filing a T1 tax return are small, he might want to consider any extra costs that would be needed to ensure the records for his expenses are acceptable to the CRA if his return is questioned. This could make filing under Part XIII the better choice, even if it costs him slightly more in taxes.

Case C
Barry is a resident of a country that does not have a tax treaty with Canada. In addition, the interest is paid on participating debt. Given these facts, the interest would be subject to Part XIII tax at the 25 percent rate and the tax would equal $1,170 [(25%)($4,680)].

Case D
Part XIII tax is applicable to interest only if the interest is paid on participating debt or is paid to a non-arm's length non-resident. The debt is not participating, and Terence is at arms' length with the Canadian bank. Given this, Part XIII tax would not be applicable and no Canadian tax would be payable.

Case E
While the Canada/U.S. tax treaty reduces the Part XIII rate on dividends, Karl is a resident of a country that does not have a tax treaty with Canada. Given this, the $8,462 in dividends would be taxed at the full 25 percent Part XIII rate and the tax would equal $2,115.50 [(25%)($8,462)].

Solution to Self Study Problem Twenty - 3

When an individual leaves Canada, there is a deemed disposition of all property owned at the time of departure at fair market value with certain exceptions. For each of the listed assets, the tax consequences that result from Mr. Rankin's departure are as follows:

City Home* Real property situated in Canada is exempted from the deemed disposition rule. There would be no deemed disposition and no tax consequences at the time of Jonathan's departure. However, the city home would be classified as Taxable Canadian Property and, as a result, any gain on the disposition of the property would be subject to Canadian taxation even though Mr. Rankin is no longer a Canadian resident.

Cottage* As was the case with the city home, for the cottage there would be no deemed disposition and no tax consequences at the time of Jonathan's departure. However, the cottage would also be classified as Taxable Canadian Property and, as a result, any gain on the disposition of the property would be subject to Canadian taxation even though Mr. Rankin is no longer a Canadian resident.

> *While this is not a required part of the solution, we would note that either the city home and/or the cottage could qualify for the principal residence exemption. However, this would require an election for a deemed disposition of the relevant property.

Automobile While gains or personal use property are taxable, losses are not deductible. Given this, there would be no tax consequences associated with the deemed disposition of the automobile.

Cash There are never any tax consequences associated with dispositions of cash.

RRSP As an "excluded right", RRSP assets are exempted from the deemed disposition rule. There would be no deemed disposition of the RRSP assets and no tax consequences when Jonathan departs from Canada. Payments from the RRSP will be taxed under Part XIII when they are withdrawn and remitted to Mr. Rankin as a non-resident.

Shares In A CCPC There is no exemption from the deemed disposition rules for any type of shares. There would be a deemed disposition of these shares on Mr. Rankin's departure resulting in a taxable capital gain of $7,500 [(1/2)($80,000 - $65,000)].

Shares In Public Companies There would be a deemed disposition of these shares, resulting in a taxable capital gain of $39,000 [(1/2)($120,000 - $42,000)].

Solution to Self Study Problem Twenty - 4

1. Foreign investment reporting is not required. Since the cottage is personal use property, the fact that its total cost is greater than $100,000 is not relevant.

2. No foreign investment reporting is required when assets are used in an active business.

3. Foreign investment reporting is required for the shares held outside of the RRSP. The cost of one-half of the shares is greater than $100,000 [(1/2)($286,000) = $143,000]. The fact that the current fair market price is below $100,000 is not relevant. Specified foreign property held in an RRSP is excluded from form T1135 reporting requirements.

4. Foreign investment reporting is not required. The total of the amount owing on the mortgage for the current year ($68,000) and the highest balance in the U.S. bank account for the year ($12,000) total less than $100,000.

5. Foreign investment reporting is not required since the yacht is not real property. In addition, it is personal use property.

6. Foreign investment reporting is not required for personal use property. If this property was used primarily for personal use (50 percent or more), it would not have to be reported. However, as the information in the problem states that it is used primarily as a rental property, it would be subject to the foreign investment reporting rules.

Solution to Self Study Problem Twenty - 5

A. Because he is a resident of Canada, the hockey player will have all US$14,000 of hockey school income subject to tax in Canada. With respect to U.S. taxation, he would not have a tax obligation in that country because his total earnings are only $7,000. The Canada/U.S. tax treaty exempts non-residents from U.S. taxation when their earnings in that country are less than $10,000.

B. Because the expert is a resident of Canada, the full $150,000 of income would be subject to tax in Canada. He would not be taxed in the U.S. because the provisions of the Canada/U.S. tax treaty exempt Canadian residents from U.S. taxation provided they are in the U.S. less than 183 days, their employer does not have a permanent establishment in the U.S., and their employer does not deduct the compensation in computing U.S. taxes. The expert was in the U.S. for only 180 days [(3)(60)], and his compensation is paid by a Canadian company.

Solution to Self Study Problem Twenty - 6

The Hispanic Ltd. tax withholding equals 25 percent ($5,750 ÷ $23,000) of the dividend paid. The Deutsch Inc. tax withholding equals 10 percent ($1,400 ÷ $14,000) of the dividend paid. As the foreign non-business tax credit is limited to 15 percent, the additional 10 percent ($2,300) withheld by Foreign Country 1 will have to be deducted in the determination of Mona's Net Income For Tax Purposes.

Net Employment Income	$ 87,000
Hispanic Ltd. Gross Dividends (No Gross Up)	23,000
Deutsch Inc. Gross Dividends (No Gross Up)	14,000
Excess Withholding [(25% - 15%)($23,000)]	(2,300)
Net Income For Tax Purposes And Taxable Income	$121,700

Using this result, her federal Tax Payable would be calculated as follows:

Tax On First $97,069		$ 17,230
Tax On Next $24,631 ($121,700 - $97,069) At 26%		6,404
Tax Payable Before Credits		$23,634
Basic Personal Credit	($13,229)	
EI	(856)	
CPP	(2,732)	
Canada Employment	(1,245)	
Total Credit Amount	($18,062)	
Applicable Rate	15%	(2,709)
Tax Otherwise Payable		$20,925
Foreign Tax Credits (See Note)		
Hispanic Ltd.		(3,450)
Deutsch Inc.		(1,400)
Federal Tax Payable		$16,075

Note The foreign non-business tax credits are calculated on a country-by-country basis (see Chapter 11).

The tax credit on the Hispanic Ltd. shares would be the lesser of:

- Amount Withheld (Limited To 15%) = [(15%)($23,000)] = $3,450

- $\left[\dfrac{\text{Foreign Non - Business Income}}{\text{Adjusted Division B Income}}\right]$(Tax Otherwise Payable)

  $= \left[\dfrac{\$23,000}{\$121,700}\right]$($20,925) = $3,954

The tax credit on the Deutsch Inc. shares would be the lesser of:

- Amount Withheld (Less Than 15%) = $1,400

- $\left[\dfrac{\text{Foreign Non - Business Income}}{\text{Adjusted Division B Income}}\right]$(Tax Otherwise Payable)

  $= \left[\dfrac{\$14,000}{\$121,700}\right]$($20,925) = $2,407

Solution to Self Study Problem Twenty - 7

Alta Inc. Dividends

As BK Inc. owns more than 10 percent of the Alta Inc. shares, Alta Inc. is a foreign affiliate of BK Inc. Alta Inc. is operating in a country with which Canada has a tax treaty. In addition, all of its income is from active business activities. Given this, all of the dividend is being paid from Exempt Surplus. This means that, while the pre-withholding amount of the dividend will be included in Net Income For Tax Purposes, this amount can be deducted in full under ITA 113(1)(a).

Bolt Ltd. Dividends

While Bolt Ltd. earns all of its income through active business activities, it is not located in a country that has a tax treaty or a TIEA with Canada. Given this, the dividend will be paid from Taxable Surplus. It will be included in Net Income For Tax Purposes and not deductible under ITA 113(1)(a). However, it will be eligible for a deduction under ITA 113(1)(b) for taxes paid by Bolt Ltd. in the foreign jurisdiction, as well as a deduction under ITA 113(1)(c) for taxes withheld on the distribution to BK Inc.

Taxable Income And Tax Payable Calculation

The required calculations for Taxable Income and Tax Payable would be as follows:

Alta Inc. Dividends (Before Withholding)	$ 34,000
Bolt Ltd. Dividends (Before Withholding)	76,000
Addition To Net Income For Tax Purposes	$110,000
Deductions:	
ITA 113(1)(a) Alta Dividends	(34,000)
ITA 113(1)(b) - Note 1	(12,000)
ITA 113(1)(c) - Note 2	(45,600)
Taxable Income	$ 18,400
Rate	25%
Canadian Tax Payable	$ 4,600

Note 1 Given Bolt's local tax rate of 5 percent, the pre-tax income that formed the base for the dividend to BK Inc. was $80,000 [$76,000 ÷ (1 - 5%)]. This means that the local taxes paid by Bolt were $4,000 [(5%)($80,000)] and that the ITA 113(1)(b) deduction would be $12,000 [($4,000)(3)]. See the text for an explanation of the relevant factor of 3.

Note 2 Taxes withheld were $11,400. Given this, the ITA 113(1)(c) deduction is equal to $45,600 [($11,400)(4)]. See the text for an explanation of the relevant factor of 4.

Verification

As indicated in the text, the goal here is to have foreign affiliate dividends paid from Taxable Surplus subject to total Canadian and foreign taxes at a rate of 25 percent. The preceding calculation has achieved this goal as supported by the following calculations:

Bolt's Pre-Tax Income [$76,000 ÷ (1 - 5%)]	$80,000
Rate	25%
Total Tax At 25% Rate	$20,000
Foreign Tax Paid On Bolt's Income [(5%)($80,000)]	$ 4,000
Taxes Withheld From Dividend	11,400
Canadian Tax Payable	4,600
Total Tax Paid	$20,000

CHAPTER 21

Chapter 21 Learning Objectives

After completing Chapter 21, you should be able to:

1. Describe, in general terms, the current transaction tax situation (GST/HST) in all of the provinces (paragraph [P hereafter] 21-1 to 21-16).
2. Describe the different ways in which transaction taxes can be assessed and the approach the GST/HST uses (P 21-17 to 21-41).
3. Explain the basic charging provision for GST/HST and the concept of supply (P 21-42 to 21-46).
4. Outline the difference between fully taxable supplies, zero-rated supplies, and exempt supplies (P 21-47 to 21-60).
5. Explain the place of supply rules and how the GST/HST is applied to tangible goods, real property, and services (P 21-61 to 21-69).

6. Explain who is responsible for collecting and remitting the GST/HST (P 21-70 to 21-73).
7. Determine whether an entity is required to register for GST and, if so, at what point in time registration is required (P 21-74 to 21-92).
8. Apply the rules for calculating input tax credits on current and capital expenditures (P 21-93 to 21-99).
9. Explain some of the basic restrictions on claiming input tax credits (P 21-100 to 21-102).
10. Discuss input tax credits as they relate to vendors of exempt supplies (P 21-103).

11. Describe the relationship between amounts determined for accounting, income tax, and GST/HST purposes (P 21-104 to 21-108).
12. Calculate the GST/HST payable or refund when fully taxable, zero-rated, and exempt supplies are provided (P 21-109 to 21-112).
13. Apply the quick method of accounting for GST/HST (P 21-113 to 21-124).
14. Apply the simplified method of accounting for input tax credits (P 21-125 to 21-130).
15. Outline the basic procedures and administration of the GST/HST (P 21-131 to 21-157).

16. Calculate the employee and partner GST/HST rebate (P 21-158 to 21-166).
17. Calculate the effects of GST/HST on the acquisition and disposition of residential property, including new homes (P 21-167 to 21-173).
18. Describe the possible GST/HST implications resulting from the sale of a business (P 21-174 to 21-187).
19. Briefly describe how the GST/HST applies to certain types of organizations, such as those included in MUSH (P 21-188 and 21-189).
20. Describe the GST/HST implications related to partner expenses, dispositions of partnership interests, transfers between a partnership and its partners and the reorganization of partnerships (P 21-190 to 21-198).
21. Explain the applicability of GST/HST legislation to trusts (P 21-199 to 21-201).

How to Work Through Chapter 21

We recommend the following approach in dealing with the material in this chapter:

Introduction To The GST/HST
- Read paragraph 21-1 to 21-7 (in the textbook).

The Current Situation And How We Will Deal With The Complexity
- Read paragraph 21-8 to 21-16.

Transaction Tax Concepts, Including VATs
- Read paragraph 21-17 to 21-41.
- Do Exercise Twenty-One-1 (in the textbook) and check the solution in this Study Guide.
- Do Self Study Problem Twenty-One-1, which is available on MyLab, and check the solution in this Study Guide.

Liability For GST/HST And The Concept Of Supply
- Read paragraph 21-42 to 21-46.

Supply Categories (Fully Taxable, Zero-Rated, And Exempt)
- Read from the Note before paragraph 21-47 to 21-60.

Applying the GST/HST Rate Using the Place Of Supply Rules
- Read paragraph 21-61 to 21-69.

Responsibility For Collection And Remittance Of GST/HST
- Read paragraph 21-70 to 21-73.

Registration - Including The Small Supplier Exemption
- Read paragraph 21-74 to 21-88.
- Do Exercise Twenty-One-2 and check the solution in this Study Guide.
- Read paragraph 21-89 to 21-92.
- Do Self Study Problem Twenty-One-2 and check the solution in this Study Guide.

Input Tax Credits
- Read paragraph 21-93 to 21-112.
- Do Exercises Twenty-One-3 to Twenty-One-5 and check the solutions in this Study Guide.
- Do Self Study Problems Twenty-One-3 and Twenty-One-4 and check the solutions in this Study Guide.

Relief For Small Businesses (Quick Method And Simplified ITC Method)
- Read paragraph 21-113 to 21-124.
- Do Exercises Twenty-One-6 and Twenty-One-7 and check the solutions in this Study Guide.
- Do Self Study Problems Twenty-One-5 and Twenty-One-6 and check the solutions in this Study Guide.
- Read paragraph 21-125 to 21-130.
- Do Exercise Twenty-One-8 and check the solution in this Study Guide.

GST/HST Procedures And Administration, Including GST/HST Returns And Payments
- Read paragraph 21-131 to 21-157.

Employee and Partner GST/HST Rebate
- Read paragraph 21-158 to 21-166.
- Do Self Study Problem Twenty-One 7 and check the solution in this Study Guide.

Residential Property and New Housing Rebate
- Read paragraph 21-167 to 21-173.
- Do Self Study Problems Twenty-One-8 and Twenty-One-9 and check the solutions in this Study Guide.

Sale of a Business
- Read paragraph 21-174 to 21-187.

Specific Applications Including Charities, Not-For-Profits, and MUSH
- Read paragraph 21-188 to 21-189.

Partnerships And GST/HST
- Read paragraph 21-190 to 21-198.

Trusts And GST/HST
- Read paragraph 21-199 to 21-201.

To Complete This Chapter
- If you would like more practice in problem solving, do the Supplementary Self Study Problems for this chapter. These problems and solutions are available on MyLab.
- Review the Key Terms Used In This Chapter in the textbook at the end of Chapter 21. Consult the Glossary for the meaning of any key terms you do not know.
- Test yourself with the Chapter 21 Glossary Flashcards available on MyLab.
- Ensure you have achieved the Chapter 21 Learning Objectives listed in this Study Guide.
- As a review, we recommend you view the PowerPoint presentation for Chapter 21 that is on MyLab.

Practice Examination
- Write the Practice Examination for Chapter 21 that is on MyLab. Mark your examination using the Practice Examination Solution that is on MyLab.

Solutions to Chapter 21 Exercises

Exercise Twenty-One - 1 Solution
Account-Based System   Under an account-based system, the 5 percent would be applied to the value added, resulting in a tax of $7,600 [(5%)($416,000 - $264,000)].

Invoice-Credit System   Alternatively, under an invoice-credit system, $20,800 [(5%) ($416,000)] would be owing on sales, but would be offset by an input tax credit of $11,650 [(5%)($233,000)] on purchases. The net tax owing in this case would be $9,150, $1,550 larger than the $7,600 tax using the accounts-based system. Note that this $1,550 is equal to 5 percent of $31,000, the difference between the $233,000 in purchases and the $264,000 cost of the merchandise sold.

Exercise Twenty-One - 2 Solution
As Ms. Salome's sales **exceed** $30,000 in the October to December 2020 quarter, she will be required to begin collecting GST on the first sale in that quarter that causes her to exceed the $30,000 threshold. This means she will have to begin collecting GST sometime between October 1 and December 31. She will be required to register within 29 days of that date.

As Mr. Laughton's sales **accumulate** to more than $30,000 ($8,000 + $13,000 + $4,000 + $17,000 = $42,000) by the end of the January to March, 2021 quarter, he is required to start collecting GST on the first sale on or after May 1, 2021, one month after the quarter in which the $30,000 threshold is reached. Registration is required within 29 days of the first sale on which GST is collected.

Exercise Twenty-One - 3 Solution
The HST payable would be calculated as follows:

HST On Sales [(13%)($1,223,000)]	$158,990
Input Tax Credits:	
Purchases [(13%)($843,000 + $126,000)]	(125,970)
Salaries	Nil
Interest	Nil
Amortization	Nil
HST Payable For The Quarter	$ 33,020

Exercise Twenty-One - 4 Solution
The HST payable would be calculated as follows:

HST On Sales [(15%)($224,000)]	$33,600
Input Tax Credits:	
Rent [(15%)($25,800)]	(3,870)
Assistant's Salary	Nil
Capital Expenditures [(15%)($36,000 + $20,000)]	(8,400)
HST Payable For The Year	$21,330

Exercise Twenty-One - 5 Solution
The pro rata input tax credit for the land and building acquisition would be $24,000 [(5%)(40%)($1,200,000)]. There would be no input tax credit for the office equipment as it is used less than 50 percent for taxable supplies.

Exercise Twenty-One - 6 Solution
The purchases made do not affect the Quick Method calculation since they are non-capital. The GST payable under the Quick Method would be calculated as follows:

Basic Tax [(1.8%)(105%)($42,500)]	$803.25
Credit On First $30,000 [(1%)($30,000)]	(300.00)
GST Payable For The Quarter	$503.25

Exercise Twenty-One - 7 Solution
If the Quick Method is not used, the HST payable (refund) would be calculated as follows:

HST On Sales [(13%)($56,100)]	$ 7,293.00
Input Tax Credits:	
Current Expenditures [(13%)($23,400)]	(3,042.00)
Capital Expenditures [(13%)($42,000)]	(5,460.00)
HST Payable (Refund) For The Quarter - Regular Method	($1,209.00)

Alternatively, under the Quick Method, the calculation would be as follows:

Basic Tax [(4.4%)(113%)($56,100)]	$2,789.29
Credit On First $30,000 [(1%)($30,000)]	(300.00)
Subtotal	$2,489.29
Input Tax Credits:	
Current Expenditures	Nil
Capital Expenditures [(13%)($42,000)]	(5,460.00)
HST Payable (Refund) For The Quarter - Quick Method	($2,970.71)

As the Quick Method produces a larger refund, it would be the preferable method. Note that input tax credits on capital expenditures are available, even when the Quick Method is used.

Exercise Twenty-One - 8 Solution

To apply the simplified method, we need to know the tax inclusive amounts of current expenditures (given in the problem), as well as the tax inclusive amounts of capital personal property expenditures. This latter figure is $52,500 [(105%)($50,000)]. Using the simplified method, the GST payable (refund) would be calculated as follows:

GST Sales [(5%)($315,000 ÷ 1.05)]	$15,000
Input Tax Credits On Purchases And Capital Personal Property [(5/105)($189,000 + $52,500)]	(11,500)
Input Tax Credits On Capital Real Property [(5%)($150,000)]	(7,500)
GST Payable (Refund) For The Year	($ 4,000)

Solution to Self Study Problem Twenty-One - 1

GST Calculation

Under the normal GST system, a 5 percent tax is applied on the selling price at each stage, and the business gets an input tax credit for the tax paid on purchased inputs. The net result is that all payments of GST by vendors are refunded as input tax credits, so there is no net out-of-pocket cost (other than administration) to vendors from the GST.

Vendor	Cost	Selling Price	GST Charged	ITC Claimed
Raw Materials Supplier		$ 100	$ 5.00	Nil
Manufacturer	$100	150	7.50	$ 5.00
Wholesaler	150	225	11.25	7.50
Distributor	225	338	16.90	11.25
Retailer	338	507	25.35	16.90
Totals		$1,320	$66.00	$40.65

The net GST charged for all stages is $25.35 ($66.00 - $40.65). The consumer bears the full cost of the tax by paying GST of $25.35 [(5%)($507)] with no opportunity to get an input tax credit.

Turnover Tax Calculation

The turnover tax is similar to the GST, as it applies to revenue. However, the turnover tax is significantly different as there is no input tax credit for tax paid at each stage on purchased goods (inputs). The tax is passed on to the purchasers in the chain, resulting in pyramiding of the tax. Because of the multiple times goods get taxed, to raise the same amount of tax revenue, the turnover tax rate of 1.92 percent (as shown in the following calculation) is much lower than the 5 percent GST rate.

$$[(\$100)(X\%)] + [(\$150)(X\%)] + [(\$225)(X\%)] + [(\$338)(X\%)] + [(\$507)(X\%)] = \$25.35$$
$$[(\$100 + \$150 + \$225 + \$338 + \$507)(X\%)] = \$25.35$$
$$[(\$1,320)(X\%)] = \$25.35$$
$$X\% = \$25.35 \div \$1,320$$
$$X\% = 1.92\%$$

As verification, the total of the selling price in the above table is $1,320. If the rate of 1.92 percent is applied to this total (the equivalent of each stage charging a turnover tax), the total tax collected would be equivalent to $25.34 (rounding error of $0.01).

Solution to Self Study Problem Twenty-One - 2

Calendar Quarter Test

Under this test, persons are required to register for the GST if taxable revenues exceed $30,000 in any single quarter. Under this test, Chantelle is not required to register.

Last Four Calendar Quarters Test (Cumulative)

Under this test, persons are required to register for the GST if their taxable revenues accumulate to more than $30,000 in any four consecutive calendar quarters. In this problem four quarters of sales accumulate to $36,500 ($6,500 + $9,000 + $9,500 + $11,500) by the end of the quarter ending December 31, 2020.

As a result, Chantelle Chance is required to start collecting GST on February 1, 2021, the first day of the second month following the quarter in which the $30,000 threshold is reached. Registration is required by March 2, 2021, 29 days after GST collection is required to begin.

Solution to Self Study Problem Twenty-One - 3

The HST refund for Norton's Variety for the current period would be calculated as follows:

HST Collected [(13%)($250,000)]	$32,500
Input Tax Credits - Current Expenditures:	
Purchases Of Fully Taxable Goods [(13%)($175,000 + $10,000)]	(24,050)
Purchases Of Zero-Rated Goods (Note 1)	Nil
Amortization Expense (Note 2)	Nil
Salaries And Wages (Note 3)	Nil
Interest Expense (Note 3)	Nil
Other Operating Expenses [(13%)(100%)($10,000)] (Note 4)	(1,300)
Input Tax Credits - Capital Expenditures:	
Building [(13%)(40%)($480,000)] (Note 5)	(24,960)
Equipment (Note 6)	Nil
HST Payable (Refund)	($17,810)

Note 1 HST is not paid on purchases of zero-rated goods. As a consequence, there are no input tax credits to be claimed on these purchases.

Note 2 Amortization expense does not affect the HST calculation.

Note 3 No HST is paid on salaries and wages or interest. As a result, no input tax credits are available.

Note 4 As more than 90 percent of the Other Expenses related to the provision of taxable supplies, the company is eligible for a 100 percent input tax credit.

Note 5 Input tax credits on real property are available based on a pro rata portion of their usage in providing taxable supplies.

Note 6 No input tax credits are available on capital expenditures other than real property if less than 50 percent of their usage is to provide fully taxable and zero-rated supplies.

Solution to Self Study Problem Twenty-One - 4

The GST refund for Lassen Ltd. for the current year would be calculated as follows:

GST Collected [(5%)($5,700,000 - $1,200,000 - $2,400,000)]	$ 105,000
Input Tax Credits:	
Purchases [(5%)($2,600,000 - $200,000)]	(120,000)
Amortization Expense	Nil
Salaries And Wages	Nil
Interest Expense	Nil
Other Pre-Tax Expenses {[5%][$370,000 - (50%)($40,000)]}	(17,500)
Income Taxes	Nil
Building [(5%)(40%)($3,000,000)]	(60,000)
Other Capital Expenditures	Nil
GST Payable (Refund)	($ 92,500)

Notes:

- The fact that GST is paid on all purchases is not unreasonable, despite the fact that the company provides both zero-rated and exempt supplies to its customers. Some zero-rated supplies, for example exports, involve selling items on which GST is paid. Exempt supplies could include the provision of certain types of services for which no purchases are required.

- Amortization expense does not affect the GST calculation.

- No GST is paid on salaries and wages, interest, or income taxes. As a result no input tax credits are available.

- The recovery of GST on meals and entertainment expenses is limited to 50 percent.

- Input tax credits on real property are available based on a pro rata portion of their usage in providing taxable supplies.

- No input tax credits are available on capital expenditures other than real property if less than 50 percent of their usage is in providing taxable and zero-rated supplies.

Solution to Self Study Problem Twenty-One - 5

The following recommendations are based solely on the minimization of the GST payment. No consideration is given to the reduction in accounting costs available through the use of the Quick Method.

Claire - Service Business
The Quick Method would be preferable in this case.

Regular Method

[($150,000 - $35,000) ÷ 1.05][5%]	$5,476

Quick Method

Basic Tax [($150,000)(3.6%)]	$5,400
Credit On First $30,000 [(1%)($30,000)]	(300)
Net GST	$5,100

Barbara - Retailer
The Regular Method is preferable in this case.

Regular Method

[($150,000 - $100,000) ÷ 1.05][5%]	$2,381

Quick Method

Basic Tax [($150,000)(1.8%)]	$2,700
Credit On First $30,000 [(1%)($30,000)]	(300)
Net GST	$2,400

Nicole - Service Business
The Quick Method would be preferable in this case.

Regular Method

[($120,000 - $35,000) ÷ 1.05][5%]	$4,048

Quick Method

Basic Tax [($120,000)(3.6%)]	$4,320
Credit On First $30,000 [(1%)($30,000)]	(300)
Net GST	$4,020

Elizabeth - Retailer
The Quick Method would be preferable in this case.

Regular Method

[($120,000 - $75,000) ÷ 1.05][5%]	$2,143

Quick Method

Basic Tax [($120,000)(1.8%)]	$2,160
Credit On First $30,000 [(1%)($30,000)]	(300)
Net GST	$1,860

Solution to Self Study Problem Twenty-One - 6

Part A
Using the regular calculations, the HST payable for Larkin Ltd. for the current year would be calculated as follows:

HST Collected [(13%)($103,000)]	$13,390
Input Tax Credits On Current Expenditures:	
Purchases [(13%)($63,000 + $6,000)]	(8,970)
Amortization Expense	Nil
Salaries And Wages	Nil
Rent [(13%)($24,000)]	(3,120)
Interest Expense	Nil
Other Operating Expenses [(13%)($12,000)]	(1,560)
Input Tax Credits On Capital Expenditures	
[(13%)(100%)($36,160 ÷ 1.13)]	(4,160)
HST Payable	($ 4,420)

Notes:

- Amortization expense does not affect the HST calculation.

- No HST is paid on salaries and wages or interest. As a result no input tax credits are available.

- Full input tax credits are available on capital expenditures other than real property if more than 50 percent of their usage is to provide fully taxable supplies.

Part B
As Larkin's HST included taxable sales of $116,390 [(113%)($103,000)] is less than $400,000 and it is not engaged in an ineligible business such as accounting, Larkin can use the Quick Method.

Part C
The Quick Method calculations would be as follows:

Basic Tax [(4.4%)(113%)($103,000)]	$5,121
Credit On First $30,000 [(1%)($30,000)]	(300)
Total Before Capital Expenditures	$4,821
Input Tax Credit On Capital Expenditures [(13%) (100%)($36,160 ÷ 1.13)]	(4,160)
HST Payable	$ 661

In this case, the regular HST calculations are preferable as it produces a refund rather than requiring a remittance.

Solution to Self Study Problem Twenty-One - 7

The maximum CCA that George can claim is as follows:

Opening UCC ($27,750 - $12,488)	$15,262
GST Rebate Claimed On Car CCA In Preceding Year	(595)
Adjusted UCC	14,667
Class 10 Rate	30%
Maximum CCA	$ 4,400

The employee GST rebate for George would be calculated as follows:

Total Expenses Other Than CCA	$28,000	
GST Exempt Purchases:		
Interest	(2,600)	
Insurance	(1,200)	
Eligible Expenses Other Than CCA	$24,200	
Rate	5/105	$1,152
Eligible CCA	$ 4,400	
Rate	5/105	210
Employee GST Rebate		$1,362

Solution to Self Study Problem Twenty-One - 8

The calculation of the new housing GST rebate is as follows:

[A][($450,000 - B) ÷ $100,000], where

A = The lesser of 36 percent of the GST paid and $6,300; and
B = The greater of $350,000 and the cost of the home.

The GST and total cost of each purchase would be as follows.

Property A

As the renovations involve more than 90 percent of the interior, they will be considered substantial. Since the renovations would be done by the vendor prior to the sale, the purchase would be deemed to be that of a "new" home. As a result, the total purchase price would be subject to GST and a new housing rebate could be claimed on the total, as follows:

GST Payable [($370,000)(5%)]	$ 18,500
Less New Housing Rebate, where	
A = the lesser of [(36%)($18,500)] = $6,660 and $6,300	
B = the greater of $350,000 and $370,000	
[$6,300][($450,000- $370,000) ÷ $100,000]	(5,040)
Net GST Payable	$ 13,460
Purchase Price	370,000
Total Cost	$383,460

Property B

As this property is a used residential unit, no GST will be payable. This means that the total cost will be $387,000.

Property C

GST will be paid on the purchase price of $323,000, plus all of the improvements. However, the new housing rebate is only available on the $10,000 cost of the improvements done by the builder in addition to the purchase price. It is not available on the additional $12,000 of costs incurred by Martin.

GST Payable [($323,000 + $10,000 + $12,000)(5%)]	$ 17,250
Less New Housing Rebate, where	
A = the lesser of [(36%)(5%)($323,000 + $10,000)] = $5,994	
and $6,300	
B = the greater of $350,000 and $345,000	
[$5,994][($450,000 - $350,000) ÷ $100,000]	(5,994)
Net GST Payable	$ 11,256
Purchase Price ($323,000 + $10,000 + $12,000)	345,000
Total Cost	$356,256

Solution to Self Study Problem Twenty-One - 9

Since in all three Cases the purchase price is less than $350,000, the new housing rebate is calculated at 36 percent of the GST paid.

Case A

To determine the total GST included in the purchase price, multiply the $200,000 price by 5/105, to arrive at the total GST amount of $9,524.

The new housing GST rebate would be $3,429 [($9,524)(36%)].

As it appears that the purchaser will be paying the GST, that individual would be entitled to the rebate.

The net GST paid would be $6,095 ($9,524 - $3,429).

Case B

The total GST that would be charged is calculated by multiplying the purchase price of $200,000 by 5 percent, to arrive at $10,000 total GST.

The new housing rebate would be $3,600 [($10,000)(36%)].

As it appears that the purchaser will be paying the GST, that individual would be entitled to the rebate.

The net GST paid would be $6,400 ($10,000 - $3,600).

Case C

Since $200,000 is equal to the price of the house including GST net of the new housing rebate, the GST excluded price can be calculated by solving the following equation for x.

$$\$200,000 = [(105\%)(x) - (36\%)(5\%)(x)]$$

The GST excluded price of the new house would be $193,798 {$200,000 ÷ [105% - (36%)(5%)]}. The total GST amount is $9,690 [($193,798)(5%)].

The new housing rebate would be $3,488 [($9,690)(36%)].

A verification of these numbers is as follows: $193,798 + $9,690 - $3,488 = $200,000.

The only GST that will be remitted is being paid by the vendor, so it can be assumed that the vendor has been assigned the rights to the GST rebate. As a consequence, the $3,488 rebate would be claimed by the vendor.

The net GST paid would be $6,202 ($9,690 - $3,488).

GLOSSARY

A

Accelerated Investment Incentive (AccII) A temporary program that encourages investments in capital assets by providing an accelerated CCA deduction on net acquisitions during the year of acquisition.

Accrual Basis A method of accounting for Income based on recording assets when the right to receive them is established and liabilities when the obligation to pay them arises.

Acquisition Of Control Acquisition of sufficient voting shares of a corporation, by a Person, or Group Of Persons, that they have the right to elect a majority of the board of directors of the Corporation.

Active Business A business carried on by a Taxpayer, other than a Specified Investment Business or a Personal Services Business.

Active Business Income Income earned by an Active Business.

Additional Refundable Tax On Investment Income (ART) A 10-2/3% tax on the Aggregate Investment Income of a CCPC.

Adjusted Active Business Income A term used in calculating the M&P Deduction, defined as the excess of a Corporation's Income from Active Business, less a Corporation's losses from Active Business. It does not appear to be a different concept than Active Business Income of a Corporation.

ADJUSTED Aggregate Investment Income A modified version of Aggregate Investment Income that is used to calculate a possible grind of the annual business limit for the small business deduction.

Adjusted Cost Base For depreciable capital property it is the cost of the property to the Taxpayer. For non-depreciable capital property it is the cost of the property to the Taxpayer, subject to ITA 53 adjustments (e.g., deduction of government grants on land purchase).

Adjusted Taxable Income Regular Taxable Income, adjusted to remove certain tax preferences. Used to calculate the Alternative Minimum Tax.

Adoption Expenses Tax Credit A credit against Tax Payable that is available to individuals with eligible adoption expenses.

Advance Tax Ruling Interpretations provided, at the request of a taxpayer, by the Income Tax Rulings Directorate as to how a particular transaction will be treated for tax purposes. Such interpretations are not binding on the CRA.

Affiliated Group Of Persons A Group Of Persons each member of which is affiliated with every other member.

Affiliated Person [ITA 251.1(1)] For an Individual, an Affiliated Person is that individual's Spouse or Common-Law Partner. For a Corporation, an Affiliated Person is a Person or an Affiliated Group Of Persons who Controls the Corporation, or the Spouse or Common-Law Partner of either the Person who Controls, or a member of the group that Controls. More complex rules apply to determine affiliation between two Corporations.

Age Tax Credit A credit against Tax Payable that is available to Individuals who are 65 years of age or older.

Aggregate Investment Income As defined in ITA 129(4), this concept of investment income includes net Taxable Capital Gains for the year reduced by any Net Capital Loss carry overs deducted in the year, Interest Income, rents, and royalties.

Alimony A term that was used at an earlier point in time to refer to both Spousal Support and Child Support.

Allowable Business Investment Loss The deductible portion (currently one-half) of a Business Investment Loss.

Allowable Capital Loss The deductible portion (currently one-half) of a Capital Loss.

Allowance   An amount paid by an employer to an Employee to provide for certain types of costs incurred by the Employee, usually travel costs or automobile costs.

Alter Ego Trust   An Inter Vivos Trust established by an Individual aged 65 years or more, subject to the conditions that the Individual must be entitled to all of the Trust's Income during his/her lifetime, and the Individual must be the only Person who can access the capital of the Trust during his/her lifetime.

Alternative Minimum Tax (AMT)   A tax, calculated at the minimum federal rate on Adjusted Taxable Income, less a basic $40,000 exemption.

Amalgamation   A Rollover provision which allows two Taxable Canadian Corporations to be combined into a single Taxable Canadian Corporation, without tax consequences.

Annual Business Limit   The maximum amount of Active Business Income that is eligible for the Small Business Deduction in a particular taxation year (currently $500,000).

Annual Child Care Expense Amount   The annual per child limit for deductible Child Care Expense. The amount is $5,000, $8,000, or $11,000, depending on the age and health of the child.

Annual Gains Limit   Taxable Capital Gains for the current year on qualified assets, less the sum of Allowable Capital Losses and Net Capital Loss Carry Overs deducted during the current year, plus Allowable Business Investment Losses realized during the current year. Used to determine the Lifetime Capital Gains Deduction for the current year.

Annuitant   This term is used to describe a Person who is receiving an Annuity. However, in tax publications this term is often (and incorrectly) used to refer to the Beneficiary of an RRSP or RPP.

Annuity   A series of periodic payments that continues for a specified period of time, or until the occurrence of some event (e.g., the death of the Annuitant).

Anti-Avoidance Provision   A provision in the *Income Tax Act* that is designed to prevent a Taxpayer from taking some action that would allow him to avoid taxes.

Apprenticeship Job Creation Tax Credit   An Investment Tax Credit that is available to eligible employers (individuals and corporations) for salaries and wages paid to qualifying apprentices.

Arm's Length   ITA 251(1) indicates that Related Persons (see definition) do not deal with each other at arm's length. Also, a taxpayer and a personal trust do not deal with each other at arm's length. In other cases, it is a question of fact as to whether an arm's length relation exists.

ART   An acronym for "additional refundable tax on investment income".

Assessment   A formal determination of taxes to be paid or refunded. A Reassessment is a form of Assessment.

Associated Corporations   Two or more Corporations that have an ownership/control arrangement that falls into one of the categories described in ITA 256(1) (e.g., two Corporations controlled by the same Person).

At-Risk Amount   A defined measure that limits the amount of deductions that can be flowed through to a Limited Partner.

At-Risk Rules   A set of rules, directed largely at Limited Partners, designed to prevent an investment from creating tax deductions that exceed the amount invested (the At-Risk Amount).

B

Basic Federal Tax Payable   An amount of individual Tax Payable that has been reduced by some, but not all of the Tax Credits available to individuals. Used in the calculation of Tax Payable of Canadian Residents who do not live in a province.

Beneficiary   The Person who will receive the benefits from a Trust.

Billed Basis   A method of determining Net Business Income based on recording inclusions when the relevant amounts are billed. Can only be used by certain specified types of professionals (e.g., accountants).

Bonus Arrangement   As used in this material, a tax planning arrangement for Employees. A Corporation declares and deducts a bonus near the end of its fiscal year. It is usually designed to be paid to the Employee early in the following calendar year. As Employment Income is taxed on a Cash Basis, the bonus will not be taxed in the employee's hands until that year.

Bonusing Down   A process of paying deductible salary to the owner-manager of a CCPC, or related parties, in order to eliminate corporate Taxable Income that is not eligible for the Small Business Deduction.

Boot   A colloquial term used by tax practitioners to refer to Non-Share Consideration.

Business A business is a self-sustaining integrated set of activities and assets conducted and managed for the purpose of providing a return to investors. A business consists of (a) inputs, (b) processes applied to those inputs, and (c) resulting outputs that are used to generate revenues.

Business Combination A transaction in which an enterprise acquires net assets that constitute a business, or acquires an equity interest in a Corporation that gives the enterprise Control over the operating, financing, and investing decisions of that Corporation.

Business Income Income that is earned through Active Business activity. This would include amounts earned by producing goods, selling goods or services, or delivering services. While usage is not always consistent, this term usually refers to a net amount (i.e., inclusions less deductions, or revenues less expenses).

Business Investment Loss A loss resulting from the Disposition of shares or debt of a Small Business Corporation.

C

Canada Caregiver Amount For Child A credit against tax payable that is available to an individual who provides care and/or support for a child under 18 years of age who has a mental or physical infirmity.

Canada Caregiver Tax Credit A credit against tax payable that is available to an individual who provides care and/or support for certain specified dependants who have a mental or physical infirmity.

Canada Child Benefit A monthly payment that is available to Individuals with children. The non-taxable payments may be reduced or eliminated if Income is in excess of a threshold amount.

Canada Disability Savings Bonds A system of grants under which the federal government makes contributions to an Individual's RDSP based on family net income.

Canada Disability Savings Grants A system of grants under which the federal government makes contributions to an Individual's RDSP based on a percentage of the contributions to that Individual's RDSP that have been made by others.

Canada Education Savings Grants A system of grants under which the federal government makes contributions to an Individual's RESP based on a percentage of the contributions to that Individual's RESP that have been made by others.

Canada Employment Credit A credit against Tax Payable that is available to individuals with employment income.

Canada Learning Bonds A system of grants under which the federal government makes contributions to an Individual's RESP based on the number of years in which the Individual's family is eligible for the National Child Benefit supplement.

Canada Pension Plan (CPP) A pension plan sponsored by the federal government. Individuals with Employment or Business Income must make contributions based on their income and, in return, receive benefits in future years.

Canada Pension Plan Tax Credit A credit against Tax Payable that is available to Individuals making contributions to the Canada Pension Plan.

Canada Training Credit A refundable credit that provides a refund to eligible individuals for a portion of training related costs.

Canada Workers Benefit A refundable credit available to low income individuals who are earning employment and business income (formerly Working Income Tax Benefit).

Canadian Controlled Private Corporation A Corporation that is controlled by Persons Resident in Canada and that does not have any of its shares listed on a designated stock exchange.

Canadian Corporation A Corporation that is resident in Canada.

Canadian Partnership A Partnership, all of the members of which are Residents of Canada at the time the term is relevant.

Capital Asset An asset that is held for the purpose of producing Income.

Capital Cost The amount paid to acquire a depreciable asset. The tax equivalent of acquisition cost in accounting.

Capital Cost Allowance (CCA) A deduction in the determination of Business or Property Income based on the capital cost of capital assets. The tax equivalent of accounting amortization.

Capital Dividend A Dividend paid out of a Private Corporation's Capital Dividend Account. It is received on a tax free basis.

Capital Dividend Account An account that tracks a group of items, defined in ITA 89(1), that can be distributed by Private Corporations to shareholders as a tax free Capital Dividend (e.g., the non-taxable portion of realized Capital Gains).

Capital Gain   The excess of proceeds resulting from the Disposition of a capital asset, over the sum of the Adjusted Cost Base of the asset plus any costs of disposition.

Capital Gains Reserve   A Reserve that is deductible against Capital Gains. It is available when some part of the Proceeds Of Disposition is not collected in the period of disposition.

Capital Gains Stripping   Procedures designed to allow a Corporation to convert a taxable capital gain resulting from the Disposition of investment shares to an arm's length party, into a tax free intercorporate Dividend.

Capital Interest (In A Trust)   All rights of the Taxpayer as a Beneficiary under the trust, other than those that are an Income Interest in the Trust.

Capital Loss   The excess of the sum of the Adjusted Cost Base of a capital asset plus any costs of disposition, over the proceeds resulting from the Disposition of the asset.

Capital Personal Property   For GST purposes, any capital property other than Real Property.

Capital Tax   A tax assessed on the capital of a Corporation, without regard to its Income.

Carry Over   As used in tax work, the ability to apply current year losses against Income in earlier or later years.

Cash Basis   A method of accounting for Income based on cash receipts and cash disbursements.

Cash Damming   Situations in which a separate bank account is established to receive all deposits of borrowed funds. Expenditures from this account are then limited to those which qualify for interest deductibility. This procedure facilitates linking the borrowed money to income producing investments.

CCPC   An acronym for "Canadian controlled private corporation".

Charitable Donations Tax Credit   A credit against Tax Payable that is available to Individuals making donations to qualifying charitable organizations.

Charitable Gifts   Donations to a registered charity, a registered Canadian amateur athletic association, a housing corporation resident in Canada that is exempt from tax under ITA 149(1)(i), a Canadian municipality, the United Nations or an agency thereof, a university outside of Canada which normally enrolls Canadian students, and a charitable organization outside of Canada to which Her Majesty in right of Canada has made a gift in the year or in the immediately preceding year.

Child Care Expenses   Costs associated with caring for an Eligible Child.

Child Support   A Support Amount that is not identified as being for the benefit of a Spouse or Common-Law Partner, or a former Spouse or Common-Law Partner.

Class   As used in tax work, a defined group of depreciable assets for which the *Income Tax Regulations* specify the CCA rate to be applied, as well as the method to be used in applying the rate.

Clawback   An income tested taxing back, or reduction, in the payment of Old Age Security benefits and Employment Insurance benefits.

Climate Action Incentive Payments   A refundable credit based on family size that is available to the residents of four provinces and two territories, specifically Manitoba, New Brunswick, Ontario, Saskatchewan, Nunavut and Yukon.

Commercial Activity   This is a GST term which refers to any business or trade carried on by a Person, or any supply of real property made by a Person. Commercial Activity does not include any activity involved with making an exempt supply or any activity engaged in by an Individual without a Reasonable Expectation Of Profit.

Commodity Tax   A type of Transaction Tax that is applied to the sale of certain types of commodities (e.g., taxes on the sale of tobacco products).

Common Shares   Corporate shares that normally have all of the rights which are provided for under the relevant corporate enabling legislation. While there may be variations in the rights of such shares, at a minimum, voting rights would have to be present for the shares to be considered Common Shares.

Common-Law Partner   A Person who cohabits in a conjugal relationship with the Taxpayer and (a) has so cohabited with the Taxpayer for a continuous period of at least one year, or (b) is a parent of a child of whom the Taxpayer is also a parent.

Comparable Uncontrolled Price   A Transfer Pricing method that bases transfer prices on the prices used in comparable transactions between arm's length buyers and sellers, operating in the same market and under the same terms and conditions.

Connected Corporation   Corporation A is connected with Corporation B if Corporation B Controls Corporation A, or if Corporation B owns more than 10% of the voting shares of Corporation A and more than 10% of the fair market value of all issued shares of Corporation A.

Consent Form   A form that is used when a taxpayer wishes to have a different person represent him in dealing with the CRA. This form (T1013) authorizes the CRA to disclose information to, and deal with, a specified representative.

Consumption Tax   A tax levied on the consumption of some product or service. This type of tax is also called a sales tax.

Contributed Capital   In accounting usage, the amount of a Corporation's Shareholders' Equity that was received in return for issuing the shares that are currently outstanding.

Control [ITA 256(1.2)(c)]   A Corporation, Person or Group Of Persons has Control of a Corporation if that Corporation, Person or Group Of Persons owns either more than 50% of the Common Shares of that Corporation or, alternatively, owns shares (common and/or preferred) with a fair market value that exceeds 50% of the fair market value of all of the outstanding shares of that Corporation.

Control (IAS 27)   Control is the power to govern the financial and operating policies of an entity so as to obtain benefits from its activities.

Controlled [ITA 251.1(3)]   Under ITA 251.1(3), Controlled means controlled, directly or indirectly in any manner whatever. [The reference here is to de facto control, which does not necessarily require majority ownership of shares.]

Controlled Foreign Affiliate   A Foreign Affiliate of the Taxpayer that was controlled by (a) the Taxpayer, (b) the Taxpayer and not more than four other Persons Resident in Canada, (c) not more than four Persons Resident in Canada, other than the Taxpayer, (d) a Person or Persons with whom the Taxpayer does not deal at arm's length, or (e) the Taxpayer and a Person or Persons with whom the Taxpayer does not deal at arm's length.

Convertible Property   A debt or equity financial instrument of a Corporation that can be exchanged for an equity financial instrument of the same Corporation, without the payment of additional consideration.

Co-Ownership   Ownership of a single real or personal property by two or more Persons.

Corporation   An artificial legal entity created through either federal or provincial legislation.

Crowdfunding   Funding a project, venture or business by raising funds from a large number of people, usually in small amounts and usually via the internet.

Crown Gifts   Gifts made to Her Majesty in right of Canada or to Her Majesty in right of a province.

Cultural Gifts   Gifts of objects that the Canadian Cultural Property Export Review Board has determined meet the criteria of the *Cultural Property And Import Act*.

Cumulative Eligible Capital (CEC)   This term was used to refer to the amortized balance of Eligible Capital Expenditures. No longer available after 2016.

Cumulative Gains Limit   Taxable Capital Gains on qualified assets that have been realized since 1984, less the sum of Allowable Capital Losses and Net Capital Loss Carry Overs deducted after 1984, plus Allowable Business Investment Losses realized after 1984, capital gains deductions claimed in previous taxation years, and the Cumulative Net Investment Loss at the end of the year. Used to determine the Lifetime Capital Gains Deduction for the current year.

Cumulative Net Investment Loss (CNIL)   The amount by which the aggregate of investment expenses for the current year and prior years ending after 1987, exceeds the aggregate of investment income for that period.

Customs Duties   A tax imposed on the importation or exportation of certain goods or services.

D

Death Benefit   All amounts in excess of $10,000 that are received by a Taxpayer in a taxation year, on or after the death of an Employee, in recognition of the Employee's service in an office or employment.

Declining Balance Method   A method of calculating CCA in which a specified rate is applied to the ending UCC balance in a depreciable asset Class in order to determine the CCA for the period.

Deemed Disposition   A requirement to assume that a Disposition has taken place when, in fact, a disposition transaction has not occurred (e.g., a change in use is deemed to be a Disposition).

Deemed Dividends   A group of capital transactions and distributions, as specified in ITA 84(1), that are deemed to be Dividend payments.

Deemed Resident An Individual who is considered a Resident of Canada because of some factor other than physical presence in Canada (e.g., members of the Canadian armed forces are deemed to be Canadian Residents under ITA 250 without regard to where they are physically located).

Deemed Year End A requirement to have a taxation year end at a specified date, or as the result of a specified event.

Deeming Rules Rules that are used to require that an item or event be given a treatment for tax purposes that is not consistent with the actual nature of the item or event (e.g., members of the Canadian armed forces are deemed to be Canadian Residents even if they are not present in Canada at any time during the year).

Deferred Income Plans A group of plans that allow Individuals to receive Income on a tax deferred basis. These include Registered Pension Plans, Deferred Profit Sharing Plans, Registered Retirement Savings Plans, and Registered Retirement Income Funds.

Deferred Profit Sharing Plan (DPSP) A trusteed plan to which employers can make deductible contributions, the amount of which is related to the profits of the enterprise, and which do not create a Taxable Benefit for the recipient employees. Earnings accumulate tax free within the plan. Withdrawals from the plan are subject to tax.

Defined Benefit Plan A retirement savings plan in which the plan sponsor (usually an employer) promises a known or determinable retirement benefit and assumes financial responsibility for providing that benefit.

Defined Contribution Plan (a.k.a., Money Purchase Plan) A retirement savings plan in which the plan sponsor (employer or individual) makes known or determinable contributions. The retirement benefit is based on the accumulated contributions and earnings on investments within the plan.

Dependant As defined in ITA 118(6), an Individual who, at any time during the year, is dependent on the taxpayer for support and is the child or grandchild of the Individual or of the individual's Spouse or Common-Law Partner, the parent, grandparent, brother, sister, uncle, aunt, niece, or nephew, if resident in Canada at any time in the year, of the Individual or of the individual's Spouse or Common-Law Partner.

Depreciable Capital Property Capital property, such as equipment or furniture and fixtures, that is subject to depreciation or amortization.

Designated Stock Exchange A stock exchange that has been designated as such by the Minister of Finance. Replaces the term "prescribed stock exchange".

Digital News Subscriptions Credit A non-refundable tax credit for individuals based on their expenditures for digital subscriptions with a Qualifying Canadian Journalism Organization.

Disability Supports Deduction A deduction available to individuals for attendant care and other disability support expenses, incurred to allow the disabled individual to work or to attend a designated educational institution.

Disability Tax Credit A credit against Tax Payable that is available to Individuals with a doctor certified severe mental or physical disability. Can be transferred to a supporting Individual.

Disability Tax Credit Supplement A supplement to the Disability Tax Credit available to individuals who are under 18 years of age at the end of the year.

Disappearing Source Rules Rules designed to provide relief to investors who have borrowed money to make an investment and subsequently sold the investment for less than the related borrowings. These rules provide that any amount of debt that remains after the proceeds of the sale are used to pay off a portion of the total balance is deemed to be debt that is used to produce income.

Discretionary Trust A Trust for which the Settlor has given the Trustee discretion to decide the amounts of income or capital to be allocated to each Beneficiary.

Disposition The disposal of an asset through sale, gift, physical destruction, conversion, expropriation, or other means.

Dividend Gross Up An amount that is based on a percentage of the Dividends from Taxable Canadian Corporations that have been received by an Individual or Trust. This amount must be included in the Net Income For Tax Purposes of the Individual or Trust.

Dividend Stripping Procedures designed to allow an Individual to remove accumulated Income from a Corporation in the form of tax-free capital gains, while still retaining Control of the Corporation.

Dividend Tax Credit   A credit against the Tax Payable of an Individual or Trust. The amount is based on a fraction of the Dividend Gross Up that has been included in Net Income For Tax Purposes.

Dividends   Amounts declared and paid, at the discretion of management, as a return on equity investments.

Dividends In Kind   Dividends, other than Stock Dividends, paid in corporate assets other than cash.

Division B Income   An alternative name for Net Income For Tax Purposes.

Double Taxation   A reference to situations in which the same stream of Income is subject to tax a second time.

Dual Resident   A taxpayer who is considered to be a Resident of two countries.

E

Earned Capital (a.k.a. Retained Earnings)   In accounting usage, the amount of a Corporation's Shareholders' Equity that resulted from the retention of earnings in the corporation.

Earned Income (Child Care Expenses)   For purposes of determining the deductible amount of Child Care Expenses, Earned Income is defined as Employment Income (gross), Business Income (not losses), and Income from scholarships, training allowances, and research grants.

Earned Income (RRSP Deduction Limit)   The sum of Employment Income (without the RPP deduction), Business Income (losses), royalties (if the taxpayer is the author, inventor, or composer), taxable (deductible) support payments, supplementary unemployment benefits, income (loss) as an active partner, net rental income (loss), research grants (net of certain expenses), and CPP disability benefits.

Earned Surplus   An archaic accounting description of what now is called Retained Earnings. However, the term continues to be found in the *Income Tax Act*.

Ecological Gifts   Gifts of land certified by the Minister of the Environment to be ecologically sensitive land, the conservation and protection of which is important to the preservation of Canada's environmental heritage.

Election   A choice that is available to a Taxpayer with respect to a particular tax outcome (e.g., a Taxpayer can elect to have the spousal Rollover provision not be applicable).

Eligible Capital Expenditure   This term was used to refer to an amount expended to acquire an intangible asset that was not eligible for CCA or deduction. No longer available after 2016.

Eligible Capital Property   An intangible asset that results from making an Eligible Capital Expenditure.

Eligible Child   With respect to the deductibility of Child Care Expenses, a child of the Taxpayer, his Spouse, or a child who is dependent on the Taxpayer or his Spouse, and whose Income does not exceed the basic personal tax credit base amount. An Eligible Child must either be under 16 years of age at some time during the year, or dependent on the Taxpayer or his Spouse by reason of physical or mental infirmity.

Eligible Dependant Tax Credit   A credit against Tax Payable that is available to a single Individual supporting a Dependant in a self-contained domestic establishment.

Eligible Dividends   Dividends that have been designated by the payor as eligible for the enhanced gross up and tax credit procedure.

Eligible Newsroom Employee   An individual who is employed by a Qualifying Canadian News Organization and who spends at least 75% of their time engaged in the production of news content, including researching, collecting information, verifying facts, photographing, writing, editing, designing, and otherwise preparing content.

Eligible RDTOH   A balance containing refundable taxes that are available for dividend refunds on eligible dividends paid.

Emigration   Leaving a country, usually in order to establish permanent residency in another country.

Employee   An Individual who has an employment relationship with an entity that provides remuneration. Whether or not an Individual is working as an Employee or a Self-Employed Individual is dependent on factors such as control, ownership of tools, chance of profit or risk of loss, and the ability to subcontract or hire an assistant.

Employee and Partner GST/HST Rebate   A provision that allows employees and partners to recover the GST paid on their employment or partnership related expenses.

Employer/Employee Relationship A written, verbal, or tacit agreement in which an Employee agrees to work on a full-time or part-time basis for an employer for a specified or indeterminate period of time, in return for Salary or wages. The employer has the right to decide where, when, and how the work will be done. In this type of relationship, a contract of services exists.

Employment Income The Salary, wages, and other remuneration, including gratuities, received by an Employee in the year (see Employer/Employee Relationship).

Employment Insurance (EI) A federal insurance plan designed to provide benefits to unemployed Individuals. In order to receive benefits, Employees must make contributions when they are employed.

Employment Insurance Tax Credit A credit against Tax Payable that is available to Employees making payments to the federal Employment Insurance plan.

Estate As the term is used in the *Income Tax Act*, the property of a deceased Individual.

Estate Freeze Procedures undertaken by an Individual in order to fix a tax value for all or part of the Individual's property, and to Transfer future growth in the value of this property to other Individuals.

Estate Planning Tax planning directed towards the distribution of an Individual's property at death.

Excessive Eligible Dividend Designation (EEDD) A balance, subject to Part III.1 tax, which reflects an inappropriate designation of an amount of dividends paid as an Eligible Dividend.

Exchange Of Shares In A Reorganization (ITA 86) A Rollover provision that allows one class of shares in a Corporation to be exchanged for a different class of shares, without tax consequences.

Excluded Business A business is an Excluded Business of a Specified Individual if that individual is actively engaged in its activities on a regular, continuous and substantial basis, either in the current taxation year or, alternatively, in any 5 prior taxation years.

Excluded Shares For shares to be classified as Excluded Shares, the Specified Individual must be aged 25 or older and must own, in terms of both fair market value and voting rights, at least 10 percent of the outstanding shares of the corporation. In addition, the corporation must not be a Professional Corporation, less than 90 percent of

its business in the previous taxation year is from services, and less than 10 percent of its income in the previous year is from a related business.

Executor A Person appointed by an Individual in their Will to oversee the administration of the Estate on their death in accordance with the terms of that Will.

Exempt Goods And Services Goods and services that are not subject to the GST. Registrants who sell Exempt Goods And Services are not eligible for Input Tax Credits for GST paid. Examples include sales of used residential housing, most medical services, and most financial services.

Exempt Surplus A surplus account that tracks certain sources of income of a Foreign Affiliate.

F

Fairness Package Replaced by the Taxpayer Relief Provisions.

Family Trust An Inter Vivos Trust, established by an Individual, with family members as Beneficiaries.

Farm Property Farm Property includes real estate and property that is used in farming activities, a share of a Corporation that is carrying on a farming business, or an interest in a Partnership that is carrying on a farming business.

Federal Tax Abatement A 10 percentage point reduction in the federal tax rate on Corporations, applicable to Income earned in a province.

Final Tax Return A term used to describe the tax return filed for an Individual for the year of their death.

First Time Home Buyer's Tax Credit A credit against Tax Payable equal to 15% of $5,000 of the cost of an individual's first Principal Residence.

First Year Rules See Half-Year Rules.

Fiscal Period A taxation year that does not exceed 53 weeks.

Fishing Property Fishing Property includes real estate and property that is used in fishing activities, a share of a Corporation that is carrying on a fishing business, or an interest in a Partnership that is carrying on a fishing business.

Fixed Term Annuity An Annuity that is paid for a specified number of periods.

Flat Tax System A tax on Income that is applied at the same rate to all Taxpayers, without regard to the level of their Income.

Foreign Accrual Property Income (FAPI)   Income of a Controlled Foreign Affiliate from property (interest, Dividends, rents, royalties), Income from inactive businesses, Taxable Capital Gains from properties not used in an Active Business, and Income from an investment business, defined as a business the principal purpose of which is to earn Property Income.

Foreign Affiliate   A non-resident Corporation in which a Canadian Taxpayer has an equity percentage of at least 1 percent. As well, the aggregate equity percentages of the Taxpayer and each Person related to the Taxpayer must be at least 10 percent.

Foreign Taxes Paid Credit   A credit against Tax Payable based on taxes withheld by a foreign taxing authority on foreign source income.

Former Business Property   Real property that is used in the operation of a business.

Fringe Benefits   Non-cash benefits provided to Employees by an employer (e.g., contributions to an Employee's Registered Pension Plan).

Full Rate Taxable Income   For purposes of calculating the General Rate Reduction, Taxable Income reduced by amounts which have received preferential treatment under some other provision (e.g., the Small Business Deduction).

Fully Taxable Goods And Services   Goods and services that are taxable at the full 5% GST rate. Registrants who sell Fully Taxable Goods And Services are entitled to Input Tax Credits for GST paid. Examples include clothing, furniture, legal fees, hydro services, building materials, and restaurant meals.

G

GAAP   An acronym for "generally accepted accounting principles".

GAAR   An acronym for "general anti-avoidance rule". This ITA 245 provision attempts, in a very generalized manner, to limit the ability of Taxpayers to avoid tax through certain types of transactions that have no bona fide purpose other than to obtain a tax benefit.

General Partner   A Partner whose personal liability for the debts and obligations of the partnership are not limited.

General Partnership   A Partnership, all of the members of which are General Partners.

General Rate Income Pool (GRIP)   A notional account that tracks amounts of a CCPC's income that can be used for the payment of Eligible Dividends.

General Rate Reduction   A percentage point deduction in the calculation of corporate Tax Payable that is designed to reduce the general corporate tax rate of 38 percent.

Gift   A voluntary Transfer of goods or services without remuneration.

Goods And Services Tax (GST)   A type of Transaction Tax that is assessed on the sale of goods and services. As it is assessed at all stages of the production/distribution chain, the tax that an enterprise must collect and pay to the government is offset by Input Tax Credits for the tax paid on the various inputs required to produce or distribute the goods and services.

Goodwill   The excess, if any, of the total fair value of a business enterprise, over the sum of the fair values of its identifiable tangible and intangible assets.

Graduated Rate Estate   A testamentary trust that is designated as a graduated rate estate. Its special features include the ability to use graduated tax rates and a non-calendar fiscal period for the 36 month period following an individual's death.

Grind   A programmed reduction in some specified tax variable (e.g. the spousal tax credit is ground down by the spouse's Net Income For Tax Purposes).

Group Of Persons   For purposes of determining Control of a Corporation, a Group Of Persons is any two or more Persons, each of whom owns shares in the Corporation.

GST   An acronym for the "goods and services tax".

GST Tax Credit   A Refundable Tax Credit that is available to all Resident Individuals aged 19 or older who file a T1 tax return. May be reduced or eliminated by a deduction of Income in excess of a threshold amount.

H

Half-Year Rules (a.k.a. First Year Rules) A group of rules which require the subtraction of one-half of the year's net additions (additions, less the amount subtracted from the class because of disposals) from the Class, prior to calculating the CCA for the year. The great majority of post-2018 capital asset acquisitions are eligible for the Accelerated Investment Incentive (AccII) so the Half-Year Rules don't apply to those acquisitions.

Harmonized Sales Tax (HST) A combined federal/provincial sales tax that is generally assessed on the same basis as the federal Goods And Services Tax (GST). The combined rate varies across the provinces and is notionally a combination of the 5% GST plus a provincial sales tax ranging from 7% to 10%.

Head Tax A tax levied on the Individuals that are included in a specified classification.

Hobby Farmer A part-time farmer who does not have a Reasonable Expectation Of Profit.

Home Accessibility Tax Credit A tax credit that is available on expenditures made for renovations that will allow seniors and disabled individuals to gain access to, or be more mobile within a dwelling.

Home Buyers' Plan (HBP) A provision that allows Individuals to make a temporary, non-taxable withdrawal from their RRSP for purposes of acquiring a residence.

I

Identical Property Rules Rules which require that, for a group of identical Capital Assets (e.g., Common Shares) acquired at different prices, the Adjusted Cost Base used to determine the gain or loss will be the average cost of the group. The rules are used when there is a partial Disposition of the group.

Immigration Entering a new country, usually for purposes of establishing permanent residence.

Imputed Interest Interest on outstanding debt calculated at a specified interest rate without regard to the actual interest rate being paid. This concept is used to determine the Taxable Benefit on loans to Employees and Shareholders.

Inadequate Consideration A term used to refer to a situation where a non-arm's length transfer of property has been made and the Proceeds Of Disposition are not equal to the fair market value.

Income A measure of either how much an entity has earned during a period or, alternatively, how much its net worth has increased during a period. As the term is used in accounting and tax, it is a rules-based calculation. In the case of accounting, the rules are referred to as generally accepted accounting principles (GAAP), while in tax the rules are found in the *Income Tax Act* and other sources.

Income Attribution The allocation of some types of Income, on assets that have been transferred to a Spouse or related minors, back to the Transferor for inclusion in the Transferor's Net Income For Tax Purposes.

Income Interest (In A Trust) A right of the Taxpayer as a Beneficiary under a Personal Trust to receive all or any part of the Income of the Trust.

Income Splitting A group of Tax Planning techniques designed to divide a given stream of Income among family members or other related parties. The value of these techniques is based on progressive tax rates which means that, if a stream of Income can be divided into a group of smaller streams, a larger portion of it will be taxed at lower rates, resulting in aggregate tax savings.

Income Tax A tax on the Income of certain defined entities.

Income Tax Application Rules A set of rules designed to deal with transitional problems associated with the introduction of Capital Gains taxation in 1972. While these rules were very important in the years immediately after 1971, they are of declining importance at this point in time.

Income Tax Folios A CRA publication providing their interpretation of various technical issues related to income taxes. These will gradually replace the CRA's Interpretation Bulletins.

Income Tax Regulations A set of rules concerning administration and enforcement of the *Income Tax Act*. One of the major issues covered here is Capital Cost Allowance rates and procedures.

Income Tax Technical News An irregularly published newsletter prepared by the Income Tax Rulings Directorate.

Income Trust A Trust that has sold its beneficial interest units to the public in order to raise funds to acquire a business operation. All cash flows from the business are distributed to the unit holders.

Indexation The process of adjusting tax brackets and some Tax Credits to reflect changes in the consumer price index.

Individual   A single human being.

Individual Pension Plan   A defined benefit pension plan established for one individual.

Information Circulars   A group of separate publications that provides information regarding procedural matters that relate to both the *Income Tax Act* and the provisions of the Canada Pension Plan.

Information Return   ITA 221(1)(d) gives the CRA the right to require any class of Taxpayer to file a return providing any class of information that it would like to have. A common example of an Information Return would be the T4 which employers are required to file in order to provide information on their Employees' earnings and withholdings.

Input Tax Credit (ITC)   An amount, claimable by a registrant, for GST paid or payable on goods or services that were acquired or imported for consumption, use, or supply in the course of the Registrant's Commercial Activity.

Instalment Threshold   An amount, currently $3,000 of net tax owing for Individuals or taxes payable for Corporations that is used to determine the need to make Instalment payments (i.e., Individuals are required to make Instalment payments if their Net Tax Owing in the current year and one of the two preceding years exceeds the Instalment Threshold of $3,000).

Instalments   Payments made during a taxation year by both Individuals and Corporations. They are designed to accumulate to an amount sufficient to cover the tax liability for the year. Individuals and Small CCPCs make quarterly Instalments. Corporations that are not Small CCPCs are required to remit monthly.

Integration   An approach to the taxation of Corporations that attempts to ensure that amounts of Income that are flowed through a Corporation to its Individual shareholders, are subject to the same amount of tax as would be the case if the Individuals had received the Income directly from its source.

Inter Vivos Transfer   A Transfer made by a living Individual, as opposed to a Transfer made subsequent to that Individual's death.

Inter Vivos Trust   A Trust that is not a Testamentary Trust.

Interest Income   An amount that represents compensation for the use of money, is calculated with reference to a principal sum, and that accrues on a continuous basis.

International Tax Treaty (a.k.a., International Tax Convention)   A bilateral agreement between two countries which establishes rules for dealing with cross-jurisdictional tax issues.

International Taxation   Income and other types of taxation related to transactions and events that take place in multiple jurisdictions.

Interpretation Bulletins   A group of over 500 individual publications which provides the CRA's interpretation of the various laws that they administer. Gradually being replaced by Income Tax Folios.

In-The-Money   A term that is used to describe stock options in situations where the fair market value of the stock exceeds the option price.

Inventory   Property, the cost or value of which is relevant in computing a taxpayer's income from a business for a taxation year. The property is being held for resale, as opposed to being held to produce income.

Investment Tax Credit   A credit against Tax Payable, calculated as a percentage of some specified type of expenditure made by the Taxpayer.

Involuntary Disposition   A Disposition of a capital property resulting from theft, destruction through natural causes, or expropriation by a statutory authority.

J

Joint Spousal Or Common-Law Partner Trust   An Inter Vivos Trust established by an Individual aged 65 years or more, subject to the conditions that the Individual and his/her Spouse or Common-Law Partner must be entitled to all of the Trust's Income during their lifetimes, and the Individual and his Spouse or Common-Law Partner must be the only Individuals who can access the capital of the Trust during his/her lifetime.

Joint Tenancy   A holding of property, either real or personal, by two or more Persons with each sharing the undivided interest that cannot be sold without the consent of all joint tenants.

Joint Venture   An arrangement in which two or more Persons work together in a limited and defined business undertaking, which does not constitute a Partnership, a Trust, or a Corporation, the expenses and revenues of which will be distributed in mutually agreed portions.

L

Labour Sponsored Funds Tax Credit A credit against Tax Payable that is available to Individuals making investments in prescribed labour sponsored venture capital corporations.

Legal Stated Capital An amount that is specified in corporate enabling legislation. In general, it is equal to the amount of consideration received for the issuance of shares.

Life Annuity An Annuity that continues until the death of the Annuitant.

Lifelong Learning Plan (LLP) A provision that allows Individuals to make temporary, non-taxable withdrawals from their RRSP when they are enrolled in a qualifying education program at a qualifying educational institution.

Lifetime Capital Gains Deduction A deduction in the calculation of the Taxable Income of an Individual. It permits the deduction of a cumulative lifetime amount of Capital Gains resulting from the Disposition of Qualified Small Business Corporation shares or Qualified Farm or Fishing Property.

Limited Liability A reference to the fact that the liability of investors in equity shares of a Corporation is limited to the amount of their invested capital.

Limited Liability Partnerships A Partnership, all of the members of which are legislatively specified professionals. The members of such Partnerships are relieved of any personal liability arising from the wrongful or negligent action of their professional Partners, as well as Employees, agents, or representatives of the Partnership who conduct partnership business.

Limited Partner As defined in most provincial legislation, a Partner whose liabilities for partnership debts is limited to the amount of his contribution to the Partnership, and who is not permitted to participate in the management of the Partnership.

Limited Partnership A Partnership composed of at least one General Partner and at least one Limited Partner. To be considered a Limited Partnership, the Partnership has to be registered as such under the appropriate provincial registry.

Limited Partnership Loss The excess of losses allocated to a Limited Partner (other than farming or capital losses), over his At-Risk Amount.

Liquidating Dividend A Dividend that represents a return of invested capital, as opposed to a distribution from earnings.

Listed Personal Property A defined subset of Personal Use Property. The included items are works of art, jewelry, rare books, stamps, and coins.

Loss Carry Back The application of a loss incurred in the current taxation year against the Income reported in a previous taxation year, resulting in a refund of taxes paid in that previous year.

Loss Carry Forward The application of a loss incurred in the current taxation year against Income reported in a subsequent taxation year, resulting in a reduction of Tax Payable in that subsequent year.

Low Rate Income Pool (LRIP) A notional account that tracks amounts of a non-CCPC's income that cannot be used for the payment of Eligible Dividends.

Lump Sum Payments Retroactive payments for Spousal or Child Support, pension benefits, EI benefits, and Employment Income (including payments for termination), that relate to prior years. Qualifying amounts of such payments are eligible for an alternative Tax Payable calculation.

M

M&P An acronym for "manufacturing and processing" usually used in connection with the calculation of the Manufacturing And Processing Profits Deduction.

Manufacturing And Processing Profits Deduction (M&P Deduction) A deduction in the calculation of corporate Tax Payable. It is equal to the General Rate Reduction rate applied to M&P Profits.

Medical Expense Tax Credit A credit against Tax Payable that is available to Individuals with qualifying medical expenses.

Merger A combination of two or more business enterprises. While widely used in the *Income Tax Act*, this term does not have a formal definition in that legislation.

Money Purchase Limit An amount, specified in tax legislation that represents the maximum amount of Employee and employer contributions that can be added, for the benefit of a given Employee, to an RPP in the specified taxation year.

Money Purchase Plan (a.k.a., Defined Contribution Plan) A retirement savings plan in which the plan sponsor (employer or Individual) makes known or determinable contributions. The retirement benefit is based on the accumulated contributions and earnings on investments within the plan.

Moving Expenses Costs, as described in ITA 62(3), that can be deducted when an Individual is moving; to a new work location, to commence full-time attendance at a post-secondary institution, to a new work location after ceasing to be a full-time student at a post-secondary institution, or to a new location to take up employment, if unemployed prior to the move.

MUSH An acronym for "municipalities, universities, schools, and hospitals". It is used in GST work to refer to the special rules applicable to these organizations.

Mutual Fund A taxable entity, either a Trust or a Corporation, that manages a portfolio of investments on behalf of its unitholders or shareholders.

N

"Negative" Adjusted Cost Base A term used to refer to situations where negative adjustments to the Adjusted Cost Base of a Capital Asset exceed its original cost plus positive adjustments. While, in general, such amounts must be taken into Income, an exception is made for Partnership Interests, for which such amounts can be carried forward.

Net Assets Assets minus the liabilities of a business enterprise.

Net Business Income As used in this text, the net of inclusions less deductions, related to Business Income, with all amounts determined as per Division B, Subdivision b, of the *Income Tax Act*.

Net Capital Loss The excess of Allowable Capital Losses over Taxable Capital Gains for the current year.

Net Income As used in this text, the net of revenues plus gains, less expenses plus losses, with all amounts determined through the application of GAAP.

Net Income For Tax Purposes The sum of Employment Income, Business and Property Income, net Taxable Capital Gains, other sources of income, and other deductions from income, determined using income tax procedures and concepts. These amounts are combined as per the rules in ITA 3. This amount is also referred to as Division B Income or simply Net Income. However, we tend to use the full Net Income For Tax Purposes title in order to avoid confusion with Net Income as determined by accounting rules.

Net Property Income As used in this text, the net of inclusions less deductions, related to Property Income, with all amounts determined as per Division B, Subdivision b, of the *Income Tax Act*.

Net Tax Owing A term, applicable to Taxpayers who are Individuals, used to describe the sum of federal and provincial taxes owing for the year, less amounts withheld for the year.

NETFILE An electronic filing system that requires the use of an approved software program. An Individual uses the Internet to transmit their return directly to the CRA, without the use of a third party.

New Housing GST/HST Rebate A provision that allows an individual to recover a portion of the GST paid on the acquisition of a new residence.

Non-Arm's Length ITA 251(1) indicates that Related Persons (see definition) do not deal with each other at arm's length. Also, a taxpayer and a personal trust do not deal with each other at arm's length. In other cases, it is a question of fact as to whether an arm's length relation exists.

Non-Capital Loss The sum of employment losses (for Individuals), business losses, property losses, Net Capital Losses deducted, and deductible Dividends received (for Corporations), less Income as calculated under ITA 3(c).

Non-Depreciable Capital Property Capital property, such as land or holdings of securities, that is not subject to depreciation or amortization.

Non-Discretionary Trust A Trust for which the Trust documents have specified the amounts of Income and capital to be allocated to each Beneficiary.

Non-Eligible Dividends Dividends that have not been designated by the payor as eligible for the enhanced gross up and tax credit procedure.

Non-Eligible RDTOH A balance containing refundable taxes that are available for dividend refunds on non-eligible dividends paid.

Non-Refundable Tax Credit A Tax Credit that can only be used against the Tax Payable of an Individual. It will not be "refunded" to Individuals without sufficient Tax Payable to make use of it.

Non-Resident A Corporation, Trust, or any other type of entity that exists, was formed or organized, or was last continued under the laws of a country, or a political subdivision of a country, other than Canada.

Non-Share Consideration Consideration received by a Taxpayer from a Corporation that is in the form of assets other than shares of the Corporation.

Northern Residents Deductions Deductions from the Taxable Income of residents of prescribed areas in northern Canada, designed to compensate them for the higher costs of living in these regions.

Notice Of Assessment A form that the CRA sends to all Taxpayers after they process their returns. It tells Taxpayers whether there were any changes made to the returns and, if so, what they are. It also informs Taxpayers of the amount of their additional tax payable or their refund.

Notice Of Objection A statement made to the CRA which provides a statement of facts and reasons, detailing why a Taxpayer or GST Registrant disagrees with an Assessment. The notice can be filed using Form T400A or by simply writing a letter to the CRA.

O

OAS Clawback A taxing back, or reduction, in the payment of Old Age Security benefits. The federal government taxes back, or retains, an amount of these payments equal to 15% of the Individual's Income in excess of an indexed threshold amount.

Old Age Security Benefits (OAS) A monthly payment to Residents of Canada who are 65 years of age or older (see also OAS Clawback).

Operating Cost Benefit A Taxable Benefit assessed to Employees whose employers pay the operating costs of an automobile provided to the Employee. It is designed to reflect, on a notional basis, the value of these operating costs.

Ordering Rule Rules which establish the sequence or order in which a group of deductions must be made.

Over Integration An application of integration procedures (e.g., gross up and dividend tax credit rates) that results in a situation where income flowed through a corporation is subject to less tax payable than the same income received directly by an individual.

P

Paid Up Capital (PUC) A balance that is, in general, equal to Legal Stated Capital as determined under the legislation governing the particular Corporation. The equivalent of Contributed Capital in accounting usage.

Parent Company A Corporation that Controls one or more Subsidiaries.

Part IV Tax A refundable tax, applicable to Private Corporations and Subject Corporations, and assessed on Portfolio Dividends received as well as some Dividends received from Connected Corporations.

Part Year Resident An Individual who either enters Canada during the year and becomes a Resident or, alternatively, an Individual who departs from Canada during the year and gives up their Resident status. In either case, the Individual will be taxed on their worldwide income for the part of the year that they were considered to be a Resident of Canada.

Partner A Person who is a member of a Partnership.

Partner and Employee GST/HST Rebate A provision that allows partners and employees to recover the GST paid on their partnership or employment related expenses.

Partnership Two or more Persons who combine forces to carry on a business together for the purpose of making a profit by contributing their skills, knowledge, labour, experience, time, or capital.

Partnership Interest A Non-Depreciable Capital Property that reflects the Partner's original cost, adjusted for earnings, withdrawals, and other factors.

Past Service Cost The cost of starting a pension plan and extending the benefits/contributions to years of service prior to the inception of the plan or, alternatively, amending the benefit/contribution formula of an existing plan and extending the change retroactively to years of service prior to the amendment.

Past Service Pension Adjustment (PSPA) An adjustment to reflect the past service benefits/contributions allocated to an Employee for years of service prior to the current year.

Penalties Amounts taxpayers or GST registrants must pay if they fail to file returns or remit or pay amounts owing on time, or if they try to evade paying or remitting tax by not filing returns. Penalties must also be paid by people who knowingly, or under circumstances amounting to gross negligence, participate in or make false statements or omissions in their returns, and by those who do not provide the information required on a prescribed form.

Pension Adjustment (PA) An adjustment reported by employers which reflects, for an individual Employee, the Employee and employer contributions to RPPs and DPSPs for the previous year (in the case of Defined Benefit RPPs, benefits are converted to an equivalent amount of contributions).

Pension Adjustment Reversal (PAR) An adjustment for amounts of benefits/contributions that were included in previously issued Pension Adjustments, but have subsequently been lost to the Individual (e.g., benefits earned during a pre-vesting period that did not ultimately vest).

Pension Income Tax Credit A credit against Tax Payable that is available to Individuals with qualifying pension income.

Periodic Child Care Expense Amount A weekly limit on deductible child care costs, defined as 1/40 of the Annual Child Care Expense Amount.

Permanent Establishment A fixed place of business of a Corporation, including an office, a branch, a mine, an oil well, a farm, a timberland, a factory, a workshop, or a warehouse.

Person A term used in the *Income Tax Act* to refer to taxable entities. For income tax purposes, the three taxable entities are Individuals, Corporations, and Trusts.

Personal Services Business A Corporation that provides the services of a Specified Shareholder [ITA 248(1)] who could reasonably be regarded as an officer or Employee of the business, and that does not have five or more other full time Employees throughout the year.

Personal Tax Credits A group of credits against Tax Payable that are specified in ITA 118(1). They include credits for Individuals, Spouses, Common-Law Partners and various Dependants, as well as credits for types of income such as pension or employment.

Personal Trust A Testamentary or Inter Vivos Trust in which no beneficial interest was acquired for consideration paid to the Trust or to a Person who contributed property to the Trust.

Personal Use Property Any property that is owned by the Taxpayer and used primarily for his enjoyment, or for the enjoyment of one or more Individuals Related to the Taxpayer.

Phased Retirement A term used to refer to situations where an individual over 55 years of age continues to earn partial pension benefits, despite the fact that he or she has started to receive pension benefits from that employer.

Political Contributions Tax Credit A credit against Tax Payable that is available to Individuals who have made contributions to a registered federal political party or to a candidate at the time of a federal election.

Pooled Registered Pension Plan A registered pension plan established by a financial institution. Eligible registrants would be employees and other individuals who are not members of a registered pension plan established by an employer.

Portfolio Dividend A Dividend received from a Corporation to which the recipient is not connected (see Connected Corporation). Usually applicable if 10% or less of the voting shares are owned.

Post-1971 Undistributed Surplus Amounts earned by a Corporation after 1971 and retained in the Corporation.

Pre-1972 Capital Surplus On Hand Capital Gains accrued before 1972 that have been realized as the result of a Disposition after 1971, less Capital Losses that accrued before 1972 that have been realized as the result of a Disposition after 1971.

Pre-1972 Undistributed Surplus Amounts earned by a Corporation prior to 1972 and retained in the Corporation.

Preferred Beneficiary An Individual who is a Beneficiary of a Trust and who is either eligible for the Disability Tax Credit or, alternatively, 18 years of age or older and can be claimed by another Individual for purposes of the dependant tax credit for Individuals who are dependant because of mental or physical infirmity.

Preferred Beneficiary Election An Election which allows trust income to be allocated to a Preferred Beneficiary without being distributed to that Beneficiary by the Trust.

Preferred Shares Shares that do not have all the rights which are provided for under the relevant corporate enabling legislation. While there are many variations in the rights that such securities have, Preferred Shares would normally have a fixed or determinable Dividend and would not have voting rights.

Prescribed Rate An interest rate which, as described in ITR 4301, changes quarterly and is based on the average interest rate paid on 90 day Treasury Bills during the first month of the preceding quarter. The basic rate is used for a variety of purposes (e.g., calculation of the Taxable Benefits on interest free loans to Employees). The basic rate, plus 2 percentage points, is used to calculate interest owing from the government to Taxpayers (e.g., interest on late payment of a tax refund). The basic rate, plus 4 percentage points, is used to calculate interest owed by Taxpayers to the government (e.g., interest on late Instalments).

Prescribed Stock Exchange   This term has been replaced by "designated stock exchange".

Principal Residence   Any accommodation owned by the Taxpayer that was ordinarily inhabited in the year by the Taxpayer, his Spouse, a former Spouse, or a dependent child, and is designated by the Taxpayer as a Principal Residence.

Private Corporation   A Corporation that is a resident of Canada, but is not a Public Corporation.

Proceeds Of Disposition   Amounts received as the result of a Disposition. Usually related to a capital property Disposition.

Professional Corporation   ITA 248(1) defines a Professional Corporation as a Corporation that carries on the professional practice of an accountant, dentist, lawyer, medical doctor, veterinarian, or chiropractor. Corporations carrying on the practice of other professionals, for example architects, do not fall within this definition.

Profit Sharing Plan   A trusteed plan to which employers can make deductible contributions, the amount of which is related to the profits of the enterprise. Both the contributions and the earnings resulting from their investment are taxed in the hands of the Employees as they occur. Payments from the plan are received by the Employees on a tax free basis.

Progressive Tax System   A tax system that applies higher effective rates for Individuals with higher Incomes and lower effective rates for Individuals with lower Incomes (e.g., personal income taxes).

Property Income   Income that is earned through the passive ownership of property. It would include rents, interest, Dividends, and some royalties (i.e., royalties paid on assets that have been purchased). While usage is not always consistent, this term usually refers to a net amount (i.e., inclusions less deductions, or revenues less expenses).

Property Tax   A tax on the ownership of some particular set of goods.

Public Corporation   A Corporation that has at least one class of its shares listed on a designated stock exchange in Canada.

PUC   An acronym for "paid up capital".

Purification Of A Small Business Corporation   A process of disposing of corporate assets that are not being used to produce Active Business Income, so that the Corporation meets the 90% of assets test required to qualify as a Small Business Corporation.

Q

Qualified Farm Property   A Qualified Farm Property is a Farm Property that, prior to its Disposition was owned by the Taxpayer, his Spouse, or his Common-Law Partner, or their children for a period of 24 months or more.

Qualified Fishing Property   A Qualified Fishing Property is a Fishing Property that, prior to its Disposition was owned by the Taxpayer, his Spouse, or his Common-Law Partner, or their children for a period of 24 months or more.

Qualified Property   Certain specified types of property that, when acquired, qualify the Taxpayer for an Investment Tax Credit.

Qualified Scientific Research And Experimental Development Expenditures   Scientific Research And Experimental Development expenditures that qualify the Taxpayer for Investment Tax Credits.

Qualified Small Business Corporation   A Small Business Corporation that, at the time of its Disposition, has been owned by no one other than the Taxpayer or a related party during the preceding 24 months, and during that 24 month period, more than 50% of the fair market value of its assets were used in an Active Business carried on primarily in Canada.

Qualifying Canadian Journalism Organization   A Canadian organization that is primarily involved in the production of written news content.

Qualifying Corporation   A CCPC throughout the year with Taxable Income in the immediately preceding year of no more than $500,000 and previous year Taxable Capital Employed In Canada of $10 million or less, thereby qualifying for the additional 15% tax credit on the first $3,000,000 of Qualified Scientific Research And Development Expenditures.

Qualifying Spousal Or Common-Law Partner Trust   A Spousal Or Common-Law Partner Trust that qualifies for the Rollover of assets into the Trust under ITA 73(1.01) for Inter Vivos Trusts or ITA 70(6) for Testamentary Trusts.

Qualitative Characteristics   This term is used in our text to refer to non-quantitative characteristics of a tax system that are considered to be desirable (e.g., fairness).

Quick Method A method of determining GST amounts payable or receivable that is available to Registrants with annual GST taxable sales, including those of associated businesses, of $400,000 or less. Specified percentages are applied to the GST inclusive sales figures to determine the GST payable or the refund. Accounting for Input Tax Credits on non-capital expenditures is not required. Input Tax Credits on capital expenditures are tracked separately.

R

RDTOH An acronym for "refundable dividend tax on hand".

Real Property Land and all appurtenances to it, including buildings, crops, and mineral rights, a.k.a., real estate.

Reasonable Expectation Of Profit (REOP) A test that involves the determination of whether a business or an investment is likely to have a profit. The CRA has tried to use this test to limit the ability of Taxpayers to deduct losses resulting from businesses and investments that fail their REOP test.

Reassessment A revision of an original Assessment (see Assessment and Notice Of Assessment).

Recapture Of CCA An inclusion in Business and Property Income that arises when deductions from a CCA Class, engendered by disposals, leave a negative balance in that Class at the end of the taxation year.

Redemption Of Shares A transaction in which a Corporation purchases some of its own outstanding shares, either in the open market, or through a direct purchase from shareholders.

Refundable Dividend Tax On Hand (RDTOH) A balance made up of refundable taxes paid, less refunds received as the result of paying Dividends. There are two separate RDTOH balances, Eligible RDTOH and Non-Eligible RDTOH.

Refundable Investment Tax Credit An Investment Tax Credit that will be paid to the Taxpayer, even if the amount resulting from the Investment Tax Credit exceeds the Taxpayer's Tax Payable.

Refundable Journalism Labour Tax Credit A refundable credit for salaries and wages paid to Eligible Newsroom Employees of a Qualifying Canadian Journalism Organization.

Refundable Medical Expense Supplement A refundable credit against Tax Payable that increases the amount available to certain low income individuals for their eligible medical expenses.

Refundable Part I Tax The portion of Part I tax that is applicable to a notional amount of Aggregate Investment Income earned by a CCPC.

Refundable Part XI.3 Tax A 50% tax that is assessed on contributions to a Retirement Compensation Arrangement and on the earnings of amounts invested in the plan. It is fully refundable when amounts are distributed from the arrangement and taxed in the hands of the recipient Employees.

Refundable Tax Credit An amount, based on a Tax Credit calculation, that will be paid to an Individual even if the amount resulting from the Tax Credit calculation exceeds the Individual's Tax Payable.

Registered Disability Savings Plan (RDSP) A trusteed arrangement that allows Individuals to make non-deductible contributions that will be invested on a tax-free basis, with the accumulated funds being used to make distributions to an individual who qualifies for the disability tax credit.

Registered Education Savings Plan (RESP) A trusteed arrangement that allows Individuals to make non-deductible contributions that will be invested on a tax-free basis, with the accumulated funds being used to provide for the post-secondary education of a child.

Registered Pension Plan (RPP) A retirement savings plan sponsored by an employer, to which the employer will make contributions which are not taxable to the Employee, and the Employee may make contributions which are deductible. Earnings accumulate tax free within the plan. Withdrawals from the plan are subject to tax.

Registered Retirement Income Fund (RRIF) A trusteed plan to which a Resident Individual can transfer balances from retirement savings plans on a tax free basis. Earnings accumulate tax free within the plan. Withdrawals from the plan are subject to tax. Unlike RRSPs, a minimum withdrawal is required each year.

Registered Retirement Savings Plan (RRSP) A trusteed plan to which a Resident Individual can make deductible contributions. Earnings accumulate tax free within the plan. Withdrawals from the plan are generally subject to tax.

Registrant An entity who is registered to collect and remit the GST.

Regressive Tax System A tax system that applies higher effective rates for Individuals with lower Incomes and lower effective rates for Individuals with higher Incomes (e.g., most sales taxes).

Related Persons ITA 251(2)(a) indicates that two Individuals are related if they are connected by blood relationship, marriage or common-law partnership, or adoption. ITA 251(2)(b) describes various situations in which a Corporation would be related to other Persons (e.g., a Corporation is related to the Person who Controls it). ITA 251(2)(c) describes various situations in which two Corporations would be related to each other (e.g., the two Corporations are controlled by the same Person).

Reorganization Of Capital (ITA 86) A Rollover provision that allows one class of shares in a Corporation to be exchanged for a different class of shares, without tax consequences.

Replacement Property Rules A set of rules which provide for the deferral of both Recapture and Capital Gains on Involuntary Dispositions and some voluntary Dispositions of capital property. Deferral is conditional on replacing the property within a specified period after the Proceeds Of Disposition are received.

Reserve A deduction in the calculation of net Business Income or net Taxable Capital Gains.

Resident A Person who is located in a place. This is the basis on which Canadian income taxes are assessed. That is, Canadian Resident Persons are liable for the payment of Canadian income tax, without regard to their citizenship or the source of their Income. While not defined in the *Income Tax Act*, IT Folio S5-F1-C1 provides guidance on the determination of residency for Individuals and IT-447 provides similar guidance for Trusts.

Residential Ties Factors that will be considered in determining whether or not an Individual is a Resident of Canada. While there are many such ties, ITF S5-F1-C1 indicates that the most commonly used would be the maintenance of a dwelling in Canada, having one's Spouse or Common-Law Partner remain in Canada, and having one's Dependants remain in Canada.

Restricted Farm Loss A farmer whose chief source of Income is not farming or a combination of farming and some other source of Income, but who has a reasonable expectation of long-run profitability, can only deduct losses to the extent of the first $2,500, plus one-half of the next $12,500. Losses in excess of this deductible amount are referred to as Restricted Farm Losses.

Restrictive Covenant An agreement entered into, an undertaking made, or a waiver of an advantage or right by the Taxpayer. This would include, but would not be limited to, non-competition agreements.

Retained Earnings (a.k.a. Earned Capital) In accounting usage, the amount of a Corporation's Shareholders' Equity that resulted from the retention of earnings in the Corporation.

Retirement Compensation Arrangement An unregistered plan to which employers make deductible contributions to provide Employees with benefits subsequent to their retirement. Both contributions and earnings are subject to a Refundable Part XI.3 Tax.

Retiring Allowance Amounts received at retirement as recognition for long service, or as the result of loss of employment.

Reversionary Trust A trust agreement under which the property held by the Trustee can revert to the Settlor.

Rights Or Things With respect to a deceased Taxpayer, these are amounts that are due, but have not been received (e.g., wages to the end of a pay period prior to death, but not yet received).

Rollover As this term is used in tax work, it refers to a tax free Transfer of assets under circumstances that, in the absence of a special Rollover provision, would be considered a taxable Transfer.

RRSP Deduction Limit The amount that is the sum of the Unused RRSP Deduction Room at the end of the preceding year, plus the amount by which the lesser of the RRSP Dollar Limit and 18% of Earned Income for the preceding year exceeds the Pension Adjustment for the preceding year. This sum is adjusted for any Past Service Pension Adjustment or Pension Adjustment Reversal. In simplified terms, it represents the maximum amount of contributions that have been made to an RRSP that can be deducted for a year.

RRSP Deduction Room The excess of the RRSP Deduction Limit, over the amount of RRSP contributions that have been deducted.

RRSP Dollar Limit Generally, the Money Purchase Limit for the preceding year.

S

Safe Income For purposes of applying ITA 55(2) to Capital Gains Stripping, Safe Income is made up of amounts earned by a Corporation after 1971, or if the investment shares in that Corporation were acquired after that date, amounts earned after the acquisition.

Salary The amount an employer pays an Employee for work done. An employer records this type of Employment Income on a T4. A common component of Employment Income.

Salary Deferral Arrangement An arrangement, whether funded or not, under which an Individual who has the right to receive compensation postpones the receipt of that compensation, and it is reasonable to assume that one of the main purposes of this postponement was to defer the payment of taxes.

Scientific Research And Experimental Development (SR&ED) Activities related to basic or applied research, and for the development of new products and processes.

Self-Employed Individual An Individual who has a business relationship with an entity. Whether or not an Individual is working as an Employee or a Self-Employed Individual is dependent on factors such as control, ownership of tools, chance of profit or risk of loss, and the ability to subcontract or hire an assistant.

Separate Class Rules Rules that require certain types of assets that would, in the absence of these special rules, be included in a single Class, be allocated to a separate balance for that Class (e.g., each rental property with a cost greater than $50,000 must be placed in a different Class 1).

Settlor The Individual who creates a Trust by contributing property to be managed and administered by a Trustee for the Beneficiaries.

Share For Share Exchange (ITA 85.1) A Rollover provision that allows one Corporation to acquire shares in another Corporation by issuing its own shares, without tax consequences to either of the Corporations or their shareholders.

Shareholders' Equity The residual interest of the shareholders of a Corporation in the Net Assets of the Corporation.

Short Fiscal Year A taxation year that is less than 12 months in duration. Can occur in the first and last years of operation, as well as certain other situations.

SIFT Partnership To be a Specified Investment Flow-Through (SIFT) partnership, (1) the partnership must be a Canadian resident partnership; (2) investments in the partnership must be publicly traded; and (3) the partnership must hold one or more non-portfolio properties.

SIFT Trust To be a Specified Investment Flow-Through (SIFT) trust, (1) the trust must be resident in Canada; (2) investments in the trust must be publicly traded; and (3) the trust must hold one or more non-portfolio properties.

Simplified ITC Accounting A method of determining Input Tax Credits available to small businesses, charities, not-for-profit organizations, and certain public service bodies. The organization must have annual GST taxable sales, including those of associated businesses, of $1,000,000 or less and annual GST taxable purchases of $4,000,000 or less. Input Tax Credits are determined by multiplying all GST inclusive purchases, except real property purchases, by 5/105 rather than using the actual GST paid. Input Tax Credits on real property are tracked separately.

Small Business Corporation A Corporation that is a Canadian Controlled Private Corporation that uses all or substantially all (90% or more) of the fair market value of its assets in an Active Business that is carried on primarily (more than 50 percent) in Canada.

Small Business Deduction A deduction in the calculation of corporate Tax Payable equal to 17.5 percentage points on the first $500,000 of Active Business Income earned by a CCPC.

Small CCPC A Canadian Controlled Private Corporation that has (1) Taxable Income in the current or previous year of $500,000 or less, (2) has Taxable Capital Employed In Canada in the current or previous year of $10 million or less, (3) is able to claim some amount of the Small Business Deduction in the current or previous year, and (4) has a perfect payment compliance record for the last 12 months.

Small Suppliers Exemption An exemption from the requirement to register for the collection and remittance of GST for those entities with less than $30,000 in taxable supplies.

Social Benefits Repayment (a.k.a., Clawback) An income tested taxing back, or reduction, in the payment of Old Age Security Benefits and Employment Insurance Benefits.

Soft Costs Costs, such as interest and property tax, on land and buildings that are incurred prior to the capital asset being used for business or income producing purposes.

Sojourner An Individual who is deemed under ITA 250 to be a Canadian Resident for the full taxation year as the result of having sojourned (i.e., been temporarily present) in Canada for 183 days or more.

Source Deductions Amounts that are withheld by an employer from the Income of Employees. The withholdings for income taxes, Canada Pension Plan contributions, and Employment Insurance premiums must be remitted to the government.

Source Individual A Source Individual (with respect to a Specified Individual) is a resident of Canada who is related to the Specified Individual.

Specified Class [ITA 256(1.1)] A class of shares that has certain specified terms and conditions, including a fixed or determinable Dividend and an absence of voting rights. Would generally be referred to as Preferred Shares.

Specified Employee An Employee who owns 10% or more of the shares of the Corporation, or who does not deal at arm's length with the Corporation.

Specified Individual Under the Tax On Split Income (TOSI) legislation a Specified Individual is an individual who is a resident of Canada and, if the individual is under 18, has a parent who is also a resident of Canada.

Specified Investment Business A Corporation that does not have five or more full time Employees throughout the year, whose principal purpose is to derive Income from property.

Specified Non-Resident Shareholder A specified shareholder who is a non-resident Person or non-resident investment company.

Specified Shareholder [(ITA 18(5)] A shareholder of a Corporation who owns, either alone or together with other related persons, more than 25% of the voting shares of a corporation or, alternatively, shares that have more than 25% of the market value of all of the corporation's shares.

Specified Shareholder [ITA 248(1)] A shareholder of a Corporation who owns, directly or indirectly, at any time in the year, not less than 10% of the issued shares of any class of the capital stock of the Corporation, or of any other Corporation that is related to the Corporation.

Split Income Certain types of Income received by a Specified Individual from non-arm's length sources that will be taxed at the maximum federal rate.

Spousal Or Common-Law Partner Trust An Inter Vivos or Testamentary Trust that has an individual's Spouse or Common-Law Partner as a Beneficiary (see also Qualifying Spousal Or Common-Law Partner Trust).

Spousal RRSP An RRSP to which the Spouse or Common-Law Partner of the Annuitant (i.e., Beneficiary of the RRSP) has made contributions that the Spouse or Common-Law Partner can deduct in calculating Net Income For Tax Purposes.

Spousal Support A Support Amount that is for the benefit of a Spouse or Common-Law Partner, or a former Spouse or Common-Law Partner.

Spousal Tax Credit A credit against Tax Payable that is available to individuals who have a Spouse or Common-Law Partner.

Spouse An Individual to whom a Taxpayer is legally married.

Standby Charge A Taxable Benefit assessed to Employees who have been provided with an automobile by their employer. It is designed to reflect, on a notional basis, the value of having the car available on a standby basis for personal usage.

Stock Dividend A pro rata distribution of corporation shares to existing shareholders of the corporation.

Stock Option A contractual arrangement which gives the holder the right to purchase a specified number of shares for a specified period of time at a specified acquisition price.

Stop Loss Rules A group of rules which, under specified conditions, prevent the deduction of a loss.

Straight-Line Method A method of calculating CCA in which a specified or determinable rate is applied to the Capital Cost of acquired assets in order to determine the CCA for the period.

Student Loan Interest Tax Credit A credit against Tax Payable that is based on the amount of interest on a loan under the *Canada Student Loans Act*, or the *Canada Student Financial Assistance Act*.

Subject Corporation For purposes of the Part IV Tax, a Public Corporation that is controlled by, or for the benefit of, an Individual or a related group of Individuals. Also used in the determination of Dividend Stripping (ITA 84.1) and share sales to non-residents (ITA 212.1) to describe a Corporation, the shares of which have been sold.

Subsidiary An enterprise that is controlled by another enterprise (the Parent Company). The Parent Company has the right and ability to obtain future economic benefits from the resources of the Subsidiary and is exposed to the related risks.

Superficial Loss (ITA 54) A loss on the Disposition of property that is disallowed for tax purposes because the Taxpayer has acquired an identical property, either 30 days before the Disposition or, alternatively, 30 days after the Disposition.

Supply A broad range of transactions between Persons. To "make a supply of property or a service" means to provide it in any way, including sale, transfer, barter, exchange, licence, rental, lease, gift, or Disposition.

Support Amount Amounts paid as the result of the separation or divorce of two Individuals who were Spouses or Common-Law Partners. Can be divided into Spousal Support and Child Support.

Surtax An additional or extra tax on something already taxed.

Syndicates A group of Persons combined or making a joint effort to undertake some specific project or to carry out a specific transaction.

T

Target Benefit Plan A hybrid pension plan that is based on defined contributions combined with a target or proposed benefit for retirees. However, unlike defined benefit plans, these plans also allow the benefit to be reduced if funding is not adequate to produce the target benefit.

Tariffs A tax imposed on the importation or exportation of certain goods or services.

Tax Avoidance The undertaking of transactions or arrangements with a view to avoiding or minimizing the payment of taxes. As the term is generally used, it refers to legitimate procedures that could also be described as Tax Planning.

Tax Base The income source, class of transaction, type of property, or other factor on which tax is assessed (e.g., sales tax is assessed on sales).

Tax Court Of Canada A court that hears appeals about income tax and GST/HST assessments. In addition, the Court has jurisdiction to hear appeals under the Canada Pension Plan Act, Employment Insurance Act, and several other Acts. The Tax Court maintains four offices (Vancouver, Ottawa, Toronto, and Montreal) and regularly conducts hearings in major centres across Canada.

Tax Credit A credit against Tax Payable.

Tax Deferral An important type of Tax Planning. The basic idea here is to find procedures that will put off the payment of taxes until a later taxation year. The value of these procedures reflects the time value of money. That is, there is a value associated with making a payment later, rather than sooner.

Tax Evasion This typically involves deliberately ignoring a specific part of the law or willfully refusing to comply with legislated reporting requirements. Tax evasion, unlike tax avoidance, has criminal consequences.

Tax Expenditures Foregone tax revenues due to special exemptions, rate reductions, rebates, and credits that reduce the amount of tax that would otherwise be payable. Often designed to encourage certain kinds of activities or to serve other objectives, such as providing assistance to lower-income Canadians.

Tax Free Savings Accounts (TFSAs) A trusteed arrangement that allows Individuals to make non-deductible contributions that will be invested in qualified assets. Earnings accumulate on a tax free basis within the plan and can be distributed to the Individual who established the plan on a tax free basis.

Tax Haven A foreign country used to avoid or reduce income taxes, especially by investors from another country.

Tax Incidence The Person who ultimately pays a tax, regardless of the legal basis of assessment (e.g., taxes paid by Corporations may be passed on to either Employees or customers).

Tax Planning The undertaking of legitimate transactions or arrangements with a view to avoiding or minimizing the payment of taxes. Some or all of such efforts could also be referred to as Tax Avoidance.

Taxable Allowance An allowance provided by an employer to an Employee that must be included in the Employee's Employment Income. The amount is included on the Employee's T4.

Taxable Benefit An amount of money, or the value of goods or services, that an employer pays or provides in addition to Salary.

Taxable Canadian Corporation A Canadian Corporation that is not exempt from Canadian income tax by way of a statutory provision.

Taxable Canadian Property   A group of assets that are listed under the definition of Taxable Canadian Property in ITA 248(1). These assets are distinguished by the fact that gains on their Disposition are taxable without regard to the residence of the selling Taxpayer. For example, if a U.S. Resident sells Canadian real estate, Canadian income tax will be assessed on any gain resulting from the sale.

Taxable Capital Employed in Canada   This amount is the GAAP-determined capital of the Corporation, less the allowance for investments in other Corporations, multiplied by the percentage of the Corporation's activity at Permanent Establishments in Canada as determined under ITR 402. It is used in a number of calculations, including the determination of a small CCPC and the calculation of the reduction of the Small Business Deduction.

Taxable Capital Gain   The taxable portion (currently one-half) of a Capital Gain.

Taxable Entity   A defined organization or Individual that is subject to tax (e.g., Corporations are taxable entities for income tax purposes).

Taxable Income   Net Income For Tax Purposes, less certain deductions that are largely specified in Division C of Part I of the *Income Tax Act*. These deductions include loss carry overs, the Lifetime Capital Gains Deduction, and for Corporations, Dividends and Charitable Gifts.

Taxable Surplus   A surplus account that tracks certain sources of Income of a Foreign Affiliate.

Taxation Year   The period that is covered by a Taxpayer's return. As defined in ITA 249, it is equal to a calendar year for Individuals and Inter Vivos Trusts, and a Fiscal Period for Corporations and Testamentary Trusts.

Taxpayer   An entity that is required to file a tax return and pay taxes. For income tax purposes, a Taxpayer is an Individual, a Corporation, or a Trust.

Taxpayer Relief Provisions   Information Circular 07-01 contains guidelines on the discretionary authority the Minister has to grant relief based on a Taxpayer's situation. An example would be a waiver of late filing interest and penalties because the Individual suffered a serious illness. It replaces the fairness provisions.

Teacher School Supply Tax Credit   A refundable tax credit available to eligible educators for up to $1,000 of eligible expenditures.

Tenancy In Common   A holding of property, either real or personal, by two or more Persons, with each having a divisible interest that can be sold.

Term Preferred Shares   Preferred Shares which have a provision which allows them to be redeemed by the issuer or redeemed at the request of the holder.

Terminal Loss   A deduction in the calculation of Business and Property Income which arises when the last asset in a CCA Class is retired and a positive balance is left in the Class.

Testamentary Trust   A Trust that arises on, and as a consequence of, the death of an Individual.

Thin Capitalization   A reference to situations where a non-resident Specified Shareholder is receiving interest on an amount of debt that exceeds two times the sum of his share of contributed capital plus 100% of Retained Earnings.

Tie-Breaker Rules   Provisions in International Tax Treaties that are designed to prevent the Double Taxation of Dual Residents.

TOSI   An acronym for Tax On Split Income. (See Split Income definition.)

Transaction Tax   A tax that is assessed on specified types of transactions. Such taxes are most commonly applied to transactions involving the sale of goods or services.

Transfer   To convey or move from one Taxpayer to a different Taxpayer.

Transfer Tax   A tax on the Transfer of property from one owner to another.

Transferee   A Taxpayer to whom a Transfer is made.

Transferor   A Taxpayer who makes a Transfer.

Trust   A relationship in which one Person holds the title to property for the benefit of another Person.

Trustee   An Individual or trust institution that holds legal title to property in trust for the benefit of the Trust Beneficiaries.

Tuition Fees Tax Credit   A credit against Tax Payable that is available to Individuals making qualifying tuition payments. The base includes specified ancillary fees and fees and ancillary costs associated with writing university examinations and required examinations in professional programs.

Twenty-One (21) Year Deemed Disposition Rule A requirement, applicable to some types of Personal Trusts, that requires a deemed disposition of the Trust's capital property at the end of every twenty-one years.

U

Undepreciated Capital Cost (UCC) The Capital Cost of a depreciable asset class, less the cumulative CCA that has been taken to date. The tax equivalent of net book value in accounting.

Under Integration An application of integration procedures (e.g., gross up and dividend tax credit rates) that results in a situation where income flowed through a corporation is subject to more tax payable than the same income received directly by an individual.

Unused RRSP Deduction Room The cumulative total of all RRSP Deduction Limits, less amounts deducted in those years. The end of the preceding year balance is used when calculating the RRSP Deduction Limit.

V

Value Added Tax (VAT) A tax based on the value added to a product at each stage of production or distribution by a particular entity. It is generally based on some accounting measurement of Income.

Vertical Amalgamation An Amalgamation of a Parent Company and one or more of its Subsidiaries.

Vested Benefit A benefit is vested if the beneficiary has an irrevocable right to receive it.

Vested Contribution A contribution is vested if the Individual making the contribution has an irrevocable right to either the amount of the contribution or a benefit of equivalent value.

Volunteer Firefighters Tax Credit A credit against Tax Payable that is available to volunteer firefighters who perform at least 200 hours of volunteer firefighting services during a taxation year.

Volunteer Search And Rescue Tax Credit A credit against Tax Payable that is available to volunteer search and rescue workers who perform at least 200 hours of volunteer search and rescue services during a taxation year.

W - Z

Wholly Dependent Person A Dependant who lives with the Taxpayer (this requirement is not applicable if the Dependant is the Taxpayer's child) in a self-contained domestic establishment and is eligible for the Eligible Dependant Tax Credit.

Will A document that is a legal declaration of an Individual's wishes as to the Disposition of his or her property after death.

Winding-Up Of A 90% Owned Subsidiary A Rollover provision that allows the asset of a 90% or more owned Subsidiary to be combined with the assets of its Parent Company, without tax consequences.

Winding-Up Of A Canadian Corporation A series of transactions that result in substantially all of the assets of a Canadian Corporation being distributed to the shareholders of that Corporation.

Zero Emission Vehicles A motor vehicle that is fully powered by electricity or hydrogen, or partially powered by electricity with a minimum battery capacity of 15 kwh.

Zero-Rated Goods And Services Goods and services that are taxable at a zero GST rate. The fact that they are designated as "taxable" means that Registrants who sell such goods and services are eligible for Input Tax Credits for the GST that they pay. Examples include basic groceries (e.g., milk, bread, and vegetables), prescription drugs, and exports.

NOTES

NOTES

NOTES